CQ's State Fact Finder

CQ's State Fact Finder 2006

Rankings Across America

Kendra A. Hovey

Harold A. Hovey

CQ PRESS

A Division of Congressional Quarterly Inc.
Washington, D.C.

To the memory of Harold A. Hovey

CQ Press
1255 22nd Street, NW, Suite 400
Washington, DC 20037

Phone: (202) 729-1900; toll-free, 1-866-427-7737 (1-866-4CQ-PRESS)

Web: www.cqpress.com

♾ The paper used in this publication exceeds the requirements of the American National Standard for Information Sciences—Permanence of Paper for Printed Library Materials, ANSI Z39.48-1992.

Printed and bound in the United States of America

10 09 08 07 06   1 2 3 4 5

ISBN 0-87289-290-5 (cloth)
ISBN 0-87289-291-3 (paper)
ISSN 1079-7149

[redacted]

Contents

Detailed Contents of Subject Rankings

Geography

Government

Federal Impacts

Taxes

Revenues and Finances

Education

Health

Crime and Law Enforcement

Transportation

Welfare

Technology

Introduction

CQ's State Fact Finder is an important source and analytical tool for anyone interested in developments and trends in the fifty U.S. states and the District of Columbia. It is an invaluable reference for researchers, whether policy specialists seeking detailed data or individuals wishing to learn more about today's social, political, and economic currents.

The U.S. economy, population, and governmental policy are constantly changing. Because these changes affect states differently, it is important that information be as up to date as possible. To meet that need, CQ Press publishes *State Fact Finder* annually. The 2006 volume is the twelfth edition.

Many readers will want to reference previous volumes to identify long- and short-term trends. The tables and statistical concepts in this edition remain similar or comparable to those found in the first edition, published in 1993. They are so closely comparable in the 1996 through 2006 editions that readers can use them for statistical analyses of changes at the state level.

Readers and libraries can receive the next edition of *State Fact Finder* as soon as it is published by establishing a standing order with CQ Press. The data in this and previous editions are also available for purchase in electronic form directly from the authors (614-262-9229, spr@columbus.rr.com).

About This Book

State Fact Finder is prepared by experts who analyze state policy and trends and compare states in ways important to policymakers, such as measuring the success of their efforts to promote economic development and the costs and apparent results of their decisions. This book differs considerably from ordinary compilations of statistics in several important ways.

First, *State Fact Finder* includes numerous statistics that are omitted from standard statistical reports of government agencies and therefore do not appear in compilations of statistics that rely solely on such published reports. For example, many of the tables in the Health and Welfare sections comparing state programs for low-income residents are based on unpublished statistics maintained by the agencies that administer these programs. Also, some tables, such as B-28, the Index of State Economic Momentum, and G-21, a comparison of state spending "needs," reflect original research by the authors.

Second, information from other sources has been converted to a basis that makes comparisons meaningful. For example, information on the headquarters of the largest companies in the United States, in Table B-16, includes the number of companies in each state in relation to population as well as the total number of companies.

Third, each table includes a ranking of the states. This makes it easy for readers to see how the state or states that interest them relate to neighboring states and to other states throughout the nation.

Fourth, the volume begins with an essay—"Finding Information Users Want to Know"—that guides researchers in the use of the data and helps them understand the scope of information available to them.

Fifth, each of the thirteen subject rankings sections begins with a brief outlook, pointing to emerging trends in that area, including issues likely to be on the front burner in the coming year. For instance, in this edition, the brief for the Revenues and Finances section highlights ways in which increased energy prices are affecting state finances. The briefs also address ongoing currents in the states. Entering 2006, these include the high costs of health care, state environmental actions on vehicle and power plant emissions, and pressures from social programs that suffered cuts during the fiscal crisis that began in 2001.

Sixth, *State Fact Finder* offers carefully documented source notes after the tables in each section. These notes cite the origins of the statistics in each table and guide researchers to sources where they can obtain additional information on the subject.

About the Publisher

State Fact Finder was first published in 1993 by Congressional Quarterly Inc., which provides comprehensive, reliable, and focused information on national public policy and political issues in the United States. *State Fact Finder* and *Governing*, a magazine covering all aspects of state government, were part of CQ's effort to offer expanded coverage of developments and trends in the states. CQ Press, a division of Congressional Quarterly, has published *State Fact Finder* since 2000.

About the Authors

Harold A. Hovey was the founder and president of State Policy Research and Kendra Hovey is the current president of the company, which government experts nationwide know as one of the most reliable and knowledgeable organizations dealing with state-level information. For more than fifteen years, the authors, through State Policy Research, published the periodicals *State Policy Reports* and *State Budget & Tax News*. For a decade they published *States in Profile*, which merged into *State Fact Finder*.

Information Development

Any data book is by definition a work in progress. What is useful one year may be less relevant the next year, as information needs change. For this reason, the authors of *State Fact Finder* welcome reactions from readers, suggestions for additional information or changes in presentation, and of course any corrections or clarifications that come to readers' attention. Please direct these to Kendra Hovey at State Policy Research (spr@columbus.rr.com).

"State Fiscal Snapshot 2006"

State tax collections are exceeding expectations in many states. Still, memories of the recent fiscal crisis should keep state officials cautious, as should the spending challenges they still face. "State Fiscal Snapshot 2006" provides a glimpse into the immediate budget situation in the states by presenting the best information as of January 2006 on state tax revenues and spending appropriations.

"Finding Information Users Want to Know"

Readers differ in their preferences on many things—from what they value in a place to live to the amount of state government spending they consider appropriate. They might also disagree on such subjects as where they should move or which state is governed best.

In this section, rather than imposing personal values as though they were facts by ranking some states as the "best places" to live or do business and so on, the authors provide guideposts on how to use the tables so that readers can obtain the information they need. Using a question-and-answer format, this section leads readers to groups of tables that can be consulted together to deal with broad issues, such as school quality or business opportunities.

This section is divided into three parts, each based on particular types of decisions that people might make. The first covers personal and family decisions, such as those concerning job opportunities. The second focuses on business decisions, such as where to locate a new plant. The third provides information about the government to assist residents in voting and in influencing public policy.

Subject Rankings

The subject rankings section forms the heart of the book. It is organized into thirteen subject areas that are challenging policymakers throughout the country: population, economies, geography, government, federal impacts, taxes, revenues and finances, education, health, crime and law enforcement, transportation, welfare, and technology. States are listed alphabetically in each table. The information also is presented in rankings that allow readers to see how each state compares with the others.

Source Notes

The source notes that follow each section are designed for use in tandem with the subject rankings to understand the specific usefulness of, and any caveats about, the data. The sources for all statistics are documented so that the calculations can be replicated or expanded upon by those who need more detail than space allows here. These source notes also help readers locate other information and sources that may be useful.

State Rankings

The state rankings section presents a composite view of each state, bringing together rankings on most of the data in the volume. This compilation provides brief summaries of states' positions in each subject area.

The Data

Rankings: There is nothing magical about rankings, though *State Fact Finder* generally follows the statistical convention of ranking from highest to lowest. Most rankings can be interpreted similarly by reversing them. For example, a table showing tax burdens from highest to lowest provides the same information when reversed to show tax burdens from lowest to highest by ranking the fiftieth state first, the forty-ninth state second, and so on.

Data Accuracy: The statistics in this volume vary greatly in their accuracy. Some, such as the land area of states or the number of state legislators, can be measured precisely. Other data, such as birth rates or finances of local governments, are estimates. The source notes generally explain how the data were developed or direct readers to the statistical providers, who usually make available detailed technical papers on their methods.

Ranking Positions and Ties: In preparing this book, the authors worked with data as presented by the statistical source. In presenting the data in tables, figures were rounded to a manageable number of digits, for example $24.5 million rather than $24,515,078. As a result, the rankings based on detailed data may show one state ranked above another even though they are apparently tied in the data published in the table.

In some tables, adding the fifty-state total to the total for the District of Columbia will not yield the U.S. total that appears in the last row. In such cases, the original source included figures for U.S. territories in the U.S. total. *State Fact Finder* cites these U.S. totals as originally recorded, without the subtraction of the territories' figures.

Junk Data: Many special interest groups have strong opinions about appropriate policies for governments. They sometimes translate these opinions into rankings of which states are "best" in their areas of interest, such as protecting the environment, providing mental health services, or maintaining a favorable climate for business. The resulting statistics are not always reliable. Sometimes they combine individually reliable statistics into measures that simply reflect the policy preferences of those who rank the composite results. *State Fact Finder* generally avoids inclusion of such reports.

Time Periods: Each table covers a specific time period, which is indicated in the heading and is normally a calendar year or span of years. In the case of fiscal data, the time periods are fiscal years that end in the year shown.

District of Columbia: The District of Columbia has a unique status in statistical compilations. It is not a state in the sense of having voting representatives in Congress—its citizens have none—and it is counted as a city, not a state, in all U.S. Census Bureau statistics on government finances. Federal agencies and private data-gathering organizations differ in how they treat the District, as well as Puerto Rico, the Virgin Islands, and other territories, in their statistics.

State Fact Finder presents information for the District of Columbia in each table but does not include it in the state rankings. The reasons are twofold. First, users of rankings find its inclusion cumbersome to explain, often having to resort to complicated explanations of rankings (such as a state being ranked fifth, fourth among states and also behind the District of Columbia). Second, the District is economically and demographically a central city with fiscal and other attributes of most central cities (such as high taxes, high crime rates, large percentages of the population in poverty and receiving government benefits, and so forth). When ranked alongside states, the District often ranks first or last in the tables, distorting other rankings.

State Fiscal Snapshot 2006

By November 2005, only four months into most of the states' 2006 fiscal year, nearly half the states had adjusted their revenue forecasts upward. Overall, collections have exceeded expectations. In the third quarter of calendar year 2005, tax revenues were up 9.2 percent over the same quarter in 2004. Research from the Rockefeller Institute of Government shows that this was the fastest third-quarter growth since at least 1991.

The outlook is not so bright in two states. In Louisiana, where the effects of Hurricane Katrina remain uncertain, officials are pessimistic. In Rhode Island, revenue is down 1.9 percent, making the budget a top priority for the state's lawmakers. In addition, sales taxes are underperforming in some northeastern and midwestern states, where consumers may be scaling back their spending due to higher fuel and home heating costs. But, even with these concerns, news on the revenue front continues to be positive for almost all of the states.

Although the revenue picture looks good, the familiar ongoing concerns—health care costs, Medicaid, and federal stipulations in the No Child Left Behind Act—will continue to put pressure on state finances. According to the National Association of State Budget Officers, states will also be pressed to deal with underfunded employee pension systems. The states are also likely to be faced with "pent-up demand" from programs that were cut during the years of fiscal crisis. At the same time, depending on actions by the federal government, states may face reduced federal funding for some social services, such as welfare-to-work, child care, and child support enforcement programs. While the federal government is poised to offer states more flexibility in the administration of Medicaid, the potential savings, though welcome, are relatively small and may result in undesirable consequences, such as increasing the number of people without health insurance.

Change in Quarterly Personal Income Tax Revenue, July to September 2004–2005

New England	6.2%
Mid-Atlantic	9.1%
Great Lakes	5.2%
Plains	10.1%
Southeast	10.3%
Southwest	11.1%
Rocky Mountain	7.2%
Far West	11.4%

Source: The Nelson A. Rockefeller Institute of Government

Inside This Section

Annual State General Fund Spending Increase, FY 2005–2006

Spending Growth	Number of States	
	FY 2005 (preliminary actual)	FY 2006 (appropriated)
Negative Growth	3	5
0.0% to 4.9%	12	14
5.0% to 9.9%	21	26
10.0% or more	14	5

Source: National Association of State Budget Officers

Revenue Outlook for the Remainder of the Fiscal Year

Outlook	Number of States	
	FY 2005 as of Nov 04	FY 2006 as of Nov 05
Optimistic	17	22
Stable	31	26
Concerned	2	1
Pessimistic	0	1

Source: National Conference of State Legislatures

The next three pages offer a snapshot of the immediate fiscal situation in the fifty states. The data are useful and timely, but differ from the rest of statistics in *State Fact Finder* in that they are best read as a measure of the situation in individual states rather than a measure for comparing states. In addition, the information collected here covers state, not state and local, taxes and spending. The data come from the Fiscal Studies Program at the Nelson A. Rockefeller Institute of Government and the National Association of State Budget Officers.

State Tax Revenues

The Nelson A. Rockefeller Institute of Government's Fiscal Studies Program collects these numbers from state taxation agencies and analyzes the data as consistently as possible. It then publishes the data in State Revenue Report, *which it updates quarterly, usually in March, June, September, and December.*

Change in Quarterly Tax Revenue by State, July to September 2004 to 2005

	%
Alabama	10.2
Alaska	5.7
Arizona	21.1
Arkansas	9.1
California	11.8
Colorado	6.6
Connecticut	4.4
Delaware	13.5
Florida	14.1
Georgia	9.4
Hawaii	16.2
Idaho	4.5 ***
Illinois	6.4
Indiana	4.7
Iowa	4.4 ***
Kansas	9.5
Kentucky	12.1
Louisiana	6.9
Maine	-2.6
Maryland	8.1
Massachusetts	7.9
Michigan	3.8
Minnesota	15.0
Mississippi	1.5
Missouri	6.0
Montana	3.6
Nebraska	13.4
Nevada	10.7
New Hampshire	11.2
New Jersey	12.6
New Mexico	No Data
New York	9.1 ***
North Carolina	8.1
North Dakota	13.0
Ohio	4.5
Oklahoma	9.3
Oregon	9.9
Pennsylvania	6.9
Rhode Island	2.9
South Carolina	8.5
South Dakota	5.7
Tennessee	10.1
Texas	9.1
Utah	10.3
Vermont	10.5
Virginia	15.2
Washington	8.2
West Virginia	3.8
Wisconsin	8.0
Wyoming	14.8
United States	9.2

Percent Change in Quarterly Tax Revenue by State, Adjusted for Legislation and Inflation, July to September 2004 to 2005

	%
Alabama	4.3
Alaska	0.0
Arizona	14.6
Arkansas	3.3
California	5.8
Colorado	0.9
Connecticut	-1.2
Delaware	7.4
Florida	7.9
Georgia	3.4
Hawaii	10.5
Idaho	6.0
Illinois	0.7
Indiana	-0.9
Iowa	0.0
Kansas	3.8
Kentucky	6.7
Louisiana	1.1
Maine	-7.8
Maryland	2.0
Massachusetts	2.1
Michigan	-1.8
Minnesota	8.7
Mississippi	-3.8
Missouri	0.3
Montana	-2.0
Nebraska	7.4
Nevada	4.7
New Hampshire	5.0
New Jersey	6.2
New Mexico	No Data
New York	4.5
North Carolina	2.4
North Dakota	6.9
Ohio	-0.6
Oklahoma	3.4
Oregon	4.1
Pennsylvania	1.1
Rhode Island	-2.8
South Carolina	2.7
South Dakota	0.0
Tennessee	3.9
Texas	3.2
Utah	4.4
Vermont	4.5
Virginia	9.8
Washington	2.4
West Virginia	-1.9
Wisconsin	2.3
Wyoming	8.6
United States	3.6

**** Indicates legislation/accounting changes significantly decreased tax receipts.*

Change in Quarterly Tax Revenue by State, July to September 2004 to 2005

	Personal Income Tax %	Corporate Income Tax %	Sales Tax %
Alabama	13.2	57.9	7.0
Alaska	n/a	83.0	n/a
Arizona	25.4	39.2	16.9
Arkansas	8.2	35.6	7.6
California	10.9	19.7	11.7
Colorado	6.2	27.3	5.5
Connecticut	7.2	-0.7	3.3
Delaware	11.4	60.7	n/a
Florida	n/a	52.8	15.1
Georgia	7.5	47.9 *	10.3
Hawaii	33.8	431.8	11.7 ***
Idaho	8.3	26.1	-0.1 ***
Illinois	7.8	19.2	8.2
Indiana	-0.7	38.6	4.7
Iowa	0.6	14.5	3.9 ***
Kansas	11.9	36.3	7.0
Kentucky	3.4 ***	64.7 *	6.5
Louisiana	0.4	64.1	12.5
Maine	2.7	25.5 *	4.1
Maryland	12.0	2.3 *	6.3
Massachusetts	7.0	20.5	5.4
Michigan	3.9	-4.9	3.6
Minnesota	9.2	33.3	6.9
Mississippi	-4.4	30.3	4.8
Missouri	7.7	85.4	3.9
Montana	2.2	43.9	n/a
Nebraska	7.6	42.2	4.8
Nevada	n/a	n/a	11.8
New Hampshire	n/a	33.9 *	n/a
New Jersey	17.4	25.4	3.0
New Mexico	No Data	No Data	No Data
New York	9.8	29.2	1.0 ***
North Carolina	10.2	-3.3	4.5
North Dakota	8.3	24.6	-0.4
Ohio	7.0 ***	-94.8 *	-3.5 *
Oklahoma	9.8	65.1	5.3
Oregon	11.8	31.1	n/a
Pennsylvania	7.7	17.8	5.5
Rhode Island	-0.5	63.5 *	4.3
South Carolina	10.3	43.1	5.1
South Dakota	n/a	n/a	5.9
Tennessee	n/a	45.8 *	8.3
Texas	n/a	n/a	11.0
Utah	9.1	46.6	8.6
Vermont	7.5	15.9	4.1
Virginia	11.6	76.1	10.5 ***
Washington	n/a	n/a	10.8
West Virginia	8.4	18.3	7.0
Wisconsin	8.3	23.4 *	4.2
Wyoming	n/a	n/a	24.0
United States	9.2	25.9	7.8

* *Indicates legislation/accounting changes significantly increased tax receipts.*
*** *Indicates legislation/accounting changes significantly decreased tax receipts.*

Double-digit growth for corporate income tax revenues continues. Personal income and sales tax revenues are also strong. Data are from the Nelson A. Rockefeller Institute of Government's Fiscal Studies Program.

Forty-seven states maintain budget stabilization funds, also called "rainy day" funds. More than half of them limit the upper amount of such funds to a certain percentage of appropriations. These reserves, together with year-ending balances, help states weather unforeseen difficulties and economic downturns. In late 2005, the National Association of State Budget Officers (NASBO) reported that "healthy state revenues, even amid substantial spending pressure, have allowed states to begin to rebuild their budget reserves." The stabilization fund and appropriations data, which reflect the budget situation at the end of 2005, are from NASBO's Fiscal Survey of the States, December 2005.

Appropriated Budget Stabilization Fund, FY 2006

	$ (in millions)
Alabama	350
Alaska	2,308
Arizona	170
Arkansas	0
California	0
Colorado	0
Connecticut	0
Delaware	161
Florida	1,080
Georgia	223
Hawaii	63
Idaho	16
Illinois	276
Indiana	328
Iowa	302
Kansas	0
Kentucky	29
Louisiana	636
Maine	0
Maryland	753
Massachusetts	2,241
Michigan	0
Minnesota	1,003
Mississippi	0
Missouri	240
Montana	0
Nebraska	274
Nevada	159
New Hampshire	31
New Jersey	288
New Mexico	1,210
New York	872
North Carolina	313
North Dakota	100
Ohio	577
Oklahoma	0
Oregon	0
Pennsylvania	337
Rhode Island	96
South Carolina	154
South Dakota	115
Tennessee	325
Texas	165
Utah	170
Vermont	52
Virginia	664
Washington	0
West Virginia	124
Wisconsin	0
Wyoming	70
United States	16,270

Percentage Change in Spending, Actual 2004–Appropriated 2005

	%
Alabama	9.8
Alaska	-0.3
Arizona	7.2
Arkansas	5.4
California	10.2
Colorado	7.3
Connecticut	0.0
Delaware	15.0
Florida	7.1
Georgia	5.9
Hawaii	10.2
Idaho	3.4
Illinois	7.5
Indiana	2.3
Iowa	7.3
Kansas	9.8
Kentucky	8.2
Louisiana	0.3
Maine	0.9
Maryland	8.0
Massachusetts	7.6
Michigan	3.7
Minnesota	2.9
Mississippi	7.6
Missouri	1.4
Montana	7.8
Nebraska	9.3
Nevada	-5.6
New Hampshire	-1.2
New Jersey	-0.9
New Mexico	0.2
New York	5.9
North Carolina	8.8
North Dakota	7.6
Ohio	2.8
Oklahoma	8.3
Oregon	20.0
Pennsylvania	5.1
Rhode Island	5.9
South Carolina	17.7
South Dakota	3.0
Tennessee	4.1
Texas	8.1
Utah	5.0
Vermont	1.5
Virginia	6.2
Washington	4.5
West Virginia	6.0
Wisconsin	5.9
Wyoming	-0.4
United States	6.3

Finding Information Users Want to Know

Most people look to state statistics to answer questions related to a decision they need to make, but they often discover in the process that the statistics they seek do not appear in the reference books they consult. Or, they may find some comparisons that seem to be relevant but then wonder whether they really are.

"Finding Information Users Want to Know"—a list of frequently asked questions—is a feature not found in other compilations of state data. The answer to each question includes information about which tables in *State Fact Finder* should be helpful and provides road maps to other statistics that might be of use. Readers are also made aware when the statistics they seek are not available or not reliable and why that is so.

This section is divided into three parts, each based on particular ways people might use state statistics: to make personal and family decisions, such as finding the states with the best job opportunities, the best health care, and even the best chances for finding a spouse; to make business decisions, such as where to locate a new business or where to find the most productive workers; and to gather information about government to assist them in their roles as voters and in influencing public policy.

About Personal Decisions on Where to Live or Visit

1. Where is the best place to find a job?

As a general rule, it is easier to get a job, better pay, and increased opportunities for advancement and building professional practices if one locates in a state with a rapidly expanding economy. Places in economic decline have fewer job opportunities, and stiff competition exists for the few positions available.

To find states with rapidly expanding economies, look at measures of recent economic growth, particularly the Index of State Economic Momentum (B-28), population growth (A-3), job growth (B-29, B-30), projections of future population growth (A-5), and new companies (B-34). The Index of State Economic Momentum (B-28) is especially useful because it summarizes the three elements of economic growth important to job seekers: population growth, income growth, and increasing numbers of jobs. For positions in high-tech industries, consult the tables in the Technology section (M). High-tech jobs (M-4) and changes in high-tech jobs (M-5) help pinpoint recent hot spots in the industry.

Growth rates are particularly important to note when seeking jobs that are inherently related to growth, such as those in the construction industry. Because the need for construction correlates with changes in the demand for homes and other buildings, there are vast differences in the availability of such jobs in fast- versus slow-growing states. For example, in 2004 there were twenty new homes being built for every 1,000 residents of Nevada, but only two homes for every 1,000 residents of Rhode Island (B-20).

When a state is classified as growing rapidly, it does not necessarily mean that all areas in the state are growing at a fast pace. For example, rapid growth in Nevada is concentrated in the Las Vegas area. To find which areas are growing and in what types of industries and jobs, consult local sources, such as state economic development departments, local chambers of commerce, or even friends familiar with the area. For nationwide statistics on growth in metropolitan areas, obtain information on recent job growth from the Bureau of Labor Statistics (www.stats.bls.gov). The Department of Commerce (www.commerce.gov) supplies somewhat less current statistics on income and other economic factors, including *County Business*

Patterns, which consists of detailed reports on major counties (www.census.gov/prod/www/abs/cbptotal.html). More general statistics can be found at "State and County QuickFacts" (quickfacts.census.gov/qfd) on the Web site of the U.S. Census Bureau.

2. Where will tax burdens be least for me and my family?

The tables in the Taxes section (F) are good guides for averaging tax burdens. Table F-1 shows what share of personal income goes toward state and local taxes. Tables F-6, F-9, and F-13 do this for each of the major taxes: property, sales, and personal income. The range among states is great. For example, New York governments take 13.1 percent of income in state and local taxes, while governments in Tennessee take 8.4 percent.

The taxes actually paid will depend on individual circumstances, such as property owned in relation to income. Note the differences in Tables F-16 and F-24. For example, wealthy retirees might prefer to live in Florida and Texas, which have no income, inheritance, or estate taxes. Young couples without much income might consider it a burden to pay those states' heavy sales taxes. If renters, they will not share in special property tax breaks for homeowners. For them, a state like Oregon, which has no sales tax but steep income taxes, might be a better deal.

While state government taxes are uniform throughout a state, local taxes vary greatly from place to place within the state. The fifty states each have on average some 1,000 different local governments, which means that there are approximately 50,000 local governments with the power to set tax rates.

Depending on the locality, property taxes may be the sum of any number of the following possibilities: individual taxes levied by a county; a municipality or township; a school district; perhaps a second school district, such as a community college or vocational district; and hosts of special districts, such as road districts, transit districts, mosquito control districts, and levee districts. Local governments in many states also levy sales taxes, and a few local governments—for example, those of Philadelphia and New York—have significant local income taxes. The state averages cited in this volume reflect all these taxes.

Local taxes vary greatly from place to place within a state. The fifty states each have on average some 1,000 different local governments, which means that there are approximately 50,000 local governments with the power to set tax rates.

To find local areas with low taxes within a state, look for places that take in large amounts of tax revenues from businesses but have a small population to serve. Also, most metropolitan areas have suburbs with concentrations of office buildings, shopping centers, and businesses and property taxes much lower than those of surrounding areas. Realtors in metropolitan regions can identify such areas. The county officials responsible for collecting property taxes can provide rate information for that locality. Most state tax departments, with offices in state capitals and major cities, publish free booklets outlining all state taxes and tax rates.

3. Which state has the best public schools?

To compare how well students do across states, consider the first five tables in the Education section (H). Use Tables H-1 and H-2 for overall comparisons, H-3 for high school students not going immediately to college, and H-4 and H-5 for how well schools are doing in preparing students to meet standards for college admission. Also use the tables to compare what states spend per student (H-15), what they pay teachers (H-16), class sizes (H-9), and more.

Except in Hawaii, all public schools are locally administrated. Great variation is found within areas in the same state; it is as important as the variation from state to state. All state education departments, located in state capitals, keep statistics on spending and the number of teachers and pupils in each school district. Because of the No Child Left Behind Act of 2001, all states issue "report cards" comparing district performance measures, such as how students do on standardized tests. Each state's department of education usually makes these available on its Web site. Use these or research locally such indicators as percentage of graduates that attend college, percentage of students winning National Merit Scholarships and other awards, and reputation for being a good (or not so good) school.

How well students do depends heavily on how much help and motivation they get at home, not just on what happens at school. Much of the difference among states results from differences among the students, not in the schools. This is true for districts within a state as well.

One key to accessing a good education for a child is getting him or her into the right school, not just the right school district. Some of the best specialized programs and some of the worst schools are both found in central cities.

Parents and guardians who want to send children to private schools should not expect much help from governments. Many states are considering "voucher" plans that help with tuition, but thus far only Florida, Ohio, Utah, Wisconsin, and the District of Columbia make these available; their programs mostly serve poor, inner-city children, except in Utah where the program serves special eduction students. Arizona, Florida, Illinois, Iowa, Minnesota, and Pennsylvania provide limited income tax breaks for private school tuition. Maine and Vermont's voucher programs serve only students in rural areas without public schools.

4. Which state is best for children?

Many tables throughout *State Fact Finder* compare states on aspects of life important to children and people raising children, including health, education, crime, and economic opportunity. The Children's Defense Fund (www.childrensdefense.org) and the Annie E. Casey Foundation (www.aecf.org) in its annual *Kids Count Data Book* provide even more detailed comparisons than the ones available here.

Children grow up in small worlds, such as school buildings and neighborhoods, so one should not rely completely on facts about states, metropolitan areas, or even individual cities and counties when researching information important to a child's life. Where a child is within one of these areas is often much more important than which larger geographical area the child is in.

5. Which is the best state for retirement?

Most people retire within twenty miles of where they lived when they stopped working. Thus, finding the right place is often more a matter of finding the right house or apartment in the right community than finding the right state. *State Fact Finder* can be helpful in finding a home in a different state, but research beyond it is necessary to make an informed decision.

In looking for a new state, it is best to start with personal preference, rather than statistical comparisons (unless the overriding concern is minimizing tax payments). Decide first what is an acceptable distance from family and friends. Next, think about climate issues, such as dealing with ice or not having a change in seasons at all. Initially making such decisions considerably narrows the range of choices. Taking a "preference inventory," such as that found in *Frommer's Retirement Places Rated,* by David Savageau, requires one to consider such things as whether being able to get a part-time job, see and hear a symphony orchestra, follow a professional sports team, and other items are important issues in terms of where one lives.

The tables in *State Fact Finder* reveal systematic differences among states in such characteristics as income and education levels of residents, living costs, crime, and taxes. Table F-25 in the Taxes section, for instance, contains information on how different state tax systems treat retirement income.

Many other books can help with retirement location decisions. A library or good bookstore should be able to recommend useful references. Some describe places to live and provide information on investments, Medicare, and estate planning. Others—for example, *Choose a College Town for Retirement,* by Joseph M. Lubow (1999)—deal only with places to retire, often with different emphases, such as culture and lifetime learning. Still others focus on specialized retirement areas, such as Florida and Hilton Head, South Carolina, but typically not New York City or any place in Ohio.

AARP is a good source for a variety of publications on retirement. The organization also posts an online retirement checklist that allows comparison among states using twenty different lifestyle factors, including housing prices, sense of community, and even cell phone coverage (www.aarpmagazine.org/bestplaces).

6. Which state universities are best?

State Fact Finder contains important statistics for selecting among state university systems. Look for them in Tables H-19 to H-27. State statistics alone cannot help in identifying which university to attend, because state systems include everything from community colleges to medical schools. California even has systems within systems. Its schools vary from the University of California (with campuses at Berkeley and elsewhere and featuring some of the finest institutions in the country) to California State University (which enjoys less of a national reputation but has outstanding specialized programs) to community colleges with diverse and varying strengths and weaknesses.

Students attend schools, not states. Consult guides and ratings of individual schools that provide information on the numbers of students, type of curriculum, costs, and attempted assessments of the quality of students and faculty.

7. Which state has the best cultural attractions and recreation?

Statistics cannot adequately measure recreational opportunities. Attempts to do so often are misleading. For example, Alaska by far has the best ratio of parkland to people, but much of the state is covered by glaciers unfit for hiking or camping by the average recreational user. Some fine experiences—the "big sky" of Montana, the bustle of the streets of New York, and the beauty of fall foliage in New England—cannot be quantified.

Fairly good statistics document how many people participate in various sports in each state. See, for example, Table C-6 on hunting. The table's notes at the end of the chapter provide information on how to obtain information on other sports. Most sports have specialized equipment stores, magazines, and guidebooks that offer information superior to state statistics for making personal recreational choices. For example, the existence of more golfers and courses per capita in a high-ranking state does not mean there would be trouble finding more than enough courses or players to make foursomes in lower-ranked states.

Guidebooks and specialized magazines often track and rate cultural opportunities. Government spending on the arts, shown in Table C-8, is not a useful indicator of the extent or the quality of arts in each state. On average, annual per capita state funding of the arts is about $1, an amount dwarfed by sales revenues, admissions, and donations.

8. Where is the best place to invest in property?

It is hard to pick a winner in a field of losers, and hard to pick a loser in a field of winners. Everybody wants to pick the right state (and area in that state) for their investment.

The old saw about the three keys to real estate investment—location, location, location—applies to states and metropolitan areas within states. For example, statistics in Table B-21, from the Office of Federal Housing Enterprise Oversight, show that in the five years from 2000 to 2005, the average house in California appreciated by 110 percent, while the average home in Indiana increased in value by 20.3 percent. Of course, how much an investment will lose or appreciate depends on the property bought, whether the price was right, and local market conditions.

Supply and demand drive real estate prices. Supply does not decrease much in poor markets; who would tear down a house or office building because of decreasing values? Supply responds to increased demand in good markets. Prices still rise because new construction often costs more than established buildings, and prices of lots and construction labor tend to rise. The most desirable locations generally already have buildings on them, so their value will tend to increase regardless of competition from new construction.

The best strategy for real estate investment is to pick an area with an expanding economy, where large numbers of new jobs are being created. See the answer to Question 1 above concerning where to find a job for tips on using *State Fact Finder* to identify such places.

9. Can picking the right states help pick winners in stocks and bonds?

Few economists or investment professionals would suggest purchasing a company's stock based on the state or states in which its headquarters or plants are found. Rather, what matters are product quality and marketing. Some successful companies operate from unlikely places. For example, farm country in South Dakota serves as the base for computer maker Gateway, and rural Maine hosts retailer L. L. Bean.

For making things, a fast-growing economy represents bad news, not good news. Fast-growing economies make it harder to get and keep good labor, workers' pay is often higher than pay in slow-growing economies, and congestion often plagues transportation facilities. Look for strong state and regional economies only when looking for regionally oriented companies that sell products, such as new homes and fast food, directly to consumers.

Most people who buy tax-exempt bonds do so through mutual funds or rely on bond-rating agencies, such as Standard & Poor's and Moody's. These professional investors rely heavily on the kinds of economic, population, and government statistics found in *State Fact Finder* and analyses of recent fiscal developments in publications like *State Policy Reports*. People who buy individual bonds or buy mutual funds of tax-exempt bonds issued by a single state can use these same statistics.

10. Which state government will interfere least with my freedom?

People occasionally say they would like to live where government interferes little in their daily lives. It is difficult to compare government intrusiveness, because governments often restrict the freedom of some citizens in order to enhance that of others. The ultimate example is capital punishment—the most intrusive of acts carried out against one person in the name of providing freedom from fear and crime for everyone else. State policies are not necessarily consistent on intrusiveness issues. For example, the states most likely to allow residents to own weapons without restriction usually prove least likely to allow residents to grow marijuana on their own property for personal consumption.

Some elements of government intrusiveness can be measured. One is taxes, measured by the many comparisons in the Taxes section (F).

Another way to look at intrusiveness involves the ratio of state and local government employees to population (D-13). For those who find local governments more accessible and less intrusive than state government, a useful measure would be the differences in state and local roles as indicated by public employees (D-15) and revenue raising (D-16).

11. Where are taxes likely to go up/down in the future?

Tax rates are set by state legislatures and local bodies (such as school boards, city councils, county commissions, etc.). Predicting where taxes will be raised or lowered would appear to be a matter of forecasting the views of those who now serve on or will subsequently be elected to these bodies. The economic and population statistics in *State Fact Finder* provide some excellent clues to future tax rates, as does commonsense thinking about why some states have higher taxes than others.

Children grow up in small worlds, such as school buildings and neighborhoods, so one should not rely completely on facts about states, metropolitan areas, or even individual cities and counties when researching information important to a child's life.

Right now, the states with the lowest taxes on residents are those that raise substantial sums of money from other sources—tourists, oil and gas, and gaming casinos, for example. Alaska, Nevada, Texas, and Wyoming are amply endowed with one or more of these sources. As a result, these four states have succeeded in maintaining low taxes while still offering extensive government services. Some states have managed to keep taxes on their residents relatively low because they attract new residents who pay substantial taxes but do not have children in public schools, which constitute a large portion of state and local spending. Fast-growing states of the Southwest and Florida are the best such examples.

These same states will, however, be under the strongest pressure to raise tax levels in the future. Mathematics dictates that as more people move to a state, the amount that its unique resource, be it oil, casinos or something else, contributes to revenues *per resident* drops. Furthermore, as time passes, state populations become more like the national average. For example, the childless young people who flocked to Florida in large numbers to work at tourist attractions and to provide health care and other services to retirees are having children in large numbers. Florida has to pay for accommodating approximately 40,000 additional students in its classrooms every year. California and Texas face similar pressures.

12. Which states have the least/most pollution?

State Fact Finder presents summary statistics on air and water pollution and hazardous waste (Tables C-10 to C-14). More important, the notes to the tables provide leads for finding more information on local areas. State averages are misleading if used to determine where to live or visit. For example, western cities, like Denver and Salt Lake City, have some of the nation's worst air pollution problems, but outside these urban areas the air is about as pure as it can get. An average for California that lumps downtown Los Angeles with the forests of northern California and the state's deserts presents a misleading overall picture as well.

13. Where do I find the best health care?

Because much more money is spent in gathering state-by-state statistics on health and health care (section I), these figures tend to be quite comprehensive compared with statistics in other fields. The statistics in *State Fact Finder* cover (1) the health of average people in a state's population, (2) apparent availability of care, (3) cost of care, and (4) government programs, which are generally oriented toward poor people. These statistics suggest strong concentrations of health professionals in northeastern states. Tables I-22 and I-23 cover the hot topic of prescription drug costs.

People seeking adequate health care for themselves and their family need not be guided by these statistics. For most people health care decisions are limited by health insurers. Because insurers will not pay for long-distance travel and hotel bills except in rare cases, doctors capable of performing all types of procedures and operations have been locating in areas wherever patients are found. One result is the development of top-flight facilities across the country, such as the University of Iowa hospital, which serves as a specialized facility for patients throughout that state, and the medical complex around Birmingham, Alabama. There is no reason for anyone to avoid an entire state because of concerns about health care, unless he or she has a very specialized medical problem. Where people decide to locate *within* a state poses the primary limits on access to health care. People who seek near-wilderness isolation by buying ranches in Colorado or residing on small islands in the Atlantic Ocean must accept the consequences of their isolation in terms of the availability of health care services.

Those utilizing public health care services, such as Medicaid, will find differences in the generosity of state programs. Despite federal minimum requirements, states retain some leeway regarding eligibility requirements, promotion of the program, and additional services offered, such as vision, dental, and prescription drug programs. Tables I-12, I-13, I-16, I-17, I-18, and I-22 are good sources of information on state Medicaid programs. Keep in mind that recent adjustments to these programs have been rapid and numerous, and that in response to burgeoning health care costs, states have been making cuts in public health care programs.

14. Where will I be safest from crime?

State statistics, and even city statistics, on crime are not much help in looking for a safe place to live. In every state, crime is most prevalent in the low-income areas of central cities. Violent crimes are most prevalent in these areas after dark. Thus, reported crime statistics overstate the risk of crime for people who do not spend evenings in low-income central city areas. A high crime rate for an entire state says more about the percentage of a state's population living in such areas than about safety in that state's suburban, small town, and rural areas as compared with similar areas in other states.

City and state crime rates are also misleading when used to consider which places are safe to visit on business or for recreation. All crime statistics that relate a crime category to population use nighttime population figures, that is, the number of people who have regular beds in a city or state. Cities have daytime commuters and business and vacation travelers. Florida, Hawaii, and Nevada, for instance, have lots of vacationers and conference goers. Adding these temporary inhabitants to the denominator would certainly decrease crime rates in cities and in these states.

15. Where is the best place to look for a mate?

People looking for a partner of the opposite sex can reasonably expect better opportunities in locations where they are outnumbered by persons of the opposite sex (A-18). Aggregate statistics can, however, be misleading for people under fifty-five looking for a partner around their own age. Because women live longer than men, the states with predominately older populations (A-7) also tend to have high ratios of women to men. Careful work by several women on the Federal Reserve Bank of Boston's research staff found the worst sex ratios—from the standpoint of women seeking men—in older northeastern cities and the states with a high percentage of jobs in health care, government, and financial services, which are disproportionately filled by women. The best ratios from the perspective of women seeking men were in booming western states, where economic growth has drawn large numbers of young men to such occupations as mining and construction.

16. Where can I find the lowest living costs?

State Fact Finder presents the best information available for use in comparative living costs (B-8), but the data must be used with care. For reasons cited in the table notes, these measures are not appropriate for what they try to measure—average living costs—but they represent the best data to be found. Also, substantial variation exists within states. All costs, except state and local taxes, run about the same in all midsize cities and rural areas throughout the nation. Taxes (see section F) and costs related to economic growth (section B) make for the biggest differences.

In booming communities and states, housing prices soar, wage rates tend to be higher, and ample and growing sales discourage everyone, from doctors to owners of corner stores, from engaging in price wars. In depressed communities and slow-growth states—for example, older industrial communities, such as Syracuse, and states like West Virginia—stagnation tends to reduce housing costs, wages, and prices.

Different people buy different things, so the costs experienced by certain types of individuals will differ from averages, often by wide margins. Business travelers have a higher cost of living because of what they buy—downtown hotel rooms, rental cars, and meals at restaurants catering to expense-account crowds. The same is true for highly paid executives with downtown jobs, particularly if they desire a short commute. The largest differentials are associated with the size of metropolitan areas, not with states. Chicago, Los Angeles, and New York are expensive places, but Rochester, Joliet, and Fresno are not.

The price of consumer goods shows little variation between states. Much of what people buy—cars, furniture, alcoholic beverages and soft drinks, packaged foods, motion pictures and videotapes, books, sports equipment, clothing, and more—is produced at distances far from them. Prices generally reflect minor differences in shipping costs among states, except in Alaska and Hawaii, where shipping increases prices more than on the mainland.

About Business Decisions on Where to Locate and Expand

1. Where is the best place to locate a business?

State Fact Finder provides useful statistics for some kinds of business but not all. Businesses that depend on local customers—from doctors' offices to fast-food franchises—will usually do better in rapidly growing areas. To use *State Fact Finder* to identify these areas, see Question 1 in the previous section. Some local businesses have specialized markets, appealing primarily to clearly defined groups, such as children or retirees. To identify areas of specific large and growing populations, review the tables in the Population (A) and Economies (B) sections.

Sophisticated investors in consumer-oriented businesses, such as franchises, often do extensive market research before committing their money. The same is true of companies deciding how and where to market consumer products, from cars to shampoo. Serious researchers generally look at areas in more geographic detail—such as on the level of zip codes, streets, and census tracts. They also rely on their own publications, most notably *American Demographics.* Many private companies specialize in providing such information and the computer software to use it. These companies advertise in related publications.

High-tech industries often locate close to academic institutions and in some cases research facilities. For instance, Silicon Valley largely grew out of Stanford University.

Some businesses, such as manufacturing companies, can produce products in locations at distances far from their consumers. Sometimes the nature of a business limits the choice of location. For example, mining and oil production companies need to be on top of their raw materials. Manufacturers need an ample supply of labor and may have special transportation requirements, such as access to a rail line or deep-water port.

Within these parameters, the factors that help determine the best location for a business relate to labor and transportation costs, state and local taxes, and electricity prices. Every firm, indeed every plant, differs in where it gets supplies, where its customers are located, how much and what kind of energy it uses, and the relative use of labor and machinery. Thus the best place to locate depends on the fit between the needs of the firm and the attractions of a potential site.

State Fact Finder contains much useful information for comparing business locations. The Population (A) and Economies (B) sections provide information about potential markets for selling products and hiring workers. The Government (D) section covers how states are governed. The Taxes (F) and Revenues and Finances (G) sections look at factors associated with each state's tax burden. The Education (H) and Transportation (K) sections examine the elements of government-provided services important to business.

In establishing a business oriented toward local economic growth, the predominant issue is what growth *will be*, not what growth *was*. Most statistics show what it *was*. The standard warning about investing in the stock market also applies to state economic growth: past performance is no guarantee of future results. Future growth depends on many factors, including fluctuations in oil prices, federal spending (particularly on defense and homeland security), and how well particular firms and industries (and thus the places where they are located) do in the marketplace. To make predictions on future growth, review trend statistics (A-3, B-29, and E-2) or the composite Index of State Economic Momentum (B-28). Forecasts can be purchased from firms specializing in forecasting, or they can be obtained inexpensively from the Department of Commerce.

2. Where is the best place to locate a high-tech business?

Some businesses require employees with specialized skill sets. For those wanting to attract high-tech or so-called creative workers, location can be essential. Tables M-4 and M-5 provide a breakdown of high-tech employment in the states. Consult the American Electronics Association for more information on state and metropolitan levels.

High-tech industries often locate close to academic institutions and in some cases research facilities. For instance, Silicon Valley largely grew out of Stanford University, and two Florida universities speared that state's High-Tech Corridor. Tables H-19 through H-29 in *State Fact Finder* provide information on higher education. Table H-29, which shows how the federal government spreads research and development money among the states, is particularly useful.

Richard Florida, a Carnegie Mellon economic development professor, pioneered what he calls a Creativity Index to attract "creative workers." In it he ranks cities using a variety of measures, including diversity. More information can be found at www.creativeclass.org.

3. Which state has the most productive workers?

Through industrial development ads in business magazines, some states try to convince firms to locate within their borders because their workers are more productive. Productivity in this context proves to be an elusive concept. Many experts doubt the accuracy of national figures about changes in worker productivity and question even more state-by-state numbers on the matter.

Employers' ideas of a productive worker vary by sector and situation. For example, software design and advertising place a premium on creativity and originality, so employees who work irregular hours can be considered highly productive. An assembly line, however, cannot work unless all workers report at the same time. Formal schooling may be necessary in the development of productive engineers, but experience may be the best education for training plumbers or people who fish for a living.

State Fact Finder has numerous statistics, particularly in the Education (H) and Health (I) sections, on factors employers may consider in determining productivity. *State Fact Finder* also includes the statistics traditionally used to calculate productivity in the states (B-7), but such data are misleading for the reasons explained in the notes to the table.

4. Which states have the lowest labor costs?

Most comparisons among states regarding labor costs are based on average annual pay (B-5), as well as annual averages in retailing (B-10) and manufacturing (B-9). Such statistics will not necessarily be useful in researching the hiring of new workers in a particular occupation in a particular location within a state. The wages that must be paid to attract competent workers in such a situation will depend upon the supply of labor and the demand for it in the local labor market. Firms looking for low-wage workers should do just the opposite of workers looking for high-paying firms, as discussed in Question 1 of the personal decisions section.

The most relevant statistic involves how much work an employer gets from a worker in relation to a dollar paid. That figure is elusive because productivity per worker is hard to calculate accurately (see Question 3 in this section). For a sophisticated attempt at calculating unit labor cost in relation to productivity, see the research of Economy.com, including its *Regional Financial Review*, which routinely analyzes the cost of doing business.

5. Where will my business pay the least taxes?

State taxes on business are a complex web of interlocking provisions made even more complex because many local governments also have separate taxes on business. These combinations affect businesses differently, depending on such factors as how profitable they are; how capital intensive they are; whether they qualify for state and local economic development incentives; and whether they are organized as proprietorships, partnerships, S (small business) corporations, or C (regular) corporations.

For entrepreneurs and businesses looking to move to a new area, there is no substitute for knowing the tax rules of the state and locality and how they will ultimately affect business plans. Such calculations are so complicated that a major consulting industry has developed to produce them.

State Fact Finder provides some good indicators of the possible results of these calculations. Start with the overall levels of taxes (F-1 to F-3). If these are high, the business will pay them somewhere—if not in taxes on the firm, then in taxes on salaries, facilities, and utility services. Next, look at the burdens of the specific taxes relevant to the business's operations. If considerable investments in property are required, such as on a plant and equipment, see Tables F-6 to F-8. If concern revolves around payroll taxes, see Tables F-13 to F-16. For taxes on sales, see Tables F-9 to F-12.

A local service business, such as a bakery or retail store, will not have to worry much about state taxes. Unless the business is situated near a border with another state, its competitors will be paying the same taxes. This may not be true concerning local taxes, so additional checking is necessary. Small businesses need not be as worried as large firms about some taxes, particularly corporate income and franchise taxes. If the concern is about taxes on individuals, such as income and estate taxes, see Tables F-16 and F-24.

Owners of nationally oriented businesses, such as manufacturing interests, may be in for some pleasant as well as unpleasant surprises about business taxes. Some states, such as New York, have high overall tax levels, but are quite competitive in taxes on manufacturing. Some states with low taxes on households, particularly those with no taxes on personal incomes, impose relatively high taxes on firms. The apportionment of corporate income among states for tax purposes dictates that for multistate firms, opening a plant in one state affects the corporate income taxes it pays in all the other states in which it has operations.

6. Which states provide the best incentives to locate in them?

The amounts and types of assistance available from state and local governments in tax breaks, grants, and loans for locating in their jurisdiction depend on the type of business. New businesses that inherently serve local customers—a car dealership, restaurant, retail store, or repair business, for example—should expect no significant help from government. Why? The business will not increase the wealth or income of the area it serves; rather it will siphon business from those companies already there and with whom it competes. Some technical assistance, and even loans, may be available, but mostly from state and local agencies administering federal small business money. Some tax breaks may exist in the right state and right locality within it, because local communities compete with each other to increase their tax base.

If a business draws money from out of state, it will likely be offered major incentives from just about any state. There are so many incentives, and their numbers are growing so quickly, that directories of them are obsolete the day of their release. Avoid trying to use national directories of this type or risk missing out on deals that states might be willing to tailor to fit a business. All states and nearly every community of any size employ "developers"—economic development professionals whose mission is to draw employers to their community or state by providing information and administering incentives. These people are eager to provide details about sites, taxes, worker availability, and state and local incentives. Look for state agencies with *development* in their titles, and find local agencies through county or city governments or chambers of commerce.

7. Which states have the lowest utility rates?

Statistics comparing state averages of electricity rates for various consumers appear in Table B-33. They are indicative of rate differentials for other fuels as well. Deregulation and restructuring have changed the energy picture, and proximity to energy sources is not necessarily the primary determinant in the price one will pay for energy. Taxes make a big difference, as do policies that determine how to charge households versus industry, as Table B-33 dramatically illustrates.

Prices vary within states among users of differing quantities of energy and among types of industrial service; for example, plants that close on high-use days may be charged cheaper rates. Concessions may also be made to firms newly locating in an area or that demonstrate that they can also obtain service from a competing utility. There is no substitute for checking the prices local utilities charge.

8. Which states regulate business the least?

There is no statistical method for comparing state and local regulation of business across the board, because government regulation touches business operations in so many different ways. The great variation in policies among states and local areas further hinders such comparison. Many of these regulatory differences are not systematic. For example, some southern states have relatively less stringent regulation of workplace conditions while imposing more stringent regulation on how corporations are governed.

9. Where is the transportation system best?

Interstate transportation systems—road, rail, air, and water lanes—form an interconnected network that allows access to every state in one way or another. Once a product or raw material embarks on this network, service is close to uniform until it leaves it. For a business with considerable shipping requirements, the key component is how easily it can connect with the national networks it needs. This varies with geography, not state lines, and is critically dependent on where the business is sited relative to transportation access points.

There are, however, systemic differences in quality among states. These appear most dramatically in measures of maintenance and construction, the condition of bridges (K-3), and highway pavement (K-2). The quality of an individual state or region's transportation system may be an important consideration for businesses. Commuting times and transportation options are key concerns for many workers in larger metropolitan areas. Tables K-7 and K-10 illustrate the numbers of workers using public transportation and how many employees support such systems.

10. Which states have pro-business attitudes?

Like most people, business owners and managers have differing needs and differing views of appropriate public policies. For example, a businessperson owning a company engaged in a low-tech, labor-intensive activity, such as poultry processing, is not much concerned with the education of the company's workers but is highly concerned with pollution control costs, state labor regulations, and taxes. A businessperson who owns a company engaged in high-tech competition for improved designs of computer chips or software is not as concerned about such state regulations or even taxes; instead, he or she is highly sensitive to how well educated employees are and whether governments maintain strong university systems and promote cultural and recreational opportunities. Thus, a state with relatively high taxes that is accustomed to paying for top-flight schools and state universities will appear anti-business to some business leaders and pro-business to others.

The phrase *business climate* was widely used in the 1980s in discussions of state policies for economic development, regulation, labor laws, and taxes. Based on characteristics found to be important to manufacturing firms that participated in state manufacturing associations, the Grant Thornton accounting firm developed statistics to rank business climate. The state rankings much favored southeastern states with low taxes, low wages, and little business regulation. The influence of these ratings on state policies encouraged the development of counter-statistics, particularly the annual *Development Report Card for the States*, published by the Corporation for Enterprise Development, or CFED, whose sponsors include many unions. As the name implies, the *Development Report Card* gives letter grades, not aggregate rankings, to reflect the complexity and controversy associated with deciding which state policies are pro-business and which are successful in promoting state economic development. The state grades are the opposite of those of the business climate rankings. In the CFED's 2004 evaluation, Connecticut, Delaware, and Massachusetts made the honor roll, while most southeastern states tended to get the lowest grades.

> *If a business draws money from out of state, it will likely be offered major incentives from just about any state. There are so many incentives, and their numbers are growing so quickly, that directories of them are obsolete the day of their release.*

The availability of these more sophisticated measures discouraged use of the old business climate rankings, which are no longer published. The term *business climate* has since been appropriated by the publishers of the business-oriented quarterly *Site Selection*. Its ranking procedure, associated with the number of new jobs (primarily in manufacturing), inherently favors large states over less populous ones. Table B-30 uses the test of which states produce the most new work and shows growth in manufacturing jobs. Tables B-16 and B-17 use the test of where large firms locate their headquarters.

11. Which states are the best places to sell business-to-business?

Many companies sell goods and services to other businesses rather than to individual consumers. Finding firms that might want to buy office supplies, parts, maintenance services, and other business-to-business offerings is different from finding individual consumers (which is discussed in Question 1 in this section). The statistics needed for finding business customers are too specialized for *State Fact Finder*, but government sources provide them in abundance. The Bureau of Labor Statistics at the Department of Labor maintains up-to-date statistics on the number of jobs in each state, with breakdowns by major industry. The Department of Commerce compiles detailed data and publishes county-level statistics in *County Business Patterns*. The department also conducts major surveys, such as the Economic Census, which includes reports on manufacturing and retail trade.

State governments collect and disseminate even more detailed information, though some do a better job than others in keeping it current and making it available in usable forms. The state agencies that administer unemployment compensation (UC)—typically called the Department of Labor or Employment Services Administration—compile details on all private firms, because they collect UC payroll taxes from them every quarter. Mom-and-pop stores and General Motors both are chartered by states and often need some kind of permit to operate in those states where they are not chartered. Secretaries of state keep such records.

Many state economic development departments have detailed statistics on businesses operating in the state, and some publish directories.

About Government and Public Policy

1. Which state is the best managed?

No one has yet found a way to use statistics to determine which states, or for that matter which private companies, are best managed. Bottom-line results—low taxes, high and growing business profits, etc.—count for something, but some states and companies face greater challenges than others in achieving them, because of circumstances beyond the control of their managers and leaders. There are awards for well-managed governments and companies, but these are like civic awards: who gets them depends on who sits on the selection committee, the criteria those particular people apply, and their personal knowledge of the candidates.

Somewhat more objective criteria can be considered in measuring state financial management. Bond rating agencies, such as Moody's, assess credit risks (G-15) much as a bank determines how much to loan a family seeking a mortgage. Like personal credit ratings, these concern only the likelihood that loans will be repaid, not whether the borrower is competent, efficient, or conducting business as he or she should.

States' financial management practices can also be compared, such as whether they conform to generally accepted accounting principles and whether they use performance-oriented budgeting. Most experts believe these practices improve the quality of state decisions. Comparisons can be found in Table G-20. For detailed comparisons of such state practices as balanced budget requirements, governors' use of the line-item veto, and the status of stabilization or "rainy day" funds, see the National Association of State Budget Officers' *Budget Processes in the States* (available at www.nasbo.org/publications/pdfs/budpro2002.pdf).

2. Which state has the fairest tax system?

Fairness in taxes depends on who one thinks should bear what share of the tax burden, or to quote the old maxim, "Where you stand depends on where you sit." The data on who pays what, where, and how are found in Tables F-6 through F-23 in the Taxes section. Also included in that section are tables on the progressivity of taxes; relative reliance on sales, income, and other tax bases; and tax burdens on high- and low-income households.

A group of experts and state officials—including governors, legislators, and tax commissioners—jointly published *Financing State Government in the 1990s,* a study of the elements of good tax systems. It is available from the National Conference of State Legislatures in Denver (www.ncsl.org). The book advocates keeping rates of all taxes as low as possible, given the money to be raised, by avoiding lots of special exemptions and by balancing reliance on property, income, and sales taxes. Look for balance in percentages of three-tax revenue in Tables F-8, F-11, and F-15.

3. Which states keep the share of taxes paid by business low?

Economists argue that all taxes, including business taxes, reduce some person's income in order to make money available for government. Part of their reasoning is that legal abstractions, such as corporations and partnerships, do not bear the burden of taxes. Instead, these entities' tax burdens find their way into prices paid by customers, lower wages paid to workers, lower prices paid to suppliers, and lower profits credited to stockholders.

Many people do not agree with this perspective. Public opinion polls usually show that voters would rather see taxes on corporations than taxes they *know* they pay, such as sales taxes and personal income taxes. While many business leaders do not agree with the economists' outlook, others share it but want to protect everyone involved—stockholders, suppliers, workers, and customers—by avoiding taxes on their businesses. As a result, comparing how states distribute tax burdens between businesses and people piques a lot of interest.

Good data to make such comparisons will never exist, because the people who might gather the information—the tax collectors—do not care about it. Most collect the same property tax on houses and stores whether they are owned by occupants, individual landlords, or a corporate landlord. When someone buys a pad of paper and pays sales tax, no one asks whether he or she is buying it to do grocery lists or for a business project. The family farm is a business as well as a home, but most states do not divide the value between the two or make the tax lower or higher if the family is organized as a sole proprietorship, partnership, or corporation. Comparisons of states on the share of taxes paid by businesses thus inherently involve guesswork and arbitrary distinctions, such as calling all severance taxes business taxes and all farm taxes people taxes. These comparisons deliberately are not included in *State Fact Finder.*

4. Which state has the highest taxes?

Tables F-1, F-2, and F-3 of the Taxes section present the three standard measures of tax burdens. While these offer general information, other tables in the Taxes section are more useful for considering what taxes are likely to be owed by an individual household or business. For that issue, see the answers to Question 2 in the personal decisions section and Question 5 in the business decisions section.

5. Which state has the best education policies?

As they do in other public policy fields, people disagree on the best education policies. To address this question, sporadic publications rank states by evaluating aggregate policies, but the results simply reflect the policy preferences of the interest group issuing them. The scores and rankings might be useful to those who share whatever the bias but misleading to those who do not. *State Fact Finder* provides statistics on education (section H) and lets the reader decide which are of most importance.

6. Which states help the poor the most?

Much disagreement surrounds what is truly helpful to poor people. For example, some people believe providing cash through welfare helps, but others argue that it hurts in the long run because it discourages working and hinders opportunities to rise out of poverty.

State Fact Finder has numerous tables on programs for poor people, including food stamps (L-4), Temporary Assistance to Needy Families (L-2, L-3, L-10, L-11, and L-19), Supplemental Security Income (L-5 and L-12), Women, Infants, and Children Program (L-6), National School Lunch Program (L-7), Medicaid (I-12, I-13, I-16, I-17, and I-18), and Head Start (H-31), as well as on tax policies affecting low-income households (L-13).

For additional information, consult the Center on Budget and Policy Priorities (www.cbpp.org), which analyzes which states are most generous toward poor people in their spending and how regressive state and local tax policies are—that is, whether they take away in taxes a larger percentage of the purchasing power of poor people than of wealthy people.

7. Which states have the best roads?

Comparing state policies on a topic such as education does not work well because different people have different ideas about what constitutes good or bad policy. Even when people can agree on desirable results (for example, how children should perform on standard reading tests), it is difficult to judge states by them because so much of the result is determined by factors governments do not control. However, when it comes to providing well-maintained roads, people generally agree on what is good and bad, and because state and local governments maintain their own roads, few extraneous factors interfere in making determinations. Highways provide a good example of how services can be compared. See Tables K-2 and K-3. Also, truckers run their own surveys, which can be found in the special-interest magazine *Overdrive*.

8. Overall, which states use tax dollars in the most cost-effective manner?

This question cannot be answered for conceptual reasons: People do not agree on what governments should do and how they should do it. For example, most people would agree that administrative costs for welfare should be kept at a minimum so that all available money can be devoted to actually assisting recipients. Most people would agree that it is bad for society if large numbers of people are allowed to cheat their governments, and most would also agree that welfare recipients should be encouraged to find jobs. These beliefs can produce contradictory results. Consider, for instance, the costs per case of administering welfare (L-19) and collecting child support (L-15). These costs are lowest if a state does little counseling and does not spend much money checking for fraud. Most people would agree that these consequences are not those desired.

Another example of a conceptual problem involves the size of elementary school classes (H-9). Some people think small classes are ideal for all schools, while others believe that small classes result in unnecessary spending.

Conceptual problems are not unique to governments. How can a company effectively measure whether its public

> *For some people, picking the state with the best policy is simple: the one with the lowest taxes or the one that spends the most on schools or taking care of the poor or is active in some other area of interest to the person making the judgment. For most people, the question is too general to be answered meaningfully.*

relations or shareholder relations departments are cost-effective?

Even if conceptual problems could be solved, enormous difficulties remain in collecting the relevant data. For many functions, good measures of effectiveness do not exist. What makes an effective police officer or an effective university professor or an effective state legislator? How could an effectiveness test be uniformly applied to every police officer, university professor, or legislator in the nation?

Often, good measures of costs are not available either, at least not ones related closely to particular services or outputs of government. Again, this problem is not unique to government. What percentage of the cost of a steer attaches to the beef and what percentage to the leather?

Most attempts to measure the cost-effectiveness of government are experimental and usually confined to activities that can be measured fairly easily, such as gathering refuse, maintaining highways, and collecting bills. For more information, see the many useful books written by Harry Hatry and published by the Urban Institute (www.urban.org).

Overall, which states use tax dollars in the most cost-effective manner? This question cannot be answered for conceptual reasons: People do not agree on what governments should do and how they should do it. Even if conceptual problems could be solved, for many functions, good measures of effectiveness do not exist.

9. Which states have the best government institutions?

Personal preference rules when it comes to deciding how governments ought to be organized, their policies established, and their leaders selected. Some people have strong opinions on these matters, which are from time to time reflected in comparisons attempting to identify states with the "best practices."

For the past thirty years, experts have advocated and states have moved toward organizing the executive branches of state government in ways that strengthen the power of governors. These moves include (1) strengthening the veto power, including allowing line-item vetoes; (2) reducing the number of executive officials—such as comptrollers, education superintendents, and insurance commissioners—selected by elections rather than appointment; (3) increasing the governor's role in preparing and administering budgets; and (4) extending governors' terms by converting two-year terms into four-year terms and allowing governors to run for reelection. Information on these developments and classifications of which states follow which practices appear in the Government section (D).

For decades state legislatures were criticized as citadels of corrupt power removed from popular control and unresponsive to the needs of citizens. One major change came with a Supreme Court decision on reapportionment, requiring "one man, one vote." Now the U.S. Senate is the only governing body in the nation where voting power is not proportional to population. The National Conference of State Legislatures, business groups, and foundations have sponsored research on "modern" legislatures emphasizing (1) longer annual sessions, (2) more staff, and (3) higher legislative pay and expenses. Three such measures of their results appear in Tables D-5, D-8, and D-9.

These ideas have come under considerable criticism recently. Some people view increases in staffing and full-time legislators as a move toward professionalizing the legislature. Others see it as a recipe for making bureaucrats out of legislators, creating "full-time politicians," and putting legislators out of touch with the people they represent. One result has been moves toward limiting the number of terms legislators can serve (D-8), in effect encouraging turnover (D-7).

Surveys show that large numbers of Americans consider corruption a common occurrence among elected officials at the state and federal levels. One cannot statistically compare ethics, but laws on conflict of interest and disclosure of personal financial information can be compared. The National Conference of State Legislatures does this, and the organization Common Cause also acts as a watchdog on this issue.

No doctrine consistently prevails on whether bigger is better for business and government. Sometimes consolidation is in fashion, forming conglomerates for business and merging regional governments to reduce the roughly 87,500 different state and local governments. Sometimes decentralization and local control come into vogue, with spin-offs for business and other special districts (for example, downtown revitalization areas, police service districts) and decentralized control of neighborhood schools within large school systems.

One way to look at differing state policies involves comparing the ratio of governments to people (D-4). Another approach examines the percentage of local government spending that local officials do not have to finance with their own taxes (D-16).

10. Overall, which states have the best policies?

For some people, picking the state with the best policy is simple: the one with the lowest taxes or the one that spends the most on schools or taking care of the poor or is active in some other area of interest to the person making the judgment.

For most people, this question is too general to be answered meaningfully, because opinions differ so markedly on what is "best." In one person's eyes, the same state may produce "good" policies on one issue but "bad" policies on another.

One thing is clear: State officials must play the hand they are dealt, balancing the needs of their population and the tax base available for revenue to meet those needs. These needs present themselves in the form of children to be educated (H-10), poor people potentially eligible for services (A-16), and more. Tax bases are apparent from economic differences, as shown in the Economies section (B). State differences in spending needs are summarized in Table G-21 and in tax bases in Table F-3.

When comparing these statistics, some conclusions become fairly obvious. For example, compared with most states, Connecticut looks pretty good, as a state with low taxes as well as high ratings on such things as spending per school pupil. Connecticut, however, has a rich tax base and a comparatively small percentage of people needing services. Mississippi faces the opposite situation.

11. All things considered, which state is run the best?

Readers are advised to ignore magazine rankings purporting to show which state governments are best or which states are governed best by the combination of state and local officials responsible for their policies. The slippery nature of such rankings becomes evident by comparing results. For example, in the mid-1990s, two financial magazines, *Worth* and *Financial World*, published a set of rankings. One held that Wyoming was the best governed, with Alaska coming in second. The other ranked Wyoming forty-third and had Alaska next to last.

For a ranking of states to be useful, pick an area where they compete for the same prize, such as jobs (B-29); where residents are judged by the same test (H-3); or where the same objective criteria are applied, such as tax levels (F-1).

There is widespread agreement on what constitutes a valuable football player or an outstanding actor. This is not true for governments. Many people think those that govern best govern least, but others think good governance produces good schools, nice roads, and quick responses from police and fire departments.

Subject Rankings

Population

From July 1, 2003, to July 1, 2004, the nation's population grew by approximately 1 percent. The Hispanic population, which passed the forty million mark during this period, experienced the largest growth rate at 3.6 percent, followed by the Asian American population at 3.4 percent. The African American population increased by 1.3 percent. The population of non-Hispanic whites, estimated at 197.8 million, increased by 0.3 percent.

Population by Race/Ethnic Groups, 2004

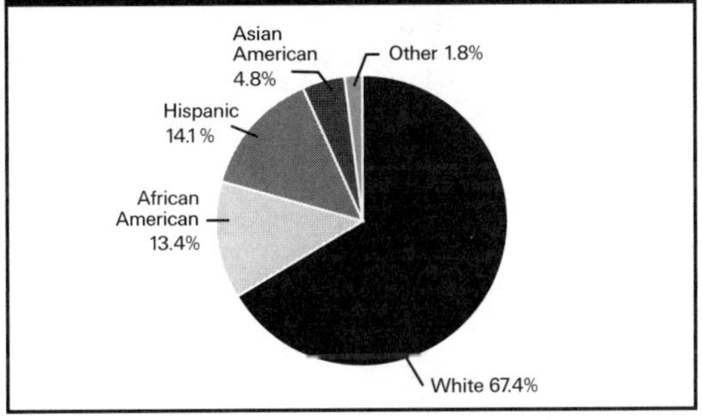

Source: U.S. Census Bureau

According to current Census Bureau projections, the growth rates of the Hispanic and Asian American populations will continue to outpace those of other racial and ethnic groups.

Population by Race/Ethnic Groups, Projected 2030

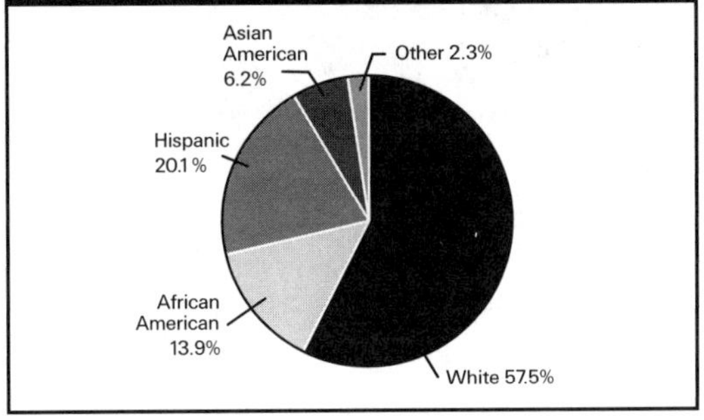

Source: U.S. Census Bureau

Twenty-five percent of the American population is under the age of 18, and 12.4 percent is age 65 or older. For Hispanics these percentages shift to 34.0 percent and 5.2 percent, respectively. The working-age population (ages 18–64) accounts for 62.7 percent of the total U.S. population. This proportion ranges from a high of 66.3 percent for Asian Americans to a low of 60.6 percent for African Americans.

A-1 Population and Percentage Distribution, 2005

State	Population 2005 (in thousands)	Percentage of national total 2005	Rank by percentage
Alabama	4,558	1.5	23
Alaska	664	0.2	47
Arizona	5,939	2.0	17
Arkansas	2,779	0.9	32
California	36,132	12.2	1
Colorado	4,665	1.6	22
Connecticut	3,510	1.2	29
Delaware	844	0.3	45
Florida	17,790	6.0	4
Georgia	9,073	3.1	9
Hawaii	1,275	0.4	42
Idaho	1,429	0.5	39
Illinois	12,763	4.3	5
Indiana	6,272	2.1	15
Iowa	2,966	1.0	30
Kansas	2,745	0.9	33
Kentucky	4,173	1.4	26
Louisiana	4,524	1.5	24
Maine	1,322	0.4	40
Maryland	5,600	1.9	19
Massachusetts	6,399	2.2	13
Michigan	10,121	3.4	8
Minnesota	5,133	1.7	21
Mississippi	2,921	1.0	31
Missouri	5,800	2.0	18
Montana	936	0.3	44
Nebraska	1,759	0.6	38
Nevada	2,415	0.8	35
New Hampshire	1,310	0.4	41
New Jersey	8,718	2.9	10
New Mexico	1,928	0.7	36
New York	19,255	6.5	3
North Carolina	8,683	2.9	11
North Dakota	637	0.2	48
Ohio	11,464	3.9	7
Oklahoma	3,548	1.2	28
Oregon	3,641	1.2	27
Pennsylvania	12,430	4.2	6
Rhode Island	1,076	0.4	43
South Carolina	4,255	1.4	25
South Dakota	776	0.3	46
Tennessee	5,963	2.0	16
Texas	22,860	7.7	2
Utah	2,470	0.8	34
Vermont	623	0.2	49
Virginia	7,567	2.6	12
Washington	6,288	2.1	14
West Virginia	1,817	0.6	37
Wisconsin	5,536	1.9	20
Wyoming	509	0.2	50
50 States	295,859	99.8	
DC	551	0.2	
United States	296,410	100.0	

Rank in order by percentage	
1	California
2	Texas
3	New York
4	Florida
5	Illinois
6	Pennsylvania
7	Ohio
8	Michigan
9	Georgia
10	New Jersey
11	North Carolina
12	Virginia
13	Massachusetts
14	Washington
15	Indiana
16	Tennessee
17	Arizona
18	Missouri
19	Maryland
20	Wisconsin
21	Minnesota
22	Colorado
23	Alabama
24	Louisiana
25	South Carolina
26	Kentucky
27	Oregon
28	Oklahoma
29	Connecticut
30	Iowa
31	Mississippi
32	Arkansas
33	Kansas
34	Utah
35	Nevada
36	New Mexico
37	West Virginia
38	Nebraska
39	Idaho
40	Maine
41	New Hampshire
42	Hawaii
43	Rhode Island
44	Montana
45	Delaware
46	South Dakota
47	Alaska
48	North Dakota
49	Vermont
50	Wyoming

Note: Numbers that appear to be identical are rounded and vary slightly in actual value. The rankings reflect the actual values before rounding. See the introduction for more details.

A-2 Population and Percentage Distribution, 2004

State	Population 2004 (in thousands)	Percentage of national total 2004	Rank by percentage
Alabama	4,530	1.5	23
Alaska	655	0.2	47
Arizona	5,744	2.0	18
Arkansas	2,753	0.9	32
California	35,894	12.2	1
Colorado	4,601	1.6	22
Connecticut	3,504	1.2	29
Delaware	830	0.3	45
Florida	17,397	5.9	4
Georgia	8,829	3.0	9
Hawaii	1,263	0.4	42
Idaho	1,393	0.5	39
Illinois	12,714	4.3	5
Indiana	6,238	2.1	14
Iowa	2,954	1.0	30
Kansas	2,736	0.9	33
Kentucky	4,146	1.4	26
Louisiana	4,516	1.5	24
Maine	1,317	0.4	40
Maryland	5,558	1.9	19
Massachusetts	6,417	2.2	13
Michigan	10,113	3.4	8
Minnesota	5,101	1.7	21
Mississippi	2,903	1.0	31
Missouri	5,755	2.0	17
Montana	927	0.3	44
Nebraska	1,747	0.6	38
Nevada	2,335	0.8	35
New Hampshire	1,300	0.4	41
New Jersey	8,699	3.0	10
New Mexico	1,903	0.6	36
New York	19,227	6.5	3
North Carolina	8,541	2.9	11
North Dakota	634	0.2	48
Ohio	11,459	3.9	7
Oklahoma	3,524	1.2	28
Oregon	3,595	1.2	27
Pennsylvania	12,406	4.2	6
Rhode Island	1,081	0.4	43
South Carolina	4,198	1.4	25
South Dakota	771	0.3	46
Tennessee	5,901	2.0	16
Texas	22,490	7.7	2
Utah	2,389	0.8	34
Vermont	621	0.2	49
Virginia	7,460	2.5	12
Washington	6,204	2.1	15
West Virginia	1,815	0.6	37
Wisconsin	5,509	1.9	20
Wyoming	507	0.2	50
50 States	293,102	99.8	
DC	554	0.2	
United States *	293,655	100.0	

**Due to rounding or data sources, the 50-state total plus D.C. may not equal the U.S. total. Please see introduction.*

Rank in order by percentage	
1	California
2	Texas
3	New York
4	Florida
5	Illinois
6	Pennsylvania
7	Ohio
8	Michigan
9	Georgia
10	New Jersey
11	North Carolina
12	Virginia
13	Massachusetts
14	Indiana
15	Washington
16	Tennessee
17	Missouri
18	Arizona
19	Maryland
20	Wisconsin
21	Minnesota
22	Colorado
23	Alabama
24	Louisiana
25	South Carolina
26	Kentucky
27	Oregon
28	Oklahoma
29	Connecticut
30	Iowa
31	Mississippi
32	Arkansas
33	Kansas
34	Utah
35	Nevada
36	New Mexico
37	West Virginia
38	Nebraska
39	Idaho
40	Maine
41	New Hampshire
42	Hawaii
43	Rhode Island
44	Montana
45	Delaware
46	South Dakota
47	Alaska
48	North Dakota
49	Vermont
50	Wyoming

Note: Numbers that appear to be identical are rounded and vary slightly in actual value. The rankings reflect the actual values before rounding. See the introduction for more details.

A-3 Percentage Change in Population, 2003-2004

State	Population 2003 (in thousands)	Percentage change in population 2003–2004	Rank by percentage change
Alabama	4,504	0.59	34
Alaska	648	1.10	17
Arizona	5,579	2.95	2
Arkansas	2,728	0.91	20
California	35,463	1.22	12
Colorado	4,548	1.18	14
Connecticut	3,487	0.48	39
Delaware	818	1.49	8
Florida	16,999	2.34	3
Georgia	8,676	1.76	5
Hawaii	1,249	1.13	16
Idaho	1,367	1.92	4
Illinois	12,649	0.51	36
Indiana	6,200	0.61	33
Iowa	2,942	0.42	40
Kansas	2,725	0.39	42
Kentucky	4,118	0.67	28
Louisiana	4,494	0.49	37
Maine	1,309	0.61	32
Maryland	5,512	0.83	24
Massachusetts	6,420	-0.06	50
Michigan	10,082	0.30	44
Minnesota	5,064	0.73	26
Mississippi	2,883	0.71	27
Missouri	5,719	0.62	31
Montana	918	0.95	19
Nebraska	1,737	0.56	35
Nevada	2,242	4.13	1
New Hampshire	1,289	0.84	23
New Jersey	8,642	0.65	29
New Mexico	1,879	1.32	10
New York	19,212	0.08	49
North Carolina	8,421	1.43	9
North Dakota	633	0.15	48
Ohio	11,438	0.19	47
Oklahoma	3,506	0.49	38
Oregon	3,564	0.85	22
Pennsylvania	12,371	0.29	45
Rhode Island	1,076	0.42	41
South Carolina	4,149	1.19	13
South Dakota	765	0.78	25
Tennessee	5,845	0.95	18
Texas	22,103	1.75	6
Utah	2,352	1.57	7
Vermont	619	0.33	43
Virginia	7,365	1.28	11
Washington	6,131	1.18	15
West Virginia	1,811	0.22	46
Wisconsin	5,474	0.63	30
Wyoming	502	0.88	21
50 States	290,231	0.99	
DC	558	-0.73	
United States	290,789	0.99	

Rank in order by percentage change	
1	Nevada
2	Arizona
3	Florida
4	Idaho
5	Georgia
6	Texas
7	Utah
8	Delaware
9	North Carolina
10	New Mexico
11	Virginia
12	California
13	South Carolina
14	Colorado
15	Washington
16	Hawaii
17	Alaska
18	Tennessee
19	Montana
20	Arkansas
21	Wyoming
22	Oregon
23	New Hampshire
24	Maryland
25	South Dakota
26	Minnesota
27	Mississippi
28	Kentucky
29	New Jersey
30	Wisconsin
31	Missouri
32	Maine
33	Indiana
34	Alabama
35	Nebraska
36	Illinois
37	Louisiana
38	Oklahoma
39	Connecticut
40	Iowa
41	Rhode Island
42	Kansas
43	Vermont
44	Michigan
45	Pennsylvania
46	West Virginia
47	Ohio
48	North Dakota
49	New York
50	Massachusetts

Note: Numbers that appear to be identical are rounded and vary slightly in actual value. The rankings reflect the actual values before rounding. See the introduction for more details.

A-4 Percentage Change in Population, 1994–2004

State	Population 1994 (in thousands)	Percentage change in population 1994–2004	Rank by percentage change
Alabama	4,260	6.3	36
Alaska	603	8.6	22
Arizona	4,245	35.3	2
Arkansas	2,494	10.4	21
California	31,484	14.0	13
Colorado	3,724	23.6	3
Connecticut	3,316	5.7	39
Delaware	718	15.7	10
Florida	14,239	22.2	5
Georgia	7,157	23.4	4
Hawaii	1,188	6.3	35
Idaho	1,145	21.7	7
Illinois	11,913	6.7	31
Indiana	5,794	7.7	27
Iowa	2,851	3.6	46
Kansas	2,581	6.0	37
Kentucky	3,849	7.7	26
Louisiana	4,347	3.9	45
Maine	1,243	6.0	38
Maryland	5,023	10.7	19
Massachusetts	6,095	5.3	43
Michigan	9,598	5.4	42
Minnesota	4,610	10.6	20
Mississippi	2,689	8.0	25
Missouri	5,324	8.1	24
Montana	861	7.6	28
Nebraska	1,639	6.6	32
Nevada	1,499	55.7	1
New Hampshire	1,143	13.7	14
New Jersey	8,014	8.5	23
New Mexico	1,682	13.1	17
New York	18,459	4.2	44
North Carolina	7,187	18.8	9
North Dakota	645	-1.6	50
Ohio	11,152	2.7	47
Oklahoma	3,281	7.4	29
Oregon	3,121	15.2	12
Pennsylvania	12,166	2.0	48
Rhode Island	1,016	6.4	34
South Carolina	3,705	13.3	15
South Dakota	731	5.5	40
Tennessee	5,231	12.8	18
Texas	18,564	21.1	8
Utah	1,960	21.9	6
Vermont	584	6.4	33
Virginia	6,593	13.1	16
Washington	5,375	15.4	11
West Virginia	1,820	-0.3	49
Wisconsin	5,134	7.3	30
Wyoming	480	5.5	41
50 States	262,537	11.6	
DC	589	-6.1	
United States *	263,126	11.6	

**Due to rounding or data sources, the 50-state total plus D.C. may not equal the U.S. total. Please see introduction.*

Rank in order by percentage change	
1	Nevada
2	Arizona
3	Colorado
4	Georgia
5	Florida
6	Utah
7	Idaho
8	Texas
9	North Carolina
10	Delaware
11	Washington
12	Oregon
13	California
14	New Hampshire
15	South Carolina
16	Virginia
17	New Mexico
18	Tennessee
19	Maryland
20	Minnesota
21	Arkansas
22	Alaska
23	New Jersey
24	Missouri
25	Mississippi
26	Kentucky
27	Indiana
28	Montana
29	Oklahoma
30	Wisconsin
31	Illinois
32	Nebraska
33	Vermont
34	Rhode Island
35	Hawaii
36	Alabama
37	Kansas
38	Maine
39	Connecticut
40	South Dakota
41	Wyoming
42	Michigan
43	Massachusetts
44	New York
45	Louisiana
46	Iowa
47	Ohio
48	Pennsylvania
49	West Virginia
50	North Dakota

Note: Numbers that appear to be identical are rounded and vary slightly in actual value. The rankings reflect the actual values before rounding. See the introduction for more details.

A-5 Projected Population, 2015, and Population Change, 2004–2015

State	Projected population 2015 (in thousands)	Percentage change in population 2004–2015	Rank by percentage change
Alabama	4,663	2.9	43
Alaska	733	11.8	13
Arizona	7,495	30.5	2
Arkansas	2,969	7.9	23
California	40,123	11.8	12
Colorado	5,049	9.7	21
Connecticut	3,635	3.8	39
Delaware	927	11.7	15
Florida	21,204	21.9	3
Georgia	10,231	15.9	8
Hawaii	1,386	9.7	20
Idaho	1,630	17.0	6
Illinois	13,097	3.0	42
Indiana	6,518	4.5	34
Iowa	3,026	2.4	45
Kansas	2,853	4.3	35
Kentucky	4,351	5.0	32
Louisiana	4,674	3.5	40
Maine	1,389	5.4	30
Maryland	6,208	11.7	14
Massachusetts	6,759	5.3	31
Michigan	10,599	4.8	33
Minnesota	5,668	11.1	17
Mississippi	3,014	3.8	38
Missouri	6,070	5.5	28
Montana	999	7.8	24
Nebraska	1,789	2.4	46
Nevada	3,058	31.0	1
New Hampshire	1,457	12.1	10
New Jersey	9,256	6.4	27
New Mexico	2,042	7.3	25
New York	19,547	1.7	47
North Carolina	10,011	17.2	5
North Dakota	635	0.1	50
Ohio	11,635	1.5	48
Oklahoma	3,662	3.9	37
Oregon	4,013	11.6	16
Pennsylvania	12,711	2.5	44
Rhode Island	1,140	5.5	29
South Carolina	4,642	10.6	18
South Dakota	797	3.4	41
Tennessee	6,502	10.2	19
Texas	26,586	18.2	4
Utah	2,783	16.5	7
Vermont	673	8.3	22
Virginia	8,467	13.5	9
Washington	6,951	12.0	11
West Virginia	1,823	0.4	49
Wisconsin	5,883	6.8	26
Wyoming	528	4.2	36
50 States	321,859	9.8	
DC	506	-8.5	
United States*	322,366	9.8	

**Due to rounding or data sources, the 50-state total plus D.C. may not equal the U.S. total. Please see introduction.*

Rank in order by percentage change	
1	Nevada
2	Arizona
3	Florida
4	Texas
5	North Carolina
6	Idaho
7	Utah
8	Georgia
9	Virginia
10	New Hampshire
11	Washington
12	California
13	Alaska
14	Maryland
15	Delaware
16	Oregon
17	Minnesota
18	South Carolina
19	Tennessee
20	Hawaii
21	Colorado
22	Vermont
23	Arkansas
24	Montana
25	New Mexico
26	Wisconsin
27	New Jersey
28	Missouri
29	Rhode Island
30	Maine
31	Massachusetts
32	Kentucky
33	Michigan
34	Indiana
35	Kansas
36	Wyoming
37	Oklahoma
38	Mississippi
39	Connecticut
40	Louisiana
41	South Dakota
42	Illinois
43	Alabama
44	Pennsylvania
45	Iowa
46	Nebraska
47	New York
48	Ohio
49	West Virginia
50	North Dakota

Note: Numbers that appear to be identical are rounded and vary slightly in actual value. The rankings reflect the actual values before rounding. See the introduction for more details.

A-6 Projected Population for the Year 2025

State	Estimated 2025 population (in thousands)	Rank
Alabama	4,800	24
Alaska	821	46
Arizona	9,532	12
Arkansas	3,151	32
California	44,305	1
Colorado	5,523	22
Connecticut	3,691	30
Delaware	991	45
Florida	25,912	3
Georgia	11,439	9
Hawaii	1,439	41
Idaho	1,853	37
Illinois	13,341	5
Indiana	6,721	18
Iowa	2,993	34
Kansas	2,919	35
Kentucky	4,490	27
Louisiana	4,762	25
Maine	1,414	42
Maryland	6,763	17
Massachusetts	6,939	16
Michigan	10,714	10
Minnesota	6,109	20
Mississippi	3,069	33
Missouri	6,315	19
Montana	1,037	44
Nebraska	1,813	38
Nevada	3,863	28
New Hampshire	1,586	40
New Jersey	9,637	11
New Mexico	2,107	36
New York	19,540	4
North Carolina	11,449	8
North Dakota	621	49
Ohio	11,606	7
Oklahoma	3,821	29
Oregon	4,536	26
Pennsylvania	12,802	6
Rhode Island	1,158	43
South Carolina	4,990	23
South Dakota	802	47
Tennessee	7,073	15
Texas	30,865	2
Utah	3,226	31
Vermont	703	48
Virginia	9,364	13
Washington	7,996	14
West Virginia	1,766	39
Wisconsin	6,088	21
Wyoming	529	50
50 States	348,984	
DC	455	
United States	349,439	

Rank in order by population	
1	California
2	Texas
3	Florida
4	New York
5	Illinois
6	Pennsylvania
7	Ohio
8	North Carolina
9	Georgia
10	Michigan
11	New Jersey
12	Arizona
13	Virginia
14	Washington
15	Tennessee
16	Massachusetts
17	Maryland
18	Indiana
19	Missouri
20	Minnesota
21	Wisconsin
22	Colorado
23	South Carolina
24	Alabama
25	Louisiana
26	Oregon
27	Kentucky
28	Nevada
29	Oklahoma
30	Connecticut
31	Utah
32	Arkansas
33	Mississippi
34	Iowa
35	Kansas
36	New Mexico
37	Idaho
38	Nebraska
39	West Virginia
40	New Hampshire
41	Hawaii
42	Maine
43	Rhode Island
44	Montana
45	Delaware
46	Alaska
47	South Dakota
48	Vermont
49	North Dakota
50	Wyoming

A-7 Population Age 65 and Over, 2004

State	Population 65 and over (in thousands)	Percentage of population 65 and over	Rank by percentage
Alabama	598	13.2	17
Alaska	42	6.4	50
Arizona	732	12.7	26
Arkansas	381	13.8	9
California	3,823	10.7	45
Colorado	451	9.8	47
Connecticut	474	13.5	12
Delaware	109	13.1	19
Florida	2,928	16.8	1
Georgia	847	9.6	48
Hawaii	172	13.6	11
Idaho	159	11.4	41
Illinois	1,521	12.0	38
Indiana	772	12.4	30
Iowa	433	14.7	5
Kansas	355	13.0	23
Kentucky	519	12.5	27
Louisiana	528	11.7	39
Maine	190	14.4	6
Maryland	635	11.4	40
Massachusetts	854	13.3	13
Michigan	1,247	12.3	31
Minnesota	615	12.1	35
Mississippi	353	12.2	32
Missouri	766	13.3	15
Montana	127	13.7	10
Nebraska	232	13.3	16
Nevada	262	11.2	44
New Hampshire	157	12.1	37
New Jersey	1,126	12.9	24
New Mexico	229	12.1	36
New York	2,493	13.0	22
North Carolina	1,032	12.1	33
North Dakota	93	14.7	4
Ohio	1,525	13.3	14
Oklahoma	464	13.2	18
Oregon	460	12.8	25
Pennsylvania	1,897	15.3	3
Rhode Island	151	13.9	8
South Carolina	520	12.4	29
South Dakota	109	14.2	7
Tennessee	738	12.5	28
Texas	2,217	9.9	46
Utah	208	8.7	49
Vermont	81	13.0	20
Virginia	847	11.4	42
Washington	703	11.3	43
West Virginia	278	15.3	2
Wisconsin	716	13.0	21
Wyoming	61	12.1	34
50 States	36,227	12.4	
DC	67	12.1	
United States	36,294	12.4	

Rank in order by percentage	
1	Florida
2	West Virginia
3	Pennsylvania
4	North Dakota
5	Iowa
6	Maine
7	South Dakota
8	Rhode Island
9	Arkansas
10	Montana
11	Hawaii
12	Connecticut
13	Massachusetts
14	Ohio
15	Missouri
16	Nebraska
17	Alabama
18	Oklahoma
19	Delaware
20	Vermont
21	Wisconsin
22	New York
23	Kansas
24	New Jersey
25	Oregon
26	Arizona
27	Kentucky
28	Tennessee
29	South Carolina
30	Indiana
31	Michigan
32	Mississippi
33	North Carolina
34	Wyoming
35	Minnesota
36	New Mexico
37	New Hampshire
38	Illinois
39	Louisiana
40	Maryland
41	Idaho
42	Virginia
43	Washington
44	Nevada
45	California
46	Texas
47	Colorado
48	Georgia
49	Utah
50	Alaska

Note: Numbers that appear to be identical are rounded and vary slightly in actual value. The rankings reflect the actual values before rounding. See the introduction for more details.

A-8 Population Age 17 and Under, 2004

State	Population 17 and under (in thousands)	Percentage of population 17 and under	Rank by percentage
Alabama	1,095	24.2	28
Alaska	188	28.7	2
Arizona	1,547	26.9	4
Arkansas	677	24.6	22
California	9,596	26.7	5
Colorado	1,179	25.6	13
Connecticut	839	23.9	31
Delaware	194	23.3	39
Florida	4,003	23.0	42
Georgia	2,333	26.4	7
Hawaii	299	23.7	35
Idaho	372	26.7	6
Illinois	3,238	25.5	14
Indiana	1,600	25.7	12
Iowa	680	23.0	41
Kansas	683	25.0	17
Kentucky	980	23.6	36
Louisiana	1,165	25.8	11
Maine	282	21.4	49
Maryland	1,395	25.1	15
Massachusetts	1,464	22.8	44
Michigan	2,533	25.1	16
Minnesota	1,240	24.3	25
Mississippi	750	25.8	10
Missouri	1,385	24.1	29
Montana	208	22.5	46
Nebraska	435	24.9	18
Nevada	604	25.9	9
New Hampshire	305	23.5	38
New Jersey	2,156	24.8	20
New Mexico	492	25.9	8
New York	4,572	23.8	32
North Carolina	2,118	24.8	19
North Dakota	139	21.9	47
Ohio	2,779	24.3	26
Oklahoma	860	24.4	24
Oregon	852	23.7	34
Pennsylvania	2,837	22.9	43
Rhode Island	244	22.6	45
South Carolina	1,025	24.4	23
South Dakota	191	24.8	21
Tennessee	1,391	23.6	37
Texas	6,267	27.9	3
Utah	740	31.0	1
Vermont	135	21.7	48
Virginia	1,805	24.2	27
Washington	1,486	24.0	30
West Virginia	385	21.2	50
Wisconsin	1,308	23.7	33
Wyoming	117	23.1	40
50 States	73,168	25.0	
DC	110	19.8	
United States	73,278	25.0	

Rank in order by percentage	
1	Utah
2	Alaska
3	Texas
4	Arizona
5	California
6	Idaho
7	Georgia
8	New Mexico
9	Nevada
10	Mississippi
11	Louisiana
12	Indiana
13	Colorado
14	Illinois
15	Maryland
16	Michigan
17	Kansas
18	Nebraska
19	North Carolina
20	New Jersey
21	South Dakota
22	Arkansas
23	South Carolina
24	Oklahoma
25	Minnesota
26	Ohio
27	Virginia
28	Alabama
29	Missouri
30	Washington
31	Connecticut
32	New York
33	Wisconsin
34	Oregon
35	Hawaii
36	Kentucky
37	Tennessee
38	New Hampshire
39	Delaware
40	Wyoming
41	Iowa
42	Florida
43	Pennsylvania
44	Massachusetts
45	Rhode Island
46	Montana
47	North Dakota
48	Vermont
49	Maine
50	West Virginia

Note: Numbers that appear to be identical are rounded and vary slightly in actual value. The rankings reflect the actual values before rounding. See the introduction for more details.

A-9 Median Age, 2004

State	Median age 2004	Rank
Alabama	37.0	22
Alaska	33.4	48
Arizona	34.1	46
Arkansas	36.6	29
California	34.2	45
Colorado	34.5	43
Connecticut	38.9	8
Delaware	37.5	16
Florida	39.3	5
Georgia	34.0	47
Hawaii	38.0	13
Idaho	34.3	44
Illinois	35.4	39
Indiana	35.7	38
Iowa	38.0	13
Kansas	36.1	34
Kentucky	37.3	19
Louisiana	35.2	40
Maine	40.7	1
Maryland	36.8	28
Massachusetts	38.1	11
Michigan	36.6	29
Minnesota	36.6	29
Mississippi	34.9	42
Missouri	37.3	19
Montana	39.6	4
Nebraska	36.0	35
Nevada	35.1	41
New Hampshire	39.2	7
New Jersey	37.8	15
New Mexico	35.8	37
New York	37.3	19
North Carolina	36.0	35
North Dakota	38.8	9
Ohio	37.5	16
Oklahoma	36.5	32
Oregon	37.0	22
Pennsylvania	39.3	5
Rhode Island	38.1	11
South Carolina	36.9	26
South Dakota	37.0	22
Tennessee	37.0	22
Texas	32.9	49
Utah	28.0	50
Vermont	40.4	2
Virginia	36.9	26
Washington	36.4	33
West Virginia	40.3	3
Wisconsin	37.5	16
Wyoming	38.4	10
50 States	n/a	
DC	35.8	
United States	36.2	

Rank in order by age	
1	Maine
2	Vermont
3	West Virginia
4	Montana
5	Florida
5	Pennsylvania
7	New Hampshire
8	Connecticut
9	North Dakota
10	Wyoming
11	Massachusetts
11	Rhode Island
13	Hawaii
13	Iowa
15	New Jersey
16	Delaware
16	Ohio
16	Wisconsin
19	Kentucky
19	Missouri
19	New York
22	Alabama
22	Oregon
22	South Dakota
22	Tennessee
26	South Carolina
26	Virginia
28	Maryland
29	Arkansas
29	Michigan
29	Minnesota
32	Oklahoma
33	Washington
34	Kansas
35	Nebraska
35	North Carolina
37	New Mexico
38	Indiana
39	Illinois
40	Louisiana
41	Nevada
42	Mississippi
43	Colorado
44	Idaho
45	California
46	Arizona
47	Georgia
48	Alaska
49	Texas
50	Utah

Note: Ties in ranking reflect ties in actual values.

A-10 African American Population, 2004

State	African American population (in thousands)	Percentage of total population	Rank by percentage of total population
Alabama	1,194	26.4	6
Alaska	24	3.6	34
Arizona	203	3.5	35
Arkansas	434	15.8	12
California	2,437	6.8	26
Colorado	189	4.1	33
Connecticut	352	10.1	21
Delaware	169	20.4	8
Florida	2,726	15.7	13
Georgia	2,613	29.6	3
Hawaii	28	2.2	40
Idaho	8	0.6	49
Illinois	1,926	15.1	14
Indiana	548	8.8	22
Iowa	68	2.3	39
Kansas	161	5.9	30
Kentucky	311	7.5	25
Louisiana	1,492	33.0	2
Maine	10	0.7	46
Maryland	1,615	29.1	5
Massachusetts	435	6.8	27
Michigan	1,451	14.3	16
Minnesota	212	4.1	32
Mississippi	1,069	36.8	1
Missouri	661	11.5	19
Montana	3	0.4	50
Nebraska	75	4.3	31
Nevada	176	7.5	24
New Hampshire	12	0.9	42
New Jersey	1,260	14.5	15
New Mexico	45	2.4	38
New York	3,361	17.5	10
North Carolina	1,861	21.8	7
North Dakota	5	0.7	47
Ohio	1,362	11.9	17
Oklahoma	272	7.7	23
Oregon	64	1.8	41
Pennsylvania	1,304	10.5	20
Rhode Island	66	6.1	28
South Carolina	1,233	29.4	4
South Dakota	6	0.8	45
Tennessee	991	16.8	11
Texas	2,633	11.7	18
Utah	23	0.9	43
Vermont	4	0.6	48
Virginia	1,483	19.9	9
Washington	216	3.5	36
West Virginia	58	3.2	37
Wisconsin	328	5.9	29
Wyoming	4	0.9	44
50 States	37,183	12.7	
DC	319	57.7	
United States	37,502	12.8	

Rank in order by percentage	
1	Mississippi
2	Louisiana
3	Georgia
4	South Carolina
5	Maryland
6	Alabama
7	North Carolina
8	Delaware
9	Virginia
10	New York
11	Tennessee
12	Arkansas
13	Florida
14	Illinois
15	New Jersey
16	Michigan
17	Ohio
18	Texas
19	Missouri
20	Pennsylvania
21	Connecticut
22	Indiana
23	Oklahoma
24	Nevada
25	Kentucky
26	California
27	Massachusetts
28	Rhode Island
29	Wisconsin
30	Kansas
31	Nebraska
32	Minnesota
33	Colorado
34	Alaska
35	Arizona
36	Washington
37	West Virginia
38	New Mexico
39	Iowa
40	Hawaii
41	Oregon
42	New Hampshire
43	Utah
44	Wyoming
45	South Dakota
46	Maine
47	North Dakota
48	Vermont
49	Idaho
50	Montana

Note: Numbers that appear to be identical are rounded and vary slightly in actual value. The rankings reflect the actual values before rounding. See the introduction for more details.

A-11 American Indian Population, 2004

State	American Indian population (in thousands)	Percentage of total population	Rank by percentage
Alabama	23.1	0.5	28
Alaska	103.6	15.8	1
Arizona	288.9	5.0	7
Arkansas	19.6	0.7	21
California	416.6	1.2	16
Colorado	52.3	1.1	17
Connecticut	11.8	0.3	37
Delaware	3.3	0.4	32
Florida	73.6	0.4	31
Georgia	27.5	0.3	40
Hawaii	4.3	0.3	36
Idaho	19.9	1.4	10
Illinois	39.0	0.3	41
Indiana	17.5	0.3	45
Iowa	10.3	0.3	35
Kansas	26.2	1.0	18
Kentucky	9.2	0.2	48
Louisiana	27.3	0.6	23
Maine	7.5	0.6	26
Maryland	17.9	0.3	39
Massachusetts	18.4	0.3	44
Michigan	60.5	0.6	24
Minnesota	59.4	1.2	15
Mississippi	13.4	0.5	29
Missouri	26.5	0.5	30
Montana	59.5	6.4	5
Nebraska	16.6	0.9	19
Nevada	33.0	1.4	11
New Hampshire	3.2	0.2	46
New Jersey	26.6	0.3	42
New Mexico	192.1	10.1	2
New York	103.4	0.5	27
North Carolina	110.2	1.3	14
North Dakota	33.0	5.2	6
Ohio	26.0	0.2	47
Oklahoma	283.8	8.1	4
Oregon	49.1	1.4	12
Pennsylvania	21.9	0.2	50
Rhode Island	6.4	0.6	25
South Carolina	15.7	0.4	34
South Dakota	66.5	8.6	3
Tennessee	17.0	0.3	43
Texas	153.4	0.7	22
Utah	32.2	1.3	13
Vermont	2.3	0.4	33
Virginia	24.3	0.3	38
Washington	101.4	1.6	9
West Virginia	3.7	0.2	49
Wisconsin	51.5	0.9	20
Wyoming	12.2	2.4	8
50 States	2,822.9	1.0	
DC	1.9	0.3	
United States	2,824.8	1.0	

Rank in order by percentage	
1	Alaska
2	New Mexico
3	South Dakota
4	Oklahoma
5	Montana
6	North Dakota
7	Arizona
8	Wyoming
9	Washington
10	Idaho
11	Nevada
12	Oregon
13	Utah
14	North Carolina
15	Minnesota
16	California
17	Colorado
18	Kansas
19	Nebraska
20	Wisconsin
21	Arkansas
22	Texas
23	Louisiana
24	Michigan
25	Rhode Island
26	Maine
27	New York
28	Alabama
29	Mississippi
30	Missouri
31	Florida
32	Delaware
33	Vermont
34	South Carolina
35	Iowa
36	Hawaii
37	Connecticut
38	Virginia
39	Maryland
40	Georgia
41	Illinois
42	New Jersey
43	Tennessee
44	Massachusetts
45	Indiana
46	New Hampshire
47	Ohio
48	Kentucky
49	West Virginia
50	Pennsylvania

Note: Numbers that appear to be identical are rounded and vary slightly in actual value. The rankings reflect the actual values before rounding. See the introduction for more details.

A-12 Asian American Population, 2004

State	Asian American population (in thousands)	Percentage of total population	Rank by percentage
Alabama	36.8	0.8	44
Alaska	29.8	4.5	9
Arizona	122.9	2.1	22
Arkansas	25.9	0.9	41
California	4,326.1	12.1	2
Colorado	116.5	2.5	19
Connecticut	107.8	3.1	15
Delaware	21.5	2.6	18
Florida	352.0	2.0	24
Georgia	229.7	2.6	17
Hawaii	527.5	41.8	1
Idaho	14.2	1.0	39
Illinois	504.6	4.0	11
Indiana	73.0	1.2	37
Iowa	42.4	1.4	31
Kansas	56.9	2.1	23
Kentucky	37.0	0.9	42
Louisiana	61.8	1.4	33
Maine	10.9	0.8	43
Maryland	257.9	4.6	7
Massachusetts	294.7	4.6	8
Michigan	220.0	2.2	20
Minnesota	172.3	3.4	13
Mississippi	21.4	0.7	45
Missouri	74.6	1.3	34
Montana	5.0	0.5	50
Nebraska	26.7	1.5	29
Nevada	128.5	5.5	6
New Hampshire	21.8	1.7	28
New Jersey	607.1	7.0	3
New Mexico	24.0	1.3	35
New York	1,249.2	6.5	4
North Carolina	148.3	1.7	27
North Dakota	4.2	0.7	47
Ohio	159.1	1.4	32
Oklahoma	53.8	1.5	30
Oregon	121.9	3.4	12
Pennsylvania	266.8	2.2	21
Rhode Island	28.8	2.7	16
South Carolina	44.4	1.1	38
South Dakota	5.2	0.7	46
Tennessee	71.1	1.2	36
Texas	718.0	3.2	14
Utah	44.6	1.9	26
Vermont	6.3	1.0	40
Virginia	329.5	4.4	10
Washington	387.8	6.3	5
West Virginia	10.2	0.6	49
Wisconsin	105.8	1.9	25
Wyoming	3.3	0.6	48
50 States	12,309.4	4.2	
DC	16.8	3.0	
United States	12,326.2	4.2	

Rank in order by percentage	
1	Hawaii
2	California
3	New Jersey
4	New York
5	Washington
6	Nevada
7	Maryland
8	Massachusetts
9	Alaska
10	Virginia
11	Illinois
12	Oregon
13	Minnesota
14	Texas
15	Connecticut
16	Rhode Island
17	Georgia
18	Delaware
19	Colorado
20	Michigan
21	Pennsylvania
22	Arizona
23	Kansas
24	Florida
25	Wisconsin
26	Utah
27	North Carolina
28	New Hampshire
29	Nebraska
30	Oklahoma
31	Iowa
32	Ohio
33	Louisiana
34	Missouri
35	New Mexico
36	Tennessee
37	Indiana
38	South Carolina
39	Idaho
40	Vermont
41	Arkansas
42	Kentucky
43	Maine
44	Alabama
45	Mississippi
46	South Dakota
47	North Dakota
48	Wyoming
49	West Virginia
50	Montana

Note: Numbers that appear to be identical are rounded and vary slightly in actual value. The rankings reflect the actual values before rounding. See the introduction for more details.

A-13 Hispanic Population, 2004

State	Hispanic population (in thousands)	Percentage of total population	Rank by percentage
Alabama	98.4	2.2	42
Alaska	32.4	4.9	28
Arizona	1,608.7	28.0	4
Arkansas	120.8	4.4	29
California	12,442.6	34.7	2
Colorado	878.8	19.1	6
Connecticut	371.8	10.6	11
Delaware	48.2	5.8	25
Florida	3,304.8	19.0	7
Georgia	598.3	6.8	21
Hawaii	99.8	7.9	18
Idaho	123.9	8.9	15
Illinois	1,774.6	14.0	10
Indiana	269.3	4.3	30
Iowa	104.1	3.5	34
Kansas	220.3	8.1	17
Kentucky	77.1	1.9	45
Louisiana	124.2	2.8	38
Maine	12.5	0.9	49
Maryland	297.7	5.4	27
Massachusetts	494.2	7.7	19
Michigan	375.0	3.7	33
Minnesota	179.3	3.5	35
Mississippi	49.1	1.7	46
Missouri	148.2	2.6	39
Montana	21.8	2.4	40
Nebraska	120.0	6.9	20
Nevada	531.9	22.8	5
New Hampshire	27.5	2.1	43
New Jersey	1,294.4	14.9	9
New Mexico	823.4	43.3	1
New York	3,076.7	16.0	8
North Carolina	517.6	6.1	24
North Dakota	9.8	1.5	47
Ohio	252.3	2.2	41
Oklahoma	223.0	6.3	23
Oregon	343.3	9.5	14
Pennsylvania	475.6	3.8	32
Rhode Island	111.8	10.3	13
South Carolina	130.4	3.1	36
South Dakota	15.1	2.0	44
Tennessee	167.0	2.8	37
Texas	7,781.2	34.6	3
Utah	253.1	10.6	12
Vermont	6.4	1.0	48
Virginia	426.2	5.7	26
Washington	526.7	8.5	16
West Virginia	14.6	0.8	50
Wisconsin	237.2	4.3	31
Wyoming	33.8	6.7	22
50 States	41,274.8	14.1	
DC	47.3	8.5	
United States	41,322.1	14.1	

Rank in order by percentage	
1	New Mexico
2	California
3	Texas
4	Arizona
5	Nevada
6	Colorado
7	Florida
8	New York
9	New Jersey
10	Illinois
11	Connecticut
12	Utah
13	Rhode Island
14	Oregon
15	Idaho
16	Washington
17	Kansas
18	Hawaii
19	Massachusetts
20	Nebraska
21	Georgia
22	Wyoming
23	Oklahoma
24	North Carolina
25	Delaware
26	Virginia
27	Maryland
28	Alaska
29	Arkansas
30	Indiana
31	Wisconsin
32	Pennsylvania
33	Michigan
34	Iowa
35	Minnesota
36	South Carolina
37	Tennessee
38	Louisiana
39	Missouri
40	Montana
41	Ohio
42	Alabama
43	New Hampshire
44	South Dakota
45	Kentucky
46	Mississippi
47	North Dakota
48	Vermont
49	Maine
50	West Virginia

Note: Numbers that appear to be identical are rounded and vary slightly in actual value. The rankings reflect the actual values before rounding. See the introduction for more details.

A-14 White (Non-Hispanic) Population, 2004

State	White population (in thousands)	Percentage of total population	Rank by percentage
Alabama	3,148	69.5	32
Alaska	438	66.9	35
Arizona	3,510	61.1	42
Arkansas	2,126	77.2	27
California	15,982	44.5	48
Colorado	3,334	72.5	30
Connecticut	2,658	75.9	28
Delaware	583	70.2	31
Florida	10,920	62.8	39
Georgia	5,319	60.2	44
Hawaii	295	23.3	50
Idaho	1,215	87.2	10
Illinois	8,414	66.2	36
Indiana	5,280	84.6	15
Iowa	2,710	91.7	5
Kansas	2,239	81.9	21
Kentucky	3,678	88.7	8
Louisiana	2,789	61.8	40
Maine	1,266	96.1	1
Maryland	3,325	59.8	46
Massachusetts	5,181	80.8	22
Michigan	7,896	78.1	25
Minnesota	4,421	86.7	12
Mississippi	1,739	59.9	45
Missouri	4,781	83.1	18
Montana	826	89.1	7
Nebraska	1,497	85.7	14
Nevada	1,429	61.2	41
New Hampshire	1,225	94.3	4
New Jersey	5,549	63.8	38
New Mexico	827	43.5	49
New York	11,746	61.1	43
North Carolina	5,861	68.6	34
North Dakota	578	91.1	6
Ohio	9,547	83.3	17
Oklahoma	2,570	72.9	29
Oregon	2,948	82.0	20
Pennsylvania	10,288	82.9	19
Rhode Island	870	80.5	23
South Carolina	2,753	65.6	37
South Dakota	671	87.1	11
Tennessee	4,611	78.1	24
Texas	11,190	49.8	47
Utah	2,003	83.8	16
Vermont	597	96.0	2
Virginia	5,122	68.7	33
Washington	4,809	77.5	26
West Virginia	1,714	94.4	3
Wisconsin	4,749	86.2	13
Wyoming	449	88.6	9
50 States	197,673	67.4	
DC	168	30.3	
United States	197,841	67.4	

Rank in order by percentage	
1	Maine
2	Vermont
3	West Virginia
4	New Hampshire
5	Iowa
6	North Dakota
7	Montana
8	Kentucky
9	Wyoming
10	Idaho
11	South Dakota
12	Minnesota
13	Wisconsin
14	Nebraska
15	Indiana
16	Utah
17	Ohio
18	Missouri
19	Pennsylvania
20	Oregon
21	Kansas
22	Massachusetts
23	Rhode Island
24	Tennessee
25	Michigan
26	Washington
27	Arkansas
28	Connecticut
29	Oklahoma
30	Colorado
31	Delaware
32	Alabama
33	Virginia
34	North Carolina
35	Alaska
36	Illinois
37	South Carolina
38	New Jersey
39	Florida
40	Louisiana
41	Nevada
42	Arizona
43	New York
44	Georgia
45	Mississippi
46	Maryland
47	Texas
48	California
49	New Mexico
50	Hawaii

Note: Numbers that appear to be identical are rounded and vary slightly in actual value. The rankings reflect the actual values before rounding. See the introduction for more details.

A-15 Mixed-Race Population, 2004

State	Mixed-race population (in thousands)	Percentage of total population	Rank by percentage
Alabama	39.4	0.9	46
Alaska	30.8	4.7	2
Arizona	85.7	1.5	12
Arkansas	32.0	1.2	30
California	855.0	2.4	6
Colorado	82.5	1.8	8
Connecticut	46.1	1.3	20
Delaware	10.8	1.3	22
Florida	209.0	1.2	28
Georgia	89.5	1.0	36
Hawaii	253.8	20.1	1
Idaho	18.6	1.3	19
Illinois	134.8	1.1	33
Indiana	66.2	1.1	32
Iowa	26.2	0.9	45
Kansas	44.5	1.6	9
Kentucky	39.9	1.0	39
Louisiana	36.7	0.8	49
Maine	11.9	0.9	44
Maryland	80.8	1.5	14
Massachusetts	82.6	1.3	23
Michigan	145.6	1.4	17
Minnesota	71.5	1.4	18
Mississippi	18.0	0.6	50
Missouri	72.8	1.3	24
Montana	13.9	1.5	11
Nebraska	18.9	1.1	31
Nevada	58.0	2.5	5
New Hampshire	12.1	0.9	42
New Jersey	108.3	1.2	25
New Mexico	27.6	1.5	16
New York	279.3	1.5	15
North Carolina	83.5	1.0	38
North Dakota	6.0	0.9	40
Ohio	139.6	1.2	27
Oklahoma	140.4	4.0	3
Oregon	83.2	2.3	7
Pennsylvania	114.7	0.9	43
Rhode Island	15.8	1.5	13
South Carolina	34.9	0.8	47
South Dakota	9.1	1.2	29
Tennessee	55.7	0.9	41
Texas	235.4	1.0	35
Utah	31.3	1.3	21
Vermont	6.6	1.1	34
Virginia	115.2	1.5	10
Washington	180.0	2.9	4
West Virginia	15.1	0.8	48
Wisconsin	55.5	1.0	37
Wyoming	6.2	1.2	26
50 States	4,430.7	1.5	
DC	8.1	1.5	
United States	4,438.8	1.5	

Rank in order by percentage	
1	Hawaii
2	Alaska
3	Oklahoma
4	Washington
5	Nevada
6	California
7	Oregon
8	Colorado
9	Kansas
10	Virginia
11	Montana
12	Arizona
13	Rhode Island
14	Maryland
15	New York
16	New Mexico
17	Michigan
18	Minnesota
19	Idaho
20	Connecticut
21	Utah
22	Delaware
23	Massachusetts
24	Missouri
25	New Jersey
26	Wyoming
27	Ohio
28	Florida
29	South Dakota
30	Arkansas
31	Nebraska
32	Indiana
33	Illinois
34	Vermont
35	Texas
36	Georgia
37	Wisconsin
38	North Carolina
39	Kentucky
40	North Dakota
41	Tennessee
42	New Hampshire
43	Pennsylvania
44	Maine
45	Iowa
46	Alabama
47	South Carolina
48	West Virginia
49	Louisiana
50	Mississippi

Note: Numbers that appear to be identical are rounded and vary slightly in actual value. The rankings reflect the actual values before rounding. See the introduction for more details.

A-16 Population in Poverty, 2004

State	Population in poverty (in thousands)	Percentage of population in poverty	Rank by percentage
Alabama	763	16.9	3
Alaska	59	9.2	43
Arizona	830	14.4	12
Arkansas	412	15.1	8
California	4,743	13.3	16
Colorado	450	10.0	34
Connecticut	348	10.0	34
Delaware	75	9.1	45
Florida	2,026	11.6	23
Georgia	1,139	13.1	18
Hawaii	105	8.4	46
Idaho	136	9.9	36
Illinois	1,534	12.2	20
Indiana	712	11.6	23
Iowa	314	10.8	32
Kansas	304	11.4	29
Kentucky	719	17.7	2
Louisiana	737	16.7	4
Maine	150	11.6	23
Maryland	545	9.8	39
Massachusetts	586	9.2	43
Michigan	1,320	13.3	16
Minnesota	358	7.0	49
Mississippi	532	18.6	1
Missouri	687	12.2	20
Montana	128	14.1	14
Nebraska	163	9.4	41
Nevada	259	10.9	31
New Hampshire	70	5.4	50
New Jersey	692	8.0	47
New Mexico	313	16.5	5
New York	2,844	15.0	9
North Carolina	1,226	14.6	11
North Dakota	61	9.7	40
Ohio	1,310	11.6	23
Oklahoma	372	10.8	32
Oregon	419	11.7	22
Pennsylvania	1,374	11.3	30
Rhode Island	121	11.5	27
South Carolina	614	14.9	10
South Dakota	101	13.4	15
Tennessee	929	15.9	7
Texas	3,674	16.5	5
Utah	236	9.9	36
Vermont	48	7.9	48
Virginia	689	9.3	42
Washington	701	11.5	27
West Virginia	254	14.2	13
Wisconsin	673	12.3	19
Wyoming	49	9.9	36
50 States	36,904	12.6	
DC	91	16.7	
United States*	36,997	12.7	

**Due to rounding or data sources, the 50-state total plus D.C. may not equal the U.S. total. Please see introduction.*

Rank in order by percentage	
1	Mississippi
2	Kentucky
3	Alabama
4	Louisiana
5	New Mexico
5	Texas
7	Tennessee
8	Arkansas
9	New York
10	South Carolina
11	North Carolina
12	Arizona
13	West Virginia
14	Montana
15	South Dakota
16	California
16	Michigan
18	Georgia
19	Wisconsin
20	Illinois
20	Missouri
22	Oregon
23	Florida
23	Indiana
23	Maine
23	Ohio
27	Rhode Island
27	Washington
29	Kansas
30	Pennsylvania
31	Nevada
32	Iowa
32	Oklahoma
34	Colorado
34	Connecticut
36	Idaho
36	Utah
36	Wyoming
39	Maryland
40	North Dakota
41	Nebraska
42	Virginia
43	Alaska
43	Massachusetts
45	Delaware
46	Hawaii
47	New Jersey
48	Vermont
49	Minnesota
50	New Hampshire

Note: Ties in ranking reflect ties in actual values.

A-17 Number and Rate of Children in Poverty, 2004

State	Number of persons under 18 in poverty (in thousands)	Percentage in poverty	Rank by percentage
Alabama	264	24.2	2
Alaska	22	12.0	40
Arizona	330	21.1	8
Arkansas	149	21.8	6
California	1,812	19.0	15
Colorado	136	11.7	41
Connecticut	102	12.2	38
Delaware	25	13.0	33
Florida	681	17.0	25
Georgia	464	19.9	12
Hawaii	27	9.6	47
Idaho	48	12.5	37
Illinois	579	18.0	19
Indiana	293	18.5	17
Iowa	87	12.8	36
Kansas	106	15.6	28
Kentucky	232	23.8	3
Louisiana	237	20.6	10
Maine	39	14.0	31
Maryland	152	11.0	43
Massachusetts	150	10.1	46
Michigan	483	19.3	13
Minnesota	112	9.0	48
Mississippi	203	26.6	1
Missouri	249	17.7	22
Montana	35	16.5	26
Nebraska	45	10.2	45
Nevada	85	13.8	32
New Hampshire	23	7.4	50
New Jersey	184	8.4	49
New Mexico	115	23.4	4
New York	969	21.3	7
North Carolina	410	19.2	14
North Dakota	17	12.1	39
Ohio	478	17.1	24
Oklahoma	120	14.1	30
Oregon	132	15.6	28
Pennsylvania	484	17.2	23
Rhode Island	46	18.3	18
South Carolina	217	21.0	9
South Dakota	35	18.6	16
Tennessee	284	20.4	11
Texas	1,452	23.2	5
Utah	100	12.9	35
Vermont	14	10.3	44
Virginia	213	11.7	41
Washington	239	15.8	27
West Virginia	70	18.0	19
Wisconsin	234	18.0	19
Wyoming	15	13.0	33
50 States	12,998	17.8	
DC	31	27.3	
United States*	13,027	17.8	

**Due to rounding or data sources, the 50-state total plus D.C. may not equal the U.S. total. Please see introduction.*

Rank in order by percentage	
1	Mississippi
2	Alabama
3	Kentucky
4	New Mexico
5	Texas
6	Arkansas
7	New York
8	Arizona
9	South Carolina
10	Louisiana
11	Tennessee
12	Georgia
13	Michigan
14	North Carolina
15	California
16	South Dakota
17	Indiana
18	Rhode Island
19	Illinois
19	West Virginia
19	Wisconsin
22	Missouri
23	Pennsylvania
24	Ohio
25	Florida
26	Montana
27	Washington
28	Kansas
28	Oregon
30	Oklahoma
31	Maine
32	Nevada
33	Delaware
33	Wyoming
35	Utah
36	Iowa
37	Idaho
38	Connecticut
39	North Dakota
40	Alaska
41	Colorado
41	Virginia
43	Maryland
44	Vermont
45	Nebraska
46	Massachusetts
47	Hawaii
48	Minnesota
49	New Jersey
50	New Hampshire

Note: Ties in ranking reflect ties in actual values.

A-18 Female and Male Populations, 2004

State	Female population (in thousands)	Male population (in thousands)	Female population as a percentage of total population	Rank by percentage female
Alabama	2,334	2,196	51.5	6
Alaska	317	339	48.3	50
Arizona	2,870	2,874	50.0	44
Arkansas	1,404	1,349	51.0	18
California	17,980	17,914	50.1	42
Colorado	2,280	2,322	49.5	48
Connecticut	1,803	1,700	51.5	7
Delaware	426	405	51.3	13
Florida	8,873	8,524	51.0	19
Georgia	4,464	4,365	50.6	32
Hawaii	633	630	50.1	41
Idaho	695	699	49.9	45
Illinois	6,470	6,243	50.9	21
Indiana	3,169	3,069	50.8	25
Iowa	1,500	1,454	50.8	28
Kansas	1,377	1,358	50.3	35
Kentucky	2,112	2,034	50.9	20
Louisiana	2,322	2,194	51.4	9
Maine	674	643	51.2	14
Maryland	2,867	2,691	51.6	4
Massachusetts	3,310	3,106	51.6	3
Michigan	5,144	4,969	50.9	22
Minnesota	2,569	2,532	50.4	34
Mississippi	1,494	1,409	51.5	8
Missouri	2,944	2,811	51.2	15
Montana	465	462	50.1	39
Nebraska	884	864	50.6	31
Nevada	1,146	1,189	49.1	49
New Hampshire	659	641	50.7	29
New Jersey	4,463	4,236	51.3	10
New Mexico	967	936	50.8	24
New York	9,923	9,305	51.6	2
North Carolina	4,342	4,199	50.8	23
North Dakota	318	317	50.1	43
Ohio	5,878	5,581	51.3	11
Oklahoma	1,783	1,740	50.6	30
Oregon	1,808	1,787	50.3	36
Pennsylvania	6,393	6,014	51.5	5
Rhode Island	559	521	51.8	1
South Carolina	2,153	2,045	51.3	12
South Dakota	388	383	50.3	37
Tennessee	3,015	2,886	51.1	17
Texas	11,289	11,201	50.2	38
Utah	1,190	1,199	49.8	46
Vermont	316	306	50.8	26
Virginia	3,788	3,671	50.8	27
Washington	3,109	3,094	50.1	40
West Virginia	928	887	51.1	16
Wisconsin	2,782	2,727	50.5	33
Wyoming	251	255	49.6	47
50 States	148,826	144,276	50.8	
DC	292	262	52.7	
United States	149,118	144,537	50.8	

Rank in order by percentage female	
1	Rhode Island
2	New York
3	Massachusetts
4	Maryland
5	Pennsylvania
6	Alabama
7	Connecticut
8	Mississippi
9	Louisiana
10	New Jersey
11	Ohio
12	South Carolina
13	Delaware
14	Maine
15	Missouri
16	West Virginia
17	Tennessee
18	Arkansas
19	Florida
20	Kentucky
21	Illinois
22	Michigan
23	North Carolina
24	New Mexico
25	Indiana
26	Vermont
27	Virginia
28	Iowa
29	New Hampshire
30	Oklahoma
31	Nebraska
32	Georgia
33	Wisconsin
34	Minnesota
35	Kansas
36	Oregon
37	South Dakota
38	Texas
39	Montana
40	Washington
41	Hawaii
42	California
43	North Dakota
44	Arizona
45	Idaho
46	Utah
47	Wyoming
48	Colorado
49	Nevada
50	Alaska

Note: Numbers that appear to be identical are rounded and vary slightly in actual value. The rankings reflect the actual values before rounding. See the introduction for more details.

A-19 Birth Rates, 2003

State	Births per 1,000 population	Rank
Alabama	13.2	32
Alaska	15.5	6
Arizona	16.3	3
Arkansas	13.9	21
California	15.2	7
Colorado	15.2	7
Connecticut	12.3	44
Delaware	13.9	21
Florida	12.5	41
Georgia	15.7	5
Hawaii	14.4	16
Idaho	16.0	4
Illinois	14.4	16
Indiana	14.0	20
Iowa	13.0	36
Kansas	14.5	13
Kentucky	13.4	29
Louisiana	14.5	13
Maine	10.6	49
Maryland	13.6	25
Massachusetts	12.5	41
Michigan	13.0	36
Minnesota	13.8	23
Mississippi	14.7	12
Missouri	13.5	26
Montana	12.4	43
Nebraska	14.9	10
Nevada	15.0	9
New Hampshire	11.2	48
New Jersey	13.5	26
New Mexico	14.8	11
New York	13.2	32
North Carolina	14.1	19
North Dakota	12.6	40
Ohio	13.1	34
Oklahoma	14.5	13
Oregon	12.9	38
Pennsylvania	11.8	46
Rhode Island	12.3	44
South Carolina	13.4	29
South Dakota	14.4	16
Tennessee	13.5	26
Texas	17.1	2
Utah	21.2	1
Vermont	10.6	49
Virginia	13.7	24
Washington	13.1	34
West Virginia	11.6	47
Wisconsin	12.8	39
Wyoming	13.4	29
50 States	n/a	
DC	13.5	
United States	14.1	

Rank in order by rate	
1	Utah
2	Texas
3	Arizona
4	Idaho
5	Georgia
6	Alaska
7	California
7	Colorado
9	Nevada
10	Nebraska
11	New Mexico
12	Mississippi
13	Kansas
13	Louisiana
13	Oklahoma
16	Hawaii
16	Illinois
16	South Dakota
19	North Carolina
20	Indiana
21	Arkansas
21	Delaware
23	Minnesota
24	Virginia
25	Maryland
26	Missouri
26	New Jersey
26	Tennessee
29	Kentucky
29	South Carolina
29	Wyoming
32	Alabama
32	New York
34	Ohio
34	Washington
36	Iowa
36	Michigan
38	Oregon
39	Wisconsin
40	North Dakota
41	Florida
41	Massachusetts
43	Montana
44	Connecticut
44	Rhode Island
46	Pennsylvania
47	West Virginia
48	New Hampshire
49	Maine
49	Vermont

Note: Ties in ranking reflect ties in actual values.

A-20 Death Rates (age-adjusted), 2003

State	Deaths per 100,000 population	Rank
Alabama	1,001.9	3
Alaska	831.3	23
Arizona	788.9	33
Arkansas	937.6	9
California	n/a	n/a
Colorado	785.3	35
Connecticut	729.5	46
Delaware	844.3	22
Florida	775.7	39
Georgia	946.4	8
Hawaii	650.1	48
Idaho	797.5	29
Illinois	n/a	n/a
Indiana	898.1	14
Iowa	769.0	41
Kansas	824.0	26
Kentucky	976.9	6
Louisiana	1,007.4	2
Maine	821.9	27
Maryland	852.9	17
Massachusetts	778.8	37
Michigan	850.3	20
Minnesota	713.4	47
Mississippi	1,015.2	1
Missouri	902.4	13
Montana	828.3	24
Nebraska	790.6	31
Nevada	925.0	11
New Hampshire	748.4	45
New Jersey	794.7	30
New Mexico	827.7	25
New York	759.8	44
North Carolina	906.8	12
North Dakota	767.5	42
Ohio	886.2	15
Oklahoma	973.9	7
Oregon	808.9	28
Pennsylvania	849.1	21
Rhode Island	786.6	34
South Carolina	934.8	10
South Dakota	790.5	32
Tennessee	982.1	5
Texas	857.2	16
Utah	782.1	36
Vermont	764.1	43
Virginia	852.8	18
Washington	776.6	38
West Virginia	994.5	4
Wisconsin	772.3	40
Wyoming	850.6	19
50 States	n/a	
DC	968.2	
United States	831.2	

Rank in order by rate	
1	Mississippi
2	Louisiana
3	Alabama
4	West Virginia
5	Tennessee
6	Kentucky
7	Oklahoma
8	Georgia
9	Arkansas
10	South Carolina
11	Nevada
12	North Carolina
13	Missouri
14	Indiana
15	Ohio
16	Texas
17	Maryland
18	Virginia
19	Wyoming
20	Michigan
21	Pennsylvania
22	Delaware
23	Alaska
24	Montana
25	New Mexico
26	Kansas
27	Maine
28	Oregon
29	Idaho
30	New Jersey
31	Nebraska
32	South Dakota
33	Arizona
34	Rhode Island
35	Colorado
36	Utah
37	Massachusetts
38	Washington
39	Florida
40	Wisconsin
41	Iowa
42	North Dakota
43	Vermont
44	New York
45	New Hampshire
46	Connecticut
47	Minnesota
48	Hawaii

A-21 Population Density, 2004

State	Persons per square mile	Rank
Alabama	89	26
Alaska	1	50
Arizona	51	36
Arkansas	53	34
California	230	11
Colorado	44	37
Connecticut	723	4
Delaware	425	6
Florida	323	8
Georgia	152	18
Hawaii	197	13
Idaho	17	44
Illinois	229	12
Indiana	174	17
Iowa	53	33
Kansas	33	40
Kentucky	104	22
Louisiana	104	23
Maine	43	38
Maryland	569	5
Massachusetts	818	3
Michigan	178	15
Minnesota	64	31
Mississippi	62	32
Missouri	84	28
Montana	6	48
Nebraska	23	42
Nevada	21	43
New Hampshire	145	19
New Jersey	1,173	1
New Mexico	16	45
New York	407	7
North Carolina	175	16
North Dakota	9	47
Ohio	280	9
Oklahoma	51	35
Oregon	37	39
Pennsylvania	277	10
Rhode Island	1,034	2
South Carolina	139	21
South Dakota	10	46
Tennessee	143	20
Texas	86	27
Utah	29	41
Vermont	67	30
Virginia	188	14
Washington	93	25
West Virginia	75	29
Wisconsin	101	24
Wyoming	5	49
50 States	83	
DC	9,074	
United States	83	

Rank in order by density	
1	New Jersey
2	Rhode Island
3	Massachusetts
4	Connecticut
5	Maryland
6	Delaware
7	New York
8	Florida
9	Ohio
10	Pennsylvania
11	California
12	Illinois
13	Hawaii
14	Virginia
15	Michigan
16	North Carolina
17	Indiana
18	Georgia
19	New Hampshire
20	Tennessee
21	South Carolina
22	Kentucky
23	Louisiana
24	Wisconsin
25	Washington
26	Alabama
27	Texas
28	Missouri
29	West Virginia
30	Vermont
31	Minnesota
32	Mississippi
33	Iowa
34	Arkansas
35	Oklahoma
36	Arizona
37	Colorado
38	Maine
39	Oregon
40	Kansas
41	Utah
42	Nebraska
43	Nevada
44	Idaho
45	New Mexico
46	South Dakota
47	North Dakota
48	Montana
49	Wyoming
50	Alaska

Note: Numbers that appear to be identical are rounded and vary slightly in actual value. The rankings reflect the actual values before rounding. See the introduction for more details.

A-22 Legal Immigrants Admitted, FY 2004

State	Legal immigrants admitted	Percentage of total legal immigrants admitted	Rank by number of legal immigrants
Alabama	2,139	0.2	40
Alaska	1,219	0.1	44
Arizona	19,297	2.0	11
Arkansas	2,251	0.2	37
California	252,920	26.7	1
Colorado	10,923	1.2	18
Connecticut	12,138	1.3	15
Delaware	1,671	0.2	41
Florida	75,644	8.0	4
Georgia	16,286	1.7	14
Hawaii	6,347	0.7	23
Idaho	2,229	0.2	38
Illinois	46,314	4.9	6
Indiana	5,929	0.6	24
Iowa	3,984	0.4	29
Kansas	4,041	0.4	28
Kentucky	3,624	0.4	31
Louisiana	2,998	0.3	34
Maine	1,264	0.1	42
Maryland	20,253	2.1	9
Massachusetts	27,676	2.9	7
Michigan	18,334	1.9	12
Minnesota	11,708	1.2	16
Mississippi	1,252	0.1	43
Missouri	6,782	0.7	22
Montana	419	0.0	49
Nebraska	2,954	0.3	35
Nevada	8,758	0.9	20
New Hampshire	2,198	0.2	39
New Jersey	50,303	5.3	5
New Mexico	3,024	0.3	33
New York	102,390	10.8	2
North Carolina	10,718	1.1	19
North Dakota	578	0.1	48
Ohio	11,599	1.2	17
Oklahoma	3,506	0.4	32
Oregon	8,389	0.9	21
Pennsylvania	18,232	1.9	13
Rhode Island	3,689	0.4	30
South Carolina	2,496	0.3	36
South Dakota	727	0.1	46
Tennessee	5,620	0.6	25
Texas	91,799	9.7	3
Utah	4,255	0.4	27
Vermont	790	0.1	45
Virginia	21,695	2.3	8
Washington	19,442	2.1	10
West Virginia	583	0.1	47
Wisconsin	5,257	0.6	26
Wyoming	295	0.0	50
50 States	936,939	99.0	
DC	2,110	0.2	
United States*	946,142	100.0	

**Due to rounding or data sources, the 50-state total plus D.C. may not equal the U.S. total. Please see introduction.*

Rank in order by number	
1	California
2	New York
3	Texas
4	Florida
5	New Jersey
6	Illinois
7	Massachusetts
8	Virginia
9	Maryland
10	Washington
11	Arizona
12	Michigan
13	Pennsylvania
14	Georgia
15	Connecticut
16	Minnesota
17	Ohio
18	Colorado
19	North Carolina
20	Nevada
21	Oregon
22	Missouri
23	Hawaii
24	Indiana
25	Tennessee
26	Wisconsin
27	Utah
28	Kansas
29	Iowa
30	Rhode Island
31	Kentucky
32	Oklahoma
33	New Mexico
34	Louisiana
35	Nebraska
36	South Carolina
37	Arkansas
38	Idaho
39	New Hampshire
40	Alabama
41	Delaware
42	Maine
43	Mississippi
44	Alaska
45	Vermont
46	South Dakota
47	West Virginia
48	North Dakota
49	Montana
50	Wyoming

A-23 Unauthorized Immigrant Population, 2000

State	Unauthorized immigrant population (in thousands)	Percentage of total unauthorized immigrant population	Rank by number of unauthorized immigrants
Alabama	24	0.3	31
Alaska	5	0.1	40
Arizona	283	4.0	6
Arkansas	27	0.4	30
California	2,209	31.6	1
Colorado	144	2.1	10
Connecticut	39	0.6	27
Delaware	10	0.1	38
Florida	337	4.8	5
Georgia	228	3.3	7
Hawaii	2	n/a	42
Idaho	19	0.3	35
Illinois	432	6.2	4
Indiana	45	0.6	24
Iowa	24	0.3	31
Kansas	47	0.7	21
Kentucky	15	0.2	37
Louisiana	5	0.1	40
Maine	<2	n/a	43
Maryland	56	0.8	19
Massachusetts	87	1.2	15
Michigan	70	1.0	16
Minnesota	60	0.9	18
Mississippi	8	0.1	39
Missouri	22	0.3	34
Montana	<2	n/a	43
Nebraska	24	0.3	31
Nevada	101	1.4	13
New Hampshire	<2	n/a	43
New Jersey	221	3.2	8
New Mexico	39	0.6	27
New York	489	7.0	3
North Carolina	206	2.9	9
North Dakota	<2	n/a	43
Ohio	40	0.6	26
Oklahoma	46	0.7	22
Oregon	90	1.3	14
Pennsylvania	49	0.7	20
Rhode Island	16	0.2	36
South Carolina	36	0.5	29
South Dakota	<2	n/a	43
Tennessee	46	0.7	22
Texas	1,041	14.9	2
Utah	65	0.9	17
Vermont	<2	n/a	43
Virginia	103	1.5	12
Washington	136	1.9	11
West Virginia	<2	n/a	43
Wisconsin	41	0.6	25
Wyoming	<2	n/a	43
50 States	6,987	99.8	
DC	7	0.1	
United States*	7,000	100.0	

**Due to rounding or data sources, the 50-state total plus D.C. may not equal the U.S. total. Please see introduction.*

Rank in order by number	
1	California
2	Texas
3	New York
4	Illinois
5	Florida
6	Arizona
7	Georgia
8	New Jersey
9	North Carolina
10	Colorado
11	Washington
12	Virginia
13	Nevada
14	Oregon
15	Massachusetts
16	Michigan
17	Utah
18	Minnesota
19	Maryland
20	Pennsylvania
21	Kansas
22	Oklahoma
22	Tennessee
24	Indiana
25	Wisconsin
26	Ohio
27	Connecticut
27	New Mexico
29	South Carolina
30	Arkansas
31	Alabama
31	Iowa
31	Nebraska
34	Missouri
35	Idaho
36	Rhode Island
37	Kentucky
38	Delaware
39	Mississippi
40	Alaska
40	Louisiana
42	Hawaii
43	Maine
43	Montana
43	New Hampshire
43	North Dakota
43	South Dakota
43	Vermont
43	West Virginia
43	Wyoming

Note: Ties in ranking reflect ties in actual values.

Source Notes for Population (Section A)

A-1 Population and Percentage Distribution, 2005: The U.S. population is counted once every decade in years ending in zero. The last such count was in 2000. For all other years, the U.S. Census Bureau prepares estimates for July 1 of each year. The 2005 estimates were released on December 21, 2005 as Table NST-EST2005-01-Annual Estimates of the Population: April 1, 2000 to July 1, 2005 and are available on the bureau's Web site (www.census.gov). Outside experts and the Census Bureau agree that the census undercounts the nation's population and that this undercount tends to be concentrated in low-income areas in major cities. The understatement of population is greatest for these communities and the states that contain them. Because population estimates are used to determine representation in Congress and how much state and local governments get from federal aid programs, some states and cities have gone to court seeking to force the federal government to use more correct estimates. In the past, the Census Bureau successfully resisted these challenges because, while it agrees the official count is inaccurate, it does not know what data might be substituted for that count.

A-2 Population and Percentage Distribution, 2004: This data is similar to the data in Table A-1 but reflects state population estimates in 2004. The numbers were released on the U.S. Census Bureau Web site (www.census.gov) on December 22, 2004 as NST-EST2004-01-Annual Estimates of the Population: April 1, 2000 to July 1, 2004.

A-3 Percentage Change in Population, 2003-2004: From the same source as Table A-2, this table shows population change over one year.

A-4 Percentage Change in Population, 1994-2004: The 1994 population data shown on this table are from intercensal state population estimates released by the U.S. Census Bureau on April 11, 2002. Comparing these numbers to 2004 estimates shows population shifts over a decade.

A-5 Projected Population, 2015, and Population Change, 2004-2015: The population projections for 2015 were made by the U.S. Census Bureau and are available on its Web site (www.census.gov). See Table A-2 for the 2004 population numbers used to calculate the projected change over time. Many private market research and economic forecasting firms also make population projections. The projections reflect recent trends, so western states are predicted to gain population rapidly while the slowest growth appears in the Northeast and the Midwest. Generally, projections for short periods are quite reliable because they are based on events that are predictable for large groups, such as the percentage of persons who will die each year and the percentage of women of childbearing age who will have babies. Over longer periods, more guesswork is involved. Major economic shifts can be caused by changes in defense spending, fluctuations in oil and gas prices, and success or failure of particular firms or industries. Those shifts affect migration of workers and ultimately where they have children and die.

A-6 Projected Population for the Year 2025: See notes to Table A-4.

A-7 Population Age 65 and Over and as a Percentage of Population, 2004: This U.S. Census Bureau estimate is available on the bureau's Web site (www.census.gov). Two kinds of states have the largest percentage of elderly citizens. First, there are states, like Florida and Arkansas, that draw large numbers of retirees from other states. Second, there are states with slow population growth, such as Pennsylvania, that lose many of their working-age younger people through migration to other states.

A-8 Population Age 17 and Under and as a Percentage of Population, 2004: This count, from the same source as Table A-7, shows the flip side of the high concentrations of elderly citizens shown in Table A-7. The highest-ranking states, typified by Utah, have a large percentage of adults of childbearing age and high birth rates.

A-9 Median Age, 2004: In each state, half the population was older than the age shown, while half was younger. This statistic, available on the U.S. Census Bureau's Web site (www.census.gov) captures age differences among states in a single number for each state.

A-10 African American Population and as a Percentage of Population, 2004: The U.S. Census Bureau identifies six race categories: White; Black or African American; American Indian and Alaska Native; Asian; Native Hawaiian and other Pacific Islander; and "some other race" (write-in answer). "Hispanic" is not considered a race by the bureau, so Hispanics are asked to classify themselves using the above six race categories, and also separately as "of Hispanic or Latino origin."

The 2000 census marked the first year respondents were able to check one or more boxes identifying race. This *State Fact Finder* table presents the number of people who classify themselves as African American or Black only. These data are from the bureau's Web site (www.census.gov). The "undercount" (see notes to Table A-1) means that statistics probably undercount African Americans and Hispanics.

A-11 American Indian Population and as a Percentage of Population, 2004: From the same source as Table A-10, this table shows the number of people who classify themselves as American Indian (including Alaska Native).

A-12 Asian American Population and as a Percentage of Population, 2004: From the same source as Table A-10, this table shows the number of people who classify themselves as Asian American.

A-13 Hispanic Population and as a Percentage of Population, 2004: See notes to Tables A-10. While the census theoretically accounts for every resident in the country, illegal immigrants (many of whom are Hispanic) have an understandable fear of being identified by any government agency. Therefore, the count of this group is probably not very accurate. The data come from the U.S. Census Bureau Web site (www.census.gov).

A-14 White (Non-Hispanic) Population and as a Percentage of Population, 2004: This data, available on the U.S. Census Bureau Web site (www.census.gov) presents the number of people who identify themselves as non-Hispanic White.

A-15 Mixed-Race Population and as a Percentage of Population, 2004: Since the 2000 census, respondents now have the option of checking two or more boxes categorizing race. This table shows the number of people who classify themselves as being of two or more races. It is from the same source as Table A-10.

A-16 Population in Poverty, 2004: The federal government has a uniform definition of the income families need to avoid poverty. The amount considered necessary varies with family size but not with rural or urban location or from state to state. The income used to calculate whether households are living in poverty does not include the value of non-cash benefits, such as medical care, provided to the poor under government programs. The estimates shown are from the U.S. Census Bureau Web site (www.census.gov). They are based in part on monthly household surveys of a small sample of the nation's population, not a full count. They reflect possible sampling errors, particularly for less populous states.

A-17 Number and Rate of Children in Poverty, 2004: These statistics are available on the U.S. Census Bureau Web site (www.census.gov) and are subject to the same caveats as similar data for persons of all ages in Table A-16. The percentage of children in poverty exceeds the percentage of all persons in poverty because households with children are often headed by a parent or parents in their early earning years, and the income needed to avoid the poverty standard is higher for families with children than for adults without children.

A-18 Female and Male Population, 2004: More than half of newly born children are male, but women tend to outlive men. The result is about equal numbers of each in the population as a whole, but disproportionate numbers of women in states with more aged population (see Table A-7). These data come from the same source as Table A-1.

A-19 Birth Rates, 2003: These data show that 14.1 children are born each year for every 1,000 people. The birth rate is nearly 66.1 per 1,000 when only women of childbearing age are considered. The data come from the National Center for Health Statistics publication, *National Vital Statistics Report* (vol. 54, no. 2, September 8, 2005) available on the Centers for Disease Control Web site (www.cdc.gov). See notes to Table A-20 below.

A-20 Death Rates (age-adjusted), 2003: Raw death rates, like raw birth rates (births related to population), are highly sensitive to the age distribution of a state's population. A state with large numbers of older persons will tend to have lower raw birth rates and higher death rates. The National Center for Health Statistics makes special calculations adjusting deaths for age and births for the numbers of women of childbearing age (called fertility rates).

State Fact Finder illustrates both approaches by using raw rates for births (Table A-19) and adjusted rates for deaths. Data showing raw rates for deaths are, like the age-adjusted death rates shown, available from the National Center for Health Statistics publication, *National Vital Statistics Report* (vol. 53, no. 15, February 28, 2005). This source also provides technical notes indicating exactly how adjustments are made. The notes also explain how a changed population standard makes these rates not directly comparable to those before data year 2000.

A-21 Population Density, 2004: This table is calculated by taking the land area estimate from the 2000 census (see Table C-1) and relating it to the 2004 population. The result is a rough measure of urban-rural characteristics of each state and is often cited as a proxy for possible crowding. However, in many states much of the land area is unusable for settlement because of lack of water, extraordinarily low or high elevation, and other factors. Consequently, much of the population of a low-density state may in fact be densely packed in a few small areas.

A-22 Legal Immigrants Admitted, FY 2004: These statistics, showing immigrants admitted by state of intended residence, are from the *2004 Statistical Yearbook of Immigration Statistics* (www.uscis.gov).

A-23 Unauthorized Immigrant Population, 2000: Counting illegal immigrants, many of whom fear being counted, is inherently difficult. These estimates are from the U.S. Citizenship and Immigration Services (www.uscis.gov). While the estimates may not be accurate, they are useful in illustrating the large differences among states.

Economies

Economic vitality, as measured by the Index of State Economic Momentum, is still strongest in the western region of the United States. Nevada has topped the Index for nine of the past ten years. In 2005, six other western states were ranked in the top ten. In fact, all the states of the West rank in the Index's top twenty. At number 22, Oklahoma, the highest ranking midwestern state, sits just above the national average. The bottom four spots are held by states on the eastern edge of the Midwest—Ohio, Indiana, Illinois, and Michigan. Layoffs in the auto industry continue to hurt manufacturing employment in this region. Additionally, households in the Midwest and the Northeast are expected to feel the pressure of increased costs for natural gas and heating oil in the winter of 2005–2006.

The good news for the Midwest is that it may be spared some of the fallout from the predicted reduction in housing activities. While the metaphors have softened—"cooling trends" have replaced the more dramatic "bursting bubbles"—analysts expect price corrections in the hottest markets. As of the end of September 2005, in sixteen states—concentrated on the coasts and in the far West—the increase in the price of homes exceeded the nation's average one-year appreciation. Over one year, prices increased by 30 percent in Arizona and 34 percent in the Phoenix-Mesa-Scottsdale area. Over the past five years, the average home in California increased in value by 113 percent, and in Indiana by a much smaller 20 percent. In contrast, the one-year appreciation in Michigan in 2005 equaled approximately 4 percent.

One-Year Change in Housing Prices, 2004–2005

United States		12.02%
West	Pacific	17.33
	Mountain	16.23
Northeast	Middle Atlantic	12.42
	New England	9.43
South	South Atlantic	16.9
	East South Central	7.06
	West South Central	6.07
Midwest	East North Central	5.99
	West North Central	6.55

Source: Office of Federal Housing Enterprise Oversight

B-1 Personal Income, 2004

State	Personal income $ (in millions)	Rank
Alabama	125,167	24
Alaska	22,340	47
Arizona	164,324	22
Arkansas	70,810	33
California	1,262,454	1
Colorado	166,153	21
Connecticut	159,435	23
Delaware	29,527	44
Florida	547,312	4
Georgia	265,538	12
Hawaii	41,176	40
Idaho	37,394	42
Illinois	441,485	5
Indiana	187,565	16
Iowa	91,500	30
Kansas	84,810	31
Kentucky	112,566	27
Louisiana	122,913	25
Maine	39,482	41
Maryland	220,261	14
Massachusetts	270,145	10
Michigan	324,134	9
Minnesota	184,515	17
Mississippi	70,770	34
Missouri	175,611	20
Montana	25,643	45
Nebraska	56,393	36
Nevada	78,876	32
New Hampshire	47,661	38
New Jersey	362,190	7
New Mexico	49,778	37
New York	737,039	2
North Carolina	250,286	13
North Dakota	18,553	49
Ohio	356,774	8
Oklahoma	98,020	29
Oregon	109,935	28
Pennsylvania	412,591	6
Rhode Island	36,936	43
South Carolina	113,988	26
South Dakota	23,602	46
Tennessee	175,885	19
Texas	690,376	3
Utah	64,376	35
Vermont	19,721	48
Virginia	269,862	11
Washington	217,240	15
West Virginia	46,619	39
Wisconsin	176,636	18
Wyoming	17,323	50
50 States	9,673,686	
DC	28,839	
United States	9,702,525	

Rank in order by $	
1	California
2	New York
3	Texas
4	Florida
5	Illinois
6	Pennsylvania
7	New Jersey
8	Ohio
9	Michigan
10	Massachusetts
11	Virginia
12	Georgia
13	North Carolina
14	Maryland
15	Washington
16	Indiana
17	Minnesota
18	Wisconsin
19	Tennessee
20	Missouri
21	Colorado
22	Arizona
23	Connecticut
24	Alabama
25	Louisiana
26	South Carolina
27	Kentucky
28	Oregon
29	Oklahoma
30	Iowa
31	Kansas
32	Nevada
33	Arkansas
34	Mississippi
35	Utah
36	Nebraska
37	New Mexico
38	New Hampshire
39	West Virginia
40	Hawaii
41	Maine
42	Idaho
43	Rhode Island
44	Delaware
45	Montana
46	South Dakota
47	Alaska
48	Vermont
49	North Dakota
50	Wyoming

B-2 Gross State Product, Total and Per Capita, 2004

State	Gross state product $ (in millions)	Per capita $	Rank per capita
Alabama	139,840	30,869	45
Alaska	34,023	51,909	3
Arizona	199,953	34,812	36
Arkansas	80,902	29,391	48
California	1,550,753	43,204	11
Colorado	199,969	43,458	10
Connecticut	185,802	53,032	2
Delaware	54,274	65,362	1
Florida	599,068	34,435	38
Georgia	343,125	38,862	21
Hawaii	50,322	39,848	17
Idaho	43,571	31,273	44
Illinois	521,900	41,050	14
Indiana	227,569	36,484	30
Iowa	111,114	37,609	26
Kansas	98,946	36,171	31
Kentucky	136,446	32,911	40
Louisiana	152,944	33,869	39
Maine	43,336	32,899	41
Maryland	227,991	41,020	15
Massachusetts	317,798	49,528	4
Michigan	372,169	36,802	28
Minnesota	223,822	43,878	9
Mississippi	76,166	26,237	50
Missouri	203,294	35,327	34
Montana	27,482	29,650	47
Nebraska	68,183	39,024	20
Nevada	100,317	42,967	12
New Hampshire	51,871	39,916	16
New Jersey	416,053	47,828	5
New Mexico	61,012	32,056	43
New York	896,739	46,639	7
North Carolina	336,398	39,385	18
North Dakota	22,687	35,763	32
Ohio	419,866	36,641	29
Oklahoma	107,600	30,537	46
Oregon	128,103	35,638	33
Pennsylvania	468,089	37,730	25
Rhode Island	41,679	38,569	22
South Carolina	136,125	32,426	42
South Dakota	29,386	38,120	24
Tennessee	217,626	36,880	27
Texas	884,136	39,312	19
Utah	82,611	34,579	37
Vermont	21,921	35,277	35
Virginia	329,332	44,147	8
Washington	261,549	42,160	13
West Virginia	49,454	27,242	49
Wisconsin	211,616	38,413	23
Wyoming	23,979	47,340	6
50 States	11,588,911	39,539	
DC	76,685	138,540	
United States*	11,665,595	39,725	

**Due to rounding or data sources, the 50-state total plus D.C. may not equal the U.S. total. Please see introduction.*

Rank in order per capita	
1	Delaware
2	Connecticut
3	Alaska
4	Massachusetts
5	New Jersey
6	Wyoming
7	New York
8	Virginia
9	Minnesota
10	Colorado
11	California
12	Nevada
13	Washington
14	Illinois
15	Maryland
16	New Hampshire
17	Hawaii
18	North Carolina
19	Texas
20	Nebraska
21	Georgia
22	Rhode Island
23	Wisconsin
24	South Dakota
25	Pennsylvania
26	Iowa
27	Tennessee
28	Michigan
29	Ohio
30	Indiana
31	Kansas
32	North Dakota
33	Oregon
34	Missouri
35	Vermont
36	Arizona
37	Utah
38	Florida
39	Louisiana
40	Kentucky
41	Maine
42	South Carolina
43	New Mexico
44	Idaho
45	Alabama
46	Oklahoma
47	Montana
48	Arkansas
49	West Virginia
50	Mississippi

B-3 Per Capita Personal Income, 2004

State	Per capita personal income $	Rank
Alabama	27,630	41
Alaska	34,085	16
Arizona	28,609	38
Arkansas	25,724	48
California	35,172	11
Colorado	36,109	9
Connecticut	45,506	1
Delaware	35,559	10
Florida	31,460	24
Georgia	30,074	32
Hawaii	32,606	19
Idaho	26,839	46
Illinois	34,725	13
Indiana	30,070	33
Iowa	30,970	27
Kansas	31,003	26
Kentucky	27,151	44
Louisiana	27,219	42
Maine	29,973	34
Maryland	39,629	4
Massachusetts	42,102	2
Michigan	32,052	22
Minnesota	36,173	8
Mississippi	24,379	50
Missouri	30,516	31
Montana	27,666	40
Nebraska	32,276	20
Nevada	33,783	17
New Hampshire	36,676	6
New Jersey	41,636	3
New Mexico	26,154	47
New York	38,333	5
North Carolina	29,303	36
North Dakota	29,247	37
Ohio	31,135	25
Oklahoma	27,819	39
Oregon	30,584	30
Pennsylvania	33,257	18
Rhode Island	34,180	15
South Carolina	27,153	43
South Dakota	30,617	29
Tennessee	29,806	35
Texas	30,697	28
Utah	26,946	45
Vermont	31,737	23
Virginia	36,175	7
Washington	35,017	12
West Virginia	25,681	49
Wisconsin	32,063	21
Wyoming	34,199	14
50 States	n/a	
DC	52,101	
United States	33,041	

Rank in order per capita	
1	Connecticut
2	Massachusetts
3	New Jersey
4	Maryland
5	New York
6	New Hampshire
7	Virginia
8	Minnesota
9	Colorado
10	Delaware
11	California
12	Washington
13	Illinois
14	Wyoming
15	Rhode Island
16	Alaska
17	Nevada
18	Pennsylvania
19	Hawaii
20	Nebraska
21	Wisconsin
22	Michigan
23	Vermont
24	Florida
25	Ohio
26	Kansas
27	Iowa
28	Texas
29	South Dakota
30	Oregon
31	Missouri
32	Georgia
33	Indiana
34	Maine
35	Tennessee
36	North Carolina
37	North Dakota
38	Arizona
39	Oklahoma
40	Montana
41	Alabama
42	Louisiana
43	South Carolina
44	Kentucky
45	Utah
46	Idaho
47	New Mexico
48	Arkansas
49	West Virginia
50	Mississippi

B-4 Personal Income from Wages and Salaries, 2004

State	Wages and salaries $ (in millions)	As percentage of personal income	Rank by percentage
Alabama	66,049	52.8	35
Alaska	13,017	58.3	6
Arizona	90,670	55.2	22
Arkansas	36,417	51.4	39
California	699,035	55.4	18
Colorado	91,863	55.3	19
Connecticut	86,577	54.3	26
Delaware	18,519	62.7	1
Florida	278,996	51.0	43
Georgia	155,166	58.4	5
Hawaii	23,715	57.6	9
Idaho	18,848	50.4	44
Illinois	253,110	57.3	10
Indiana	103,540	55.2	21
Iowa	48,134	52.6	36
Kansas	45,847	54.1	27
Kentucky	61,792	54.9	25
Louisiana	63,861	52.0	38
Maine	20,191	51.1	41
Maryland	112,383	51.0	42
Massachusetts	160,157	59.3	3
Michigan	180,245	55.6	15
Minnesota	110,065	59.7	2
Mississippi	34,276	48.4	46
Missouri	97,382	55.5	17
Montana	12,156	47.4	49
Nebraska	30,431	54.0	29
Nevada	45,171	57.3	11
New Hampshire	25,064	52.6	37
New Jersey	194,057	53.6	32
New Mexico	26,497	53.2	33
New York	431,455	58.5	4
North Carolina	141,282	56.4	12
North Dakota	10,294	55.5	16
Ohio	201,274	56.4	13
Oklahoma	47,309	48.3	47
Oregon	59,334	54.0	28
Pennsylvania	222,267	53.9	30
Rhode Island	18,892	51.1	40
South Carolina	61,311	53.8	31
South Dakota	11,357	48.1	48
Tennessee	97,109	55.2	20
Texas	380,354	55.1	23
Utah	37,268	57.9	7
Vermont	10,459	53.0	34
Virginia	155,881	57.8	8
Washington	119,265	54.9	24
West Virginia	22,027	47.2	50
Wisconsin	99,120	56.1	14
Wyoming	8,405	48.5	45
50 States	5,337,896	55.2	
DC	45,863	159.0	
United States	5,383,759	55.5	

Rank in order by percentage	
1	Delaware
2	Minnesota
3	Massachusetts
4	New York
5	Georgia
6	Alaska
7	Utah
8	Virginia
9	Hawaii
10	Illinois
11	Nevada
12	North Carolina
13	Ohio
14	Wisconsin
15	Michigan
16	North Dakota
17	Missouri
18	California
19	Colorado
20	Tennessee
21	Indiana
22	Arizona
23	Texas
24	Washington
25	Kentucky
26	Connecticut
27	Kansas
28	Oregon
29	Nebraska
30	Pennsylvania
31	South Carolina
32	New Jersey
33	New Mexico
34	Vermont
35	Alabama
36	Iowa
37	New Hampshire
38	Louisiana
39	Arkansas
40	Rhode Island
41	Maine
42	Maryland
43	Florida
44	Idaho
45	Wyoming
46	Mississippi
47	Oklahoma
48	South Dakota
49	Montana
50	West Virginia

Note: Numbers that appear to be identical are rounded and vary slightly in actual value. The rankings reflect the actual values before rounding. See the introduction for more details.

B-5 Average Annual Pay, 2004

State	Average annual pay $	Rank
Alabama	33,414	31
Alaska	39,062	15
Arizona	36,646	21
Arkansas	30,245	45
California	44,641	5
Colorado	40,276	12
Connecticut	51,007	1
Delaware	42,487	7
Florida	35,186	25
Georgia	37,866	18
Hawaii	35,198	24
Idaho	29,871	46
Illinois	42,277	8
Indiana	34,694	30
Iowa	32,097	36
Kansas	32,738	34
Kentucky	33,165	33
Louisiana	31,880	38
Maine	31,906	37
Maryland	42,579	6
Massachusetts	48,916	3
Michigan	40,373	11
Minnesota	40,398	10
Mississippi	28,535	48
Missouri	34,845	27
Montana	27,830	50
Nebraska	31,507	40
Nevada	37,106	20
New Hampshire	39,176	14
New Jersey	48,064	4
New Mexico	31,411	41
New York	49,941	2
North Carolina	34,791	28
North Dakota	28,987	47
Ohio	36,441	22
Oklahoma	30,743	43
Oregon	35,630	23
Pennsylvania	38,555	16
Rhode Island	37,651	19
South Carolina	31,839	39
South Dakota	28,281	49
Tennessee	34,925	26
Texas	38,511	17
Utah	32,171	35
Vermont	33,274	32
Virginia	40,534	9
Washington	39,361	13
West Virginia	30,382	44
Wisconsin	34,743	29
Wyoming	31,210	42
50 States	n/a	
DC	63,887	
United States	39,354	

Rank in order by $	
1	Connecticut
2	New York
3	Massachusetts
4	New Jersey
5	California
6	Maryland
7	Delaware
8	Illinois
9	Virginia
10	Minnesota
11	Michigan
12	Colorado
13	Washington
14	New Hampshire
15	Alaska
16	Pennsylvania
17	Texas
18	Georgia
19	Rhode Island
20	Nevada
21	Arizona
22	Ohio
23	Oregon
24	Hawaii
25	Florida
26	Tennessee
27	Missouri
28	North Carolina
29	Wisconsin
30	Indiana
31	Alabama
32	Vermont
33	Kentucky
34	Kansas
35	Utah
36	Iowa
37	Maine
38	Louisiana
39	South Carolina
40	Nebraska
41	New Mexico
42	Wyoming
43	Oklahoma
44	West Virginia
45	Arkansas
46	Idaho
47	North Dakota
48	Mississippi
49	South Dakota
50	Montana

B-6 Average Hourly Earnings, 2005

State	Average hourly earnings $	Rank
Alabama	14.96	36
Alaska	15.34	29
Arizona	14.80	37
Arkansas	13.89	44
California	15.73	25
Colorado	15.92	22
Connecticut	18.92	3
Delaware	17.80	7
Florida	13.93	43
Georgia	14.52	39
Hawaii	13.65	47
Idaho	15.02	35
Illinois	15.87	23
Indiana	18.30	5
Iowa	16.23	19
Kansas	17.19	14
Kentucky	16.76	16
Louisiana	17.24	12
Maine	17.60	10
Maryland	17.27	11
Massachusetts	17.74	8
Michigan	21.36	1
Minnesota	16.39	18
Mississippi	13.58	48
Missouri	17.12	15
Montana	15.64	26
Nebraska	15.44	28
Nevada	15.09	34
New Hampshire	15.97	21
New Jersey	15.79	24
New Mexico	13.73	46
New York	17.87	6
North Carolina	14.36	41
North Dakota	15.23	32
Ohio	19.13	2
Oklahoma	14.62	38
Oregon	15.52	27
Pennsylvania	15.27	31
Rhode Island	13.15	50
South Carolina	15.32	30
South Dakota	13.33	49
Tennessee	13.85	45
Texas	13.94	42
Utah	14.45	40
Vermont	15.16	33
Virginia	16.41	17
Washington	18.87	4
West Virginia	17.20	13
Wisconsin	16.14	20
Wyoming	17.63	9
50 States	n/a	
DC	n/a	
United States	16.60	

Rank in order by $	
1	Michigan
2	Ohio
3	Connecticut
4	Washington
5	Indiana
6	New York
7	Delaware
8	Massachusetts
9	Wyoming
10	Maine
11	Maryland
12	Louisiana
13	West Virginia
14	Kansas
15	Missouri
16	Kentucky
17	Virginia
18	Minnesota
19	Iowa
20	Wisconsin
21	New Hampshire
22	Colorado
23	Illinois
24	New Jersey
25	California
26	Montana
27	Oregon
28	Nebraska
29	Alaska
30	South Carolina
31	Pennsylvania
32	North Dakota
33	Vermont
34	Nevada
35	Idaho
36	Alabama
37	Arizona
38	Oklahoma
39	Georgia
40	Utah
41	North Carolina
42	Texas
43	Florida
44	Arkansas
45	Tennessee
46	New Mexico
47	Hawaii
48	Mississippi
49	South Dakota
50	Rhode Island

B-7 Value Added in Manufacturing, 2003

State	Value added $ (in millions)	Per capita $	Rank per capita
Alabama	29,768	6,610	24
Alaska	1,413	2,180	48
Arizona	29,017	5,201	36
Arkansas	22,730	8,333	10
California	197,547	5,571	34
Colorado	17,243	3,792	42
Connecticut	25,771	7,391	17
Delaware	4,607	5,630	31
Florida	42,391	2,494	46
Georgia	58,683	6,764	23
Hawaii	1,224	981	50
Idaho	7,701	5,634	30
Illinois	93,534	7,395	16
Indiana	80,988	13,063	1
Iowa	32,739	11,128	3
Kansas	20,429	7,497	15
Kentucky	35,562	8,635	9
Louisiana	30,605	6,811	22
Maine	7,377	5,635	29
Maryland	18,490	3,354	44
Massachusetts	46,266	7,206	18
Michigan	97,552	9,676	5
Minnesota	41,451	8,185	11
Mississippi	17,169	5,956	28
Missouri	43,120	7,540	14
Montana	1,794	1,953	49
Nebraska	11,844	6,817	21
Nevada	5,040	2,248	47
New Hampshire	8,909	6,913	20
New Jersey	51,979	6,014	27
New Mexico	6,150	3,274	45
New York	80,199	4,174	40
North Carolina	89,017	10,571	4
North Dakota	2,520	3,978	41
Ohio	109,282	9,555	6
Oklahoma	17,686	5,044	37
Oregon	25,109	7,045	19
Pennsylvania	93,777	7,581	13
Rhode Island	6,039	5,612	32
South Carolina	39,228	9,455	7
South Dakota	3,776	4,936	38
Tennessee	51,130	8,747	8
Texas	123,846	5,603	33
Utah	12,720	5,408	35
Vermont	4,972	8,027	12
Virginia	46,849	6,361	25
Washington	38,896	6,344	26
West Virginia	8,205	4,529	39
Wisconsin	65,355	11,938	2
Wyoming	1,722	3,429	43
50 States	1,909,420	6,579	
DC	196	351	
United States*	1,909,616	6,567	

**Due to rounding or data sources, the 50-state total plus D.C. may not equal the U.S. total. Please see introduction.*

Rank in order per capita	
1	Indiana
2	Wisconsin
3	Iowa
4	North Carolina
5	Michigan
6	Ohio
7	South Carolina
8	Tennessee
9	Kentucky
10	Arkansas
11	Minnesota
12	Vermont
13	Pennsylvania
14	Missouri
15	Kansas
16	Illinois
17	Connecticut
18	Massachusetts
19	Oregon
20	New Hampshire
21	Nebraska
22	Louisiana
23	Georgia
24	Alabama
25	Virginia
26	Washington
27	New Jersey
28	Mississippi
29	Maine
30	Idaho
31	Delaware
32	Rhode Island
33	Texas
34	California
35	Utah
36	Arizona
37	Oklahoma
38	South Dakota
39	West Virginia
40	New York
41	North Dakota
42	Colorado
43	Wyoming
44	Maryland
45	New Mexico
46	Florida
47	Nevada
48	Alaska
49	Montana
50	Hawaii

B-8 Cost of Living, 2005

State	Cost of living index	Rank by index
Alabama	91.0	40
Alaska	128.6	6
Arizona	101.5	19
Arkansas	86.9	48
California	136.3	2
Colorado	97.2	24
Connecticut	127.4	7
Delaware	102.4	18
Florida	101.0	20
Georgia	90.4	42
Hawaii	157.8	1
Idaho	92.5	35
Illinois	95.3	30
Indiana	93.7	32
Iowa	95.3	29
Kansas	91.7	37
Kentucky	92.1	36
Louisiana	96.2	26
Maine	n/a	n/a
Maryland	126.1	8
Massachusetts	130.5	4
Michigan	100.6	22
Minnesota	100.1	23
Mississippi	90.5	41
Missouri	91.6	38
Montana	100.7	21
Nebraska	89.7	43
Nevada	113.0	11
New Hampshire	n/a	n/a
New Jersey	134.4	3
New Mexico	107.3	13
New York	129.9	5
North Carolina	95.4	27
North Dakota	91.4	39
Ohio	96.7	25
Oklahoma	88.1	47
Oregon	105.3	14
Pennsylvania	104.1	15
Rhode Island	125.4	9
South Carolina	94.3	31
South Dakota	93.6	33
Tennessee	89.4	46
Texas	89.4	45
Utah	93.5	34
Vermont	114.7	10
Virginia	103.4	16
Washington	108.5	12
West Virginia	89.6	44
Wisconsin	95.4	28
Wyoming	102.7	17
50 States	n/a	
DC	141.4	
United States	100.0	

Rank in order by index	
1	Hawaii
2	California
3	New Jersey
4	Massachusetts
5	New York
6	Alaska
7	Connecticut
8	Maryland
9	Rhode Island
10	Vermont
11	Nevada
12	Washington
13	New Mexico
14	Oregon
15	Pennsylvania
16	Virginia
17	Wyoming
18	Delaware
19	Arizona
20	Florida
21	Montana
22	Michigan
23	Minnesota
24	Colorado
25	Ohio
26	Louisiana
27	North Carolina
28	Wisconsin
29	Iowa
30	Illinois
31	South Carolina
32	Indiana
33	South Dakota
34	Utah
35	Idaho
36	Kentucky
37	Kansas
38	Missouri
39	North Dakota
40	Alabama
41	Mississippi
42	Georgia
43	Nebraska
44	West Virginia
45	Texas
46	Tennessee
47	Oklahoma
48	Arkansas

Note: Numbers that appear to be identical are rounded and vary slightly in actual value. The rankings reflect the actual values before rounding. See the introduction for more details.

B-9 Average Annual Pay in Manufacturing, 2004

State	Average annual pay in manufacturing $	Rank
Alabama	39,581	39
Alaska	33,712	46
Arizona	52,723	7
Arkansas	33,258	48
California	56,531	4
Colorado	52,632	8
Connecticut	61,071	1
Delaware	50,550	12
Florida	42,473	27
Georgia	41,473	34
Hawaii	32,576	50
Idaho	41,538	33
Illinois	48,639	15
Indiana	47,638	17
Iowa	42,189	29
Kansas	43,030	24
Kentucky	43,246	23
Louisiana	47,961	16
Maine	40,990	35
Maryland	53,365	6
Massachusetts	60,886	2
Michigan	56,073	5
Minnesota	49,117	14
Mississippi	33,254	49
Missouri	42,668	26
Montana	35,347	45
Nebraska	35,786	44
Nevada	42,459	28
New Hampshire	50,638	11
New Jersey	59,153	3
New Mexico	40,591	38
New York	50,256	13
North Carolina	41,727	32
North Dakota	36,016	43
Ohio	47,506	18
Oklahoma	38,650	42
Oregon	46,905	19
Pennsylvania	45,953	20
Rhode Island	40,810	36
South Carolina	40,783	37
South Dakota	33,526	47
Tennessee	42,048	30
Texas	51,328	10
Utah	38,710	41
Vermont	45,355	21
Virginia	41,988	31
Washington	51,805	9
West Virginia	42,769	25
Wisconsin	44,153	22
Wyoming	39,090	40
50 States	n/a	
DC	74,421	
United States	47,861	

Rank in order by $	
1	Connecticut
2	Massachusetts
3	New Jersey
4	California
5	Michigan
6	Maryland
7	Arizona
8	Colorado
9	Washington
10	Texas
11	New Hampshire
12	Delaware
13	New York
14	Minnesota
15	Illinois
16	Louisiana
17	Indiana
18	Ohio
19	Oregon
20	Pennsylvania
21	Vermont
22	Wisconsin
23	Kentucky
24	Kansas
25	West Virginia
26	Missouri
27	Florida
28	Nevada
29	Iowa
30	Tennessee
31	Virginia
32	North Carolina
33	Idaho
34	Georgia
35	Maine
36	Rhode Island
37	South Carolina
38	New Mexico
39	Alabama
40	Wyoming
41	Utah
42	Oklahoma
43	North Dakota
44	Nebraska
45	Montana
46	Alaska
47	South Dakota
48	Arkansas
49	Mississippi
50	Hawaii

B-10 Average Annual Pay in Retailing, 2004

State	Average annual pay in retailing $	Rank
Alabama	21,737	35
Alaska	25,770	10
Arizona	26,429	8
Arkansas	19,515	49
California	28,930	1
Colorado	25,070	12
Connecticut	28,535	2
Delaware	23,991	20
Florida	24,825	14
Georgia	24,125	18
Hawaii	24,576	15
Idaho	22,274	32
Illinois	24,394	17
Indiana	21,446	36
Iowa	20,376	44
Kansas	20,841	38
Kentucky	20,890	37
Louisiana	20,523	43
Maine	21,925	33
Maryland	26,212	9
Massachusetts	27,029	5
Michigan	23,561	22
Minnesota	23,056	25
Mississippi	19,644	48
Missouri	21,777	34
Montana	20,686	42
Nebraska	20,265	45
Nevada	27,167	4
New Hampshire	25,556	11
New Jersey	28,415	3
New Mexico	22,586	28
New York	26,513	7
North Carolina	22,474	29
North Dakota	19,802	47
Ohio	22,741	27
Oklahoma	20,719	41
Oregon	24,039	19
Pennsylvania	22,809	26
Rhode Island	24,478	16
South Carolina	22,321	31
South Dakota	19,872	46
Tennessee	23,577	21
Texas	24,853	13
Utah	22,434	30
Vermont	23,438	23
Virginia	23,371	24
Washington	26,612	6
West Virginia	19,493	50
Wisconsin	20,812	39
Wyoming	20,734	40
50 States	n/a	
DC	27,813	
United States	24,415	

Rank in order by $	
1	California
2	Connecticut
3	New Jersey
4	Nevada
5	Massachusetts
6	Washington
7	New York
8	Arizona
9	Maryland
10	Alaska
11	New Hampshire
12	Colorado
13	Texas
14	Florida
15	Hawaii
16	Rhode Island
17	Illinois
18	Georgia
19	Oregon
20	Delaware
21	Tennessee
22	Michigan
23	Vermont
24	Virginia
25	Minnesota
26	Pennsylvania
27	Ohio
28	New Mexico
29	North Carolina
30	Utah
31	South Carolina
32	Idaho
33	Maine
34	Missouri
35	Alabama
36	Indiana
37	Kentucky
38	Kansas
39	Wisconsin
40	Wyoming
41	Oklahoma
42	Montana
43	Louisiana
44	Iowa
45	Nebraska
46	South Dakota
47	North Dakota
48	Mississippi
49	Arkansas
50	West Virginia

B-11 Labor Force, 2005

State	Labor force (in thousands)	Labor force as percentage of population	Rank by percentage
Alabama	2,173	48.0	47
Alaska	345	52.6	22
Arizona	2,848	49.6	40
Arkansas	1,357	49.3	43
California	17,905	49.9	38
Colorado	2,542	55.2	10
Connecticut	1,822	52.0	25
Delaware	439	52.9	18
Florida	8,730	50.2	36
Georgia	4,546	51.5	30
Hawaii	644	51.0	33
Idaho	735	52.7	19
Illinois	6,510	51.2	31
Indiana	3,224	51.7	28
Iowa	1,652	55.9	7
Kansas	1,466	53.6	13
Kentucky	2,015	48.6	46
Louisiana	1,980	43.8	50
Maine	717	54.4	11
Maryland	2,952	53.1	16
Massachusetts	3,382	52.7	20
Michigan	5,126	50.7	35
Minnesota	2,940	57.6	1
Mississippi	1,292	44.5	48
Missouri	3,021	52.5	23
Montana	494	53.3	15
Nebraska	986	56.4	5
Nevada	1,228	52.6	21
New Hampshire	742	57.1	3
New Jersey	4,486	51.6	29
New Mexico	940	49.4	41
New York	9,494	49.4	42
North Carolina	4,347	50.9	34
North Dakota	356	56.1	6
Ohio	5,939	51.8	27
Oklahoma	1,734	49.2	44
Oregon	1,865	51.9	26
Pennsylvania	6,341	51.1	32
Rhode Island	579	53.6	12
South Carolina	2,089	49.8	39
South Dakota	430	55.8	8
Tennessee	2,903	49.2	45
Texas	11,245	50.0	37
Utah	1,243	52.0	24
Vermont	356	57.2	2
Virginia	3,955	53.0	17
Washington	3,314	53.4	14
West Virginia	803	44.2	49
Wisconsin	3,048	55.3	9
Wyoming	286	56.5	4
50 States	149,562	51.0	
DC	300	54.2	
United States	149,862	51.0	

Rank in order by percentage	
1	Minnesota
2	Vermont
3	New Hampshire
4	Wyoming
5	Nebraska
6	North Dakota
7	Iowa
8	South Dakota
9	Wisconsin
10	Colorado
11	Maine
12	Rhode Island
13	Kansas
14	Washington
15	Montana
16	Maryland
17	Virginia
18	Delaware
19	Idaho
20	Massachusetts
21	Nevada
22	Alaska
23	Missouri
24	Utah
25	Connecticut
26	Oregon
27	Ohio
28	Indiana
29	New Jersey
30	Georgia
31	Illinois
32	Pennsylvania
33	Hawaii
34	North Carolina
35	Michigan
36	Florida
37	Texas
38	California
39	South Carolina
40	Arizona
41	New Mexico
42	New York
43	Arkansas
44	Oklahoma
45	Tennessee
46	Kentucky
47	Alabama
48	Mississippi
49	West Virginia
50	Louisiana

Note: Numbers that appear to be identical are rounded and vary slightly in actual value. The rankings reflect the actual values before rounding. See the introduction for more details.

B-12 Unemployed and Unemployment Rate, 2005

State	Unemployed (in thousands)	Unemployment rate (percentage of labor force unemployed)	Rank by rate
Alabama	86.2	4.0	40
Alaska	23.3	6.8	3
Arizona	141.6	5.0	26
Arkansas	77.0	5.7	11
California	905.7	5.1	24
Colorado	130.6	5.1	22
Connecticut	95.1	5.2	20
Delaware	18.1	4.1	38
Florida	302.8	3.5	49
Georgia	241.9	5.3	18
Hawaii	17.5	2.7	50
Idaho	26.0	3.5	48
Illinois	374.0	5.7	8
Indiana	169.8	5.3	19
Iowa	74.5	4.5	33
Kansas	73.6	5.0	25
Kentucky	115.1	5.7	9
Louisiana	227.1	11.5	1
Maine	38.3	5.3	17
Maryland	121.6	4.1	37
Massachusetts	159.2	4.7	30
Michigan	327.8	6.4	5
Minnesota	111.9	3.8	44
Mississippi	124.0	9.6	2
Missouri	145.2	4.8	29
Montana	22.0	4.5	34
Nebraska	38.5	3.9	42
Nevada	51.2	4.2	36
New Hampshire	28.4	3.8	43
New Jersey	194.3	4.3	35
New Mexico	51.5	5.5	15
New York	495.3	5.2	21
North Carolina	237.3	5.5	16
North Dakota	12.8	3.6	46
Ohio	347.4	5.8	7
Oklahoma	85.8	4.9	27
Oregon	114.1	6.1	6
Pennsylvania	306.8	4.8	28
Rhode Island	32.7	5.6	12
South Carolina	137.3	6.6	4
South Dakota	16.9	3.9	41
Tennessee	147.5	5.1	23
Texas	642.1	5.7	10
Utah	57.6	4.6	31
Vermont	13.1	3.7	45
Virginia	140.2	3.5	47
Washington	186.3	5.6	14
West Virginia	45.2	5.6	13
Wisconsin	140.1	4.6	32
Wyoming	11.7	4.1	39
50 States	7,684.0	5.1	
DC	18.4	6.1	
United States	7,702.4	5.1	

Rank in order by rate	
1	Louisiana
2	Mississippi
3	Alaska
4	South Carolina
5	Michigan
6	Oregon
7	Ohio
8	Illinois
9	Kentucky
10	Texas
11	Arkansas
12	Rhode Island
13	West Virginia
14	Washington
15	New Mexico
16	North Carolina
17	Maine
18	Georgia
19	Indiana
20	Connecticut
21	New York
22	Colorado
23	Tennessee
24	California
25	Kansas
26	Arizona
27	Oklahoma
28	Pennsylvania
29	Missouri
30	Massachusetts
31	Utah
32	Wisconsin
33	Iowa
34	Montana
35	New Jersey
36	Nevada
37	Maryland
38	Delaware
39	Wyoming
40	Alabama
41	South Dakota
42	Nebraska
43	New Hampshire
44	Minnesota
45	Vermont
46	North Dakota
47	Virginia
48	Idaho
49	Florida
50	Hawaii

Note: Numbers that appear to be identical are rounded and vary slightly in actual value. The rankings reflect the actual values before rounding. See the introduction for more details.

B-13 Employment and Employment Rate, 2005

State	Employed (in thousands)	Employment rate (percentage of labor force employed)	Rank by rate
Alabama	2,087	96.0	11
Alaska	321	93.2	48
Arizona	2,706	95.0	25
Arkansas	1,280	94.3	40
California	16,999	94.9	27
Colorado	2,411	94.9	29
Connecticut	1,727	94.8	31
Delaware	421	95.9	13
Florida	8,427	96.5	2
Georgia	4,304	94.7	33
Hawaii	627	97.3	1
Idaho	709	96.5	3
Illinois	6,136	94.3	43
Indiana	3,055	94.7	32
Iowa	1,578	95.5	18
Kansas	1,393	95.0	26
Kentucky	1,900	94.3	42
Louisiana	1,753	88.5	50
Maine	679	94.7	34
Maryland	2,830	95.9	14
Massachusetts	3,222	95.3	21
Michigan	4,798	93.6	46
Minnesota	2,828	96.2	7
Mississippi	1,168	90.4	49
Missouri	2,876	95.2	22
Montana	472	95.5	17
Nebraska	947	96.1	9
Nevada	1,177	95.8	15
New Hampshire	714	96.2	8
New Jersey	4,291	95.7	16
New Mexico	889	94.5	36
New York	8,998	94.8	30
North Carolina	4,110	94.5	35
North Dakota	343	96.4	5
Ohio	5,592	94.2	44
Oklahoma	1,648	95.1	24
Oregon	1,750	93.9	45
Pennsylvania	6,034	95.2	23
Rhode Island	547	94.4	39
South Carolina	1,952	93.4	47
South Dakota	413	96.1	10
Tennessee	2,755	94.9	28
Texas	10,603	94.3	41
Utah	1,185	95.4	20
Vermont	343	96.3	6
Virginia	3,815	96.5	4
Washington	3,128	94.4	37
West Virginia	758	94.4	38
Wisconsin	2,908	95.4	19
Wyoming	275	95.9	12
50 States	141,878	94.9	
DC	281	93.9	
United States	142,159	94.9	

Rank in order by rate	
1	Hawaii
2	Florida
3	Idaho
4	Virginia
5	North Dakota
6	Vermont
7	Minnesota
8	New Hampshire
9	Nebraska
10	South Dakota
11	Alabama
12	Wyoming
13	Delaware
14	Maryland
15	Nevada
16	New Jersey
17	Montana
18	Iowa
19	Wisconsin
20	Utah
21	Massachusetts
22	Missouri
23	Pennsylvania
24	Oklahoma
25	Arizona
26	Kansas
27	California
28	Tennessee
29	Colorado
30	New York
31	Connecticut
32	Indiana
33	Georgia
34	Maine
35	North Carolina
36	New Mexico
37	Washington
38	West Virginia
39	Rhode Island
40	Arkansas
41	Texas
42	Kentucky
43	Illinois
44	Ohio
45	Oregon
46	Michigan
47	South Carolina
48	Alaska
49	Mississippi
50	Louisiana

Note: Numbers that appear to be identical are rounded and vary slightly in actual value. The rankings reflect the actual values before rounding. See the introduction for more details.

B-14 Government Employment, 2005

State	Government employment (in thousands)	Percentage of total employment	Rank by percentage
Alabama	359	18.6	13
Alaska	81	26.2	1
Arizona	408	16.4	32
Arkansas	205	17.5	20
California	2,407	16.3	33
Colorado	368	16.5	30
Connecticut	242	14.5	41
Delaware	60	13.9	46
Florida	1,094	14.0	45
Georgia	649	16.5	29
Hawaii	121	20.0	9
Idaho	113	18.5	14
Illinois	841	14.3	43
Indiana	427	14.4	42
Iowa	245	16.6	28
Kansas	242	18.0	17
Kentucky	311	17.1	25
Louisiana	379	22.5	4
Maine	105	17.1	26
Maryland	469	18.2	15
Massachusetts	410	12.8	49
Michigan	679	15.6	36
Minnesota	415	15.2	37
Mississippi	242	22.5	5
Missouri	430	15.8	35
Montana	86	20.5	8
Nebraska	163	17.3	23
Nevada	144	11.6	50
New Hampshire	90	14.1	44
New Jersey	645	15.9	34
New Mexico	203	25.1	2
New York	1,489	17.4	21
North Carolina	657	16.9	27
North Dakota	75	21.8	6
Ohio	797	14.7	39
Oklahoma	314	20.9	7
Oregon	271	16.4	31
Pennsylvania	755	13.2	48
Rhode Island	66	13.2	47
South Carolina	331	18.1	16
South Dakota	75	19.2	11
Tennessee	415	15.2	38
Texas	1,672	17.4	22
Utah	204	17.7	19
Vermont	54	17.3	24
Virginia	657	18.0	18
Washington	529	19.1	12
West Virginia	144	19.3	10
Wisconsin	412	14.6	40
Wyoming	65	24.8	3
50 States	21,614	16.3	
DC	230	33.8	
United States	21,844	16.4	

Rank in order by percentage	
1	Alaska
2	New Mexico
3	Wyoming
4	Louisiana
5	Mississippi
6	North Dakota
7	Oklahoma
8	Montana
9	Hawaii
10	West Virginia
11	South Dakota
12	Washington
13	Alabama
14	Idaho
15	Maryland
16	South Carolina
17	Kansas
18	Virginia
19	Utah
20	Arkansas
21	New York
22	Texas
23	Nebraska
24	Vermont
25	Kentucky
26	Maine
27	North Carolina
28	Iowa
29	Georgia
30	Colorado
31	Oregon
32	Arizona
33	California
34	New Jersey
35	Missouri
36	Michigan
37	Minnesota
38	Tennessee
39	Ohio
40	Wisconsin
41	Connecticut
42	Indiana
43	Illinois
44	New Hampshire
45	Florida
46	Delaware
47	Rhode Island
48	Pennsylvania
49	Massachusetts
50	Nevada

Note: Numbers that appear to be identical are rounded and vary slightly in actual value. The rankings reflect the actual values before rounding. See the introduction for more details.

B-15 Manufacturing Employment, 2005

State	Manufacturing employment (in thousands)	Percentage of total employment	Rank by percentage
Alabama	296	15.3	7
Alaska	15	4.6	45
Arizona	176	7.1	40
Arkansas	203	17.1	3
California	1,551	10.5	25
Colorado	153	6.8	41
Connecticut	197	11.8	19
Delaware	34	7.8	38
Florida	392	5.0	44
Georgia	444	11.3	22
Hawaii	15	2.6	50
Idaho	63	10.1	28
Illinois	693	11.7	20
Indiana	574	19.2	1
Iowa	229	15.4	6
Kansas	180	13.4	13
Kentucky	266	14.5	11
Louisiana	140	8.3	35
Maine	62	9.9	29
Maryland	139	5.4	43
Massachusetts	314	9.7	30
Michigan	677	15.4	5
Minnesota	349	12.8	14
Mississippi	168	15.6	4
Missouri	317	11.5	21
Montana	19	4.5	47
Nebraska	102	10.8	24
Nevada	48	3.8	48
New Hampshire	82	12.6	16
New Jersey	328	8.1	37
New Mexico	37	4.6	46
New York	582	6.8	42
North Carolina	573	14.6	10
North Dakota	26	7.3	39
Ohio	823	15.1	8
Oklahoma	143	9.5	31
Oregon	210	12.6	15
Pennsylvania	681	11.9	18
Rhode Island	55	11.0	23
South Carolina	264	14.3	12
South Dakota	40	10.2	27
Tennessee	412	15.0	9
Texas	894	9.3	32
Utah	118	10.2	26
Vermont	38	12.1	17
Virginia	299	8.2	36
Washington	258	9.3	33
West Virginia	62	8.3	34
Wisconsin	505	17.7	2
Wyoming	10	3.7	49
50 States	14,247	10.7	
DC	3	0.4	
United States	14,250	10.7	

Rank in order by percentage	
1	Indiana
2	Wisconsin
3	Arkansas
4	Mississippi
5	Michigan
6	Iowa
7	Alabama
8	Ohio
9	Tennessee
10	North Carolina
11	Kentucky
12	South Carolina
13	Kansas
14	Minnesota
15	Oregon
16	New Hampshire
17	Vermont
18	Pennsylvania
19	Connecticut
20	Illinois
21	Missouri
22	Georgia
23	Rhode Island
24	Nebraska
25	California
26	Utah
27	South Dakota
28	Idaho
29	Maine
30	Massachusetts
31	Oklahoma
32	Texas
33	Washington
34	West Virginia
35	Louisiana
36	Virginia
37	New Jersey
38	Delaware
39	North Dakota
40	Arizona
41	Colorado
42	New York
43	Maryland
44	Florida
45	Alaska
46	New Mexico
47	Montana
48	Nevada
49	Wyoming
50	Hawaii

Note: Numbers that appear to be identical are rounded and vary slightly in actual value. The rankings reflect the actual values before rounding. See the introduction for more details.

B-16 *Fortune* 500 Companies, 2005

State	Number of *Fortune* 500 companies	*Fortune* 500 companies per million population	Rank per million
Alabama	2	0.4	35
Alaska	0	n/a	n/a
Arizona	3	0.5	34
Arkansas	5	1.8	17
California	52	1.4	22
Colorado	10	2.2	12
Connecticut	14	4.0	1
Delaware	2	2.4	8
Florida	14	0.8	30
Georgia	17	1.9	14
Hawaii	0	n/a	n/a
Idaho	2	1.4	24
Illinois	33	2.6	6
Indiana	6	1.0	29
Iowa	2	0.7	33
Kansas	2	0.7	32
Kentucky	6	1.4	23
Louisiana	1	0.2	39
Maine	0	n/a	n/a
Maryland	6	1.1	28
Massachusetts	11	1.7	19
Michigan	22	2.2	11
Minnesota	18	3.5	2
Mississippi	0	n/a	n/a
Missouri	11	1.9	15
Montana	0	n/a	n/a
Nebraska	4	2.3	9
Nevada	3	1.3	26
New Hampshire	1	0.8	31
New Jersey	24	2.8	4
New Mexico	0	n/a	n/a
New York	54	2.8	3
North Carolina	14	1.6	20
North Dakota	0	n/a	n/a
Ohio	30	2.6	5
Oklahoma	5	1.4	25
Oregon	1	0.3	37
Pennsylvania	27	2.2	10
Rhode Island	2	1.9	16
South Carolina	1	0.2	38
South Dakota	0	n/a	n/a
Tennessee	7	1.2	27
Texas	48	2.1	13
Utah	1	0.4	36
Vermont	0	n/a	n/a
Virginia	18	2.4	7
Washington	9	1.5	21
West Virginia	0	n/a	n/a
Wisconsin	10	1.8	18
Wyoming	0	n/a	n/a
50 States	498	1.7	
DC	2	3.6	
United States	500	1.7	

Rank in order per million	
1	Connecticut
2	Minnesota
3	New York
4	New Jersey
5	Ohio
6	Illinois
7	Virginia
8	Delaware
9	Nebraska
10	Pennsylvania
11	Michigan
12	Colorado
13	Texas
14	Georgia
15	Missouri
16	Rhode Island
17	Arkansas
18	Wisconsin
19	Massachusetts
20	North Carolina
21	Washington
22	California
23	Kentucky
24	Idaho
25	Oklahoma
26	Nevada
27	Tennessee
28	Maryland
29	Indiana
30	Florida
31	New Hampshire
32	Kansas
33	Iowa
34	Arizona
35	Alabama
36	Utah
37	Oregon
38	South Carolina
39	Louisiana

Note: Numbers that appear to be identical are rounded and vary slightly in actual value. The rankings reflect the actual values before rounding. See the introduction for more details.

B-17 *Forbes* 500 Companies, 2003

State	Number of *Forbes* 500 companies	*Forbes* 500 companies per million companies	Rank per million
Alabama	12	2.7	19
Alaska	0	n/a	n/a
Arizona	8	1.4	38
Arkansas	5	1.8	29
California	109	3.1	14
Colorado	13	2.9	18
Connecticut	26	7.5	1
Delaware	3	3.7	7
Florida	22	1.3	39
Georgia	19	2.2	25
Hawaii	2	1.6	34
Idaho	4	2.9	16
Illinois	48	3.8	4
Indiana	12	1.9	26
Iowa	5	1.7	32
Kansas	5	1.8	28
Kentucky	6	1.5	37
Louisiana	7	1.6	35
Maine	2	1.5	36
Maryland	13	2.4	22
Massachusetts	23	3.6	9
Michigan	26	2.6	20
Minnesota	22	4.3	2
Mississippi	2	0.7	44
Missouri	18	3.2	12
Montana	0	n/a	n/a
Nebraska	5	2.9	17
Nevada	5	2.2	23
New Hampshire	1	0.8	43
New Jersey	32	3.7	6
New Mexico	1	0.5	46
New York	82	4.3	3
North Carolina	16	1.9	27
North Dakota	2	3.2	13
Ohio	41	3.6	8
Oklahoma	6	1.7	31
Oregon	4	1.1	40
Pennsylvania	44	3.6	10
Rhode Island	4	3.7	5
South Carolina	4	1.0	41
South Dakota	0	n/a	n/a
Tennessee	10	1.7	30
Texas	65	2.9	15
Utah	2	0.9	42
Vermont	1	1.6	33
Virginia	25	3.4	11
Washington	15	2.4	21
West Virginia	1	0.6	45
Wisconsin	12	2.2	24
Wyoming	0	n/a	n/a
50 States	790	2.7	
DC	6	10.6	
United States*	802	2.8	

**Due to rounding or data sources, the 50-state total plus D.C. may not equal the U.S. total. Please see introduction.*

Rank in order per million	
1	Connecticut
2	Minnesota
3	New York
4	Illinois
5	Rhode Island
6	New Jersey
7	Delaware
8	Ohio
9	Massachusetts
10	Pennsylvania
11	Virginia
12	Missouri
13	North Dakota
14	California
15	Texas
16	Idaho
17	Nebraska
18	Colorado
19	Alabama
20	Michigan
21	Washington
22	Maryland
23	Nevada
24	Wisconsin
25	Georgia
26	Indiana
27	North Carolina
28	Kansas
29	Arkansas
30	Tennessee
31	Oklahoma
32	Iowa
33	Vermont
34	Hawaii
35	Louisiana
36	Maine
37	Kentucky
38	Arizona
39	Florida
40	Oregon
41	South Carolina
42	Utah
43	New Hampshire
44	Mississippi
45	West Virginia
46	New Mexico

Note: Numbers that appear to be identical are rounded and vary slightly in actual value. The rankings reflect the actual values before rounding. See the introduction for more details.

B-18 Tourism Spending, 2003

State	Tourism spending $ (in millions)	Percentage of U.S. total	Per capita $	Rank per capita
Alabama	5,549	1.1	1,232	44
Alaska	1,380	0.3	2,129	8
Arizona	9,153	1.9	1,641	23
Arkansas	3,973	0.8	1,456	35
California	61,075	12.4	1,722	19
Colorado	9,193	1.9	2,022	10
Connecticut	6,709	1.4	1,924	14
Delaware	1,135	0.2	1,387	39
Florida	42,893	8.7	2,523	4
Georgia	14,524	3.0	1,674	22
Hawaii	7,487	1.5	5,995	2
Idaho	2,206	0.4	1,613	25
Illinois	21,595	4.4	1,707	20
Indiana	6,689	1.4	1,079	49
Iowa	4,629	0.9	1,574	29
Kansas	3,846	0.8	1,412	38
Kentucky	5,433	1.1	1,319	41
Louisiana	9,055	1.8	2,015	11
Maine	1,988	0.4	1,519	33
Maryland	9,012	1.8	1,635	24
Massachusetts	9,952	2.0	1,550	32
Michigan	11,990	2.4	1,189	47
Minnesota	7,952	1.6	1,570	30
Mississippi	5,432	1.1	1,885	16
Missouri	9,177	1.9	1,605	26
Montana	2,059	0.4	2,242	5
Nebraska	2,773	0.6	1,596	27
Nevada	19,319	3.9	8,616	1
New Hampshire	2,688	0.5	2,086	9
New Jersey	14,728	3.0	1,704	21
New Mexico	4,076	0.8	2,170	7
New York	27,726	5.6	1,443	36
North Carolina	12,632	2.6	1,500	34
North Dakota	1,237	0.3	1,953	13
Ohio	12,419	2.5	1,086	48
Oklahoma	4,208	0.9	1,200	46
Oregon	5,557	1.1	1,559	31
Pennsylvania	15,237	3.1	1,232	45
Rhode Island	1,427	0.3	1,326	40
South Carolina	7,215	1.5	1,739	18
South Dakota	1,521	0.3	1,989	12
Tennessee	10,580	2.2	1,810	17
Texas	31,471	6.4	1,424	37
Utah	3,725	0.8	1,584	28
Vermont	1,372	0.3	2,215	6
Virginia	13,890	2.8	1,886	15
Washington	8,040	1.6	1,311	42
West Virginia	1,798	0.4	993	50
Wisconsin	7,157	1.5	1,307	43
Wyoming	1,708	0.3	3,402	3
50 States	486,590	99.1	1,677	
DC	4,280	0.9	7,675	
United States	490,870	100.0	1,688	

Rank in order per capita	
1	Nevada
2	Hawaii
3	Wyoming
4	Florida
5	Montana
6	Vermont
7	New Mexico
8	Alaska
9	New Hampshire
10	Colorado
11	Louisiana
12	South Dakota
13	North Dakota
14	Connecticut
15	Virginia
16	Mississippi
17	Tennessee
18	South Carolina
19	California
20	Illinois
21	New Jersey
22	Georgia
23	Arizona
24	Maryland
25	Idaho
26	Missouri
27	Nebraska
28	Utah
29	Iowa
30	Minnesota
31	Oregon
32	Massachusetts
33	Maine
34	North Carolina
35	Arkansas
36	New York
37	Texas
38	Kansas
39	Delaware
40	Rhode Island
41	Kentucky
42	Washington
43	Wisconsin
44	Alabama
45	Pennsylvania
46	Oklahoma
47	Michigan
48	Ohio
49	Indiana
50	West Virginia

Note: Numbers that appear to be identical are rounded and vary slightly in actual value. The rankings reflect the actual values before rounding. See the introduction for more details.

B-19 Exports, 2005

State	Exports $ (millions)	Exports per capita $	Rank per capita
Alabama	7,533	1,663	29
Alaska	2,967	4,527	2
Arizona	10,747	1,871	22
Arkansas	2,716	987	43
California	85,511	2,382	13
Colorado	4,962	1,078	40
Connecticut	7,063	2,016	18
Delaware	1,771	2,133	15
Florida	24,666	1,418	30
Georgia	15,676	1,775	26
Hawaii	627	497	50
Idaho	2,376	1,706	27
Illinois	26,371	2,074	17
Indiana	16,016	2,568	8
Iowa	5,487	1,857	23
Kansas	4,909	1,795	24
Kentucky	10,955	2,642	7
Louisiana	14,384	3,185	5
Maine	1,635	1,241	37
Maryland	5,355	964	44
Massachusetts	16,307	2,541	10
Michigan	27,647	2,734	6
Minnesota	10,768	2,111	16
Mississippi	3,001	1,034	41
Missouri	7,458	1,296	35
Montana	543	586	49
Nebraska	2,236	1,280	36
Nevada	2,788	1,194	39
New Hampshire	1,841	1,417	31
New Jersey	15,559	1,789	25
New Mexico	1,794	943	45
New York	37,412	1,946	20
North Carolina	14,430	1,690	28
North Dakota	889	1,401	32
Ohio	25,748	2,247	14
Oklahoma	3,051	866	47
Oregon	8,980	2,498	11
Pennsylvania	16,359	1,319	33
Rhode Island	935	865	48
South Carolina	10,717	2,553	9
South Dakota	706	915	46
Tennessee	14,088	2,387	12
Texas	95,283	4,237	4
Utah	4,543	1,901	21
Vermont	3,184	5,124	1
Virginia	9,053	1,214	38
Washington	27,642	4,456	3
West Virginia	2,355	1,297	34
Wisconsin	10,975	1,992	19
Wyoming	504	995	42
50 States	628,521	2,144	
DC	590	1,065	
United States*	666,566	2,270	

**Due to rounding or data sources, the 50-state total plus D.C. may not equal the U.S. total. Please see introduction.*

Rank in order per capita	
1	Vermont
2	Alaska
3	Washington
4	Texas
5	Louisiana
6	Michigan
7	Kentucky
8	Indiana
9	South Carolina
10	Massachusetts
11	Oregon
12	Tennessee
13	California
14	Ohio
15	Delaware
16	Minnesota
17	Illinois
18	Connecticut
19	Wisconsin
20	New York
21	Utah
22	Arizona
23	Iowa
24	Kansas
25	New Jersey
26	Georgia
27	Idaho
28	North Carolina
29	Alabama
30	Florida
31	New Hampshire
32	North Dakota
33	Pennsylvania
34	West Virginia
35	Missouri
36	Nebraska
37	Maine
38	Virginia
39	Nevada
40	Colorado
41	Mississippi
42	Wyoming
43	Arkansas
44	Maryland
45	New Mexico
46	South Dakota
47	Oklahoma
48	Rhode Island
49	Montana
50	Hawaii

B-20 Housing Permits, 2004

State	Housing permits	Permits per 10,000 population	Rank per 10,000
Alabama	27,411	60.5	27
Alaska	3,133	47.8	41
Arizona	90,644	157.8	2
Arkansas	15,855	57.6	30
California	207,390	57.8	28
Colorado	46,499	101.1	9
Connecticut	11,837	33.8	47
Delaware	7,858	94.6	10
Florida	255,893	147.1	3
Georgia	108,356	122.7	5
Hawaii	9,034	71.5	19
Idaho	18,108	130.0	4
Illinois	59,753	47.0	42
Indiana	39,233	62.9	25
Iowa	16,345	55.3	32
Kansas	13,301	48.6	39
Kentucky	22,623	54.6	33
Louisiana	22,989	50.9	36
Maine	8,771	66.6	21
Maryland	27,382	49.3	38
Massachusetts	22,477	35.0	46
Michigan	54,721	54.1	34
Minnesota	41,843	82.0	13
Mississippi	14,532	50.1	37
Missouri	32,791	57.0	31
Montana	4,975	53.7	35
Nebraska	10,920	62.5	26
Nevada	44,556	190.8	1
New Hampshire	8,653	66.6	20
New Jersey	35,936	41.3	44
New Mexico	12,555	66.0	22
New York	53,497	27.8	49
North Carolina	93,077	109.0	6
North Dakota	4,033	63.6	24
Ohio	51,695	45.1	43
Oklahoma	17,068	48.4	40
Oregon	27,309	76.0	15
Pennsylvania	49,665	40.0	45
Rhode Island	2,532	23.4	50
South Carolina	43,230	103.0	7
South Dakota	5,839	75.7	17
Tennessee	44,791	75.9	16
Texas	188,842	84.0	12
Utah	24,267	101.6	8
Vermont	3,588	57.7	29
Virginia	63,220	84.7	11
Washington	50,089	80.7	14
West Virginia	5,716	31.5	48
Wisconsin	39,992	72.6	18
Wyoming	3,317	65.5	23
50 States	2,068,141	70.6	
DC	1,936	35.0	
United States	2,070,077	70.5	

Rank in order per 10,000 population	
1	Nevada
2	Arizona
3	Florida
4	Idaho
5	Georgia
6	North Carolina
7	South Carolina
8	Utah
9	Colorado
10	Delaware
11	Virginia
12	Texas
13	Minnesota
14	Washington
15	Oregon
16	Tennessee
17	South Dakota
18	Wisconsin
19	Hawaii
20	New Hampshire
21	Maine
22	New Mexico
23	Wyoming
24	North Dakota
25	Indiana
26	Nebraska
27	Alabama
28	California
29	Vermont
30	Arkansas
31	Missouri
32	Iowa
33	Kentucky
34	Michigan
35	Montana
36	Louisiana
37	Mississippi
38	Maryland
39	Kansas
40	Oklahoma
41	Alaska
42	Illinois
43	Ohio
44	New Jersey
45	Pennsylvania
46	Massachusetts
47	Connecticut
48	West Virginia
49	New York
50	Rhode Island

Note: Numbers that appear to be identical are rounded and vary slightly in actual value. The rankings reflect the actual values before rounding. See the introduction for more details.

B-21 Percentage Change in Home Prices, 2000–2005

State	Percentage change in price	Rank
Alabama	26.15	39
Alaska	42.16	23
Arizona	66.96	12
Arkansas	29.25	35
California	109.68	1
Colorado	30.69	32
Connecticut	62.59	15
Delaware	63.76	14
Florida	90.24	5
Georgia	29.72	34
Hawaii	92.62	4
Idaho	36.56	25
Illinois	40.14	24
Indiana	20.34	50
Iowa	25.28	41
Kansas	26.52	37
Kentucky	25.12	42
Louisiana	29.95	33
Maine	66.56	13
Maryland	86.75	6
Massachusetts	70.70	11
Michigan	25.50	40
Minnesota	53.75	17
Mississippi	22.86	47
Missouri	34.10	29
Montana	46.60	19
Nebraska	22.38	48
Nevada	94.05	3
New Hampshire	71.41	9
New Jersey	80.49	7
New Mexico	35.59	27
New York	71.16	10
North Carolina	24.21	44
North Dakota	35.07	28
Ohio	22.94	46
Oklahoma	26.30	38
Oregon	44.69	21
Pennsylvania	49.59	18
Rhode Island	100.70	2
South Carolina	28.96	36
South Dakota	30.79	31
Tennessee	24.76	43
Texas	23.37	45
Utah	21.75	49
Vermont	60.16	16
Virginia	73.30	8
Washington	44.96	20
West Virginia	32.39	30
Wisconsin	36.41	26
Wyoming	44.29	22
50 States	n/a	
DC	113.10	
United States	53.29	

Rank in order by percentage	
1	California
2	Rhode Island
3	Nevada
4	Hawaii
5	Florida
6	Maryland
7	New Jersey
8	Virginia
9	New Hampshire
10	New York
11	Massachusetts
12	Arizona
13	Maine
14	Delaware
15	Connecticut
16	Vermont
17	Minnesota
18	Pennsylvania
19	Montana
20	Washington
21	Oregon
22	Wyoming
23	Alaska
24	Illinois
25	Idaho
26	Wisconsin
27	New Mexico
28	North Dakota
29	Missouri
30	West Virginia
31	South Dakota
32	Colorado
33	Louisiana
34	Georgia
35	Arkansas
36	South Carolina
37	Kansas
38	Oklahoma
39	Alabama
40	Michigan
41	Iowa
42	Kentucky
43	Tennessee
44	North Carolina
45	Texas
46	Ohio
47	Mississippi
48	Nebraska
49	Utah
50	Indiana

B-22 Net Farm Income, 2004

State	Net farm income $ (in thousands)	Net farm income per capita $	Rank by total income
Alabama	2,034,116	449	13
Alaska	15,790	24	50
Arizona	1,399,446	244	22
Arkansas	3,242,643	1,178	6
California	12,249,636	341	1
Colorado	1,298,832	282	23
Connecticut	102,286	29	45
Delaware	349,790	421	38
Florida	2,373,158	136	11
Georgia	2,844,610	322	8
Hawaii	121,943	97	42
Idaho	1,536,468	1,103	18
Illinois	4,022,264	316	4
Indiana	2,360,081	378	12
Iowa	5,683,117	1,924	3
Kansas	1,466,321	536	19
Kentucky	1,083,229	261	26
Louisiana	822,428	182	30
Maine	111,362	85	44
Maryland	587,940	106	35
Massachusetts	75,715	12	46
Michigan	1,056,863	105	27
Minnesota	2,645,305	519	9
Mississippi	1,801,653	621	17
Missouri	2,491,980	433	10
Montana	721,730	779	32
Nebraska	3,459,064	1,980	5
Nevada	127,664	55	41
New Hampshire	36,670	28	48
New Jersey	157,786	18	40
New Mexico	862,414	453	29
New York	638,475	33	33
North Carolina	2,989,725	350	7
North Dakota	971,069	1,531	28
Ohio	1,417,299	124	21
Oklahoma	1,451,903	412	20
Oregon	1,293,222	360	24
Pennsylvania	1,272,526	103	25
Rhode Island	18,424	17	49
South Carolina	772,536	184	31
South Dakota	2,012,435	2,611	14
Tennessee	457,656	78	36
Texas	6,722,369	299	2
Utah	381,757	160	37
Vermont	117,823	190	43
Virginia	627,643	84	34
Washington	2,012,080	324	15
West Virginia	37,540	21	47
Wisconsin	1,979,478	359	16
Wyoming	223,381	441	39
50 States	82,539,640	282	
DC	n/a	n/a	
United States*	82,539,641	281	

**Due to rounding or data sources, the 50-state total plus D.C. may not equal the U.S. total. Please see introduction.*

Rank in order by total income	
1	California
2	Texas
3	Iowa
4	Illinois
5	Nebraska
6	Arkansas
7	North Carolina
8	Georgia
9	Minnesota
10	Missouri
11	Florida
12	Indiana
13	Alabama
14	South Dakota
15	Washington
16	Wisconsin
17	Mississippi
18	Idaho
19	Kansas
20	Oklahoma
21	Ohio
22	Arizona
23	Colorado
24	Oregon
25	Pennsylvania
26	Kentucky
27	Michigan
28	North Dakota
29	New Mexico
30	Louisiana
31	South Carolina
32	Montana
33	New York
34	Virginia
35	Maryland
36	Tennessee
37	Utah
38	Delaware
39	Wyoming
40	New Jersey
41	Nevada
42	Hawaii
43	Vermont
44	Maine
45	Connecticut
46	Massachusetts
47	West Virginia
48	New Hampshire
49	Rhode Island
50	Alaska

B-23 Financial Institution Assets, 2004

State	Total assets $ (in millions)	Per capita assets $	Rank per capita
Alabama	237,299	52,382	8
Alaska	3,893	5,940	49
Arizona	59,322	10,328	42
Arkansas	40,687	14,781	32
California	838,479	23,360	20
Colorado	39,397	8,562	44
Connecticut	60,729	17,333	26
Delaware	436,011	525,084	2
Florida	127,319	7,318	47
Georgia	224,677	25,447	16
Hawaii	33,843	26,799	12
Idaho	5,462	3,920	50
Illinois	340,636	26,793	13
Indiana	102,752	16,473	28
Iowa	51,092	17,293	27
Kansas	57,820	21,137	23
Kentucky	51,470	12,415	38
Louisiana	59,778	13,238	34
Maine	43,005	32,647	10
Maryland	46,227	8,317	45
Massachusetts	224,188	34,939	9
Michigan	194,650	19,248	25
Minnesota	63,483	12,445	37
Mississippi	42,051	14,486	33
Missouri	91,787	15,950	30
Montana	14,646	15,802	31
Nebraska	46,087	26,377	15
Nevada	56,086	24,022	19
New Hampshire	31,234	24,035	18
New Jersey	167,720	19,281	24
New Mexico	15,823	8,314	46
New York	1,166,151	60,651	7
North Carolina	1,302,251	152,467	4
North Dakota	15,413	24,297	17
Ohio	1,579,724	137,859	5
Oklahoma	56,422	16,013	29
Oregon	23,600	6,565	48
Pennsylvania	330,986	26,679	14
Rhode Island	246,069	227,708	3
South Carolina	44,476	10,594	41
South Dakota	442,451	573,954	1
Tennessee	133,491	22,622	21
Texas	215,441	9,579	43
Utah	193,304	80,913	6
Vermont	7,867	12,660	35
Virginia	221,222	29,655	11
Washington	78,503	12,654	36
West Virginia	19,846	10,932	40
Wisconsin	118,361	21,485	22
Wyoming	5,689	11,231	39
50 States	10,008,920	34,148	
DC	899	1,624	
United States*	10,104,623	34,410	

**Due to rounding or data sources, the 50-state total plus D.C. may not equal the U.S. total. Please see introduction.*

Rank in order per capita	
1	South Dakota
2	Delaware
3	Rhode Island
4	North Carolina
5	Ohio
6	Utah
7	New York
8	Alabama
9	Massachusetts
10	Maine
11	Virginia
12	Hawaii
13	Illinois
14	Pennsylvania
15	Nebraska
16	Georgia
17	North Dakota
18	New Hampshire
19	Nevada
20	California
21	Tennessee
22	Wisconsin
23	Kansas
24	New Jersey
25	Michigan
26	Connecticut
27	Iowa
28	Indiana
29	Oklahoma
30	Missouri
31	Montana
32	Arkansas
33	Mississippi
34	Louisiana
35	Vermont
36	Washington
37	Minnesota
38	Kentucky
39	Wyoming
40	West Virginia
41	South Carolina
42	Arizona
43	Texas
44	Colorado
45	Maryland
46	New Mexico
47	Florida
48	Oregon
49	Alaska
50	Idaho

B-24 Bankruptcy Filings by Individuals and Businesses, 2005

State	Bankruptcy petitions	Petitions per 1,000 residents	Rank per 1,000
Alabama	42,640	9.41	2
Alaska	1,608	2.45	50
Arizona	32,425	5.65	22
Arkansas	25,469	9.25	3
California	122,588	3.42	45
Colorado	30,244	6.57	18
Connecticut	11,772	3.36	46
Delaware	3,597	4.33	36
Florida	85,849	4.93	30
Georgia	77,300	8.75	5
Hawaii	3,182	2.52	49
Idaho	9,690	6.95	13
Illinois	83,551	6.57	19
Indiana	55,884	8.96	4
Iowa	14,308	4.84	31
Kansas	17,342	6.34	20
Kentucky	29,206	7.04	10
Louisiana	31,100	6.89	15
Maine	4,702	3.57	44
Maryland	28,503	5.13	27
Massachusetts	19,624	3.06	47
Michigan	68,512	6.77	17
Minnesota	19,353	3.79	40
Mississippi	21,822	7.52	9
Missouri	39,176	6.81	16
Montana	4,413	4.76	32
Nebraska	9,645	5.52	23
Nevada	16,262	6.97	12
New Hampshire	4,886	3.76	42
New Jersey	40,719	4.68	33
New Mexico	10,053	5.28	24
New York	81,739	4.25	37
North Carolina	37,543	4.40	34
North Dakota	2,455	3.87	39
Ohio	95,762	8.36	7
Oklahoma	28,204	8.00	8
Oregon	25,304	7.04	11
Pennsylvania	62,262	5.02	29
Rhode Island	4,449	4.12	38
South Carolina	15,224	3.63	43
South Dakota	2,914	3.78	41
Tennessee	60,848	10.31	1
Texas	97,516	4.34	35
Utah	20,514	8.59	6
Vermont	1,746	2.81	48
Virginia	38,788	5.20	26
Washington	37,743	6.08	21
West Virginia	12,574	6.93	14
Wisconsin	29,043	5.27	25
Wyoming	2,549	5.03	28
50 States	1,622,602	5.54	
DC	1,892	3.42	
United States*	1,637,254	5.58	

**Due to rounding or data sources, the 50-state total plus D.C. may not equal the U.S. total. Please see introduction.*

Rank in order per 1,000 residents	
1	Tennessee
2	Alabama
3	Arkansas
4	Indiana
5	Georgia
6	Utah
7	Ohio
8	Oklahoma
9	Mississippi
10	Kentucky
11	Oregon
12	Nevada
13	Idaho
14	West Virginia
15	Louisiana
16	Missouri
17	Michigan
18	Colorado
19	Illinois
20	Kansas
21	Washington
22	Arizona
23	Nebraska
24	New Mexico
25	Wisconsin
26	Virginia
27	Maryland
28	Wyoming
29	Pennsylvania
30	Florida
31	Iowa
32	Montana
33	New Jersey
34	North Carolina
35	Texas
36	Delaware
37	New York
38	Rhode Island
39	North Dakota
40	Minnesota
41	South Dakota
42	New Hampshire
43	South Carolina
44	Maine
45	California
46	Connecticut
47	Massachusetts
48	Vermont
49	Hawaii
50	Alaska

Note: Numbers that appear to be identical are rounded and vary slightly in actual value. The rankings reflect the actual values before rounding. See the introduction for more details.

B-25 Patents Issued, FY 2004

State	Patents issued	Patents per 100,000 population	Rank per 100,000
Alabama	454	10.0	43
Alaska	58	8.8	46
Arizona	1,746	30.4	20
Arkansas	172	6.2	49
California	22,389	62.4	4
Colorado	2,366	51.4	8
Connecticut	1,760	50.2	9
Delaware	411	49.5	10
Florida	3,144	18.1	30
Georgia	1,504	17.0	31
Hawaii	106	8.4	47
Idaho	1,831	131.4	1
Illinois	3,994	31.4	19
Indiana	1,596	25.6	25
Iowa	771	26.1	24
Kansas	512	18.7	29
Kentucky	491	11.8	41
Louisiana	428	9.5	45
Maine	161	12.2	39
Maryland	1,517	27.3	23
Massachusetts	4,109	64.0	3
Michigan	4,260	42.1	11
Minnesota	3,178	62.3	5
Mississippi	164	5.6	50
Missouri	961	16.7	33
Montana	144	15.5	35
Nebraska	255	14.6	37
Nevada	482	20.6	28
New Hampshire	699	53.8	7
New Jersey	3,517	40.4	13
New Mexico	394	20.7	27
New York	6,788	35.3	15
North Carolina	2,122	24.8	26
North Dakota	61	9.6	44
Ohio	3,678	32.1	17
Oklahoma	545	15.5	36
Oregon	1,970	54.8	6
Pennsylvania	3,397	27.4	22
Rhode Island	362	33.5	16
South Carolina	609	14.5	38
South Dakota	89	11.5	42
Tennessee	956	16.2	34
Texas	6,424	28.6	21
Utah	763	31.9	18
Vermont	442	71.1	2
Virginia	1,255	16.8	32
Washington	2,544	41.0	12
West Virginia	116	6.4	48
Wisconsin	2,051	37.2	14
Wyoming	60	11.8	40
50 States	97,806	33.4	
DC	78	14.1	
United States*	97,913	33.3	

**Due to rounding or data sources, the 50-state total plus D.C. may not equal the U.S. total. Please see introduction.*

Rank in order per 100,000 population	
1	Idaho
2	Vermont
3	Massachusetts
4	California
5	Minnesota
6	Oregon
7	New Hampshire
8	Colorado
9	Connecticut
10	Delaware
11	Michigan
12	Washington
13	New Jersey
14	Wisconsin
15	New York
16	Rhode Island
17	Ohio
18	Utah
19	Illinois
20	Arizona
21	Texas
22	Pennsylvania
23	Maryland
24	Iowa
25	Indiana
26	North Carolina
27	New Mexico
28	Nevada
29	Kansas
30	Florida
31	Georgia
32	Virginia
33	Missouri
34	Tennessee
35	Montana
36	Oklahoma
37	Nebraska
38	South Carolina
39	Maine
40	Wyoming
41	Kentucky
42	South Dakota
43	Alabama
44	North Dakota
45	Louisiana
46	Alaska
47	Hawaii
48	West Virginia
49	Arkansas
50	Mississippi

Note: Numbers that appear to be identical are rounded and vary slightly in actual value. The rankings reflect the actual values before rounding. See the introduction for more details.

B-26 Workers' Compensation Temporary Disability Payments, 2005

State	Maximum weekly benefit $	Rank
Alabama	607.00	28
Alaska	832.00	10
Arizona	374.01	49
Arkansas	466.00	44
California	840.00	9
Colorado	674.59	21
Connecticut	931.00	4
Delaware	523.83	39
Florida	626.00	25
Georgia	425.00	47
Hawaii	622.00	26
Idaho	488.77	43
Illinois	1,034.56	3
Indiana	588.00	31
Iowa	1,133.00	1
Kansas	449.00	45
Kentucky	607.23	27
Louisiana	438.00	46
Maine	523.20	40
Maryland	770.00	11
Massachusetts	918.78	5
Michigan	689.00	18
Minnesota	750.00	13
Mississippi	351.41	50
Missouri	675.90	20
Montana	504.00	42
Nebraska	579.00	33
Nevada	633.08	24
New Hampshire	1,069.50	2
New Jersey	666.00	22
New Mexico	563.32	35
New York	400.00	48
North Carolina	704.00	17
North Dakota	577.00	34
Ohio	678.00	19
Oklahoma	528.00	38
Oregon	915.78	6
Pennsylvania	716.00	14
Rhode Island	760.00	12
South Carolina	592.56	29
South Dakota	513.00	41
Tennessee	638.00	23
Texas	539.00	37
Utah	589.00	30
Vermont	915.00	7
Virginia	706.00	16
Washington	905.17	8
West Virginia	545.36	36
Wisconsin	711.00	15
Wyoming	586.00	32
50 States	n/a	
DC	1,022.00	
United States	n/a	

Rank in order by $	
1	Iowa
2	New Hampshire
3	Illinois
4	Connecticut
5	Massachusetts
6	Oregon
7	Vermont
8	Washington
9	California
10	Alaska
11	Maryland
12	Rhode Island
13	Minnesota
14	Pennsylvania
15	Wisconsin
16	Virginia
17	North Carolina
18	Michigan
19	Ohio
20	Missouri
21	Colorado
22	New Jersey
23	Tennessee
24	Nevada
25	Florida
26	Hawaii
27	Kentucky
28	Alabama
29	South Carolina
30	Utah
31	Indiana
32	Wyoming
33	Nebraska
34	North Dakota
35	New Mexico
36	West Virginia
37	Texas
38	Oklahoma
39	Delaware
40	Maine
41	South Dakota
42	Montana
43	Idaho
44	Arkansas
45	Kansas
46	Louisiana
47	Georgia
48	New York
49	Arizona
50	Mississippi

B-27 Average Unemployment Compensation Benefit, 2005

State	Average weekly unemployment compensation benefit $	Rank
Alabama	182.50	50
Alaska	196.59	47
Arizona	194.34	48
Arkansas	230.39	36
California	284.30	11
Colorado	307.49	7
Connecticut	296.58	8
Delaware	247.16	30
Florida	225.24	38
Georgia	248.03	29
Hawaii	343.11	2
Idaho	232.29	35
Illinois	277.06	13
Indiana	272.93	16
Iowa	270.31	17
Kansas	278.71	12
Kentucky	256.67	26
Louisiana	198.24	46
Maine	245.26	32
Maryland	259.36	24
Massachusetts	358.24	1
Michigan	290.21	10
Minnesota	314.38	6
Mississippi	190.73	49
Missouri	206.94	45
Montana	210.51	44
Nebraska	221.75	40
Nevada	263.11	20
New Hampshire	261.68	23
New Jersey	328.87	4
New Mexico	226.30	37
New York	276.69	14
North Carolina	261.77	22
North Dakota	236.34	33
Ohio	257.19	25
Oklahoma	225.09	39
Oregon	267.30	18
Pennsylvania	291.98	9
Rhode Island	340.91	3
South Carolina	221.58	41
South Dakota	211.46	43
Tennessee	215.84	42
Texas	262.74	21
Utah	265.23	19
Vermont	274.88	15
Virginia	251.67	27
Washington	315.79	5
West Virginia	235.17	34
Wisconsin	248.89	28
Wyoming	246.78	31
50 States	n/a	
DC	274.96	
United States	263.75	

Rank in order by $	
1	Massachusetts
2	Hawaii
3	Rhode Island
4	New Jersey
5	Washington
6	Minnesota
7	Colorado
8	Connecticut
9	Pennsylvania
10	Michigan
11	California
12	Kansas
13	Illinois
14	New York
15	Vermont
16	Indiana
17	Iowa
18	Oregon
19	Utah
20	Nevada
21	Texas
22	North Carolina
23	New Hampshire
24	Maryland
25	Ohio
26	Kentucky
27	Virginia
28	Wisconsin
29	Georgia
30	Delaware
31	Wyoming
32	Maine
33	North Dakota
34	West Virginia
35	Idaho
36	Arkansas
37	New Mexico
38	Florida
39	Oklahoma
40	Nebraska
41	South Carolina
42	Tennessee
43	South Dakota
44	Montana
45	Missouri
46	Louisiana
47	Alaska
48	Arizona
49	Mississippi
50	Alabama

B-28 Index of State Economic Momentum, September 2005

State	Index of state economic momentum September 2005	Rank
Alabama	-0.09	24
Alaska	0.14	20
Arizona	2.44	2
Arkansas	-0.17	27
California	0.15	19
Colorado	0.51	14
Connecticut	-0.20	29
Delaware	0.41	16
Florida	1.73	3
Georgia	0.13	21
Hawaii	1.21	6
Idaho	1.69	4
Illinois	-1.35	49
Indiana	-0.97	48
Iowa	-0.67	44
Kansas	-0.39	35
Kentucky	-0.58	41
Louisiana	-0.62	42
Maine	-0.64	43
Maryland	0.34	17
Massachusetts	-0.85	46
Michigan	-2.09	50
Minnesota	-0.33	31
Mississippi	-0.11	25
Missouri	-0.52	40
Montana	0.46	15
Nebraska	-0.75	45
Nevada	4.18	1
New Hampshire	0.26	18
New Jersey	-0.23	30
New Mexico	0.80	8
New York	-0.44	39
North Carolina	0.53	12
North Dakota	-0.14	26
Ohio	-0.97	47
Oklahoma	0.02	22
Oregon	0.52	13
Pennsylvania	-0.37	34
Rhode Island	-0.39	36
South Carolina	-0.36	33
South Dakota	-0.42	37
Tennessee	-0.19	28
Texas	0.60	10
Utah	1.36	5
Vermont	-0.02	23
Virginia	0.70	9
Washington	0.55	11
West Virginia	-0.35	32
Wisconsin	-0.44	38
Wyoming	0.84	7
50 States	0.00	
DC	-0.34	
United States	-0.00	

Rank in order by index	
1	Nevada
2	Arizona
3	Florida
4	Idaho
5	Utah
6	Hawaii
7	Wyoming
8	New Mexico
9	Virginia
10	Texas
11	Washington
12	North Carolina
13	Oregon
14	Colorado
15	Montana
16	Delaware
17	Maryland
18	New Hampshire
19	California
20	Alaska
21	Georgia
22	Oklahoma
23	Vermont
24	Alabama
25	Mississippi
26	North Dakota
27	Arkansas
28	Tennessee
29	Connecticut
30	New Jersey
31	Minnesota
32	West Virginia
33	South Carolina
34	Pennsylvania
35	Kansas
36	Rhode Island
37	South Dakota
38	Wisconsin
39	New York
40	Missouri
41	Kentucky
42	Louisiana
43	Maine
44	Iowa
45	Nebraska
46	Massachusetts
47	Ohio
48	Indiana
49	Illinois
50	Michigan

Note: Numbers that appear to be identical are rounded and vary slightly in actual value. The rankings reflect the actual values before rounding. See the introduction for more details.

B-29 Employment Change, 2004–2005

State	Change in number of jobs July 2004–2005 (in thousands)	Percentage change in employment	Rank by percentage change
Alabama	20.2	1.06	34
Alaska	4.6	1.41	23
Arizona	98.9	4.26	2
Arkansas	11.9	1.03	35
California	220.0	1.52	19
Colorado	45.7	2.09	11
Connecticut	20.5	1.25	26
Delaware	8.6	2.01	14
Florida	245.0	3.31	5
Georgia	24.0	0.62	45
Hawaii	17.0	2.94	7
Idaho	22.9	3.86	3
Illinois	38.2	0.65	43
Indiana	24.7	0.85	40
Iowa	16.6	1.14	30
Kansas	12.3	0.93	38
Kentucky	22.0	1.23	28
Louisiana	8.0	0.42	47
Maine	3.9	0.62	44
Maryland	59.4	2.34	10
Massachusetts	18.9	0.59	46
Michigan	-30.5	-0.70	50
Minnesota	40.5	1.51	20
Mississippi	16.4	1.47	21
Missouri	29.2	1.09	33
Montana	6.9	1.65	17
Nebraska	8.2	0.89	39
Nevada	73.5	6.37	1
New Hampshire	13.0	2.06	13
New Jersey	50.9	1.26	25
New Mexico	16.3	2.07	12
New York	85.0	1.01	36
North Carolina	55.7	1.47	22
North Dakota	3.7	1.11	32
Ohio	14.5	0.27	48
Oklahoma	25.8	1.77	15
Oregon	50.2	3.15	6
Pennsylvania	63.4	1.13	31
Rhode Island	5.8	1.19	29
South Carolina	-3.6	-0.20	49
South Dakota	6.7	1.73	16
Tennessee	21.8	0.81	41
Texas	117.5	1.25	27
Utah	38.1	3.47	4
Vermont	4.8	1.61	18
Virginia	49.0	1.36	24
Washington	68.0	2.51	9
West Virginia	7.2	0.97	37
Wisconsin	22.4	0.79	42
Wyoming	7.1	2.70	8
50 States	1,810.8	1.39	
DC	11.3	1.67	
United States	1,822.1	1.39	

Rank in order by percentage change	
1	Nevada
2	Arizona
3	Idaho
4	Utah
5	Florida
6	Oregon
7	Hawaii
8	Wyoming
9	Washington
10	Maryland
11	Colorado
12	New Mexico
13	New Hampshire
14	Delaware
15	Oklahoma
16	South Dakota
17	Montana
18	Vermont
19	California
20	Minnesota
21	Mississippi
22	North Carolina
23	Alaska
24	Virginia
25	New Jersey
26	Connecticut
27	Texas
28	Kentucky
29	Rhode Island
30	Iowa
31	Pennsylvania
32	North Dakota
33	Missouri
34	Alabama
35	Arkansas
36	New York
37	West Virginia
38	Kansas
39	Nebraska
40	Indiana
41	Tennessee
42	Wisconsin
43	Illinois
44	Maine
45	Georgia
46	Massachusetts
47	Louisiana
48	Ohio
49	South Carolina
50	Michigan

Note: Numbers that appear to be identical are rounded and vary slightly in actual value. The rankings reflect the actual values before rounding. See the introduction for more details.

B-30 Manufacturing Employment Change, 2004-2005

State	Change in number of manufacturing jobs July 2004–2005 (in thousands)	Percentage change in manufacturing employment	Rank by percentage change
Alabama	5.4	1.85	7
Alaska	0.5	2.36	3
Arizona	-0.7	-0.40	29
Arkansas	-1.5	-0.73	34
California	-3.0	-0.19	27
Colorado	-2.7	-1.73	43
Connecticut	-0.3	-0.15	26
Delaware	-1.8	-5.13	49
Florida	3.8	0.98	17
Georgia	-5.5	-1.23	39
Hawaii	-0.2	-1.29	40
Idaho	1.2	1.92	6
Illinois	-6.8	-0.97	36
Indiana	2.1	0.37	21
Iowa	3.1	1.37	13
Kansas	0.7	0.39	20
Kentucky	1.7	0.66	19
Louisiana	-1.8	-1.19	38
Maine	-1.6	-2.54	46
Maryland	-5.2	-3.61	48
Massachusetts	-1.9	-0.60	31
Michigan	-15.7	-2.35	45
Minnesota	4.6	1.33	14
Mississippi	1.5	0.84	18
Missouri	3.2	1.05	16
Montana	0.3	1.54	10
Nebraska	-0.5	-0.49	30
Nevada	1.4	3.01	2
New Hampshire	1.1	1.37	12
New Jersey	-10.3	-3.04	47
New Mexico	0.1	0.28	22
New York	-12.6	-2.13	44
North Carolina	-6.9	-1.19	37
North Dakota	0.4	1.57	9
Ohio	-1.2	-0.15	25
Oklahoma	-1.1	-0.77	35
Oregon	6.2	3.02	1
Pennsylvania	-11.6	-1.67	41
Rhode Island	-2.9	-5.26	50
South Carolina	-4.5	-1.68	42
South Dakota	0.8	2.02	5
Tennessee	-1.1	-0.27	28
Texas	-0.8	-0.09	24
Utah	1.9	1.64	8
Vermont	0.4	1.07	15
Virginia	-2.0	-0.67	33
Washington	3.7	1.38	11
West Virginia	-0.4	-0.63	32
Wisconsin	1.4	0.28	23
Wyoming	0.2	2.08	4
50 States	-58.9	-0.41	
DC	0.1	4.00	
United States	-58.8	-0.41	

Rank in order by percentage change	
1	Oregon
2	Nevada
3	Alaska
4	Wyoming
5	South Dakota
6	Idaho
7	Alabama
8	Utah
9	North Dakota
10	Montana
11	Washington
12	New Hampshire
13	Iowa
14	Minnesota
15	Vermont
16	Missouri
17	Florida
18	Mississippi
19	Kentucky
20	Kansas
21	Indiana
22	New Mexico
23	Wisconsin
24	Texas
25	Ohio
26	Connecticut
27	California
28	Tennessee
29	Arizona
30	Nebraska
31	Massachusetts
32	West Virginia
33	Virginia
34	Arkansas
35	Oklahoma
36	Illinois
37	North Carolina
38	Louisiana
39	Georgia
40	Hawaii
41	Pennsylvania
42	South Carolina
43	Colorado
44	New York
45	Michigan
46	Maine
47	New Jersey
48	Maryland
49	Delaware
50	Rhode Island

Note: Numbers that appear to be identical are rounded and vary slightly in actual value. The rankings reflect the actual values before rounding. See the introduction for more details.

B-31 Home Ownership, 2004

State	Home ownership rate (as percentage)	Rank
Alabama	78.0	2
Alaska	67.2	42
Arizona	68.7	40
Arkansas	69.1	37
California	59.7	49
Colorado	71.1	30
Connecticut	71.7	26
Delaware	77.3	3
Florida	72.2	23
Georgia	70.9	32
Hawaii	60.6	48
Idaho	73.7	12
Illinois	72.7	20
Indiana	75.8	7
Iowa	73.2	17
Kansas	69.9	35
Kentucky	73.3	14
Louisiana	70.6	33
Maine	74.7	10
Maryland	72.1	24
Massachusetts	63.8	46
Michigan	77.1	4
Minnesota	76.4	5
Mississippi	74.0	11
Missouri	72.4	21
Montana	72.4	21
Nebraska	71.2	29
Nevada	65.7	44
New Hampshire	73.3	14
New Jersey	68.8	39
New Mexico	71.5	28
New York	54.8	50
North Carolina	69.8	36
North Dakota	70.0	34
Ohio	73.1	18
Oklahoma	71.1	30
Oregon	69.0	38
Pennsylvania	74.9	8
Rhode Island	61.5	47
South Carolina	76.2	6
South Dakota	68.5	41
Tennessee	71.6	27
Texas	65.5	45
Utah	74.9	8
Vermont	72.0	25
Virginia	73.4	13
Washington	66.0	43
West Virginia	80.3	1
Wisconsin	73.3	14
Wyoming	72.8	19
50 States	n/a	
DC	45.6	
United States	69.0	

Rank in order by rate	
1	West Virginia
2	Alabama
3	Delaware
4	Michigan
5	Minnesota
6	South Carolina
7	Indiana
8	Pennsylvania
8	Utah
10	Maine
11	Mississippi
12	Idaho
13	Virginia
14	Kentucky
14	New Hampshire
14	Wisconsin
17	Iowa
18	Ohio
19	Wyoming
20	Illinois
21	Missouri
21	Montana
23	Florida
24	Maryland
25	Vermont
26	Connecticut
27	Tennessee
28	New Mexico
29	Nebraska
30	Colorado
30	Oklahoma
32	Georgia
33	Louisiana
34	North Dakota
35	Kansas
36	North Carolina
37	Arkansas
38	Oregon
39	New Jersey
40	Arizona
41	South Dakota
42	Alaska
43	Washington
44	Nevada
45	Texas
46	Massachusetts
47	Rhode Island
48	Hawaii
49	California
50	New York

Note: Ties in ranking reflect ties in actual values.

B-32 Annual Electricity Use Per Residential Customer, 2003

State	Average annual kwh use per residential customer	Rank
Alabama	14,797	3
Alaska	8,047	40
Arizona	12,809	14
Arkansas	12,765	15
California	6,646	49
Colorado	8,208	39
Connecticut	9,385	34
Delaware	11,733	22
Florida	14,660	4
Georgia	13,159	10
Hawaii	7,848	42
Idaho	12,290	20
Illinois	8,808	36
Indiana	11,673	24
Iowa	10,028	30
Kansas	10,718	27
Kentucky	13,446	9
Louisiana	15,328	1
Maine	6,412	50
Maryland	12,945	13
Massachusetts	7,705	43
Michigan	7,971	41
Minnesota	9,581	33
Mississippi	14,618	5
Missouri	12,298	19
Montana	9,763	32
Nebraska	11,727	23
Nevada	11,601	25
New Hampshire	7,547	44
New Jersey	8,386	38
New Mexico	7,076	47
New York	6,853	48
North Carolina	13,060	11
North Dakota	12,402	18
Ohio	10,260	28
Oklahoma	12,966	12
Oregon	11,836	21
Pennsylvania	10,132	29
Rhode Island	7,112	46
South Carolina	14,145	7
South Dakota	11,106	26
Tennessee	15,143	2
Texas	14,289	6
Utah	8,817	35
Vermont	7,331	45
Virginia	13,979	8
Washington	12,483	17
West Virginia	12,534	16
Wisconsin	8,734	37
Wyoming	9,845	31
50 States	n/a	
DC	9,476	
United States	10,876	

Rank in order by average use	
1	Louisiana
2	Tennessee
3	Alabama
4	Florida
5	Mississippi
6	Texas
7	South Carolina
8	Virginia
9	Kentucky
10	Georgia
11	North Carolina
12	Oklahoma
13	Maryland
14	Arizona
15	Arkansas
16	West Virginia
17	Washington
18	North Dakota
19	Missouri
20	Idaho
21	Oregon
22	Delaware
23	Nebraska
24	Indiana
25	Nevada
26	South Dakota
27	Kansas
28	Ohio
29	Pennsylvania
30	Iowa
31	Wyoming
32	Montana
33	Minnesota
34	Connecticut
35	Utah
36	Illinois
37	Wisconsin
38	New Jersey
39	Colorado
40	Alaska
41	Michigan
42	Hawaii
43	Massachusetts
44	New Hampshire
45	Vermont
46	Rhode Island
47	New Mexico
48	New York
49	California
50	Maine

B-33 Average Cost Per Kilowatt Hour, 2003

State	Average cost for industrial customer (cents per kwh)	Average cost for residential customer (cents per kwh)	Residential cost as percentage of industrial cost	Rank by residential as percentage of industrial
Alabama	4.0	7.4	185.6	8
Alaska	7.9	12.0	152.4	38
Arizona	5.4	8.3	155.3	35
Arkansas	4.0	7.2	179.3	14
California	9.8	12.0	121.9	50
Colorado	5.1	8.1	159.6	30
Connecticut	7.9	11.3	142.7	42
Delaware	5.1	8.6	167.0	23
Florida	5.4	8.6	158.1	32
Georgia	4.0	7.7	191.7	6
Hawaii	12.2	16.7	137.2	44
Idaho	4.2	6.2	150.1	40
Illinois	4.9	8.4	170.6	20
Indiana	3.9	7.0	179.4	13
Iowa	4.2	8.6	206.0	1
Kansas	4.6	7.7	167.0	24
Kentucky	3.2	5.8	181.2	12
Louisiana	5.6	7.8	140.7	43
Maine	6.4	12.4	194.8	4
Maryland	4.9	7.7	158.0	33
Massachusetts	9.1	11.7	128.2	47
Michigan	5.0	8.4	168.3	22
Minnesota	4.4	7.7	175.6	15
Mississippi	4.5	7.6	169.6	21
Missouri	4.5	7.0	154.8	36
Montana	4.0	7.6	188.5	7
Nebraska	4.2	6.9	164.3	26
Nevada	7.3	9.0	123.4	49
New Hampshire	9.4	12.0	127.6	48
New Jersey	7.5	10.7	143.2	41
New Mexico	5.0	8.7	175.6	16
New York	7.1	14.3	200.5	2
North Carolina	4.8	8.3	173.6	18
North Dakota	4.0	6.5	163.8	27
Ohio	4.8	8.3	172.7	19
Oklahoma	4.6	7.5	162.8	29
Oregon	4.6	7.1	152.4	39
Pennsylvania	6.1	9.6	155.7	34
Rhode Island	9.1	11.6	128.2	46
South Carolina	4.0	8.0	200.5	3
South Dakota	4.5	7.5	165.7	25
Tennessee	4.3	6.5	152.7	37
Texas	5.3	9.2	173.6	17
Utah	3.8	6.9	182.0	11
Vermont	8.0	12.8	159.4	31
Virginia	4.2	7.8	183.6	10
Washington	4.8	6.3	132.4	45
West Virginia	3.8	6.2	163.6	28
Wisconsin	4.7	8.7	184.0	9
Wyoming	3.7	7.0	192.7	5
50 States	n/a	n/a	n/a	
DC	5.6	7.7	136.3	
United States	5.1	8.7	169.5	

Rank in order by percentage	
1	Iowa
2	New York
3	South Carolina
4	Maine
5	Wyoming
6	Georgia
7	Montana
8	Alabama
9	Wisconsin
10	Virginia
11	Utah
12	Kentucky
13	Indiana
14	Arkansas
15	Minnesota
16	New Mexico
17	Texas
18	North Carolina
19	Ohio
20	Illinois
21	Mississippi
22	Michigan
23	Delaware
24	Kansas
25	South Dakota
26	Nebraska
27	North Dakota
28	West Virginia
29	Oklahoma
30	Colorado
31	Vermont
32	Florida
33	Maryland
34	Pennsylvania
35	Arizona
36	Missouri
37	Tennessee
38	Alaska
39	Oregon
40	Idaho
41	New Jersey
42	Connecticut
43	Louisiana
44	Hawaii
45	Washington
46	Rhode Island
47	Massachusetts
48	New Hampshire
49	Nevada
50	California

Note: Numbers that appear to be identical are rounded and vary slightly in actual value. The rankings reflect the actual values before rounding. See the introduction for more details.

B-34 New Companies, 2004

State	New companies	New companies per 1,000 employees	Rank per 1,000 employees
Alabama	9,413	4.6	45
Alaska	1,848	6.0	26
Arizona	12,421	4.7	43
Arkansas	7,852	6.4	22
California	117,016	7.1	15
Colorado	23,694	9.9	4
Connecticut	9,064	5.3	33
Delaware	3,270	8.1	10
Florida	77,754	9.7	6
Georgia	29,547	7.1	16
Hawaii	3,698	6.2	24
Idaho	7,814	11.7	1
Illinois	28,453	4.7	42
Indiana	13,906	4.6	46
Iowa	5,954	3.9	50
Kansas	6,742	4.9	41
Kentucky	8,807	4.7	44
Louisiana	9,875	5.1	39
Maine	4,300	6.4	21
Maryland	21,751	7.9	11
Massachusetts	18,822	5.8	27
Michigan	24,625	5.2	36
Minnesota	15,167	5.4	32
Mississippi	6,141	4.9	40
Missouri	16,155	5.7	30
Montana	4,588	9.9	5
Nebraska	4,849	5.1	37
Nevada	10,483	9.3	7
New Hampshire	4,865	7.0	17
New Jersey	35,895	8.6	9
New Mexico	5,683	6.6	19
New York	62,854	7.1	14
North Carolina	23,387	5.8	28
North Dakota	1,747	5.1	38
Ohio	22,725	4.1	48
Oklahoma	9,263	5.7	29
Oregon	13,481	7.8	12
Pennsylvania	33,188	5.6	31
Rhode Island	3,932	7.4	13
South Carolina	11,745	6.2	25
South Dakota	1,691	4.1	49
Tennessee	17,415	6.3	23
Texas	54,098	5.2	35
Utah	11,357	10.0	3
Vermont	2,322	6.8	18
Virginia	24,134	6.6	20
Washington	31,955	10.5	2
West Virginia	3,937	5.3	34
Wisconsin	13,093	4.5	47
Wyoming	2,519	9.3	8
50 States	895,295	6.4	
DC	4,393	16.0	
United States*	904,607	6.5	

**Due to rounding or data sources, the 50-state total plus D.C. may not equal the U.S. total. Please see introduction.*

Rank in order per 1,000 employees	
1	Idaho
2	Washington
3	Utah
4	Colorado
5	Montana
6	Florida
7	Nevada
8	Wyoming
9	New Jersey
10	Delaware
11	Maryland
12	Oregon
13	Rhode Island
14	New York
15	California
16	Georgia
17	New Hampshire
18	Vermont
19	New Mexico
20	Virginia
21	Maine
22	Arkansas
23	Tennessee
24	Hawaii
25	South Carolina
26	Alaska
27	Massachusetts
28	North Carolina
29	Oklahoma
30	Missouri
31	Pennsylvania
32	Minnesota
33	Connecticut
34	West Virginia
35	Texas
36	Michigan
37	Nebraska
38	North Dakota
39	Louisiana
40	Mississippi
41	Kansas
42	Illinois
43	Arizona
44	Kentucky
45	Alabama
46	Indiana
47	Wisconsin
48	Ohio
49	South Dakota
50	Iowa

Note: Numbers that appear to be identical are rounded and vary slightly in actual value. The rankings reflect the actual values before rounding. See the introduction for more details.

Source Notes for Economies (Section B)

B-1 Personal Income, 2004: These data reflect income of residents of each state, including pensions, dividends, interest, and rent as well as amounts received from employers as wages and salaries. These estimates are made by the Department of Commerce each quarter. The calendar year 2004 estimates were released in September of 2005 and are available on the department's Web site (www.bea.doc.gov).

B-2 Gross State Product, Total and Per Capita, 2004: The gross state product is the state counterpart of the gross national product (now called the gross domestic product). This is the single best measure of the size of a state's economy. It is the sum of all the value of production of goods and services. While estimates of national data are released on a current basis, state-by-state estimates are made by the Department of Commerce only with a substantial lag. These 2004 data were released in October 2005 and come from the same source as Table B-1.

B-3 Per Capita Personal Income, 2004: These data, from the same source as Table B-1, reflect personal income in relation to population. They are a common measure of the relative affluence of each state. The data are also used to determine what percentage of each state's Medicaid costs the federal government pays .

B-4 Personal Income from Wages and Salaries, 2004: These data, from the same source as Table B-1, show the portion of personal income that comes from wages and salaries. The percentages, calculated for *State Fact Finder*, indicate relative reliance of states' economies on current work, as distinct from investments and government payments.

B-5 Average Annual Pay, 2004: These data reflect the average pay of workers in each state. They are from the Department of Labor's Quarterly Census of Employment and Wages (www.bls.gov/cew/home.htm).

B-6 Average Hourly Earnings, 2005: These data are often used to compare wage costs of the states. They are prepared monthly by the Department of Labor and released in the publication *Employment and Earnings*. These August 2005 data appeared in the October 2005 edition. These data only cover production workers, excluding service and retailing employees as well as government employees.

B-7 Value Added in Manufacturing, 2003: This table measures the value that is added by manufacturing operations in each state. Value added is calculated by subtracting the value of inputs to production from the value of the outputs. For example, the value of manufacturing a car is the value of the car minus the value of components, such as engines, purchased to manufacture it. These data are from the U.S. Census Bureau's *2003 Annual Survey of Manufacturers* issued in May of 2005. Value added per worker can be calculated from this report. This per worker statistic is sometimes used to compare the productivity of state work forces but is a misleading statistic because capital investments in machinery make massive contributions to adding values in highly automated operations such as chemical manufacturing.

B-8 Cost of Living, 2005: The federal government has not attempted to produce measures that compare living costs since the 1980s and, even then, provided the data only for selected large metropolitan areas, not states. Some researchers periodically try to produce such indices, but they are of doubtful statistical validity. The one shown is from the Missouri Economic Research and Information Center and is based on voluntary surveys of chambers of commerce taken by ACCRA, a non-profit economic and community development research organization. The data cover the second quarter of calendar year 2005.

B-9 Average Annual Pay in Manufacturing, 2004: This is the manufacturing component of the data described for Table B-5, from the same source. States with many jobs in high-wage industries, like chemical or vehicle manufacturing, rank highest.

B-10 Average Annual Pay in Retailing, 2004: This is the retailing component of the data described for Table B-5, from the same source. Because most retailing jobs are entry-level positions requiring little experience or formal training, these data are a good measure of the costs of obtaining new workers in the states.

B-11 Labor Force, 2005: About 149.9 million people, 51 percent of Americans, are either working or looking for work but not working (unemployed). These two groups make up the labor force. The rest of the population are not in the labor force because they are retired, too young to work, disabled, or have opted not to work. This group includes "discouraged workers" who indicate that they would like to work but have given up hope of finding a job.

The labor force data are available on the Web site of the Bureau of Labor Statistics (www.bls.gov). They are also available in its monthly publication *Regional and State Employment and Unemployment* released on October 21, 2005, with preliminary estimates for September. The data are seasonally adjusted to make month-to-month comparisons possible despite fluctuations associated with time of the year such as hiring by retail stores for the December holiday season and summertime hiring of students. The 2004 population estimates come from the U.S. Census Bureau (see Table A-1). Labor force as a percentage of population varies among states because of differences in the percentage of population at working-age and the percentage of people who want to work—the labor force participation rate.

B-12 Unemployed and Unemployment Rate, 2005: The estimates of persons unemployed and the unemployment rate (percentage of labor force unemployed) are from the same source as Table B-11.

B-13 Employment and Employment Rate, 2005: The Bureau of Labor Statistics faces a perpetual dilemma in presenting statistics on employment and unemployment. It must make national unemployment estimates based on a survey of households in which people are asked whether they are looking for work. This *household survey* also provides the national estimate of the people who are employed. But the sample is too small to provide reliable estimates of employment for less populous states. To provide estimates for those states, the bureau obtains monthly reports from employers, called the *establishment survey*. The national totals from the two different surveys often diverge by hundreds of thousands of workers. Periodically, the bureau "benchmarks" the totals and revises past estimates to make them consistent.

To make the matter even more complicated, the bureau attempts in various complex ways to use the results of one survey to guide estimating procedures for the other. How this is done is explained in detail in various technical publications available from the bureau. The net effect harmonizes the results of the two approaches better for large states than small ones. For example, the employment in Wyoming implicit in the bureau's estimates is the labor force (Table B-11) minus the unemployed (Table B-12)—275,000— but the employment published in a different table in the report (see notes to Table B-11) is 263,300. For Table B-13 *State Fact Finder* uses the implicit estimate, employment is thus derived by subtracting the number of unemployed from the labor force. The employment rate is the relationship between the employment shown and the labor force on Table B-11.

Because *State Fact Finder* contains many tables relying on employment data for individual states, it uses the best employment estimates available, those from the establishment survey, in Table B-14 and other tables showing state-by-state details of employment.

B-14 Government Employment, 2005: This table, from the same source as Table B-11, uses seasonally adjusted data from the establishment survey (see notes to Table B-13 on differences between the household and establishment surveys) which were made available by the Bureau of Labor Statistics on October 21, 2005, with preliminary estimates for September. The employment reported on this table includes federal, state, and local employees.

These Bureau of Labor Statistics data on government employment covering 2005 are more current than data provided by the U.S. Census Bureau. The latest Census Bureau data, published in 2005, cover information on March 2004 payrolls. But the Census Bureau data are used often in *State Fact Finder* because the Bureau of Labor Statistics data do not include such details as how much employees are paid and the type of service (for example, education, transportation) they provide.

B-15 Manufacturing Employment, 2005: These data are comparable to those shown in Table B-14 but cover manufacturing.

B-16 *Fortune* 500 Companies, 2005: Two major business magazines—*Fortune* and *Forbes*—provide annual listings of the largest companies in America, using somewhat different criteria. This table reflects the list as published in *Fortune* (April 5, 2005). Because large states tend to have the most large companies, the rankings are based on a calculation of the representation of these companies' headquarters in each state in relation to population of that state.

B-17 *Forbes* 500 Companies, 2003: This table is the counterpart of Table B-16. This listing was published in *Forbes* magazine (March 28, 2003). Because *Forbes* uses four separate criteria for its listings, 802 American companies are included in the "500" list.

B-18 Tourism Spending, 2003: The travel industry is a major factor in the economies of all states and a dominant factor in a few. However, data on it are elusive. Many trips combine business and pleasure, so separating tourism from business is difficult. Other trips combine an activity, such as coming home for the holidays, with a tourist activity, such as visiting a museum. Restaurants and gift shops do not normally know whether their customers are tourists or local customers. Consequently, estimates of tourism spending have more guesswork than most of the statistics in *State Fact Finder*. The 2003 data shown in the table are the most up-to-date. They are prepared by the Travel Industry Association of America (TIA) and are published in *Tourism Works for America*. The data are based on the Travel Industry Association's Travel Economic Impact Model. The state tourism offices may use a different methodology and the data and results may not be comparable to this TIA table.

B-19 Exports, 2005: National estimates of exports are made quarterly by the Department of Commerce to develop estimates of gross domestic product and balance of payments with other nations. Relatively current estimates by state are also made by the department but are of doubtful reliability because of data-gathering limitations and conceptual problems. For example, does a shipment from a New York port of a product from an Ohio plant of items made from components from Ohio and Mississippi contained in boxes produced in South Carolina constitute an export from New York, Ohio, or somewhere else? The data shown came from the U.S. Census Bureau Web site (www.census.gov).

B-20 Housing Permits, 2004: No state-by-state system exists to report completion of single-family houses and apartment and condominium units, but there are good data on the issuance of permits for such construction. Although some builders obtain permits and then don't build, permits are expensive so most permits are followed by construction. The data shown were compiled by the National Association of Home Builders (NAHB) and are available on its Web site (www.nahb.org). The relationship to population shows which states have rapidly growing populations and which are more stagnant.

B-21 Percentage Change in Home Prices, 2000–2005: Most people are interested in changes in housing prices because of the implications for a specific existing home—usually the one they own. The data often cited in the media, which come from realtors' sales records, come from averages of homes sold. As a result, they include large percentages of new (and typically larger, better equipped, and more expensive) homes in fast-growing states. A preferable way to measure price changes is to examine prices for successive sales of the same homes. This has recently become possible with improvements in computing capacity and the increasing importance of secondary mortgage lenders, who buy massive numbers of mortgages from banks and other lenders. The data in the table reflect this approach.

The information comes from *House Price Index Second Quarter 2005* published by the Office of Federal Housing Enterprise Oversight and available on its Web site (www.ofheo.gov).

B-22 Net Farm Income, 2004: These data reflect the net income derived from farming—the value of farm sales minus the cost of production. They are estimates made by the Department of Agriculture and are available on its Web site (www.ers.usda.gov). The *State Fact Finder* calculation of per capita amounts provides a basis for comparing the importance of agriculture to the economies of each state.

B-23 Financial Institution Assets, 2004: This table shows total assets of banks, trust companies, and savings institutions. These data, from the Federal Deposit Insurance Corporation's *Statistics on Banking: 2004* (www2.fdic.gov), provide a good measure of the importance of banking in each state. However, they provide no indication of the wealth of individuals in a state as deposits flow freely across state lines. States that have successfully tried to draw financial institutions, like Delaware and South Dakota, show large per capita amounts, as do regional banking centers, such as the Boston banks that serve customers throughout New England.

B-24 Bankruptcy Filings by Individuals and Businesses, 2005: These data show how new bankruptcy cases (mostly individuals rather than businesses) were distributed among the states. These data cover the twelve-month period ending June 30, 2005, and come from the Web site of the Administrative Office of the U.S. Courts (www.uscourts.gov).

B-25 Patents Issued, FY 2004: The United States Patent and Trademark Office issued 97,913 new patents in fiscal year 2004 to residents (corporations and individuals) in the states shown. When related to population, this statistic is often used to compare states in the degree to which they are on the forefront of new technology. The data come from the United States Patent and Trademark Office and are available on its Web site (www.uspto.gov) as *Performance and Accountability Report Fiscal Year 2004*. Because patent applications are often made by or for companies, headquarters of companies (for example, DuPont in Delaware and 3M in Minnesota) affect the results.

B-26 Workers' Compensation Temporary Disability Payments, 2005: All states maintain a program that provides compensation for workers who are injured on the job. These programs differ massively from state to state in how much money is paid for certain injuries, how hard it is to prove disability and its relationship to the job, and how employers are forced to pay program costs. These differences, set by state policy, are not captured by aggregate statistics on workers' compensation costs because some industries (like construction and logging) are inherently more hazardous than others (like banking), so state-by-state costs will vary with the mix of industries. This table compares one major dimension of benefit generosity/parsimony, the maximum payment per month to a worker who is temporarily unable to work because of a job-related injury. The data come from the Department of Labor publication dated January 2005, *State Workers' Compensation Laws*.

B-27 Average Unemployment Compensation Benefit, 2005: All states maintain a federally supervised program of unemployment compensation. States have wide discretion in determining how large unemployment compensation payments will be, how long they will last, and how costs are distributed among employers. This table from the Web site of the Department of Labor Employment and Training Administration (ows.doleta.gov) shows the average weekly benefit paid in each state in September 2005.

B-28 Index of State Economic Momentum, September 2005: Each quarter *State Policy Reports* publishes its Index of State Economic Momentum, a statistic created by State Policy Research to compare the recent economic performance of each state in relation to the national average. A state growing at the national average rate would show an index of 0.0 while one growing roughly 1.0 percent faster would show an index of 1.0. Negative numbers show states lagging behind national average growth. The index combines (with equal weights) the most recent known one-year changes in (1) employment, (2) personal income, and (3) population.

B-29 Employment Change, 2004–2005: This table uses Department of Labor data from July 2004 and July 2005 (not seasonally adjusted) to show the change in the number of jobs in each state. The data, from the Bureau of Labor Statistics Web site (www.bls.gov), are one component of the state economic momentum index shown in Table B-28.

B-30 Manufacturing Employment Change, 2004–2005: This table uses Department of Labor (see source for Table B-29) data from July 2004 to July 2005 (not seasonally adjusted) to show the states experiencing job loss and those experiencing job growth in manufacturing. These data are released monthly and revised often, but differences in state economic performance tend to persist from month to month.

B-31 Home Ownership, 2004: These data show the percentage of households living in homes they own. The data come from the *Housing Vacancy Survey*, available on the U.S. Census Bureau Web site (www.census.gov). Because of the relatively small samples, the margin of error for less populous states is relatively large.

B-32 Annual Electricity Use Per Residential Customer, 2003: These data from the Edison Electric Institute (EEI) show differences in electricity use among the states. The results are heavily influenced by the relative importance of heating and air conditioning and the mix of fuels used for heating. These data are not strictly comparable to earlier EEI data. Since 2001, EEI has included data for retail customers serviced by alternative power suppliers.

B-33 Average Cost Per Kilowatt Hour, 2003: These data also come from the Edison Electric Institute (see source for Table B-32), which maintains additional details on other years, types of consumers, and more. The data have many uses. The cost per kilowatt hour permits comparisons among states of electricity costs for households and businesses. The residential rate as a percentage of industrial rate is a useful indicator of the extent to which state regulatory policy (which controls rates charged by private companies) is tilted toward providing low industrial rates to stimulate economic development or low residential rates to keep prices low for voters/consumers at the potential expense of loss of industry. Based on costs of service, industrial users should pay less because they are cheaper per kilowatt to bill and often agree to have service curtailed when there is a shortage of power. See source for Table B-33 for information to consider when comparing 2001 and later data to Edison Electric Institute data from previous years.

B-34 New Companies, 2004: These data show the number of companies that applied for new account numbers from state employment services. These data were made available to *State Fact Finder* by the Department of Labor Unemployment Insurance Service in an e-mail dated November 16, 2005. *State Fact Finder* then related these numbers to the total number of workers in each state. These employment numbers are annual averages and were released on the Bureau of Labor Statistics Web site (www.bls.gov) on March 10, 2005.

Geography

Passage of a national omnibus energy bill looked as if it would happen in 2003 and then again in 2004, but it was August 2005 before such a bill became law. Key to the passage was the removal of two controversial provisions. A liability shield for the makers of a gasoline additive called MTBE was dropped, as was language that would have opened the Arctic National Wildlife Refuge (ANWR) to drilling. Neither of these issues appears ready to go away. Drilling in ANWR quickly became a contentious issue again when it was tacked on (and then stripped from) a defense appropriations bill.

The energy bill passed in 2005 does not set new fuel-efficiency standards nor does it lay out a plan to reduce U.S. dependence on foreign oil. It does establish a diesel emissions reduction program—largely through grants and loans for voluntary retrofits—and allocates funds for conservation and for renewable energy sources such as wind and solar power.

While the federal government remains silent on the issue of greenhouse gases, a handful of states continue to address the problem by opting for higher vehicle emissions standards (Connecticut, Maine, Massachusetts, New Jersey, New York, Rhode Island, and Vermont are following California's lead) and regulating power plant emissions of carbon dioxide (Delaware, Connecticut, Maine, New Hampshire, New Jersey, New York, and Vermont).

Individuals, businesses, and governments are feeling the pinch of rising energy costs. A few energy-producing states are actually reaping some benefits from escalating prices, but overall, energy issues are becoming a major factor negatively affecting economic conditions in the states.

Energy Consumption by Region, 2005	
Per capita energy consumption (in million BTUs)	
Northeast	270
Midwest	378
South	399
West	280
United States	343

Source: Energy Information Administration

C-1 Total Land Area, 2000

State	Land area (in square miles)	Rank
Alabama	50,744	28
Alaska	571,951	1
Arizona	113,635	6
Arkansas	52,068	27
California	155,959	3
Colorado	103,718	8
Connecticut	4,845	48
Delaware	1,954	49
Florida	53,927	26
Georgia	57,906	21
Hawaii	6,423	47
Idaho	82,747	11
Illinois	55,584	24
Indiana	35,867	38
Iowa	55,869	23
Kansas	81,815	13
Kentucky	39,728	36
Louisiana	43,562	33
Maine	30,862	39
Maryland	9,774	42
Massachusetts	7,840	45
Michigan	56,804	22
Minnesota	79,610	14
Mississippi	46,907	31
Missouri	68,886	18
Montana	145,552	4
Nebraska	76,872	15
Nevada	109,826	7
New Hampshire	8,968	44
New Jersey	7,417	46
New Mexico	121,356	5
New York	47,214	30
North Carolina	48,711	29
North Dakota	68,976	17
Ohio	40,948	35
Oklahoma	68,667	19
Oregon	95,997	10
Pennsylvania	44,817	32
Rhode Island	1,045	50
South Carolina	30,110	40
South Dakota	75,885	16
Tennessee	41,217	34
Texas	261,797	2
Utah	82,144	12
Vermont	9,250	43
Virginia	39,594	37
Washington	66,544	20
West Virginia	24,078	41
Wisconsin	54,310	25
Wyoming	97,100	9
50 States	3,537,380	
DC	61	
United States	3,537,441	

Rank in order by square mile	
1	Alaska
2	Texas
3	California
4	Montana
5	New Mexico
6	Arizona
7	Nevada
8	Colorado
9	Wyoming
10	Oregon
11	Idaho
12	Utah
13	Kansas
14	Minnesota
15	Nebraska
16	South Dakota
17	North Dakota
18	Missouri
19	Oklahoma
20	Washington
21	Georgia
22	Michigan
23	Iowa
24	Illinois
25	Wisconsin
26	Florida
27	Arkansas
28	Alabama
29	North Carolina
30	New York
31	Mississippi
32	Pennsylvania
33	Louisiana
34	Tennessee
35	Ohio
36	Kentucky
37	Virginia
38	Indiana
39	Maine
40	South Carolina
41	West Virginia
42	Maryland
43	Vermont
44	New Hampshire
45	Massachusetts
46	New Jersey
47	Hawaii
48	Connecticut
49	Delaware
50	Rhode Island

C-2 Land Owned by Federal Government, 2004

State	Total acres of federally owned land (in thousands)	Percentage of land federally owned	Rank by total acres
Alabama	514	1.6	38
Alaska	252,496	69.1	1
Arizona	34,933	48.1	4
Arkansas	2,408	7.2	20
California	45,393	45.3	3
Colorado	24,355	36.6	11
Connecticut	14	0.4	49
Delaware	26	2.0	48
Florida	2,859	8.2	18
Georgia	1,409	3.8	26
Hawaii	797	19.4	31
Idaho	26,565	50.2	9
Illinois	642	1.8	35
Indiana	463	2.0	39
Iowa	274	0.8	42
Kansas	631	1.2	36
Kentucky	1,379	5.4	27
Louisiana	1,475	5.1	25
Maine	208	1.1	44
Maryland	179	2.8	45
Massachusetts	94	1.9	47
Michigan	3,638	10.0	14
Minnesota	2,874	5.6	17
Mississippi	2,197	7.3	22
Missouri	2,225	5.0	21
Montana	27,910	29.9	8
Nebraska	665	1.4	34
Nevada	59,363	84.5	2
New Hampshire	776	13.5	32
New Jersey	148	3.1	46
New Mexico	32,484	41.8	6
New York	234	0.8	43
North Carolina	3,710	11.8	13
North Dakota	1,186	2.7	28
Ohio	448	1.7	40
Oklahoma	1,586	3.6	24
Oregon	32,716	53.1	5
Pennsylvania	720	2.5	33
Rhode Island	3	0.4	50
South Carolina	561	2.9	37
South Dakota	3,028	6.2	16
Tennessee	866	3.2	30
Texas	3,130	1.9	15
Utah	30,272	57.5	7
Vermont	443	7.5	41
Virginia	2,534	9.9	19
Washington	12,950	30.3	12
West Virginia	1,146	7.4	29
Wisconsin	1,972	5.6	23
Wyoming	26,391	42.3	10
50 States	653,289	28.8	
DC	10	24.7	
United States	653,299	28.8	

Rank in order by total acres	
1	Alaska
2	Nevada
3	California
4	Arizona
5	Oregon
6	New Mexico
7	Utah
8	Montana
9	Idaho
10	Wyoming
11	Colorado
12	Washington
13	North Carolina
14	Michigan
15	Texas
16	South Dakota
17	Minnesota
18	Florida
19	Virginia
20	Arkansas
21	Missouri
22	Mississippi
23	Wisconsin
24	Oklahoma
25	Louisiana
26	Georgia
27	Kentucky
28	North Dakota
29	West Virginia
30	Tennessee
31	Hawaii
32	New Hampshire
33	Pennsylvania
34	Nebraska
35	Illinois
36	Kansas
37	South Carolina
38	Alabama
39	Indiana
40	Ohio
41	Vermont
42	Iowa
43	New York
44	Maine
45	Maryland
46	New Jersey
47	Massachusetts
48	Delaware
49	Connecticut
50	Rhode Island

C-3 State Park Acreage, FY 2005

State	State park acreage	Acreage per 1,000 population	Rank by total acreage
Alabama	49,710	11.0	42
Alaska	3,353,485	5,116.4	1
Arizona	60,921	10.6	38
Arkansas	52,610	19.1	41
California	1,492,622	41.6	3
Colorado	356,688	77.5	8
Connecticut	203,480	58.1	16
Delaware	24,366	29.3	47
Florida	613,701	35.3	4
Georgia	83,809	9.5	32
Hawaii	27,117	21.5	46
Idaho	45,337	32.5	43
Illinois	479,175	37.7	6
Indiana	179,220	28.7	18
Iowa	63,432	21.5	37
Kansas	32,900	12.0	45
Kentucky	58,291	14.1	40
Louisiana	41,204	9.1	44
Maine	98,533	74.8	30
Maryland	268,176	48.2	12
Massachusetts	297,517	46.4	9
Michigan	285,573	28.2	11
Minnesota	221,274	43.4	15
Mississippi	24,287	8.4	48
Missouri	140,318	24.4	22
Montana	59,644	64.4	39
Nebraska	134,681	77.1	24
Nevada	132,524	56.8	26
New Hampshire	232,006	178.5	14
New Jersey	388,569	44.7	7
New Mexico	90,693	47.7	31
New York	1,542,630	80.2	2
North Carolina	174,862	20.5	19
North Dakota	17,401	27.4	49
Ohio	164,406	14.3	20
Oklahoma	71,579	20.3	34
Oregon	99,030	27.5	29
Pennsylvania	290,129	23.4	10
Rhode Island	8,748	8.1	50
South Carolina	80,734	19.2	33
South Dakota	105,396	136.7	28
Tennessee	136,403	23.1	23
Texas	601,558	26.7	5
Utah	149,667	62.6	21
Vermont	68,858	110.8	35
Virginia	64,277	8.6	36
Washington	259,684	41.9	13
West Virginia	195,831	107.9	17
Wisconsin	132,829	24.1	25
Wyoming	119,266	235.5	27
50 States	13,875,151	47.3	
DC	n/a	n/a	
United States	13,875,151	47.2	

Rank in order by total acreage	
1	Alaska
2	New York
3	California
4	Florida
5	Texas
6	Illinois
7	New Jersey
8	Colorado
9	Massachusetts
10	Pennsylvania
11	Michigan
12	Maryland
13	Washington
14	New Hampshire
15	Minnesota
16	Connecticut
17	West Virginia
18	Indiana
19	North Carolina
20	Ohio
21	Utah
22	Missouri
23	Tennessee
24	Nebraska
25	Wisconsin
26	Nevada
27	Wyoming
28	South Dakota
29	Oregon
30	Maine
31	New Mexico
32	Georgia
33	South Carolina
34	Oklahoma
35	Vermont
36	Virginia
37	Iowa
38	Arizona
39	Montana
40	Kentucky
41	Arkansas
42	Alabama
43	Idaho
44	Louisiana
45	Kansas
46	Hawaii
47	Delaware
48	Mississippi
49	North Dakota
50	Rhode Island

C-4 State Park Visitors, FY 2005

State	State park total visitors (in thousands)	Visitors per capita	Rank per capita
Alabama	4,397	1.0	46
Alaska	4,003	6.1	5
Arizona	2,196	0.4	50
Arkansas	9,805	3.6	14
California	82,032	2.3	25
Colorado	12,146	2.6	23
Connecticut	6,573	1.9	31
Delaware	3,927	4.7	9
Florida	19,118	1.1	43
Georgia	12,765	1.4	41
Hawaii	9,221	7.3	3
Idaho	2,782	2.0	29
Illinois	43,328	3.4	15
Indiana	18,341	2.9	17
Iowa	14,628	5.0	7
Kansas	7,281	2.7	22
Kentucky	7,598	1.8	32
Louisiana	2,087	0.5	48
Maine	2,226	1.7	35
Maryland	10,743	1.9	30
Massachusetts	10,051	1.6	39
Michigan	20,452	2.0	27
Minnesota	7,820	1.5	40
Mississippi	3,128	1.1	45
Missouri	17,047	3.0	16
Montana	1,485	1.6	38
Nebraska	9,886	5.7	6
Nevada	4,149	1.8	33
New Hampshire	2,851	2.2	26
New Jersey	14,124	1.6	37
New Mexico	3,840	2.0	28
New York	53,525	2.8	20
North Carolina	11,275	1.3	42
North Dakota	1,049	1.7	36
Ohio	53,371	4.7	10
Oklahoma	14,086	4.0	13
Oregon	45,144	12.6	1
Pennsylvania	34,692	2.8	19
Rhode Island	3,072	2.8	18
South Carolina	7,367	1.8	34
South Dakota	9,217	12.0	2
Tennessee	28,162	4.8	8
Texas	9,716	0.4	49
Utah	5,867	2.5	24
Vermont	680	1.1	44
Virginia	6,126	0.8	47
Washington	40,410	6.5	4
West Virginia	7,833	4.3	12
Wisconsin	14,967	2.7	21
Wyoming	2,274	4.5	11
50 States	718,858	2.5	
DC	n/a	n/a	
United States	718,858	2.4	

Rank in order per capita	
1	Oregon
2	South Dakota
3	Hawaii
4	Washington
5	Alaska
6	Nebraska
7	Iowa
8	Tennessee
9	Delaware
10	Ohio
11	Wyoming
12	West Virginia
13	Oklahoma
14	Arkansas
15	Illinois
16	Missouri
17	Indiana
18	Rhode Island
19	Pennsylvania
20	New York
21	Wisconsin
22	Kansas
23	Colorado
24	Utah
25	California
26	New Hampshire
27	Michigan
28	New Mexico
29	Idaho
30	Maryland
31	Connecticut
32	Kentucky
33	Nevada
34	South Carolina
35	Maine
36	North Dakota
37	New Jersey
38	Montana
39	Massachusetts
40	Minnesota
41	Georgia
42	North Carolina
43	Florida
44	Vermont
45	Mississippi
46	Alabama
47	Virginia
48	Louisiana
49	Texas
50	Arizona

Note: Numbers that appear to be identical are rounded and vary slightly in actual value. The rankings reflect the actual values before rounding. See the introduction for more details.

C-5 Percentage of Population Not Physically Active, 2004

State	Percentage reporting not to be physically active	Rank
Alabama	29.6	5
Alaska	20.6	35
Arizona	24.2	18
Arkansas	26.5	7
California	22.7	25
Colorado	18.7	42
Connecticut	18.9	40
Delaware	21.8	28
Florida	23.6	22
Georgia	25.8	10
Hawaii	n/a	n/a
Idaho	19.1	38
Illinois	24.9	13
Indiana	25.3	12
Iowa	21.3	32
Kansas	23.2	23
Kentucky	29.8	2
Louisiana	29.8	2
Maine	21.5	31
Maryland	21.8	28
Massachusetts	20.0	37
Michigan	22.1	26
Minnesota	15.9	49
Mississippi	31.3	1
Missouri	24.8	14
Montana	18.9	40
Nebraska	21.6	30
Nevada	24.2	18
New Hampshire	18.5	43
New Jersey	25.7	11
New Mexico	21.2	34
New York	26.5	7
North Carolina	24.7	15
North Dakota	21.3	32
Ohio	23.0	24
Oklahoma	27.8	6
Oregon	17.2	47
Pennsylvania	24.4	17
Rhode Island	24.2	18
South Carolina	23.8	21
South Dakota	19.0	39
Tennessee	29.7	4
Texas	26.1	9
Utah	16.9	48
Vermont	18.1	45
Virginia	21.9	27
Washington	17.3	46
West Virginia	24.5	16
Wisconsin	18.5	43
Wyoming	20.1	36
50 States	n/a	
DC	22.3	
United States	22.9	

Rank in order by percentage	
1	Mississippi
2	Kentucky
2	Louisiana
4	Tennessee
5	Alabama
6	Oklahoma
7	Arkansas
7	New York
9	Texas
10	Georgia
11	New Jersey
12	Indiana
13	Illinois
14	Missouri
15	North Carolina
16	West Virginia
17	Pennsylvania
18	Arizona
18	Nevada
18	Rhode Island
21	South Carolina
22	Florida
23	Kansas
24	Ohio
25	California
26	Michigan
27	Virginia
28	Delaware
28	Maryland
30	Nebraska
31	Maine
32	Iowa
32	North Dakota
34	New Mexico
35	Alaska
36	Wyoming
37	Massachusetts
38	Idaho
39	South Dakota
40	Connecticut
40	Montana
42	Colorado
43	New Hampshire
43	Wisconsin
45	Vermont
46	Washington
47	Oregon
48	Utah
49	Minnesota

Note: Ties in ranking reflect ties in actual values.

C-6 Hunters with Firearms, 2003

State	Hunters with firearms (in thousands)	Percentage of population	Rank by percentage
Alabama	357	7.9	21
Alaska	n/a	n/a	n/a
Arizona	252	4.5	34
Arkansas	469	17.2	4
California	981	2.8	45
Colorado	204	4.5	36
Connecticut	21	0.6	48
Delaware	70	8.6	18
Florida	660	3.9	38
Georgia	801	9.2	16
Hawaii	n/a	n/a	n/a
Idaho	269	19.7	3
Illinois	445	3.5	39
Indiana	287	4.6	33
Iowa	208	7.1	26
Kansas	182	6.7	27
Kentucky	504	12.2	9
Louisiana	479	10.7	11
Maine	129	9.9	14
Maryland	237	4.3	37
Massachusetts	156	2.4	46
Michigan	995	9.9	15
Minnesota	423	8.4	20
Mississippi	208	7.2	25
Missouri	486	8.5	19
Montana	355	38.7	2
Nebraska	175	10.1	13
Nevada	68	3.0	44
New Hampshire	101	7.8	22
New Jersey	272	3.1	43
New Mexico	193	10.3	12
New York	991	5.2	30
North Carolina	620	7.4	24
North Dakota	248	39.1	1
Ohio	381	3.3	41
Oklahoma	315	9.0	17
Oregon	175	4.9	31
Pennsylvania	1,353	10.9	10
Rhode Island	22	2.0	47
South Carolina	195	4.7	32
South Dakota	122	16.0	5
Tennessee	330	5.6	29
Texas	1,472	6.7	28
Utah	77	3.3	42
Vermont	46	7.4	23
Virginia	254	3.4	40
Washington	275	4.5	35
West Virginia	248	13.7	7
Wisconsin	712	13.0	8
Wyoming	80	16.0	6
50 States	17,823	6.1	
DC	n/a	n/a	
United States*	17,901	6.2	

**Due to rounding or data sources, the 50-state total plus D.C. may not equal the U.S. total. Please see introduction.*

Rank in order by percentage	
1	North Dakota
2	Montana
3	Idaho
4	Arkansas
5	South Dakota
6	Wyoming
7	West Virginia
8	Wisconsin
9	Kentucky
10	Pennsylvania
11	Louisiana
12	New Mexico
13	Nebraska
14	Maine
15	Michigan
16	Georgia
17	Oklahoma
18	Delaware
19	Missouri
20	Minnesota
21	Alabama
22	New Hampshire
23	Vermont
24	North Carolina
25	Mississippi
26	Iowa
27	Kansas
28	Texas
29	Tennessee
30	New York
31	Oregon
32	South Carolina
33	Indiana
34	Arizona
35	Washington
36	Colorado
37	Maryland
38	Florida
39	Illinois
40	Virginia
41	Ohio
42	Utah
43	New Jersey
44	Nevada
45	California
46	Massachusetts
47	Rhode Island
48	Connecticut

Note: Numbers that appear to be identical are rounded and vary slightly in actual value. The rankings reflect the actual values before rounding. See the introduction for more details.

C-7 Registered Boats, 2004

State	Registered boats	Registered boats per 1,000 population	Rank by total number of boats
Alabama	264,006	58	17
Alaska	49,225	75	45
Arizona	147,294	26	30
Arkansas	205,745	75	26
California	894,884	25	3
Colorado	98,079	21	34
Connecticut	111,992	32	31
Delaware	51,797	62	43
Florida	946,072	54	1
Georgia	322,252	36	14
Hawaii	13,205	10	50
Idaho	83,639	60	36
Illinois	393,856	31	10
Indiana	213,309	34	21
Iowa	228,140	77	20
Kansas	98,512	36	33
Kentucky	174,463	42	28
Louisiana	309,950	69	15
Maine	94,582	72	35
Maryland	206,681	37	24
Massachusetts	150,683	23	29
Michigan	944,800	93	2
Minnesota	853,448	167	4
Mississippi	209,216	72	23
Missouri	326,210	57	13
Montana	59,271	64	40
Nebraska	77,636	44	37
Nevada	57,612	25	41
New Hampshire	101,626	78	32
New Jersey	209,678	24	22
New Mexico	38,439	20	47
New York	519,066	27	7
North Carolina	356,946	42	11
North Dakota	52,961	83	42
Ohio	414,938	36	8
Oklahoma	206,049	58	25
Oregon	190,119	53	27
Pennsylvania	354,079	29	12
Rhode Island	43,671	40	46
South Carolina	397,458	95	9
South Dakota	51,604	67	44
Tennessee	261,465	44	18
Texas	616,779	27	5
Utah	74,293	31	38
Vermont	32,498	52	48
Virginia	242,642	33	19
Washington	266,056	43	16
West Virginia	63,504	35	39
Wisconsin	605,467	110	6
Wyoming	25,897	51	49
50 States	12,711,794	43	
DC	2,908	5	
United States*	12,781,476	44	

**Due to rounding or data sources, the 50-state total plus D.C. may not equal the U.S. total. Please see introduction.*

Rank in order by total number	
1	Florida
2	Michigan
3	California
4	Minnesota
5	Texas
6	Wisconsin
7	New York
8	Ohio
9	South Carolina
10	Illinois
11	North Carolina
12	Pennsylvania
13	Missouri
14	Georgia
15	Louisiana
16	Washington
17	Alabama
18	Tennessee
19	Virginia
20	Iowa
21	Indiana
22	New Jersey
23	Mississippi
24	Maryland
25	Oklahoma
26	Arkansas
27	Oregon
28	Kentucky
29	Massachusetts
30	Arizona
31	Connecticut
32	New Hampshire
33	Kansas
34	Colorado
35	Maine
36	Idaho
37	Nebraska
38	Utah
39	West Virginia
40	Montana
41	Nevada
42	North Dakota
43	Delaware
44	South Dakota
45	Alaska
46	Rhode Island
47	New Mexico
48	Vermont
49	Wyoming
50	Hawaii

C-8 State Spending on State Arts Agencies, FY 2005

State	State spending for the arts $ (in thousands)	Per capita $	Rank per capita
Alabama	3,169	0.70	29
Alaska	461	0.70	28
Arizona	3,523	0.61	33
Arkansas	1,461	0.53	39
California	2,047	0.06	50
Colorado	500	0.11	48
Connecticut	7,538	2.15	5
Delaware	1,709	2.06	6
Florida	15,810	0.91	20
Georgia	3,629	0.41	41
Hawaii	5,906	4.68	1
Idaho	836	0.60	34
Illinois	18,865	1.48	9
Indiana	3,617	0.58	35
Iowa	1,350	0.46	40
Kansas	1,517	0.55	37
Kentucky	4,211	1.02	17
Louisiana	4,935	1.09	15
Maine	856	0.65	31
Maryland	11,002	1.98	7
Massachusetts	8,347	1.30	11
Michigan	11,719	1.16	13
Minnesota	8,593	1.68	8
Mississippi	1,662	0.57	36
Missouri	450	0.08	49
Montana	290	0.31	45
Nebraska	1,119	0.64	32
Nevada	1,726	0.74	27
New Hampshire	691	0.53	38
New Jersey	28,680	3.30	2
New Mexico	1,478	0.78	25
New York	44,455	2.31	4
North Carolina	5,920	0.69	30
North Dakota	512	0.81	23
Ohio	11,376	0.99	19
Oklahoma	3,924	1.11	14
Oregon	584	0.16	47
Pennsylvania	14,500	1.17	12
Rhode Island	2,644	2.45	3
South Carolina	3,321	0.79	24
South Dakota	588	0.76	26
Tennessee	5,947	1.01	18
Texas	4,510	0.20	46
Utah	2,565	1.07	16
Vermont	520	0.84	22
Virginia	3,002	0.40	42
Washington	2,307	0.37	44
West Virginia	2,378	1.31	10
Wisconsin	2,160	0.39	43
Wyoming	432	0.85	21
50 States	269,339	0.92	
DC	3,817	6.90	
United States*	303,066	1.02	

Due to rounding or data sources, the 50-state total plus D.C. may not equal the U.S. total. Please see introduction.

Rank in order per capita	
1	Hawaii
2	New Jersey
3	Rhode Island
4	New York
5	Connecticut
6	Delaware
7	Maryland
8	Minnesota
9	Illinois
10	West Virginia
11	Massachusetts
12	Pennsylvania
13	Michigan
14	Oklahoma
15	Louisiana
16	Utah
17	Kentucky
18	Tennessee
19	Ohio
20	Florida
21	Wyoming
22	Vermont
23	North Dakota
24	South Carolina
25	New Mexico
26	South Dakota
27	Nevada
28	Alaska
29	Alabama
30	North Carolina
31	Maine
32	Nebraska
33	Arizona
34	Idaho
35	Indiana
36	Mississippi
37	Kansas
38	New Hampshire
39	Arkansas
40	Iowa
41	Georgia
42	Virginia
43	Wisconsin
44	Washington
45	Montana
46	Texas
47	Oregon
48	Colorado
49	Missouri
50	California

Note: Numbers that appear to be identical are rounded and vary slightly in actual value. The rankings reflect the actual values before rounding. See the introduction for more details.

C-9 Energy Consumption, Total and Per Capita, 2001

State	Energy consumption (in trillion BTUs)	BTUs per capita	Rank per capita
Alabama	1,942.6	434,692	9
Alaska	736.6	1,162,508	1
Arizona	1,353.0	254,948	43
Arkansas	1,106.3	410,547	11
California	7,853.4	226,974	48
Colorado	1,270.0	286,618	39
Connecticut	853.1	248,384	45
Delaware	292.5	367,186	21
Florida	4,134.8	252,533	44
Georgia	2,880.6	342,697	26
Hawaii	282.2	229,987	47
Idaho	501.0	379,377	19
Illinois	3,870.2	309,116	35
Indiana	2,801.7	457,290	7
Iowa	1,150.7	392,467	14
Kansas	1,043.7	386,252	15
Kentucky	1,879.5	461,928	6
Louisiana	3,499.5	782,821	3
Maine	490.7	382,025	16
Maryland	1,420.4	263,717	41
Massachusetts	1,548.8	241,956	46
Michigan	3,120.0	311,805	34
Minnesota	1,744.5	349,982	23
Mississippi	1,172.6	410,038	12
Missouri	1,815.0	321,962	29
Montana	365.6	403,807	13
Nebraska	627.1	364,585	22
Nevada	629.4	300,040	37
New Hampshire	322.2	255,844	42
New Jersey	2,500.4	293,781	38
New Mexico	679.2	370,958	20
New York	4,134.6	216,649	49
North Carolina	2,590.5	315,680	33
North Dakota	406.9	639,227	4
Ohio	3,982.3	349,638	24
Oklahoma	1,539.5	443,714	8
Oregon	1,064.3	306,411	36
Pennsylvania	3,922.5	318,822	31
Rhode Island	227.3	214,503	50
South Carolina	1,548.8	381,278	18
South Dakota	248.0	327,037	28
Tennessee	2,195.4	381,849	17
Texas	12,028.8	562,857	5
Utah	725.4	318,338	32
Vermont	163.6	266,894	40
Virginia	2,314.6	321,617	30
Washington	2,033.9	339,357	27
West Virginia	761.7	422,938	10
Wisconsin	1,863.4	344,694	25
Wyoming	439.1	889,309	2
50 States	96,077.9	337,419	
DC	168.2	293,122	
United States*	96,275.3	337,432	

**Due to rounding or data sources, the 50-state total plus D.C. may not equal the U.S. total. Please see introduction.*

Rank in order per capita	
1	Alaska
2	Wyoming
3	Louisiana
4	North Dakota
5	Texas
6	Kentucky
7	Indiana
8	Oklahoma
9	Alabama
10	West Virginia
11	Arkansas
12	Mississippi
13	Montana
14	Iowa
15	Kansas
16	Maine
17	Tennessee
18	South Carolina
19	Idaho
20	New Mexico
21	Delaware
22	Nebraska
23	Minnesota
24	Ohio
25	Wisconsin
26	Georgia
27	Washington
28	South Dakota
29	Missouri
30	Virginia
31	Pennsylvania
32	Utah
33	North Carolina
34	Michigan
35	Illinois
36	Oregon
37	Nevada
38	New Jersey
39	Colorado
40	Vermont
41	Maryland
42	New Hampshire
43	Arizona
44	Florida
45	Connecticut
46	Massachusetts
47	Hawaii
48	California
49	New York
50	Rhode Island

C-10 Toxic Chemical Release, 2003

State	Toxic chemical release in pounds (in thousands)	Per capita release in pounds	Rank per capita
Alabama	118,449	26.3	12
Alaska	539,644	832.4	1
Arizona	48,214	8.6	34
Arkansas	40,602	14.9	21
California	57,872	1.6	46
Colorado	22,518	5.0	40
Connecticut	5,384	1.5	47
Delaware	13,613	16.6	19
Florida	126,452	7.4	37
Georgia	126,651	14.6	22
Hawaii	3,118	2.5	44
Idaho	61,328	44.9	6
Illinois	132,401	10.5	29
Indiana	234,766	37.9	8
Iowa	37,402	12.7	25
Kansas	28,864	10.6	28
Kentucky	90,582	22.0	15
Louisiana	126,845	28.2	11
Maine	9,305	7.1	38
Maryland	45,500	8.3	36
Massachusetts	9,013	1.4	48
Michigan	101,605	10.1	31
Minnesota	31,449	6.2	39
Mississippi	63,077	21.9	16
Missouri	102,499	17.9	18
Montana	45,207	49.2	5
Nebraska	51,471	29.6	10
Nevada	409,054	182.4	2
New Hampshire	5,944	4.6	41
New Jersey	23,124	2.7	43
New Mexico	17,899	9.5	32
New York	44,027	2.3	45
North Carolina	129,146	15.3	20
North Dakota	23,639	37.3	9
Ohio	251,597	22.0	14
Oklahoma	29,968	8.5	35
Oregon	42,129	11.8	27
Pennsylvania	166,918	13.5	23
Rhode Island	892	0.8	49
South Carolina	83,708	20.2	17
South Dakota	10,320	13.5	24
Tennessee	142,540	24.4	13
Texas	261,905	11.8	26
Utah	241,995	102.9	3
Vermont	347	0.6	50
Virginia	74,230	10.1	30
Washington	22,880	3.7	42
West Virginia	102,170	56.4	4
Wisconsin	50,798	9.3	33
Wyoming	19,263	38.4	7
50 States	4,428,322	15.3	
DC	14	0.0	
United States*	4,438,720	15.3	

**Due to rounding or data sources, the 50-state total plus D.C. may not equal the U.S. total. Please see introduction.*

Rank in order per capita	
1	Alaska
2	Nevada
3	Utah
4	West Virginia
5	Montana
6	Idaho
7	Wyoming
8	Indiana
9	North Dakota
10	Nebraska
11	Louisiana
12	Alabama
13	Tennessee
14	Ohio
15	Kentucky
16	Mississippi
17	South Carolina
18	Missouri
19	Delaware
20	North Carolina
21	Arkansas
22	Georgia
23	Pennsylvania
24	South Dakota
25	Iowa
26	Texas
27	Oregon
28	Kansas
29	Illinois
30	Virginia
31	Michigan
32	New Mexico
33	Wisconsin
34	Arizona
35	Oklahoma
36	Maryland
37	Florida
38	Maine
39	Minnesota
40	Colorado
41	New Hampshire
42	Washington
43	New Jersey
44	Hawaii
45	New York
46	California
47	Connecticut
48	Massachusetts
49	Rhode Island
50	Vermont

Note: Numbers that appear to be identical are rounded and vary slightly in actual value. The rankings reflect the actual values before rounding. See the introduction for more details.

C-11 Hazardous Waste Sites, 2005

State	Hazardous waste sites #	Rank
Alabama	13	28
Alaska	6	43
Arizona	9	41
Arkansas	10	38
California	93	3
Colorado	17	20
Connecticut	14	23
Delaware	14	23
Florida	50	6
Georgia	15	22
Hawaii	3	45
Idaho	6	43
Illinois	41	9
Indiana	29	14
Iowa	11	34
Kansas	10	38
Kentucky	14	23
Louisiana	11	34
Maine	12	30
Maryland	17	20
Massachusetts	31	11
Michigan	66	5
Minnesota	24	18
Mississippi	3	45
Missouri	26	16
Montana	14	23
Nebraska	12	30
Nevada	1	49
New Hampshire	20	19
New Jersey	113	1
New Mexico	12	30
New York	87	4
North Carolina	31	11
North Dakota	0	50
Ohio	30	13
Oklahoma	10	38
Oregon	11	34
Pennsylvania	94	2
Rhode Island	12	30
South Carolina	26	16
South Dakota	2	47
Tennessee	13	28
Texas	43	8
Utah	14	23
Vermont	11	34
Virginia	29	14
Washington	46	7
West Virginia	9	41
Wisconsin	37	10
Wyoming	2	47
50 States	1,224	
DC	1	
United States*	1,239	

**Due to rounding or data sources, the 50-state total plus D.C. may not equal the U.S. total. Please see introduction.*

Rank in order by #	
1	New Jersey
2	Pennsylvania
3	California
4	New York
5	Michigan
6	Florida
7	Washington
8	Texas
9	Illinois
10	Wisconsin
11	Massachusetts
11	North Carolina
13	Ohio
14	Indiana
14	Virginia
16	Missouri
16	South Carolina
18	Minnesota
19	New Hampshire
20	Colorado
20	Maryland
22	Georgia
23	Connecticut
23	Delaware
23	Kentucky
23	Montana
23	Utah
28	Alabama
28	Tennessee
30	Maine
30	Nebraska
30	New Mexico
30	Rhode Island
34	Iowa
34	Louisiana
34	Oregon
34	Vermont
38	Arkansas
38	Kansas
38	Oklahoma
41	Arizona
41	West Virginia
43	Alaska
43	Idaho
45	Hawaii
45	Mississippi
47	South Dakota
47	Wyoming
49	Nevada
50	North Dakota

Note: Ties in ranking reflect ties in actual values.

C-12 Drinking Water Quality, FY 2004

State	Percentage of community water systems with health violations	Rank
Alabama	1.8	49
Alaska	17.0	3
Arizona	13.4	8
Arkansas	13.2	9
California	5.7	37
Colorado	6.7	30
Connecticut	11.6	16
Delaware	10.6	21
Florida	6.2	33
Georgia	2.7	45
Hawaii	2.6	47
Idaho	11.8	14
Illinois	11.3	19
Indiana	11.3	18
Iowa	5.1	39
Kansas	10.6	20
Kentucky	9.6	23
Louisiana	8.9	26
Maine	19.0	2
Maryland	5.0	40
Massachusetts	7.8	28
Michigan	4.8	42
Minnesota	2.2	48
Mississippi	1.6	50
Missouri	12.7	11
Montana	11.5	17
Nebraska	22.1	1
Nevada	9.1	25
New Hampshire	14.5	6
New Jersey	2.6	46
New Mexico	12.7	12
New York	4.1	43
North Carolina	12.1	13
North Dakota	6.9	29
Ohio	6.0	35
Oklahoma	14.2	7
Oregon	15.2	4
Pennsylvania	5.8	36
Rhode Island	6.0	34
South Carolina	10.0	22
South Dakota	9.4	24
Tennessee	3.7	44
Texas	6.2	32
Utah	8.6	27
Vermont	14.7	5
Virginia	12.8	10
Washington	11.6	15
West Virginia	6.3	31
Wisconsin	5.0	41
Wyoming	5.4	38
50 States	8.3	
DC	33.3	
United States	8.3	

Rank in order by percentage	
1	Nebraska
2	Maine
3	Alaska
4	Oregon
5	Vermont
6	New Hampshire
7	Oklahoma
8	Arizona
9	Arkansas
10	Virginia
11	Missouri
12	New Mexico
13	North Carolina
14	Idaho
15	Washington
16	Connecticut
17	Montana
18	Indiana
19	Illinois
20	Kansas
21	Delaware
22	South Carolina
23	Kentucky
24	South Dakota
25	Nevada
26	Louisiana
27	Utah
28	Massachusetts
29	North Dakota
30	Colorado
31	West Virginia
32	Texas
33	Florida
34	Rhode Island
35	Ohio
36	Pennsylvania
37	California
38	Wyoming
39	Iowa
40	Maryland
41	Wisconsin
42	Michigan
43	New York
44	Tennessee
45	Georgia
46	New Jersey
47	Hawaii
48	Minnesota
49	Alabama
50	Mississippi

Note: Numbers that appear to be identical are rounded and vary slightly in actual value. The rankings reflect the actual values before rounding. See the introduction for more details.

C-13 Expired Surface Water Pollution Discharge Permits, 2005

State	Percentage of major facilities with expired Clean Water Act permits	Rank
Alabama	8.7	32
Alaska	32.4	8
Arizona	27.3	11
Arkansas	1.8	45
California	16.1	20
Colorado	11.4	26
Connecticut	28.4	10
Delaware	47.6	4
Florida	16.7	19
Georgia	15.9	22
Hawaii	21.1	17
Idaho	57.1	2
Illinois	10.5	30
Indiana	29.5	9
Iowa	25.2	14
Kansas	3.6	43
Kentucky	37.9	7
Louisiana	12.5	25
Maine	8.0	34
Maryland	8.4	33
Massachusetts	25.8	13
Michigan	10.2	31
Minnesota	5.6	38
Mississippi	0.0	46
Missouri	26.4	12
Montana	61.0	1
Nebraska	1.9	44
Nevada	0.0	46
New Hampshire	44.8	6
New Jersey	16.1	20
New Mexico	22.2	16
New York	5.2	39
North Carolina	10.6	28
North Dakota	0.0	46
Ohio	12.6	24
Oklahoma	7.3	35
Oregon	56.6	3
Pennsylvania	7.1	36
Rhode Island	24.0	15
South Carolina	3.8	42
South Dakota	17.2	18
Tennessee	14.1	23
Texas	10.6	28
Utah	0.0	46
Vermont	6.1	37
Virginia	10.8	27
Washington	44.9	5
West Virginia	4.1	41
Wisconsin	4.6	40
Wyoming	0.0	46
50 States	n/a	
DC	0.0	
United States	15.2	

Rank in order by percentage	
1	Montana
2	Idaho
3	Oregon
4	Delaware
5	Washington
6	New Hampshire
7	Kentucky
8	Alaska
9	Indiana
10	Connecticut
11	Arizona
12	Missouri
13	Massachusetts
14	Iowa
15	Rhode Island
16	New Mexico
17	Hawaii
18	South Dakota
19	Florida
20	California
20	New Jersey
22	Georgia
23	Tennessee
24	Ohio
25	Louisiana
26	Colorado
27	Virginia
28	North Carolina
28	Texas
30	Illinois
31	Michigan
32	Alabama
33	Maryland
34	Maine
35	Oklahoma
36	Pennsylvania
37	Vermont
38	Minnesota
39	New York
40	Wisconsin
41	West Virginia
42	South Carolina
43	Kansas
44	Nebraska
45	Arkansas
46	Mississippi
46	Nevada
46	North Dakota
46	Utah
46	Wyoming

Note: Ties in ranking reflect ties in actual values.

C-14 Air Pollution Emissions, 2001

State	Emissions in short tons (in thousands)	Per capita	Rank by total emissions
Alabama	4,367	1.0	15
Alaska	553	0.9	47
Arizona	2,847	0.5	31
Arkansas	2,666	1.0	33
California	12,096	0.4	2
Colorado	2,944	0.7	27
Connecticut	1,456	0.4	41
Delaware	549	0.7	48
Florida	11,502	0.7	3
Georgia	7,019	0.8	8
Hawaii	511	0.4	49
Idaho	2,321	1.8	34
Illinois	7,095	0.6	7
Indiana	6,265	1.0	11
Iowa	2,962	1.0	26
Kansas	3,055	1.1	25
Kentucky	3,793	0.9	19
Louisiana	3,922	0.9	18
Maine	1,048	0.8	44
Maryland	2,935	0.5	28
Massachusetts	2,923	0.5	29
Michigan	6,627	0.7	9
Minnesota	4,595	0.9	13
Mississippi	2,910	1.0	30
Missouri	5,045	0.9	12
Montana	1,598	1.8	38
Nebraska	1,973	1.2	37
Nevada	1,413	0.7	42
New Hampshire	793	0.6	45
New Jersey	3,437	0.4	21
New Mexico	2,736	1.5	32
New York	7,585	0.4	5
North Carolina	6,269	0.8	10
North Dakota	1,503	2.4	39
Ohio	8,106	0.7	4
Oklahoma	3,434	1.0	22
Oregon	3,476	1.0	20
Pennsylvania	7,410	0.6	6
Rhode Island	384	0.4	50
South Carolina	3,219	0.8	24
South Dakota	1,100	1.5	43
Tennessee	4,528	0.8	14
Texas	14,808	0.7	1
Utah	1,994	0.9	36
Vermont	587	1.0	46
Virginia	4,358	0.6	16
Washington	3,398	0.6	23
West Virginia	2,255	1.3	35
Wisconsin	3,939	0.7	17
Wyoming	1,501	3.0	40
50 States	193,811	0.7	
DC	144	0.3	
United States*	193,956	0.7	

**Due to rounding or data sources, the 50-state total plus D.C. may not equal the U.S. total. Please see introduction.*

Rank in order by total emissions	
1	Texas
2	California
3	Florida
4	Ohio
5	New York
6	Pennsylvania
7	Illinois
8	Georgia
9	Michigan
10	North Carolina
11	Indiana
12	Missouri
13	Minnesota
14	Tennessee
15	Alabama
16	Virginia
17	Wisconsin
18	Louisiana
19	Kentucky
20	Oregon
21	New Jersey
22	Oklahoma
23	Washington
24	South Carolina
25	Kansas
26	Iowa
27	Colorado
28	Maryland
29	Massachusetts
30	Mississippi
31	Arizona
32	New Mexico
33	Arkansas
34	Idaho
35	West Virginia
36	Utah
37	Nebraska
38	Montana
39	North Dakota
40	Wyoming
41	Connecticut
42	Nevada
43	South Dakota
44	Maine
45	New Hampshire
46	Vermont
47	Alaska
48	Delaware
49	Hawaii
50	Rhode Island

Source Notes for Geography (Section C)

C-1 Total Land Area, 2000: This statistic comes from the 2000 census and is prepared by the geography division of the U.S. Census Bureau. It can be combined with population statistics to calculate the population "density" of each state (see Table A-21).

C-2 Land Owned by Federal Government, 2004: The federal government owns land for its buildings, military installations, and other facilities in every state, but these holdings are not major factors in the land use patterns of most states. The federal government also owns massive areas as part of the National Park Service and the Forest Service, and public lands managed by the Department of the Interior, primarily arid lands in western states. These federal land holdings, measured in land area—not land usefulness—are more than half of the land in some states. The data are maintained by the individual federal agencies that own the land, and they are compiled in the General Services Administration's (GSA) publication, *Federal Real Property Profile as of January 30, 2004.* The report can be found on the GSA Web site (www.gsa.gov).

C-3 State Park Acreage, FY 2005: These statistics show the acres of state parks and the number of acres of state parks per one thousand people. The data cover the year ending June 30, 2005. They come from the National Association of State Park Directors (www.naspd.org). The ratio was calculated by *State Fact Finder.*

C-4 State Park Visitors, FY 2005: State park agencies make estimates of the number of visitors to state parks maintained by the National Association of State Park Directors (see source for Table C-3). *State Fact Finder* related these visits to population using Census data. The data can be viewed as indicating that the average person visits a state park about 2.5 times a year.

C-5 Percentage of Population Not Physically Active, 2004: There are few reliable data on a state level on the participation of citizens in various forms of recreational activities, as no one maintains records of who hikes, plays tennis, or fishes except when they use facilities requiring admission. These data are from a survey of the Centers for Disease Control and Prevention (CDC). The data reflect the percentage of those surveyed who answered "no" to the question "During the past month, did you participate in any physical activities?" The numbers are available on the CDC Web site (www.cdc.gov) as part of the Behavioral Risk Factor Surveillance System.

C-6 Hunters with Firearms, 2003: These data show the sharp differences among states in the use of firearms for hunting—statistics highly relevant to debates over use and control of firearms. Note that the participant for the state listed is a resident of that state even though they may not have hunted in that state. That is, a hunter with firearms in Texas is a resident of Texas even though he or she may have hunted in Louisiana. Estimates by state are made by the National Sporting Goods Association (Mt. Prospect, Illinois 60056) for all major recreation activities.

C-7 Registered Boats, 2004: All states require registration of motorboats and some require registration of other boats, such as canoes and sailboats. These data, collected from state authorities by the U.S. Coast Guard, show the number of registered boats and the relationship between the number of boats and population. The data come from the Consumer Affairs and Analysis Branch of the U.S. Coast Guard and were provided to *State Fact Finder* on November 29, 2005.

C-8 State Spending on State Arts Agencies, FY 2005: Each of the fifty states and six jurisdictional governments supports an arts agency as the primary means of funding the arts and encouraging cultural participation. These agencies receive the bulk of their funding from state level legislative appropriations, with additional support from the National Endowment for the Arts and other sources (governmental, private, and earned). This table measures legislative support for state arts agencies in fiscal year 2005. The National Assembly of State Arts Agencies collects and publishes this information and provided it to *State Fact Finder* on June 29, 2005.

C-9 Energy Consumption, Total and Per Capita, 2001: At the time of the "energy crisis" of the 1970s, the federal government established a Department of Energy (DOE) and a vast data collection mechanism covering production and consumption of all forms of energy, including coal, oil, gas, nuclear power, and renewables. This table from the Energy Information Administration (EIA) of the DOE shows total energy consumption and relates it to the population of each state.

These data show consumption by all users, including businesses, by the state where energy is used, not necessarily where it is produced. States with relatively small populations and intensive energy use for mining and petrochemical manufacturing show the largest use. The EIA has detailed data by state on sources of energy and use in categories, such as residential and industrial. The data, which includes renewable energy sources—solar, wind, hydroelectric, geothermal, ethanol, and wood and waste—are published on the EIA Web site (www.eia.doe.gov). The EIA also publishes an annual report, *State Energy Data Report,* with detailed information regarding energy consumption and prices.

C-10 Toxic Chemical Release, 2003: The U.S. Environmental Protection Agency (EPA) requires detailed reporting of what it defines as "toxic" chemical releases into the atmosphere.

These data, from the *2003 Toxics Release Inventory*, available on the EPA Web site (www.epa.gov), are frequently cited by the media as indicators of health risks and air pollution in particular states. They are of limited value for this purpose. The effects of releases in a particular state often are not felt in that state because they are carried to an adjacent state or the oceans.

C-11 Hazardous Waste Sites, 2005: This table shows the number of sites the Environmental Protection Agency (EPA) has designated for cleanup under the Superfund program. The program and the designations are highly controversial, but the data are often cited as indicators of the relative prevalence of hazardous waste problems in particular states. The data are available on the EPA Web site (www.epa.gov).

C-12 Drinking Water Quality, FY 2004: Under the Safe Drinking Water Act (SDWA), each state reports to the Environmental Protection Agency (EPA) on the status of its community water systems. This table shows what percentage of these systems in each state had reported health-based violations in fiscal year 2004.

C-13 Expired Surface Water Pollution Discharge Permits, 2005: Under the Clean Water Act a system of permits was created to regulate and reduce toxic discharges. These permits are issued to factories, utilities, sewage treatment plants, and any other private or public entity that releases pollutants into the nation's waters. Permits come up for renewal at least every five years, at which time new requirements for pollution reduction or better treatment technologies are generally required. This table based on data from the Environmental Protection Agency's National Pollutant Discharge Elimination System (NPDES) and available on its Web site (www.cfpub.epa.gov/npdes/home.cfm?program_id=3) provides a measure of the permit backlog in each state. Environmental groups argue that while permits remain in limbo, a water pollution program cannot be operated effectively. The EPA has put forth the goal of reducing backlog to 10 percent (the amount determined by the EPA to be acceptable). In September of 2005, nineteen states had reached or exceeded this goal.

C-14 Air Pollution Emissions, 2001: Despite many years and millions of dollars put into efforts to measure air pollution on a state-by-state basis, no satisfactory method has been found to develop a summary measure. There are many problems. Air pollution affects people where they breathe, so for some purposes the relevant measure is what's in the ambient air, but there is little interest in measuring air quality in places with few or no people like mountains and deserts. So, such measures focus on metropolitan areas, not states. Within each state, there are dramatic differences in pollution levels associated with such factors as proximity to prevailing winds and pollution sources and elevation.

Air pollution can only be controlled where it originates, so measurement related to enforcement concentrates on place of origin, which is often not the same as the state where people are affected. Airborne pollutants don't recognize state lines, so the relevant concept is airsheds, not states.

State Fact Finder developed this table primarily to lead users to the vast quantities of data available. The table reflects added estimates of short tons of pollution emissions in each state for six pollutants — carbon monoxide, nitrogen oxide, volatile organic compounds, sulfur dioxide, particulate matter, and ammonia. The per capita calculation is provided only as a subject of possible interest. The ranking based on total tons of emissions is not a proxy for the seriousness of air pollution to the residents of the states listed and not a recognized measure of how effectively states control pollution.

The data on each pollutant by state and major causes (for example, transportation, farming, utility operation) come from the Emission Factor and Inventory Group at the Environmental Protection Agency Office of Air Quality Planning and Standards and were released to *State Fact Finder* on November 3, 2004. This office is a good source for other information useful to readers interested in comparing air pollution emissions of the various states.

Government

In 2005, new governors were elected in New Jersey and Virginia. Both are Democrats replacing Democrats, so Republicans continue to control twenty-eight governorships to the Democrats' twenty-two. In 2006, thirty-six states will hold gubernatorial elections.

States Electing Governors in 2006

Alabama	Iowa	Ohio
Alaska	Kansas	Oklahoma
Arizona	Maine	Oregon
Arkansas	Maryland	Pennsylvania
California	Massachusetts	Rhode Island
Colorado	Michigan	South Carolina
Connecticut	Minnesota	South Dakota
Florida	Nebraska	Tennessee
Georgia	Nevada	Texas
Hawaii	New Hampshire	Vermont
Idaho	New Mexico	Wisconsin
Illinois	New York	Wyoming

The November 2005 legislative elections—held only in New Jersey and Virginia—did not shift control in the statehouses. Democrats retained control of the House and Senate in nineteen states and Republicans held onto power in twenty states. Power is split in ten states, and Nebraska's unicameral legislature is nonpartisan. Almost 84 percent of the nation's state legislative seats will be up for election in 2006, and in seventeen states, all seats in both chambers will be decided. Only Virginia, New Jersey, Mississippi, and Louisiana will not hold state legislative elections in 2006.

States in Which All Seats Are Up For Election in 2006

Alabama	Minnesota
Arizona	New Hampshire
Connecticut	New York
Georgia	North Carolina
Idaho	Rhode Island
Maine	South Carolina
Maryland	South Dakota
Massachusetts	Vermont
Michigan	

D-1 Members of the United States House, 2006

State	Number of House members	Change from 1990 census	Rank
Alabama	7	0	22
Alaska	1	0	44
Arizona	8	+2	18
Arkansas	4	0	31
California	53	+1	1
Colorado	7	+1	22
Connecticut	5	-1	27
Delaware	1	0	44
Florida	25	+2	4
Georgia	13	+2	9
Hawaii	2	0	39
Idaho	2	0	39
Illinois	19	-1	5
Indiana	9	-1	14
Iowa	5	0	27
Kansas	4	0	31
Kentucky	6	0	25
Louisiana	7	0	22
Maine	2	0	39
Maryland	8	0	18
Massachusetts	10	0	13
Michigan	15	-1	8
Minnesota	8	0	18
Mississippi	4	-1	31
Missouri	9	0	14
Montana	1	0	44
Nebraska	3	0	34
Nevada	3	+1	34
New Hampshire	2	0	39
New Jersey	13	0	9
New Mexico	3	0	34
New York	29	-2	3
North Carolina	13	+1	9
North Dakota	1	0	44
Ohio	18	-1	7
Oklahoma	5	-1	27
Oregon	5	0	27
Pennsylvania	19	-2	5
Rhode Island	2	0	39
South Carolina	6	0	25
South Dakota	1	0	44
Tennessee	9	0	14
Texas	32	+2	2
Utah	3	0	34
Vermont	1	0	44
Virginia	11	0	12
Washington	9	0	14
West Virginia	3	0	34
Wisconsin	8	-1	18
Wyoming	1	0	44
50 States	435		
DC	n/a		
United States	435		

Rank in order by #	
1	California
2	Texas
3	New York
4	Florida
5	Illinois
5	Pennsylvania
7	Ohio
8	Michigan
9	Georgia
9	New Jersey
9	North Carolina
12	Virginia
13	Massachusetts
14	Indiana
14	Missouri
14	Tennessee
14	Washington
18	Arizona
18	Maryland
18	Minnesota
18	Wisconsin
22	Alabama
22	Colorado
22	Louisiana
25	Kentucky
25	South Carolina
27	Connecticut
27	Iowa
27	Oklahoma
27	Oregon
31	Arkansas
31	Kansas
31	Mississippi
34	Nebraska
34	Nevada
34	New Mexico
34	Utah
34	West Virginia
39	Hawaii
39	Idaho
39	Maine
39	New Hampshire
39	Rhode Island
44	Alaska
44	Delaware
44	Montana
44	North Dakota
44	South Dakota
44	Vermont
44	Wyoming

Note: Ties in ranking reflect ties in actual values.

D-2 Members of State Legislatures, 2006

State	Senate members	House members	Total members	Rank by total members
Alabama	35	105	140	27
Alaska	20	40	60	49
Arizona	30	60	90	43
Arkansas	35	100	135	30
California	40	80	120	35
Colorado	35	65	100	42
Connecticut	36	151	187	9
Delaware	21	41	62	48
Florida	40	120	160	18
Georgia	56	180	236	3
Hawaii	25	51	76	46
Idaho	35	70	105	39
Illinois	59	118	177	13
Indiana	50	100	150	19
Iowa	50	100	150	19
Kansas	40	125	165	17
Kentucky	38	100	138	29
Louisiana	39	105	144	25
Maine	35	151	186	10
Maryland	47	141	188	8
Massachusetts	40	160	200	6
Michigan	38	110	148	23
Minnesota	67	134	201	5
Mississippi	52	122	174	14
Missouri	34	163	197	7
Montana	50	100	150	19
Nebraska	49	n/a	49	50
Nevada	21	42	63	47
New Hampshire	24	400	424	1
New Jersey	40	80	120	35
New Mexico	42	70	112	38
New York	62	150	212	4
North Carolina	50	120	170	15
North Dakota	47	94	141	26
Ohio	33	99	132	32
Oklahoma	48	101	149	22
Oregon	30	60	90	43
Pennsylvania	50	203	253	2
Rhode Island	38	75	113	37
South Carolina	46	124	170	15
South Dakota	35	70	105	39
Tennessee	33	99	132	32
Texas	31	150	181	11
Utah	29	75	104	41
Vermont	30	150	180	12
Virginia	40	100	140	27
Washington	49	98	147	24
West Virginia	34	100	134	31
Wisconsin	33	99	132	32
Wyoming	30	60	90	43
50 States	1,971	5,411	7,382	
DC	n/a	n/a	n/a	
United States	1,971	5,411	7,382	

Rank in order by total members	
1	New Hampshire
2	Pennsylvania
3	Georgia
4	New York
5	Minnesota
6	Massachusetts
7	Missouri
8	Maryland
9	Connecticut
10	Maine
11	Texas
12	Vermont
13	Illinois
14	Mississippi
15	North Carolina
15	South Carolina
17	Kansas
18	Florida
19	Indiana
19	Iowa
19	Montana
22	Oklahoma
23	Michigan
24	Washington
25	Louisiana
26	North Dakota
27	Alabama
27	Virginia
29	Kentucky
30	Arkansas
31	West Virginia
32	Ohio
32	Tennessee
32	Wisconsin
35	California
35	New Jersey
37	Rhode Island
38	New Mexico
39	Idaho
39	South Dakota
41	Utah
42	Colorado
43	Arizona
43	Oregon
43	Wyoming
46	Hawaii
47	Nevada
48	Delaware
49	Alaska
50	Nebraska

Note: Ties in ranking reflect ties in actual values.

D-3 State Legislators Per Million Population, 2006

State	Legislators per million population	Rank
Alabama	31	29
Alaska	92	9
Arizona	16	42
Arkansas	49	19
California	3	50
Colorado	22	38
Connecticut	53	17
Delaware	75	11
Florida	9	48
Georgia	27	32
Hawaii	60	14
Idaho	75	10
Illinois	14	44
Indiana	24	34
Iowa	51	18
Kansas	60	13
Kentucky	33	26
Louisiana	32	27
Maine	141	6
Maryland	34	25
Massachusetts	31	28
Michigan	15	43
Minnesota	39	23
Mississippi	60	15
Missouri	34	24
Montana	162	5
Nebraska	28	30
Nevada	27	31
New Hampshire	326	1
New Jersey	14	45
New Mexico	59	16
New York	11	47
North Carolina	20	40
North Dakota	222	3
Ohio	12	46
Oklahoma	42	21
Oregon	25	33
Pennsylvania	20	39
Rhode Island	105	8
South Carolina	40	22
South Dakota	136	7
Tennessee	22	37
Texas	8	49
Utah	44	20
Vermont	290	2
Virginia	19	41
Washington	24	36
West Virginia	74	12
Wisconsin	24	35
Wyoming	178	4
50 States	25	
DC	n/a	
United States	25	

Rank in order per million population	
1	New Hampshire
2	Vermont
3	North Dakota
4	Wyoming
5	Montana
6	Maine
7	South Dakota
8	Rhode Island
9	Alaska
10	Idaho
11	Delaware
12	West Virginia
13	Kansas
14	Hawaii
15	Mississippi
16	New Mexico
17	Connecticut
18	Iowa
19	Arkansas
20	Utah
21	Oklahoma
22	South Carolina
23	Minnesota
24	Missouri
25	Maryland
26	Kentucky
27	Louisiana
28	Massachusetts
29	Alabama
30	Nebraska
31	Nevada
32	Georgia
33	Oregon
34	Indiana
35	Wisconsin
36	Washington
37	Tennessee
38	Colorado
39	Pennsylvania
40	North Carolina
41	Virginia
42	Arizona
43	Michigan
44	Illinois
45	New Jersey
46	Ohio
47	New York
48	Florida
49	Texas
50	California

Note: Numbers that appear to be identical are rounded and vary slightly in actual value. The rankings reflect the actual values before rounding. See the introduction for more details.

D-4 Units of Government, 2002

State	Number of government units	Units per 10,000 population	Rank per 10,000 population
Alabama	1,172	2.6	31
Alaska	176	2.7	30
Arizona	639	1.2	42
Arkansas	1,589	5.9	13
California	4,410	1.3	41
Colorado	1,929	4.3	20
Connecticut	581	1.7	37
Delaware	340	4.2	21
Florida	1,192	0.7	48
Georgia	1,449	1.7	36
Hawaii	20	0.2	50
Idaho	1,159	8.6	8
Illinois	6,904	5.5	15
Indiana	3,086	5.0	17
Iowa	1,976	6.7	10
Kansas	3,888	14.3	5
Kentucky	1,440	3.5	25
Louisiana	474	1.1	45
Maine	827	6.4	11
Maryland	266	0.5	49
Massachusetts	842	1.3	40
Michigan	2,805	2.8	29
Minnesota	3,483	6.9	9
Mississippi	1,001	3.5	26
Missouri	3,423	6.0	12
Montana	1,128	12.4	6
Nebraska	2,792	16.2	3
Nevada	211	1.0	46
New Hampshire	560	4.4	19
New Jersey	1,413	1.6	38
New Mexico	859	4.6	18
New York	3,421	1.8	34
North Carolina	961	1.2	43
North Dakota	2,736	43.2	1
Ohio	3,637	3.2	27
Oklahoma	1,799	5.2	16
Oregon	1,440	4.1	22
Pennsylvania	5,032	4.1	23
Rhode Island	119	1.1	44
South Carolina	702	1.7	35
South Dakota	1,867	24.6	2
Tennessee	931	1.6	39
Texas	4,785	2.2	33
Utah	606	2.6	32
Vermont	734	11.9	7
Virginia	522	0.7	47
Washington	1,788	2.9	28
West Virginia	687	3.8	24
Wisconsin	3,049	5.6	14
Wyoming	723	14.5	4
50 States	87,573	3.0	
DC	2	0.0	
United States*	87,576	3.0	

**Due to rounding or data sources, the 50-state total plus D.C. may not equal the U.S. total. Please see introduction.*

Rank in order per 10,000 population	
1	North Dakota
2	South Dakota
3	Nebraska
4	Wyoming
5	Kansas
6	Montana
7	Vermont
8	Idaho
9	Minnesota
10	Iowa
11	Maine
12	Missouri
13	Arkansas
14	Wisconsin
15	Illinois
16	Oklahoma
17	Indiana
18	New Mexico
19	New Hampshire
20	Colorado
21	Delaware
22	Oregon
23	Pennsylvania
24	West Virginia
25	Kentucky
26	Mississippi
27	Ohio
28	Washington
29	Michigan
30	Alaska
31	Alabama
32	Utah
33	Texas
34	New York
35	South Carolina
36	Georgia
37	Connecticut
38	New Jersey
39	Tennessee
40	Massachusetts
41	California
42	Arizona
43	North Carolina
44	Rhode Island
45	Louisiana
46	Nevada
47	Virginia
48	Florida
49	Maryland
50	Hawaii

Note: Numbers that appear to be identical are rounded and vary slightly in actual value. The rankings reflect the actual values before rounding. See the introduction for more details.

D-5 State Legislator Compensation, 2005

State	Salary $	Per diem during session $	Rank by salary
Alabama	1,050	2,280/month	48
Alaska	24,012	156-200/day	20
Arizona	24,000	35-60/day	21
Arkansas	14,067	110/day	31
California	110,880	138/day	1
Colorado	30,000	45-99/day	17
Connecticut	28,000	0	19
Delaware	39,785	0	11
Florida	29,916	117/day	18
Georgia	16,524	128/day	25
Hawaii	34,200	10-80/day	14
Idaho	15,646	38-99/day	28
Illinois	57,619	102/day	5
Indiana	11,600	134/day	36
Iowa	21,381	65-86/day	22
Kansas	8,376	91/day	41
Kentucky	14,464	100/day	30
Louisiana	16,800	113/day	24
Maine	10,020	70/day	39
Maryland	40,500	128-225/day	10
Massachusetts	55,569	10-100/day	7
Michigan	79,650	12,000/year	2
Minnesota	31,140	66/day	16
Mississippi	10,000	91/day	40
Missouri	31,351	77/day	15
Montana	8,371	90/day	42
Nebraska	12,000	31-91/day	35
Nevada	7,800	federal rate	44
New Hampshire	100	0	49
New Jersey	49,000	0	8
New Mexico	0	146/day	50
New York	79,500	varies	3
North Carolina	13,951	104/day	32
North Dakota	13,500	900/month	33
Ohio	56,261	0	6
Oklahoma	38,400	116/day	12
Oregon	16,284	91/day	27
Pennsylvania	69,647	128/day	4
Rhode Island	12,646	0	34
South Carolina	10,400	95/day	38
South Dakota	6,000	110/day	46
Tennessee	16,500	141/day	26
Texas	7,200	128/day	45
Utah	5,400	118/day	47
Vermont	11,023	35-104/day	37
Virginia	18,000	117/day	23
Washington	34,227	90/day	13
West Virginia	15,000	115/day	29
Wisconsin	45,569	88/day	9
Wyoming	7,950	85/day	43
50 States (average)	26,226	n/a	
DC	92,500	0	
United States (average)	27,525	n/a	

Rank in order by salary	
1	California
2	Michigan
3	New York
4	Pennsylvania
5	Illinois
6	Ohio
7	Massachusetts
8	New Jersey
9	Wisconsin
10	Maryland
11	Delaware
12	Oklahoma
13	Washington
14	Hawaii
15	Missouri
16	Minnesota
17	Colorado
18	Florida
19	Connecticut
20	Alaska
21	Arizona
22	Iowa
23	Virginia
24	Louisiana
25	Georgia
26	Tennessee
27	Oregon
28	Idaho
29	West Virginia
30	Kentucky
31	Arkansas
32	North Carolina
33	North Dakota
34	Rhode Island
35	Nebraska
36	Indiana
37	Vermont
38	South Carolina
39	Maine
40	Mississippi
41	Kansas
42	Montana
43	Wyoming
44	Nevada
45	Texas
46	South Dakota
47	Utah
48	Alabama
49	New Hampshire
50	New Mexico

D-6 Percentage of Legislators Who Are Female, 2006

State	Percentage of female legislators	Rank
Alabama	10.7	49
Alaska	18.3	32
Arizona	33.3	3
Arkansas	16.3	38
California	30.8	10
Colorado	33.0	7
Connecticut	29.4	14
Delaware	33.9	2
Florida	24.4	22
Georgia	18.2	33
Hawaii	30.3	12
Idaho	27.6	17
Illinois	27.7	16
Indiana	17.3	36
Iowa	20.0	29
Kansas	32.7	8
Kentucky	12.3	48
Louisiana	17.4	34
Maine	23.1	23
Maryland	35.6	1
Massachusetts	25.0	19
Michigan	20.3	27
Minnesota	29.9	13
Mississippi	12.6	47
Missouri	20.8	26
Montana	24.7	20
Nebraska	24.5	21
Nevada	33.3	3
New Hampshire	30.4	11
New Jersey	15.8	41
New Mexico	31.3	9
New York	22.2	25
North Carolina	22.9	24
North Dakota	16.3	38
Ohio	19.7	30
Oklahoma	14.8	44
Oregon	27.8	15
Pennsylvania	13.4	46
Rhode Island	16.8	37
South Carolina	8.2	50
South Dakota	16.2	40
Tennessee	17.4	34
Texas	19.3	31
Utah	20.2	28
Vermont	33.3	3
Virginia	15.0	43
Washington	33.3	3
West Virginia	15.7	42
Wisconsin	25.8	18
Wyoming	14.4	45
50 States	22.6	
DC	n/a	
United States	22.6	

Rank in order by percentage	
1	Maryland
2	Delaware
3	Arizona
3	Nevada
3	Vermont
3	Washington
7	Colorado
8	Kansas
9	New Mexico
10	California
11	New Hampshire
12	Hawaii
13	Minnesota
14	Connecticut
15	Oregon
16	Illinois
17	Idaho
18	Wisconsin
19	Massachusetts
20	Montana
21	Nebraska
22	Florida
23	Maine
24	North Carolina
25	New York
26	Missouri
27	Michigan
28	Utah
29	Iowa
30	Ohio
31	Texas
32	Alaska
33	Georgia
34	Tennessee
34	Louisiana
36	Indiana
37	Rhode Island
38	North Dakota
38	Arkansas
40	South Dakota
41	New Jersey
42	West Virginia
43	Virginia
44	Oklahoma
45	Wyoming
46	Pennsylvania
47	Mississippi
48	Kentucky
49	Alabama
50	South Carolina

Note: Ties in ranking reflect ties in actual values.

D-7 Turnover in Legislatures, 2005

State	Percentage of new legislators	Rank
Alabama	n/a	n/a
Alaska	18.3	22
Arizona	28.9	8
Arkansas	29.6	7
California	28.3	9
Colorado	24.0	15
Connecticut	12.3	34
Delaware	8.1	42
Florida	13.1	32
Georgia	25.8	12
Hawaii	14.5	29
Idaho	19.0	19
Illinois	6.2	44
Indiana	9.3	38
Iowa	13.3	31
Kansas	24.8	14
Kentucky	13.0	33
Louisiana	n/a	n/a
Maine	39.8	1
Maryland	n/a	n/a
Massachusetts	8.5	41
Michigan	36.4	3
Minnesota	19.4	18
Mississippi	n/a	n/a
Missouri	24.9	13
Montana	34.7	5
Nebraska	16.3	25
Nevada	27.0	10
New Hampshire	32.5	6
New Jersey	n/a	n/a
New Mexico	15.2	28
New York	9.0	39
North Carolina	18.8	20
North Dakota	8.5	40
Ohio	15.9	26
Oklahoma	36.9	2
Oregon	26.7	11
Pennsylvania	6.7	43
Rhode Island	14.2	30
South Carolina	10.0	36
South Dakota	35.2	4
Tennessee	12.1	35
Texas	9.9	37
Utah	18.3	23
Vermont	21.1	17
Virginia	n/a	n/a
Washington	18.4	21
West Virginia	15.7	27
Wisconsin	18.2	24
Wyoming	23.3	16
50 States	19.7	
DC	n/a	
United States	19.7	

Rank in order by percentage	
1	Maine
2	Oklahoma
3	Michigan
4	South Dakota
5	Montana
6	New Hampshire
7	Arkansas
8	Arizona
9	California
10	Nevada
11	Oregon
12	Georgia
13	Missouri
14	Kansas
15	Colorado
16	Wyoming
17	Vermont
18	Minnesota
19	Idaho
20	North Carolina
21	Washington
22	Alaska
23	Utah
24	Wisconsin
25	Nebraska
26	Ohio
27	West Virginia
28	New Mexico
29	Hawaii
30	Rhode Island
31	Iowa
32	Florida
33	Kentucky
34	Connecticut
35	Tennessee
36	South Carolina
37	Texas
38	Indiana
39	New York
40	North Dakota
41	Massachusetts
42	Delaware
43	Pennsylvania
44	Illinois

Note: Numbers that appear to be identical are rounded and vary slightly in actual value. The rankings reflect the actual values before rounding. See the introduction for more details.

D-8 Term Limits (in years), 2006

State	Consecutive term limits Governor	Consecutive term limits House	Consecutive term limits Senate	Rank by House members
Alabama	8	n/a	n/a	n/a
Alaska	8	n/a	n/a	n/a
Arizona	8	8	8	4
Arkansas	8	6	8	13
California	8	6	8	13
Colorado	8	8	8	4
Connecticut	n/a	n/a	n/a	n/a
Delaware	8	n/a	n/a	n/a
Florida	8	8	8	4
Georgia	8	n/a	n/a	n/a
Hawaii	8	n/a	n/a	n/a
Idaho	n/a	n/a	n/a	n/a
Illinois	n/a	n/a	n/a	n/a
Indiana	8	n/a	n/a	n/a
Iowa	n/a	n/a	n/a	n/a
Kansas	8	n/a	n/a	n/a
Kentucky	8	n/a	n/a	n/a
Louisiana	8	12	12	1
Maine	8	8	8	4
Maryland	8	n/a	n/a	n/a
Massachusetts	n/a	n/a	n/a	n/a
Michigan	8	6	8	13
Minnesota	n/a	n/a	n/a	n/a
Mississippi	8	n/a	n/a	n/a
Missouri	8	8	8	4
Montana	8	8	8	4
Nebraska	8	unicameral	8	4
Nevada	8	12	12	1
New Hampshire	n/a	n/a	n/a	n/a
New Jersey	8	n/a	n/a	n/a
New Mexico	8	n/a	n/a	n/a
New York	n/a	n/a	n/a	n/a
North Carolina	8	n/a	n/a	n/a
North Dakota	n/a	n/a	n/a	n/a
Ohio	8	8	8	4
Oklahoma	8	12	12	1
Oregon	n/a	n/a	n/a	n/a
Pennsylvania	8	n/a	n/a	n/a
Rhode Island	8	n/a	n/a	n/a
South Carolina	8	n/a	n/a	n/a
South Dakota	8	8	8	4
Tennessee	8	n/a	n/a	n/a
Texas	n/a	n/a	n/a	n/a
Utah	12	n/a	n/a	n/a
Vermont	n/a	n/a	n/a	n/a
Virginia	4	n/a	n/a	n/a
Washington	n/a	n/a	n/a	n/a
West Virginia	8	n/a	n/a	n/a
Wisconsin	n/a	n/a	n/a	n/a
Wyoming	8	n/a	n/a	n/a
50 States	n/a	n/a	n/a	
DC	n/a	n/a	n/a	
United States	n/a	n/a	n/a	

Rank in order by House members	
1	Louisiana
1	Nevada
1	Oklahoma
4	Arizona
4	Colorado
4	Florida
4	Maine
4	Missouri
4	Montana
4	Nebraska
4	Ohio
4	South Dakota
13	Arkansas
13	California
13	Michigan

Note: Ties in ranking reflect ties in actual values.

D-9 Legislative Session Length, 2006

State	Legislative length in calendar days #	Rank
Alabama	105	13
Alaska	121	8
Arizona	103	14
Arkansas	no regular session	n/a
California	240	1
Colorado	120	9
Connecticut	85	23
Delaware	172	3
Florida	60	30
Georgia	66	27
Hawaii	110	10
Idaho	72	26
Illinois	no limit	n/a
Indiana	65	28
Iowa	103	14
Kansas	103	14
Kentucky	103	14
Louisiana	85	23
Maine	106	12
Maryland	90	21
Massachusetts	no limit	n/a
Michigan	no limit	n/a
Minnesota	83	25
Mississippi	90	21
Missouri	147	5
Montana	no regular session	n/a
Nebraska	102	18
Nevada	no regular session	n/a
New Hampshire	179	2
New Jersey	no limit	n/a
New Mexico	30	35
New York	no limit	n/a
North Carolina	92	20
North Dakota	no regular session	n/a
Ohio	no limit	n/a
Oklahoma	110	10
Oregon	no regular session	n/a
Pennsylvania	no limit	n/a
Rhode Island	170	4
South Carolina	143	6
South Dakota	65	28
Tennessee	102	18
Texas	no regular session	n/a
Utah	45	34
Vermont	125	7
Virginia	60	30
Washington	60	30
West Virginia	60	30
Wisconsin	no limit	n/a
Wyoming	23	36
50 States	n/a	
DC	no limit	
United States	n/a	

Rank in order by #	
1	California
2	New Hampshire
3	Delaware
4	Rhode Island
5	Missouri
6	South Carolina
7	Vermont
8	Alaska
9	Colorado
10	Hawaii
10	Oklahoma
12	Maine
13	Alabama
14	Arizona
14	Iowa
14	Kansas
14	Kentucky
18	Nebraska
18	Tennessee
20	North Carolina
21	Maryland
21	Mississippi
23	Connecticut
23	Louisiana
25	Minnesota
26	Idaho
27	Georgia
28	Indiana
28	South Dakota
30	Florida
30	Virginia
30	Washington
30	West Virginia
34	Utah
35	New Mexico
36	Wyoming

Note: Ties in ranking reflect ties in actual values.

D-10 Party Control of State Legislatures, 2006

State	Democrats in legislature	Republicans in legislature	Legislative control	Percentage of members Democratic	Rank by percentage Democratic
Alabama	88	52	D	62.9	9
Alaska	22	38	R	36.7	41
Arizona	34	56	R	37.8	39
Arkansas	99	36	D	73.3	4
California	73	47	D	60.8	11
Colorado	53	47	D	53.0	20
Connecticut	123	64	D	65.8	7
Delaware	28	34	S	45.2	30
Florida	50	110	R	31.3	44
Georgia	104	132	R	44.1	32
Hawaii	61	15	D	80.3	3
Idaho	20	85	R	19.0	49
Illinois	96	80	D	54.2	18
Indiana	65	85	R	43.3	33
Iowa	74	76	S	49.3	27
Kansas	52	113	R	31.5	43
Kentucky	72	66	S	52.2	22
Louisiana	94	49	D	65.3	8
Maine	94	90	D	50.5	24
Maryland	131	57	D	69.7	5
Massachusetts	173	26	D	86.5	1
Michigan	68	80	R	45.9	29
Minnesota	101	99	S	50.2	25
Mississippi	103	71	D	59.2	12
Missouri	77	120	R	39.1	38
Montana	77	73	S	51.3	23
Nebraska	0	0	n/a	n/a	n/a
Nevada	35	28	S	55.6	16
New Hampshire	155	269	R	36.6	42
New Jersey	70	50	D	58.3	13
New Mexico	65	47	D	58.0	14
New York	131	80	S	61.8	10
North Carolina	92	78	D	54.1	19
North Dakota	41	98	R	29.1	45
Ohio	49	83	R	37.1	40
Oklahoma	70	79	S	47.0	28
Oregon	45	45	S	50.0	26
Pennsylvania	113	140	R	44.7	31
Rhode Island	92	21	D	81.4	2
South Carolina	69	101	R	40.6	35
South Dakota	29	76	R	27.6	46
Tennessee	69	63	S	52.3	21
Texas	75	106	R	41.4	34
Utah	27	77	R	26.0	47
Vermont	104	69	D	57.8	15
Virginia	55	82	R	39.3	37
Washington	81	66	D	55.1	17
West Virginia	89	45	D	66.4	6
Wisconsin	53	79	R	40.2	36
Wyoming	21	69	R	23.3	48
50 States	3,662	3,652	19 D, 20 R, 10 S	49.9	
DC	n/a	n/a	n/a	n/a	
United States	3,658	3,656	19 D, 20 R, 10 S	49.6	

Rank in order by percentage Democratic	
1	Massachusetts
2	Rhode Island
3	Hawaii
4	Arkansas
5	Maryland
6	West Virginia
7	Connecticut
8	Louisiana
9	Alabama
10	New York
11	California
12	Mississippi
13	New Jersey
14	New Mexico
15	Vermont
16	Nevada
17	Washington
18	Illinois
19	North Carolina
20	Colorado
21	Tennessee
22	Kentucky
23	Montana
24	Maine
25	Minnesota
26	Oregon
27	Iowa
28	Oklahoma
29	Michigan
30	Delaware
31	Pennsylvania
32	Georgia
33	Indiana
34	Texas
35	South Carolina
36	Wisconsin
37	Virginia
38	Missouri
39	Arizona
40	Ohio
41	Alaska
42	New Hampshire
43	Kansas
44	Florida
45	North Dakota
46	South Dakota
47	Utah
48	Wyoming
49	Idaho

D-11 Governors' Institutional Power Rating, 2006

State	Power rating	Rank
Alabama	2.8	46
Alaska	4.1	1
Arizona	3.4	29
Arkansas	3.1	39
California	3.2	35
Colorado	3.6	17
Connecticut	3.6	17
Delaware	3.5	26
Florida	3.6	17
Georgia	3.2	35
Hawaii	3.4	29
Idaho	3.5	26
Illinois	3.8	8
Indiana	3.1	39
Iowa	3.7	14
Kansas	3.3	32
Kentucky	3.5	26
Louisiana	3.4	29
Maine	3.6	17
Maryland	3.8	8
Massachusetts	3.6	17
Michigan	3.6	17
Minnesota	3.8	8
Mississippi	2.9	44
Missouri	3.6	17
Montana	3.6	17
Nebraska	3.8	8
Nevada	3.0	42
New Hampshire	2.8	46
New Jersey	4.1	1
New Mexico	3.7	14
New York	4.1	1
North Carolina	2.9	44
North Dakota	3.9	6
Ohio	3.9	6
Oklahoma	2.8	46
Oregon	3.3	32
Pennsylvania	3.7	14
Rhode Island	2.6	49
South Carolina	3.0	42
South Dakota	3.8	8
Tennessee	3.8	8
Texas	3.2	35
Utah	4.0	5
Vermont	2.5	50
Virginia	3.2	35
Washington	3.6	17
West Virginia	4.1	1
Wisconsin	3.3	32
Wyoming	3.1	39
50 States	3.5	
DC	n/a	
United States	3.5	

Rank in order by rating	
1	Alaska
1	New Jersey
1	New York
1	West Virginia
5	Utah
6	North Dakota
6	Ohio
8	Illinois
8	Maryland
8	Minnesota
8	Nebraska
8	South Dakota
8	Tennessee
14	Iowa
14	New Mexico
14	Pennsylvania
17	Colorado
17	Connecticut
17	Florida
17	Maine
17	Massachusetts
17	Michigan
17	Missouri
17	Montana
17	Washington
26	Delaware
26	Idaho
26	Kentucky
29	Arizona
29	Hawaii
29	Louisiana
32	Kansas
32	Oregon
32	Wisconsin
35	California
35	Georgia
35	Texas
35	Virginia
39	Arkansas
39	Indiana
39	Wyoming
42	Nevada
42	South Carolina
44	Mississippi
44	North Carolina
46	Alabama
46	New Hampshire
46	Oklahoma
49	Rhode Island
50	Vermont

Note: Ties in ranking reflect ties in actual values.

D-12 Number of Statewide Elected Officials, 2004

State	Elected officials #	Rank
Alabama	8	9
Alaska	2	45
Arizona	5	34
Arkansas	6	22
California	9	6
Colorado	5	34
Connecticut	6	22
Delaware	6	22
Florida	7	15
Georgia	11	2
Hawaii	2	45
Idaho	9	6
Illinois	6	22
Indiana	8	9
Iowa	8	9
Kansas	6	22
Kentucky	8	9
Louisiana	8	9
Maine	1	48
Maryland	4	41
Massachusetts	6	22
Michigan	4	41
Minnesota	5	34
Mississippi	9	6
Missouri	6	22
Montana	7	15
Nebraska	6	22
Nevada	6	22
New Hampshire	1	48
New Jersey	1	48
New Mexico	7	15
New York	4	41
North Carolina	10	3
North Dakota	12	1
Ohio	7	15
Oklahoma	8	9
Oregon	6	22
Pennsylvania	5	34
Rhode Island	5	34
South Carolina	10	3
South Dakota	7	15
Tennessee	2	45
Texas	5	34
Utah	5	34
Vermont	7	15
Virginia	3	44
Washington	10	3
West Virginia	6	22
Wisconsin	7	15
Wyoming	6	22
50 States	n/a	
DC	n/a	
United States	n/a	

Rank in order by #	
1	North Dakota
2	Georgia
3	North Carolina
3	South Carolina
3	Washington
6	California
6	Idaho
6	Mississippi
9	Alabama
9	Indiana
9	Iowa
9	Kentucky
9	Louisiana
9	Oklahoma
15	Florida
15	Montana
15	New Mexico
15	Ohio
15	South Dakota
15	Vermont
15	Wisconsin
22	Arkansas
22	Connecticut
22	Delaware
22	Illinois
22	Kansas
22	Massachusetts
22	Missouri
22	Nebraska
22	Nevada
22	Oregon
22	West Virginia
22	Wyoming
34	Arizona
34	Colorado
34	Minnesota
34	Pennsylvania
34	Rhode Island
34	Texas
34	Utah
41	Maryland
41	Michigan
41	New York
44	Virginia
45	Alaska
45	Hawaii
45	Tennessee
48	Maine
48	New Hampshire
48	New Jersey

Note: Ties in ranking reflect ties in actual values.

D-13 State and Local Government Employees, 2004

State	Government employees #	Per 10,000 population	Rank per 10,000 population
Alabama	270,632	597	12
Alaska	50,841	776	2
Arizona	270,719	471	47
Arkansas	151,938	552	25
California	1,776,132	495	45
Colorado	248,404	540	30
Connecticut	181,617	518	39
Delaware	47,879	577	16
Florida	824,337	474	46
Georgia	500,305	567	20
Hawaii	70,932	562	24
Idaho	78,310	562	23
Illinois	635,760	500	43
Indiana	329,581	528	35
Iowa	184,552	625	9
Kansas	179,546	656	4
Kentucky	237,217	572	17
Louisiana	282,311	625	8
Maine	77,055	585	14
Maryland	282,362	508	40
Massachusetts	323,067	503	41
Michigan	504,272	499	44
Minnesota	275,067	539	31
Mississippi	188,369	649	6
Missouri	311,206	541	29
Montana	54,272	586	13
Nebraska	114,767	657	3
Nevada	96,376	413	50
New Hampshire	68,484	527	36
New Jersey	495,189	569	19
New Mexico	124,642	655	5
New York	1,184,394	616	10
North Carolina	453,940	531	34
North Dakota	40,884	644	7
Ohio	623,226	544	27
Oklahoma	200,939	570	18
Oregon	179,817	500	42
Pennsylvania	570,379	460	49
Rhode Island	50,521	468	48
South Carolina	243,004	579	15
South Dakota	43,549	565	22
Tennessee	317,514	538	32
Texas	1,271,164	565	21
Utah	127,595	534	33
Vermont	38,149	614	11
Virginia	410,885	551	26
Washington	322,991	521	38
West Virginia	98,232	541	28
Wisconsin	287,256	521	37
Wyoming	43,533	859	1
50 States	15,744,113	537	
DC	44,671	807	
United States	15,788,784	538	

Rank in order by 10,000 population	
1	Wyoming
2	Alaska
3	Nebraska
4	Kansas
5	New Mexico
6	Mississippi
7	North Dakota
8	Louisiana
9	Iowa
10	New York
11	Vermont
12	Alabama
13	Montana
14	Maine
15	South Carolina
16	Delaware
17	Kentucky
18	Oklahoma
19	New Jersey
20	Georgia
21	Texas
22	South Dakota
23	Idaho
24	Hawaii
25	Arkansas
26	Virginia
27	Ohio
28	West Virginia
29	Missouri
30	Colorado
31	Minnesota
32	Tennessee
33	Utah
34	North Carolina
35	Indiana
36	New Hampshire
37	Wisconsin
38	Washington
39	Connecticut
40	Maryland
41	Massachusetts
42	Oregon
43	Illinois
44	Michigan
45	California
46	Florida
47	Arizona
48	Rhode Island
49	Pennsylvania
50	Nevada

Note: Numbers that appear to be identical are rounded and vary slightly in actual value. The rankings reflect the actual values before rounding. See the introduction for more details.

D-14 Average Salaries of State and Local Government Employees, 2004

State	Average salary $	Rank
Alabama	34,813	37
Alaska	48,004	6
Arizona	40,050	21
Arkansas	31,905	48
California	55,461	1
Colorado	43,634	15
Connecticut	50,688	4
Delaware	42,495	18
Florida	39,298	22
Georgia	35,833	33
Hawaii	41,508	19
Idaho	34,371	41
Illinois	43,713	14
Indiana	36,619	28
Iowa	37,859	25
Kansas	35,312	35
Kentucky	34,478	38
Louisiana	32,807	47
Maine	34,914	36
Maryland	46,958	9
Massachusetts	47,854	8
Michigan	44,247	12
Minnesota	44,304	11
Mississippi	30,979	50
Missouri	34,323	42
Montana	33,377	45
Nebraska	36,600	29
Nevada	46,636	10
New Hampshire	37,388	26
New Jersey	52,825	2
New Mexico	33,580	44
New York	51,612	3
North Carolina	37,336	27
North Dakota	36,104	32
Ohio	40,702	20
Oklahoma	31,735	49
Oregon	42,567	17
Pennsylvania	43,802	13
Rhode Island	48,832	5
South Carolina	34,423	40
South Dakota	33,355	46
Tennessee	34,469	39
Texas	36,269	31
Utah	36,510	30
Vermont	38,336	24
Virginia	38,781	23
Washington	47,942	7
West Virginia	33,702	43
Wisconsin	42,814	16
Wyoming	35,585	34
50 States	42,462	
DC	54,903	
United States	42,497	

Rank in order by $	
1	California
2	New Jersey
3	New York
4	Connecticut
5	Rhode Island
6	Alaska
7	Washington
8	Massachusetts
9	Maryland
10	Nevada
11	Minnesota
12	Michigan
13	Pennsylvania
14	Illinois
15	Colorado
16	Wisconsin
17	Oregon
18	Delaware
19	Hawaii
20	Ohio
21	Arizona
22	Florida
23	Virginia
24	Vermont
25	Iowa
26	New Hampshire
27	North Carolina
28	Indiana
29	Nebraska
30	Utah
31	Texas
32	North Dakota
33	Georgia
34	Wyoming
35	Kansas
36	Maine
37	Alabama
38	Kentucky
39	Tennessee
40	South Carolina
41	Idaho
42	Missouri
43	West Virginia
44	New Mexico
45	Montana
46	South Dakota
47	Louisiana
48	Arkansas
49	Oklahoma
50	Mississippi

D-15 Local Employment, 2004

State	Number of local employees	Local share of state and local employees %	Rank by percentage
Alabama	184,985	68.4	32
Alaska	26,184	51.5	48
Arizona	204,693	75.6	10
Arkansas	97,933	64.5	41
California	1,383,075	77.9	5
Colorado	182,752	73.6	14
Connecticut	122,969	67.7	37
Delaware	23,625	49.3	49
Florida	641,072	77.8	6
Georgia	378,779	75.7	7
Hawaii	14,392	20.3	50
Idaho	55,112	70.4	27
Illinois	502,088	79.0	2
Indiana	239,177	72.6	17
Iowa	131,261	71.1	21
Kansas	135,759	75.6	9
Kentucky	157,736	66.5	38
Louisiana	191,711	67.9	35
Maine	55,335	71.8	19
Maryland	191,680	67.9	36
Massachusetts	235,016	72.7	16
Michigan	371,447	73.7	13
Minnesota	200,524	72.9	15
Mississippi	131,401	69.8	29
Missouri	220,476	70.8	25
Montana	35,701	65.8	39
Nebraska	81,105	70.7	26
Nevada	71,097	73.8	12
New Hampshire	48,529	70.9	24
New Jersey	345,815	69.8	28
New Mexico	75,356	60.5	45
New York	938,009	79.2	1
North Carolina	321,830	70.9	23
North Dakota	23,130	56.6	47
Ohio	487,185	78.2	4
Oklahoma	136,845	68.1	33
Oregon	122,394	68.1	34
Pennsylvania	409,290	71.8	20
Rhode Island	30,363	60.1	46
South Carolina	167,401	68.9	31
South Dakota	30,348	69.7	30
Tennessee	235,609	74.2	11
Texas	1,002,992	78.9	3
Utah	78,695	61.7	44
Vermont	24,227	63.5	42
Virginia	291,568	71.0	22
Washington	210,253	65.1	40
West Virginia	60,649	61.7	43
Wisconsin	217,422	75.7	8
Wyoming	31,470	72.3	18
50 States	11,556,465	73.4	
DC	44,671	100.0	
United States	11,601,136	73.5	

Rank in order by percentage	
1	New York
2	Illinois
3	Texas
4	Ohio
5	California
6	Florida
7	Georgia
8	Wisconsin
9	Kansas
10	Arizona
11	Tennessee
12	Nevada
13	Michigan
14	Colorado
15	Minnesota
16	Massachusetts
17	Indiana
18	Wyoming
19	Maine
20	Pennsylvania
21	Iowa
22	Virginia
23	North Carolina
24	New Hampshire
25	Missouri
26	Nebraska
27	Idaho
28	New Jersey
29	Mississippi
30	South Dakota
31	South Carolina
32	Alabama
33	Oklahoma
34	Oregon
35	Louisiana
36	Maryland
37	Connecticut
38	Kentucky
39	Montana
40	Washington
41	Arkansas
42	Vermont
43	West Virginia
44	Utah
45	New Mexico
46	Rhode Island
47	North Dakota
48	Alaska
49	Delaware
50	Hawaii

Note: Numbers that appear to be identical are rounded and vary slightly in actual value. The rankings reflect the actual values before rounding. See the introduction for more details.

D-16 Local Spending Accountability, FY 2002

State	Percentage of local spending raised by local government	Rank
Alabama	61.9	26
Alaska	55.5	40
Arizona	57.6	37
Arkansas	45.6	47
California	53.1	43
Colorado	70.3	3
Connecticut	68.8	7
Delaware	47.8	46
Florida	70.3	4
Georgia	66.2	10
Hawaii	69.5	5
Idaho	60.2	30
Illinois	62.1	24
Indiana	64.5	16
Iowa	62.4	21
Kansas	65.0	14
Kentucky	58.4	33
Louisiana	64.5	15
Maine	73.2	1
Maryland	73.1	2
Massachusetts	58.4	34
Michigan	44.5	48
Minnesota	53.8	41
Mississippi	56.4	39
Missouri	64.2	17
Montana	56.8	38
Nebraska	68.9	6
Nevada	62.3	23
New Hampshire	63.0	20
New Jersey	68.5	8
New Mexico	42.5	50
New York	62.0	25
North Carolina	57.9	36
North Dakota	61.0	27
Ohio	60.7	29
Oklahoma	58.0	35
Oregon	53.5	42
Pennsylvania	59.4	32
Rhode Island	65.9	12
South Carolina	62.3	22
South Dakota	65.9	11
Tennessee	64.1	18
Texas	68.3	9
Utah	60.1	31
Vermont	43.8	49
Virginia	61.0	28
Washington	63.5	19
West Virginia	52.3	44
Wisconsin	50.3	45
Wyoming	65.4	13
50 States	60.5	
DC	66.1	
United States	60.6	

Rank in order by percentage	
1	Maine
2	Maryland
3	Colorado
4	Florida
5	Hawaii
6	Nebraska
7	Connecticut
8	New Jersey
9	Texas
10	Georgia
11	South Dakota
12	Rhode Island
13	Wyoming
14	Kansas
15	Louisiana
16	Indiana
17	Missouri
18	Tennessee
19	Washington
20	New Hampshire
21	Iowa
22	South Carolina
23	Nevada
24	Illinois
25	New York
26	Alabama
27	North Dakota
28	Virginia
29	Ohio
30	Idaho
31	Utah
32	Pennsylvania
33	Kentucky
34	Massachusetts
35	Oklahoma
36	North Carolina
37	Arizona
38	Montana
39	Mississippi
40	Alaska
41	Minnesota
42	Oregon
43	California
44	West Virginia
45	Wisconsin
46	Delaware
47	Arkansas
48	Michigan
49	Vermont
50	New Mexico

Note: Numbers that appear to be identical are rounded and vary slightly in actual value. The rankings reflect the actual values before rounding. See the introduction for more details.

D-17 Percentage of Eligible Voters Registered, November 2004

State	Percentage of registered voters	Rank
Alabama	83.16	29
Alaska	104.93	1
Arizona	76.88	40
Arkansas	81.94	33
California	79.78	38
Colorado	93.59	10
Connecticut	87.99	22
Delaware	92.17	13
Florida	86.54	25
Georgia	69.26	44
Hawaii	73.80	41
Idaho	69.54	43
Illinois	88.26	21
Indiana	93.76	9
Iowa	96.19	5
Kansas	86.38	26
Kentucky	89.16	19
Louisiana	87.31	24
Maine	n/a	n/a
Maryland	81.63	34
Massachusetts	91.06	15
Michigan	98.29	3
Minnesota	81.33	35
Mississippi	n/a	n/a
Missouri	99.16	2
Montana	90.05	18
Nebraska	92.37	11
Nevada	61.91	45
New Hampshire	90.86	16
New Jersey	87.79	23
New Mexico	79.54	39
New York	94.73	6
North Carolina	88.64	20
North Dakota	n/a	n/a
Ohio	94.03	8
Oklahoma	83.07	30
Oregon	82.96	31
Pennsylvania	90.10	17
Rhode Island	91.42	14
South Carolina	72.33	42
South Dakota	97.09	4
Tennessee	83.60	28
Texas	92.26	12
Utah	80.55	36
Vermont	94.48	7
Virginia	85.41	27
Washington	80.41	37
West Virginia	82.13	32
Wisconsin	n/a	n/a
Wyoming	61.16	46
50 States	n/a	
DC	98.19	
United States	86.84	

Rank in order by percentage	
1	Alaska
2	Missouri
3	Michigan
4	South Dakota
5	Iowa
6	New York
7	Vermont
8	Ohio
9	Indiana
10	Colorado
11	Nebraska
12	Texas
13	Delaware
14	Rhode Island
15	Massachusetts
16	New Hampshire
17	Pennsylvania
18	Montana
19	Kentucky
20	North Carolina
21	Illinois
22	Connecticut
23	New Jersey
24	Louisiana
25	Florida
26	Kansas
27	Virginia
28	Tennessee
29	Alabama
30	Oklahoma
31	Oregon
32	West Virginia
33	Arkansas
34	Maryland
35	Minnesota
36	Utah
37	Washington
38	California
39	New Mexico
40	Arizona
41	Hawaii
42	South Carolina
43	Idaho
44	Georgia
45	Nevada
46	Wyoming

Note: Numbers that appear to be identical are rounded and vary slightly in actual value. The rankings reflect the actual values before rounding. See the introduction for more details.

D-18 Percentage of Population Voting, November 2004

State	Percentage voting in general election*	Percentage casting ballot for U.S. Senate	Percentage casting ballot for U.S. House	Percentage casting ballot for Governor	Rank by percentage voting in general election
Alabama	55.1	53.8	52.4	n/a	39
Alaska	69.9	68.8	67.1	n/a	6
Arizona	53.4	52.1	49.7	n/a	44
Arkansas	51.2	50.5	41.3	n/a	49
California	59.8	58.1	56.0	n/a	30
Colorado	65.0	64.4	62.3	n/a	14
Connecticut	66.1	59.6	59.8	n/a	12
Delaware	62.4	n/a	59.2	60.7	24
Florida	63.9	61.0	47.3	n/a	19
Georgia	53.8	52.5	48.3	n/a	43
Hawaii	48.9	47.4	47.5	n/a	50
Idaho	60.8	51.2	58.1	n/a	28
Illinois	61.7	60.2	58.4	n/a	26
Indiana	54.0	53.1	52.9	53.6	42
Iowa	68.8	67.5	66.6	n/a	7
Kansas	60.8	57.8	59.2	n/a	27
Kentucky	57.3	55.0	52.2	n/a	35
Louisiana	58.7	55.8	46.7	n/a	32
Maine	75.3	n/a	72.2	n/a	2
Maryland	62.7	60.4	59.2	n/a	22
Massachusetts	64.6	n/a	38.5	n/a	16
Michigan	66.4	n/a	63.5	n/a	10
Minnesota	77.3	n/a	74.4	n/a	1
Mississippi	52.9	n/a	51.8	n/a	46
Missouri	64.4	63.8	62.9	64.1	17
Montana	63.5	n/a	62.7	62.9	20
Nebraska	62.0	n/a	60.9	n/a	25
Nevada	54.3	53.0	51.8	n/a	41
New Hampshire	71.9	69.9	69.1	70.2	4
New Jersey	63.3	n/a	57.1	n/a	21
New Mexico	57.2	n/a	56.2	n/a	36
New York	59.2	53.6	49.8	n/a	31
North Carolina	56.4	55.9	55.0	56.2	38
North Dakota	64.8	64.3	64.4	64.2	15
Ohio	66.3	63.9	63.0	n/a	11
Oklahoma	56.7	56.1	53.3	n/a	37
Oregon	71.2	69.0	68.7	n/a	5
Pennsylvania	62.5	60.6	55.8	n/a	23
Rhode Island	58.1	n/a	53.5	n/a	34
South Carolina	51.9	51.2	46.1	n/a	48
South Dakota	68.2	68.8	68.5	n/a	8
Tennessee	54.6	n/a	49.7	n/a	40
Texas	52.2	n/a	48.7	n/a	47
Utah	58.5	57.5	57.3	58.0	33
Vermont	66.5	65.4	64.9	65.8	9
Virginia	60.5	n/a	56.8	n/a	29
Washington	65.4	64.5	62.5	64.3	13
West Virginia	53.1	n/a	51.0	51.6	45
Wisconsin	73.9	72.7	69.6	n/a	3
Wyoming	64.1	n/a	62.9	n/a	18
50 States	n/a	n/a	n/a	n/a	
DC	58.2	n/a	45.9	n/a	
United States	60.7	58.8	55.3	59.4	

** general turnout is based on the Presidential vote*

Rank in order by percentage	
1	Minnesota
2	Maine
3	Wisconsin
4	New Hampshire
5	Oregon
6	Alaska
7	Iowa
8	South Dakota
9	Vermont
10	Michigan
11	Ohio
12	Connecticut
13	Washington
14	Colorado
15	North Dakota
16	Massachusetts
17	Missouri
18	Wyoming
19	Florida
20	Montana
21	New Jersey
22	Maryland
23	Pennsylvania
24	Delaware
25	Nebraska
26	Illinois
27	Kansas
28	Idaho
29	Virginia
30	California
31	New York
32	Louisiana
33	Utah
34	Rhode Island
35	Kentucky
36	New Mexico
37	Oklahoma
38	North Carolina
39	Alabama
40	Tennessee
41	Nevada
42	Indiana
43	Georgia
44	Arizona
45	West Virginia
46	Mississippi
47	Texas
48	South Carolina
49	Arkansas
50	Hawaii

Note: Numbers that appear to be identical are rounded and vary slightly in actual value. The rankings reflect the actual values before rounding. See the introduction for more details.

D-19 Statewide Initiatives and Popular Referenda, 2005

State	Number of initiatives	Initiatives approved by voters	Rank by number of initiatives
Alabama	0	n/a	n/a
Alaska	0	n/a	n/a
Arizona	0	n/a	n/a
Arkansas	0	n/a	n/a
California	8	0	1
Colorado	0	n/a	n/a
Connecticut	0	n/a	n/a
Delaware	0	n/a	n/a
Florida	0	n/a	n/a
Georgia	0	n/a	n/a
Hawaii	0	n/a	n/a
Idaho	0	n/a	n/a
Illinois	0	n/a	n/a
Indiana	0	n/a	n/a
Iowa	0	n/a	n/a
Kansas	0	n/a	n/a
Kentucky	0	n/a	n/a
Louisiana	0	n/a	n/a
Maine	1	0	4
Maryland	0	n/a	n/a
Massachusetts	0	n/a	n/a
Michigan	0	n/a	n/a
Minnesota	0	n/a	n/a
Mississippi	0	n/a	n/a
Missouri	0	n/a	n/a
Montana	0	n/a	n/a
Nebraska	0	n/a	n/a
Nevada	0	n/a	n/a
New Hampshire	0	n/a	n/a
New Jersey	0	n/a	n/a
New Mexico	0	n/a	n/a
New York	0	n/a	n/a
North Carolina	0	n/a	n/a
North Dakota	0	n/a	n/a
Ohio	4	0	3
Oklahoma	1	0	4
Oregon	0	n/a	n/a
Pennsylvania	0	n/a	n/a
Rhode Island	0	n/a	n/a
South Carolina	0	n/a	n/a
South Dakota	0	n/a	n/a
Tennessee	0	n/a	n/a
Texas	0	n/a	n/a
Utah	0	n/a	n/a
Vermont	0	n/a	n/a
Virginia	0	n/a	n/a
Washington	5	2	2
West Virginia	0	n/a	n/a
Wisconsin	0	n/a	n/a
Wyoming	0	n/a	n/a
50 States	19	2	
DC	n/a	n/a	
United States	19	2	

Rank in order by #	
1	California
2	Washington
3	Ohio
4	Oklahoma
4	Maine

Note: Ties in ranking reflect ties in actual values.

D-20 Campaign Costs Per Vote in Most Recent Gubernatorial Election, 2001, 2002, 2003, or 2004

State	Number of candidates and election year	Winning party and margin of victory %	Partisan shift (yes or no) and type of race (incumbent or open seat)	Total costs $ (in millions)	Cost per vote $	Rank by cost per vote
Alabama	9 in 2002	R-0.3	Y-I*	33.2	24.3	8
Alaska	18 in 2002	R-15	Y-O	5.6	24.8	6
Arizona	17 in 2002	D-1	Y-O	8.0	6.5	35
Arkansas	5 in 2002	R-6	N-I	4.7	5.9	36
California	16 in 2002	D-5	N-I	115.1	15.4	17
Colorado	5 in 2002	R-29	N-I	6.4	4.5	44
Connecticut	2 in 2002	R-12	N-I	8.3	8.1	32
Delaware	5 in 2004	D-5	N-I	2.6	7.3	33
Florida	6 in 2002	R-13	N-I	18.0	3.5	47
Georgia	5 in 2002	R-5	Y-I*	25.5	12.6	24
Hawaii	18 in 2002	R-4	Y-O	9.9	26.0	5
Idaho	8 in 2002	R-14	N-I	2.3	5.7	37
Illinois	7 in 2002	D-8	Y-O	51.2	14.5	20
Indiana	5 in 2004	R-5	Y-I*	32.0	13.1	22
Iowa	6 in 2002	D-8	N-I	13.8	13.5	21
Kansas	7 in 2002	D-8	Y-O	16.0	19.2	12
Kentucky	9 in 2003	R-10	Y-O	11.7	10.8	27
Louisiana	13 in 2003	D-4	Y-O	40.0	28.4	3
Maine	8 in 2002	D-6	Y-O	4.5	9.0	29
Maryland	6 in 2002	R-4	Y-O	5.4	3.2	49
Massachusetts	9 in 2002	R-5	N-O	32.1	14.5	19
Michigan	9 in 2002	D-4	Y-O	15.2	4.8	42
Minnesota	9 in 2002	R-8	Y-O	6.3	2.8	50
Mississippi	11 in 2003	R-7	Y-I*	20.1	22.5	9
Missouri	14 in 2004	R-3	Y-I*	15.5	5.7	37
Montana	8 in 2004	D-4	Y-O	3.8	8.5	31
Nebraska	5 in 2002	R-41	N-I	1.7	3.5	48
Nevada	15 in 2002	R-46	N-I	2.9	5.7	39
New Hampshire	6 in 2004	D-2	Y-I*	5.7	8.6	30
New Jersey	11 in 2001	D-15	Y-O	39.0	17.5	15
New Mexico	7 in 2002	D-17	Y-O	10.5	21.7	11
New York	9 in 2002	R-16	N-I	154.2	32.9	1
North Carolina	9 in 2004	D-13	N-I	18.2	5.2	40
North Dakota	3 in 2004	R-44	N-I	1.4	4.5	44
Ohio	5 in 2002	R-20	N-I	15.2	4.7	43
Oklahoma	9 in 2002	D-0.7	Y-O	11.8	11.4	25
Oregon	12 in 2002	D-3	N-O	15.9	12.6	23
Pennsylvania	5 in 2002	D-9	Y-O	68.4	19.1	14
Rhode Island	6 in 2002	R-10	N-O	7.3	21.9	10
South Carolina	8 in 2002	R-6	Y-I*	31.1	28.3	4
South Dakota	9 in 2002	R-15	N-O	9.7	29.1	2
Tennessee	12 in 2002	D-3	Y-O	18.1	10.9	26
Texas	9 in 2002	R-18	N-I	110.9	24.4	7
Utah	5 in 2004	R-16	N-I	6.3	6.9	34
Vermont	6 in 2004	R-21	N-I	1.2	3.9	46
Virginia	4 in 2001	D-5	Y-O	36.1	19.1	13
Washington	15 in 2004	D-0.005	N-O	14.6	5.2	41
West Virginia	26 in 2004	D-30	N-O	11.6	15.5	16
Wisconsin	12 in 2002	D-4	Y-I*	18.0	10.1	28
Wyoming	10 in 2002	D-2	Y-O	2.7	14.6	18
50 States Avg.	9.2	11	n/a	1128.0	13.3	
DC	n/a	n/a	n/a	n/a	n/a	
United States Avg.	9.2	11	n/a	1128.0	13.3	

* *incumbent did not win*

Rank in order by cost per vote	
1	New York
2	So. Dakota
3	Louisiana
4	So. Carolina
5	Hawaii
6	Alaska
7	Texas
8	Alabama
9	Mississippi
10	Rhode Island
11	New Mexico
12	Kansas
13	Virginia
14	Pennsylvania
15	New Jersey
16	West Virginia
17	California
18	Wyoming
19	Massachusetts
20	Illinois
21	Iowa
22	Indiana
23	Oregon
24	Georgia
25	Oklahoma
26	Tennessee
27	Kentucky
28	Wisconsin
29	Maine
30	New Hampshire
31	Montana
32	Connecticut
33	Delaware
34	Utah
35	Arizona
36	Arkansas
37	Idaho
37	Missouri
39	Nevada
40	No. Carolina
41	Washington
42	Michigan
43	Ohio
44	Colorado
44	No. Dakota
46	Vermont
47	Florida
48	Nebraska
49	Maryland
50	Minnesota

Note: Ties in ranking reflect ties in actual values.

Source Notes for Government (Section D)

D-1 Members of the United States House, 2006: Each state is allocated two senators and representation in the House of Representatives based on population, as determined by the census, which is taken in every year ending in zero (for example, 2000 and 2010).

The data in the table list the number of representatives as of 2006, based on unadjusted population numbers (see notes to Table A-1) from the 2000 census. Reapportionment of the 435 House seats resulted in gains in some western and southern states and loses in some northeastern and midwestern states. This allocation will prevail until seats are reapportioned based on the results of the 2010 census.

D-2 Members of State Legislatures, 2006: Like the Congress, state legislatures—except Nebraska's one-house legislature—have an upper and lower house, generally called senates and assemblies. These data come from the organization of legislators nationwide, the National Conference of State Legislatures.

D-3 State Legislators Per Million Population, 2006: Some small population states, like New Hampshire, have large legislatures. Some large states, like California, have relatively small ones. This table highlights the differences by relating the number of legislators (see Table D-2) to the most recent population estimates (see Table A-1).

D-4 Units of Government, 2002: There are more than eighty-seven thousand units of government in the United States, including counties, cities, towns, townships, school districts, and special districts that provide water, maintain sewage systems, build and maintain roads, control mosquitoes, and more. There are so many that they are only counted every five years in the U.S. Census Bureau's Census of Governments, the most recent of which was in 2002. The data are available on the Census Bureau Web site (www.census.gov) as *Government Organization* (GC02(1)-1).

D-5 State Legislator Compensation, 2005: These data show the major sources of cash compensation of legislators, annual salaries, and per diem amounts. The data were drawn from the National Conference of State Legislatures Web site (www.ncsl.org).

Comparisons of legislative pay from state to state are nearly impossible. Some states pay their legislators like most employers pay their employees—a regular salary plus reimbursement of employment-related travel expenses while on official business away from the normal place of work. In addition, because most legislators live in their districts, they are paid expenses when staying overnight in the state capitol. Some states compensate legislators at a per diem rate, often adding an expense allowance that can exceed expenses actually incurred. Additionally, some legislatures provide extra pay for committee chairpersons and legislative leaders. Pensions for legislative service are nonexistent or negligible in some states, while pension and other benefits, such as employer-paid health care, are an important part of legislative compensation in other states.

D-6 Percentage of Legislators Who Are Female, 2006: The percentage of legislators who are women passed 20 percent in 1993 from less than 10 percent in the 1970s and less than 5 percent in the 1960s. The percentages for each state were calculated by the National Conference of State Legislatures and are available on its Web site (www.ncsl.org).

D-7 Turnover in Legislatures, 2005: This table, from Tim Storey of the National Conference of State Legislatures, shows the percentage of new state legislators taking office after the 2004 elections.

D-8 Term Limits (in years), 2006: This table, from the same source as Table D-7 shows the maximum number of consecutive years governors and legislators can serve. The states shown with no limits allow elected officials to serve as long as voters approve. The states are ranked, with many ties, somewhat arbitrarily. Those with the longest allowable terms for members of their lower house are ranked highest.

D-9 Legislative Session Length, 2006: Many states have constitutional limits on the length of time the legislature meets in its regular sessions. Those shown in the table are calendar days (for example, a sixty-day limit would be about two months). Many of the states with short sessions exercise the option of having special sessions called by the legislative leadership or governor. These data are available on the Web site of the National Conference of State Legislatures (www.ncsl.org).

It is difficult to compare the varying practices of the states. While most meet annually, some meet biannually, and some meet throughout the year.

D-10 Party Control of State Legislatures, 2006: These data, developed by the National Conference of State Legislatures shortly after the November 2005 election, show the party affiliation of legislators taking office in 2006. The states are ranked by the percentage of Democrats (reading top to bottom) or Republicans (bottom to top) in the combined legislative houses. S represents a split in party control.

D-11 Governors' Institutional Power Rating, 2006: This table presents the results of an update of the on-going study by Dr. Thad Beyle of the University of North Carolina at Chapel Hill, included in *Politics in the American States: A Comparative Analysis* published by CQ Press. The ranking is based on six measures of institutional power—tenure, appointment power, the number of other statewide elected officials, budget power, veto power, and party control. Those interested in more detailed data on this and earlier studies of the governor's powers should visit Dr. Thad Beyle's Web site (www.unc.edu/~beyle).

D-12 Number of Statewide Elected Officials, 2004: The federal pattern of holding nationwide elections for only the chief executive and running mate (president and vice president) is not followed by the states. States often elect the attorneys general, secretaries of state, comptrollers, treasurers, and auditors. The count in the table, using information collected in the Council of State Government's *The Book of the States* (vol. 36, 2004 Edition), excludes judges, who are also elected in many states.

D-13 State and Local Government Employees, 2004: These statistics, from the U.S. Census Bureau's count of public employees available on the bureau's Web site (www.census.gov), express the full-time equivalent of part-time workers plus full-time workers in state and local governments and relate the totals to population.

D-14 Average Salaries of State and Local Government Employees, 2004: These statistics, from the same source as Table D-13, show annual average state and local government salaries, which were obtained by dividing compensation in March 2004 by the number of employees in 2004 and multiplying by twelve.

D-15 Local Employment, 2004: The count of local employees identified is substantially larger than the number of state employees. The table shows the percentage of local employees. See Table D-13 for the source of these data.

D-16 Local Spending Accountability, FY 2002: Since 1970 there has been a massive growth in both federal and state aid to local governments. As a result, local officials finance over one-third of what they spend with money they do not raise by their own local taxes and fees. Critics say this encourages government spending to be excessive because the elected officials who spend the money do not have to account to taxpayers for raising it. The Wisconsin Taxpayers Association has dubbed this difference "the accountability gap." The table shows a measure of this gap, as calculated by State Policy Research using data from the U.S. Census Bureau (see source note to Table F-1 for important details). The numbers reflect the percentage of their spending local officials raised.

D-17 Percentage of Eligible Voters Registered, November 2004: These statistics were compiled from each state's chief election officer by the Committee for the Study of the American Electorate (CSAE), a non-partisan, non-profit research organization based in Washington, D.C. The table shows the best available data on the percentage of persons presumably eligible to vote in each state, based on the voting-age population in relation to the number who have complied with that state's requirements to vote. Presumably the over 100 percent of registered voters in Alaska is a fiction. According to CSAE, "in any given election the official registration figures provided by the states are inaccurate." This is because registration rolls often contain the names of people who have died or have moved. As part of the Motor-Voter law, states are required to maintain those who have moved or died on the registration rolls for at least two federal elections, though the names, if the election administration has knowledge of them, can be moved to an inactive list.

The accuracy of a state's registration count is related to the practices of a state's election administration—specifically, how often and how thorough the state conducts a so-called list cleaning. CSAE estimates that even after accounting for "inactives," registration rolls nationwide can be assumed to be inflated by approximately 10 percent.

Data are not available for North Dakota because the state has no voter registration. Wisconsin has election day registration at the polls. Maine and Mississippi had incomplete registration counts.

D-18 Percentage of Population Voting, November 2004: Not all persons legally old enough to vote actually do so. The table shows the percentage of eligible U.S citizens who voted in the elections of November 2004. The first column contains total turnout percentages. Because general turnout is based on the presidential vote, these figures also represent the percentage of voters casting ballots for president. The second column shows the percentage of voters casting ballots for the U.S. Senate in the thirty-four states with Senate elections. The third column shows the percentage casting ballots for the U.S. House, and the fourth column shows the percentage of voters casting ballots for governor in the eleven states with gubernatorial elections in 2004.

The data come from the Committee for the Study of the American Electorate (CSAE). The figures for most states are final, but not all are certified by the chief election officer in each state. In January 2005, CSAE reported that in California, Oregon, and Washington at least four million absentee and mail votes were still to be counted. In addition, CSAE estimates, "between one and two million other votes still to be counted in other states." Also, because it is based on the presidential vote, general turnout is likely to understate actual turnout. In any election, some voters cast ballots but do not vote for president or they cast invalid ballots. CSAE reports that only thirty-one states also count actual ballots cast. In the past comparing actual ballots cast to the presidental vote yields a difference of approximately one percentage point. Because of the intense interest in the 2004 presidential race, CSAE predicts this differential to be even smaller.

D-19 Statewide Initiatives and Popular Referenda, 2005: In most states, voters select candidates to make policy for them as legislators but never vote directly on policy except when changes in the state constitution are being made. Some states allow "direct democracy," including allowing voters to put up a measure for popular vote by collecting a minimum number of signatures (voter initiatives). This tabulation shows the number of such initiatives on state ballots in elections in 2005.

The numbers reflect (1) whether initiatives are permitted in the state; (2) the difficulty of putting measures on the ballot, as affected by the number for signatures required and other factors in the constitutions of each state; and (3) voter interest in making state policy by this direct democracy approach.

These statistics come from a compilation of ballot measure results from the National Conference of State Legislatures (www.ncsl.org).

D-20 Campaign Costs Per Vote in Most Recent Gubernatorial Election, 2001, 2002, 2003, or 2004: This table was created by Dr. Thad Beyle, Department of Political Science, University of North Carolina at Chapel Hill, NC 27599-3265, and Dr. Jennifer M. Jensen, Department of Political Science, Binghamton University at SUNY, Binghamton, NY 13902-6000. The authors compiled data from the specific agency in each state that regulates elections and campaign finances. The result is a measure of the gubernatorial campaign costs (converted to 2004 dollars) in each state per vote in each state. Variables that have potential effects on these costs are also presented in this table. These variables include (1) the number of candidates seeking office, (2) the election year, (3) the party that won the office, (4) by what margin of victory, (5) whether or not the election resulted in a partisan shift, (6) whether or not an incumbent was seeking reelection, and (7) whether or not the incumbent won. Anyone interested in more detailed data on these elections should visit Dr. Beyle's Web site (www.unc.edu/~beyle).

Federal Impacts

In fiscal year 2002, federal outlays exceeded revenues, and so began the current budget deficit. One possible fix—raising taxes—is not under consideration, and the other—cutting spending—is proving to be difficult. The budget cuts that the House and Senate fought over in late 2005 are not large enough to make much of a dent in the deficit, especially if expiring tax cuts are extended. Moreover, as *State Policy Reports* editor Marcia Howard explains, there is every reason to believe that in the short run spending needs will only increase:

> The imminent retirement of the first wave of Baby Boomers will put pressure on both Social Security and Medicare. New prescription drug coverage will exacerbate the pressures on Medicare. As the Baby Boomers age, many of them will become eligible for—and dependent on—Medicaid. Defense spending will continue to grow as long as the country must finance its military operations in Iraq and Afghanistan. Finally, interest on the federal debt must be paid. It could grow larger if interest rates increase or if deficits grow rather than shrink; it could contract if the opposite situations develop.

For a short summary of ideas on how to deal with the deficit see the November 2005 issue of *State Policy Reports* (Volume 23, Issue 22).

Recent data show that federal outlays in the first two months of fiscal year 2006 were 11.4 percent higher than in the first two months of fiscal year 2005. Interest on the debt is up nearly 40 percent over the same period, partly because of higher inflation and interest rates.

Federal Outlays, Preliminary 2006

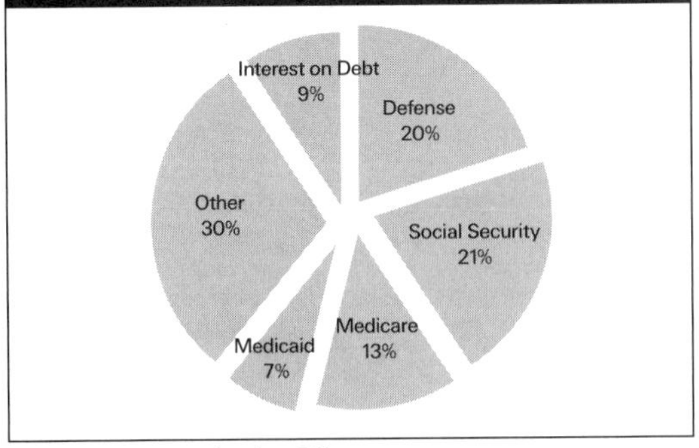

Source: Congressional Budget Office

E-1 Federal Spending, Total and Per Capita, FY 2004

State	Total federal spending $ (in millions)	Per capita federal spending $	Rank per capita
Alabama	39,047	8,619	9
Alaska	8,445	12,885	1
Arizona	41,979	7,309	24
Arkansas	19,489	7,080	28
California	232,387	6,474	34
Colorado	30,060	6,533	33
Connecticut	30,304	8,649	8
Delaware	5,253	6,326	39
Florida	121,934	7,009	29
Georgia	55,153	6,247	41
Hawaii	12,187	9,650	5
Idaho	8,968	6,437	36
Illinois	76,828	6,043	45
Indiana	37,918	6,079	44
Iowa	19,473	6,591	32
Kansas	19,131	6,994	30
Kentucky	31,714	7,649	18
Louisiana	32,954	7,298	25
Maine	10,865	8,248	13
Maryland	64,726	11,645	3
Massachusetts	53,120	8,279	12
Michigan	60,488	5,981	46
Minnesota	28,791	5,644	49
Mississippi	22,338	7,695	17
Missouri	45,730	7,947	15
Montana	7,494	8,085	14
Nebraska	11,795	6,751	31
Nevada	12,769	5,469	50
New Hampshire	7,959	6,125	42
New Jersey	55,264	6,353	38
New Mexico	19,864	10,437	4
New York	143,903	7,484	22
North Carolina	55,233	6,467	35
North Dakota	6,035	9,513	6
Ohio	73,195	6,388	37
Oklahoma	26,644	7,562	21
Oregon	21,871	6,084	43
Pennsylvania	94,900	7,649	19
Rhode Island	8,245	7,630	20
South Carolina	30,051	7,158	27
South Dakota	6,602	8,564	10
Tennessee	45,441	7,701	16
Texas	141,858	6,308	40
Utah	13,684	5,728	47
Vermont	4,633	7,456	23
Virginia	90,638	12,150	2
Washington	44,841	7,228	26
West Virginia	15,183	8,364	11
Wisconsin	31,554	5,728	48
Wyoming	4,393	8,673	7
50 States	2,083,331	7,108	
DC	37,630	67,983	
United States*	2,162,204	7,223	

**Due to rounding or data sources, the 50-state total plus D.C. may not equal the U.S. total. Please see introduction.*

Rank in order per capita	
1	Alaska
2	Virginia
3	Maryland
4	New Mexico
5	Hawaii
6	North Dakota
7	Wyoming
8	Connecticut
9	Alabama
10	South Dakota
11	West Virginia
12	Massachusetts
13	Maine
14	Montana
15	Missouri
16	Tennessee
17	Mississippi
18	Kentucky
19	Pennsylvania
20	Rhode Island
21	Oklahoma
22	New York
23	Vermont
24	Arizona
25	Louisiana
26	Washington
27	South Carolina
28	Arkansas
29	Florida
30	Kansas
31	Nebraska
32	Iowa
33	Colorado
34	California
35	North Carolina
36	Idaho
37	Ohio
38	New Jersey
39	Delaware
40	Texas
41	Georgia
42	New Hampshire
43	Oregon
44	Indiana
45	Illinois
46	Michigan
47	Utah
48	Wisconsin
49	Minnesota
50	Nevada

Note: Numbers that appear to be identical are rounded and vary slightly in actual value. The rankings reflect the actual values before rounding. See the introduction for more details.

E-2 Increase in Total Federal Spending, FY 1999–2004

State	Total federal spending FY 1999 $ (in millions)	Percentage increase in federal spending	Rank by percentage increase
Alabama	26,904	45.1	15
Alaska	5,291	59.6	1
Arizona	27,075	55.0	4
Arkansas	13,706	42.2	19
California	168,676	37.8	30
Colorado	21,940	37.0	33
Connecticut	19,644	54.3	5
Delaware	3,816	37.7	31
Florida	87,716	39.0	26
Georgia	39,415	39.9	23
Hawaii	8,660	40.7	21
Idaho	6,207	44.5	16
Illinois	56,646	35.6	38
Indiana	27,013	40.4	22
Iowa	15,708	24.0	49
Kansas	14,520	31.8	47
Kentucky	22,374	41.7	20
Louisiana	24,558	34.2	41
Maine	7,456	45.7	14
Maryland	42,339	52.9	6
Massachusetts	38,820	36.8	34
Michigan	44,128	37.1	32
Minnesota	21,897	31.5	48
Mississippi	16,564	34.9	40
Missouri	33,474	36.6	35
Montana	6,251	19.9	50
Nebraska	8,844	33.4	44
Nevada	8,013	59.4	2
New Hampshire	5,389	47.7	8
New Jersey	41,204	34.1	42
New Mexico	13,616	45.9	13
New York	103,393	39.2	25
North Carolina	37,482	47.4	9
North Dakota	4,578	31.8	46
Ohio	53,772	36.1	37
Oklahoma	19,298	38.1	29
Oregon	15,759	38.8	27
Pennsylvania	69,996	35.6	39
Rhode Island	6,250	31.9	45
South Carolina	20,952	43.4	18
South Dakota	4,943	33.6	43
Tennessee	30,982	46.7	11
Texas	98,488	44.0	17
Utah	9,294	47.2	10
Vermont	3,168	46.2	12
Virginia	58,168	55.8	3
Washington	32,156	39.4	24
West Virginia	11,135	36.4	36
Wisconsin	22,757	38.7	28
Wyoming	2,931	49.9	7
50 States	1,483,366	40.4	
DC	26,232	43.5	
United States*	1,555,651	39.0	

**Due to rounding or data sources, the 50-state total plus D.C. may not equal the U.S. total. Please see introduction.*

Rank in order by percentage increase	
1	Alaska
2	Nevada
3	Virginia
4	Arizona
5	Connecticut
6	Maryland
7	Wyoming
8	New Hampshire
9	North Carolina
10	Utah
11	Tennessee
12	Vermont
13	New Mexico
14	Maine
15	Alabama
16	Idaho
17	Texas
18	South Carolina
19	Arkansas
20	Kentucky
21	Hawaii
22	Indiana
23	Georgia
24	Washington
25	New York
26	Florida
27	Oregon
28	Wisconsin
29	Oklahoma
30	California
31	Delaware
32	Michigan
33	Colorado
34	Massachusetts
35	Missouri
36	West Virginia
37	Ohio
38	Illinois
39	Pennsylvania
40	Mississippi
41	Louisiana
42	New Jersey
43	South Dakota
44	Nebraska
45	Rhode Island
46	North Dakota
47	Kansas
48	Minnesota
49	Iowa
50	Montana

Note: Numbers that appear to be identical are rounded and vary slightly in actual value. The rankings reflect the actual values before rounding. See the introduction for more details.

E-3 Federal Spending on Grants, Total and Per Capita, FY 2004

State	Federal grants to state and local governments $ (in millions)	Per capita federal grants to state and local government $	Rank per capita
Alabama	7,008	1,547	22
Alaska	3,217	4,908	1
Arizona	8,364	1,456	30
Arkansas	4,683	1,701	16
California	54,534	1,519	23
Colorado	5,643	1,226	46
Connecticut	5,556	1,586	21
Delaware	1,241	1,495	26
Florida	19,610	1,127	48
Georgia	11,759	1,332	39
Hawaii	2,158	1,709	15
Idaho	1,995	1,432	35
Illinois	16,531	1,300	42
Indiana	7,436	1,192	47
Iowa	4,039	1,367	37
Kansas	3,469	1,268	43
Kentucky	6,743	1,626	18
Louisiana	7,787	1,724	14
Maine	2,758	2,094	11
Maryland	8,837	1,590	20
Massachusetts	13,876	2,163	7
Michigan	13,227	1,308	40
Minnesota	7,209	1,413	36
Mississippi	5,379	1,853	13
Missouri	8,734	1,518	24
Montana	1,997	2,155	9
Nebraska	2,531	1,449	31
Nevada	2,322	995	50
New Hampshire	1,879	1,446	32
New Jersey	11,333	1,303	41
New Mexico	4,663	2,450	4
New York	50,009	2,601	3
North Carolina	12,574	1,472	27
North Dakota	1,515	2,388	5
Ohio	16,514	1,441	34
Oklahoma	5,271	1,496	25
Oregon	5,185	1,442	33
Pennsylvania	19,916	1,605	19
Rhode Island	2,329	2,155	8
South Carolina	6,145	1,464	29
South Dakota	1,620	2,101	10
Tennessee	9,863	1,671	17
Texas	27,792	1,236	44
Utah	2,948	1,234	45
Vermont	1,423	2,290	6
Virginia	7,991	1,071	49
Washington	9,083	1,464	28
West Virginia	3,701	2,039	12
Wisconsin	7,484	1,358	38
Wyoming	1,636	3,230	2
50 States	449,517	1,534	
DC	4,205	7,597	
United States*	460,152	1,410	

**Due to rounding or data sources, the 50-state total plus D.C. may not equal the U.S. total. Please see introduction.*

Rank in order per capita	
1	Alaska
2	Wyoming
3	New York
4	New Mexico
5	North Dakota
6	Vermont
7	Massachusetts
8	Rhode Island
9	Montana
10	South Dakota
11	Maine
12	West Virginia
13	Mississippi
14	Louisiana
15	Hawaii
16	Arkansas
17	Tennessee
18	Kentucky
19	Pennsylvania
20	Maryland
21	Connecticut
22	Alabama
23	California
24	Missouri
25	Oklahoma
26	Delaware
27	North Carolina
28	Washington
29	South Carolina
30	Arizona
31	Nebraska
32	New Hampshire
33	Oregon
34	Ohio
35	Idaho
36	Minnesota
37	Iowa
38	Wisconsin
39	Georgia
40	Michigan
41	New Jersey
42	Illinois
43	Kansas
44	Texas
45	Utah
46	Colorado
47	Indiana
48	Florida
49	Virginia
50	Nevada

Note: Numbers that appear to be identical are rounded and vary slightly in actual value. The rankings reflect the actual values before rounding. See the introduction for more details.

E-4 Federal Spending on Procurement, FY 2004

State	Total spending on procurement $ (in millions)	Per capita procurement spending $	Rank per capita
Alabama	7,600	1,678	7
Alaska	1,700	2,594	5
Arizona	9,797	1,706	6
Arkansas	848	308	50
California	40,254	1,121	15
Colorado	5,747	1,249	13
Connecticut	9,509	2,714	4
Delaware	265	319	49
Florida	11,447	658	33
Georgia	5,813	658	32
Hawaii	2,066	1,636	8
Idaho	1,373	985	19
Illinois	6,583	518	40
Indiana	4,002	642	34
Iowa	1,599	541	39
Kansas	2,242	820	22
Kentucky	4,637	1,118	17
Louisiana	3,418	757	28
Maine	1,711	1,299	12
Maryland	20,804	3,743	2
Massachusetts	9,127	1,422	9
Michigan	4,119	407	46
Minnesota	2,329	457	45
Mississippi	2,372	817	23
Missouri	7,991	1,389	10
Montana	587	633	35
Nebraska	697	399	47
Nevada	1,600	685	31
New Hampshire	985	758	27
New Jersey	6,132	705	30
New Mexico	5,973	3,138	3
New York	8,889	462	43
North Carolina	3,933	460	44
North Dakota	503	793	26
Ohio	6,936	605	36
Oklahoma	2,804	796	24
Oregon	1,283	357	48
Pennsylvania	9,311	751	29
Rhode Island	559	517	41
South Carolina	4,193	999	18
South Dakota	438	568	38
Tennessee	8,118	1,376	11
Texas	26,969	1,199	14
Utah	2,304	964	20
Vermont	541	871	21
Virginia	35,325	4,735	1
Washington	6,946	1,120	16
West Virginia	1,041	573	37
Wisconsin	2,641	479	42
Wyoming	403	796	25
50 States	306,464	1,046	
DC	13,347	24,113	
United States*	339,681	882	

**Due to rounding or data sources, the 50-state total plus D.C. may not equal the U.S. total. Please see introduction.*

Rank in order per capita	
1	Virginia
2	Maryland
3	New Mexico
4	Connecticut
5	Alaska
6	Arizona
7	Alabama
8	Hawaii
9	Massachusetts
10	Missouri
11	Tennessee
12	Maine
13	Colorado
14	Texas
15	California
16	Washington
17	Kentucky
18	South Carolina
19	Idaho
20	Utah
21	Vermont
22	Kansas
23	Mississippi
24	Oklahoma
25	Wyoming
26	North Dakota
27	New Hampshire
28	Louisiana
29	Pennsylvania
30	New Jersey
31	Nevada
32	Georgia
33	Florida
34	Indiana
35	Montana
36	Ohio
37	West Virginia
38	South Dakota
39	Iowa
40	Illinois
41	Rhode Island
42	Wisconsin
43	New York
44	North Carolina
45	Minnesota
46	Michigan
47	Nebraska
48	Oregon
49	Delaware
50	Arkansas

Note: Numbers that appear to be identical are rounded and vary slightly in actual value. The rankings reflect the actual values before rounding. See the introduction for more details.

E-5 Federal Spending on Payments to Individuals, FY 2004

State	Total federal payments to individuals $ (in millions)	Per capita federal payments to individuals $	Rank per capita
Alabama	20,947	4,624	6
Alaska	1,800	2,746	49
Arizona	20,211	3,519	40
Arkansas	12,449	4,523	7
California	115,570	3,220	45
Colorado	14,213	3,089	48
Connecticut	13,637	3,892	27
Delaware	3,253	3,918	25
Florida	80,482	4,626	5
Georgia	29,257	3,314	44
Hawaii	4,809	3,808	31
Idaho	4,702	3,375	42
Illinois	46,708	3,674	35
Indiana	24,023	3,851	29
Iowa	12,586	4,260	13
Kansas	11,213	4,099	21
Kentucky	17,102	4,125	20
Louisiana	18,931	4,192	14
Maine	5,439	4,129	19
Maryland	24,562	4,419	8
Massachusetts	26,560	4,139	18
Michigan	39,532	3,909	26
Minnesota	16,950	3,323	43
Mississippi	12,493	4,304	11
Missouri	24,963	4,338	10
Montana	4,023	4,340	9
Nebraska	7,269	4,160	16
Nevada	7,501	3,213	47
New Hampshire	4,440	3,417	41
New Jersey	33,471	3,848	30
New Mexico	7,157	3,760	32
New York	75,935	3,949	23
North Carolina	31,529	3,691	34
North Dakota	3,230	5,092	1
Ohio	44,169	3,855	28
Oklahoma	15,107	4,287	12
Oregon	13,500	3,756	33
Pennsylvania	59,064	4,761	4
Rhode Island	4,529	4,191	15
South Carolina	16,558	3,944	24
South Dakota	3,779	4,902	3
Tennessee	23,984	4,064	22
Texas	72,407	3,220	46
Utah	6,281	2,629	50
Vermont	2,264	3,643	37
Virginia	30,979	4,153	17
Washington	22,754	3,668	36
West Virginia	9,084	5,004	2
Wisconsin	19,534	3,546	39
Wyoming	1,833	3,619	38
50 States	1,122,773	3,831	
DC	4,552	8,224	
United States*	1,136,769	3,871	

**Due to rounding or data sources, the 50-state total plus D.C. may not equal the U.S. total. Please see introduction.*

Rank in order per capita	
1	North Dakota
2	West Virginia
3	South Dakota
4	Pennsylvania
5	Florida
6	Alabama
7	Arkansas
8	Maryland
9	Montana
10	Missouri
11	Mississippi
12	Oklahoma
13	Iowa
14	Louisiana
15	Rhode Island
16	Nebraska
17	Virginia
18	Massachusetts
19	Maine
20	Kentucky
21	Kansas
22	Tennessee
23	New York
24	South Carolina
25	Delaware
26	Michigan
27	Connecticut
28	Ohio
29	Indiana
30	New Jersey
31	Hawaii
32	New Mexico
33	Oregon
34	North Carolina
35	Illinois
36	Washington
37	Vermont
38	Wyoming
39	Wisconsin
40	Arizona
41	New Hampshire
42	Idaho
43	Minnesota
44	Georgia
45	California
46	Texas
47	Nevada
48	Colorado
49	Alaska
50	Utah

Note: Numbers that appear to be identical are rounded and vary slightly in actual value. The rankings reflect the actual values before rounding. See the introduction for more details.

E-6 Federal Spending on Social Security and Medicare, FY 2004

State	Total Social Security and Medicare spending $ (in millions)	Per capita spending $	Rank per capita
Alabama	14,836	3,275	4
Alaska	895	1,366	50
Arizona	14,313	2,492	36
Arkansas	8,615	3,130	10
California	86,266	2,403	41
Colorado	9,091	1,976	48
Connecticut	11,278	3,219	6
Delaware	2,411	2,903	21
Florida	61,831	3,554	3
Georgia	19,742	2,236	45
Hawaii	3,073	2,433	38
Idaho	3,149	2,260	44
Illinois	35,196	2,768	24
Indiana	17,841	2,860	22
Iowa	8,763	2,966	19
Kansas	7,682	2,808	23
Kentucky	12,709	3,065	14
Louisiana	13,918	3,082	11
Maine	3,925	2,980	18
Maryland	14,100	2,537	35
Massachusetts	20,962	3,267	5
Michigan	31,705	3,135	9
Minnesota	12,314	2,414	39
Mississippi	8,828	3,041	15
Missouri	17,706	3,077	13
Montana	2,490	2,687	29
Nebraska	4,496	2,573	34
Nevada	5,176	2,217	46
New Hampshire	3,350	2,578	33
New Jersey	26,779	3,078	12
New Mexico	4,436	2,331	43
New York	60,875	3,166	8
North Carolina	22,449	2,628	32
North Dakota	1,755	2,767	25
Ohio	34,538	3,014	16
Oklahoma	10,294	2,922	20
Oregon	9,508	2,645	31
Pennsylvania	46,028	3,710	2
Rhode Island	3,455	3,197	7
South Carolina	11,510	2,742	27
South Dakota	2,050	2,660	30
Tennessee	17,615	2,985	17
Texas	48,716	2,166	47
Utah	3,946	1,652	49
Vermont	1,679	2,702	28
Virginia	17,540	2,351	42
Washington	14,951	2,410	40
West Virginia	6,949	3,828	1
Wisconsin	15,160	2,752	26
Wyoming	1,236	2,441	37
50 States	818,131	2,791	
DC	1,637	2,957	
United States*	826,683	2,815	

**Due to rounding or data sources, the 50-state total plus D.C. may not equal the U.S. total. Please see introduction.*

Rank in order per capita	
1	West Virginia
2	Pennsylvania
3	Florida
4	Alabama
5	Massachusetts
6	Connecticut
7	Rhode Island
8	New York
9	Michigan
10	Arkansas
11	Louisiana
12	New Jersey
13	Missouri
14	Kentucky
15	Mississippi
16	Ohio
17	Tennessee
18	Maine
19	Iowa
20	Oklahoma
21	Delaware
22	Indiana
23	Kansas
24	Illinois
25	North Dakota
26	Wisconsin
27	South Carolina
28	Vermont
29	Montana
30	South Dakota
31	Oregon
32	North Carolina
33	New Hampshire
34	Nebraska
35	Maryland
36	Arizona
37	Wyoming
38	Hawaii
39	Minnesota
40	Washington
41	California
42	Virginia
43	New Mexico
44	Idaho
45	Georgia
46	Nevada
47	Texas
48	Colorado
49	Utah
50	Alaska

E-7 Social Security Benefits Paid, FY 2004

State	Social Security amounts paid $ (in thousands)	Number of recipients	Average monthly benefit $	Rank by average benefit
Alabama	722,714	884,410	817	43
Alaska	51,917	63,440	818	42
Arizona	794,247	888,460	894	16
Arkansas	436,581	546,080	799	48
California	3,876,601	4,411,970	879	26
Colorado	493,571	571,470	864	28
Connecticut	566,578	584,090	970	2
Delaware	137,822	148,860	926	5
Florida	2,985,634	3,381,970	883	22
Georgia	1,004,376	1,192,050	843	36
Hawaii	175,645	199,240	882	23
Idaho	187,314	219,250	854	32
Illinois	1,722,772	1,883,750	915	8
Indiana	950,014	1,038,130	915	7
Iowa	480,250	545,990	880	24
Kansas	401,416	447,140	898	13
Kentucky	632,483	784,910	806	45
Louisiana	582,293	739,180	788	49
Maine	213,717	265,470	805	46
Maryland	681,245	761,160	895	15
Massachusetts	946,394	1,066,620	887	17
Michigan	1,603,478	1,716,290	934	3
Minnesota	686,336	775,050	886	19
Mississippi	422,221	545,710	774	50
Missouri	898,963	1,046,110	859	30
Montana	139,775	165,910	842	37
Nebraska	251,213	290,580	865	27
Nevada	307,626	340,680	903	11
New Hampshire	197,646	219,080	902	12
New Jersey	1,341,270	1,370,440	979	1
New Mexico	243,013	303,610	800	47
New York	2,821,845	3,045,290	927	4
North Carolina	1,251,605	1,467,400	853	33
North Dakota	94,123	114,720	820	41
Ohio	1,723,337	1,950,740	883	21
Oklahoma	522,890	623,160	839	39
Oregon	548,081	611,490	896	14
Pennsylvania	2,180,687	2,405,080	907	10
Rhode Island	170,040	191,710	887	18
South Carolina	635,980	750,970	847	34
South Dakota	113,123	139,770	809	44
Tennessee	895,689	1,069,600	837	40
Texas	2,406,126	2,864,870	840	38
Utah	230,695	262,330	879	25
Vermont	94,676	110,180	859	31
Virginia	959,592	1,114,210	861	29
Washington	837,606	913,040	917	6
West Virginia	343,345	407,460	843	35
Wisconsin	850,099	937,490	907	9
Wyoming	72,944	82,510	884	20
50 States	40,887,608	46,459,120	880	
DC	54,878	71,670	766	
United States*	41,591,855	47,707,380	872	

**Due to rounding or data sources, the 50-state total plus D.C. may not equal the U.S. total. Please see introduction.*

Rank in order by average benefit	
1	New Jersey
2	Connecticut
3	Michigan
4	New York
5	Delaware
6	Washington
7	Indiana
8	Illinois
9	Wisconsin
10	Pennsylvania
11	Nevada
12	New Hampshire
13	Kansas
14	Oregon
15	Maryland
16	Arizona
17	Massachusetts
18	Rhode Island
19	Minnesota
20	Wyoming
21	Ohio
22	Florida
23	Hawaii
24	Iowa
25	Utah
26	California
27	Nebraska
28	Colorado
29	Virginia
30	Missouri
31	Vermont
32	Idaho
33	North Carolina
34	South Carolina
35	West Virginia
36	Georgia
37	Montana
38	Texas
39	Oklahoma
40	Tennessee
41	North Dakota
42	Alaska
43	Alabama
44	South Dakota
45	Kentucky
46	Maine
47	New Mexico
48	Arkansas
49	Louisiana
50	Mississippi

Note: Numbers that appear to be identical are rounded and vary slightly in actual value. The rankings reflect the actual values before rounding. See the introduction for more details.

E-8 Federal Spending on Employee Wages and Salaries, FY 2004

State	Total federal spending on wages and salaries $ (in millions)	Per capita spending on wages and salaries $	Rank per capita
Alabama	3,492	771	18
Alaska	1,728	2,636	1
Arizona	3,608	628	29
Arkansas	1,509	548	38
California	22,029	614	31
Colorado	4,457	969	11
Connecticut	1,602	457	45
Delaware	494	595	33
Florida	10,395	598	32
Georgia	8,324	943	13
Hawaii	3,154	2,498	2
Idaho	898	645	28
Illinois	7,007	551	37
Indiana	2,457	394	48
Iowa	1,249	423	47
Kansas	2,208	807	16
Kentucky	3,231	779	17
Louisiana	2,818	624	30
Maine	957	727	23
Maryland	10,523	1,893	4
Massachusetts	3,557	554	36
Michigan	3,610	357	49
Minnesota	2,302	451	46
Mississippi	2,094	721	24
Missouri	4,042	702	25
Montana	886	956	12
Nebraska	1,298	743	22
Nevada	1,347	577	35
New Hampshire	654	503	41
New Jersey	4,328	498	42
New Mexico	2,072	1,089	6
New York	9,070	472	44
North Carolina	7,197	843	15
North Dakota	787	1,241	5
Ohio	5,576	487	43
Oklahoma	3,463	983	9
Oregon	1,903	529	40
Pennsylvania	6,609	533	39
Rhode Island	829	767	19
South Carolina	3,156	752	20
South Dakota	765	992	8
Tennessee	3,476	589	34
Texas	14,690	653	26
Utah	2,150	900	14
Vermont	405	652	27
Virginia	16,342	2,191	3
Washington	6,058	977	10
West Virginia	1,358	748	21
Wisconsin	1,895	344	50
Wyoming	521	1,029	7
50 States	204,580	698	
DC	15,526	28,049	
United States*	225,601	675	

**Due to rounding or data sources, the 50-state total plus D.C. may not equal the U.S. total. Please see introduction.*

Rank in order per capita	
1	Alaska
2	Hawaii
3	Virginia
4	Maryland
5	North Dakota
6	New Mexico
7	Wyoming
8	South Dakota
9	Oklahoma
10	Washington
11	Colorado
12	Montana
13	Georgia
14	Utah
15	North Carolina
16	Kansas
17	Kentucky
18	Alabama
19	Rhode Island
20	South Carolina
21	West Virginia
22	Nebraska
23	Maine
24	Mississippi
25	Missouri
26	Texas
27	Vermont
28	Idaho
29	Arizona
30	Louisiana
31	California
32	Florida
33	Delaware
34	Tennessee
35	Nevada
36	Massachusetts
37	Illinois
38	Arkansas
39	Pennsylvania
40	Oregon
41	New Hampshire
42	New Jersey
43	Ohio
44	New York
45	Connecticut
46	Minnesota
47	Iowa
48	Indiana
49	Michigan
50	Wisconsin

Note: Numbers that appear to be identical are rounded and vary slightly in actual value. The rankings reflect the actual values before rounding. See the introduction for more details.

E-9 Federal Spending on Defense, FY 2004

State	Total spending on defense $ (in millions)	Per capita defense spending	Rank per capita
Alabama	8,725	1,926	7
Alaska	2,522	3,847	2
Arizona	11,135	1,939	6
Arkansas	1,596	580	41
California	42,723	1,190	20
Colorado	6,182	1,343	12
Connecticut	9,735	2,778	4
Delaware	629	758	32
Florida	17,419	1,001	26
Georgia	10,175	1,152	22
Hawaii	4,772	3,779	3
Idaho	744	534	42
Illinois	5,918	466	43
Indiana	4,465	716	35
Iowa	1,262	427	45
Kansas	2,948	1,078	23
Kentucky	5,132	1,238	18
Louisiana	4,433	982	27
Maine	2,297	1,744	8
Maryland	13,796	2,482	5
Massachusetts	8,240	1,284	16
Michigan	3,783	374	49
Minnesota	2,112	414	46
Mississippi	3,624	1,249	17
Missouri	8,585	1,492	9
Montana	658	710	36
Nebraska	1,321	756	33
Nevada	1,612	690	37
New Hampshire	1,125	866	29
New Jersey	5,843	672	38
New Mexico	2,471	1,298	15
New York	7,555	393	48
North Carolina	8,679	1,016	24
North Dakota	833	1,312	14
Ohio	7,539	658	39
Oklahoma	4,279	1,214	19
Oregon	1,311	365	50
Pennsylvania	9,037	728	34
Rhode Island	1,022	946	28
South Carolina	4,881	1,163	21
South Dakota	658	853	30
Tennessee	3,770	639	40
Texas	31,895	1,418	10
Utah	3,305	1,384	11
Vermont	623	1,003	25
Virginia	38,533	5,165	1
Washington	8,321	1,341	13
West Virginia	734	404	47
Wisconsin	2,414	438	44
Wyoming	412	814	31
50 States	331,783	n/a	
DC	5,264	9,509	
United States*	347,689	1,148	

**Due to rounding or data sources, the 50-state total plus D.C. may not equal the U.S. total. Please see introduction.*

Rank in order per capita	
1	Virginia
2	Alaska
3	Hawaii
4	Connecticut
5	Maryland
6	Arizona
7	Alabama
8	Maine
9	Missouri
10	Texas
11	Utah
12	Colorado
13	Washington
14	North Dakota
15	New Mexico
16	Massachusetts
17	Mississippi
18	Kentucky
19	Oklahoma
20	California
21	South Carolina
22	Georgia
23	Kansas
24	North Carolina
25	Vermont
26	Florida
27	Louisiana
28	Rhode Island
29	New Hampshire
30	South Dakota
31	Wyoming
32	Delaware
33	Nebraska
34	Pennsylvania
35	Indiana
36	Montana
37	Nevada
38	New Jersey
39	Ohio
40	Tennessee
41	Arkansas
42	Idaho
43	Illinois
44	Wisconsin
45	Iowa
46	Minnesota
47	West Virginia
48	New York
49	Michigan
50	Oregon

E-10 Homeland Security Grants, Total and Per Capita, FY 2005

State	Homeland security grants $ (in thousands)	Per capita	Rank per capita
Alabama	17,689	3.90	28
Alaska	9,369	14.29	4
Arizona	20,022	3.49	35
Arkansas	13,855	5.03	19
California	84,614	2.36	50
Colorado	17,797	3.87	29
Connecticut	15,491	4.42	22
Delaware	9,733	11.72	6
Florida	44,728	2.57	47
Georgia	26,726	3.03	42
Hawaii	10,684	8.46	9
Idaho	10,918	7.84	12
Illinois	35,299	2.78	46
Indiana	21,350	3.42	36
Iowa	14,326	4.85	21
Kansas	13,850	5.06	18
Kentucky	16,862	4.07	25
Louisiana	17,679	3.91	27
Maine	10,788	8.19	11
Maryland	19,866	3.57	32
Massachusetts	21,863	3.41	38
Michigan	29,740	2.94	43
Minnesota	18,895	3.70	30
Mississippi	14,191	4.89	20
Missouri	20,289	3.53	33
Montana	9,949	10.73	7
Nebraska	11,724	6.71	13
Nevada	12,808	5.49	16
New Hampshire	10,749	8.27	10
New Jersey	26,626	3.06	40
New Mexico	12,016	6.31	15
New York	49,418	2.57	48
North Carolina	26,127	3.06	41
North Dakota	9,336	14.72	3
Ohio	32,669	2.85	44
Oklahoma	15,552	4.41	23
Oregon	15,656	4.36	24
Pennsylvania	34,677	2.80	45
Rhode Island	10,292	9.52	8
South Carolina	16,925	4.03	26
South Dakota	9,618	12.48	5
Tennessee	20,585	3.49	34
Texas	55,743	2.48	49
Utah	13,046	5.46	17
Vermont	9,304	14.97	2
Virginia	23,922	3.21	39
Washington	21,211	3.42	37
West Virginia	11,878	6.54	14
Wisconsin	19,787	3.59	31
Wyoming	9,050	17.87	1
50 States	1,025,292	3.50	
DC	9,184	16.59	
United States*	1,100,000	3.75	

**Due to rounding or data sources, the 50-state total plus D.C. may not equal the U.S. total. Please see introduction.*

Rank in order per capita	
1	Wyoming
2	Vermont
3	North Dakota
4	Alaska
5	South Dakota
6	Delaware
7	Montana
8	Rhode Island
9	Hawaii
10	New Hampshire
11	Maine
12	Idaho
13	Nebraska
14	West Virginia
15	New Mexico
16	Nevada
17	Utah
18	Kansas
19	Arkansas
20	Mississippi
21	Iowa
22	Connecticut
23	Oklahoma
24	Oregon
25	Kentucky
26	South Carolina
27	Louisiana
28	Alabama
29	Colorado
30	Minnesota
31	Wisconsin
32	Maryland
33	Missouri
34	Tennessee
35	Arizona
36	Indiana
37	Washington
38	Massachusetts
39	Virginia
40	New Jersey
41	North Carolina
42	Georgia
43	Michigan
44	Ohio
45	Pennsylvania
46	Illinois
47	Florida
48	New York
49	Texas
50	California

Note: Numbers that appear to be identical are rounded and vary slightly in actual value. The rankings reflect the actual values before rounding. See the introduction for more details.

E-11 Federal Grant Spending Per Dollar of State Tax Revenue, FY 2002

State	Federal aid per dollar of state tax revenue $	Rank
Alabama	0.89	9
Alaska	1.42	1
Arizona	0.58	34
Arkansas	0.65	22
California	0.53	36
Colorado	0.55	35
Connecticut	0.41	46
Delaware	0.41	45
Florida	0.50	38
Georgia	0.62	25
Hawaii	0.40	48
Idaho	0.58	31
Illinois	0.46	42
Indiana	0.58	33
Iowa	0.66	21
Kansas	0.62	27
Kentucky	0.64	23
Louisiana	0.81	11
Maine	0.69	18
Maryland	0.49	41
Massachusetts	0.34	49
Michigan	0.51	37
Minnesota	0.40	47
Mississippi	0.92	6
Missouri	0.77	14
Montana	0.98	5
Nebraska	0.59	30
Nevada	0.32	50
New Hampshire	0.63	24
New Jersey	0.45	43
New Mexico	0.76	15
New York	0.74	16
North Carolina	0.61	29
North Dakota	0.92	7
Ohio	0.61	28
Oklahoma	0.67	20
Oregon	1.09	2
Pennsylvania	0.62	26
Rhode Island	0.77	13
South Carolina	0.83	10
South Dakota	1.07	3
Tennessee	0.91	8
Texas	0.72	17
Utah	0.58	32
Vermont	0.69	19
Virginia	0.42	44
Washington	0.49	40
West Virginia	0.80	12
Wisconsin	0.50	39
Wyoming	1.02	4
50 States	0.59	
DC	n/a	
United States	0.59	

Rank in order by $	
1	Alaska
2	Oregon
3	South Dakota
4	Wyoming
5	Montana
6	Mississippi
7	North Dakota
8	Tennessee
9	Alabama
10	South Carolina
11	Louisiana
12	West Virginia
13	Rhode Island
14	Missouri
15	New Mexico
16	New York
17	Texas
18	Maine
19	Vermont
20	Oklahoma
21	Iowa
22	Arkansas
23	Kentucky
24	New Hampshire
25	Georgia
26	Pennsylvania
27	Kansas
28	Ohio
29	North Carolina
30	Nebraska
31	Idaho
32	Utah
33	Indiana
34	Arizona
35	Colorado
36	California
37	Michigan
38	Florida
39	Wisconsin
40	Washington
41	Maryland
42	Illinois
43	New Jersey
44	Virginia
45	Delaware
46	Connecticut
47	Minnesota
48	Hawaii
49	Massachusetts
50	Nevada

Note: Numbers that appear to be identical are rounded and vary slightly in actual value. The rankings reflect the actual values before rounding. See the introduction for more details.

E-12 State and Local General Revenue from Federal Government, FY 2002

State	Total general revenue from federal government $ (in millions)	Percentage of revenue from federal government	Rank by percentage
Alabama	6,263	26.4	13
Alaska	1,789	24.8	18
Arizona	5,719	22.4	23
Arkansas	3,645	27.5	11
California	48,250	21.3	28
Colorado	4,269	16.4	46
Connecticut	4,039	17.7	43
Delaware	959	17.1	45
Florida	14,956	17.3	44
Georgia	9,357	21.1	31
Hawaii	1,547	20.8	34
Idaho	1,415	21.4	27
Illinois	12,717	18.4	40
Indiana	6,283	19.4	38
Iowa	3,626	21.5	26
Kansas	3,098	21.2	29
Kentucky	5,414	25.5	14
Louisiana	6,485	24.9	17
Maine	1,901	23.5	20
Maryland	5,927	18.3	42
Massachusetts	6,176	15.8	49
Michigan	12,543	21.6	25
Minnesota	6,088	18.3	41
Mississippi	4,625	30.2	2
Missouri	7,329	25.2	15
Montana	1,590	31.0	1
Nebraska	1,973	20.1	36
Nevada	1,632	14.3	50
New Hampshire	1,296	20.2	35
New Jersey	8,949	16.2	47
New Mexico	3,124	28.7	7
New York	36,186	23.3	21
North Carolina	10,241	23.2	22
North Dakota	1,156	28.9	6
Ohio	13,863	21.1	30
Oklahoma	4,413	24.4	19
Oregon	6,438	29.8	3
Pennsylvania	16,026	22.3	24
Rhode Island	1,766	26.6	12
South Carolina	5,333	25.1	16
South Dakota	1,150	29.5	5
Tennessee	7,604	27.7	10
Texas	22,915	21.0	32
Utah	2,613	20.9	33
Vermont	1,087	28.2	8
Virginia	6,235	16.0	48
Washington	7,042	19.4	39
West Virginia	2,999	29.7	4
Wisconsin	6,456	19.8	37
Wyoming	1,187	28.0	9
50 States	357,694	21.3	
DC	2,840	41.0	
United States	360,534	21.4	

Rank in order by percentage	
1	Montana
2	Mississippi
3	Oregon
4	West Virginia
5	South Dakota
6	North Dakota
7	New Mexico
8	Vermont
9	Wyoming
10	Tennessee
11	Arkansas
12	Rhode Island
13	Alabama
14	Kentucky
15	Missouri
16	South Carolina
17	Louisiana
18	Alaska
19	Oklahoma
20	Maine
21	New York
22	North Carolina
23	Arizona
24	Pennsylvania
25	Michigan
26	Iowa
27	Idaho
28	California
29	Kansas
30	Ohio
31	Georgia
32	Texas
33	Utah
34	Hawaii
35	New Hampshire
36	Nebraska
37	Wisconsin
38	Indiana
39	Washington
40	Illinois
41	Minnesota
42	Maryland
43	Connecticut
44	Florida
45	Delaware
46	Colorado
47	New Jersey
48	Virginia
49	Massachusetts
50	Nevada

Note: Numbers that appear to be identical are rounded and vary slightly in actual value. The rankings reflect the actual values before rounding. See the introduction for more details.

E-13 Federal Tax Burden, Total and Per Capita, FY 2003

State	Federal tax burden total $ (in millions)	Federal tax burden per capita $	Rank per capita
Alabama	20,480	4,542	43
Alaska	3,870	5,978	20
Arizona	28,473	5,111	37
Arkansas	11,705	4,285	47
California	258,053	7,280	7
Colorado	32,305	7,051	9
Connecticut	36,126	10,401	1
Delaware	5,419	6,642	13
Florida	103,526	6,110	18
Georgia	49,084	5,646	24
Hawaii	6,536	5,231	31
Idaho	6,302	4,633	39
Illinois	88,378	6,978	10
Indiana	33,183	5,357	30
Iowa	15,113	5,131	35
Kansas	15,127	5,543	27
Kentucky	18,998	4,615	41
Louisiana	19,764	4,396	46
Maine	6,782	5,221	33
Maryland	39,554	7,195	8
Massachusetts	60,191	9,318	2
Michigan	60,967	6,041	19
Minnesota	34,372	6,794	12
Mississippi	11,147	3,857	50
Missouri	31,079	5,447	28
Montana	4,160	4,550	42
Nebraska	9,635	5,544	26
Nevada	14,118	6,309	15
New Hampshire	9,972	7,746	4
New Jersey	76,020	8,795	3
New Mexico	7,229	3,862	49
New York	144,645	7,524	5
North Carolina	44,065	5,228	32
North Dakota	3,061	4,833	38
Ohio	62,295	5,442	29
Oklahoma	15,744	4,480	45
Oregon	19,970	5,610	25
Pennsylvania	76,683	6,209	17
Rhode Island	6,762	6,293	16
South Carolina	19,133	4,615	40
South Dakota	3,918	5,128	36
Tennessee	30,264	5,171	34
Texas	127,200	5,761	22
Utah	10,564	4,494	44
Vermont	3,565	5,752	23
Virginia	48,705	6,619	14
Washington	44,674	7,282	6
West Virginia	7,218	4,010	48
Wisconsin	31,877	5,827	21
Wyoming	3,438	6,871	11
50 States	1,821,449	6,329	
DC	5,162	9,069	
United States*	1,826,604	6,282	

**Due to rounding or data sources, the 50-state total plus D.C. may not equal the U.S. total. Please see introduction.*

Rank in order per capita	
1	Connecticut
2	Massachusetts
3	New Jersey
4	New Hampshire
5	New York
6	Washington
7	California
8	Maryland
9	Colorado
10	Illinois
11	Wyoming
12	Minnesota
13	Delaware
14	Virginia
15	Nevada
16	Rhode Island
17	Pennsylvania
18	Florida
19	Michigan
20	Alaska
21	Wisconsin
22	Texas
23	Vermont
24	Georgia
25	Oregon
26	Nebraska
27	Kansas
28	Missouri
29	Ohio
30	Indiana
31	Hawaii
32	North Carolina
33	Maine
34	Tennessee
35	Iowa
36	South Dakota
37	Arizona
38	North Dakota
39	Idaho
40	South Carolina
41	Kentucky
42	Montana
43	Alabama
44	Utah
45	Oklahoma
46	Louisiana
47	Arkansas
48	West Virginia
49	New Mexico
50	Mississippi

Note: Numbers that appear to be identical are rounded and vary slightly in actual value. The rankings reflect the actual values before rounding. See the introduction for more details.

E-14 Federal Spending Per Dollar of Taxes Paid, FY 2003

State	Spending per dollar of taxes paid $	Rank
Alabama	1.69	6
Alaska	1.89	2
Arizona	1.23	21
Arkansas	1.47	13
California	0.78	43
Colorado	0.80	41
Connecticut	0.65	48
Delaware	0.82	40
Florida	1.00	32
Georgia	0.95	36
Hawaii	1.58	9
Idaho	1.32	18
Illinois	0.73	45
Indiana	0.96	35
Iowa	1.06	29
Kansas	1.13	25
Kentucky	1.52	10
Louisiana	1.47	14
Maine	1.36	16
Maryland	1.34	17
Massachusetts	0.78	44
Michigan	0.86	38
Minnesota	0.70	47
Mississippi	1.83	3
Missouri	1.31	19
Montana	1.60	7
Nebraska	1.06	30
Nevada	0.70	46
New Hampshire	0.64	49
New Jersey	0.57	50
New Mexico	1.99	1
New York	0.80	42
North Carolina	1.09	26
North Dakota	1.75	5
Ohio	1.02	31
Oklahoma	1.48	12
Oregon	1.00	33
Pennsylvania	1.08	27
Rhode Island	1.06	28
South Carolina	1.36	15
South Dakota	1.49	11
Tennessee	1.29	20
Texas	0.98	34
Utah	1.19	22
Vermont	1.14	23
Virginia	1.58	8
Washington	0.90	37
West Virginia	1.82	4
Wisconsin	0.84	39
Wyoming	1.13	24
50 States	n/a	
DC	6.59	
United States	1.00	

Rank in order by $	
1	New Mexico
2	Alaska
3	Mississippi
4	West Virginia
5	North Dakota
6	Alabama
7	Montana
8	Virginia
9	Hawaii
10	Kentucky
11	South Dakota
12	Oklahoma
13	Arkansas
14	Louisiana
15	South Carolina
16	Maine
17	Maryland
18	Idaho
19	Missouri
20	Tennessee
21	Arizona
22	Utah
23	Vermont
24	Wyoming
25	Kansas
26	North Carolina
27	Pennsylvania
28	Rhode Island
29	Iowa
30	Nebraska
31	Ohio
32	Florida
33	Oregon
34	Texas
35	Indiana
36	Georgia
37	Washington
38	Michigan
39	Wisconsin
40	Delaware
41	Colorado
42	New York
43	California
44	Massachusetts
45	Illinois
46	Nevada
47	Minnesota
48	Connecticut
49	New Hampshire
50	New Jersey

Note: Numbers that appear to be identical are rounded and vary slightly in actual value. The rankings reflect the actual values before rounding. See the introduction for more details.

E-15 Highway Charges Returned to States, FY 2004

State	Percentage of charges returned to states	Rank
Alabama	116	21
Alaska	695	1
Arizona	103	43
Arkansas	119	18
California	111	24
Colorado	110	27
Connecticut	161	12
Delaware	194	9
Florida	107	34
Georgia	108	31
Hawaii	227	7
Idaho	165	11
Illinois	99	48
Indiana	99	48
Iowa	109	29
Kansas	124	17
Kentucky	107	34
Louisiana	106	38
Maine	103	43
Maryland	110	27
Massachusetts	117	19
Michigan	106	38
Minnesota	91	50
Mississippi	103	43
Missouri	107	34
Montana	250	3
Nebraska	114	22
Nevada	102	46
New Hampshire	129	15
New Jersey	108	31
New Mexico	126	16
New York	141	13
North Carolina	104	41
North Dakota	231	5
Ohio	100	47
Oklahoma	108	31
Oregon	112	23
Pennsylvania	141	13
Rhode Island	263	2
South Carolina	109	29
South Dakota	230	6
Tennessee	104	41
Texas	107	34
Utah	111	24
Vermont	234	4
Virginia	106	38
Washington	111	24
West Virginia	198	8
Wisconsin	117	19
Wyoming	178	10
50 States	n/a	
DC	486	
United States	116	

Rank in order by percentage	
1	Alaska
2	Rhode Island
3	Montana
4	Vermont
5	North Dakota
6	South Dakota
7	Hawaii
8	West Virginia
9	Delaware
10	Wyoming
11	Idaho
12	Connecticut
13	New York
13	Pennsylvania
15	New Hampshire
16	New Mexico
17	Kansas
18	Arkansas
19	Massachusetts
19	Wisconsin
21	Alabama
22	Nebraska
23	Oregon
24	California
24	Utah
24	Washington
27	Colorado
27	Maryland
29	Iowa
29	South Carolina
31	Georgia
31	New Jersey
31	Oklahoma
34	Florida
34	Kentucky
34	Missouri
34	Texas
38	Louisiana
38	Michigan
38	Virginia
41	North Carolina
41	Tennessee
43	Arizona
43	Maine
43	Mississippi
46	Nevada
47	Ohio
48	Illinois
48	Indiana
50	Minnesota

Note: Ties in ranking reflect ties in actual values.

E-16 Terms of Trade with the Federal Government, FY 2004

State	Federal grants to state and local governments $ (in millions)	Terms of trade, ratio of federal grants to federal taxes paid	Rank by ratio
Alabama	7,008	1.38	16
Alaska	3,217	3.35	1
Arizona	8,364	1.18	22
Arkansas	4,683	1.61	10
California	54,534	0.85	40
Colorado	5,643	0.70	46
Connecticut	5,556	0.62	49
Delaware	1,241	0.92	35
Florida	19,610	0.76	43
Georgia	11,759	0.96	31
Hawaii	2,158	1.33	18
Idaho	1,995	1.27	21
Illinois	16,531	0.75	45
Indiana	7,436	0.90	36
Iowa	4,039	1.08	26
Kansas	3,469	0.92	34
Kentucky	6,743	1.43	13
Louisiana	7,787	1.59	12
Maine	2,758	1.64	9
Maryland	8,837	0.90	37
Massachusetts	13,876	0.93	33
Michigan	13,227	0.87	39
Minnesota	7,209	0.84	41
Mississippi	5,379	1.94	5
Missouri	8,734	1.13	24
Montana	1,997	1.93	6
Nebraska	2,531	1.06	28
Nevada	2,322	0.66	47
New Hampshire	1,879	0.76	44
New Jersey	11,333	0.60	50
New Mexico	4,663	2.60	2
New York	50,009	1.39	14
North Carolina	12,574	1.15	23
North Dakota	1,515	1.99	4
Ohio	16,514	1.07	27
Oklahoma	5,271	1.35	17
Oregon	5,185	1.05	30
Pennsylvania	19,916	1.05	29
Rhode Island	2,329	1.39	15
South Carolina	6,145	1.29	20
South Dakota	1,620	1.66	8
Tennessee	9,863	1.31	19
Texas	27,792	0.88	38
Utah	2,948	1.12	25
Vermont	1,423	1.61	11
Virginia	7,991	0.66	48
Washington	9,083	0.82	42
West Virginia	3,701	2.06	3
Wisconsin	7,484	0.95	32
Wyoming	1,636	1.92	7
50 States	449,517	0.99	
DC	4,205	3.28	
United States*	460,152	1.00	

**Due to rounding or data sources, the 50-state total plus D.C. may not equal the U.S. total. Please see introduction.*

Rank in order by ratio	
1	Alaska
2	New Mexico
3	West Virginia
4	North Dakota
5	Mississippi
6	Montana
7	Wyoming
8	South Dakota
9	Maine
10	Arkansas
11	Vermont
12	Louisiana
13	Kentucky
14	New York
15	Rhode Island
16	Alabama
17	Oklahoma
18	Hawaii
19	Tennessee
20	South Carolina
21	Idaho
22	Arizona
23	North Carolina
24	Missouri
25	Utah
26	Iowa
27	Ohio
28	Nebraska
29	Pennsylvania
30	Oregon
31	Georgia
32	Wisconsin
33	Massachusetts
34	Kansas
35	Delaware
36	Indiana
37	Maryland
38	Texas
39	Michigan
40	California
41	Minnesota
42	Washington
43	Florida
44	New Hampshire
45	Illinois
46	Colorado
47	Nevada
48	Virginia
49	Connecticut
50	New Jersey

Note: Numbers that appear to be identical are rounded and vary slightly in actual value. The rankings reflect the actual values before rounding. See the introduction for more details.

E-17 Federal Personal Income Taxes, 2003

State	Federal tax liability $ (in millions)	Federal tax liability per capita $	Rank per capita
Alabama	8.40	1,864	39
Alaska	1.92	2,957	13
Arizona	12.13	2,174	31
Arkansas	4.45	1,632	48
California	108.08	3,048	11
Colorado	13.50	2,969	12
Connecticut	17.99	5,158	1
Delaware	2.42	2,953	15
Florida	46.60	2,742	18
Georgia	20.25	2,334	24
Hawaii	2.94	2,351	23
Idaho	2.34	1,711	47
Illinois	39.14	3,094	9
Indiana	13.70	2,210	29
Iowa	5.87	1,994	37
Kansas	6.12	2,248	27
Kentucky	7.47	1,815	40
Louisiana	8.05	1,791	42
Maine	2.72	2,077	35
Maryland	18.76	3,404	5
Massachusetts	25.77	4,015	3
Michigan	25.20	2,500	20
Minnesota	14.96	2,954	14
Mississippi	4.15	1,441	50
Missouri	12.58	2,200	30
Montana	1.62	1,767	45
Nebraska	3.76	2,163	32
Nevada	7.08	3,155	8
New Hampshire	4.26	3,309	6
New Jersey	36.27	4,196	2
New Mexico	3.24	1,726	46
New York	67.84	3,531	4
North Carolina	17.74	2,107	34
North Dakota	1.26	1,985	38
Ohio	26.15	2,287	26
Oklahoma	6.26	1,786	43
Oregon	7.64	2,142	33
Pennsylvania	32.65	2,639	19
Rhode Island	2.97	2,760	17
South Carolina	7.52	1,813	41
South Dakota	1.59	2,075	36
Tennessee	13.09	2,240	28
Texas	55.19	2,497	21
Utah	4.19	1,782	44
Vermont	1.44	2,333	25
Virginia	23.35	3,170	7
Washington	18.89	3,081	10
West Virginia	2.79	1,541	49
Wisconsin	13.54	2,474	22
Wyoming	1.47	2,928	16
50 States	787.33	2,713	
DC	2.52	4,526	
United States	789.85	2,716	

Rank in order per capita	
1	Connecticut
2	New Jersey
3	Massachusetts
4	New York
5	Maryland
6	New Hampshire
7	Virginia
8	Nevada
9	Illinois
10	Washington
11	California
12	Colorado
13	Alaska
14	Minnesota
15	Delaware
16	Wyoming
17	Rhode Island
18	Florida
19	Pennsylvania
20	Michigan
21	Texas
22	Wisconsin
23	Hawaii
24	Georgia
25	Vermont
26	Ohio
27	Kansas
28	Tennessee
29	Indiana
30	Missouri
31	Arizona
32	Nebraska
33	Oregon
34	North Carolina
35	Maine
36	South Dakota
37	Iowa
38	North Dakota
39	Alabama
40	Kentucky
41	South Carolina
42	Louisiana
43	Oklahoma
44	Utah
45	Montana
46	New Mexico
47	Idaho
48	Arkansas
49	West Virginia
50	Mississippi

E-18 Federal Share of Medicaid, FY 2006–2007

State	2006 federal cost-sharing percentages for Medicaid %	2007 federal cost-sharing percentages for Medicaid %	Rank by 2006
Alabama	69.51	68.85	9
Alaska	50.16	51.07	37
Arizona	66.98	66.47	13
Arkansas	73.77	73.37	2
California	50.00	50.00	39
Colorado	50.00	50.00	39
Connecticut	50.00	50.00	39
Delaware	50.09	50.00	38
Florida	58.89	58.76	28
Georgia	60.60	61.97	24
Hawaii	58.81	57.55	29
Idaho	69.91	70.36	7
Illinois	50.00	50.00	39
Indiana	62.98	62.61	19
Iowa	63.61	61.98	17
Kansas	60.41	60.25	25
Kentucky	69.26	69.58	11
Louisiana	69.79	69.69	8
Maine	62.90	63.27	20
Maryland	50.00	50.00	39
Massachusetts	50.00	50.00	39
Michigan	56.59	56.38	32
Minnesota	50.00	50.00	39
Mississippi	76.00	75.89	1
Missouri	61.93	61.60	21
Montana	70.54	69.11	6
Nebraska	59.68	57.93	27
Nevada	54.76	53.93	34
New Hampshire	50.00	50.00	39
New Jersey	50.00	50.00	39
New Mexico	71.15	71.93	4
New York	50.00	50.00	39
North Carolina	63.49	64.52	18
North Dakota	65.85	64.72	14
Ohio	59.88	59.66	26
Oklahoma	67.91	68.14	12
Oregon	61.57	61.07	22
Pennsylvania	55.05	54.39	33
Rhode Island	54.45	52.35	35
South Carolina	69.32	69.54	10
South Dakota	65.07	62.92	15
Tennessee	63.99	63.65	16
Texas	60.66	60.78	23
Utah	70.76	70.14	5
Vermont	58.49	58.93	30
Virginia	50.00	50.00	39
Washington	50.00	50.12	39
West Virginia	72.99	72.82	3
Wisconsin	57.65	57.47	31
Wyoming	54.23	52.91	36
50 States	n/a	n/a	
DC	70.00	70.00	
United States	n/a	n/a	

Rank in order by 2006 percentage	
1	Mississippi
2	Arkansas
3	West Virginia
4	New Mexico
5	Utah
6	Montana
7	Idaho
8	Louisiana
9	Alabama
10	South Carolina
11	Kentucky
12	Oklahoma
13	Arizona
14	North Dakota
15	South Dakota
16	Tennessee
17	Iowa
18	North Carolina
19	Indiana
20	Maine
21	Missouri
22	Oregon
23	Texas
24	Georgia
25	Kansas
26	Ohio
27	Nebraska
28	Florida
29	Hawaii
30	Vermont
31	Wisconsin
32	Michigan
33	Pennsylvania
34	Nevada
35	Rhode Island
36	Wyoming
37	Alaska
38	Delaware
39	California
39	Colorado
39	Connecticut
39	Illinois
39	Maryland
39	Massachusetts
39	Minnesota
39	New Hampshire
39	New Jersey
39	New York
39	Virginia
39	Washington

Note: Ties in ranking reflect ties in actual values.

Source Notes for Federal Impacts (Section E)

E-1 Federal Spending, Total and Per Capita, FY 2004: The federal government affects state economies and state finances through its massive spending, accounting for nearly one-quarter of all economic activity in the United States. The primary components of that spending are grants to state and local governments; payments to individuals, such as Social Security; wages and salaries of federal employees; and purchases of goods and services, such as weapons for the Department of Defense.

Details of where these funds are spent are compiled by federal agencies and summarized by the U.S. Census Bureau in *Consolidated Federal Funds Report for Fiscal Year 2004.* Many tables in this section reflect the latest version of this report, covering federal spending in fiscal year 2004, which for the federal government ended in September 2004.

This table reflects total federal spending of $2.2 trillion, along with the results of dividing each state's total by its population to permit meaningful comparisons among states. The federal figures exclude certain forms of federal spending that cannot reasonably be associated with particular states, primarily interest on the federal debt and money spent in other countries.

E-2 Increase in Total Federal Spending, FY 1999–2004: This table uses the U.S. Census Bureau reports for federal fiscal years 1999 and 2004 to show the percentage change in total federal spending in each state over a five-year period. The data come from the federal report described in the notes to Table E-1.

E-3 Federal Spending on Grants, Total and Per Capita, FY 2004: This table reflects the federal spending for grants that help state and local governments finance welfare, Medicaid, highway construction, and other activities. The data come from the federal report described in the notes to Table E-1.

E-4 Federal Spending on Procurement, Total and Per Capita, FY 2004: This table reflects the federal spending for purchases ranging from tanks and space shuttles to gasoline for federal vehicles. The data come from the federal report described in the notes to Table E-1.

E-5 Federal Spending on Payments to Individuals, FY 2004: This table reflects the federal spending for payments to individuals. The primary components are Social Security pensions, Medicare payments to health care providers, pensions for retired federal workers, and food stamps. The data come from the federal report described in the notes to Table E-1.

E-6 Federal Spending on Social Security and Medicare, FY 2004: This table reflects the federal spending for Social Security pensions and Medicare payments to health care providers. This spending is a part of the total covered by Table E-5. The per capita amounts suggest the massive impact that this flow of funds has among states. While revenues from payroll taxes are concentrated in states that are showing strong economic growth, states with slower growth receive large portions of personal income from these retirement-related federal payments and private pensions. The data come from the federal report described in the notes to Table E-1.

E-7 Social Security Benefits Paid, FY 2004: This table provides another perspective on Social Security payments, using tabulations for December 2004 payments prepared by the Social Security Administration and available on the SSA Web site (www.ssa.gov).

This agency can provide additional details on benefits paid in each state, such as the amounts paid to retired workers, to deceased workers' beneficiaries, and to workers and their families based on disability. Besides the amounts paid and number of recipient households, the table shows the average benefit per household. This amount is appreciably higher in states where salaries have been high (such as in the Northeast) than where they have been low (such as in the South).

E-8 Federal Spending on Employee Wages and Salaries, FY 2004: This table reflects the federal spending on payments for salaries of civilian and military federal employees. The largest amounts are found in states with major federal installations, such as military bases. Because the Postal Service is included and some agencies, such as the Department of Agriculture, which operate in every state, even states without major installations show substantial federal spending. The data come from the federal report described in the notes to Table E-1.

E-9 Federal Spending on Defense, FY 2004: This table reflects federal spending on defense on everything from payroll, to procurement, to military retirees. The data come from the federal report described in the notes to Table E-1.

E-10 Homeland Security Grants, Total and Per Capita, FY 2005: The creation of the Department of Homeland Security (DHS), established to "detect, prepare for, prevent, protect against, respond to, and recover from terrorist attacks," involved a substantial reorganization of the federal government. Many pre-existing public safety programs such as the Federal Emergency Management Agency (FEMA) and the Transportation Security Administration were transferred to the new department. Immigration and Naturalization Services was eliminated and the Bureau of Citizenship and Immigration Services was formed in its place.

The table shows how grants for homeland security were distributed amongst the states in fiscal year 2005. Because there is a generous minimum allocation for each state, less populous areas of the country show high per capita amounts. The data on homeland security grants comes from a special compilation by Federal Funds Information for States (www.ffis.org).

E-11 Federal Grant Spending Per Dollar of State Tax Revenue, FY 2002: Most federal grant spending is now concentrated on state-administered programs, such as welfare and Medicaid. The amounts are substantial when compared with the amount that states raise from state taxes, as shown by the table, which relates the amounts provided by federal grants to the amounts states raised from taxes. The data for fiscal year 2002 are from "Government Finances," available on the U.S. Census Bureau Web site (www.census.gov).

E-12 State and Local General Revenue from Federal Government, FY 2002: These data, covering both state and local government, show the amount of federal aid contributing to "general revenue" as defined by the U.S. Census Bureau in its annual survey of government finances. It excludes certain trust funds, such as unemployment insurance, but includes others, such as those used for highway construction. The data are calculated from the bureau's "State and Local Government Finances: FY 2002" available on the bureau's Web site (www.census.gov).

E-13 Federal Tax Burden, Total and Per Capita, FY 2003: This table shows where the burdens of federal taxes fell in federal fiscal year 2003. The data come from the Tax Foundation's *Special Report* (no. 124, July 2003), which uses formulas to spread the burden of certain taxes, such as the corporate income tax, among states and actual data from federal tax collectors to show the sources of major tax revenues, such as those from personal income and payroll taxes.

E-14 Federal Spending Per Dollar of Taxes Paid, FY 2003: These data relate how much taxpayers in each state pay in federal taxes to the amounts the federal government spends in each state. The information comes from calculations by the Tax Foundation using allocations of tax burdens (see Table E-13) and the U.S. Census Bureau report on federal spending (see Table E-1).

Many states get more than a dollar back in federal spending for every dollar sent to the federal government in taxes. This occurs primarily in states where federal installations and/or purchasing is concentrated. Because a substantial portion of federal spending is financed by borrowing (deficit spending), the nationwide total would show more money returned as spending than paid as taxes, so the Tax Foundation adjusted spending to eliminate the deficit-financed portion.

E-15 Highway Charges Returned to States, FY 2004: Federal spending for highways is financed by special user charges, such as federal taxes on gasoline and diesel fuel. Some states, such as Alaska and Hawaii, receive much more federal highway aid than federal user charges collected in their states. Others, which highway officials call "donor states," can receive less than a dollar of aid from every dollar in federal highway taxes collected within their boundaries. Some states will appear as particularly large "donee states" because of expansive interstate projects underway in a particular period. Which states should "donate" how much is a subject of perpetual controversy in the Congress. The controversy spawns many different ways to measure the federal redistribution of highway revenues.

In fiscal year 2004, federal collections of highway user charges were about $30 billion while allocations of spending authority to states were $34.6 billion. Federal spending for highways is financed by special "user charges," such as federal taxes on gasoline and diesel fuel.

This table is parallel to Table E-12 but covers only highway spending. It was developed by the Federal Highway Administration and is published in *2004 Highway Statistics*. Data from this book and earlier editions of *Highway Statistics* are available on the FHWA Web site (www.fhwa.dot.gov).

E-16 Terms of Trade with the Federal Government, FY 2004: This table was developed by State Policy Research to show the relationship between amounts paid by taxpayers in each state to the federal grants to state and local government financed by their federal taxes. The table shows federal grants, identical to the amounts shown in Table E-3. Because all grants, even those paid currently out of money the federal government raises by borrowing, are ultimately paid for by taxpayers, the total federal tax revenue to pay for grants was stipulated as equal to the grants for the fifty states and the District of Columbia.

To determine how this tax burden to pay for grants was distributed among states, the total tax burden for grants was allocated based on the percentage of all federal taxes paid by citizens and corporations in each state, using the Tax Foundation's logic (also used to prepare Table E-13). The result is that the sum of grants and of taxes are identical for the fifty states plus the District of Columbia.

However, the amounts are by no means equal for individual states. States with relatively high personal incomes (and thus federal tax liabilities) but low grants will show ratios below one. Conceptually, for example, 0.95 can be considered as getting 95 cents back in grants for every dollar in federal taxes paid, or a 95 percent return. Conversely, states with lower incomes and high grants will show a ratio above one.

E-17 Federal Personal Income Taxes, 2003: This table shows how much households in each state were required to pay in federal income taxes on their income during 2003, as reported in tax returns filed in January through December of 2004. The data were reported in the *SOI Bulletin* (Spring 2005) available on the Web site of the Internal Revenue Service (www.irs.gov).

E-18 Federal Share of Medicaid, FY 2006–2007: The federal grants to states for Medicaid are based on multiplying the total costs of these programs by the federal cost-sharing percentages shown in the table. The formula used to determine each state's share provides the largest federal shares for the states with the lowest per capita incomes. A special rule overrides the calculation for more affluent states, so no state has less than 50 percent of these costs paid by the federal government.

As part of the Jobs and Growth Tax Relief Reconciliation Act of 2003 federal medical assistance percentages were temporarily increased for the last two quarters of fiscal year 2003 and the first three quarters of fiscal year 2004. This fiscal relief ended in fiscal year 2005. All fifty states received federal medical assistance percentage decreases. The largest reductions were experienced in Wyoming, Vermont, Maine, Montana, and Pennsylvania.

The percentages were published in Federal Funds Information for States' (FFIS) *Issue Brief 05-39,* released September 28, 2005.

Taxes

State tax revenues were remarkably strong in the second half of 2005. Returns were so good that half the states have revised their revenue forecasts upward, according to a November 2005 survey conducted by the National Conference of State Legislatures. Corporate income tax revenue has shown the most dramatic increase. Personal income and sales tax revenues are also strong.

Percent Change in State Tax Revenue Third Quarter 2004-Third Quarter 2005

Type of Tax	Percent
Personal Income	9.2
Corporate Income	25.9
Sales	7.8
Total	9.2

Source: The Nelson A. Rockefeller Institute of Government

With such strong returns, there will likely be some talk of state-level tax cuts. Yet, state officials may find themselves feeling cautious so soon after the recent fiscal crisis. In addition, state governments are still not holding on to enough revenue to return government services to their pre-recession levels. A December 2005 analysis from the Center on Budget and Policy Priorities asserts, "State revenues would have to grow by more than 9 percent per year between now and 2008 in order to generate enough funds simply to restore the level of services that prevailed in fiscal year 2000."

Year-Over-Year Change in Quarterly State Tax Revenue, Adjusted for Legislated Tax Changes and Inflation, 2001-2005

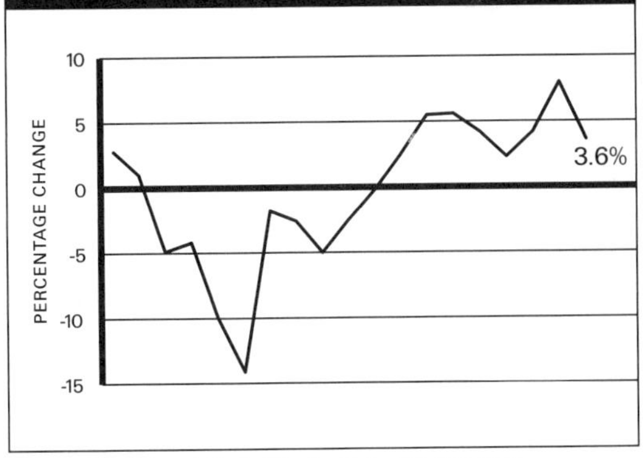

Source: The Nelson A. Rockefeller Institute of Government

F-1 State and Local Tax Revenue, FY 2002

State	State and local taxes $ (in millions)	State and local taxes as a percentage of personal income	Rank by percentage
Alabama	9,719	8.8	48
Alaska	2,070	10.3	28
Arizona	14,420	10.4	19
Arkansas	6,460	10.4	22
California	120,416	10.6	17
Colorado	13,900	9.2	45
Connecticut	15,125	10.4	27
Delaware	2,687	10.7	15
Florida	44,840	9.4	44
Georgia	24,058	10.0	34
Hawaii	4,240	12.1	4
Idaho	3,291	10.0	36
Illinois	41,570	10.1	29
Indiana	16,987	10.0	33
Iowa	8,330	10.4	24
Kansas	7,975	10.4	26
Kentucky	10,781	10.6	16
Louisiana	12,182	11.1	10
Maine	4,541	13.0	2
Maryland	19,874	10.4	20
Massachusetts	23,895	9.6	40
Michigan	30,644	10.4	25
Minnesota	18,456	11.3	7
Mississippi	6,524	10.4	23
Missouri	15,123	9.6	39
Montana	2,135	9.8	38
Nebraska	5,316	10.8	14
Nevada	6,433	10.1	30
New Hampshire	3,599	8.5	49
New Jersey	34,629	10.4	21
New Mexico	4,878	11.1	9
New York	88,878	13.1	1
North Carolina	22,576	10.0	35
North Dakota	1,729	10.5	18
Ohio	36,165	11.1	11
Oklahoma	8,782	10.0	37
Oregon	9,003	9.1	46
Pennsylvania	37,627	10.1	31
Rhode Island	3,622	11.4	6
South Carolina	9,752	9.6	41
South Dakota	1,841	9.0	47
Tennessee	12,974	8.4	50
Texas	58,981	9.5	42
Utah	6,026	10.8	13
Vermont	1,965	11.1	12
Virginia	22,131	9.5	43
Washington	19,514	10.1	32
West Virginia	4,641	11.2	8
Wisconsin	18,610	11.7	5
Wyoming	1,818	12.2	3
50 States	901,734	10.4	
DC	3,228	12.4	
United States	904,962	10.4	

Rank in order by percentage	
1	New York
2	Maine
3	Wyoming
4	Hawaii
5	Wisconsin
6	Rhode Island
7	Minnesota
8	West Virginia
9	New Mexico
10	Louisiana
11	Ohio
12	Vermont
13	Utah
14	Nebraska
15	Delaware
16	Kentucky
17	California
18	North Dakota
19	Arizona
20	Maryland
21	New Jersey
22	Arkansas
23	Mississippi
24	Iowa
25	Michigan
26	Kansas
27	Connecticut
28	Alaska
29	Illinois
30	Nevada
31	Pennsylvania
32	Washington
33	Indiana
34	Georgia
35	North Carolina
36	Idaho
37	Oklahoma
38	Montana
39	Missouri
40	Massachusetts
41	South Carolina
42	Texas
43	Virginia
44	Florida
45	Colorado
46	Oregon
47	South Dakota
48	Alabama
49	New Hampshire
50	Tennessee

Note: Numbers that appear to be identical are rounded and vary slightly in actual value. The rankings reflect the actual values before rounding. See the introduction for more details.

F-2 Per Capita State and Local Tax Revenue, FY 2002

State	State and local taxes per capita $	State taxes per capita $	Local taxes per capita $	Rank by state and local taxes per capita
Alabama	2,166	1,451	715	50
Alaska	3,215	1,692	1,523	16
Arizona	2,643	1,554	1,089	36
Arkansas	2,384	1,928	455	45
California	3,429	2,214	1,215	9
Colorado	3,084	1,536	1,548	19
Connecticut	4,371	2,610	1,760	2
Delaware	3,328	2,692	636	13
Florida	2,683	1,517	1,166	34
Georgia	2,810	1,609	1,202	28
Hawaii	3,406	2,748	658	11
Idaho	2,454	1,693	761	43
Illinois	3,299	1,784	1,515	14
Indiana	2,758	1,656	1,102	29
Iowa	2,837	1,705	1,132	26
Kansas	2,936	1,770	1,166	25
Kentucky	2,634	1,948	686	37
Louisiana	2,718	1,641	1,076	31
Maine	3,508	2,029	1,479	8
Maryland	3,641	1,983	1,659	7
Massachusetts	3,718	2,306	1,412	4
Michigan	3,049	2,175	874	22
Minnesota	3,677	2,634	1,042	5
Mississippi	2,272	1,647	625	48
Missouri	2,666	1,539	1,127	35
Montana	2,348	1,586	761	47
Nebraska	3,074	1,731	1,344	20
Nevada	2,960	1,815	1,144	24
New Hampshire	2,823	1,488	1,335	27
New Jersey	4,031	2,134	1,897	3
New Mexico	2,629	1,956	674	38
New York	4,639	2,258	2,381	1
North Carolina	2,713	1,867	846	32
North Dakota	2,726	1,762	964	30
Ohio	3,166	1,763	1,404	18
Oklahoma	2,514	1,732	781	42
Oregon	2,557	1,466	1,090	41
Pennsylvania	3,050	1,795	1,256	21
Rhode Island	3,386	1,989	1,397	12
South Carolina	2,374	1,482	892	46
South Dakota	2,420	1,283	1,136	44
Tennessee	2,238	1,345	893	49
Texas	2,708	1,316	1,392	33
Utah	2,602	1,695	907	39
Vermont	3,187	2,463	724	17
Virginia	3,034	1,752	1,282	23
Washington	3,215	2,081	1,134	15
West Virginia	2,576	1,971	605	40
Wisconsin	3,420	2,171	1,249	10
Wyoming	3,646	2,194	1,452	6
50 States	3,133	1,860	1,273	
DC	5,654	0	5,654	
United States	3,138	1,856	1,282	

Rank in order by state and local taxes per capita	
1	New York
2	Connecticut
3	New Jersey
4	Massachusetts
5	Minnesota
6	Wyoming
7	Maryland
8	Maine
9	California
10	Wisconsin
11	Hawaii
12	Rhode Island
13	Delaware
14	Illinois
15	Washington
16	Alaska
17	Vermont
18	Ohio
19	Colorado
20	Nebraska
21	Pennsylvania
22	Michigan
23	Virginia
24	Nevada
25	Kansas
26	Iowa
27	New Hampshire
28	Georgia
29	Indiana
30	North Dakota
31	Louisiana
32	North Carolina
33	Texas
34	Florida
35	Missouri
36	Arizona
37	Kentucky
38	New Mexico
39	Utah
40	West Virginia
41	Oregon
42	Oklahoma
43	Idaho
44	South Dakota
45	Arkansas
46	South Carolina
47	Montana
48	Mississippi
49	Tennessee
50	Alabama

Note: Numbers that appear to be identical are rounded and vary slightly in actual value. The rankings reflect the actual values before rounding. See the introduction for more details.

F-3 State and Local Tax Effort, FY 1999

State	Tax effort %	Rank
Alabama	82	45
Alaska	87	40
Arizona	87	41
Arkansas	91	36
California	96	23
Colorado	95	26
Connecticut	119	2
Delaware	89	39
Florida	86	42
Georgia	94	29
Hawaii	95	27
Idaho	97	22
Illinois	101	15
Indiana	93	31
Iowa	93	32
Kansas	99	16
Kentucky	97	21
Louisiana	98	20
Maine	118	4
Maryland	103	11
Massachusetts	106	10
Michigan	103	12
Minnesota	113	7
Mississippi	99	17
Missouri	92	33
Montana	82	44
Nebraska	94	28
Nevada	76	50
New Hampshire	76	49
New Jersey	113	6
New Mexico	99	18
New York	143	1
North Carolina	92	35
North Dakota	92	34
Ohio	103	13
Oklahoma	98	19
Oregon	80	46
Pennsylvania	107	9
Rhode Island	119	3
South Carolina	90	38
South Dakota	79	47
Tennessee	78	48
Texas	91	37
Utah	95	25
Vermont	102	14
Virginia	94	30
Washington	96	24
West Virginia	110	8
Wisconsin	115	5
Wyoming	86	43
50 States	n/a	
DC	151	
United States	100	

Rank in order by tax effort	
1	New York
2	Connecticut
3	Rhode Island
4	Maine
5	Wisconsin
6	New Jersey
7	Minnesota
8	West Virginia
9	Pennsylvania
10	Massachusetts
11	Maryland
12	Michigan
13	Ohio
14	Vermont
15	Illinois
16	Kansas
17	Mississippi
18	New Mexico
19	Oklahoma
20	Louisiana
21	Kentucky
22	Idaho
23	California
24	Washington
25	Utah
26	Colorado
27	Hawaii
28	Nebraska
29	Georgia
30	Virginia
31	Indiana
32	Iowa
33	Missouri
34	North Dakota
35	North Carolina
36	Arkansas
37	Texas
38	South Carolina
39	Delaware
40	Alaska
41	Arizona
42	Florida
43	Wyoming
44	Montana
45	Alabama
46	Oregon
47	South Dakota
48	Tennessee
49	New Hampshire
50	Nevada

Note: Numbers that appear to be identical are rounded and vary slightly in actual value. The rankings reflect the actual values before rounding. See the introduction for more details.

F-4 State and Local Tax Capacity, FY 1999

State	Tax capacity %	Rank
Alabama	82	46
Alaska	109	11
Arizona	98	23
Arkansas	81	47
California	111	8
Colorado	105	15
Connecticut	127	2
Delaware	123	3
Florida	103	18
Georgia	98	23
Hawaii	116	4
Idaho	84	44
Illinois	104	16
Indiana	94	30
Iowa	96	28
Kansas	92	34
Kentucky	85	43
Louisiana	83	45
Maine	92	35
Maryland	104	17
Massachusetts	114	7
Michigan	99	20
Minnesota	108	13
Mississippi	74	49
Missouri	93	33
Montana	94	31
Nebraska	98	22
Nevada	129	1
New Hampshire	114	6
New Jersey	114	5
New Mexico	87	41
New York	106	14
North Carolina	97	25
North Dakota	96	27
Ohio	94	32
Oklahoma	79	48
Oregon	108	12
Pennsylvania	92	37
Rhode Island	91	38
South Carolina	86	42
South Dakota	96	29
Tennessee	92	36
Texas	90	39
Utah	90	40
Vermont	99	21
Virginia	102	19
Washington	110	10
West Virginia	72	50
Wisconsin	96	26
Wyoming	111	9
50 States	n/a	
DC	127	
United States	100	

Rank in order by tax capacity	
1	Nevada
2	Connecticut
3	Delaware
4	Hawaii
5	New Jersey
6	New Hampshire
7	Massachusetts
8	California
9	Wyoming
10	Washington
11	Alaska
12	Oregon
13	Minnesota
14	New York
15	Colorado
16	Illinois
17	Maryland
18	Florida
19	Virginia
20	Michigan
21	Vermont
22	Nebraska
23	Arizona
24	Georgia
25	North Carolina
26	Wisconsin
27	North Dakota
28	Iowa
29	South Dakota
30	Indiana
31	Montana
32	Ohio
33	Missouri
34	Kansas
35	Maine
36	Tennessee
37	Pennsylvania
38	Rhode Island
39	Texas
40	Utah
41	New Mexico
42	South Carolina
43	Kentucky
44	Idaho
45	Louisiana
46	Alabama
47	Arkansas
48	Oklahoma
49	Mississippi
50	West Virginia

Note: Numbers that appear to be identical are rounded and vary slightly in actual value. The rankings reflect the actual values before rounding. See the introduction for more details.

F-5 Change in State and Local Taxes, FY 1997-2002

State	Percentage change in state and local taxes	Percentage change per capita	Change as a percentage of personal income	Rank by percentage change in state and local taxes
Alabama	22.1	17.6	-4.0	24
Alaska	-14.2	-18.7	-32.8	50
Arizona	38.3	15.4	-4.0	3
Arkansas	26.2	17.4	-1.1	16
California	33.0	21.9	-4.9	7
Colorado	37.6	18.9	-8.6	4
Connecticut	10.1	3.9	-17.6	48
Delaware	24.7	13.5	-3.6	20
Florida	25.8	10.5	-6.6	17
Georgia	32.4	15.8	-4.5	8
Hawaii	10.2	5.5	-4.7	47
Idaho	21.0	9.1	-11.2	30
Illinois	21.4	15.5	-4.5	28
Indiana	15.4	9.9	-9.4	42
Iowa	15.8	12.5	-6.6	41
Kansas	17.9	12.9	-7.9	38
Kentucky	21.2	15.8	-6.6	29
Louisiana	26.5	22.9	1.5	14
Maine	27.8	22.6	-3.2	12
Maryland	33.9	25.0	-0.9	6
Massachusetts	18.8	13.0	-14.1	35
Michigan	15.1	12.0	-7.1	43
Minnesota	17.3	9.5	-12.2	40
Mississippi	21.7	15.7	-5.2	26
Missouri	20.1	14.5	-5.4	32
Montana	10.6	6.9	-13.7	46
Nebraska	18.3	13.4	-5.0	36
Nevada	40.8	8.8	-4.0	2
New Hampshire	30.8	20.2	-7.0	10
New Jersey	26.4	18.5	-6.2	15
New Mexico	14.9	6.8	-12.7	44
New York	17.8	11.6	-8.0	39
North Carolina	27.3	13.7	-5.3	13
North Dakota	9.5	10.7	-9.4	49
Ohio	24.4	21.9	0.8	21
Oklahoma	23.2	17.2	-7.4	23
Oregon	11.6	2.8	-14.8	45
Pennsylvania	18.0	14.9	-5.4	37
Rhode Island	24.2	14.6	-3.3	22
South Carolina	25.0	15.3	-6.3	19
South Dakota	25.8	22.0	-1.9	18
Tennessee	22.1	13.1	-5.8	25
Texas	35.4	20.5	-6.0	5
Utah	28.8	14.9	-6.5	11
Vermont	21.5	16.0	-10.6	27
Virginia	31.5	21.5	-3.9	9
Washington	19.2	10.3	-14.1	33
West Virginia	20.5	21.4	-2.1	31
Wisconsin	19.1	13.8	-8.5	34
Wyoming	46.6	41.1	4.3	1
50 States	24.2	15.3	-6.7	
DC	22.4	13.6	-12.6	
United States	24.2	15.3	-6.7	

Rank in order by percentage change	
1	Wyoming
2	Nevada
3	Arizona
4	Colorado
5	Texas
6	Maryland
7	California
8	Georgia
9	Virginia
10	New Hampshire
11	Utah
12	Maine
13	North Carolina
14	Louisiana
15	New Jersey
16	Arkansas
17	Florida
18	South Dakota
19	South Carolina
20	Delaware
21	Ohio
22	Rhode Island
23	Oklahoma
24	Alabama
25	Tennessee
26	Mississippi
27	Vermont
28	Illinois
29	Kentucky
30	Idaho
31	West Virginia
32	Missouri
33	Washington
34	Wisconsin
35	Massachusetts
36	Nebraska
37	Pennsylvania
38	Kansas
39	New York
40	Minnesota
41	Iowa
42	Indiana
43	Michigan
44	New Mexico
45	Oregon
46	Montana
47	Hawaii
48	Connecticut
49	North Dakota
50	Alaska

Note: Numbers that appear to be identical are rounded and vary slightly in actual value. The rankings reflect the actual values before rounding. See the introduction for more details.

F-6 Property Taxes, FY 2002

State	Property taxes $ (in millions)	Property taxes as a percentage of personal income	Rank by percentage
Alabama	1,474	1.33	50
Alaska	830	4.12	7
Arizona	4,254	3.08	26
Arkansas	1,003	1.61	48
California	30,234	2.66	36
Colorado	4,162	2.76	34
Connecticut	5,995	4.10	8
Delaware	400	1.60	49
Florida	15,754	3.29	19
Georgia	6,640	2.77	33
Hawaii	615	1.75	45
Idaho	959	2.91	30
Illinois	15,873	3.87	13
Indiana	5,976	3.53	16
Iowa	2,878	3.59	14
Kansas	2,525	3.28	20
Kentucky	1,977	1.95	43
Louisiana	1,940	1.77	44
Maine	1,912	5.48	1
Maryland	5,412	2.84	32
Massachusetts	8,722	3.50	17
Michigan	9,793	3.32	18
Minnesota	5,215	3.20	24
Mississippi	1,647	2.62	37
Missouri	3,880	2.46	39
Montana	852	3.91	12
Nebraska	1,749	3.54	15
Nevada	1,702	2.68	35
New Hampshire	2,169	5.10	2
New Jersey	16,050	4.83	3
New Mexico	756	1.73	46
New York	26,826	3.95	11
North Carolina	5,422	2.41	40
North Dakota	532	3.24	23
Ohio	10,643	3.27	22
Oklahoma	1,482	1.68	47
Oregon	3,139	3.17	25
Pennsylvania	10,911	2.93	29
Rhode Island	1,462	4.59	6
South Carolina	3,096	3.04	27
South Dakota	668	3.28	21
Tennessee	3,453	2.23	41
Texas	24,521	3.97	10
Utah	1,420	2.55	38
Vermont	824	4.64	5
Virginia	6,711	2.89	31
Washington	5,791	2.99	28
West Virginia	901	2.17	42
Wisconsin	6,466	4.07	9
Wyoming	692	4.64	4
50 States	278,309	3.21	
DC	803	3.10	
United States	279,112	3.21	

Rank in order by percentage	
1	Maine
2	New Hampshire
3	New Jersey
4	Wyoming
5	Vermont
6	Rhode Island
7	Alaska
8	Connecticut
9	Wisconsin
10	Texas
11	New York
12	Montana
13	Illinois
14	Iowa
15	Nebraska
16	Indiana
17	Massachusetts
18	Michigan
19	Florida
20	Kansas
21	South Dakota
22	Ohio
23	North Dakota
24	Minnesota
25	Oregon
26	Arizona
27	South Carolina
28	Washington
29	Pennsylvania
30	Idaho
31	Virginia
32	Maryland
33	Georgia
34	Colorado
35	Nevada
36	California
37	Mississippi
38	Utah
39	Missouri
40	North Carolina
41	Tennessee
42	West Virginia
43	Kentucky
44	Louisiana
45	Hawaii
46	New Mexico
47	Oklahoma
48	Arkansas
49	Delaware
50	Alabama

Note: Numbers that appear to be identical are rounded and vary slightly in actual value. The rankings reflect the actual values before rounding. See the introduction for more details.

F-7 Property Taxes Per Capita, FY 2002

State	Property tax per capita $	Rank
Alabama	328	50
Alaska	1,289	10
Arizona	780	33
Arkansas	370	49
California	861	30
Colorado	924	25
Connecticut	1,733	2
Delaware	495	43
Florida	943	21
Georgia	776	34
Hawaii	494	44
Idaho	715	36
Illinois	1,260	11
Indiana	970	19
Iowa	980	17
Kansas	930	24
Kentucky	483	45
Louisiana	433	46
Maine	1,477	4
Maryland	992	16
Massachusetts	1,357	8
Michigan	974	18
Minnesota	1,039	14
Mississippi	573	41
Missouri	684	37
Montana	937	22
Nebraska	1,011	15
Nevada	783	32
New Hampshire	1,701	3
New Jersey	1,868	1
New Mexico	408	48
New York	1,400	5
North Carolina	652	38
North Dakota	840	31
Ohio	932	23
Oklahoma	424	47
Oregon	891	27
Pennsylvania	885	28
Rhode Island	1,367	7
South Carolina	754	35
South Dakota	878	29
Tennessee	596	40
Texas	1,126	13
Utah	613	39
Vermont	1,336	9
Virginia	920	26
Washington	954	20
West Virginia	500	42
Wisconsin	1,188	12
Wyoming	1,388	6
50 States	967	
DC	1,407	
United States	968	

Rank in order per capita	
1	New Jersey
2	Connecticut
3	New Hampshire
4	Maine
5	New York
6	Wyoming
7	Rhode Island
8	Massachusetts
9	Vermont
10	Alaska
11	Illinois
12	Wisconsin
13	Texas
14	Minnesota
15	Nebraska
16	Maryland
17	Iowa
18	Michigan
19	Indiana
20	Washington
21	Florida
22	Montana
23	Ohio
24	Kansas
25	Colorado
26	Virginia
27	Oregon
28	Pennsylvania
29	South Dakota
30	California
31	North Dakota
32	Nevada
33	Arizona
34	Georgia
35	South Carolina
36	Idaho
37	Missouri
38	North Carolina
39	Utah
40	Tennessee
41	Mississippi
42	West Virginia
43	Delaware
44	Hawaii
45	Kentucky
46	Louisiana
47	Oklahoma
48	New Mexico
49	Arkansas
50	Alabama

F-8 Property Tax Revenue as a Percentage of Three-Tax Revenue, FY 2002

State	Property tax as a percentage of three-tax revenue	Rank
Alabama	17.5	48
Alaska	72.8	2
Arizona	31.7	31
Arkansas	17.0	49
California	28.8	37
Colorado	32.2	29
Connecticut	42.2	11
Delaware	26.8	40
Florida	40.7	14
Georgia	29.5	36
Hawaii	15.5	50
Idaho	32.6	27
Illinois	42.6	9
Indiana	38.3	16
Iowa	38.0	17
Kansas	33.9	24
Kentucky	21.0	44
Louisiana	18.2	47
Maine	45.2	8
Maryland	30.0	35
Massachusetts	39.6	15
Michigan	36.8	21
Minnesota	31.5	32
Mississippi	28.0	39
Missouri	28.0	38
Montana	48.9	5
Nebraska	37.0	20
Nevada	30.7	34
New Hampshire	76.2	1
New Jersey	50.6	3
New Mexico	18.6	46
New York	33.7	25
North Carolina	26.4	41
North Dakota	37.5	19
Ohio	32.1	30
Oklahoma	20.5	45
Oregon	40.8	13
Pennsylvania	34.4	23
Rhode Island	42.4	10
South Carolina	34.9	22
South Dakota	41.8	12
Tennessee	31.2	33
Texas	46.1	6
Utah	25.2	42
Vermont	45.6	7
Virginia	33.6	26
Washington	32.6	28
West Virginia	23.0	43
Wisconsin	37.7	18
Wyoming	50.0	4
50 States	34.6	
DC	29.9	
United States	34.6	

Rank in order by percentage	
1	New Hampshire
2	Alaska
3	New Jersey
4	Wyoming
5	Montana
6	Texas
7	Vermont
8	Maine
9	Illinois
10	Rhode Island
11	Connecticut
12	South Dakota
13	Oregon
14	Florida
15	Massachusetts
16	Indiana
17	Iowa
18	Wisconsin
19	North Dakota
20	Nebraska
21	Michigan
22	South Carolina
23	Pennsylvania
24	Kansas
25	New York
26	Virginia
27	Idaho
28	Washington
29	Colorado
30	Ohio
31	Arizona
32	Minnesota
33	Tennessee
34	Nevada
35	Maryland
36	Georgia
37	California
38	Missouri
39	Mississippi
40	Delaware
41	North Carolina
42	Utah
43	West Virginia
44	Kentucky
45	Oklahoma
46	New Mexico
47	Louisiana
48	Alabama
49	Arkansas
50	Hawaii

Note: Numbers that appear to be identical are rounded and vary slightly in actual value. The rankings reflect the actual values before rounding. See the introduction for more details.

F-9 Sales Taxes, FY 2002

State	State and local sales taxes $ (in millions)	State and local taxes as a percentage of personal income	Rank by percentage
Alabama	4,800	4.33	16
Alaska	311	1.54	47
Arizona	7,081	5.13	8
Arkansas	3,340	5.38	5
California	41,560	3.66	24
Colorado	5,302	3.52	30
Connecticut	4,516	3.09	40
Delaware	326	1.30	49
Florida	22,936	4.79	10
Georgia	9,395	3.92	19
Hawaii	2,244	6.39	1
Idaho	1,135	3.44	33
Illinois	13,876	3.38	34
Indiana	5,522	3.26	38
Iowa	2,886	3.60	27
Kansas	3,066	3.99	18
Kentucky	3,942	3.88	21
Louisiana	6,949	6.35	2
Maine	1,242	3.56	29
Maryland	4,974	2.61	44
Massachusetts	5,363	2.15	45
Michigan	10,238	3.47	32
Minnesota	5,918	3.63	26
Mississippi	3,255	5.19	7
Missouri	6,044	3.84	22
Montana	374	1.72	46
Nebraska	1,819	3.69	23
Nevada	3,840	6.04	4
New Hampshire	605	1.42	48
New Jersey	8,804	2.65	43
New Mexico	2,319	5.30	6
New York	22,491	3.31	36
North Carolina	7,852	3.48	31
North Dakota	689	4.19	17
Ohio	10,766	3.30	37
Oklahoma	3,446	3.91	20
Oregon	889	0.90	50
Pennsylvania	11,291	3.03	41
Rhode Island	1,164	3.65	25
South Carolina	3,425	3.37	35
South Dakota	930	4.56	15
Tennessee	7,461	4.82	9
Texas	28,639	4.64	14
Utah	2,619	4.71	12
Vermont	573	3.22	39
Virginia	6,542	2.81	42
Washington	11,976	6.19	3
West Virginia	1,980	4.76	11
Wisconsin	5,698	3.59	28
Wyoming	691	4.64	13
50 States	323,104	3.72	
DC	936	3.61	
United States	324,040	3.72	

Rank in order by percentage	
1	Hawaii
2	Louisiana
3	Washington
4	Nevada
5	Arkansas
6	New Mexico
7	Mississippi
8	Arizona
9	Tennessee
10	Florida
11	West Virginia
12	Utah
13	Wyoming
14	Texas
15	South Dakota
16	Alabama
17	North Dakota
18	Kansas
19	Georgia
20	Oklahoma
21	Kentucky
22	Missouri
23	Nebraska
24	California
25	Rhode Island
26	Minnesota
27	Iowa
28	Wisconsin
29	Maine
30	Colorado
31	North Carolina
32	Michigan
33	Idaho
34	Illinois
35	South Carolina
36	New York
37	Ohio
38	Indiana
39	Vermont
40	Connecticut
41	Pennsylvania
42	Virginia
43	New Jersey
44	Maryland
45	Massachusetts
46	Montana
47	Alaska
48	New Hampshire
49	Delaware
50	Oregon

Note: Numbers that appear to be identical are rounded and vary slightly in actual value. The rankings reflect the actual values before rounding. See the introduction for more details.

F-10 Sales Taxes Per Capita, FY 2002

State	Sales taxes per capita $	Rank per capita
Alabama	1,070	26
Alaska	482	46
Arizona	1,298	9
Arkansas	1,233	12
California	1,184	14
Colorado	1,177	16
Connecticut	1,305	8
Delaware	404	49
Florida	1,372	6
Georgia	1,098	23
Hawaii	1,803	2
Idaho	847	43
Illinois	1,101	21
Indiana	897	42
Iowa	983	33
Kansas	1,129	20
Kentucky	963	34
Louisiana	1,550	4
Maine	959	35
Maryland	911	40
Massachusetts	834	44
Michigan	1,019	31
Minnesota	1,179	15
Mississippi	1,134	18
Missouri	1,065	27
Montana	411	48
Nebraska	1,052	28
Nevada	1,767	3
New Hampshire	475	47
New Jersey	1,025	30
New Mexico	1,250	11
New York	1,174	17
North Carolina	944	36
North Dakota	1,086	25
Ohio	943	37
Oklahoma	986	32
Oregon	252	50
Pennsylvania	915	39
Rhode Island	1,089	24
South Carolina	834	45
South Dakota	1,222	13
Tennessee	1,287	10
Texas	1,315	7
Utah	1,131	19
Vermont	929	38
Virginia	897	41
Washington	1,973	1
West Virginia	1,099	22
Wisconsin	1,047	29
Wyoming	1,387	5
50 States	1,123	
DC	1,639	
United States	1,124	

Rank in order per capita	
1	Washington
2	Hawaii
3	Nevada
4	Louisiana
5	Wyoming
6	Florida
7	Texas
8	Connecticut
9	Arizona
10	Tennessee
11	New Mexico
12	Arkansas
13	South Dakota
14	California
15	Minnesota
16	Colorado
17	New York
18	Mississippi
19	Utah
20	Kansas
21	Illinois
22	West Virginia
23	Georgia
24	Rhode Island
25	North Dakota
26	Alabama
27	Missouri
28	Nebraska
29	Wisconsin
30	New Jersey
31	Michigan
32	Oklahoma
33	Iowa
34	Kentucky
35	Maine
36	North Carolina
37	Ohio
38	Vermont
39	Pennsylvania
40	Maryland
41	Virginia
42	Indiana
43	Idaho
44	Massachusetts
45	South Carolina
46	Alaska
47	New Hampshire
48	Montana
49	Delaware
50	Oregon

Note: Numbers that appear to be identical are rounded and vary slightly in actual value. The rankings reflect the actual values before rounding. See the introduction for more details.

F-11 Sales Tax Revenue as a Percentage of Three-Tax Revenue, FY 2002

State	Sales taxes as a percentage of three-tax revenue	Rank
Alabama	57.1	8
Alaska	27.2	45
Arizona	52.7	13
Arkansas	56.5	9
California	39.6	24
Colorado	41.0	23
Connecticut	31.8	39
Delaware	21.9	47
Florida	59.3	5
Georgia	41.7	21
Hawaii	56.5	10
Idaho	38.7	25
Illinois	37.3	31
Indiana	35.4	34
Iowa	38.1	30
Kansas	41.2	22
Kentucky	41.9	20
Louisiana	65.1	4
Maine	29.4	41
Maryland	27.6	44
Massachusetts	24.4	46
Michigan	38.4	28
Minnesota	35.7	32
Mississippi	55.3	11
Missouri	43.6	19
Montana	21.4	48
Nebraska	38.5	27
Nevada	69.3	1
New Hampshire	21.3	49
New Jersey	27.8	43
New Mexico	57.2	7
New York	28.3	42
North Carolina	38.2	29
North Dakota	48.5	16
Ohio	32.4	38
Oklahoma	47.8	17
Oregon	11.5	50
Pennsylvania	35.6	33
Rhode Island	33.8	35
South Carolina	38.6	26
South Dakota	58.2	6
Tennessee	67.5	2
Texas	53.9	12
Utah	46.4	18
Vermont	31.7	40
Virginia	32.8	37
Washington	67.4	3
West Virginia	50.6	14
Wisconsin	33.2	36
Wyoming	50.0	15
50 States	40.2	
DC	34.8	
United States	40.2	

Rank in order by percentage	
1	Nevada
2	Tennessee
3	Washington
4	Louisiana
5	Florida
6	South Dakota
7	New Mexico
8	Alabama
9	Arkansas
10	Hawaii
11	Mississippi
12	Texas
13	Arizona
14	West Virginia
15	Wyoming
16	North Dakota
17	Oklahoma
18	Utah
19	Missouri
20	Kentucky
21	Georgia
22	Kansas
23	Colorado
24	California
25	Idaho
26	South Carolina
27	Nebraska
28	Michigan
29	North Carolina
30	Iowa
31	Illinois
32	Minnesota
33	Pennsylvania
34	Indiana
35	Rhode Island
36	Wisconsin
37	Virginia
38	Ohio
39	Connecticut
40	Vermont
41	Maine
42	New York
43	New Jersey
44	Maryland
45	Alaska
46	Massachusetts
47	Delaware
48	Montana
49	New Hampshire
50	Oregon

Note: Numbers that appear to be identical are rounded and vary slightly in actual value. The rankings reflect the actual values before rounding. See the introduction for more details.

F-12 Sales Tax Rates and Reach, 2006

State	State sales tax rate 2006 %	Number of services subject to sales tax 2004	Estimated losses from failure to tax e-commerce 2003 $ (in millions)	Rank by sales tax rate
Alabama	4.00	37	205.9	38
Alaska	n/a	1	n/a	n/a
Arizona	5.60	58	377.3	22
Arkansas	6.00	72	165.8	10
California	6.25	23	2,129.3	7
Colorado	2.90	14	248.2	45
Connecticut	6.00	80	226.9	10
Delaware	n/a	143	n/a	n/a
Florida	6.00	64	1,072.7	10
Georgia	4.00	36	511.4	38
Hawaii	4.00	160	112.6	38
Idaho	6.00	30	57.6	10
Illinois	6.25	17	501.3	7
Indiana	6.00	23	279.3	10
Iowa	5.00	94	125.4	25
Kansas	5.30	71	156.8	24
Kentucky	6.00	29	187.4	10
Louisiana	4.00	55	366.5	38
Maine	5.00	24	58.9	25
Maryland	5.00	39	232.8	25
Massachusetts	5.00	19	245.7	25
Michigan	6.00	26	500.6	10
Minnesota	6.50	67	331.2	4
Mississippi	7.00	74	167.7	1
Missouri	4.23	28	272.8	37
Montana	n/a	19	n/a	n/a
Nebraska	5.50	76	109.4	23
Nevada	6.50	15	159.1	4
New Hampshire	n/a	11	n/a	n/a
New Jersey	6.00	55	404.6	10
New Mexico	5.00	156	124.0	25
New York	4.25	56	1,098.3	36
North Carolina	4.50	30	341.8	34
North Dakota	5.00	27	31.9	25
Ohio	6.00	68	525.7	10
Oklahoma	4.50	32	167.9	35
Oregon	n/a	0	n/a	n/a
Pennsylvania	6.00	55	509.1	10
Rhode Island	7.00	29	51.5	1
South Carolina	5.00	34	179.4	25
South Dakota	4.00	146	42.0	38
Tennessee	7.00	67	436.3	1
Texas	6.25	81	1,419.4	7
Utah	4.75	57	129.1	33
Vermont	6.00	29	25.4	10
Virginia	4.00	18	256.0	38
Washington	6.50	157	488.2	4
West Virginia	6.00	110	77.5	10
Wisconsin	5.00	74	264.3	25
Wyoming	4.00	62	36.8	38
50 States	n/a	n/a	15,411.8	
DC	5.75	70	43.9	
United States	5.60	168	15,455.7	

Rank in order by rate	
1	Mississippi
1	Rhode Island
1	Tennessee
4	Minnesota
4	Nevada
4	Washington
7	California
7	Illinois
7	Texas
10	Arkansas
10	Connecticut
10	Florida
10	Idaho
10	Indiana
10	Kentucky
10	Michigan
10	New Jersey
10	Ohio
10	Pennsylvania
10	Vermont
10	West Virginia
22	Arizona
23	Nebraska
24	Kansas
25	Iowa
25	Maine
25	Maryland
25	Massachusetts
25	New Mexico
25	North Dakota
25	South Carolina
25	Wisconsin
33	Utah
34	North Carolina
35	Oklahoma
36	New York
37	Missouri
38	Alabama
38	Georgia
38	Hawaii
38	Louisiana
38	South Dakota
38	Virginia
38	Wyoming
45	Colorado

Note: Ties in ranking reflect ties in actual values.

F-13 Individual Income Taxes, FY 2002

State	Individual income tax $ (in millions)	Income tax as a percentage of personal income	Rank by percentage
Alabama	2,127	1.92	36
Alaska	0	n/a	n/a
Arizona	2,091	1.51	40
Arkansas	1,566	2.52	22
California	33,047	2.91	13
Colorado	3,476	2.31	30
Connecticut	3,685	2.52	21
Delaware	763	3.05	12
Florida	0	n/a	n/a
Georgia	6,488	2.71	16
Hawaii	1,112	3.16	9
Idaho	842	2.56	19
Illinois	7,471	1.82	37
Indiana	4,121	2.44	25
Iowa	1,814	2.26	32
Kansas	1,855	2.41	26
Kentucky	3,496	3.44	5
Louisiana	1,789	1.63	38
Maine	1,073	3.08	11
Maryland	7,644	4.02	2
Massachusetts	7,913	3.17	8
Michigan	6,598	2.24	34
Minnesota	5,443	3.34	6
Mississippi	985	1.57	39
Missouri	3,929	2.50	23
Montana	518	2.38	27
Nebraska	1,153	2.34	28
Nevada	0	n/a	n/a
New Hampshire	71	0.17	42
New Jersey	6,867	2.07	35
New Mexico	983	2.25	33
New York	30,208	4.45	1
North Carolina	7,265	3.22	7
North Dakota	200	1.21	41
Ohio	11,794	3.62	4
Oklahoma	2,286	2.59	17
Oregon	3,675	3.71	3
Pennsylvania	9,510	2.55	20
Rhode Island	824	2.58	18
South Carolina	2,349	2.31	29
South Dakota	0	n/a	n/a
Tennessee	146	0.09	43
Texas	0	n/a	n/a
Utah	1,605	2.89	14
Vermont	408	2.30	31
Virginia	6,711	2.89	15
Washington	0	n/a	n/a
West Virginia	1,035	2.49	24
Wisconsin	4,974	3.13	10
Wyoming	0	n/a	n/a
50 States	201,909	2.33	
DC	949	3.66	
United States	202,858	2.33	

Rank in order by percentage	
1	New York
2	Maryland
3	Oregon
4	Ohio
5	Kentucky
6	Minnesota
7	North Carolina
8	Massachusetts
9	Hawaii
10	Wisconsin
11	Maine
12	Delaware
13	California
14	Utah
15	Virginia
16	Georgia
17	Oklahoma
18	Rhode Island
19	Idaho
20	Pennsylvania
21	Connecticut
22	Arkansas
23	Missouri
24	West Virginia
25	Indiana
26	Kansas
27	Montana
28	Nebraska
29	South Carolina
30	Colorado
31	Vermont
32	Iowa
33	New Mexico
34	Michigan
35	New Jersey
36	Alabama
37	Illinois
38	Louisiana
39	Mississippi
40	Arizona
41	North Dakota
42	New Hampshire
43	Tennessee

Note: Numbers that appear to be identical are rounded and vary slightly in actual value. The rankings reflect the actual values before rounding. See the introduction for more details.

F-14 Individual Income Taxes Per Capita, FY 2002

State	Income taxes per capita $	Rank per capita
Alabama	474	37
Alaska	0	n/a
Arizona	383	39
Arkansas	578	32
California	941	9
Colorado	771	17
Connecticut	1,065	5
Delaware	946	8
Florida	0	n/a
Georgia	758	20
Hawaii	893	12
Idaho	628	29
Illinois	593	31
Indiana	669	24
Iowa	618	30
Kansas	683	23
Kentucky	854	14
Louisiana	399	38
Maine	829	15
Maryland	1,401	2
Massachusetts	1,231	3
Michigan	656	27
Minnesota	1,084	4
Mississippi	343	40
Missouri	693	22
Montana	569	35
Nebraska	667	25
Nevada	0	n/a
New Hampshire	56	42
New Jersey	799	16
New Mexico	530	36
New York	1,577	1
North Carolina	873	13
North Dakota	315	41
Ohio	1,033	7
Oklahoma	654	28
Oregon	1,044	6
Pennsylvania	771	18
Rhode Island	770	19
South Carolina	572	34
South Dakota	0	n/a
Tennessee	25	43
Texas	0	n/a
Utah	693	21
Vermont	661	26
Virginia	920	10
Washington	0	n/a
West Virginia	574	33
Wisconsin	914	11
Wyoming	0	n/a
50 States	702	
DC	1,663	
United States	703	

Rank in order per capita	
1	New York
2	Maryland
3	Massachusetts
4	Minnesota
5	Connecticut
6	Oregon
7	Ohio
8	Delaware
9	California
10	Virginia
11	Wisconsin
12	Hawaii
13	North Carolina
14	Kentucky
15	Maine
16	New Jersey
17	Colorado
18	Pennsylvania
19	Rhode Island
20	Georgia
21	Utah
22	Missouri
23	Kansas
24	Indiana
25	Nebraska
26	Vermont
27	Michigan
28	Oklahoma
29	Idaho
30	Iowa
31	Illinois
32	Arkansas
33	West Virginia
34	South Carolina
35	Montana
36	New Mexico
37	Alabama
38	Louisiana
39	Arizona
40	Mississippi
41	North Dakota
42	New Hampshire
43	Tennessee

Note: Numbers that appear to be identical are rounded and vary slightly in actual value. The rankings reflect the actual values before rounding. See the introduction for more details.

F-15 Individual Income Tax Revenue as a Percentage of Three-Tax Revenue, FY 2002

State	Income tax as a percentage of three-tax revenue	Rank
Alabama	25.3	28
Alaska	n/a	n/a
Arizona	15.6	40
Arkansas	26.5	22
California	31.5	12
Colorado	26.9	21
Connecticut	26.0	26
Delaware	51.3	1
Florida	n/a	n/a
Georgia	28.8	16
Hawaii	28.0	20
Idaho	28.7	17
Illinois	20.1	37
Indiana	26.4	25
Iowa	23.9	33
Kansas	24.9	29
Kentucky	37.1	5
Louisiana	16.8	38
Maine	25.4	27
Maryland	42.4	3
Massachusetts	36.0	6
Michigan	24.8	30
Minnesota	32.8	10
Mississippi	16.7	39
Missouri	28.4	19
Montana	29.7	14
Nebraska	24.4	31
Nevada	n/a	n/a
New Hampshire	2.5	42
New Jersey	21.6	36
New Mexico	24.2	32
New York	38.0	4
North Carolina	35.4	8
North Dakota	14.0	41
Ohio	35.5	7
Oklahoma	31.7	11
Oregon	47.7	2
Pennsylvania	30.0	13
Rhode Island	23.9	34
South Carolina	26.5	23
South Dakota	n/a	n/a
Tennessee	1.3	43
Texas	n/a	n/a
Utah	28.4	18
Vermont	22.6	35
Virginia	33.6	9
Washington	n/a	n/a
West Virginia	26.4	24
Wisconsin	29.0	15
Wyoming	n/a	n/a
50 States	25.1	
DC	35.3	
United States	25.2	

Rank in order by percentage	
1	Delaware
2	Oregon
3	Maryland
4	New York
5	Kentucky
6	Massachusetts
7	Ohio
8	North Carolina
9	Virginia
10	Minnesota
11	Oklahoma
12	California
13	Pennsylvania
14	Montana
15	Wisconsin
16	Georgia
17	Idaho
18	Utah
19	Missouri
20	Hawaii
21	Colorado
22	Arkansas
23	South Carolina
24	West Virginia
25	Indiana
26	Connecticut
27	Maine
28	Alabama
29	Kansas
30	Michigan
31	Nebraska
32	New Mexico
33	Iowa
34	Rhode Island
35	Vermont
36	New Jersey
37	Illinois
38	Louisiana
39	Mississippi
40	Arizona
41	North Dakota
42	New Hampshire
43	Tennessee

Note: Numbers that appear to be identical are rounded and vary slightly in actual value. The rankings reflect the actual values before rounding. See the introduction for more details.

F-16 Highest Personal Income Tax Rate, 2005

State	Highest rate %	Rank
Alabama	3.02	40
Alaska	no tax	n/a
Arizona	5.04	30
Arkansas	7.00	13
California	9.30	3
Colorado	4.63	34
Connecticut	5.00	31
Delaware	5.95	24
Florida	no tax	n/a
Georgia	6.00	22
Hawaii	8.25	7
Idaho	7.80	10
Illinois	3.00	41
Indiana	3.40	38
Iowa	5.42	28
Kansas	6.45	21
Kentucky	6.00	22
Louisiana	3.62	36
Maine	8.50	6
Maryland	4.75	33
Massachusetts	5.30	29
Michigan	3.90	35
Minnesota	7.85	9
Mississippi	5.00	31
Missouri	3.62	36
Montana	6.64	19
Nebraska	6.84	15
Nevada	no tax	n/a
New Hampshire	no tax	n/a
New Jersey	8.97	5
New Mexico	6.80	16
New York	7.70	11
North Carolina	8.25	7
North Dakota	5.54	27
Ohio	7.50	12
Oklahoma	6.65	18
Oregon	9.00	4
Pennsylvania	3.07	39
Rhode Island	9.90	1
South Carolina	7.00	13
South Dakota	no tax	n/a
Tennessee	no tax	n/a
Texas	no tax	n/a
Utah	5.61	26
Vermont	9.50	2
Virginia	5.75	25
Washington	no tax	n/a
West Virginia	6.50	20
Wisconsin	6.75	17
Wyoming	no tax	n/a
50 States	n/a	
DC	9.30	
United States	n/a	

Rank in order by percentage	
1	Rhode Island
2	Vermont
3	California
4	Oregon
5	New Jersey
6	Maine
7	Hawaii
7	North Carolina
9	Minnesota
10	Idaho
11	New York
12	Ohio
13	Arkansas
13	South Carolina
15	Nebraska
16	New Mexico
17	Wisconsin
18	Oklahoma
19	Montana
20	West Virginia
21	Kansas
22	Georgia
22	Kentucky
24	Delaware
25	Virginia
26	Utah
27	North Dakota
28	Iowa
29	Massachusetts
30	Arizona
31	Connecticut
31	Mississippi
33	Maryland
34	Colorado
35	Michigan
36	Louisiana
36	Missouri
38	Indiana
39	Pennsylvania
40	Alabama
41	Illinois

Note: Ties in ranking reflect ties in actual values.

F-17 Corporate Income Taxes, Total and Per Capita, FY 2002

State	Corporate income taxes $ (in millions)	Corporate income taxes per capita $	Rank per capita
Alabama	323	72	21
Alaska	269	418	1
Arizona	346	63	28
Arkansas	177	65	27
California	5,333	152	6
Colorado	205	46	39
Connecticut	149	43	41
Delaware	252	312	2
Florida	1,219	73	20
Georgia	568	66	25
Hawaii	53	42	43
Idaho	77	57	33
Illinois	1,384	110	11
Indiana	709	115	10
Iowa	88	30	45
Kansas	122	45	40
Kentucky	302	74	19
Louisiana	264	59	32
Maine	77	60	31
Maryland	359	66	26
Massachusetts	812	126	8
Michigan	2,065	205	5
Minnesota	534	106	12
Mississippi	196	68	22
Missouri	300	53	36
Montana	68	75	18
Nebraska	108	62	29
Nevada	0	n/a	n/a
New Hampshire	377	296	3
New Jersey	1,101	128	7
New Mexico	124	67	23
New York	5,075	265	4
North Carolina	668	80	16
North Dakota	50	79	17
Ohio	761	67	24
Oklahoma	174	50	37
Oregon	196	56	34
Pennsylvania	1,198	97	13
Rhode Island	28	26	46
South Carolina	160	39	44
South Dakota	41	53	35
Tennessee	503	87	14
Texas	0	n/a	n/a
Utah	111	48	38
Vermont	37	61	30
Virginia	309	42	42
Washington	0	n/a	n/a
West Virginia	220	122	9
Wisconsin	445	82	15
Wyoming	0	n/a	n/a
50 States	27,941	97	
DC	211	370	
United States	28,152	98	

Rank in order per capita	
1	Alaska
2	Delaware
3	New Hampshire
4	New York
5	Michigan
6	California
7	New Jersey
8	Massachusetts
9	West Virginia
10	Indiana
11	Illinois
12	Minnesota
13	Pennsylvania
14	Tennessee
15	Wisconsin
16	North Carolina
17	North Dakota
18	Montana
19	Kentucky
20	Florida
21	Alabama
22	Mississippi
23	New Mexico
24	Ohio
25	Georgia
26	Maryland
27	Arkansas
28	Arizona
29	Nebraska
30	Vermont
31	Maine
32	Louisiana
33	Idaho
34	Oregon
35	South Dakota
36	Missouri
37	Oklahoma
38	Utah
39	Colorado
40	Kansas
41	Connecticut
42	Virginia
43	Hawaii
44	South Carolina
45	Iowa
46	Rhode Island

Note: Numbers that appear to be identical are rounded and vary slightly in actual value. The rankings reflect the actual values before rounding. See the introduction for more details.

F-18 Motor Fuel Taxes

State	Gasoline tax 2005 cents/gallons	Motor fuel taxes FY 2002 $ (in millions)	Fuel taxes as a percentage of personal income	Rank by gas tax
Alabama	18.00	557	0.50	36
Alaska	8.00	40	0.20	49
Arizona	18.00	625	0.45	36
Arkansas	21.50	414	0.67	22
California	18.00	3,296	0.29	36
Colorado	22.00	569	0.38	20
Connecticut	25.00	425	0.29	11
Delaware	23.00	108	0.43	18
Florida	14.50	2,379	0.50	46
Georgia	7.50	650	0.27	50
Hawaii	16.00	143	0.41	44
Idaho	25.00	214	0.65	11
Illinois	20.10	1,562	0.38	27
Indiana	18.00	742	0.44	36
Iowa	20.50	343	0.43	26
Kansas	24.00	377	0.49	14
Kentucky	17.40	461	0.45	41
Louisiana	20.00	559	0.51	28
Maine	25.20	192	0.55	10
Maryland	23.50	703	0.37	16
Massachusetts	21.00	667	0.27	24
Michigan	19.00	1,090	0.37	33
Minnesota	20.00	620	0.38	28
Mississippi	18.40	417	0.66	35
Missouri	17.03	695	0.44	42
Montana	27.00	191	0.88	5
Nebraska	26.30	308	0.62	8
Nevada	23.00	414	0.65	18
New Hampshire	19.50	120	0.28	32
New Jersey	14.50	524	0.16	46
New Mexico	18.90	200	0.46	34
New York	23.20	492	0.07	17
North Carolina	26.85	1,209	0.54	7
North Dakota	21.00	111	0.67	24
Ohio	26.00	1,376	0.42	9
Oklahoma	17.00	410	0.47	43
Oregon	24.00	409	0.41	14
Pennsylvania	30.00	1,753	0.47	2
Rhode Island	31.00	130	0.41	1
South Carolina	16.00	411	0.40	44
South Dakota	22.00	123	0.61	20
Tennessee	21.40	814	0.53	23
Texas	20.00	2,835	0.46	28
Utah	24.50	336	0.61	13
Vermont	20.00	71	0.40	28
Virginia	17.50	849	0.36	40
Washington	28.00	743	0.38	4
West Virginia	27.00	300	0.72	5
Wisconsin	29.90	955	0.60	3
Wyoming	14.00	75	0.50	48
50 States	n/a	33,009	0.38	
DC	22.50	35	0.14	
United States	n/a	33,044	0.38	

Rank in order by gas tax	
1	Rhode Island
2	Pennsylvania
3	Wisconsin
4	Washington
5	Montana
5	West Virginia
7	North Carolina
8	Nebraska
9	Ohio
10	Maine
11	Connecticut
11	Idaho
13	Utah
14	Kansas
14	Oregon
16	Maryland
17	New York
18	Delaware
18	Nevada
20	Colorado
20	South Dakota
22	Arkansas
23	Tennessee
24	Massachusetts
24	North Dakota
26	Iowa
27	Illinois
28	Louisiana
28	Minnesota
28	Texas
28	Vermont
32	New Hampshire
33	Michigan
34	New Mexico
35	Mississippi
36	Alabama
36	Arizona
36	California
36	Indiana
40	Virginia
41	Kentucky
42	Missouri
43	Oklahoma
44	Hawaii
44	South Carolina
46	Florida
46	New Jersey
48	Wyoming
49	Alaska
50	Georgia

Note: Ties in ranking reflect ties in actual values.

F-19 Motor Vehicle Fees and Taxes, 2005

State	Motor vehicle registration fees $	Motor vehicle sales and excise taxes %	Rank by registration fees
Alabama	23.00	2.00	35
Alaska	34.00	n/a	19
Arizona	8.00	5.60	49
Arkansas	25.00	5.13	30
California	30.00	6.00	24
Colorado	28.74	2.90	28
Connecticut	35.00	6.00	18
Delaware	20.00	2.75	38
Florida	32.50	6.00	22
Georgia	20.00	4.00	38
Hawaii	46.42	4.00	11
Idaho	48.00	5.00	10
Illinois	78.00	6.25	6
Indiana	12.00	5.00	46
Iowa	93.00	5.00	2
Kansas	25.00	4.90	30
Kentucky	12.00	6.00	46
Louisiana	26.50	4.00	29
Maine	25.00	5.00	30
Maryland	64.00	5.00	7
Massachusetts	25.00	5.00	30
Michigan	n/a	6.00	n/a
Minnesota	108.75	6.50	1
Mississippi	15.00	5.00	42
Missouri	39.00	4.23	16
Montana	18.75	n/a	41
Nebraska	15.00	5.50	42
Nevada	33.00	6.50	21
New Hampshire	31.20	n/a	23
New Jersey	81.00	6.00	4
New Mexico	42.00	3.00	13
New York	22.50	4.25	36
North Carolina	20.00	3.00	38
North Dakota	79.00	5.00	5
Ohio	39.50	6.00	15
Oklahoma	93.00	3.25	2
Oregon	15.00	n/a	42
Pennsylvania	36.00	6.00	17
Rhode Island	30.00	7.00	24
South Carolina	12.00	5.00	46
South Dakota	42.00	3.00	13
Tennessee	21.50	7.00	37
Texas	59.80	6.25	8
Utah	24.50	4.75	34
Vermont	43.00	6.00	12
Virginia	29.50	3.00	27
Washington	33.75	6.80	20
West Virginia	30.00	5.00	24
Wisconsin	55.00	5.00	9
Wyoming	15.00	3.00	42
50 States	n/a	n/a	
DC	115.00	6.00	
United States	n/a	n/a	

Rank in order by $	
1	Minnesota
2	Iowa
2	Oklahoma
4	New Jersey
5	North Dakota
6	Illinois
7	Maryland
8	Texas
9	Wisconsin
10	Idaho
11	Hawaii
12	Vermont
13	New Mexico
13	South Dakota
15	Ohio
16	Missouri
17	Pennsylvania
18	Connecticut
19	Alaska
20	Washington
21	Nevada
22	Florida
23	New Hampshire
24	California
24	Rhode Island
24	West Virginia
27	Virginia
28	Colorado
29	Louisiana
30	Arkansas
30	Kansas
30	Maine
30	Massachusetts
34	Utah
35	Alabama
36	New York
37	Tennessee
38	Delaware
38	Georgia
38	North Carolina
41	Montana
42	Mississippi
42	Nebraska
42	Oregon
42	Wyoming
46	Indiana
46	Kentucky
46	South Carolina
49	Arizona

Note: Ties in ranking reflect ties in actual values.

F-20 Tobacco Taxes

State	Cigarette tax rate 2005 cents/pack	Tobacco taxes FY 2002 $ (in millions)	Tobacco taxes as a percentage of personal income	Rank by tax rate
Alabama	42.5	79.1	0.07	38
Alaska	160.0	51.4	0.26	5
Arizona	118.0	161.8	0.12	14
Arkansas	59.0	93.1	0.15	29
California	87.0	1,102.9	0.10	21
Colorado	84.0	66.2	0.04	22
Connecticut	151.0	158.3	0.11	6
Delaware	55.0	27.7	0.11	32
Florida	33.9	466.5	0.10	43
Georgia	37.0	94.1	0.04	40
Hawaii	140.0	65.5	0.19	10
Idaho	57.0	28.4	0.09	30
Illinois	98.0	530.2	0.13	19
Indiana	55.5	123.2	0.07	31
Iowa	36.0	94.5	0.12	41
Kansas	79.0	52.3	0.07	24
Kentucky	30.0	16.8	0.02	44
Louisiana	36.0	128.5	0.12	41
Maine	100.0	94.1	0.27	17
Maryland	100.0	209.9	0.11	17
Massachusetts	151.0	275.0	0.11	6
Michigan	200.0	670.0	0.23	3
Minnesota	48.0	173.5	0.11	36
Mississippi	18.0	55.6	0.09	48
Missouri	17.0	123.6	0.08	49
Montana	170.0	13.3	0.06	4
Nebraska	64.0	44.2	0.09	27
Nevada	80.0	63.7	0.10	23
New Hampshire	52.0	82.6	0.19	35
New Jersey	240.0	406.9	0.12	2
New Mexico	91.0	17.8	0.04	20
New York	150.0	1,038.4	0.15	8
North Carolina	30.0	41.5	0.02	44
North Dakota	44.0	21.6	0.13	37
Ohio	125.0	285.8	0.09	12
Oklahoma	103.0	71.5	0.08	16
Oregon	118.0	176.1	0.18	14
Pennsylvania	135.0	317.4	0.09	11
Rhode Island	246.0	83.1	0.26	1
South Carolina	7.0	26.6	0.03	50
South Dakota	53.0	18.7	0.09	34
Tennessee	20.0	83.6	0.05	47
Texas	41.0	540.1	0.09	39
Utah	69.5	51.0	0.09	26
Vermont	119.0	26.6	0.15	13
Virginia	30.0	52.1	0.02	44
Washington	142.5	330.7	0.17	9
West Virginia	55.0	32.2	0.08	32
Wisconsin	77.0	302.7	0.19	25
Wyoming	60.0	5.1	0.03	28
50 States	n/a	9,075.7	0.10	
DC	100.0	17.2	0.07	
United States	n/a	9,092.9	0.10	

Rank in order by tax rate	
1	Rhode Island
2	New Jersey
3	Michigan
4	Montana
5	Alaska
6	Connecticut
6	Massachusetts
8	New York
9	Washington
10	Hawaii
11	Pennsylvania
12	Ohio
13	Vermont
14	Arizona
14	Oregon
16	Oklahoma
17	Maine
17	Maryland
19	Illinois
20	New Mexico
21	California
22	Colorado
23	Nevada
24	Kansas
25	Wisconsin
26	Utah
27	Nebraska
28	Wyoming
29	Arkansas
30	Idaho
31	Indiana
32	Delaware
32	West Virginia
34	South Dakota
35	New Hampshire
36	Minnesota
37	North Dakota
38	Alabama
39	Texas
40	Georgia
41	Iowa
41	Louisiana
43	Florida
44	Kentucky
44	North Carolina
44	Virginia
47	Tennessee
48	Mississippi
49	Missouri
50	South Carolina

Note: Ties in ranking reflect ties in actual values.

F-21 State and Local Taxes on High-Income Families, 2004

State	Taxes for family with $150,000/year income $	Percentage of income	Rank by $
Alabama	11,677	7.8	38
Alaska	5,711	3.8	49
Arizona	11,371	7.6	39
Arkansas	14,423	9.6	23
California	19,048	12.7	4
Colorado	11,098	7.4	41
Connecticut	21,364	14.2	2
Delaware	12,085	8.1	37
Florida	6,791	4.5	48
Georgia	16,839	11.2	10
Hawaii	13,700	9.1	31
Idaho	14,984	10.0	18
Illinois	14,380	9.6	24
Indiana	15,423	10.3	16
Iowa	14,219	9.5	25
Kansas	12,429	8.3	35
Kentucky	15,536	10.4	15
Louisiana	14,802	9.9	21
Maine	18,120	12.1	7
Maryland	17,769	11.8	8
Massachusetts	14,833	9.9	20
Michigan	16,377	10.9	13
Minnesota	14,528	9.7	22
Mississippi	13,409	8.9	33
Missouri	14,059	9.4	27
Montana	12,373	8.2	36
Nebraska	15,626	10.4	14
Nevada	6,806	4.5	47
New Hampshire	9,574	6.4	43
New Jersey	18,785	12.5	5
New Mexico	13,887	9.3	30
New York	22,635	15.1	1
North Carolina	14,914	9.9	19
North Dakota	11,194	7.5	40
Ohio	16,458	11.0	12
Oklahoma	13,421	8.9	32
Oregon	17,562	11.7	9
Pennsylvania	19,077	12.7	3
Rhode Island	18,335	12.2	6
South Carolina	15,215	10.1	17
South Dakota	7,457	5.0	46
Tennessee	8,664	5.8	45
Texas	9,145	6.1	44
Utah	14,210	9.5	26
Vermont	13,943	9.3	28
Virginia	12,863	8.6	34
Washington	9,581	6.4	42
West Virginia	13,922	9.3	29
Wisconsin	16,687	11.1	11
Wyoming	5,410	3.6	50
50 States	n/a	n/a	
DC	16,327	10.9	
United States	13,903	9.3	

Rank in order by $	
1	New York
2	Connecticut
3	Pennsylvania
4	California
5	New Jersey
6	Rhode Island
7	Maine
8	Maryland
9	Oregon
10	Georgia
11	Wisconsin
12	Ohio
13	Michigan
14	Nebraska
15	Kentucky
16	Indiana
17	South Carolina
18	Idaho
19	North Carolina
20	Massachusetts
21	Louisiana
22	Minnesota
23	Arkansas
24	Illinois
25	Iowa
26	Utah
27	Missouri
28	Vermont
29	West Virginia
30	New Mexico
31	Hawaii
32	Oklahoma
33	Mississippi
34	Virginia
35	Kansas
36	Montana
37	Delaware
38	Alabama
39	Arizona
40	North Dakota
41	Colorado
42	Washington
43	New Hampshire
44	Texas
45	Tennessee
46	South Dakota
47	Nevada
48	Florida
49	Alaska
50	Wyoming

F-22 State and Local Taxes in the Largest City in Each State, 2004

State	Taxes for family with $50,000/year income $	Percentage of income	Rank by $
Alabama	3,933	7.9	29
Alaska	2,142	4.3	48
Arizona	3,321	6.6	42
Arkansas	4,021	8.0	27
California	4,719	9.4	15
Colorado	3,395	6.8	40
Connecticut	5,819	11.6	4
Delaware	3,461	6.9	39
Florida	1,956	3.9	49
Georgia	4,949	9.9	12
Hawaii	3,941	7.9	28
Idaho	3,670	7.3	33
Illinois	4,865	9.7	13
Indiana	5,221	10.4	9
Iowa	4,410	8.8	19
Kansas	3,335	6.7	41
Kentucky	4,854	9.7	14
Louisiana	3,607	7.2	35
Maine	4,956	9.9	11
Maryland	5,681	11.4	5
Massachusetts	4,713	9.4	17
Michigan	5,253	10.5	8
Minnesota	4,160	8.3	23
Mississippi	3,802	7.6	32
Missouri	4,387	8.8	20
Montana	2,770	5.5	46
Nebraska	4,325	8.7	21
Nevada	2,596	5.2	47
New Hampshire	3,518	7.0	38
New Jersey	5,962	11.9	3
New Mexico	3,840	7.7	31
New York	6,143	12.3	2
North Carolina	4,215	8.4	22
North Dakota	3,566	7.1	36
Ohio	4,715	9.4	16
Oklahoma	4,096	8.2	24
Oregon	5,398	10.8	7
Pennsylvania	6,237	12.5	1
Rhode Island	5,489	11.0	6
South Carolina	3,641	7.3	34
South Dakota	2,826	5.7	45
Tennessee	3,219	6.4	44
Texas	3,295	6.6	43
Utah	4,607	9.2	18
Vermont	4,073	8.1	25
Virginia	4,056	8.1	26
Washington	3,561	7.1	37
West Virginia	3,858	7.7	30
Wisconsin	5,107	10.2	10
Wyoming	1,938	3.9	50
50 States	n/a	n/a	
DC	4,584	9.2	
United States	4,161	8.3	

Rank in order by $	
1	Pennsylvania
2	New York
3	New Jersey
4	Connecticut
5	Maryland
6	Rhode Island
7	Oregon
8	Michigan
9	Indiana
10	Wisconsin
11	Maine
12	Georgia
13	Illinois
14	Kentucky
15	California
16	Ohio
17	Massachusetts
18	Utah
19	Iowa
20	Missouri
21	Nebraska
22	North Carolina
23	Minnesota
24	Oklahoma
25	Vermont
26	Virginia
27	Arkansas
28	Hawaii
29	Alabama
30	West Virginia
31	New Mexico
32	Mississippi
33	Idaho
34	South Carolina
35	Louisiana
36	North Dakota
37	Washington
38	New Hampshire
39	Delaware
40	Colorado
41	Kansas
42	Arizona
43	Texas
44	Tennessee
45	South Dakota
46	Montana
47	Nevada
48	Alaska
49	Florida
50	Wyoming

F-23 Progressivity of Major State and Local Taxes, 2004

State	Progressivity index %	Rank by most progressive to least
Alabama	95.1	41
Alaska	122.7	46
Arizona	71.1	19
Arkansas	70.1	15
California	76.1	27
Colorado	70.2	17
Connecticut	80.7	33
Delaware	71.0	18
Florida	59.7	6
Georgia	70.1	15
Hawaii	75.7	25
Idaho	48.9	4
Illinois	94.7	40
Indiana	93.5	39
Iowa	76.1	27
Kansas	51.9	5
Kentucky	81.7	34
Louisiana	43.4	2
Maine	65.7	10
Maryland	64.7	9
Massachusetts	74.5	23
Michigan	89.4	35
Minnesota	59.7	6
Mississippi	69.9	14
Missouri	76.0	26
Montana	59.9	8
Nebraska	73.9	20
Nevada	132.0	50
New Hampshire	119.9	44
New Jersey	99.3	42
New Mexico	68.6	12
New York	48.8	3
North Carolina	66.7	11
North Dakota	93.0	38
Ohio	79.5	31
Oklahoma	80.5	32
Oregon	77.9	29
Pennsylvania	89.9	37
Rhode Island	75.1	23
South Carolina	41.3	1
South Dakota	127.6	49
Tennessee	124.5	48
Texas	110.3	43
Utah	74.3	22
Vermont	74.0	21
Virginia	88.9	35
Washington	123.2	47
West Virginia	78.0	30
Wisconsin	68.9	13
Wyoming	116.6	44
50 States	n/a	
DC	60.0	
United States	80.5	

Rank in order by percentage	
1	South Carolina
2	Louisiana
3	New York
4	Idaho
5	Kansas
6	Florida
6	Minnesota
8	Montana
9	Maryland
10	Maine
11	North Carolina
12	New Mexico
13	Wisconsin
14	Mississippi
15	Arkansas
15	Georgia
17	Colorado
18	Delaware
19	Arizona
20	Nebraska
21	Vermont
22	Utah
23	Massachusetts
23	Rhode Island
25	Hawaii
26	Missouri
27	California
27	Iowa
29	Oregon
30	West Virginia
31	Ohio
32	Oklahoma
33	Connecticut
34	Kentucky
35	Virginia
35	Michigan
37	Pennsylvania
38	North Dakota
39	Indiana
40	Illinois
41	Alabama
42	New Jersey
43	Texas
44	Wyoming
44	New Hampshire
46	Alaska
47	Washington
48	Tennessee
49	South Dakota
50	Nevada

Note: Ties in ranking reflect ties in actual values.

F-24 State Estate Taxes, 2005

State	Type of state death tax 2005	State revenue "picked-up" from the federal estate tax FY 2001 $ (in millions)	Per capita state revenue from the federal estate tax $	Rank per capita
Alabama	Pick-up	45.80	10.26	39
Alaska	Pick-up	2.70	4.25	47
Arizona	Pick-up	74.65	14.07	29
Arkansas	Pick-up	26.10	9.70	41
California	Pick-up	934.00	27.07	8
Colorado	Pick-up	82.60	18.70	17
Connecticut	Inheritance	68.00	19.85	14
Delaware	Pick-up	41.20	51.75	1
Florida	Pick-up	767.10	46.78	2
Georgia	Pick-up	127.50	15.21	24
Hawaii	Pick-up	17.50	14.29	27
Idaho	Pick-up	41.40	31.34	5
Illinois	Pick-up	361.00	28.92	6
Indiana	Inheritance	29.00	4.74	45
Iowa	Inheritance	38.50	13.17	32
Kansas	Pick-up	41.20	15.29	23
Kentucky	Inheritance	45.10	11.09	37
Louisiana	Inheritance	20.30	4.55	46
Maine	Pick-up	30.60	23.78	10
Maryland	Inheritance	103.40	19.24	15
Massachusetts	Pick-up	203.30	31.87	4
Michigan	Pick-up	155.30	15.54	22
Minnesota	Pick-up	53.00	10.66	38
Mississippi	Pick-up	27.60	9.66	42
Missouri	Pick-up	156.80	27.85	7
Montana	Pick-up	10.10	11.17	36
Nebraska	Inheritance	27.90	16.28	20
Nevada	Pick-up	42.50	20.18	13
New Hampshire	Pick-up	24.00	19.06	16
New Jersey	Inheritance	202.00	23.81	9
New Mexico	Pick-up	25.30	13.83	30
New York	Pick-up	720.00	37.87	3
North Carolina	Pick-up	123.10	15.04	26
North Dakota	Pick-up	5.30	8.35	43
Ohio	Estate	35.00	3.08	48
Oklahoma	Estate	0.00	0.00	50
Oregon	Pick-up	43.70	12.58	33
Pennsylvania	Inheritance	60.00	4.88	44
Rhode Island	Pick-up	22.00	20.78	11
South Carolina	Pick-up	49.00	12.06	34
South Dakota	Pick-up	8.60	11.37	35
Tennessee	Inheritance	9.60	1.67	49
Texas	Pick-up	322.40	15.12	25
Utah	Pick-up	30.50	13.44	31
Vermont	Pick-up	12.70	20.71	12
Virginia	Pick-up	125.00	17.39	19
Washington	Estate	107.10	17.89	18
West Virginia	Pick-up	17.50	9.71	40
Wisconsin	Pick-up	77.00	14.25	28
Wyoming	Pick-up	7.90	15.98	21
50 States	n/a	5,601.85	19.71	
DC	Pick-up	51.50	90.06	
United States*	n/a	5,653.40	19.85	

**Due to rounding or data sources, the 50-state total plus D.C. may not equal the U.S. total. Please see introduction.*

Rank in order per capita	
1	Delaware
2	Florida
3	New York
4	Massachusetts
5	Idaho
6	Illinois
7	Missouri
8	California
9	New Jersey
10	Maine
11	Rhode Island
12	Vermont
13	Nevada
14	Connecticut
15	Maryland
16	New Hampshire
17	Colorado
18	Washington
19	Virginia
20	Nebraska
21	Wyoming
22	Michigan
23	Kansas
24	Georgia
25	Texas
26	North Carolina
27	Hawaii
28	Wisconsin
29	Arizona
30	New Mexico
31	Utah
32	Iowa
33	Oregon
34	South Carolina
35	South Dakota
36	Montana
37	Kentucky
38	Minnesota
39	Alabama
40	West Virginia
41	Arkansas
42	Mississippi
43	North Dakota
44	Pennsylvania
45	Indiana
46	Louisiana
47	Alaska
48	Ohio
49	Tennessee
50	Oklahoma

F-25 State Taxes on Retirement Income, 2003

State	Exclusion for state and local pension $	Exclusion for federal civilian pension $	Exclusion for military pension $	Exclusion for Social Security $	Exclusion for private pension $
Alabama	full	full	full	full	varies
Alaska	n/a	n/a	n/a	n/a	n/a
Arizona	2,500	2,500	2,500	full	none
Arkansas	6,000	6,000	6,000	full	6,000
California	none	none	none	full	none
Colorado	20,000–24,000	20,000–24,000	20,000–24,000	20,000–24,000	20,000–24,000
Connecticut	none	none	none	income threshold	none
Delaware	2,000–12,500	2,000–12,500	2,000–12,500	full	2,000–12,500
Florida	n/a	n/a	n/a	n/a	n/a
Georgia	15,000	15,000	15,000	full	15,000
Hawaii	full	full	full	full	varies
Idaho	none–19,920*	none–19,920*	none–19,920*	full	none
Illinois	full	full	full	full	varies
Indiana	none	2,000*	none	full	none
Iowa	6,000	6,000	6,000	income threshold	6,000
Kansas	full	full	full	taxed at fed level	none
Kentucky	up to 36,414	up to 36,414	up to 36,414	income threshold	up to 36,414
Louisiana	full	full	full	full	6,000
Maine	6,000*	6,000*	6,000*	full	6,000*
Maryland	18,500*	18,500*	18,500*	full	18,500*
Massachusetts	full	full	full	full	none
Michigan	full	full	full	full	34,920
Minnesota	14,500	14,500	14,500	taxed at fed level	14,500
Mississippi	full	full	full	full	varies
Missouri	6,000 or under	6,000 or under	6,000 or under	taxed at fed level	4,000
Montana	up to 3,600	up to 3,600	up to 3,600	income threshold	up to 3,600
Nebraska	none	none	none	taxed at fed level	none
Nevada	n/a	n/a	n/a	n/a	n/a
New Hampshire	n/a	n/a	n/a	n/a	n/a
New Jersey	15,000	15,000	full	full	15,000
New Mexico	none–8,000	none–8,000	none–8,000	full	none–8,000
New York	full	full	full	full	20,000
North Carolina	4,000	4,000	4,000	full	2,000
North Dakota	none–5,000*	5,000*	5,000*	taxed at fed level	none
Ohio	200 credit	200 credit	200 credit	full	200 credit
Oklahoma	5,500	5,500	5,500	full	none–4,400
Oregon	9% credit	9% credit	9% credit	full	9% credit
Pennsylvania	full	full	full	full	full
Rhode Island	none	none	none	taxed at fed level	none
South Carolina	3,000–10,000	3,000–10,000	3,000–10,000	full	3,000–10,000
South Dakota	n/a	n/a	n/a	n/a	n/a
Tennessee	n/a	n/a	n/a	n/a	n/a
Texas	n/a	n/a	n/a	n/a	n/a
Utah	4,800–7,500	4,800–7,500	4,800–7,500	4,800–7,500	4,800–7,500
Vermont	none	none	none	taxed at fed level	none
Virginia	6,000–12,000	6,000–12,000	6,000–12,000	full	6,000–12,000
Washington	n/a	n/a	n/a	n/a	n/a
West Virginia	2,000–full	2,000	2,000–32,000	full	none
Wisconsin	none	none	full	50% exempt	none
Wyoming	n/a	n/a	n/a	n/a	n/a
50 States	n/a	n/a	n/a	n/a	n/a
DC	3,000	3,000	3,000	full	none
United States	n/a	n/a	n/a	n/a	n/a

** reduced by the amount of Social Security received*

Source Notes for Taxes (Section F)

F-1 State and Local Tax Revenue, Total and as a Percentage of Personal Income, FY 2002: This is the most common definition of the tax burdens of state and local governments. It is the tax component of "general revenue" used by the U.S. Census Bureau in its annual survey of government finances. It excludes taxes used to finance certain trust funds, such as unemployment insurance taxes, but includes other earmarked revenues, such as gasoline tax revenues for highway construction. Tax revenues are related to personal income as a common proxy for tax base or "ability to pay."

For decades, state officials, media, scholars, taxpayer groups, and others have been comparing tax burdens and spending patterns of states using data published by the U.S. Census Bureau in its annual volume *Governmental Finances*. These data were also republished in many secondary sources such as *Significant Features of Fiscal Federalism*, published by the Advisory Commission on Intergovernmental Relations; *Statistical Abstract of the United States*, published by the U.S. Census Bureau and U.S. Government Printing Office; and other secondary sources.

The bureau and other federal statistical agencies have been responding to tight budgets by limiting the number of their printed publications and analyses, both statistical and narrative, of the data they produce. This has allowed them to concentrate their resources on what only they can do—collecting and refining the underlying data. Beginning with the data for 1993, the bureau has stopped publishing state and local fiscal data in printed reports such as *Governmental Finances*, making them available only electronically. Also the bureau has discontinued making popular analytical calculations such as those comparing taxes and spending with personal income and population. This change and budget restrictions have eliminated some secondary sources, such as *Significant Features*.

Anyone with access to the Internet, computer capability, and the ability to unzip and download the Census data can make calculations such as taxes as a percentage of personal income and per capita spending on particular state and/or local functions. However, not everyone has these capabilities, and those that do can produce different data unless they are careful to follow particular complex conventions covering such matters as which concepts of taxing and spending to use, which revision of often-revised government data to use, and which years of population and personal income estimates to use.

No government agency, including the U.S. Census Bureau, will certify the resulting differing numbers as the appropriate ones or vouch for their accuracy in applying past concepts for calculating them. However, many users will demand that comparative numbers be consistent from user to user, from year to year, and from state to state. As a result, some publications are becoming more authoritative than others. Congressional Quarterly Inc., in conjunction with State Policy Research, is committed to publishing these comparative data annually in such widely used publications as *State Fact Finder, State Policy Reports*, and *Governing* magazine. It is likely that these sources, which are using identical data, will become the standard sources for most users.

All of the tables in *State Fact Finder* that rely on U.S. Census Bureau data covering government finances in 2002 use the same conventions, based on past practices of the bureau. The underlying data on tax revenues and spending come from the bureau Web site (www.census.gov). These data reflect fiscal information for varying government fiscal years ending in 2002, which for most states is a fiscal year ending on June 30, 2002, and for many local governments is a fiscal year ending on December 31, 2002.

Following the historical practice of the bureau not to use revised personal income and population numbers, the personal income numbers used for comparison with these fiscal data are calendar year data for 2001 representing the original 2001 estimates released by the Bureau of Economic Analysis. The population data used to calculate per capita amounts are estimates for July 1, 2002, as originally released by the bureau in 2003.

The data on tax burdens and spending in relation to personal income and per capita are comparable with those of prior years, as published by the U.S. Census Bureau and secondary sources, to exactly the degree that bureau data for earlier years have been comparable. Data for any year are not recalculated. While underlying data on government revenues and spending are not normally revised, the U.S. Census Bureau and Bureau of Economic Analysis do re-estimate historical estimates of population and personal income.

F-2 Per Capita State and Local Tax Revenue, FY 2002: This table relates total tax revenue to population, providing another measure of relative tax burdens (see Table F-1). It also shows the division of tax revenues between state and local governments in each state.

F-3 State and Local Tax Effort, FY 1999: The revenue-raising ability of states and their local governments varies markedly among the states. For example, Alaska and Texas get massive revenues by taxing oil and gas, and Nevada gets large revenues from taxing casino gambling, but most states get no revenue from these sources. What states will collect from particular tax rates applied to property, sales, and income is higher in states with more affluent citizens. Because of these differences, the revenue collected (see Tables F-1 and F-2) is not a good indicator of how high tax rates are in each state.

A more appropriate way to compare the relative burden of state and local taxes, or what is often called "tax effort," is to consider what each state would raise if it and its local governments applied national average tax rates to their own tax bases. Unfortunately, this methodology, known as the "representative tax system," is tedious and expensive to apply. The Advisory Commission on Intergovernmental Relations historically did this work but stopped with the 1991 calculations. The commission was phased out in 1996, and no one had stepped forward to do the work until recently, when a report, based on the fiscal year 1994 U.S. Census Bureau data on state and local finances, was issued by the Federal Reserve Bank of Boston. Robert Tannenwald, the author of that report and assistant vice president and economist at the Federal Reserve Bank of Boston, has published subsequent updates. The latest, co-authored with Nicholas Turner, covers fiscal year 1999. "Interstate Fiscal Disparity in State Fiscal Year 1999," published by the Federal Reserve Bank of Boston in Public Policy Discussion Papers (No. 04-9), is the source for the tax effort statistics shown in this table.

The values reflect differences in tax effort. For example, New York state and local governments have taxes that raise 43 percent more than would be raised if tax rates in that state were equal to the national average.

While the best available data on tax effort and tax capacity are those appearing in Tables F-3 and F-4, they must be used with caution. For states which are quite close to the national average and to each other, the results are not what statisticians call "robust." The measurements of tax base and tax revenues are quite reliable, but not so reliable that they prevent a point or two difference in the index from potentially being explained by errors. Also the differences in tax rates associated with small differences in tax effort are likely to be too small to affect decisions of households and businesses. Finally, the data are for fiscal year 1999, while decisions made today are in fiscal year 2005. The relevant data, which are unavailable, would reflect changes already made and others already underway.

So, for example, the differences among Kansas (99), Oklahoma (98), and Illinois (101) and among Arkansas (91), Missouri (92), and South Carolina (90) cannot appropriately be used as an argument for changing public policy in those states. This being said, large differences among the states and extreme differences from the national average permit substantial conclusions about differing state policies and their effects.

F-4 State and Local Tax Capacity, FY 1999: The representative tax system (see notes to Table F-3) also permits a comparison of the tax base, or fiscal capacity, of individual states. This is presented in what can be viewed either as percentages of the national average or as index numbers. Either way, the table indicates, for example, that if it applied national average tax rates, Alabama would raise only 82 percent of the amount that those same rates would in the average state. For reasons indicated in the notes to Table F-3, these data are not available for any year more recent than 1999.

F-5 Change in State and Local Taxes, FY 1997–2002: In the five years covered by the table, the U.S. Census Bureau reports for each year indicate that state and local tax revenues have increased by just over 24 percent. However, growth has been much faster in some states than others. See Table F-1 for the source for 2002 figures; 1997 numbers come from *State Fact Finder 2001*.

The table shows increases in state and local taxes as would be expected because the nation's population has been growing and prices have increased due to inflation. Predictably, the increases tend to be largest in states where population and government workloads, such as children in public schools, have grown most rapidly, such as Nevada. However, on average, tax burdens (taxes in relation to personal income) have declined.

F-6 Property Taxes, Total and as a Percentage of Personal Income, FY 2002: This and subsequent tables deal with the total revenues raised by particular state and local taxes. They start with the revenues from those taxes as indicated by U.S. Census Bureau data (see notes to Table F-1). Those revenues are then related to both population and personal income to provide the two most common measures of the levels, or burdens, of those taxes in each state.

F-7 Property Taxes Per Capita, FY 2002: See notes to Table F-6.

F-8 Property Tax Revenue as a Percentage of Three-Tax Revenue, FY 2002: Some people feel that their total state and local taxes are too high, while others may not be sure about total tax burdens but feel that a particular revenue source, such as property taxes, is too heavily used in their state. This table, using Census data (see notes to Table F-1), relates the amount raised from taxing property with the amounts raised from the other two major tax bases—sales and income.

F-9 Sales Taxes, Total and as a Percentage of Personal Income, FY 2002: All states, including those which do not have state sales taxes, show some sales tax revenues. The U.S. Census Bureau counts as sales tax revenues both revenues from sales taxes levied on sales of most goods and special excise taxes on particular goods, such as tobacco and alcoholic beverages. See notes to Table F-6.

F-10 Sales Taxes Per Capita, FY 2002: See notes to Tables F-6 and F-9.

F-11 Sales Tax Revenue as a Percentage of Three-Tax Revenue, FY 2002: See notes to Tables F-8 and F-9.

F-12 Sales Tax Rates and Reach, 2006: Many of the "goods" of today's economy are beyond the reach of the sales tax as it is currently structured. For instance, cars and clothing are taxed, but services such as barbering and landscaping generally are not. Neither are out-of-state mail order or e-commerce purchases. Because of the limited reach of the sales tax, without rate hikes sales tax collections would fall.

Many experts suggest that the sales tax would be fairer and a more productive revenue source if it applied equally to both goods *and* services; bricks-and-mortar *and* Internet shopping. A current debate centers around how to extend the reach of the sales tax, if indeed it should be extended at all. This table provides three elements relevant to that debate. The first column of information shows each state's statewide sales tax rate at the beginning of 2006 (localities may levy additional taxes). The second column shows the number of services covered in 2004 by the sales tax in each state. The table includes states, such as New Hampshire, that have no general sales tax and ones, such as Alaska, that may have special excise taxes on a few services. This count, along with the sales tax rates, was compiled by the Federation of Tax Administrators (FTA) and is available on its Web site (www.taxadmin.org).

The third column shows the estimated state and local revenue losses from e-commerce in 2003. The data come from a study conducted by two economists, Dr. Donald Bruce and Dr. William F. Fox, at the Center for Business and Economic Research (CBER) at the University of Tennessee. The study is titled "State and Local Sales Tax Revenue Losses from E-Commerce: Estimates as of July 2004" and is available on the CBER Web site (cber.bus.utk.edu/ecomm.htm). For general information on the efforts of some states to simplify and unify the sales tax consult the Streamlined Sales Tax Project.

F-13 Individual Income Taxes, Total and as a Percentage of Personal Income, FY 2002: Some states that do not tax personal income from wages and salaries do have taxes based on income from other sources, such as dividends, interest, rent, and capital gains. Revenues from all these taxes appear in the table. For the source, see notes to Table F-6.

F-14 Individual Income Taxes Per Capita, FY 2002: See notes to Tables F-6 and F-13.

F-15 Individual Income Tax Revenue as a Percentage of Three-Tax Revenue, FY 2002: See notes to Tables F-8 and F-13.

F-16 Highest Personal Income Tax Rate, 2005: While some states have no income tax at all, the rates paid by high-income households in a few other states can go as high as 9 percent. This table, developed by State Policy Research from compilations of state tax laws published by CCH, Inc., shows the highest state personal income tax rates. A few states use low flat-rate income taxes with few deductions and exemptions, so the same rate is applicable to all taxable income. Most states use a graduated rate schedule. In most of the states showing the highest rates in the table, this "marginal" or "top bracket" rate is paid only on income exceeding a threshold of $100,000 or more.

The rates shown were those in effect in December 2005 on income earned in 2005, to be reported on tax returns filed in early 2006.

F-17 Corporate Income Taxes, Total and Per Capita, FY 2002: See notes to Table F-6. This table is now the best of many unsatisfactory ways of comparing corporate income taxes in the fifty states. However, since 2002 states have made more changes in corporate income taxes (tax base, tax rates, tax credits) than in any other single tax affecting business.

Because of the widespread use of special tax credits for investment, research and development, job expansion, and other purposes and because of differences among states in how much income of multistate corporations is attributed to the taxing state, comparisons of corporate income tax rates are not particularly meaningful.

The most appropriate way to compare corporate income taxes of states is to make calculations of tax liability for individual hypothetical corporations. Such calculations reflect the different state definitions of the tax base, different tax rates, and different tax credits as well as different characteristics of firms in particular industries which affect tax liability. These calculations are complex because taxes levied by one state depend in part on taxes levied by other states. Such calculations have been made in special studies prepared for individual states, but they are typically made only for those ten to twenty states that the requesting state considers to be its major competitors in economic development.

F-18 Motor Fuel Taxes: States tax motor fuels, such as gasoline and diesel fuel, mostly to provide funds for road construction and maintenance. The table shows the tax rate on gasoline from a special compilation prepared by the Federation of Tax Administrators (FTA), covering rates in effect January 1, 2005. This statistic is available on the FTA Web site (www.taxadmin.org). The table also includes total state and local revenues from motor fuel taxes in fiscal year 2002, compiled by the U.S. Census Bureau and available on its Web site (see notes to Table F-1). *State Fact Finder* related those revenues to personal income.

F-19 Motor Vehicle Fees and Taxes, 2005: States assess vehicle registration fees annually. The amounts shown in this table are those that would be assessed on a 4-door, 6-passenger, 8-cylinder automobile, bought new at $7,900 and weighing 3,522 pounds. In most states, vehicle sales or excise taxes are also assessed on vehicles at the point of sale or titling. The table shows the percentage of fair market value assessed in each state. In some states the tax is capped at a dollar amount.

F-20 Tobacco Taxes: These data come from the same sources as those of Table F-18 but cover cigarette and related tobacco taxes. Over the last three years more than half of the states increased cigarette excise taxes. The rates shown on the table were in effect January, 2005.

F-21 State and Local Taxes on High-Income Families, 2004: The amounts shown are the liability to be faced by a hypothetical family with an adjusted yearly gross income of $150,000. The estimates are based on taxes incurred in the largest city in each state, as calculated by the District of Columbia Department of Finance and Revenue in *Tax Rates and Tax Burdens in the District of Columbia: A Nationwide Comparison.* The calculations for each state's largest city are not necessarily representative of statewide averages.

F-22 State and Local Taxes in the Largest City in Each State, 2004: These data show the costs of state and local taxes in the largest city in each state to typical families with incomes of $50,000. The calculations for each state's largest city are not necessarily representative of statewide averages. For the source of the data see the notes to Table F-21.

F-23 Progressivity of Major State and Local Taxes, 2004: These data compare the tax burdens as a percentage of income on households of two income levels ($25,000 and $150,000), using data from the analysis described in the notes to Table F-21. Low numbers indicate that the percentage paid by higher-income households is significantly higher than the percentage paid by low-income households, making the state and local tax structure "progressive." States with no personal income tax and high reliance on sales and property taxes, such as Nevada, have tax systems that can be called regressive. Their progressivity percentages over one hundred indicate that poorer households pay a larger percentage of their income on state and local taxes than do higher-income households.

F-24 State Estate Taxes, 2005: The federal government levies taxes on the estates of persons when they die. State governments also tax estates either directly by taxing the amount left to heirs (estate taxes) or by taxing the amounts received by particular heirs (inheritance taxes). Some of the state tax liability is allowed by the federal government as a 100 percent credit against federal taxes owed. This means that states can levy taxes up to the amount of the credit without making taxpayers pay more, so all states levy such "pick-up" taxes. Some states levy additional taxes, though the trend has been to eliminate the extra taxes out of fear that they encourage affluent older residents to move to other states. The table shows which states levy these extra taxes and the type of tax they used in 2005. For more detailed information on estate taxes in individual states go to the estate planning section of CCH's Financial Planning Toolkit on its Web site (www.finance.cch.com/text/c50s15d170.asp).

The table also shows how much revenue the states collected from pick-up taxes—$5.7 billion in fiscal year 2001—and ranks this amount per capita. These data show how the phase out and eventual repeal of the federal estate tax will affect budgets in states that do not "decouple" from federal changes. The revenue numbers, plus a discussion of how states can avoid losing this income, are found in a report from the Center on Budget and Policy Priorities titled, "States Can Retain Their Estate Taxes Even as the Federal Estate Tax is Phased Out" available on its Web site (www.cbpp.org).

F-25 State Taxes on Retirement Income, 2003: Many of the forty-one states that levy a broad-based personal income tax exempt some or all retirement income. Generally, the purpose is to aid those no longer earning income through engagement in work, and to attract, or retain, retired people.

The table shows how retirement income is treated by the fifty states and the District of Columbia. The exclusions shown are based on a taxpayer filing as an individual for income received in 2003. Ranges, such as that shown for Colorado ($20,000–$24,000) reflect either differences based on the age or the total income of the taxpayer, and, in a few cases, the type of job from which the taxpayer retired.

Four states tax Social Security benefits above a specific income threshold. Seven tax this income at the same level it is taxed by the federal government.

The table shows that states tend to be more generous in their tax treatment of public pensions and Social Security benefits than in their treatment of private pensions. Pennsylvania is the only state to fully exempt income from private pension plans. The table shows that the exclusion for private plans "varies" in four states. Each of these states has particular calculations based on the type of retirement plan. Alabama, for example, excludes income from defined benefit plans. Hawaii does this for contributory plans, while Illinois and Mississippi exempt income from "qualified" retirement plans. There are many details associated with each state's taxation policy on retirement income, both public and private. See the National Conference of State Legislature's "State Personal Income Taxes on Pensions and Retirement Income: Tax Year 2003" for more detailed information.

Revenues and Finances

"While the fiscal future is certainly brighter, it's not cloudless." This conclusion from a November 2005 survey by the National Conference of State Legislatures (NCSL) of legislative fiscal offices sums up the situation in most states at the start of 2006. Overall, revenues are above forecasts, but this fiscal good news is accompanied by ongoing uncertainties on the spending front.

Medicaid continues to consume budget dollars, although it looks as if states will be offered more flexibility in how they administer the program—including the option of increased premiums. Spending overruns in education and corrections will be an issue in some states. In addition, higher energy costs, already affecting consumers, will put some pressure on state budgets. Although energy-producing states, particularly Alaska and Louisiana, may see their revenues benefit from higher energy prices, many other states are looking for ways to offset energy costs. The NCSL report highlights how increased energy prices are having an effect on state finances:

- As many as seventeen states expect to consider or make supplemental appropriations to address higher fuel and heating costs. In Ohio, for instance, the governor asked that Temporary Assistance to Needy Families (TANF) funds be used to supplement the Home Energy Assistance Program.

- At least six states expect agencies will need to absorb extra energy costs into their existing budgets.

- At least three states are focusing on conservation measures. Georgia's governor, for example, has implemented a variety of programs including alternative work schedules and telecommuting for state employees.

- Two states—Ohio and South Carolina—will allow school districts to use school bus acquisition funds for fuel expenses.

- In at least two states higher energy costs will affect the budgets for transportation projects as the costs for certain oil-based products (like asphalt) rise.

G-1 State and Local Total Revenue, FY 2002

State	Total revenue $ (in millions)	Per capita total revenue $	Total revenue as a percentage of personal income	Rank per capita
Alabama	24,740	5,514	22.3	39
Alaska	6,993	10,862	34.7	1
Arizona	30,083	5,513	21.8	40
Arkansas	13,616	5,024	21.9	50
California	250,701	7,139	22.1	6
Colorado	25,657	5,693	17.0	35
Connecticut	24,831	7,176	17.0	5
Delaware	5,972	7,397	23.8	4
Florida	92,631	5,542	19.4	37
Georgia	46,166	5,393	19.3	44
Hawaii	7,452	5,986	21.2	26
Idaho	6,873	5,125	20.8	49
Illinois	73,588	5,840	17.9	32
Indiana	34,221	5,556	20.2	36
Iowa	17,601	5,993	21.9	25
Kansas	15,985	5,886	20.8	30
Kentucky	22,475	5,491	22.1	41
Louisiana	27,374	6,107	25.0	22
Maine	8,019	6,195	23.0	20
Maryland	33,468	6,132	17.6	21
Massachusetts	41,925	6,523	16.8	13
Michigan	63,099	6,278	21.4	18
Minnesota	35,131	6,999	21.5	7
Mississippi	15,905	5,538	25.3	38
Missouri	30,621	5,398	19.5	43
Montana	5,511	6,059	25.3	24
Nebraska	12,031	6,957	24.4	8
Nevada	12,809	5,893	20.2	29
New Hampshire	6,729	5,277	15.8	46
New Jersey	54,835	6,383	16.5	15
New Mexico	11,503	6,201	26.3	19
New York	170,982	8,925	25.2	2
North Carolina	48,597	5,841	21.6	31
North Dakota	4,227	6,665	25.7	10
Ohio	72,627	6,359	22.3	16
Oklahoma	19,161	5,484	21.7	42
Oregon	23,201	6,588	23.4	11
Pennsylvania	73,694	5,974	19.8	27
Rhode Island	6,863	6,415	21.5	14
South Carolina	24,985	6,083	24.6	23
South Dakota	3,964	5,209	19.5	48
Tennessee	33,483	5,776	21.7	33
Texas	114,018	5,235	18.5	47
Utah	13,789	5,953	24.8	28
Vermont	4,046	6,561	22.8	12
Virginia	38,780	5,317	16.7	45
Washington	42,124	6,941	21.8	9
West Virginia	11,345	6,296	27.3	17
Wisconsin	31,424	5,775	19.8	34
Wyoming	4,346	8,715	29.2	3
50 States	1,800,199	6,255	20.7	
DC	7,352	12,878	28.3	
United States	1,807,551	6,268	20.8	

Rank in order per capita	
1	Alaska
2	New York
3	Wyoming
4	Delaware
5	Connecticut
6	California
7	Minnesota
8	Nebraska
9	Washington
10	North Dakota
11	Oregon
12	Vermont
13	Massachusetts
14	Rhode Island
15	New Jersey
16	Ohio
17	West Virginia
18	Michigan
19	New Mexico
20	Maine
21	Maryland
22	Louisiana
23	South Carolina
24	Montana
25	Iowa
26	Hawaii
27	Pennsylvania
28	Utah
29	Nevada
30	Kansas
31	North Carolina
32	Illinois
33	Tennessee
34	Wisconsin
35	Colorado
36	Indiana
37	Florida
38	Mississippi
39	Alabama
40	Arizona
41	Kentucky
42	Oklahoma
43	Missouri
44	Georgia
45	Virginia
46	New Hampshire
47	Texas
48	South Dakota
49	Idaho
50	Arkansas

G-2 State and Local General Revenue, FY 2002

State	General revenue $ (in millions)	Per capita general revenue $	General revenue as a percentage of personal income	Rank per capita
Alabama	23,741	5,292	21.4	35
Alaska	7,209	11,198	35.8	1
Arizona	25,524	4,678	18.5	50
Arkansas	13,259	4,892	21.3	48
California	226,605	6,453	20.0	7
Colorado	26,041	5,779	17.3	22
Connecticut	22,805	6,590	15.6	6
Delaware	5,600	6,936	22.3	4
Florida	86,663	5,185	18.1	39
Georgia	44,360	5,182	18.5	40
Hawaii	7,429	5,967	21.1	17
Idaho	6,620	4,936	20.1	47
Illinois	69,098	5,484	16.8	29
Indiana	32,363	5,254	19.1	36
Iowa	16,871	5,745	21.0	24
Kansas	14,635	5,389	19.0	31
Kentucky	21,231	5,187	20.9	38
Louisiana	26,049	5,811	23.8	21
Maine	8,077	6,239	23.1	11
Maryland	32,319	5,921	17.0	18
Massachusetts	39,002	6,068	15.6	14
Michigan	57,942	5,765	19.6	23
Minnesota	33,193	6,613	20.3	5
Mississippi	15,293	5,325	24.4	33
Missouri	29,062	5,123	18.5	44
Montana	5,122	5,632	23.5	27
Nebraska	9,821	5,680	19.9	26
Nevada	11,417	5,253	18.0	37
New Hampshire	6,406	5,024	15.1	45
New Jersey	55,256	6,432	16.6	8
New Mexico	10,868	5,858	24.8	19
New York	155,541	8,119	22.9	3
North Carolina	44,165	5,308	19.6	34
North Dakota	3,994	6,299	24.3	9
Ohio	65,568	5,741	20.1	25
Oklahoma	18,061	5,170	20.5	42
Oregon	21,625	6,141	21.8	13
Pennsylvania	71,961	5,834	19.3	20
Rhode Island	6,637	6,205	20.8	12
South Carolina	21,239	5,171	20.9	41
South Dakota	3,902	5,127	19.1	43
Tennessee	27,484	4,741	17.8	49
Texas	109,128	5,011	17.7	46
Utah	12,499	5,396	22.5	30
Vermont	3,857	6,256	21.7	10
Virginia	39,026	5,351	16.8	32
Washington	36,345	5,989	18.8	15
West Virginia	10,111	5,611	24.3	28
Wisconsin	32,555	5,983	20.5	16
Wyoming	4,237	8,496	28.4	2
50 States	1,677,816	5,830	19.3	
DC	6,922	12,125	26.7	
United States	1,684,738	5,842	19.4	

Rank in order per capita	
1	Alaska
2	Wyoming
3	New York
4	Delaware
5	Minnesota
6	Connecticut
7	California
8	New Jersey
9	North Dakota
10	Vermont
11	Maine
12	Rhode Island
13	Oregon
14	Massachusetts
15	Washington
16	Wisconsin
17	Hawaii
18	Maryland
19	New Mexico
20	Pennsylvania
21	Louisiana
22	Colorado
23	Michigan
24	Iowa
25	Ohio
26	Nebraska
27	Montana
28	West Virginia
29	Illinois
30	Utah
31	Kansas
32	Virginia
33	Mississippi
34	North Carolina
35	Alabama
36	Indiana
37	Nevada
38	Kentucky
39	Florida
40	Georgia
41	South Carolina
42	Oklahoma
43	South Dakota
44	Missouri
45	New Hampshire
46	Texas
47	Idaho
48	Arkansas
49	Tennessee
50	Arizona

G-3 State and Local "Own-Source" General Revenue, FY 2002

State	"Own-source"general revenue $ (in millions)	Per capita "own-source" general revenue $	"Own-source" general revenue as a percentage of personal income	Rank per capita
Alabama	17,478	3,896	15.7	40
Alaska	5,420	8,418	26.9	1
Arizona	19,805	3,630	14.3	47
Arkansas	9,613	3,547	15.5	49
California	178,355	5,079	15.7	9
Colorado	21,772	4,831	14.5	11
Connecticut	18,766	5,423	12.8	5
Delaware	4,641	5,748	18.5	4
Florida	71,707	4,290	15.0	29
Georgia	35,002	4,089	14.6	34
Hawaii	5,881	4,724	16.7	15
Idaho	5,204	3,881	15.8	42
Illinois	56,382	4,475	13.7	26
Indiana	26,080	4,234	15.4	32
Iowa	13,245	4,510	16.5	21
Kansas	11,537	4,248	15.0	31
Kentucky	15,817	3,865	15.6	44
Louisiana	19,564	4,364	17.9	27
Maine	6,176	4,771	17.7	14
Maryland	26,391	4,835	13.9	10
Massachusetts	32,826	5,107	13.2	8
Michigan	45,398	4,517	15.4	20
Minnesota	27,105	5,400	16.6	6
Mississippi	10,667	3,715	17.0	46
Missouri	21,733	3,831	13.8	45
Montana	3,532	3,883	16.2	41
Nebraska	7,848	4,539	15.9	17
Nevada	9,785	4,502	15.4	22
New Hampshire	5,110	4,008	12.0	36
New Jersey	46,307	5,391	13.9	7
New Mexico	7,744	4,175	17.7	33
New York	119,356	6,230	17.6	2
North Carolina	33,924	4,077	15.1	35
North Dakota	2,838	4,475	17.3	25
Ohio	51,704	4,527	15.9	19
Oklahoma	13,648	3,906	15.5	39
Oregon	15,187	4,313	15.3	28
Pennsylvania	55,935	4,535	15.0	18
Rhode Island	4,871	4,554	15.3	16
South Carolina	15,907	3,873	15.6	43
South Dakota	2,752	3,616	13.5	48
Tennessee	19,880	3,429	12.9	50
Texas	86,214	3,958	14.0	37
Utah	9,886	4,268	17.8	30
Vermont	2,770	4,493	15.6	24
Virginia	32,791	4,496	14.1	23
Washington	29,303	4,828	15.2	12
West Virginia	7,112	3,947	17.1	38
Wisconsin	26,100	4,797	16.4	13
Wyoming	3,050	6,115	20.5	3
50 States	1,320,121	4,587	15.2	
DC	4,082	7,151	15.7	
United States	1,324,203	4,592	15.2	

Rank in order per capita	
1	Alaska
2	New York
3	Wyoming
4	Delaware
5	Connecticut
6	Minnesota
7	New Jersey
8	Massachusetts
9	California
10	Maryland
11	Colorado
12	Washington
13	Wisconsin
14	Maine
15	Hawaii
16	Rhode Island
17	Nebraska
18	Pennsylvania
19	Ohio
20	Michigan
21	Iowa
22	Nevada
23	Virginia
24	Vermont
25	North Dakota
26	Illinois
27	Louisiana
28	Oregon
29	Florida
30	Utah
31	Kansas
32	Indiana
33	New Mexico
34	Georgia
35	North Carolina
36	New Hampshire
37	Texas
38	West Virginia
39	Oklahoma
40	Alabama
41	Montana
42	Idaho
43	South Carolina
44	Kentucky
45	Missouri
46	Mississippi
47	Arizona
48	South Dakota
49	Arkansas
50	Tennessee

Note: Numbers that appear to be identical are rounded and vary slightly in actual value. The rankings reflect the actual values before rounding. See the introduction for more details.

G-4 State and Local Non-Tax "Own-Source" Revenue, FY 2002

State	Non-tax "own-source" revenue $ (in millions)	Per capita non-tax "own-source" revenue $	Non-tax "own-source" revenue as a percentage of personal income	Rank per capita
Alabama	7,759	1,729	7.0	7
Alaska	3,350	5,203	16.6	1
Arizona	5,385	987	3.9	50
Arkansas	3,154	1,164	5.1	48
California	57,939	1,650	5.1	11
Colorado	7,872	1,747	5.2	6
Connecticut	3,641	1,052	2.5	49
Delaware	1,954	2,420	7.8	3
Florida	26,867	1,608	5.6	14
Georgia	10,944	1,278	4.6	37
Hawaii	1,642	1,319	4.7	34
Idaho	1,913	1,427	5.8	26
Illinois	14,812	1,176	3.6	45
Indiana	9,093	1,476	5.4	21
Iowa	4,915	1,673	6.1	9
Kansas	3,562	1,312	4.6	35
Kentucky	5,037	1,231	5.0	40
Louisiana	7,382	1,647	6.7	12
Maine	1,635	1,263	4.7	38
Maryland	6,517	1,194	3.4	42
Massachusetts	8,930	1,389	3.6	28
Michigan	14,754	1,468	5.0	22
Minnesota	8,649	1,723	5.3	8
Mississippi	4,144	1,443	6.6	25
Missouri	6,610	1,165	4.2	47
Montana	1,397	1,536	6.4	18
Nebraska	2,532	1,464	5.1	23
Nevada	3,352	1,542	5.3	17
New Hampshire	1,511	1,185	3.6	44
New Jersey	11,678	1,359	3.5	33
New Mexico	2,867	1,545	6.5	16
New York	30,477	1,591	4.5	15
North Carolina	11,348	1,364	5.0	31
North Dakota	1,109	1,749	6.7	5
Ohio	15,539	1,361	4.8	32
Oklahoma	4,866	1,393	5.5	27
Oregon	6,184	1,756	6.2	4
Pennsylvania	18,308	1,484	4.9	20
Rhode Island	1,249	1,168	3.9	46
South Carolina	6,155	1,499	6.0	19
South Dakota	910	1,196	4.5	41
Tennessee	6,906	1,191	4.5	43
Texas	27,233	1,250	4.4	39
Utah	3,860	1,667	6.9	10
Vermont	805	1,306	4.5	36
Virginia	10,660	1,462	4.6	24
Washington	9,790	1,613	5.1	13
West Virginia	2,471	1,371	5.9	30
Wisconsin	7,490	1,377	4.7	29
Wyoming	1,231	2,469	8.3	2
50 States	418,388	1,454	4.8	
DC	854	1,496	3.3	
United States	419,242	1,454	4.8	

Rank in order per capita	
1	Alaska
2	Wyoming
3	Delaware
4	Oregon
5	North Dakota
6	Colorado
7	Alabama
8	Minnesota
9	Iowa
10	Utah
11	California
12	Louisiana
13	Washington
14	Florida
15	New York
16	New Mexico
17	Nevada
18	Montana
19	South Carolina
20	Pennsylvania
21	Indiana
22	Michigan
23	Nebraska
24	Virginia
25	Mississippi
26	Idaho
27	Oklahoma
28	Massachusetts
29	Wisconsin
30	West Virginia
31	North Carolina
32	Ohio
33	New Jersey
34	Hawaii
35	Kansas
36	Vermont
37	Georgia
38	Maine
39	Texas
40	Kentucky
41	South Dakota
42	Maryland
43	Tennessee
44	New Hampshire
45	Illinois
46	Rhode Island
47	Missouri
48	Arkansas
49	Connecticut
50	Arizona

Note: Numbers that appear to be identical are rounded and vary slightly in actual value. The rankings reflect the actual values before rounding. See the introduction for more details.

G-5 State and Local Total Expenditures, FY 2002

State	Total expenditures $ (in millions)	Per capita total expenditures $	Total expenditures as a percentage of personal income	Rank per capita
Alabama	28,532	6,359	25.7	31
Alaska	9,397	14,597	46.7	1
Arizona	31,308	5,738	22.7	46
Arkansas	14,570	5,376	23.5	50
California	292,412	8,327	25.7	4
Colorado	31,891	7,077	21.2	16
Connecticut	27,592	7,973	18.9	7
Delaware	5,947	7,366	23.7	13
Florida	99,307	5,942	20.8	43
Georgia	52,310	6,111	21.8	37
Hawaii	9,402	7,552	26.8	10
Idaho	7,565	5,641	22.9	47
Illinois	87,402	6,936	21.3	19
Indiana	36,302	5,894	21.5	44
Iowa	19,294	6,570	24.1	28
Kansas	16,718	6,156	21.7	36
Kentucky	24,839	6,069	24.5	38
Louisiana	27,664	6,171	25.3	35
Maine	8,677	6,703	24.9	24
Maryland	35,577	6,518	18.7	29
Massachusetts	51,146	7,957	20.5	8
Michigan	69,533	6,918	23.6	20
Minnesota	40,516	8,071	24.8	6
Mississippi	17,285	6,019	27.5	39
Missouri	33,036	5,824	21.0	45
Montana	5,616	6,175	25.8	34
Nebraska	12,492	7,224	25.3	14
Nevada	13,971	6,428	22.0	30
New Hampshire	7,066	5,542	16.6	49
New Jersey	64,289	7,484	19.3	11
New Mexico	12,689	6,840	29.0	23
New York	198,536	10,363	29.2	2
North Carolina	51,839	6,230	23.0	33
North Dakota	4,190	6,608	25.5	27
Ohio	79,972	7,002	24.5	17
Oklahoma	20,776	5,947	23.5	42
Oregon	27,731	7,875	28.0	9
Pennsylvania	86,262	6,993	23.1	18
Rhode Island	7,928	7,411	24.9	12
South Carolina	28,106	6,843	27.6	21
South Dakota	4,276	5,618	21.0	48
Tennessee	36,638	6,320	23.7	32
Texas	129,874	5,963	21.0	41
Utah	15,523	6,702	27.9	25
Vermont	4,218	6,841	23.7	22
Virginia	43,688	5,990	18.8	40
Washington	50,431	8,310	26.1	5
West Virginia	11,930	6,621	28.7	26
Wisconsin	39,262	7,216	24.7	15
Wyoming	4,337	8,697	29.1	3
50 States	2,039,862	7,088	23.5	
DC	7,832	13,719	30.2	
United States	2,047,694	7,101	23.5	

Rank in order per capita	
1	Alaska
2	New York
3	Wyoming
4	California
5	Washington
6	Minnesota
7	Connecticut
8	Massachusetts
9	Oregon
10	Hawaii
11	New Jersey
12	Rhode Island
13	Delaware
14	Nebraska
15	Wisconsin
16	Colorado
17	Ohio
18	Pennsylvania
19	Illinois
20	Michigan
21	South Carolina
22	Vermont
23	New Mexico
24	Maine
25	Utah
26	West Virginia
27	North Dakota
28	Iowa
29	Maryland
30	Nevada
31	Alabama
32	Tennessee
33	North Carolina
34	Montana
35	Louisiana
36	Kansas
37	Georgia
38	Kentucky
39	Mississippi
40	Virginia
41	Texas
42	Oklahoma
43	Florida
44	Indiana
45	Missouri
46	Arizona
47	Idaho
48	South Dakota
49	New Hampshire
50	Arkansas

G-6 State and Local General Expenditures, FY 2002

State	General expenditures $ (in millions)	General expenditures as a percentage of personal income	Rank by percentage
Alabama	24,606	22.2	15
Alaska	8,443	41.9	1
Arizona	25,252	18.3	40
Arkansas	13,068	21.0	23
California	235,486	20.7	24
Colorado	27,099	18.0	43
Connecticut	24,199	16.6	48
Delaware	5,357	21.4	20
Florida	87,082	18.2	41
Georgia	44,951	18.8	36
Hawaii	8,289	23.6	8
Idaho	6,804	20.6	25
Illinois	73,819	18.0	44
Indiana	32,796	19.4	33
Iowa	17,186	21.4	17
Kansas	14,876	19.3	34
Kentucky	21,591	21.3	21
Louisiana	24,317	22.2	14
Maine	7,948	22.8	13
Maryland	31,796	16.7	47
Massachusetts	42,347	17.0	45
Michigan	60,723	20.6	27
Minnesota	34,933	21.4	19
Mississippi	15,384	24.5	4
Missouri	29,045	18.4	39
Montana	5,051	23.2	11
Nebraska	9,745	19.7	31
Nevada	11,766	18.5	38
New Hampshire	6,343	14.9	50
New Jersey	54,387	16.4	49
New Mexico	11,436	26.1	2
New York	161,130	23.7	5
North Carolina	44,540	19.8	30
North Dakota	3,886	23.6	7
Ohio	67,047	20.6	28
Oklahoma	18,154	20.6	26
Oregon	22,990	23.2	10
Pennsylvania	73,312	19.7	32
Rhode Island	6,761	21.2	22
South Carolina	23,820	23.4	9
South Dakota	3,885	19.1	35
Tennessee	28,952	18.7	37
Texas	111,604	18.1	42
Utah	12,861	23.1	12
Vermont	3,805	21.4	18
Virginia	39,267	16.9	46
Washington	38,646	20.0	29
West Virginia	9,848	23.7	6
Wisconsin	34,003	21.4	16
Wyoming	3,853	25.8	3
50 States	1,724,489	19.9	
DC	6,180	23.8	
United States	1,730,669	19.9	

Rank in order by percentage	
1	Alaska
2	New Mexico
3	Wyoming
4	Mississippi
5	New York
6	West Virginia
7	North Dakota
8	Hawaii
9	South Carolina
10	Oregon
11	Montana
12	Utah
13	Maine
14	Louisiana
15	Alabama
16	Wisconsin
17	Iowa
18	Vermont
19	Minnesota
20	Delaware
21	Kentucky
22	Rhode Island
23	Arkansas
24	California
25	Idaho
26	Oklahoma
27	Michigan
28	Ohio
29	Washington
30	North Carolina
31	Nebraska
32	Pennsylvania
33	Indiana
34	Kansas
35	South Dakota
36	Georgia
37	Tennessee
38	Nevada
39	Missouri
40	Arizona
41	Florida
42	Texas
43	Colorado
44	Illinois
45	Massachusetts
46	Virginia
47	Maryland
48	Connecticut
49	New Jersey
50	New Hampshire

Note: Numbers that appear to be identical are rounded and vary slightly in actual value. The rankings reflect the actual values before rounding. See the introduction for more details.

G-7 State and Local General Expenditures Per Capita, FY 2002

State	State and local general expenditure per capita $	State general expenditure per capita $	Local general expenditure per capita $	Rank by state and local general expenditure per capita
Alabama	5,484	2,689	2,795	30
Alaska	13,115	8,771	4,344	1
Arizona	4,628	1,700	2,928	50
Arkansas	4,822	2,791	2,031	49
California	6,706	2,379	4,327	6
Colorado	6,013	2,300	3,713	20
Connecticut	6,993	3,988	3,005	4
Delaware	6,635	4,224	2,411	8
Florida	5,210	1,988	3,222	41
Georgia	5,251	2,164	3,087	40
Hawaii	6,659	5,264	1,395	7
Idaho	5,073	2,399	2,674	46
Illinois	5,858	2,348	3,510	23
Indiana	5,325	2,278	3,047	38
Iowa	5,852	2,761	3,091	24
Kansas	5,477	2,447	3,030	31
Kentucky	5,275	3,131	2,144	39
Louisiana	5,425	2,676	2,749	33
Maine	6,140	3,600	2,540	17
Maryland	5,826	2,834	2,991	25
Massachusetts	6,588	3,452	3,136	9
Michigan	6,042	2,464	3,578	19
Minnesota	6,959	3,029	3,930	5
Mississippi	5,357	2,788	2,569	36
Missouri	5,120	2,404	2,717	44
Montana	5,554	3,160	2,394	28
Nebraska	5,636	2,544	3,092	27
Nevada	5,414	1,753	3,661	34
New Hampshire	4,975	2,351	2,623	48
New Jersey	6,331	2,749	3,582	12
New Mexico	6,165	3,474	2,690	16
New York	8,411	3,004	5,407	2
North Carolina	5,353	2,414	2,939	37
North Dakota	6,129	3,512	2,616	18
Ohio	5,870	2,391	3,479	22
Oklahoma	5,196	2,727	2,469	42
Oregon	6,528	3,030	3,498	10
Pennsylvania	5,943	2,786	3,158	21
Rhode Island	6,320	3,827	2,494	13
South Carolina	5,800	3,118	2,681	26
South Dakota	5,104	2,691	2,413	45
Tennessee	4,994	2,417	2,577	47
Texas	5,124	2,070	3,054	43
Utah	5,552	3,010	2,542	29
Vermont	6,171	3,847	2,324	15
Virginia	5,384	2,355	3,029	35
Washington	6,368	3,024	3,344	11
West Virginia	5,465	3,389	2,076	32
Wisconsin	6,249	2,499	3,751	14
Wyoming	7,727	3,277	4,450	3
50 States	5,992	2,587	3,405	
DC	10,824	n/a	10,824	
United States	6,002	2,582	3,420	

Rank in order by state and local per capita	
1	Alaska
2	New York
3	Wyoming
4	Connecticut
5	Minnesota
6	California
7	Hawaii
8	Delaware
9	Massachusetts
10	Oregon
11	Washington
12	New Jersey
13	Rhode Island
14	Wisconsin
15	Vermont
16	New Mexico
17	Maine
18	North Dakota
19	Michigan
20	Colorado
21	Pennsylvania
22	Ohio
23	Illinois
24	Iowa
25	Maryland
26	South Carolina
27	Nebraska
28	Montana
29	Utah
30	Alabama
31	Kansas
32	West Virginia
33	Louisiana
34	Nevada
35	Virginia
36	Mississippi
37	North Carolina
38	Indiana
39	Kentucky
40	Georgia
41	Florida
42	Oklahoma
43	Texas
44	Missouri
45	South Dakota
46	Idaho
47	Tennessee
48	New Hampshire
49	Arkansas
50	Arizona

G-8 Percentage Change in State and Local Expenditures, FY 1997–2002

State	Percentage change	Rank
Alabama	42.8	8
Alaska	28.0	48
Arizona	42.1	10
Arkansas	38.8	20
California	48.3	5
Colorado	55.2	1
Connecticut	36.1	32
Delaware	35.9	33
Florida	37.3	29
Georgia	37.6	27
Hawaii	23.6	50
Idaho	39.6	13
Illinois	39.0	19
Indiana	40.4	12
Iowa	34.0	36
Kansas	34.8	35
Kentucky	38.5	21
Louisiana	29.2	44
Maine	37.7	26
Maryland	39.3	15
Massachusetts	34.0	37
Michigan	32.5	41
Minnesota	39.1	16
Mississippi	38.5	22
Missouri	42.0	11
Montana	29.2	45
Nebraska	31.2	42
Nevada	48.7	4
New Hampshire	28.6	46
New Jersey	33.1	40
New Mexico	36.5	30
New York	28.6	47
North Carolina	42.7	9
North Dakota	29.5	43
Ohio	39.4	14
Oklahoma	49.1	3
Oregon	39.0	18
Pennsylvania	38.5	23
Rhode Island	39.0	17
South Carolina	49.4	2
South Dakota	33.4	39
Tennessee	36.3	31
Texas	46.0	6
Utah	42.9	7
Vermont	37.3	28
Virginia	37.7	25
Washington	34.0	38
West Virginia	27.2	49
Wisconsin	35.2	34
Wyoming	37.7	24
50 States	38.7	
DC	42.5	
United States	38.7	

Rank in order by percentage	
1	Colorado
2	South Carolina
3	Oklahoma
4	Nevada
5	California
6	Texas
7	Utah
8	Alabama
9	North Carolina
10	Arizona
11	Missouri
12	Indiana
13	Idaho
14	Ohio
15	Maryland
16	Minnesota
17	Rhode Island
18	Oregon
19	Illinois
20	Arkansas
21	Kentucky
22	Mississippi
23	Pennsylvania
24	Wyoming
25	Virginia
26	Maine
27	Georgia
28	Vermont
29	Florida
30	New Mexico
31	Tennessee
32	Connecticut
33	Delaware
34	Wisconsin
35	Kansas
36	Iowa
37	Massachusetts
38	Washington
39	South Dakota
40	New Jersey
41	Michigan
42	Nebraska
43	North Dakota
44	Louisiana
45	Montana
46	New Hampshire
47	New York
48	Alaska
49	West Virginia
50	Hawaii

Note: Numbers that appear to be identical are rounded and vary slightly in actual value. The rankings reflect the actual values before rounding. See the introduction for more details.

G-9 State Government General Revenue, FY 2003

State	State government general revenue $ (in millions)	State government general revenue per capita $	Rank per capita
Alabama	16,575	3,680	33
Alaska	6,099	9,407	1
Arizona	16,890	3,027	47
Arkansas	10,731	3,934	24
California	147,998	4,173	19
Colorado	13,999	3,078	45
Connecticut	16,217	4,651	11
Delaware	4,721	5,770	3
Florida	49,584	2,917	50
Georgia	26,320	3,034	46
Hawaii	6,377	5,107	6
Idaho	4,617	3,377	41
Illinois	40,816	3,227	44
Indiana	21,675	3,496	39
Iowa	11,097	3,772	27
Kansas	9,752	3,579	36
Kentucky	16,526	4,013	22
Louisiana	18,276	4,067	21
Maine	6,093	4,654	10
Maryland	20,539	3,726	29
Massachusetts	27,012	4,207	18
Michigan	43,010	4,266	17
Minnesota	23,072	4,556	13
Mississippi	11,873	4,119	20
Missouri	19,135	3,346	42
Montana	3,968	4,321	15
Nebraska	6,750	3,885	25
Nevada	6,548	2,921	49
New Hampshire	4,566	3,543	37
New Jersey	38,819	4,492	14
New Mexico	9,007	4,795	8
New York	98,842	5,145	5
North Carolina	30,171	3,583	35
North Dakota	3,036	4,792	9
Ohio	42,422	3,709	32
Oklahoma	12,903	3,680	34
Oregon	13,283	3,727	28
Pennsylvania	46,905	3,792	26
Rhode Island	5,172	4,806	7
South Carolina	15,409	3,714	31
South Dakota	2,683	3,507	38
Tennessee	19,278	3,298	43
Texas	66,458	3,007	48
Utah	8,759	3,724	30
Vermont	3,352	5,413	4
Virginia	25,528	3,466	40
Washington	24,134	3,936	23
West Virginia	8,317	4,591	12
Wisconsin	23,433	4,281	16
Wyoming	3,603	7,176	2
50 States	1,112,349	3,833	
DC	n/a	n/a	
United States	1,112,349	3,833	

Rank in order per capita	
1	Alaska
2	Wyoming
3	Delaware
4	Vermont
5	New York
6	Hawaii
7	Rhode Island
8	New Mexico
9	North Dakota
10	Maine
11	Connecticut
12	West Virginia
13	Minnesota
14	New Jersey
15	Montana
16	Wisconsin
17	Michigan
18	Massachusetts
19	California
20	Mississippi
21	Louisiana
22	Kentucky
23	Washington
24	Arkansas
25	Nebraska
26	Pennsylvania
27	Iowa
28	Oregon
29	Maryland
30	Utah
31	South Carolina
32	Ohio
33	Alabama
34	Oklahoma
35	North Carolina
36	Kansas
37	New Hampshire
38	South Dakota
39	Indiana
40	Virginia
41	Idaho
42	Missouri
43	Tennessee
44	Illinois
45	Colorado
46	Georgia
47	Arizona
48	Texas
49	Nevada
50	Florida

Note: Numbers that appear to be identical are rounded and vary slightly in actual value. The rankings reflect the actual values before rounding. See the introduction for more details.

G-10 State Government General Spending, FY 2003

State	State government general spending $ (in millions)	State government general spending per capita	Rank per capita
Alabama	17,010	3,777	32
Alaska	7,111	10,970	1
Arizona	17,503	3,137	47
Arkansas	11,081	4,062	23
California	173,158	4,883	10
Colorado	14,793	3,253	46
Connecticut	17,885	5,129	8
Delaware	4,376	5,349	5
Florida	50,218	2,954	50
Georgia	29,291	3,376	43
Hawaii	6,852	5,487	4
Idaho	4,759	3,482	39
Illinois	43,954	3,475	41
Indiana	21,295	3,435	42
Iowa	11,715	3,982	25
Kansas	9,843	3,613	36
Kentucky	16,858	4,093	22
Louisiana	16,323	3,632	34
Maine	6,072	4,638	12
Maryland	21,789	3,953	27
Massachusetts	27,871	4,341	17
Michigan	44,522	4,416	14
Minnesota	25,384	5,012	9
Mississippi	12,095	4,196	21
Missouri	19,137	3,346	44
Montana	3,917	4,266	18
Nebraska	6,494	3,737	33
Nevada	6,706	2,991	49
New Hampshire	4,592	3,563	38
New Jersey	34,860	4,034	24
New Mexico	9,714	5,171	7
New York	101,825	5,300	6
North Carolina	30,428	3,613	35
North Dakota	2,898	4,575	13
Ohio	44,614	3,901	29
Oklahoma	13,306	3,795	31
Oregon	14,130	3,964	26
Pennsylvania	48,252	3,901	30
Rhode Island	5,026	4,671	11
South Carolina	17,685	4,263	19
South Dakota	2,663	3,482	40
Tennessee	19,387	3,317	45
Texas	66,804	3,022	48
Utah	9,176	3,901	28
Vermont	3,594	5,803	2
Virginia	26,289	3,569	37
Washington	26,021	4,244	20
West Virginia	7,998	4,415	15
Wisconsin	23,813	4,350	16
Wyoming	2,881	5,739	3
50 States	1,163,968	4,010	
DC	n/a	n/a	
United States	1,163,968	4,010	

Rank in order per capita	
1	Alaska
2	Vermont
3	Wyoming
4	Hawaii
5	Delaware
6	New York
7	New Mexico
8	Connecticut
9	Minnesota
10	California
11	Rhode Island
12	Maine
13	North Dakota
14	Michigan
15	West Virginia
16	Wisconsin
17	Massachusetts
18	Montana
19	South Carolina
20	Washington
21	Mississippi
22	Kentucky
23	Arkansas
24	New Jersey
25	Iowa
26	Oregon
27	Maryland
28	Utah
29	Ohio
30	Pennsylvania
31	Oklahoma
32	Alabama
33	Nebraska
34	Louisiana
35	North Carolina
36	Kansas
37	Virginia
38	New Hampshire
39	Idaho
40	South Dakota
41	Illinois
42	Indiana
43	Georgia
44	Missouri
45	Tennessee
46	Colorado
47	Arizona
48	Texas
49	Nevada
50	Florida

Note: Numbers that appear to be identical are rounded and vary slightly in actual value. The rankings reflect the actual values before rounding. See the introduction for more details.

G-11 State Government General Fund Spending, FY 2003

State	State government general fund spending $ (in millions)	As a percentage of personal income	Rank by percentage
Alabama	16,012	13.5	24
Alaska	6,496	30.1	2
Arizona	19,550	13.0	27
Arkansas	12,631	19.1	7
California	161,512	13.6	22
Colorado	13,213	8.4	49
Connecticut	20,533	13.6	23
Delaware	5,825	21.4	5
Florida	48,560	9.5	45
Georgia	27,981	11.0	39
Hawaii	8,029	20.9	6
Idaho	4,359	12.5	33
Illinois	37,653	9.0	48
Indiana	19,288	10.8	41
Iowa	13,480	16.1	11
Kansas	10,083	12.5	32
Kentucky	18,376	16.9	10
Louisiana	16,989	14.5	17
Maine	6,064	16.1	12
Maryland	23,037	11.2	38
Massachusetts	26,058	10.3	44
Michigan	39,844	12.7	31
Minnesota	23,099	13.4	25
Mississippi	11,708	17.4	9
Missouri	17,460	10.5	42
Montana	3,649	15.4	14
Nebraska	6,809	12.9	28
Nevada	5,756	8.2	50
New Hampshire	4,065	9.1	47
New Jersey	36,217	10.5	43
New Mexico	11,464	24.0	4
New York	89,056	12.8	29
North Carolina	28,780	12.1	36
North Dakota	2,520	13.9	19
Ohio	46,905	13.7	21
Oklahoma	12,922	13.9	20
Oregon	15,086	14.7	16
Pennsylvania	47,292	12.1	37
Rhode Island	5,509	16.0	13
South Carolina	16,704	15.4	15
South Dakota	2,861	13.2	26
Tennessee	20,275	12.2	35
Texas	59,057	9.2	46
Utah	7,542	12.7	30
Vermont	2,674	14.1	18
Virginia	26,925	10.8	40
Washington	25,137	12.3	34
West Virginia	15,678	35.1	1
Wisconsin	31,770	18.9	8
Wyoming	4,201	26.0	3
50 States	1,136,694	12.5	
DC	n/a	n/a	
United States	1,136,694	12.4	

Rank in order by percentage	
1	West Virginia
2	Alaska
3	Wyoming
4	New Mexico
5	Delaware
6	Hawaii
7	Arkansas
8	Wisconsin
9	Mississippi
10	Kentucky
11	Iowa
12	Maine
13	Rhode Island
14	Montana
15	South Carolina
16	Oregon
17	Louisiana
18	Vermont
19	North Dakota
20	Oklahoma
21	Ohio
22	California
23	Connecticut
24	Alabama
25	Minnesota
26	South Dakota
27	Arizona
28	Nebraska
29	New York
30	Utah
31	Michigan
32	Kansas
33	Idaho
34	Washington
35	Tennessee
36	North Carolina
37	Pennsylvania
38	Maryland
39	Georgia
40	Virginia
41	Indiana
42	Missouri
43	New Jersey
44	Massachusetts
45	Florida
46	Texas
47	New Hampshire
48	Illinois
49	Colorado
50	Nevada

Note: Numbers that appear to be identical are rounded and vary slightly in actual value. The rankings reflect the actual values before rounding. See the introduction for more details.

G-12 State and Local Debt, FY 2002

State	State and local debt $ (in millions)	State and local debt per capita $	State and local debt as a percentage of personal income	Rank per capita
Alabama	19,057	4,248	17.2	41
Alaska	8,646	13,429	42.9	1
Arizona	26,606	4,876	19.3	27
Arkansas	8,754	3,230	14.1	49
California	209,371	5,962	18.4	15
Colorado	26,678	5,920	17.7	16
Connecticut	27,767	8,024	19.0	4
Delaware	5,533	6,853	22.1	8
Florida	90,276	5,401	18.9	22
Georgia	34,301	4,007	14.3	43
Hawaii	8,448	6,786	24.0	11
Idaho	3,985	2,972	12.1	50
Illinois	80,936	6,423	19.7	13
Indiana	24,071	3,908	14.2	44
Iowa	9,494	3,233	11.8	48
Kansas	12,313	4,534	16.0	36
Kentucky	28,994	7,084	28.6	7
Louisiana	21,009	4,687	19.2	31
Maine	6,346	4,903	18.2	26
Maryland	25,663	4,702	13.5	30
Massachusetts	65,322	10,162	26.2	3
Michigan	54,195	5,392	18.4	23
Minnesota	32,010	6,377	19.6	14
Mississippi	9,934	3,459	15.8	47
Missouri	24,244	4,274	15.4	40
Montana	3,963	4,357	18.2	39
Nebraska	7,906	4,572	16.0	34
Nevada	15,773	7,257	24.8	6
New Hampshire	7,221	5,663	17.0	18
New Jersey	57,590	6,704	17.3	12
New Mexico	8,603	4,638	19.7	32
New York	197,195	10,293	29.0	2
North Carolina	33,461	4,022	14.8	42
North Dakota	2,905	4,581	17.7	33
Ohio	51,344	4,495	15.8	37
Oklahoma	12,508	3,580	14.2	46
Oregon	18,827	5,346	19.0	24
Pennsylvania	83,809	6,794	22.5	10
Rhode Island	7,312	6,835	22.9	9
South Carolina	22,873	5,569	22.5	21
South Dakota	3,451	4,534	16.9	35
Tennessee	21,128	3,644	13.7	45
Texas	122,810	5,639	19.9	19
Utah	13,250	5,720	23.8	17
Vermont	3,028	4,910	17.0	25
Virginia	35,422	4,857	15.2	28
Washington	45,561	7,507	23.6	5
West Virginia	8,085	4,487	19.5	38
Wisconsin	30,327	5,574	19.1	20
Wyoming	2,388	4,788	16.0	29
50 States	1,680,692	5,840	19.4	
DC	5,436	9,522	21.0	
United States	1,686,128	5,847	19.4	

Rank in order per capita	
1	Alaska
2	New York
3	Massachusetts
4	Connecticut
5	Washington
6	Nevada
7	Kentucky
8	Delaware
9	Rhode Island
10	Pennsylvania
11	Hawaii
12	New Jersey
13	Illinois
14	Minnesota
15	California
16	Colorado
17	Utah
18	New Hampshire
19	Texas
20	Wisconsin
21	South Carolina
22	Florida
23	Michigan
24	Oregon
25	Vermont
26	Maine
27	Arizona
28	Virginia
29	Wyoming
30	Maryland
31	Louisiana
32	New Mexico
33	North Dakota
34	Nebraska
35	South Dakota
36	Kansas
37	Ohio
38	West Virginia
39	Montana
40	Missouri
41	Alabama
42	North Carolina
43	Georgia
44	Indiana
45	Tennessee
46	Oklahoma
47	Mississippi
48	Iowa
49	Arkansas
50	Idaho

Note: Numbers that appear to be identical are rounded and vary slightly in actual value. The rankings reflect the actual values before rounding. See the introduction for more details.

G-13 State and Local Debt Related to Revenue, FY 2002

State	State and local debt as a percentage of general revenue	Rank
Alabama	77.0	30
Alaska	123.6	3
Arizona	88.4	23
Arkansas	64.3	45
California	83.5	26
Colorado	104.0	15
Connecticut	111.8	8
Delaware	92.6	19
Florida	97.5	16
Georgia	74.3	36
Hawaii	113.4	7
Idaho	58.0	48
Illinois	110.0	9
Indiana	70.3	40
Iowa	53.9	50
Kansas	77.0	31
Kentucky	129.0	2
Louisiana	76.7	32
Maine	79.1	29
Maryland	76.7	33
Massachusetts	155.8	1
Michigan	85.9	25
Minnesota	91.1	22
Mississippi	62.5	47
Missouri	79.2	28
Montana	71.9	37
Nebraska	65.7	43
Nevada	123.1	4
New Hampshire	107.3	12
New Jersey	105.0	14
New Mexico	74.8	35
New York	115.3	5
North Carolina	68.9	41
North Dakota	68.7	42
Ohio	70.7	39
Oklahoma	65.3	44
Oregon	81.1	27
Pennsylvania	113.7	6
Rhode Island	106.5	13
South Carolina	91.5	20
South Dakota	87.0	24
Tennessee	63.1	46
Texas	107.7	11
Utah	96.1	18
Vermont	74.8	34
Virginia	91.3	21
Washington	108.2	10
West Virginia	71.3	38
Wisconsin	96.5	17
Wyoming	54.9	49
50 States	93.4	
DC	73.9	
United States	93.3	

Rank in order by percentage	
1	Massachusetts
2	Kentucky
3	Alaska
4	Nevada
5	New York
6	Pennsylvania
7	Hawaii
8	Connecticut
9	Illinois
10	Washington
11	Texas
12	New Hampshire
13	Rhode Island
14	New Jersey
15	Colorado
16	Florida
17	Wisconsin
18	Utah
19	Delaware
20	South Carolina
21	Virginia
22	Minnesota
23	Arizona
24	South Dakota
25	Michigan
26	California
27	Oregon
28	Missouri
29	Maine
30	Alabama
31	Kansas
32	Louisiana
33	Maryland
34	Vermont
35	New Mexico
36	Georgia
37	Montana
38	West Virginia
39	Ohio
40	Indiana
41	North Carolina
42	North Dakota
43	Nebraska
44	Oklahoma
45	Arkansas
46	Tennessee
47	Mississippi
48	Idaho
49	Wyoming
50	Iowa

Note: Numbers that appear to be identical are rounded and vary slightly in actual value. The rankings reflect the actual values before rounding. See the introduction for more details.

G-14 State and Local Full Faith and Credit Debt, FY 2002

State	Full faith and credit debt $ (in millions)	Per capita $	As a percentage of personal income	Rank per capita
Alabama	7,086	1,579	6.4	30
Alaska	2,729	4,238	13.5	5
Arizona	9,469	1,735	6.9	26
Arkansas	2,525	932	4.1	41
California	60,746	1,730	5.3	27
Colorado	8,432	1,871	5.6	22
Connecticut	18,045	5,214	12.4	1
Delaware	1,593	1,973	6.4	18
Florida	16,702	999	3.5	40
Georgia	16,123	1,883	6.7	20
Hawaii	5,901	4,740	16.8	3
Idaho	888	662	2.7	45
Illinois	41,601	3,301	10.1	8
Indiana	3,313	538	2.0	48
Iowa	3,509	1,195	4.4	38
Kansas	5,103	1,879	6.6	21
Kentucky	2,877	703	2.8	44
Louisiana	6,663	1,486	6.1	33
Maine	1,900	1,468	5.4	36
Maryland	11,307	2,072	5.9	16
Massachusetts	29,011	4,513	11.6	4
Michigan	20,173	2,007	6.8	17
Minnesota	16,326	3,252	10.0	9
Mississippi	5,662	1,972	9.0	19
Missouri	6,044	1,065	3.8	39
Montana	600	660	2.8	46
Nebraska	2,297	1,328	4.7	37
Nevada	10,572	4,864	16.6	2
New Hampshire	2,363	1,853	5.6	23
New Jersey	19,573	2,278	5.9	14
New Mexico	2,739	1,476	6.3	34
New York	70,528	3,681	10.4	6
North Carolina	12,219	1,469	5.4	35
North Dakota	506	798	3.1	43
Ohio	18,693	1,637	5.7	28
Oklahoma	2,205	631	2.5	47
Oregon	8,714	2,474	8.8	12
Pennsylvania	33,191	2,691	8.9	11
Rhode Island	1,948	1,821	6.1	24
South Carolina	8,916	2,171	8.8	15
South Dakota	651	856	3.2	42
Tennessee	10,113	1,744	6.5	25
Texas	51,853	2,381	8.4	13
Utah	3,492	1,508	6.3	32
Vermont	975	1,581	5.5	29
Virginia	11,429	1,567	4.9	31
Washington	21,163	3,487	10.9	7
West Virginia	922	512	2.2	49
Wisconsin	15,362	2,823	9.7	10
Wyoming	216	432	1.4	50
50 States	614,967	2,137	7.1	
DC	3,919	6,864	15.1	
United States	618,886	2,146	7.1	

Rank in order per capita	
1	Connecticut
2	Nevada
3	Hawaii
4	Massachusetts
5	Alaska
6	New York
7	Washington
8	Illinois
9	Minnesota
10	Wisconsin
11	Pennsylvania
12	Oregon
13	Texas
14	New Jersey
15	South Carolina
16	Maryland
17	Michigan
18	Delaware
19	Mississippi
20	Georgia
21	Kansas
22	Colorado
23	New Hampshire
24	Rhode Island
25	Tennessee
26	Arizona
27	California
28	Ohio
29	Vermont
30	Alabama
31	Virginia
32	Utah
33	Louisiana
34	New Mexico
35	North Carolina
36	Maine
37	Nebraska
38	Iowa
39	Missouri
40	Florida
41	Arkansas
42	South Dakota
43	North Dakota
44	Kentucky
45	Idaho
46	Montana
47	Oklahoma
48	Indiana
49	West Virginia
50	Wyoming

G-15 State Government Bond Ratings, 2005

State	State bond ratings	Rank
Alabama	Aa2	3
Alaska	Aa2	3
Arizona	no general obligation debt	n/a
Arkansas	Aa2	3
California	A2	6
Colorado	no general obligation debt	n/a
Connecticut	Aa3	4
Delaware	Aaa	1
Florida	Aa1	2
Georgia	Aaa	1
Hawaii	Aa2	3
Idaho	no general obligation debt	n/a
Illinois	Aa3	4
Indiana	no general obligation debt	n/a
Iowa	no general obligation debt	n/a
Kansas	no general obligation debt	n/a
Kentucky	no general obligation debt	n/a
Louisiana	A2	6
Maine	Aa3	4
Maryland	Aaa	1
Massachusetts	Aa2	3
Michigan	Aa2	3
Minnesota	Aa1	2
Mississippi	Aa3	4
Missouri	Aaa	1
Montana	Aa3	4
Nebraska	no general obligation debt	n/a
Nevada	Aa1	2
New Hampshire	Aa2	3
New Jersey	Aa3	4
New Mexico	Aa1	2
New York	A1	5
North Carolina	Aa1	2
North Dakota	no general obligation debt	n/a
Ohio	Aa1	2
Oklahoma	Aa3	4
Oregon	Aa3	4
Pennsylvania	Aa2	3
Rhode Island	Aa3	4
South Carolina	Aaa	1
South Dakota	no general obligation debt	n/a
Tennessee	Aa2	3
Texas	Aa1	2
Utah	Aaa	1
Vermont	Aa1	2
Virginia	Aaa	1
Washington	Aa1	2
West Virginia	Aa3	4
Wisconsin	Aa3	4
Wyoming	no general obligation debt	n/a
50 States	n/a	
DC	A2	
United States	n/a	

Rank in order by rating	
1	Delaware
1	Georgia
1	Maryland
1	Missouri
1	South Carolina
1	Utah
1	Virginia
2	Florida
2	Minnesota
2	Nevada
2	New Mexico
2	North Carolina
2	Ohio
2	Texas
2	Vermont
2	Washington
3	Alabama
3	Alaska
3	Arkansas
3	Hawaii
3	Massachusetts
3	Michigan
3	New Hampshire
3	Pennsylvania
3	Tennessee
4	Connecticut
4	Illinois
4	Maine
4	Mississippi
4	Montana
4	New Jersey
4	Oklahoma
4	Oregon
4	Rhode Island
4	West Virginia
4	Wisconsin
5	New York
6	California
6	Louisiana

Note: Ties in ranking reflect ties in actual values.

G-16 State Solvency Index, 2003

State	State solvency index	Rank by index
Alabama	-1,072	27
Alaska	37,398	1
Arizona	-126	14
Arkansas	-701	22
California	-962	25
Colorado	-1,470	33
Connecticut	-5,012	50
Delaware	138	8
Florida	35	12
Georgia	56	11
Hawaii	-4,176	48
Idaho	123	9
Illinois	-3,659	46
Indiana	-674	20
Iowa	-490	19
Kansas	-1,389	32
Kentucky	-1,348	30
Louisiana	-1,795	35
Maine	-2,044	38
Maryland	-1,377	31
Massachusetts	-4,996	49
Michigan	-1,172	28
Minnesota	-934	24
Mississippi	-2,358	42
Missouri	-1,011	26
Montana	-360	16
Nebraska	91	10
Nevada	-2,082	39
New Hampshire	-1,583	34
New Jersey	-906	23
New Mexico	4,194	3
New York	-3,163	45
North Carolina	1,271	5
North Dakota	2,349	4
Ohio	-2,560	43
Oklahoma	-2,239	41
Oregon	-257	15
Pennsylvania	-691	21
Rhode Island	-4,160	47
South Carolina	-2,216	40
South Dakota	813	7
Tennessee	-37	13
Texas	859	6
Utah	-1,346	29
Vermont	-402	17
Virginia	-424	18
Washington	-1,909	37
West Virginia	-2,933	44
Wisconsin	-1,877	36
Wyoming	5,012	2
50 States	-1,083	
DC	n/a	
United States	-1,081	

Rank in order by index	
1	Alaska
2	Wyoming
3	New Mexico
4	North Dakota
5	North Carolina
6	Texas
7	South Dakota
8	Delaware
9	Idaho
10	Nebraska
11	Georgia
12	Florida
13	Tennessee
14	Arizona
15	Oregon
16	Montana
17	Vermont
18	Virginia
19	Iowa
20	Indiana
21	Pennsylvania
22	Arkansas
23	New Jersey
24	Minnesota
25	California
26	Missouri
27	Alabama
28	Michigan
29	Utah
30	Kentucky
31	Maryland
32	Kansas
33	Colorado
34	New Hampshire
35	Louisiana
36	Wisconsin
37	Washington
38	Maine
39	Nevada
40	South Carolina
41	Oklahoma
42	Mississippi
43	Ohio
44	West Virginia
45	New York
46	Illinois
47	Rhode Island
48	Hawaii
49	Massachusetts
50	Connecticut

G-17 Assets of State-Administered Pension Plans, FY 2004

State	Total assets $ (in millions)	Total membership #	Average assets per member	Rank by average
Alabama	24,990	255,573	97,779	37
Alaska	12,540	68,115	184,095	7
Arizona	30,602	381,682	80,176	42
Arkansas	14,810	138,658	106,810	32
California	477,760	2,115,457	225,843	2
Colorado	36,863	323,414	113,979	27
Connecticut	24,505	148,195	165,359	11
Delaware	5,966	42,049	141,871	15
Florida	128,638	763,472	168,491	10
Georgia	61,546	538,677	114,253	26
Hawaii	8,559	67,074	127,604	18
Idaho	7,559	71,564	105,632	33
Illinois	112,287	938,508	119,644	21
Indiana	20,056	270,619	74,111	45
Iowa	19,854	269,188	73,755	46
Kansas	11,553	192,602	59,983	50
Kentucky	25,635	293,476	87,348	39
Louisiana	30,689	260,817	117,666	25
Maine	8,310	48,514	171,286	9
Maryland	40,583	276,651	146,695	13
Massachusetts	46,847	377,915	123,963	19
Michigan	67,376	485,046	138,906	16
Minnesota	44,799	499,580	89,673	38
Mississippi	18,383	272,219	67,531	48
Missouri	47,364	324,179	146,103	14
Montana	6,097	73,568	82,873	40
Nebraska	8,376	74,782	112,007	30
Nevada	18,022	85,311	211,254	4
New Hampshire	4,435	59,071	75,075	44
New Jersey	53,508	515,224	103,854	34
New Mexico	17,508	155,094	112,887	28
New York	296,211	1,265,263	234,111	1
North Carolina	60,240	534,613	112,680	29
North Dakota	2,863	34,700	82,511	41
Ohio	134,912	1,214,227	111,109	31
Oklahoma	18,957	161,093	117,676	24
Oregon	46,815	211,055	221,815	3
Pennsylvania	88,175	560,538	157,305	12
Rhode Island	7,878	45,161	174,452	8
South Carolina	24,260	361,017	67,198	49
South Dakota	5,868	49,575	118,363	22
Tennessee	33,008	256,417	128,726	17
Texas	139,552	1,396,125	99,957	36
Utah	14,563	120,471	120,885	20
Vermont	2,590	32,877	78,789	43
Virginia	47,967	471,499	101,733	35
Washington	47,190	253,177	186,391	5
West Virginia	4,921	71,994	68,350	47
Wisconsin	75,656	409,595	184,709	6
Wyoming	4,992	42,302	118,009	23
50 States	2,492,638	17,877,993	139,425	
DC	2,125	12,513	169,818	
United States	2,157,991	17,890,506	120,622	

Rank in order by average	
1	New York
2	California
3	Oregon
4	Nevada
5	Washington
6	Wisconsin
7	Alaska
8	Rhode Island
9	Maine
10	Florida
11	Connecticut
12	Pennsylvania
13	Maryland
14	Missouri
15	Delaware
16	Michigan
17	Tennessee
18	Hawaii
19	Massachusetts
20	Utah
21	Illinois
22	South Dakota
23	Wyoming
24	Oklahoma
25	Louisiana
26	Georgia
27	Colorado
28	New Mexico
29	North Carolina
30	Nebraska
31	Ohio
32	Arkansas
33	Idaho
34	New Jersey
35	Virginia
36	Texas
37	Alabama
38	Minnesota
39	Kentucky
40	Montana
41	North Dakota
42	Arizona
43	Vermont
44	New Hampshire
45	Indiana
46	Iowa
47	West Virginia
48	Mississippi
49	South Carolina
50	Kansas

G-18 State Reserves at the End of FY 2005

State	Balances as a percentage of expenditures	Rank
Alabama	13.8	9
Alaska	74.9	1
Arizona	10.5	15
Arkansas	0.0	48
California	9.2	19
Colorado	2.5	46
Connecticut	4.4	35
Delaware	24.8	2
Florida	15.7	6
Georgia	7.5	24
Hawaii	12.9	11
Idaho	10.9	14
Illinois	3.5	40
Indiana	3.7	37
Iowa	6.6	29
Kansas	10.3	17
Kentucky	3.7	37
Louisiana	6.5	30
Maine	2.9	42
Maryland	15.1	7
Massachusetts	10.5	15
Michigan	0.0	48
Minnesota	6.9	28
Mississippi	2.9	43
Missouri	7.5	24
Montana	21.8	3
Nebraska	21.3	4
Nevada	8.4	21
New Hampshire	7.5	24
New Jersey	2.3	47
New Mexico	14.4	8
New York	2.8	45
North Carolina	5.1	33
North Dakota	18.6	5
Ohio	2.9	43
Oklahoma	9.5	18
Oregon	6.2	32
Pennsylvania	3.0	41
Rhode Island	4.5	34
South Carolina	9.2	19
South Dakota	13.6	10
Tennessee	7.7	23
Texas	12.5	13
Utah	3.7	37
Vermont	4.4	35
Virginia	7.5	24
Washington	8.0	22
West Virginia	12.9	11
Wisconsin	0.0	48
Wyoming	6.3	31
50 States	n/a	
DC	n/a	
United States	6.9	

Rank in order by percentage	
1	Alaska
2	Delaware
3	Montana
4	Nebraska
5	North Dakota
6	Florida
7	Maryland
8	New Mexico
9	Alabama
10	South Dakota
11	Hawaii
11	West Virginia
13	Texas
14	Idaho
15	Arizona
15	Massachusetts
17	Kansas
18	Oklahoma
19	California
19	South Carolina
21	Nevada
22	Washington
23	Tennessee
24	Georgia
24	Missouri
24	New Hampshire
24	Virginia
28	Minnesota
29	Iowa
30	Louisiana
31	Wyoming
32	Oregon
33	North Carolina
34	Rhode Island
35	Connecticut
35	Vermont
37	Indiana
37	Kentucky
37	Utah
40	Illinois
41	Pennsylvania
42	Maine
43	Mississippi
43	Ohio
45	New York
46	Colorado
47	New Jersey
48	Arkansas
48	Michigan
48	Wisconsin

Note: Ties in ranking reflect ties in actual values.

G-19 State and Local Capital Outlays and Interest, FY 2002

State	Outlays and interest per capita $	Capital outlays per capita $	Interest per capita $	Rank by outlays and interest per capita
Alabama	978	775	204	34
Alaska	2,979	2,262	717	1
Arizona	1,212	958	255	16
Arkansas	775	606	169	50
California	1,104	794	310	24
Colorado	1,465	1,148	317	7
Connecticut	1,281	859	422	14
Delaware	1,338	927	411	11
Florida	1,252	954	298	15
Georgia	1,210	1,011	199	17
Hawaii	1,366	903	464	10
Idaho	828	667	162	46
Illinois	1,334	1,004	330	12
Indiana	867	665	202	43
Iowa	1,061	920	141	27
Kansas	937	688	248	37
Kentucky	1,075	692	382	25
Louisiana	900	653	247	39
Maine	820	557	264	48
Maryland	1,043	782	261	30
Massachusetts	1,596	1,035	561	4
Michigan	1,036	785	251	31
Minnesota	1,419	1,103	316	8
Mississippi	808	622	186	49
Missouri	958	762	196	35
Montana	923	683	239	38
Nebraska	1,398	1,167	231	9
Nevada	1,504	1,127	377	6
New Hampshire	864	538	327	44
New Jersey	1,062	778	285	26
New Mexico	995	776	219	33
New York	1,857	1,326	530	2
North Carolina	946	734	212	36
North Dakota	1,192	945	246	20
Ohio	1,048	798	250	29
Oklahoma	889	701	188	40
Oregon	1,053	821	233	28
Pennsylvania	1,136	784	352	22
Rhode Island	828	519	309	47
South Carolina	1,209	859	349	18
South Dakota	1,111	874	237	23
Tennessee	840	651	189	45
Texas	1,197	917	280	19
Utah	1,292	1,008	285	13
Vermont	871	583	288	41
Virginia	1,017	765	252	32
Washington	1,577	1,216	362	5
West Virginia	869	609	260	42
Wisconsin	1,158	877	280	21
Wyoming	1,651	1,371	281	3
50 States	1,185	884	301	
DC	3,464	3,029	435	
United States	1,189	888	302	

Rank in order per capita	
1	Alaska
2	New York
3	Wyoming
4	Massachusetts
5	Washington
6	Nevada
7	Colorado
8	Minnesota
9	Nebraska
10	Hawaii
11	Delaware
12	Illinois
13	Utah
14	Connecticut
15	Florida
16	Arizona
17	Georgia
18	South Carolina
19	Texas
20	North Dakota
21	Wisconsin
22	Pennsylvania
23	South Dakota
24	California
25	Kentucky
26	New Jersey
27	Iowa
28	Oregon
29	Ohio
30	Maryland
31	Michigan
32	Virginia
33	New Mexico
34	Alabama
35	Missouri
36	North Carolina
37	Kansas
38	Montana
39	Louisiana
40	Oklahoma
41	Vermont
42	West Virginia
43	Indiana
44	New Hampshire
45	Tennessee
46	Idaho
47	Rhode Island
48	Maine
49	Mississippi
50	Arkansas

G-20 Index of State Budget Process Quality, 2002

State	Index of state budget process quality	Rank
Alabama	56.9	40
Alaska	49.0	45
Arizona	48.6	46
Arkansas	52.0	42
California	60.5	35
Colorado	73.7	14
Connecticut	72.4	15
Delaware	67.0	21
Florida	76.0	13
Georgia	93.0	1
Hawaii	77.0	12
Idaho	37.9	47
Illinois	81.2	3
Indiana	29.9	49
Iowa	72.2	16
Kansas	59.0	39
Kentucky	65.5	26
Louisiana	80.5	6
Maine	62.0	31
Maryland	77.1	11
Massachusetts	79.2	7
Michigan	81.4	2
Minnesota	80.8	5
Mississippi	60.3	37
Missouri	70.9	18
Montana	66.0	24
Nebraska	64.0	28
Nevada	71.0	17
New Hampshire	27.5	50
New Jersey	77.5	9
New Mexico	78.0	8
New York	68.4	20
North Carolina	53.0	41
North Dakota	60.4	36
Ohio	60.6	34
Oklahoma	69.0	19
Oregon	66.8	22
Pennsylvania	65.7	25
Rhode Island	77.3	10
South Carolina	62.7	29
South Dakota	66.4	23
Tennessee	61.5	32
Texas	62.7	29
Utah	81.2	3
Vermont	37.7	48
Virginia	52.0	42
Washington	61.1	33
West Virginia	59.6	38
Wisconsin	51.9	44
Wyoming	64.2	27
50 States	64.6	
DC	n/a	
United States	64.6	

Rank in order by index	
1	Georgia
2	Michigan
3	Illinois
3	Utah
5	Minnesota
6	Louisiana
7	Massachusetts
8	New Mexico
9	New Jersey
10	Rhode Island
11	Maryland
12	Hawaii
13	Florida
14	Colorado
15	Connecticut
16	Iowa
17	Nevada
18	Missouri
19	Oklahoma
20	New York
21	Delaware
22	Oregon
23	South Dakota
24	Montana
25	Pennsylvania
26	Kentucky
27	Wyoming
28	Nebraska
29	South Carolina
29	Texas
31	Maine
32	Tennessee
33	Washington
34	Ohio
35	California
36	North Dakota
37	Mississippi
38	West Virginia
39	Kansas
40	Alabama
41	North Carolina
42	Arkansas
42	Virginia
44	Wisconsin
45	Alaska
46	Arizona
47	Idaho
48	Vermont
49	Indiana
50	New Hampshire

Note: Ties in ranking reflect ties in actual values.

G-21 Relative State Spending "Needs," FY 1999

State	Additional spending needed to meet national average %	Rank by least "need" to most
Alabama	3	40
Alaska	10	49
Arizona	3	41
Arkansas	0	34
California	7	48
Colorado	-3	20
Connecticut	-2	26
Delaware	-4	13
Florida	-8	5
Georgia	5	45
Hawaii	-10	1
Idaho	2	37
Illinois	-1	27
Indiana	-4	14
Iowa	-10	2
Kansas	-2	25
Kentucky	-1	28
Louisiana	6	47
Maine	-9	4
Maryland	-3	17
Massachusetts	-4	11
Michigan	4	42
Minnesota	-2	24
Mississippi	4	44
Missouri	-4	15
Montana	1	35
Nebraska	-4	12
Nevada	0	32
New Hampshire	-7	6
New Jersey	-3	18
New Mexico	12	50
New York	1	36
North Carolina	0	33
North Dakota	2	38
Ohio	-2	21
Oklahoma	-1	30
Oregon	0	31
Pennsylvania	-6	7
Rhode Island	-6	8
South Carolina	-2	23
South Dakota	-5	10
Tennessee	-2	22
Texas	5	46
Utah	4	43
Vermont	-9	3
Virginia	-3	16
Washington	-3	19
West Virginia	-1	29
Wisconsin	-6	9
Wyoming	2	39
50 States	n/a	
DC	18	
United States	0	

Rank in order by percentage	
1	Hawaii
2	Iowa
3	Vermont
4	Maine
5	Florida
6	New Hampshire
7	Pennsylvania
8	Rhode Island
9	Wisconsin
10	South Dakota
11	Massachusetts
12	Nebraska
13	Delaware
14	Indiana
15	Missouri
16	Virginia
17	Maryland
18	New Jersey
19	Washington
20	Colorado
21	Ohio
22	Tennessee
23	South Carolina
24	Minnesota
25	Kansas
26	Connecticut
27	Illinois
28	Kentucky
29	West Virginia
30	Oklahoma
31	Oregon
32	Nevada
33	North Carolina
34	Arkansas
35	Montana
36	New York
37	Idaho
38	North Dakota
39	Wyoming
40	Alabama
41	Arizona
42	Michigan
43	Utah
44	Mississippi
45	Georgia
46	Texas
47	Louisiana
48	California
49	Alaska
50	New Mexico

Note: Numbers that appear to be identical are rounded and vary slightly in actual value. The rankings reflect the actual values before rounding. See the introduction for more details.

G-22 Structural Deficits

State	Projected state and local surplus or shortfall in 2009 as a percentage of baseline revenues	Rank
Alabama	-7.0	37
Alaska	-11.1	42
Arizona	-16.6	49
Arkansas	-6.6	32
California	0.4	14
Colorado	-6.8	35
Connecticut	3.5	5
Delaware	2.6	6
Florida	-12.4	45
Georgia	-8.5	39
Hawaii	-12.8	47
Idaho	-12.7	46
Illinois	-0.3	17
Indiana	-3.9	28
Iowa	-2.7	26
Kansas	-2.3	24
Kentucky	-4.6	30
Louisiana	-0.5	19
Maine	1.3	10
Maryland	1.2	11
Massachusetts	4.8	2
Michigan	-0.1	15
Minnesota	-0.9	21
Mississippi	-6.9	36
Missouri	-2.8	27
Montana	-0.3	17
Nebraska	-5.3	31
Nevada	-20.9	50
New Hampshire	3.7	3
New Jersey	3.7	3
New Mexico	-8.6	40
New York	1.2	11
North Carolina	-6.7	34
North Dakota	0.6	13
Ohio	-2.6	25
Oklahoma	2.4	8
Oregon	-11.4	43
Pennsylvania	-0.1	15
Rhode Island	-0.6	20
South Carolina	-7.7	38
South Dakota	-4.1	29
Tennessee	-11.5	44
Texas	-6.6	32
Utah	-10.1	41
Vermont	1.4	9
Virginia	-1.5	23
Washington	-15.0	48
West Virginia	2.6	6
Wisconsin	-1.0	22
Wyoming	7.9	1
50 States	n/a	
DC	n/a	
United States	-3.5	

Rank in order by percentage	
1	Wyoming
2	Massachusetts
3	New Jersey
3	New Hampshire
5	Connecticut
6	Delaware
6	West Virginia
8	Oklahoma
9	Vermont
10	Maine
11	New York
11	Maryland
13	North Dakota
14	California
15	Michigan
15	Pennsylvania
17	Montana
17	Illinois
19	Louisiana
20	Rhode Island
21	Minnesota
22	Wisconsin
23	Virginia
24	Kansas
25	Ohio
26	Iowa
27	Missouri
28	Indiana
29	South Dakota
30	Kentucky
31	Nebraska
32	Arkansas
32	Texas
34	North Carolina
35	Colorado
36	Mississippi
37	Alabama
38	South Carolina
39	Georgia
40	New Mexico
41	Utah
42	Alaska
43	Oregon
44	Tennessee
45	Florida
46	Idaho
47	Hawaii
48	Washington
49	Arizona
50	Nevada

Note: Ties in ranking reflect ties in actual values.

Source Notes for Revenues and Finances (Section G)

G-1 State and Local Total Revenue, FY 2002: This table and many others in this section of *State Fact Finder* rely on analysis of data collected by the U.S. Census Bureau for fiscal year 2002. For sources of the fiscal data and the population and personal income estimates used to build the tables, see the extensive note associated with Table F-1.

Total revenue, shown in this table, is the most inclusive definition of the financial size of state and local governments used by the bureau in its annual survey of government finances. It includes utilities run by state and local governments and many categories of trust funds. Such funds typically collect revenues, such as unemployment insurance taxes, for a particular purpose, such as paying unemployment compensation benefits, and are not commingled with other public funds. The revenues included come from state and local taxes, fees such as hospital charges and university tuition, and from the federal government.

G-2 State and Local General Revenue, FY 2002: From the same source as Table F-1, this table relates general revenue to population and personal income in each state. Because general revenue eliminates difficult to compare proprietary functions, such as utility and trust fund revenues, it allows for more appropriate state-by-state comparisons.

G-3 State and Local "Own-Source" General Revenue, FY 2002: These data reflect the concept often used to measure the fiscal burdens associated with state and local activity. Revenues from federal aid are excluded, along with the revenues of trust funds and utilities. For source see the notes to Table F-1.

G-4 State and Local Non-Tax "Own-Source" Revenue, FY 2002: The principal sources of non-tax revenues are (1) fees related to use of state facilities and services, such as those charged by public hospitals and universities, and (2) interest earned on money held by governments in anticipation of spending. For source see the notes to Table F-1.

G-5 State and Local Total Expenditures, FY 2002: This is the spending counterpart of the revenues shown on Table G-1. For source see the notes to Table F-1.

G-6 State and Local General Expenditures, FY 2002: This concept of "general" spending (see notes to Table G-2) is the most appropriate for comparing spending among states. For source see the notes to Table F-1.

G-7 State and Local General Expenditures Per Capita, FY 2002: This table relates general expenditures to population with separate totals for state governments and local governments. State aid to local governments is included only when local officials spend the resources, to avoid double counting. For source see the notes to Table F-1.

G-8 Percentage Change in State and Local Expenditures, FY 1997–2002: This statistic shows the differences among states in the five-year growth of state and local spending. The changes shown are not adjusted for factors that might account for some of the differences in growth rates, such as growth in population and other factors affecting needs for government services. Fiscal year 1997 data are from the U.S. Census Bureau and are published in *State Fact Finder 2001*. For fiscal year 2002 data, see source for Table F-1.

G-9 State Government General Revenue, FY 2003: Unlike Tables G-1 through G-8, these data deal with state governments alone, not state and local governments combined. They are from the 2003 version of "State Government Finances," available on the U.S. Census Bureau Web site (www.census.gov).

For most purposes, comparisons of finances among states need to include state and local revenues and spending because of major differences in the division of state and local responsibilities between states. For example, New York local governments pay nearly half of all state and local welfare costs, but local governments in most other states have almost no responsibility for paying these costs. Comparisons of states alone would make New York spending look artificially small. In Hawaii, the state alone pays for schools, while in other states local governments pay half these costs. Comparisons of states alone would make Hawaii's spending look artificially large.

However, comparisons of state governments alone are useful for those attempting to evaluate state officeholders and aspirants and for discussions of state government spending priorities and tax burdens.

This table and Table G-10 show "general" revenues and expenditures, a less inclusive measure than "total" expenditures. The difference is primarily associated with enterprises run by some state governments and not others, particularly liquor sales monopolies run by about a third of the states and the electric power marketing operations run by a few states. State impacts on utility services and liquor prices and sales are similar from state to state but some states achieve them by directly managing these functions. Because huge amounts of money are involved, inclusion of these operations in state comparisons would artificially distort the spending comparisons, so the concepts of general expenditures and general revenues exclude them.

G-10 State Government General Spending, FY 2003: See notes to Table G-9.

G-11 State Government General Fund Spending, FY 2003: These data reflect other estimates of state government spending. They come from a survey of state executive branch budget offices reported in the *2003 State Expenditure Report* by the National Association of State Budget Officers (NASBO). They reflect state fiscal year 2003 definitions. The year ended on June 30, 2003, for forty-six states, while one state ended the fiscal year in the spring and three ended in the fall.

The NASBO report differs from the U.S. Census Bureau reports in many ways. The bureau reports include all funds, while the NASBO report covers primarily funds subject to appropriation by legislatures and therefore for most states excludes funds of quasi-independent entities such as toll highway authorities. The bureau does not distinguish among funds within state government, while the NASBO report presents data separately for state general funds, federal funds, and other state funds. The data shown in the table reflect the total of all reported funds. The NASBO data use different definitions of spending categories than do the U.S. Census Bureau data. See the notes for Table G-9 on the hazards of considering state spending without also considering local spending.

G-12 State and Local Debt, FY 2002: These data, from the U.S. Census Bureau (see notes to Table F-1), reflect the total debt of all state and local governments at the end of fiscal year 2002, including debt of special authorities.

G-13 State and Local Debt Related to Revenue, FY 2002: This table relates total debt (see Table G-12) to total revenue (see Table G-1). Consequently, it offers a measure of how state and local budgets are strained by the costs of paying principal and interest on past obligations.

G-14 State and Local Full Faith and Credit Debt, FY 2002: These data reflect the component of total debt (see Table G-12) that is backed by the "full faith and credit" of the governments that issued the debt. This debt, commonly known as "general obligation" debt, is backed by all revenue sources of the issuing government. The debt not included in these totals, often known as revenue bonds, is backed only by specified revenues, not general taxes.

G-15 State Government Bond Ratings, 2005: Because thousands of individual state and local governments issue bonds, purchasers such as individuals and mutual funds find it difficult to analyze the risks associated with each individual issue. As a result, three rating agencies (Fitch, Moody's, and Standard & Poor's) evaluate the quality of individual bond issues. The ratings of revenue bonds are unique to the bonds and the revenue sources that back them. The ratings of general obligation bonds shown in this table are reflections of the fiscal soundness of state governments overall. As a result, they affect perceptions of fiscal soundness of states by voters as well as by potential bond purchasers.

The ratings shown come from Moody's and are dated December 12, 2005. Ratings from the other two agencies would show about the same ranking of states. Moody's system considers Aaa highest, followed by Aa1, Aa2, Aa3, A1, A2, and so on, down to lower ratings, which are awarded to some local governments but no states, which are generally considered good credit risks. Some states have so little general obligation debt that they have no recent ratings and therefore are not ranked in this table. While there is no clearly appropriate way to insert them in the rankings, many of these states have strong credit and would rank above many of the states shown in the rankings.

G-16 State Solvency Index, 2003: While state financial reports and U.S. Census Bureau data provide substantial detail about state finances, they do not provide answers to some common sense questions about state financial status. One of these questions is equivalent to "net worth," a fundamental concept in viewing the finances of individuals and companies. This table reflects a special study created by State Policy Research using data from a variety of dates as close to late 2003 as possible. See *State Policy Reports* (vol. 20, no. 20) for more on the Solvency Index.

Conceptually, the number shown is an answer to the question: If each state were to cease operations tomorrow and pay off all debts (including pension promises to employees), how much money would be left over? For some states, the answer is that nothing would be left. Instead, they would have to levy a special assessment on each citizen (the amounts shown as negative numbers) in order to cease operations. Some states, particularly Alaska with its large reserves built from oil revenues, would have money left over that could be distributed to taxpayers. The calculations exclude the value of physical assets, such as state park lands, trucks, and computers.

G-17 Assets of State-Administered Pension Plans, FY 2004: States run pension plans for their own employees and, in most states, for teachers, city workers, and other local employees as well. To be considered actuarially sound, these plans must have built up enough assets from contributions of employees and their government employers to be able to cover the amounts needed to pay retired workers plus current workers when they retire. How much this amounts to depends on many factors, such as the exact benefits promised and the life expectancy of workers. There is no substitute for actuarial studies of each plan for determining the right amount each plan should have to cover future obligations. This table shows the assets of state-administered plans and the persons who are considered members of these plans—retirees and active workers accruing retirement benefits. Dividing these two numbers produces average assets per member, which is a rough measure of the relative solvency of the public pension plans in each state. The data come from the U.S. Census Bureau Web site (www.census.gov).

G-18 State Reserves at the End of FY 2005: These data reflect the projected cash reserves of state governments as they finished fiscal year 2005, generally in the summer of 2005. These reserves come in two primary forms—balances (equivalent to the balances people show in their checkbooks) and "rainy day" or stabilization funds (formal reserves, somewhat akin to the savings accounts maintained by individuals). The data come from a survey of state budget officers by the National Association of State Budget Officers (NASBO) published in December 2005, titled *The Fiscal Survey of States*, and available on the NASBO Web site (www.nasbo.org).

Relating balances to spending provides a basis for comparisons among states of different sizes and financial responsibilities. Nationwide, this table indicates that states have enough in reserve to pay their normal bills for about 6.9 percent of their fiscal years, or roughly twenty-five days, with no additional revenue coming in.

G-19 State and Local Capital Outlays and Interest, FY 2002: This table, from the same source as Table F-1, shows per capita amounts of spending in fiscal year 2002 for interest and capital outlays. The outlays reflect the pace of activity in financing new facilities, such as roads and schools. The interest reflects the extent to which taxpayers of each state are seeing their tax funds used to pay interest on past spending, normally borrowing to finance capital outlays.

G-20 Index of State Budget Process Quality, 2002: Experts in public administration and budgeting generally agree on criteria of best budgeting practices, such as considering the impacts of spending and tax decisions over a longer period than one year. The numbers shown in the table are scores, with a perfect score being 100, developed by State Policy Research by comparing these criteria with actual state budget practices, as reported by the National Association of State Budget Officers in its special report *Budget Processes in the States* (January 2002).

G-21 Relative State Spending "Needs," FY 1999: Individual states have quite different population characteristics, as shown by many of the tables in *State Fact Finder*. For example, school-age children are an extraordinarily large proportion of the population of Utah, but a smaller-than-average proportion of Pennsylvania's population. As a result, some states would have higher per capita spending than others, even if all states spent identical amounts per pupil, had identical welfare payments, and identical levels of other services. These differences are important to consider in viewing differences in per capita spending among states.

The table was created by Robert Tannenwald and Nicholas Turner and published in "Interstate Fiscal Disparity in State Fiscal Year 1999," Public Policy Discussion Papers, The Federal Reserve Bank of Boston (no. 04-9). Tannenwald and Turner calculated what state and local governments in each state would have to spend if they applied national average spending (for example, spending per pupil) to their own particular mix of population using government services. For example, to match national average spending patterns, Louisiana would have to spend 7 percent more than the national average. Why? Because the state has extra burdens associated with large percentages of welfare recipients and school-age children.

These data are conceptually similar to concepts of tax capacity shown in Table F-4. Together, these data reflect a consistent pattern of strains that circumstances put on taxpayers and decision makers of individual states. More affluent states, such as Connecticut, often combine above-average tax bases with below-average spending needs while less affluent states, like Mississippi, show the reverse.

G-22 Structural Deficits: In addition to their current budget problems, many state officials worry about *structural* deficits—long-term shortfalls because revenues from current taxes will be insufficient to cover the spending needed to maintain current programs. If such deficits exist, they would be obscured by extraordinary performance of the economy and tax collections, but would be magnified by *cyclical* deficits during any economic downturn.

This table shows the result of subtracting projected spending from projected revenues eight years from now. A budget gap or structural deficit is indicated by all the negative results. A value of zero indicates that state and local governments could cover the future costs of their current policies, including adjustments for inflation and workload changes, with revenues from their current tax system, with no change in tax rates or the definition of bases. A positive value means covering costs with money left.

The methodology used to derive this table was created by State Policy Research. An explanation of the methodology and the original calculations are published in *The Outlook for State and Local Finances*, National Education Association. The National Education Association updated the data in March 2003 (unpublished).

Education

State officials and other citizens worried about costs to states of the No Child Left Behind (NCLB) law received discouraging news in late 2005. First, the state of Michigan's lawsuit, filed on the grounds that NCLB constituted an illegal unfunded mandate on state and local school districts, was dismissed. A similar case is pending in Connecticut. Other states, unhappy with aspects of the program, may yet take legal action.

Second, according to the report releasing the National Assessment of Educational Progress (NAEP) reading test scores in late 2005,"between 1992 and 2005, there was no significant change in the percentage of fourth-graders performing at or above Basic." Eighth-graders showed some improvement over the same period, but performance declined by one percentage point from 2003 to 2005. The mathematics report, released at the same time, offered some better news. Fourth-graders' average score was 3 points higher and eighth-graders' average score was 1 point higher in 2005 than in 2003.

Percent Scoring Below Basic on NAEP Test, 2005

	Reading	Mathematics
Fourth Grade	36	20
Eighth Grade	27	31

Source: National Assessment of Educational Progress

Marcia Howard, editor of *State Policy Reports* notes, "To date, there is not much evidence that the stringent new requirements of the law are having an effect on student performance." The NAEP test is seen as a "barometer of the effectiveness No Child Left Behind legislation," according to Howard. NCLB "specifies remedies that schools must offer if their test scores do not improve sufficiently, a costly provision that states would prefer to avoid if necessary. Therefore, improving their performance on the NAEP is a fiscal imperative for many states."

Regionally, scores tend to be better in northern states and worse in southern states, with the notable exception of Virginia.

H-1 Average Proficiency in Math, Eighth Grade, 2005

State	Average math score	Percent at or above basic	Rank by score
Alabama	262	53	49
Alaska	279	69	29
Arizona	274	64	35
Arkansas	272	64	38
California	269	57	44
Colorado	281	70	20
Connecticut	281	70	20
Delaware	281	72	20
Florida	274	65	35
Georgia	272	62	38
Hawaii	266	56	47
Idaho	281	73	20
Illinois	278	68	31
Indiana	282	74	16
Iowa	284	75	10
Kansas	284	77	10
Kentucky	274	64	35
Louisiana	268	59	46
Maine	281	74	20
Maryland	278	66	31
Massachusetts	292	80	1
Michigan	277	68	33
Minnesota	290	79	2
Mississippi	262	52	49
Missouri	276	68	34
Montana	286	80	6
Nebraska	284	75	10
Nevada	270	60	43
New Hampshire	285	77	7
New Jersey	284	74	10
New Mexico	263	53	48
New York	280	70	28
North Carolina	282	72	16
North Dakota	287	81	3
Ohio	283	74	15
Oklahoma	271	63	41
Oregon	282	72	16
Pennsylvania	281	72	20
Rhode Island	272	63	38
South Carolina	281	71	20
South Dakota	287	80	3
Tennessee	271	61	41
Texas	281	72	20
Utah	279	71	29
Vermont	287	78	3
Virginia	284	75	10
Washington	285	75	7
West Virginia	269	60	44
Wisconsin	285	76	7
Wyoming	282	76	16
50 States	n/a	n/a	
DC	245	31	
United States	278	68	

Rank in order by score	
1	Massachusetts
2	Minnesota
3	North Dakota
3	South Dakota
3	Vermont
6	Montana
7	New Hampshire
7	Washington
7	Wisconsin
10	Iowa
10	Kansas
10	Nebraska
10	New Jersey
10	Virginia
15	Ohio
16	Indiana
16	North Carolina
16	Oregon
16	Wyoming
20	Colorado
20	Connecticut
20	Delaware
20	Idaho
20	Maine
20	Pennsylvania
20	South Carolina
20	Texas
28	New York
29	Alaska
29	Utah
31	Illinois
31	Maryland
33	Michigan
34	Missouri
35	Arizona
35	Florida
35	Kentucky
38	Arkansas
38	Georgia
38	Rhode Island
41	Oklahoma
41	Tennessee
43	Nevada
44	California
44	West Virginia
46	Louisiana
47	Hawaii
48	New Mexico
49	Alabama
49	Mississippi

Note: Ties in ranking reflect ties in actual values.

H-2 Average Proficiency in Reading, Eighth Grade, 2005

State	Reading score	Percent at or above basic	Rank by score
Alabama	252	63	46
Alaska	259	70	34
Arizona	255	65	42
Arkansas	258	69	36
California	250	60	49
Colorado	265	75	19
Connecticut	264	74	23
Delaware	266	80	17
Florida	256	66	41
Georgia	257	67	39
Hawaii	249	58	50
Idaho	264	76	23
Illinois	264	75	23
Indiana	261	73	29
Iowa	267	79	12
Kansas	267	78	12
Kentucky	264	75	23
Louisiana	253	64	44
Maine	270	81	2
Maryland	261	69	29
Massachusetts	274	83	1
Michigan	261	73	29
Minnesota	268	80	9
Mississippi	251	60	47
Missouri	265	76	19
Montana	269	82	5
Nebraska	267	80	12
Nevada	253	63	44
New Hampshire	270	80	2
New Jersey	269	80	5
New Mexico	251	62	47
New York	265	75	19
North Carolina	258	69	36
North Dakota	270	83	2
Ohio	267	78	12
Oklahoma	260	72	33
Oregon	263	74	27
Pennsylvania	267	77	12
Rhode Island	261	71	29
South Carolina	257	67	39
South Dakota	269	82	5
Tennessee	259	71	34
Texas	258	69	36
Utah	262	73	28
Vermont	269	79	5
Virginia	268	78	9
Washington	265	75	19
West Virginia	255	67	42
Wisconsin	266	77	17
Wyoming	268	81	9
50 States	n/a	n/a	
DC	238	45	
United States	260	71	

Rank in order by score	
1	Massachusetts
2	Maine
2	New Hampshire
2	North Dakota
5	Montana
5	New Jersey
5	South Dakota
5	Vermont
9	Minnesota
9	Virginia
9	Wyoming
12	Iowa
12	Kansas
12	Nebraska
12	Ohio
12	Pennsylvania
17	Delaware
17	Wisconsin
19	Colorado
19	Missouri
19	New York
19	Washington
23	Connecticut
23	Idaho
23	Illinois
23	Kentucky
27	Oregon
28	Utah
29	Indiana
29	Maryland
29	Michigan
29	Rhode Island
33	Oklahoma
34	Alaska
34	Tennessee
36	Arkansas
36	North Carolina
36	Texas
39	Georgia
39	South Carolina
41	Florida
42	Arizona
42	West Virginia
44	Louisiana
44	Nevada
46	Alabama
47	Mississippi
47	New Mexico
49	California
50	Hawaii

Note: Ties in ranking reflect ties in actual values.

H-3 Armed Forces Qualification Test Ranks, FY 2003

State	AFQT rank	Rank
Alabama	59.0	46
Alaska	65.4	4
Arizona	62.7	23
Arkansas	59.3	45
California	60.5	40
Colorado	64.6	10
Connecticut	61.8	29
Delaware	60.9	36
Florida	60.8	37
Georgia	59.4	44
Hawaii	58.5	48
Idaho	65.1	7
Illinois	62.0	28
Indiana	64.2	13
Iowa	64.0	16
Kansas	63.6	18
Kentucky	60.1	42
Louisiana	57.3	49
Maine	64.3	12
Maryland	61.1	35
Massachusetts	63.1	21
Michigan	62.4	25
Minnesota	65.0	8
Mississippi	57.0	50
Missouri	61.6	30
Montana	63.5	19
Nebraska	64.1	15
Nevada	63.0	22
New Hampshire	67.2	1
New Jersey	60.4	41
New Mexico	59.9	43
New York	61.2	34
North Carolina	60.7	38
North Dakota	65.2	6
Ohio	63.4	20
Oklahoma	61.6	30
Oregon	65.9	3
Pennsylvania	62.7	23
Rhode Island	62.4	25
South Carolina	58.9	47
South Dakota	63.9	17
Tennessee	61.4	32
Texas	61.3	33
Utah	64.5	11
Vermont	66.9	2
Virginia	62.3	27
Washington	65.3	5
West Virginia	60.6	39
Wisconsin	64.2	13
Wyoming	64.9	9
50 States	n/a	
DC	55.9	
United States	61.7	

Rank in order by rank	
1	New Hampshire
2	Vermont
3	Oregon
4	Alaska
5	Washington
6	North Dakota
7	Idaho
8	Minnesota
9	Wyoming
10	Colorado
11	Utah
12	Maine
13	Indiana
13	Wisconsin
15	Nebraska
16	Iowa
17	South Dakota
18	Kansas
19	Montana
20	Ohio
21	Massachusetts
22	Nevada
23	Arizona
23	Pennsylvania
25	Michigan
25	Rhode Island
27	Virginia
28	Illinois
29	Connecticut
30	Missouri
30	Oklahoma
32	Tennessee
33	Texas
34	New York
35	Maryland
36	Delaware
37	Florida
38	North Carolina
39	West Virginia
40	California
41	New Jersey
42	Kentucky
43	New Mexico
44	Georgia
45	Arkansas
46	Alabama
47	South Carolina
48	Hawaii
49	Louisiana
50	Mississippi

Note: Ties in ranking reflect ties in actual values.

H-4 SAT Scores, 2005

State	Average SAT score	Percentage of graduates tested	Rank by score
Alabama	n/a	n/a	n/a
Alaska	1,042	52	6
Arizona	1,056	33	2
Arkansas	n/a	n/a	n/a
California	1,026	50	10
Colorado	n/a	n/a	n/a
Connecticut	1,034	86	8
Delaware	1,005	74	20
Florida	996	65	22
Georgia	993	75	24
Hawaii	1,006	61	19
Idaho	n/a	n/a	n/a
Illinois	n/a	n/a	n/a
Indiana	1,012	66	15
Iowa	n/a	n/a	n/a
Kansas	n/a	n/a	n/a
Kentucky	n/a	n/a	n/a
Louisiana	n/a	n/a	n/a
Maine	1,014	75	14
Maryland	1,026	71	10
Massachusetts	1,047	86	5
Michigan	n/a	n/a	n/a
Minnesota	n/a	n/a	n/a
Mississippi	n/a	n/a	n/a
Missouri	n/a	n/a	n/a
Montana	n/a	n/a	n/a
Nebraska	n/a	n/a	n/a
Nevada	1,021	39	12
New Hampshire	1,050	81	4
New Jersey	1,020	86	13
New Mexico	n/a	n/a	n/a
New York	1,008	92	17
North Carolina	1,010	74	16
North Dakota	n/a	n/a	n/a
Ohio	n/a	n/a	n/a
Oklahoma	n/a	n/a	n/a
Oregon	1,054	59	3
Pennsylvania	1,004	75	21
Rhode Island	1,008	72	17
South Carolina	993	64	24
South Dakota	n/a	n/a	n/a
Tennessee	n/a	n/a	n/a
Texas	995	54	23
Utah	n/a	n/a	n/a
Vermont	1,038	67	7
Virginia	1,030	73	9
Washington	1,066	55	1
West Virginia	n/a	n/a	n/a
Wisconsin	n/a	n/a	n/a
Wyoming	n/a	n/a	n/a
50 States	n/a	n/a	
DC	968	79	
United States	1,028	49	

Rank in order by score	
1	Washington
2	Arizona
3	Oregon
4	New Hampshire
5	Massachusetts
6	Alaska
7	Vermont
8	Connecticut
9	Virginia
10	California
10	Maryland
12	Nevada
13	New Jersey
14	Maine
15	Indiana
16	North Carolina
17	New York
17	Rhode Island
19	Hawaii
20	Delaware
21	Pennsylvania
22	Florida
23	Texas
24	Georgia
24	South Carolina

Note: Ties in ranking reflect ties in actual values.

H-5 ACT Scores, 2005

State	ACT composite scores	Percentage of graduates tested	Rank by score
Alabama	20.2	77	21
Alaska	n/a	n/a	n/a
Arizona	n/a	n/a	n/a
Arkansas	20.3	76	19
California	n/a	n/a	n/a
Colorado	20.2	100	21
Connecticut	n/a	n/a	n/a
Delaware	n/a	n/a	n/a
Florida	n/a	n/a	n/a
Georgia	n/a	n/a	n/a
Hawaii	n/a	n/a	n/a
Idaho	21.3	58	13
Illinois	20.3	100	19
Indiana	n/a	n/a	n/a
Iowa	22.0	66	3
Kansas	21.7	76	6
Kentucky	20.4	76	16
Louisiana	19.8	85	24
Maine	n/a	n/a	n/a
Maryland	n/a	n/a	n/a
Massachusetts	n/a	n/a	n/a
Michigan	21.4	69	10
Minnesota	22.3	68	1
Mississippi	18.7	94	25
Missouri	21.6	70	7
Montana	21.8	57	4
Nebraska	21.8	76	4
Nevada	n/a	n/a	n/a
New Hampshire	n/a	n/a	n/a
New Jersey	n/a	n/a	n/a
New Mexico	20.0	61	23
New York	n/a	n/a	n/a
North Carolina	n/a	n/a	n/a
North Dakota	21.3	82	13
Ohio	21.4	66	10
Oklahoma	20.4	69	16
Oregon	n/a	n/a	n/a
Pennsylvania	n/a	n/a	n/a
Rhode Island	n/a	n/a	n/a
South Carolina	n/a	n/a	n/a
South Dakota	21.5	76	8
Tennessee	20.5	92	15
Texas	n/a	n/a	n/a
Utah	21.5	68	8
Vermont	n/a	n/a	n/a
Virginia	n/a	n/a	n/a
Washington	n/a	n/a	n/a
West Virginia	20.4	65	16
Wisconsin	22.2	69	2
Wyoming	21.4	69	10
50 States	n/a	n/a	
DC	n/a	n/a	
United States	20.9	40	

Rank in order by score	
1	Minnesota
2	Wisconsin
3	Iowa
4	Montana
4	Nebraska
6	Kansas
7	Missouri
8	South Dakota
8	Utah
10	Michigan
10	Ohio
10	Wyoming
13	Idaho
13	North Dakota
15	Tennessee
16	Kentucky
16	Oklahoma
16	West Virginia
19	Arkansas
19	Illinois
21	Alabama
21	Colorado
23	New Mexico
24	Louisiana
25	Mississippi

Note: Ties in ranking reflect ties in actual values.

H-6 Percentage of Population over 25 with a High School Diploma, 2004

State	High school graduates %	Rank by percentage
Alabama	82.4	42
Alaska	90.2	8
Arizona	84.4	37
Arkansas	79.2	48
California	81.3	44
Colorado	88.3	16
Connecticut	88.8	13
Delaware	86.5	30
Florida	85.9	33
Georgia	85.2	35
Hawaii	88.0	18
Idaho	87.9	19
Illinois	86.8	29
Indiana	87.2	26
Iowa	89.8	9
Kansas	89.6	11
Kentucky	81.8	43
Louisiana	78.7	49
Maine	87.1	27
Maryland	87.4	24
Massachusetts	86.9	28
Michigan	87.9	19
Minnesota	92.3	1
Mississippi	83.0	39
Missouri	87.9	21
Montana	91.9	2
Nebraska	91.3	4
Nevada	86.3	32
New Hampshire	90.8	6
New Jersey	87.6	22
New Mexico	82.9	40
New York	85.4	34
North Carolina	80.9	46
North Dakota	89.5	12
Ohio	88.1	17
Oklahoma	85.2	35
Oregon	87.4	24
Pennsylvania	86.5	30
Rhode Island	81.1	45
South Carolina	83.6	38
South Dakota	87.5	23
Tennessee	82.9	40
Texas	78.3	50
Utah	91.0	5
Vermont	90.8	6
Virginia	88.4	15
Washington	89.7	10
West Virginia	80.9	46
Wisconsin	88.8	13
Wyoming	91.9	2
50 States	n/a	
DC	86.4	
United States	85.0	

Rank in order by percentage	
1	Minnesota
2	Montana
2	Wyoming
4	Nebraska
5	Utah
6	New Hampshire
6	Vermont
8	Alaska
9	Iowa
10	Washington
11	Kansas
12	North Dakota
13	Connecticut
13	Wisconsin
15	Virginia
16	Colorado
17	Ohio
18	Hawaii
19	Idaho
19	Michigan
21	Missouri
22	New Jersey
23	South Dakota
24	Maryland
24	Oregon
26	Indiana
27	Maine
28	Massachusetts
29	Illinois
30	Delaware
30	Pennsylvania
32	Nevada
33	Florida
34	New York
35	Georgia
35	Oklahoma
37	Arizona
38	South Carolina
39	Mississippi
40	New Mexico
40	Tennessee
42	Alabama
43	Kentucky
44	California
45	Rhode Island
46	North Carolina
46	West Virginia
48	Arkansas
49	Louisiana
50	Texas

Note: Ties in ranking reflect ties in actual values.

H-7 Students in Private Schools, 2001–2002

State	Private school enrollment	Percentage of total enrollment	Rank by percentage
Alabama	76,634	9.5	24
Alaska	6,747	4.8	44
Arizona	44,360	4.6	46
Arkansas	29,290	6.2	39
California	655,502	9.6	23
Colorado	54,450	6.8	38
Connecticut	71,147	11.1	16
Delaware	26,365	18.6	1
Florida	303,093	10.8	17
Georgia	117,229	7.4	35
Hawaii	40,199	17.9	2
Idaho	10,291	4.0	48
Illinois	293,290	12.4	13
Indiana	111,257	10.0	21
Iowa	47,647	8.9	27
Kansas	41,027	8.1	31
Kentucky	72,819	10.3	20
Louisiana	137,266	15.8	3
Maine	18,779	8.4	29
Maryland	153,861	15.1	5
Massachusetts	140,810	12.6	11
Michigan	177,026	9.3	25
Minnesota	101,180	10.5	18
Mississippi	52,565	9.6	22
Missouri	124,326	12.3	14
Montana	9,941	6.1	40
Nebraska	43,137	13.2	10
Nevada	16,623	4.5	47
New Hampshire	24,750	10.5	19
New Jersey	218,187	14.0	8
New Mexico	23,637	6.9	37
New York	492,518	14.8	6
North Carolina	103,219	7.2	36
North Dakota	6,782	5.8	41
Ohio	256,427	12.4	12
Oklahoma	30,579	4.7	45
Oregon	45,448	7.6	33
Pennsylvania	331,471	15.4	4
Rhode Island	26,125	14.2	7
South Carolina	58,937	8.1	30
South Dakota	10,950	8.0	32
Tennessee	92,099	9.2	26
Texas	241,674	5.5	42
Utah	16,814	3.4	49
Vermont	13,058	11.5	15
Virginia	109,993	8.7	28
Washington	82,189	7.4	34
West Virginia	15,737	5.3	43
Wisconsin	141,812	13.9	9
Wyoming	2,209	2.5	50
50 States	5,321,476	10.1	
DC	20,043	22.6	
United States*	5,341,516	10.1	

Due to rounding or data sources, the 50-state total plus D.C. may not equal the U.S. total. Please see introduction.

Rank in order by percentage	
1	Delaware
2	Hawaii
3	Louisiana
4	Pennsylvania
5	Maryland
6	New York
7	Rhode Island
8	New Jersey
9	Wisconsin
10	Nebraska
11	Massachusetts
12	Ohio
13	Illinois
14	Missouri
15	Vermont
16	Connecticut
17	Florida
18	Minnesota
19	New Hampshire
20	Kentucky
21	Indiana
22	Mississippi
23	California
24	Alabama
25	Michigan
26	Tennessee
27	Iowa
28	Virginia
29	Maine
30	South Carolina
31	Kansas
32	South Dakota
33	Oregon
34	Washington
35	Georgia
36	North Carolina
37	New Mexico
38	Colorado
39	Arkansas
40	Montana
41	North Dakota
42	Texas
43	West Virginia
44	Alaska
45	Oklahoma
46	Arizona
47	Nevada
48	Idaho
49	Utah
50	Wyoming

Note: Numbers that appear to be identical are rounded and vary slightly in actual value. The rankings reflect the actual values before rounding. See the introduction for more details.

H-8 High School Graduation Rates, 2001

State	Graduation rates %	Rank
Alabama	61	42
Alaska	64	38
Arizona	67	33
Arkansas	71	26
California	69	31
Colorado	69	31
Connecticut	77	10
Delaware	64	38
Florida	53	49
Georgia	56	47
Hawaii	66	34
Idaho	80	2
Illinois	75	14
Indiana	72	23
Iowa	78	6
Kansas	74	16
Kentucky	65	35
Louisiana	65	35
Maine	72	23
Maryland	75	14
Massachusetts	71	26
Michigan	74	16
Minnesota	79	4
Mississippi	58	45
Missouri	73	22
Montana	77	10
Nebraska	77	10
Nevada	55	48
New Hampshire	74	16
New Jersey	86	1
New Mexico	61	42
New York	61	42
North Carolina	64	38
North Dakota	80	2
Ohio	71	26
Oklahoma	70	30
Oregon	74	16
Pennsylvania	76	13
Rhode Island	74	16
South Carolina	51	50
South Dakota	79	4
Tennessee	58	45
Texas	65	35
Utah	78	6
Vermont	78	6
Virginia	74	16
Washington	63	41
West Virginia	71	26
Wisconsin	78	6
Wyoming	72	23
50 States	n/a	
DC	65	
United States	n/a	

Rank in order by percentage	
1	New Jersey
2	Idaho
2	North Dakota
4	Minnesota
4	South Dakota
6	Iowa
6	Utah
6	Vermont
6	Wisconsin
10	Connecticut
10	Montana
10	Nebraska
13	Pennsylvania
14	Illinois
14	Maryland
16	Kansas
16	Michigan
16	New Hampshire
16	Oregon
16	Rhode Island
16	Virginia
22	Missouri
23	Indiana
23	Maine
23	Wyoming
26	Arkansas
26	Massachusetts
26	Ohio
26	West Virginia
30	Oklahoma
31	California
31	Colorado
33	Arizona
34	Hawaii
35	Kentucky
35	Louisiana
35	Texas
38	Alaska
38	Delaware
38	North Carolina
41	Washington
42	Alabama
42	New Mexico
42	New York
45	Mississippi
45	Tennessee
47	Georgia
48	Nevada
49	Florida
50	South Carolina

Note: Ties in ranking reflect ties in actual values.

H-9 Pupil-Teacher Ratio, 2004–2005

State	Pupils per teacher in public K-12 schools	Rank by ratio
Alabama	15.7	19
Alaska	16.8	11
Arizona	21.5	2
Arkansas	13.8	36
California	19.9	3
Colorado	17.0	9
Connecticut	13.3	41
Delaware	14.9	25
Florida	16.6	12
Georgia	14.8	27
Hawaii	16.1	14
Idaho	17.6	8
Illinois	15.9	16
Indiana	16.9	10
Iowa	13.8	36
Kansas	14.3	33
Kentucky	15.9	16
Louisiana	14.8	27
Maine	11.9	47
Maryland	15.4	22
Massachusetts	14.6	31
Michigan	17.8	7
Minnesota	16.0	15
Mississippi	15.8	18
Missouri	13.3	41
Montana	14.3	33
Nebraska	13.8	36
Nevada	19.4	5
New Hampshire	13.5	40
New Jersey	12.7	44
New Mexico	15.0	23
New York	12.7	44
North Carolina	14.8	27
North Dakota	12.9	43
Ohio	16.2	13
Oklahoma	15.6	20
Oregon	19.8	4
Pennsylvania	15.0	23
Rhode Island	11.3	49
South Carolina	14.6	31
South Dakota	13.6	39
Tennessee	15.6	20
Texas	14.9	25
Utah	22.6	1
Vermont	10.9	50
Virginia	11.8	48
Washington	19.3	6
West Virginia	14.1	35
Wisconsin	14.7	30
Wyoming	12.6	46
50 States	n/a	
DC	12.4	
United States	15.6	

Rank in order by ratio	
1	Utah
2	Arizona
3	California
4	Oregon
5	Nevada
6	Washington
7	Michigan
8	Idaho
9	Colorado
10	Indiana
11	Alaska
12	Florida
13	Ohio
14	Hawaii
15	Minnesota
16	Illinois
16	Kentucky
18	Mississippi
19	Alabama
20	Oklahoma
20	Tennessee
22	Maryland
23	New Mexico
23	Pennsylvania
25	Delaware
25	Texas
27	Georgia
27	Louisiana
27	North Carolina
30	Wisconsin
31	Massachusetts
31	South Carolina
33	Kansas
33	Montana
35	West Virginia
36	Arkansas
36	Iowa
36	Nebraska
39	South Dakota
40	New Hampshire
41	Connecticut
41	Missouri
43	North Dakota
44	New Jersey
44	New York
46	Wyoming
47	Maine
48	Virginia
49	Rhode Island
50	Vermont

Note: Ties in ranking reflect ties in actual values.

H-10 Public School Enrollment, 2004-2005

State	Enrollment (in thousands)	Percentage of total population	Rank by percentage
Alabama	731	16.1	25
Alaska	133	20.3	2
Arizona	986	17.2	8
Arkansas	452	16.4	20
California	6,322	17.6	6
Colorado	767	16.7	14
Connecticut	576	16.5	18
Delaware	119	14.3	50
Florida	2,630	15.1	45
Georgia	1,553	17.6	7
Hawaii	183	14.5	49
Idaho	250	17.9	4
Illinois	2,098	16.5	17
Indiana	1,021	16.4	21
Iowa	478	16.2	23
Kansas	469	17.1	10
Kentucky	637	15.4	41
Louisiana	724	16.0	27
Maine	199	15.1	44
Maryland	866	15.6	37
Massachusetts	976	15.2	43
Michigan	1,726	17.1	12
Minnesota	838	16.4	19
Mississippi	485	16.7	13
Missouri	892	15.5	38
Montana	147	15.8	32
Nebraska	285	16.3	22
Nevada	401	17.2	9
New Hampshire	207	15.9	31
New Jersey	1,392	16.0	28
New Mexico	325	17.1	11
New York	2,822	14.7	47
North Carolina	1,345	15.7	34
North Dakota	99	15.7	36
Ohio	1,847	16.1	26
Oklahoma	629	17.9	5
Oregon	552	15.4	40
Pennsylvania	1,815	14.6	48
Rhode Island	161	14.9	46
South Carolina	670	16.0	30
South Dakota	122	15.8	33
Tennessee	929	15.7	35
Texas	4,384	19.5	3
Utah	494	20.7	1
Vermont	95	15.3	42
Virginia	1,205	16.2	24
Washington	1,024	16.5	15
West Virginia	279	15.4	39
Wisconsin	881	16.0	29
Wyoming	84	16.5	16
50 States	48,305	16.5	
DC	62	11.3	
United States	48,367	16.5	

Rank in order by percentage	
1	Utah
2	Alaska
3	Texas
4	Idaho
5	Oklahoma
6	California
7	Georgia
8	Arizona
9	Nevada
10	Kansas
11	New Mexico
12	Michigan
13	Mississippi
14	Colorado
15	Washington
16	Wyoming
17	Illinois
18	Connecticut
19	Minnesota
20	Arkansas
21	Indiana
22	Nebraska
23	Iowa
24	Virginia
25	Alabama
26	Ohio
27	Louisiana
28	New Jersey
29	Wisconsin
30	South Carolina
31	New Hampshire
32	Montana
33	South Dakota
34	North Carolina
35	Tennessee
36	North Dakota
37	Maryland
38	Missouri
39	West Virginia
40	Oregon
41	Kentucky
42	Vermont
43	Massachusetts
44	Maine
45	Florida
46	Rhode Island
47	New York
48	Pennsylvania
49	Hawaii
50	Delaware

Note: Numbers that appear to be identical are rounded and vary slightly in actual value. The rankings reflect the actual values before rounding. See the introduction for more details.

H-11 Public Library Holdings Per Capita, FY 2002

State	Holdings per capita	Rank per capita
Alabama	2.0	40
Alaska	3.5	19
Arizona	1.7	50
Arkansas	2.1	37
California	2.0	40
Colorado	2.7	29
Connecticut	4.2	9
Delaware	1.9	44
Florida	1.8	48
Georgia	1.9	44
Hawaii	2.5	32
Idaho	3.1	23
Illinois	3.7	16
Indiana	4.2	9
Iowa	3.9	14
Kansas	4.8	4
Kentucky	2.0	40
Louisiana	2.5	32
Maine	5.1	1
Maryland	3.0	24
Massachusetts	4.9	2
Michigan	3.2	21
Minnesota	3.2	21
Mississippi	2.1	37
Missouri	3.6	18
Montana	2.9	25
Nebraska	4.4	8
Nevada	1.9	44
New Hampshire	4.5	7
New Jersey	3.7	16
New Mexico	2.5	32
New York	4.2	9
North Carolina	2.0	40
North Dakota	4.1	13
Ohio	4.2	9
Oklahoma	2.2	36
Oregon	2.8	27
Pennsylvania	2.4	35
Rhode Island	3.9	14
South Carolina	2.1	37
South Dakota	4.7	5
Tennessee	1.8	48
Texas	1.9	44
Utah	2.7	29
Vermont	4.7	5
Virginia	2.7	29
Washington	2.9	25
West Virginia	2.8	27
Wisconsin	3.5	19
Wyoming	4.9	2
50 States	n/a	
DC	4.6	
United States	2.8	

Rank in order per capita	
1	Maine
2	Massachusetts
2	Wyoming
4	Kansas
5	South Dakota
5	Vermont
7	New Hampshire
8	Nebraska
9	Connecticut
9	Indiana
9	New York
9	Ohio
13	North Dakota
14	Iowa
14	Rhode Island
16	Illinois
16	New Jersey
18	Missouri
19	Alaska
19	Wisconsin
21	Michigan
21	Minnesota
23	Idaho
24	Maryland
25	Montana
25	Washington
27	Oregon
27	West Virginia
29	Colorado
29	Utah
29	Virginia
32	Hawaii
32	Louisiana
32	New Mexico
35	Pennsylvania
36	Oklahoma
37	Arkansas
37	Mississippi
37	South Carolina
40	Alabama
40	California
40	Kentucky
40	North Carolina
44	Delaware
44	Georgia
44	Nevada
44	Texas
48	Florida
48	Tennessee
50	Arizona

Note: Ties in ranking reflect ties in actual values.

H-12 Children with Disabilities, 2004

State	Children with disabilities #	Percentage of public school enrollment	Rank by percentage
Alabama	93,402	12.8	39
Alaska	18,134	13.6	35
Arizona	119,841	12.2	43
Arkansas	68,088	15.1	21
California	675,417	10.7	50
Colorado	83,249	10.9	49
Connecticut	73,028	12.7	40
Delaware	18,698	15.7	14
Florida	400,001	15.2	19
Georgia	195,928	12.6	41
Hawaii	22,711	12.4	42
Idaho	28,880	11.6	48
Illinois	322,982	15.4	16
Indiana	175,205	17.2	5
Iowa	73,637	15.4	17
Kansas	65,290	13.9	33
Kentucky	106,916	16.8	6
Louisiana	102,498	14.2	29
Maine	37,573	18.9	2
Maryland	112,404	13.0	38
Massachusetts	161,993	16.6	8
Michigan	242,083	14.0	31
Minnesota	115,491	13.8	34
Mississippi	68,883	14.2	28
Missouri	142,872	16.0	12
Montana	19,515	13.3	36
Nebraska	45,712	16.1	10
Nevada	47,015	11.7	46
New Hampshire	31,675	15.3	18
New Jersey	245,878	17.7	4
New Mexico	51,464	15.8	13
New York	452,312	16.0	11
North Carolina	193,377	14.4	27
North Dakota	14,681	14.8	22
Ohio	260,710	14.1	30
Oklahoma	95,022	15.1	20
Oregon	77,094	14.0	32
Pennsylvania	282,356	15.6	15
Rhode Island	31,532	19.6	1
South Carolina	111,509	16.6	7
South Dakota	17,921	14.7	23
Tennessee	122,643	13.2	37
Texas	514,236	11.7	47
Utah	59,840	12.1	44
Vermont	13,894	14.6	25
Virginia	174,417	14.5	26
Washington	124,067	12.1	45
West Virginia	50,377	18.0	3
Wisconsin	129,179	14.7	24
Wyoming	13,565	16.2	9
50 States	6,705,195	13.9	
DC	13,424	21.5	
United States	6,726,670	13.9	

Rank in order by percentage	
1	Rhode Island
2	Maine
3	West Virginia
4	New Jersey
5	Indiana
6	Kentucky
7	South Carolina
8	Massachusetts
9	Wyoming
10	Nebraska
11	New York
12	Missouri
13	New Mexico
14	Delaware
15	Pennsylvania
16	Illinois
17	Iowa
18	New Hampshire
19	Florida
20	Oklahoma
21	Arkansas
22	North Dakota
23	South Dakota
24	Wisconsin
25	Vermont
26	Virginia
27	North Carolina
28	Mississippi
29	Louisiana
30	Ohio
31	Michigan
32	Oregon
33	Kansas
34	Minnesota
35	Alaska
36	Montana
37	Tennessee
38	Maryland
39	Alabama
40	Connecticut
41	Georgia
42	Hawaii
43	Arizona
44	Utah
45	Washington
46	Nevada
47	Texas
48	Idaho
49	Colorado
50	California

Note: Numbers that appear to be identical are rounded and vary slightly in actual value. The rankings reflect the actual values before rounding. See the introduction for more details.

H-13 State and Local Education Spending, FY 2002

State	Education spending $ (in millions)	Education spending per capita	Education spending as a percentage of personal income	Rank per capita
Alabama	8,320	1,855	7.5	38
Alaska	2,107	3,272	10.5	1
Arizona	8,796	1,612	6.4	49
Arkansas	4,783	1,765	7.7	45
California	76,827	2,188	6.8	16
Colorado	9,011	2,000	6.0	29
Connecticut	7,852	2,269	5.4	9
Delaware	1,937	2,399	7.7	4
Florida	25,795	1,543	5.4	50
Georgia	17,366	2,029	7.2	27
Hawaii	2,257	1,813	6.4	40
Idaho	2,423	1,806	7.3	41
Illinois	25,953	2,060	6.3	24
Indiana	12,193	1,980	7.2	30
Iowa	6,467	2,202	8.1	14
Kansas	5,501	2,026	7.2	28
Kentucky	6,878	1,680	6.8	47
Louisiana	7,994	1,783	7.3	43
Maine	2,491	1,924	7.1	35
Maryland	12,142	2,225	6.4	13
Massachusetts	13,443	2,091	5.4	20
Michigan	23,745	2,363	8.0	7
Minnesota	11,266	2,244	6.9	11
Mississippi	5,101	1,776	8.1	44
Missouri	10,556	1,861	6.7	37
Montana	1,792	1,970	8.2	32
Nebraska	3,797	2,196	7.7	15
Nevada	3,679	1,693	5.8	46
New Hampshire	2,439	1,913	5.7	36
New Jersey	20,544	2,391	6.2	5
New Mexico	4,176	2,251	9.5	10
New York	47,723	2,491	7.0	3
North Carolina	15,262	1,834	6.8	39
North Dakota	1,311	2,068	8.0	23
Ohio	23,623	2,068	7.2	22
Oklahoma	6,904	1,976	7.8	31
Oregon	7,543	2,142	7.6	17
Pennsylvania	24,296	1,970	6.5	33
Rhode Island	2,180	2,038	6.8	26
South Carolina	8,380	2,040	8.2	25
South Dakota	1,360	1,787	6.7	42
Tennessee	9,468	1,633	6.1	48
Texas	45,703	2,098	7.4	19
Utah	5,196	2,243	9.3	12
Vermont	1,460	2,368	8.2	6
Virginia	15,149	2,077	6.5	21
Washington	12,866	2,120	6.7	18
West Virginia	3,519	1,953	8.5	34
Wisconsin	12,565	2,309	7.9	8
Wyoming	1,277	2,562	8.6	2
50 States	593,416	2,062	6.8	
DC	1,175	2,058	4.5	
United States	594,591	2,062	6.8	

Rank in order per capita	
1	Alaska
2	Wyoming
3	New York
4	Delaware
5	New Jersey
6	Vermont
7	Michigan
8	Wisconsin
9	Connecticut
10	New Mexico
11	Minnesota
12	Utah
13	Maryland
14	Iowa
15	Nebraska
16	California
17	Oregon
18	Washington
19	Texas
20	Massachusetts
21	Virginia
22	Ohio
23	North Dakota
24	Illinois
25	South Carolina
26	Rhode Island
27	Georgia
28	Kansas
29	Colorado
30	Indiana
31	Oklahoma
32	Montana
33	Pennsylvania
34	West Virginia
35	Maine
36	New Hampshire
37	Missouri
38	Alabama
39	North Carolina
40	Hawaii
41	Idaho
42	South Dakota
43	Louisiana
44	Mississippi
45	Arkansas
46	Nevada
47	Kentucky
48	Tennessee
49	Arizona
50	Florida

Note: Numbers that appear to be identical are rounded and vary slightly in actual value. The rankings reflect the actual values before rounding. See the introduction for more details.

H-14 State and Local Education Spending as a Percentage of General Spending, FY 2002

State	Education spending as a percentage of general spending	Rank by percentage
Alabama	33.8	29
Alaska	25.0	50
Arizona	34.8	27
Arkansas	36.6	16
California	32.6	39
Colorado	33.3	32
Connecticut	32.4	40
Delaware	36.2	19
Florida	29.6	47
Georgia	38.6	5
Hawaii	27.2	49
Idaho	35.6	21
Illinois	35.2	25
Indiana	37.2	13
Iowa	37.6	12
Kansas	37.0	14
Kentucky	31.9	43
Louisiana	32.9	36
Maine	31.3	45
Maryland	38.2	9
Massachusetts	31.7	44
Michigan	39.1	3
Minnesota	32.3	41
Mississippi	33.2	33
Missouri	36.3	18
Montana	35.5	22
Nebraska	39.0	4
Nevada	31.3	46
New Hampshire	38.5	7
New Jersey	37.8	11
New Mexico	36.5	17
New York	29.6	48
North Carolina	34.3	28
North Dakota	33.7	30
Ohio	35.2	23
Oklahoma	38.0	10
Oregon	32.8	37
Pennsylvania	33.1	35
Rhode Island	32.2	42
South Carolina	35.2	24
South Dakota	35.0	26
Tennessee	32.7	38
Texas	41.0	1
Utah	40.4	2
Vermont	38.4	8
Virginia	38.6	6
Washington	33.3	31
West Virginia	35.7	20
Wisconsin	37.0	15
Wyoming	33.2	34
50 States	34.4	
DC	19.0	
United States	34.4	

Rank in order by percentage	
1	Texas
2	Utah
3	Michigan
4	Nebraska
5	Georgia
6	Virginia
7	New Hampshire
8	Vermont
9	Maryland
10	Oklahoma
11	New Jersey
12	Iowa
13	Indiana
14	Kansas
15	Wisconsin
16	Arkansas
17	New Mexico
18	Missouri
19	Delaware
20	West Virginia
21	Idaho
22	Montana
23	Ohio
24	South Carolina
25	Illinois
26	South Dakota
27	Arizona
28	North Carolina
29	Alabama
30	North Dakota
31	Washington
32	Colorado
33	Mississippi
34	Wyoming
35	Pennsylvania
36	Louisiana
37	Oregon
38	Tennessee
39	California
40	Connecticut
41	Minnesota
42	Rhode Island
43	Kentucky
44	Massachusetts
45	Maine
46	Nevada
47	Florida
48	New York
49	Hawaii
50	Alaska

Note: Numbers that appear to be identical are rounded and vary slightly in actual value. The rankings reflect the actual values before rounding. See the introduction for more details.

H-15 Spending Per Pupil, 2004-2005

State	Spending per pupil $	Rank
Alabama	6,886	42
Alaska	10,042	10
Arizona	5,474	49
Arkansas	6,202	48
California	7,815	31
Colorado	8,337	24
Connecticut	11,893	3
Delaware	11,016	6
Florida	7,035	40
Georgia	8,451	23
Hawaii	8,622	21
Idaho	6,743	44
Illinois	9,591	15
Indiana	8,723	20
Iowa	7,477	36
Kansas	7,558	35
Kentucky	7,906	28
Louisiana	7,589	34
Maine	10,723	7
Maryland	9,762	11
Massachusetts	11,681	4
Michigan	8,909	19
Minnesota	9,249	18
Mississippi	6,452	46
Missouri	7,451	37
Montana	8,025	27
Nebraska	7,608	33
Nevada	6,525	45
New Hampshire	9,642	12
New Jersey	13,370	1
New Mexico	8,236	25
New York	12,879	2
North Carolina	7,350	38
North Dakota	7,033	41
Ohio	9,557	16
Oklahoma	6,269	47
Oregon	7,842	30
Pennsylvania	9,638	13
Rhode Island	10,641	8
South Carolina	8,161	26
South Dakota	7,618	32
Tennessee	6,856	43
Texas	7,142	39
Utah	5,245	50
Vermont	11,608	5
Virginia	8,577	22
Washington	7,858	29
West Virginia	9,448	17
Wisconsin	9,619	14
Wyoming	10,198	9
50 States	n/a	
DC	15,073	
United States	8,618	

Rank in order by $	
1	New Jersey
2	New York
3	Connecticut
4	Massachusetts
5	Vermont
6	Delaware
7	Maine
8	Rhode Island
9	Wyoming
10	Alaska
11	Maryland
12	New Hampshire
13	Pennsylvania
14	Wisconsin
15	Illinois
16	Ohio
17	West Virginia
18	Minnesota
19	Michigan
20	Indiana
21	Hawaii
22	Virginia
23	Georgia
24	Colorado
25	New Mexico
26	South Carolina
27	Montana
28	Kentucky
29	Washington
30	Oregon
31	California
32	South Dakota
33	Nebraska
34	Louisiana
35	Kansas
36	Iowa
37	Missouri
38	North Carolina
39	Texas
40	Florida
41	North Dakota
42	Alabama
43	Tennessee
44	Idaho
45	Nevada
46	Mississippi
47	Oklahoma
48	Arkansas
49	Arizona
50	Utah

H-16 Average Teacher Salary, 2004–2005

State	Average teacher salary $	Rank
Alabama	38,186	46
Alaska	52,424	10
Arizona	42,905	27
Arkansas	40,495	34
California	57,876	2
Colorado	43,949	23
Connecticut	58,688	1
Delaware	50,869	12
Florida	41,587	31
Georgia	46,526	17
Hawaii	46,149	18
Idaho	42,122	29
Illinois	55,629	6
Indiana	46,591	16
Iowa	39,284	40
Kansas	39,175	41
Kentucky	40,522	33
Louisiana	38,880	43
Maine	39,610	37
Maryland	52,331	11
Massachusetts	54,325	7
Michigan	56,973	3
Minnesota	46,906	15
Mississippi	36,590	48
Missouri	38,971	42
Montana	38,485	44
Nebraska	39,456	38
Nevada	43,394	25
New Hampshire	43,941	24
New Jersey	56,682	4
New Mexico	39,391	39
New York	56,200	5
North Carolina	43,348	26
North Dakota	36,449	49
Ohio	48,692	13
Oklahoma	37,879	47
Oregon	48,330	14
Pennsylvania	53,258	9
Rhode Island	53,473	8
South Carolina	42,207	28
South Dakota	34,040	50
Tennessee	42,072	30
Texas	41,009	32
Utah	39,965	36
Vermont	44,535	21
Virginia	44,763	20
Washington	45,724	19
West Virginia	38,360	45
Wisconsin	44,299	22
Wyoming	40,392	35
50 States	n/a	
DC	58,456	
United States	47,808	

Rank in order by $	
1	Connecticut
2	California
3	Michigan
4	New Jersey
5	New York
6	Illinois
7	Massachusetts
8	Rhode Island
9	Pennsylvania
10	Alaska
11	Maryland
12	Delaware
13	Ohio
14	Oregon
15	Minnesota
16	Indiana
17	Georgia
18	Hawaii
19	Washington
20	Virginia
21	Vermont
22	Wisconsin
23	Colorado
24	New Hampshire
25	Nevada
26	North Carolina
27	Arizona
28	South Carolina
29	Idaho
30	Tennessee
31	Florida
32	Texas
33	Kentucky
34	Arkansas
35	Wyoming
36	Utah
37	Maine
38	Nebraska
39	New Mexico
40	Iowa
41	Kansas
42	Missouri
43	Louisiana
44	Montana
45	West Virginia
46	Alabama
47	Oklahoma
48	Mississippi
49	North Dakota
50	South Dakota

H-17 Sources of School Funds, 2004–2005

State	Percentage from federal	Percentage from state	Percentage from local	Rank by percentage local
Alabama	11.8	57.4	30.8	36
Alaska	12.5	63.5	23.9	46
Arizona	7.7	51.2	41.0	27
Arkansas	11.3	51.8	36.9	33
California	10.8	63.7	25.5	44
Colorado	7.0	43.3	49.7	14
Connecticut	6.0	39.2	54.8	9
Delaware	10.0	63.0	27.0	43
Florida	10.8	42.7	46.6	19
Georgia	9.1	45.2	45.7	21
Hawaii	10.5	87.2	2.3	50
Idaho	9.6	60.1	30.4	38
Illinois	8.5	29.2	62.3	1
Indiana	6.8	50.3	42.9	23
Iowa	7.3	46.2	46.4	20
Kansas	8.1	52.8	39.2	30
Kentucky	11.8	58.5	29.7	39
Louisiana	13.5	48.6	37.8	32
Maine	9.6	40.8	49.7	15
Maryland	7.2	37.3	55.5	7
Massachusetts	6.2	41.1	52.7	11
Michigan	7.4	64.0	28.7	41
Minnesota	6.8	69.5	23.7	47
Mississippi	15.1	54.2	30.7	37
Missouri	9.1	32.4	58.5	5
Montana	12.2	47.1	40.7	29
Nebraska	7.4	37.8	54.8	8
Nevada	7.6	31.6	60.8	2
New Hampshire	6.2	51.8	41.9	25
New Jersey	3.3	37.7	59.0	4
New Mexico	18.0	69.7	12.3	48
New York	6.6	45.3	48.1	17
North Carolina	11.6	63.6	24.8	45
North Dakota	14.2	35.7	50.0	13
Ohio	6.3	46.0	47.8	18
Oklahoma	13.1	53.6	33.2	34
Oregon	10.1	49.1	40.8	28
Pennsylvania	8.3	35.6	56.1	6
Rhode Island	3.4	36.7	59.9	3
South Carolina	11.5	44.8	43.7	22
South Dakota	16.4	34.4	49.2	16
Tennessee	12.1	45.8	42.1	24
Texas	11.6	37.3	51.1	12
Utah	9.5	57.7	32.9	35
Vermont	8.0	85.9	6.1	49
Virginia	7.3	38.2	54.5	10
Washington	10.3	61.6	28.1	42
West Virginia	11.9	59.3	28.8	40
Wisconsin	6.8	52.0	41.2	26
Wyoming	9.5	51.4	39.0	31
50 States	n/a	n/a	n/a	
DC	14.8	0.0	85.2	
United States	8.9	48.3	42.7	

Rank in order by percentage local	
1	Illinois
2	Nevada
3	Rhode Island
4	New Jersey
5	Missouri
6	Pennsylvania
7	Maryland
8	Nebraska
9	Connecticut
10	Virginia
11	Massachusetts
12	Texas
13	North Dakota
14	Colorado
15	Maine
16	South Dakota
17	New York
18	Ohio
19	Florida
20	Iowa
21	Georgia
22	South Carolina
23	Indiana
24	Tennessee
25	New Hampshire
26	Wisconsin
27	Arizona
28	Oregon
29	Montana
30	Kansas
31	Wyoming
32	Louisiana
33	Arkansas
34	Oklahoma
35	Utah
36	Alabama
37	Mississippi
38	Idaho
39	Kentucky
40	West Virginia
41	Michigan
42	Washington
43	Delaware
44	California
45	North Carolina
46	Alaska
47	Minnesota
48	New Mexico
49	Vermont
50	Hawaii

Note: Numbers that appear to be identical are rounded and vary slightly in actual value. The rankings reflect the actual values before rounding. See the introduction for more details.

H-18 State Aid Per Pupil in Average Daily Attendance, 2004-2005

State	State aid per pupil $ (in thousands)	Rank
Alabama	4,478	28
Alaska	7,197	7
Arizona	4,069	39
Arkansas	4,802	25
California	6,632	9
Colorado	4,076	37
Connecticut	5,493	18
Delaware	7,863	4
Florida	3,963	41
Georgia	4,614	27
Hawaii	11,507	2
Idaho	4,272	34
Illinois	3,089	48
Indiana	5,486	20
Iowa	4,422	30
Kansas	5,504	17
Kentucky	5,595	15
Louisiana	4,394	31
Maine	4,866	23
Maryland	4,305	32
Massachusetts	5,532	16
Michigan	8,184	3
Minnesota	7,742	5
Mississippi	4,302	33
Missouri	3,268	45
Montana	4,709	26
Nebraska	3,380	44
Nevada	2,557	50
New Hampshire	5,785	14
New Jersey	5,398	21
New Mexico	7,203	6
New York	6,286	11
North Carolina	4,860	24
North Dakota	3,216	47
Ohio	5,487	19
Oklahoma	4,070	38
Oregon	4,946	22
Pennsylvania	4,222	35
Rhode Island	3,727	42
South Carolina	4,445	29
South Dakota	3,084	49
Tennessee	3,528	43
Texas	3,265	46
Utah	4,098	36
Vermont	12,949	1
Virginia	4,057	40
Washington	5,879	13
West Virginia	6,311	10
Wisconsin	6,021	12
Wyoming	6,637	8
50 States	5,067	
DC	n/a	
United States	5,056	

Rank in order by $	
1	Vermont
2	Hawaii
3	Michigan
4	Delaware
5	Minnesota
6	New Mexico
7	Alaska
8	Wyoming
9	California
10	West Virginia
11	New York
12	Wisconsin
13	Washington
14	New Hampshire
15	Kentucky
16	Massachusetts
17	Kansas
18	Connecticut
19	Ohio
20	Indiana
21	New Jersey
22	Oregon
23	Maine
24	North Carolina
25	Arkansas
26	Montana
27	Georgia
28	Alabama
29	South Carolina
30	Iowa
31	Louisiana
32	Maryland
33	Mississippi
34	Idaho
35	Pennsylvania
36	Utah
37	Colorado
38	Oklahoma
39	Arizona
40	Virginia
41	Florida
42	Rhode Island
43	Tennessee
44	Nebraska
45	Missouri
46	Texas
47	North Dakota
48	Illinois
49	South Dakota
50	Nevada

H-19 State and Local Spending for Higher Education (Census Definition), FY 2002

State	Higher education spending $ (in millions)	Per capita $	Percentage of personal income	Rank per capita
Alabama	2,720	606	2.5	21
Alaska	487	757	2.4	6
Arizona	2,703	495	2.0	36
Arkansas	1,438	531	2.3	30
California	20,376	580	1.8	25
Colorado	2,856	634	1.9	19
Connecticut	1,555	449	1.1	43
Delaware	629	780	2.5	5
Florida	5,792	347	1.2	50
Georgia	3,891	455	1.6	42
Hawaii	792	636	2.3	18
Idaho	692	516	2.1	33
Illinois	6,506	516	1.6	32
Indiana	3,614	587	2.1	24
Iowa	2,328	793	2.9	3
Kansas	1,770	652	2.3	14
Kentucky	2,403	587	2.4	23
Louisiana	2,092	467	1.9	40
Maine	559	432	1.6	46
Maryland	3,531	647	1.9	15
Massachusetts	2,517	392	1.0	48
Michigan	7,296	726	2.5	7
Minnesota	2,947	587	1.8	22
Mississippi	1,841	641	2.9	16
Missouri	2,645	466	1.7	41
Montana	506	557	2.3	28
Nebraska	1,192	689	2.4	11
Nevada	810	373	1.3	49
New Hampshire	561	440	1.3	45
New Jersey	4,028	469	1.2	38
New Mexico	1,462	788	3.3	4
New York	7,983	417	1.2	47
North Carolina	5,148	619	2.3	20
North Dakota	510	805	3.1	2
Ohio	5,834	511	1.8	34
Oklahoma	2,228	638	2.5	17
Oregon	2,538	721	2.6	9
Pennsylvania	5,770	468	1.5	39
Rhode Island	480	448	1.5	44
South Carolina	2,130	519	2.1	31
South Dakota	362	476	1.8	37
Tennessee	2,958	510	1.9	35
Texas	12,482	573	2.0	26
Utah	2,131	920	3.8	1
Vermont	429	695	2.4	10
Virginia	4,154	570	1.8	27
Washington	3,982	656	2.1	13
West Virginia	1,000	555	2.4	29
Wisconsin	3,710	682	2.3	12
Wyoming	360	723	2.4	8
50 States	156,731	545	1.8	
DC	79	139	0.3	
United States	156,810	544	1.8	

Rank in order per capita	
1	Utah
2	North Dakota
3	Iowa
4	New Mexico
5	Delaware
6	Alaska
7	Michigan
8	Wyoming
9	Oregon
10	Vermont
11	Nebraska
12	Wisconsin
13	Washington
14	Kansas
15	Maryland
16	Mississippi
17	Oklahoma
18	Hawaii
19	Colorado
20	North Carolina
21	Alabama
22	Minnesota
23	Kentucky
24	Indiana
25	California
26	Texas
27	Virginia
28	Montana
29	West Virginia
30	Arkansas
31	South Carolina
32	Illinois
33	Idaho
34	Ohio
35	Tennessee
36	Arizona
37	South Dakota
38	New Jersey
39	Pennsylvania
40	Louisiana
41	Missouri
42	Georgia
43	Connecticut
44	Rhode Island
45	New Hampshire
46	Maine
47	New York
48	Massachusetts
49	Nevada
50	Florida

Note: Numbers that appear to be identical are rounded and vary slightly in actual value. The rankings reflect the actual values before rounding. See the introduction for more details.

H-20 State and Local Spending for Higher Education as a Percentage of General Spending, FY 2002

State	Higher education spending as a percentage of general spending	Rank
Alabama	11.1	16
Alaska	5.8	49
Arizona	10.7	21
Arkansas	11.0	19
California	8.7	38
Colorado	10.5	23
Connecticut	6.4	47
Delaware	11.8	10
Florida	6.7	46
Georgia	8.7	37
Hawaii	9.6	29
Idaho	10.2	26
Illinois	8.8	35
Indiana	11.0	18
Iowa	13.5	2
Kansas	11.9	9
Kentucky	11.1	14
Louisiana	8.6	39
Maine	7.0	44
Maryland	11.1	15
Massachusetts	5.9	48
Michigan	12.0	7
Minnesota	8.4	40
Mississippi	12.0	8
Missouri	9.1	32
Montana	10.0	28
Nebraska	12.2	6
Nevada	6.9	45
New Hampshire	8.8	34
New Jersey	7.4	42
New Mexico	12.8	4
New York	5.0	50
North Carolina	11.6	11
North Dakota	13.1	3
Ohio	8.7	36
Oklahoma	12.3	5
Oregon	11.0	17
Pennsylvania	7.9	41
Rhode Island	7.1	43
South Carolina	8.9	33
South Dakota	9.3	31
Tennessee	10.2	25
Texas	11.2	13
Utah	16.6	1
Vermont	11.3	12
Virginia	10.6	22
Washington	10.3	24
West Virginia	10.2	27
Wisconsin	10.9	20
Wyoming	9.4	30
50 States	9.1	
DC	1.3	
United States	9.1	

Rank in order by percentage	
1	Utah
2	Iowa
3	North Dakota
4	New Mexico
5	Oklahoma
6	Nebraska
7	Michigan
8	Mississippi
9	Kansas
10	Delaware
11	North Carolina
12	Vermont
13	Texas
14	Kentucky
15	Maryland
16	Alabama
17	Oregon
18	Indiana
19	Arkansas
20	Wisconsin
21	Arizona
22	Virginia
23	Colorado
24	Washington
25	Tennessee
26	Idaho
27	West Virginia
28	Montana
29	Hawaii
30	Wyoming
31	South Dakota
32	Missouri
33	South Carolina
34	New Hampshire
35	Illinois
36	Ohio
37	Georgia
38	California
39	Louisiana
40	Minnesota
41	Pennsylvania
42	New Jersey
43	Rhode Island
44	Maine
45	Nevada
46	Florida
47	Connecticut
48	Massachusetts
49	Alaska
50	New York

Note: Numbers that appear to be identical are rounded and vary slightly in actual value. The rankings reflect the actual values before rounding. See the introduction for more details.

H-21 Public Higher Education Enrollment, 2003

State	Higher education enrollment #	Percentage of total population	Rank
Alabama	255,183	5.7	29
Alaska	31,451	4.9	47
Arizona	437,620	7.8	2
Arkansas	138,407	5.1	43
California	2,410,306	6.8	10
Colorado	306,370	6.7	11
Connecticut	179,103	5.1	42
Delaware	50,319	6.2	19
Florida	894,088	5.3	39
Georgia	422,067	4.9	46
Hawaii	68,072	5.5	37
Idaho	76,442	5.6	32
Illinois	809,721	6.4	15
Indiana	353,158	5.7	27
Iowa	215,624	7.3	5
Kansas	194,422	7.1	6
Kentucky	237,766	5.8	23
Louisiana	252,063	5.6	31
Maine	65,107	5.0	45
Maryland	316,307	5.7	26
Massachusetts	445,633	6.9	7
Michigan	627,358	6.2	18
Minnesota	339,731	6.7	13
Mississippi	149,665	5.2	40
Missouri	363,792	6.4	16
Montana	47,412	5.2	41
Nebraska	120,305	6.9	8
Nevada	101,804	4.5	49
New Hampshire	70,438	5.5	36
New Jersey	391,669	4.5	50
New Mexico	127,768	6.8	9
New York	1,157,256	6.0	22
North Carolina	468,025	5.6	33
North Dakota	48,641	7.7	3
Ohio	620,351	5.4	38
Oklahoma	221,797	6.3	17
Oregon	202,346	5.7	28
Pennsylvania	696,770	5.6	30
Rhode Island	81,415	7.6	4
South Carolina	209,080	5.0	44
South Dakota	49,157	6.4	14
Tennessee	281,080	4.8	48
Texas	1,225,807	5.5	34
Utah	191,218	8.1	1
Vermont	37,915	6.1	20
Virginia	424,316	5.8	24
Washington	353,198	5.8	25
West Virginia	100,242	5.5	35
Wisconsin	331,153	6.0	21
Wyoming	33,750	6.7	12
50 States	17,232,688	5.9	
DC	96,774	17.4	
United States	17,329,462	6.0	

Rank in order by percentage	
1	Utah
2	Arizona
3	North Dakota
4	Rhode Island
5	Iowa
6	Kansas
7	Massachusetts
8	Nebraska
9	New Mexico
10	California
11	Colorado
12	Wyoming
13	Minnesota
14	South Dakota
15	Illinois
16	Missouri
17	Oklahoma
18	Michigan
19	Delaware
20	Vermont
21	Wisconsin
22	New York
23	Kentucky
24	Virginia
25	Washington
26	Maryland
27	Indiana
28	Oregon
29	Alabama
30	Pennsylvania
31	Louisiana
32	Idaho
33	North Carolina
34	Texas
35	West Virginia
36	New Hampshire
37	Hawaii
38	Ohio
39	Florida
40	Mississippi
41	Montana
42	Connecticut
43	Arkansas
44	South Carolina
45	Maine
46	Georgia
47	Alaska
48	Tennessee
49	Nevada
50	New Jersey

Note: Numbers that appear to be identical are rounded and vary slightly in actual value. The rankings reflect the actual values before rounding. See the introduction for more details.

H-22 Per Pupil State Support of Higher Education, FY 2005

State	Per pupil support $	Rank
Alabama	4,749	11
Alaska	7,420	1
Arizona	2,088	46
Arkansas	4,942	9
California	3,772	23
Colorado	1,931	49
Connecticut	4,294	14
Delaware	4,044	18
Florida	3,491	30
Georgia	4,510	13
Hawaii	6,019	3
Idaho	4,220	15
Illinois	3,278	37
Indiana	4,014	20
Iowa	3,445	31
Kansas	3,682	25
Kentucky	4,709	12
Louisiana	5,026	7
Maine	3,681	26
Maryland	3,681	27
Massachusetts	1,976	48
Michigan	3,152	41
Minnesota	3,748	24
Mississippi	5,279	6
Missouri	2,368	44
Montana	3,218	39
Nebraska	4,202	16
Nevada	4,978	8
New Hampshire	1,636	50
New Jersey	4,838	10
New Mexico	5,306	5
New York	3,499	29
North Carolina	5,616	4
North Dakota	4,121	17
Ohio	3,391	33
Oklahoma	3,435	32
Oregon	2,899	42
Pennsylvania	2,888	43
Rhode Island	2,140	45
South Carolina	3,192	40
South Dakota	3,302	36
Tennessee	3,873	22
Texas	3,983	21
Utah	3,272	38
Vermont	2,084	47
Virginia	3,509	28
Washington	4,042	19
West Virginia	3,386	34
Wisconsin	3,333	35
Wyoming	6,279	2
50 States	3,656	
DC	n/a	
United States	3,636	

Rank in order by $	
1	Alaska
2	Wyoming
3	Hawaii
4	North Carolina
5	New Mexico
6	Mississippi
7	Louisiana
8	Nevada
9	Arkansas
10	New Jersey
11	Alabama
12	Kentucky
13	Georgia
14	Connecticut
15	Idaho
16	Nebraska
17	North Dakota
18	Delaware
19	Washington
20	Indiana
21	Texas
22	Tennessee
23	California
24	Minnesota
25	Kansas
26	Maine
27	Maryland
28	Virginia
29	New York
30	Florida
31	Iowa
32	Oklahoma
33	Ohio
34	West Virginia
35	Wisconsin
36	South Dakota
37	Illinois
38	Utah
39	Montana
40	South Carolina
41	Michigan
42	Oregon
43	Pennsylvania
44	Missouri
45	Rhode Island
46	Arizona
47	Vermont
48	Massachusetts
49	Colorado
50	New Hampshire

Note: Numbers that appear to be identical are rounded and vary slightly in actual value. The rankings reflect the actual values before rounding. See the introduction for more details.

H-23 Average In-State Tuition and Fees at Public Universities, 2004–2005

State	Average in-state tuition and fees $	Rank
Alabama	4,497	29
Alaska	3,525	45
Arizona	4,078	35
Arkansas	4,602	27
California	4,262	33
Colorado	3,583	42
Connecticut	6,290	12
Delaware	6,626	8
Florida	3,048	49
Georgia	3,517	46
Hawaii	3,581	43
Idaho	3,623	41
Illinois	6,446	10
Indiana	5,859	16
Iowa	5,407	19
Kansas	4,206	34
Kentucky	4,472	30
Louisiana	3,641	40
Maine	5,652	17
Maryland	6,424	11
Massachusetts	7,060	6
Michigan	6,187	13
Minnesota	6,599	9
Mississippi	4,002	36
Missouri	6,009	14
Montana	4,449	31
Nebraska	4,809	25
Nevada	2,850	50
New Hampshire	8,173	4
New Jersey	8,108	5
New Mexico	3,534	44
New York	5,036	23
North Carolina	3,651	39
North Dakota	4,603	26
Ohio	8,364	3
Oklahoma	3,814	37
Oregon	5,117	20
Pennsylvania	8,698	2
Rhode Island	5,931	15
South Carolina	6,646	7
South Dakota	4,504	28
Tennessee	4,335	32
Texas	5,075	21
Utah	3,402	47
Vermont	9,036	1
Virginia	5,554	18
Washington	4,925	24
West Virginia	3,700	38
Wisconsin	5,051	22
Wyoming	3,243	48
50 States	n/a	
DC	2,520	
United States	5,143	

Rank in order by $	
1	Vermont
2	Pennsylvania
3	Ohio
4	New Hampshire
5	New Jersey
6	Massachusetts
7	South Carolina
8	Delaware
9	Minnesota
10	Illinois
11	Maryland
12	Connecticut
13	Michigan
14	Missouri
15	Rhode Island
16	Indiana
17	Maine
18	Virginia
19	Iowa
20	Oregon
21	Texas
22	Wisconsin
23	New York
24	Washington
25	Nebraska
26	North Dakota
27	Arkansas
28	South Dakota
29	Alabama
30	Kentucky
31	Montana
32	Tennessee
33	California
34	Kansas
35	Arizona
36	Mississippi
37	Oklahoma
38	West Virginia
39	North Carolina
40	Louisiana
41	Idaho
42	Colorado
43	Hawaii
44	New Mexico
45	Alaska
46	Georgia
47	Utah
48	Wyoming
49	Florida
50	Nevada

H-24 Average Out-of-State Tuition and Fees at Public Universities, 2004–2005

State	Average out-of-state tuition and fees $	Rank
Alabama	12,664	34
Alaska	11,338	45
Arizona	13,067	31
Arkansas	12,425	36
California	22,912	3
Colorado	21,669	5
Connecticut	19,322	11
Delaware	16,640	21
Florida	15,672	25
Georgia	15,588	27
Hawaii	10,061	47
Idaho	11,652	42
Illinois	20,864	6
Indiana	18,085	14
Iowa	16,048	23
Kansas	12,691	33
Kentucky	12,019	40
Louisiana	11,092	46
Maine	15,784	24
Maryland	18,726	12
Massachusetts	17,861	16
Michigan	26,027	1
Minnesota	19,659	10
Mississippi	9,264	50
Missouri	16,547	22
Montana	12,787	32
Nebraska	13,478	30
Nevada	11,524	43
New Hampshire	20,256	8
New Jersey	15,599	26
New Mexico	12,447	35
New York	12,217	38
North Carolina	17,549	19
North Dakota	11,522	44
Ohio	18,033	15
Oklahoma	11,658	41
Oregon	17,646	18
Pennsylvania	20,784	7
Rhode Island	18,338	13
South Carolina	16,784	20
South Dakota	9,296	48
Tennessee	14,529	28
Texas	13,634	29
Utah	12,410	37
Vermont	23,866	2
Virginia	22,700	4
Washington	17,811	17
West Virginia	12,060	39
Wisconsin	19,862	9
Wyoming	9,273	49
50 States	n/a	
DC	n/a	
United States	15,675	

Rank in order by $	
1	Michigan
2	Vermont
3	California
4	Virginia
5	Colorado
6	Illinois
7	Pennsylvania
8	New Hampshire
9	Wisconsin
10	Minnesota
11	Connecticut
12	Maryland
13	Rhode Island
14	Indiana
15	Ohio
16	Massachusetts
17	Washington
18	Oregon
19	North Carolina
20	South Carolina
21	Delaware
22	Missouri
23	Iowa
24	Maine
25	Florida
26	New Jersey
27	Georgia
28	Tennessee
29	Texas
30	Nebraska
31	Arizona
32	Montana
33	Kansas
34	Alabama
35	New Mexico
36	Arkansas
37	Utah
38	New York
39	West Virginia
40	Kentucky
41	Oklahoma
42	Idaho
43	Nevada
44	North Dakota
45	Alaska
46	Louisiana
47	Hawaii
48	South Dakota
49	Wyoming
50	Mississippi

H-25 Percentage Change in Tuition and Fees at Public Universities, 2004–2005

State	Average in-state tuition and fees $	Average out-of-state tuition and fees $	Rank by in-state $
Alabama	10.7	12.1	13
Alaska	-1.6	18.3	50
Arizona	13.3	5.7	8
Arkansas	9.9	7.9	18
California	14.5	17.7	6
Colorado	2.6	6.6	48
Connecticut	6.8	9.8	33
Delaware	7.4	3.8	30
Florida	4.9	13.5	43
Georgia	3.2	4.9	47
Hawaii	3.3	1.2	46
Idaho	7.7	8.5	28
Illinois	13.2	15.6	9
Indiana	4.9	7.6	43
Iowa	8.3	5	24
Kansas	11.2	9.6	11
Kentucky	15.6	7.1	4
Louisiana	6.5	19.9	35
Maine	6.9	8	32
Maryland	9.4	7.4	21
Massachusetts	7.6	9.3	29
Michigan	10.9	5	12
Minnesota	4.5	4.9	45
Mississippi	5.6	5	40
Missouri	10.2	3.4	15
Montana	8.5	7.8	23
Nebraska	10.1	9.1	17
Nevada	5.6	3.3	40
New Hampshire	6.0	6.5	38
New Jersey	7.0	8	31
New Mexico	6.8	4.1	33
New York	0.7	3.5	49
North Carolina	11.8	10.2	10
North Dakota	18.2	16.4	3
Ohio	21.9	10	2
Oklahoma	9.5	13.7	20
Oregon	10.3	3.4	14
Pennsylvania	8.3	10.4	24
Rhode Island	8.7	12.4	22
South Carolina	15.2	11	5
South Dakota	5.8	4.3	39
Tennessee	6.5	7.4	35
Texas	27.8	6.4	1
Utah	8.3	9.9	24
Vermont	6.2	5.2	37
Virginia	9.8	3.3	19
Washington	7.9	11.2	27
West Virginia	10.2	12	15
Wisconsin	13.5	3.8	7
Wyoming	5.0	3.7	42
50 States	n/a	n/a	
DC	0.0	n/a	
United States	10.6	8.1	

Rank in order by in-state $	
1	Texas
2	Ohio
3	North Dakota
4	Kentucky
5	South Carolina
6	California
7	Wisconsin
8	Arizona
9	Illinois
10	North Carolina
11	Kansas
12	Michigan
13	Alabama
14	Oregon
15	Missouri
15	West Virginia
17	Nebraska
18	Arkansas
19	Virginia
20	Oklahoma
21	Maryland
22	Rhode Island
23	Montana
24	Iowa
24	Pennsylvania
24	Utah
27	Washington
28	Idaho
29	Massachusetts
30	Delaware
31	New Jersey
32	Maine
33	Connecticut
33	New Mexico
35	Louisiana
35	Tennessee
37	Vermont
38	New Hampshire
39	South Dakota
40	Mississippi
40	Nevada
42	Wyoming
43	Florida
43	Indiana
45	Minnesota
46	Hawaii
47	Georgia
48	Colorado
49	New York
50	Alaska

Note: Ties in ranking reflect ties in actual values.

H-26 Higher Education Affordability Index, 2004

State	Affordability index (100=most affordable)	Rank
Alabama	45	45
Alaska	57	19
Arizona	51	35
Arkansas	55	25
California	83	1
Colorado	61	11
Connecticut	53	27
Delaware	51	35
Florida	52	33
Georgia	53	27
Hawaii	63	7
Idaho	62	10
Illinois	66	4
Indiana	63	7
Iowa	55	25
Kansas	58	18
Kentucky	60	14
Louisiana	53	27
Maine	43	46
Maryland	53	27
Massachusetts	51	35
Michigan	57	19
Minnesota	72	3
Mississippi	51	35
Missouri	53	27
Montana	42	48
Nebraska	59	15
Nevada	52	33
New Hampshire	41	50
New Jersey	64	6
New Mexico	59	15
New York	56	21
North Carolina	61	11
North Dakota	51	35
Ohio	46	43
Oklahoma	56	21
Oregon	43	46
Pennsylvania	59	15
Rhode Island	42	48
South Carolina	46	43
South Dakota	50	40
Tennessee	48	42
Texas	63	7
Utah	74	2
Vermont	53	27
Virginia	61	11
Washington	56	21
West Virginia	50	40
Wisconsin	65	5
Wyoming	56	21
50 States	n/a	
DC	n/a	
United States	n/a	

Rank in order by index	
1	California
2	Utah
3	Minnesota
4	Illinois
5	Wisconsin
6	New Jersey
7	Hawaii
7	Indiana
7	Texas
10	Idaho
11	Colorado
11	North Carolina
11	Virginia
14	Kentucky
15	Nebraska
15	New Mexico
15	Pennsylvania
18	Kansas
19	Alaska
19	Michigan
21	New York
21	Oklahoma
21	Washington
21	Wyoming
25	Arkansas
25	Iowa
27	Connecticut
27	Georgia
27	Louisiana
27	Maryland
27	Missouri
27	Vermont
33	Florida
33	Nevada
35	Arizona
35	Delaware
35	Massachusetts
35	Mississippi
35	North Dakota
40	South Dakota
40	West Virginia
42	Tennessee
43	Ohio
43	South Carolina
45	Alabama
46	Maine
46	Oregon
48	Montana
48	Rhode Island
50	New Hampshire

Note: Ties in ranking reflect ties in actual values.

H-27 Average Salary of Associate Professors at "Flagship" State Universities, 2004-2005

State	Associate professor average salary $ (in thousands)	Rank
Alabama	64.0	36
Alaska	59.9	44
Arizona	68.9	24
Arkansas	63.0	37
California	78.1	4
Colorado	72.7	14
Connecticut	79.0	3
Delaware	76.1	9
Florida	69.1	22
Georgia	64.7	34
Hawaii	68.0	27
Idaho	57.6	48
Illinois	75.1	12
Indiana	70.7	18
Iowa	69.1	22
Kansas	65.2	32
Kentucky	64.1	35
Louisiana	61.7	42
Maine	63.0	37
Maryland	76.3	8
Massachusetts	82.1	1
Michigan	81.6	2
Minnesota	70.7	18
Mississippi	65.1	33
Missouri	65.9	29
Montana	53.2	50
Nebraska	68.1	26
Nevada	75.6	10
New Hampshire	71.6	16
New Jersey	77.7	6
New Mexico	59.8	45
New York	70.8	17
North Carolina	77.2	7
North Dakota	60.0	43
Ohio	72.1	15
Oklahoma	61.9	41
Oregon	59.0	47
Pennsylvania	75.4	11
Rhode Island	62.3	40
South Carolina	65.7	30
South Dakota	56.8	49
Tennessee	68.9	24
Texas	70.3	20
Utah	66.2	28
Vermont	65.3	31
Virginia	78.1	4
Washington	70.2	21
West Virginia	59.8	45
Wisconsin	73.4	13
Wyoming	62.4	39
50 States	68.3	
DC	82.8	
United States	68.6	

Rank in order by $	
1	Massachusetts
2	Michigan
3	Connecticut
4	California
4	Virginia
6	New Jersey
7	North Carolina
8	Maryland
9	Delaware
10	Nevada
11	Pennsylvania
12	Illinois
13	Wisconsin
14	Colorado
15	Ohio
16	New Hampshire
17	New York
18	Indiana
18	Minnesota
20	Texas
21	Washington
22	Florida
22	Iowa
24	Arizona
24	Tennessee
26	Nebraska
27	Hawaii
28	Utah
29	Missouri
30	South Carolina
31	Vermont
32	Kansas
33	Mississippi
34	Georgia
35	Kentucky
36	Alabama
37	Arkansas
37	Maine
39	Wyoming
40	Rhode Island
41	Oklahoma
42	Louisiana
43	North Dakota
44	Alaska
45	New Mexico
45	West Virginia
47	Oregon
48	Idaho
49	South Dakota
50	Montana

Note: Ties in ranking reflect ties in actual values.

H-28 State and Local Education Employees, 2004

State	Education employees #	Per 10,000 population	Rank per 10,000 population
Alabama	99,361	219	33
Alaska	20,138	307	3
Arizona	108,639	189	45
Arkansas	66,236	241	23
California	668,278	186	46
Colorado	96,848	210	39
Connecticut	87,786	251	15
Delaware	17,545	211	38
Florida	304,553	175	47
Georgia	234,625	266	7
Hawaii	26,752	212	37
Idaho	32,029	230	28
Illinois	270,386	213	36
Indiana	135,658	217	34
Iowa	75,821	257	13
Kansas	78,210	286	5
Kentucky	109,035	263	9
Louisiana	112,646	249	17
Maine	38,193	290	4
Maryland	113,739	205	41
Massachusetts	152,853	238	25
Michigan	230,899	228	30
Minnesota	123,413	242	22
Mississippi	75,368	260	10
Missouri	129,396	225	31
Montana	23,150	250	16
Nebraska	44,283	253	14
Nevada	36,761	157	50
New Hampshire	33,518	258	11
New Jersey	224,001	258	12
New Mexico	46,805	246	19
New York	471,257	245	20
North Carolina	162,612	190	44
North Dakota	14,836	234	26
Ohio	263,302	230	29
Oklahoma	86,059	244	21
Oregon	62,722	174	48
Pennsylvania	245,088	198	43
Rhode Island	21,761	201	42
South Carolina	100,136	239	24
South Dakota	20,301	263	8
Tennessee	127,810	217	35
Texas	625,993	278	6
Utah	49,427	207	40
Vermont	19,631	316	2
Virginia	184,437	247	18
Washington	99,871	161	49
West Virginia	42,115	232	27
Wisconsin	120,836	219	32
Wyoming	16,731	330	1
50 States	6,551,850	224	
DC	11,132	201	
United States	6,562,982	223	

Rank in order per 10,000 population	
1	Wyoming
2	Vermont
3	Alaska
4	Maine
5	Kansas
6	Texas
7	Georgia
8	South Dakota
9	Kentucky
10	Mississippi
11	New Hampshire
12	New Jersey
13	Iowa
14	Nebraska
15	Connecticut
16	Montana
17	Louisiana
18	Virginia
19	New Mexico
20	New York
21	Oklahoma
22	Minnesota
23	Arkansas
24	South Carolina
25	Massachusetts
26	North Dakota
27	West Virginia
28	Idaho
29	Ohio
30	Michigan
31	Missouri
32	Wisconsin
33	Alabama
34	Indiana
35	Tennessee
36	Illinois
37	Hawaii
38	Delaware
39	Colorado
40	Utah
41	Maryland
42	Rhode Island
43	Pennsylvania
44	North Carolina
45	Arizona
46	California
47	Florida
48	Oregon
49	Washington
50	Nevada

Note: Numbers that appear to be identical are rounded and vary slightly in actual value. The rankings reflect the actual values before rounding. See the introduction for more details.

H-29 Federal Research and Development Spending, FY 2003

State	Federal R&D spending $ (in thousands)	Federal R&D spending per capita $	Rank per capita
Alabama	2,932,910	651	5
Alaska	246,021	379	10
Arizona	1,856,783	333	13
Arkansas	139,716	51	50
California	17,410,257	491	7
Colorado	1,612,002	354	12
Connecticut	2,067,969	593	6
Delaware	91,384	112	39
Florida	2,522,054	148	35
Georgia	1,514,260	175	28
Hawaii	349,644	280	17
Idaho	216,120	158	33
Illinois	1,900,260	150	34
Indiana	561,238	91	43
Iowa	465,249	158	32
Kansas	189,979	70	48
Kentucky	232,097	56	49
Louisiana	441,902	98	42
Maine	144,936	111	40
Maryland	7,804,386	1,416	2
Massachusetts	5,156,530	803	4
Michigan	1,673,200	166	30
Minnesota	861,269	170	29
Mississippi	1,173,860	407	9
Missouri	1,269,896	222	19
Montana	129,548	141	36
Nebraska	146,325	84	44
Nevada	409,308	183	26
New Hampshire	363,118	282	16
New Jersey	1,785,820	207	23
New Mexico	2,850,052	1,517	1
New York	3,972,873	207	22
North Carolina	1,610,868	191	25
North Dakota	101,753	161	31
Ohio	2,396,000	209	21
Oklahoma	274,349	78	46
Oregon	480,234	135	37
Pennsylvania	3,787,926	306	14
Rhode Island	523,349	486	8
South Carolina	411,723	99	41
South Dakota	54,788	72	47
Tennessee	1,039,274	178	27
Texas	4,757,023	215	20
Utah	650,187	276	18
Vermont	181,870	294	15
Virginia	6,212,933	844	3
Washington	2,292,132	374	11
West Virginia	367,393	203	24
Wisconsin	657,170	120	38
Wyoming	41,096	82	45
50 States	88,331,034	304	
DC	2,916,133	5,230	
United States*	91,525,003	315	

**Due to rounding or data sources, the 50-state total plus D.C. may not equal the U.S. total. Please see introduction.*

Rank in order per capita	
1	New Mexico
2	Maryland
3	Virginia
4	Massachusetts
5	Alabama
6	Connecticut
7	California
8	Rhode Island
9	Mississippi
10	Alaska
11	Washington
12	Colorado
13	Arizona
14	Pennsylvania
15	Vermont
16	New Hampshire
17	Hawaii
18	Utah
19	Missouri
20	Texas
21	Ohio
22	New York
23	New Jersey
24	West Virginia
25	North Carolina
26	Nevada
27	Tennessee
28	Georgia
29	Minnesota
30	Michigan
31	North Dakota
32	Iowa
33	Idaho
34	Illinois
35	Florida
36	Montana
37	Oregon
38	Wisconsin
39	Delaware
40	Maine
41	South Carolina
42	Louisiana
43	Indiana
44	Nebraska
45	Wyoming
46	Oklahoma
47	South Dakota
48	Kansas
49	Kentucky
50	Arkansas

Note: Numbers that appear to be identical are rounded and vary slightly in actual value. The rankings reflect the actual values before rounding. See the introduction for more details.

H-30 Total Library Operating Expenditures, FY 2002

State	Library spending $ (in thousands)	Library spending per capita	Rank per capita
Alabama	69,748	15.68	46
Alaska	23,401	36.35	10
Arizona	117,262	22.11	34
Arkansas	35,297	13.75	49
California	888,570	25.38	26
Colorado	164,480	38.21	9
Connecticut	140,198	40.93	5
Delaware	15,567	19.87	37
Florida	381,661	22.92	32
Georgia	151,841	19.13	39
Hawaii	25,176	20.52	36
Idaho	26,439	22.85	33
Illinois	465,046	41.03	4
Indiana	240,705	42.41	3
Iowa	74,408	25.51	25
Kansas	81,320	36.14	11
Kentucky	76,540	19.00	40
Louisiana	104,007	23.20	31
Maine	29,005	24.36	29
Maryland	183,270	35.19	14
Massachusetts	226,680	35.71	12
Michigan	295,024	29.75	18
Minnesota	157,846	31.45	16
Mississippi	36,381	13.14	50
Missouri	140,942	27.56	22
Montana	14,965	16.62	44
Nebraska	36,668	26.45	24
Nevada	57,121	26.79	23
New Hampshire	36,546	28.93	19
New Jersey	325,279	39.02	7
New Mexico	29,918	18.32	41
New York	845,217	44.65	2
North Carolina	147,598	18.03	42
North Dakota	8,910	16.16	45
Ohio	612,287	53.93	1
Oklahoma	60,186	21.28	35
Oregon	122,428	38.94	8
Pennsylvania	289,667	24.18	30
Rhode Island	36,972	35.27	13
South Carolina	78,721	19.38	38
South Dakota	14,903	24.74	27
Tennessee	80,659	14.17	47
Texas	323,760	16.69	43
Utah	62,697	28.08	21
Vermont	14,064	24.38	28
Virginia	199,725	28.28	20
Washington	235,572	39.87	6
West Virginia	25,186	13.93	48
Wisconsin	170,683	31.30	17
Wyoming	16,222	32.81	15
50 States	7,996,768	n/a	
DC	27,366	47.84	
United States	8,024,133	28.94	

Rank in order per capita	
1	Ohio
2	New York
3	Indiana
4	Illinois
5	Connecticut
6	Washington
7	New Jersey
8	Oregon
9	Colorado
10	Alaska
11	Kansas
12	Massachusetts
13	Rhode Island
14	Maryland
15	Wyoming
16	Minnesota
17	Wisconsin
18	Michigan
19	New Hampshire
20	Virginia
21	Utah
22	Missouri
23	Nevada
24	Nebraska
25	Iowa
26	California
27	South Dakota
28	Vermont
29	Maine
30	Pennsylvania
31	Louisiana
32	Florida
33	Idaho
34	Arizona
35	Oklahoma
36	Hawaii
37	Delaware
38	South Carolina
39	Georgia
40	Kentucky
41	New Mexico
42	North Carolina
43	Texas
44	Montana
45	North Dakota
46	Alabama
47	Tennessee
48	West Virginia
49	Arkansas
50	Mississippi

H-31 Head Start Enrollment and Funding, 2004

State	Head Start enrollment #	Head Start spending per enrollee $	Rank by $ per enrollee
Alabama	16,374	6,443	44
Alaska	1,634	7,560	11
Arizona	13,215	7,720	9
Arkansas	10,879	5,865	49
California	98,933	8,326	6
Colorado	9,820	6,892	27
Connecticut	7,148	7,191	19
Delaware	2,197	5,813	50
Florida	35,574	7,317	15
Georgia	23,450	7,115	21
Hawaii	3,063	7,400	13
Idaho	2,957	7,579	10
Illinois	39,672	6,733	34
Indiana	14,234	6,681	35
Iowa	7,775	6,566	42
Kansas	7,949	6,345	46
Kentucky	16,071	6,645	37
Louisiana	21,982	6,573	41
Maine	3,979	6,872	29
Maryland	10,344	7,471	12
Massachusetts	13,011	8,247	7
Michigan	35,124	6,611	39
Minnesota	10,339	6,879	28
Mississippi	26,754	5,985	47
Missouri	17,473	6,744	33
Montana	2,945	7,045	22
Nebraska	5,080	7,029	23
Nevada	2,754	8,605	3
New Hampshire	1,632	8,123	8
New Jersey	15,130	8,444	5
New Mexico	7,451	6,951	25
New York	49,300	8,724	2
North Carolina	19,098	7,297	16
North Dakota	2,353	7,229	17
Ohio	38,029	6,419	45
Oklahoma	13,474	5,956	48
Oregon	8,716	6,757	32
Pennsylvania	30,868	7,322	14
Rhode Island	3,150	6,921	26
South Carolina	12,248	6,672	36
South Dakota	2,827	6,595	40
Tennessee	16,437	7,192	18
Texas	67,785	6,994	24
Utah	5,518	6,778	31
Vermont	1,569	8,559	4
Virginia	13,768	7,128	20
Washington	11,118	9,012	1
West Virginia	7,650	6,556	43
Wisconsin	13,532	6,635	38
Wyoming	1,793	6,833	30
50 States	804,176	7,217	
DC	3,403	7,307	
United States*	905,851	7,222	

**Due to rounding or data sources, the 50-state total plus D.C. may not equal the U.S. total. Please see introduction.*

Rank in order $ per enrollee	
1	Washington
2	New York
3	Nevada
4	Vermont
5	New Jersey
6	California
7	Massachusetts
8	New Hampshire
9	Arizona
10	Idaho
11	Alaska
12	Maryland
13	Hawaii
14	Pennsylvania
15	Florida
16	North Carolina
17	North Dakota
18	Tennessee
19	Connecticut
20	Virginia
21	Georgia
22	Montana
23	Nebraska
24	Texas
25	New Mexico
26	Rhode Island
27	Colorado
28	Minnesota
29	Maine
30	Wyoming
31	Utah
32	Oregon
33	Missouri
34	Illinois
35	Indiana
36	South Carolina
37	Kentucky
38	Wisconsin
39	Michigan
40	South Dakota
41	Louisiana
42	Iowa
43	West Virginia
44	Alabama
45	Ohio
46	Kansas
47	Mississippi
48	Oklahoma
49	Arkansas
50	Delaware

Source Notes for Education (Section H)

H-1 Average Proficiency in Math, Eighth Grade, 2005: These statistics reflect scores on national tests administered to eighth graders to determine their ability to deal with basic concepts of mathematics. The statistics were developed through the National Assessment of Educational Progress, as administered by the Department of Education. They are available as the *NAEP 2005 Mathematics Report Card* (nces.ed.gov).

Statistics comparing the educational achievements of students in individual states, school districts, and schools are a central component of The No Child Left Behind Act. Supporters of these statistics and tests argue that it is much more appropriate to compare results in education programs than the common statistics that just compare costs, such as how much is spent per pupil. Statistics on test results measure achievement of pupils, not that of teachers or school systems. Experts disagree on the relative influence of factors affecting student achievement, but all agree that it is heavily influenced by such out-of-school factors as early childhood training in the home, children's physical and mental health, and participation of parents in the educational process.

H-2 Average Proficiency in Reading, Eighth Grade, 2005: These data are comparable to those shown in Table H-1, except they cover reading. These statistics come from the *NAEP 2005 Reading Report Card* (nces.ed.gov).

H-3 Armed Forces Qualification Test Ranks, FY 2003: Many employers test potential employees to determine their suitability for work, as indicated by such factors as ability to read and understand instructions and perform simple calculations. One of the most widely used tests is offered nationwide to persons seeking to enlist in the armed forces. These data reflect average scores of test-takers in the period from October 2002 to the end of September 2003. These data are prepared by the Department of Defense and published annually, along with other information about persons in uniform, in *Population Representation in the Military Services.*

The Department of Defense, which does not want to become an arbitrator of which states prepare students best for jobs, tries to discourage the use of these results to rank states. Regardless, the results provide the best single measure of performance of high school graduates being tested by an employer using criteria approximating aptitude for work.

H-4 SAT Scores, 2005: College-bound students are generally required to take an achievement test to gain admission to the college or university of their choice. There are two major tests used for this purpose, the Scholastic Aptitude Test (SAT), which is administered by the College Board (www.collegeboard.com), and the ACT test, which is administered by the American College Testing Program (www.act.org). Both organizations seek to discourage the use of their test scores as a way to compare education systems of states, but they are commonly used because of the lack of other comparisons indicating how well states and individual school districts and schools compare in meeting these standards for college admissions. The test scores are presented here and in Table H-5, with neither table including all states. Each state's results are given only for the test that is most often taken in that state. Failure to sort in this way would produce highly misleading results. For example, many southern states rely primarily on the ACT, but their students who seek admission to exclusive private universities in the northeast and California must take the SAT. As a result, the SAT is taken by a small fraction of high school graduates, but those who take it score extraordinarily high.

H-5 ACT Scores, 2005: See notes to Table H-4.

H-6 Percentage of Population over 25 with a High School Diploma, 2004: These data reflect the percentage of the total population over age twenty-five that has a high school diploma. Because each generation of Americans has, on average, attended school longer than its predecessors, the states with the highest ranks tend to be those with the fastest growth and thus youngest population. The source is the U.S. Census Bureau (www.census.gov).

H-7 Students in Private Schools, 2001–2002: Just over five million students in kindergarten through the twelfth grade attend private schools. The private enrollment statistics were released in October 2004 by the Department of Education, National Center for Education Statistics (NCES). The data are posted on the NCES Web site (nces.ed.gov). Private enrollment statistics are gathered every two years as part of the National Education Association's Private School Survey (PSS).

H-8 High School Graduation Rates, 2001: As part of the federal No Child Left Behind Act, states are required to track and improve high school graduation rates. States report these rates to the Department of Education. For a variety of reasons—states may not have adequate systems in place to count graduates and the Department of Education does not require uniform reporting procedures—the validity of these state-reported rates is questionable. In this table, *State Fact Finder* presents graduation rates as calculated by an independent source, using what is called the Cumulative Promotion Index (CPI). The CPI uses enrollment and diploma-count data covering all four high school grade levels to arrive at an estimated graduation rate. It was developed by Christopher Swanson and is published in the Education Trust's report, *Getting Honest About Grad Rates: Too Many States Hide Behind False Data.* The report also contains the state-reported graduation rates for 2002-2003 and detailed information on state-reported rates and the CPI. At the National Governors' Association meeting in the fall of 2005, forty-six states pledged to work towards implementation of a standard and accurate measure to determine graduation rates.

H-9 Pupil-Teacher Ratio, 2004–2005: Small classes are generally believed to be more beneficial to students than large ones, so pupil-teacher ratios are commonly used as a proxy measure of educational quality. The statistic shows a ratio lower than typical class sizes because some specialized teachers, such as those teaching art or special education, are included. These data come from the National Education Association's *Rankings and Estimates, A Report of School Statistics Update* released in Fall of 2005 on the NEA Web site (www.nea.org).

For these and other commonly used educational statistics comparing states, there are three primary sources: the Department of Education, the National Education Association (NEA), and the American Federation of Teachers (which, like the NEA, represents teachers). These organizations produce somewhat different data, using different concepts and different schedules. However, the rankings of states on any particular indicator are about the same regardless of the source used.

H-10 Public School Enrollment, 2004–2005: These statistics, from the same source as Table H-9, show how the nation's 48.4 million public school pupils are distributed among the states. The comparison with each state's population is a rough indicator of the differences among states in the financial burdens of providing free public education.

H-11 Public Library Holdings Per Capita, FY 2002: These data, from *Public Libraries Survey, FY 2002* published by the National Center of Educational Statistics, relate the holdings of books (and related materials) to the population of each state. Nationally, public libraries hold about three books for every person. The reports exclude significant sources of reading materials not in public libraries, such as collections of private and university libraries and certain public school systems.

H-12 Children with Disabilities, 2004: A substantial percentage of the nation's public school students are given special financing by state and federal programs because of something unique about them. The table reflects a Department of Education count of students in 2004 classified as disabled or receiving extra school money because of poverty. These data come from the Department of Education, Office of Special Education Programs, Data Analysis System (*www.ed.gov*).

H-13 State and Local Education Spending, FY 2002: This table relates spending data to population and personal income in each state. The data come from the U.S. Census Bureau's electronic publication "State and Local Government Finance Estimates, by State," available on the bureau's Web site (www.census.gov). Population numbers, also from the Census, are as of July 1, 2002, and personal income numbers are from the Department of Commerce. Based on census historical practices, *State Fact Finder* used calendar year 2001 numbers. See notes to Table F-1 for more extensive information on the source of the data.

H-14 State and Local Education Spending as a Percentage of General Spending, FY 2002: This table, from the same source as Table H-13, shows the relative importance of education spending in state and local budgets. It is derived by comparing this spending with total "general" spending. General spending includes essentially all other spending, except municipal electric and other utilities and trust funds, such as those for workers' compensation.

H-15 Spending Per Pupil, 2004–2005: This table, from the same source as Table H-9, shows spending in public schools for operations (excluding capital outlays) in relation to the number of pupils enrolled.

H-16 Average Teacher Salary, 2004–2005: These average salary calculations, from the same source as Table H-9, show the average gross wage of teachers, not including special pay for leading student activities or teaching in summer sessions.

H-17 Sources of School Funds, 2004–2005: Federal aid covers just under 9 percent of the costs of educating public school students. State and local governments divide the remainder in proportions that vary considerably from state to state, as shown in the table. The data come from the same source as Table H-9.

H-18 State Aid Per Pupil in Average Daily Attendance, 2004–2005: These data, calculated from statistics in the National Education Association's 2005 release *Rankings and Estimates* and the Fall 2005 update, show the amount each state government spends on supporting local public schools, expressed in relation to the number of pupils attending school.

H-19 State and Local Spending for Higher Education (Census Definition), FY 2002: This table relates spending data to population and personal income in each state. For source, see notes to Table H-13. For more statisitics, with slightly different assumptions, on higher education finance see publications from the State Higher Education Executive Officers (www.sheeo.org).

H-20 State and Local Spending for Higher Education as a Percentage of General Spending, FY 2002: This table, from the same source as Table H-13, shows the relative importance of higher education in state and local budgets. It is derived by comparing this spending with total "general" spending. General spending includes essentially all other spending excepting municipal electric and other utilities and trust funds, such as those for workers' compensation.

H-21 Public Higher Education Enrollment, 2003: This table shows the total number of students enrolled in public universities and colleges in fall 2003 and relates this number to the total population of each state. This percentage is an indicator of the relative costs of supporting public higher education in each state. The enrollment data were made available to *State Fact Finder* by the Department of Education, National Center for Education Statistics, Postsecondary Studies Division.

H-22 Per Pupil State Support of Higher Education, FY 2005: There are a variety of different statistics seeking to measure state outlays for higher education on a per pupil basis. None are totally satisfactory for complex reasons, such as the difficulty in classifying pupils as private or public in institutions that receive public support for some of their programs but are truly private in financing other programs. This table relates state government spending for fiscal year 2005 to the latest available enrollment data for all Title IV institutions of higher education. The amount of state support comes from a survey of fiscal year 2005 state appropriations for higher education conducted by the Center for the Study of Education Policy at Illinois State University (www.coe.ilstu.edu/grapevine).

H-23 Average In-State Tuition and Fees at Public Universities, 2004–2005: These data reflect a composite of average in-state tuition and general fees charged by public four-year institutions of higher education in the 2004–2005 academic year. They are from the *2004-2005 College Board Annual Survey of Colleges* and are printed in *2004-2005 Student Charges and Financial Aid* from the American Association of State Colleges and Universities and the National Association of State Universities and Land-Grant Colleges.

H-24 Average Out-of-State Tuition and Fees at Public Universities, 2004–2005: These data are similar to those in Table H-23, but cover out-of-state tuition. They are printed in *2004–2005 Washington State Tuition and Fee Report* from the Washington Higher Education Coordinating Board.

H-25 Percentage Change in Tuition and Fees at Public Universities, 2004–2005: This table shows one-year increases in public higher education tuition. See notes to Table H-23 for the source of in-state increases and the notes to Table H-24 for out-of-state tuition increases.

H-26 Higher Education Affordability Index, 2004: These affordability scores and rankings were developed by The National Center for Public Policy and Higher Education (www.highereducation.org) and collected in *Measuring Up 2004: The National Report Card on Higher Education.* They reflect a composite of indicators, including the percent of income needed to pay for college expenses for all income groups at public, private, and community colleges; availability of state and Pell grants, and other financial aid; and average loan amount borrowed by undergraduates. In the report, the results are presented in both letter grades and index scores, 100 equalling the most affordable.

H-27 Average Salary of Associate Professors at "Flagship" State Universities, 2004–2005: These statistics were developed for *State Fact Finder* based on detailed salary surveys by the American Association of University Professors as printed in its magazine *Academe* (March/April 2005).

To make the comparisons, the "flagship" university salary for an associate professor was used. Usually the "flagship" is the largest, oldest state university, but in some states several institutions can be considered flagships, such as the University of Michigan and Michigan State. In those cases, *State Fact Finder* generally selected the university originally constituted as the general land-grant institution (for example, the University of Michigan) rather than the one initially designated as an agricultural and mechanical school (for example, Michigan State).

H-28 State and Local Education Employees, 2004: This statistic comes from "Public Employment,"a U.S. Census Bureau survey of state and local government employment, available on the Internet (www.census.gov). It covers employees of public schools, from janitors to principals, but it does not include higher education employees.

H-29 Federal Research and Development Spending, FY 2003: The federal government is a major supplier of funds for research and development of new products and processes. This federally supported research provides an important source of income for state and private universities and a base from which state economies can develop in high technology industries. The table shows how federal research and development spending in fiscal year 2003 was distributed among the states and relates that spending to the population of each state. The data were developed by the National Science Foundation.

H-30 Total Library Operating Expenditures, FY 2002: These data are from the same source as Table H-11.

H-31 Head Start Enrollment and Funding, 2004: Head Start is a federally-funded program designed to prepare disadvantaged students for the experience of K-12 school. Grants are awarded directly to local public agencies, private organizations, Indian tribes, and school systems. These data are from the Administration for Children and Families (ACF) Web site (www.acf.hhs.gov).

Health

A decline in job-based benefits—due to job losses, shifts to self-employment or to small firms, and increased premiums—has added to the number of people without medical insurance in America. Between 2000 and 2004 employer-sponsored coverage fell nearly 5 percent for both adults and children. While 6.3 million more adults were uninsured in 2004 than in 2000, expanded State Children's Health Insurance Program (SCHIP) coverage helped keep more children insured.

Number of Non-Elderly Uninsured Americans, 2000–2004 (in millions)

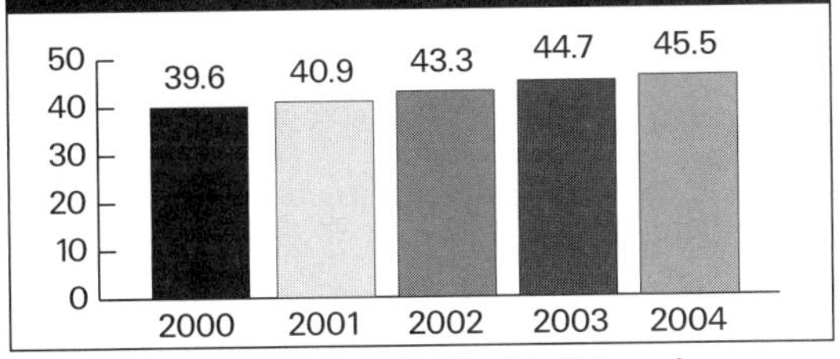

Source: Kaiser Commission on Medicaid and the Uninsured

Health care spending is expected to increase 7.3 percent in 2006, to equal 16 percent of the U.S. gross domestic product.

Projected 2006 Health Care Spending

Who Pays

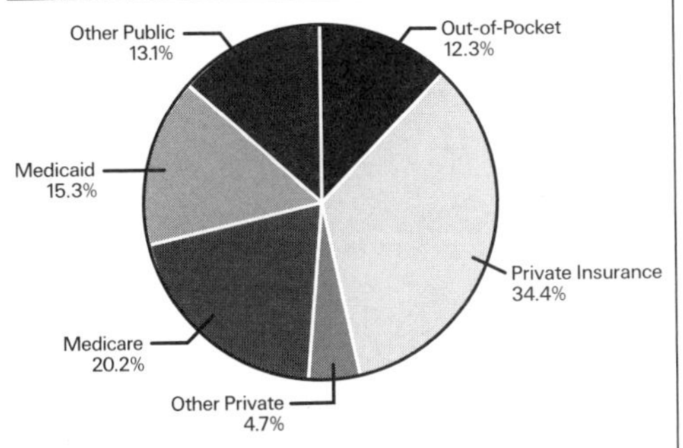

Where It Goes

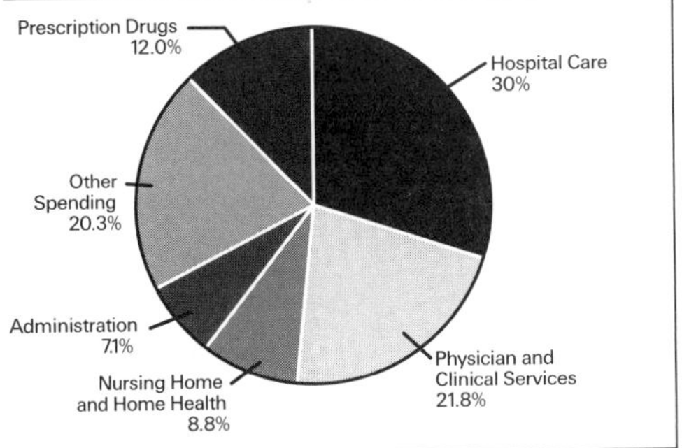

Source: Centers for Medicare & Medicaid Services

I-1 Immunization Rates, 2004

State	Vaccination coverage %	Rank
Alabama	84.1	26
Alaska	78.2	50
Arizona	81.8	38
Arkansas	84.9	20
California	84.1	26
Colorado	80.1	44
Connecticut	88.9	7
Delaware	86.4	13
Florida	90.1	3
Georgia	86.7	11
Hawaii	83.4	29
Idaho	82.8	33
Illinois	86.4	13
Indiana	81.3	40
Iowa	88.0	8
Kansas	80.6	42
Kentucky	80.4	43
Louisiana	76.9	45
Maine	86.2	17
Maryland	81.3	40
Massachusetts	91.5	1
Michigan	83.1	30
Minnesota	86.5	12
Mississippi	86.4	13
Missouri	86.0	18
Montana	82.6	35
Nebraska	83.0	32
Nevada	71.3	49
New Hampshire	89.5	5
New Jersey	84.1	26
New Mexico	84.8	22
New York	84.6	24
North Carolina	82.5	36
North Dakota	84.7	23
Ohio	83.1	30
Oklahoma	74.8	48
Oregon	81.8	38
Pennsylvania	87.3	10
Rhode Island	90.9	2
South Carolina	82.8	33
South Dakota	89.2	6
Tennessee	84.3	25
Texas	75.4	46
Utah	75.4	46
Vermont	89.6	4
Virginia	85.6	19
Washington	82.4	37
West Virginia	87.7	9
Wisconsin	86.3	16
Wyoming	84.9	20
50 States	n/a	
DC	86.3	
United States	83.5	

Rank in order by percentage	
1	Massachusetts
2	Rhode Island
3	Florida
4	Vermont
5	New Hampshire
6	South Dakota
7	Connecticut
8	Iowa
9	West Virginia
10	Pennsylvania
11	Georgia
12	Minnesota
13	Delaware
13	Illinois
13	Mississippi
16	Wisconsin
17	Maine
18	Missouri
19	Virginia
20	Arkansas
20	Wyoming
22	New Mexico
23	North Dakota
24	New York
25	Tennessee
26	Alabama
26	California
26	New Jersey
29	Hawaii
30	Michigan
30	Ohio
32	Nebraska
33	Idaho
33	South Carolina
35	Montana
36	North Carolina
37	Washington
38	Arizona
38	Oregon
40	Indiana
40	Maryland
42	Kansas
43	Kentucky
44	Colorado
45	Louisiana
46	Texas
46	Utah
48	Oklahoma
49	Nevada
50	Alaska

Note: Ties in ranking reflect ties in actual values.

I-2 Infant Mortality Rates, 2005

State	Infant deaths per 1,000 live births	Rank
Alabama	8.5	7
Alaska	6.3	28
Arizona	6.6	24
Arkansas	8.7	4
California	5.1	43
Colorado	6.6	24
Connecticut	5.6	36
Delaware	6.9	19
Florida	6.9	19
Georgia	7.9	12
Hawaii	4.5	48
Idaho	6.8	22
Illinois	7.1	17
Indiana	8.6	6
Iowa	5.1	43
Kansas	6.5	26
Kentucky	6.7	23
Louisiana	9.6	2
Maine	6.1	31
Maryland	8.1	10
Massachusetts	4.4	50
Michigan	7.4	14
Minnesota	4.9	47
Mississippi	9.3	3
Missouri	7.3	16
Montana	5.6	36
Nebraska	6.3	28
Nevada	6.0	34
New Hampshire	5.2	41
New Jersey	5.0	46
New Mexico	6.2	30
New York	6.1	31
North Carolina	8.2	9
North Dakota	5.4	39
Ohio	7.7	13
Oklahoma	8.0	11
Oregon	5.6	36
Pennsylvania	6.9	19
Rhode Island	5.2	41
South Carolina	8.3	8
South Dakota	7.4	14
Tennessee	8.7	4
Texas	5.9	35
Utah	5.1	43
Vermont	4.5	48
Virginia	7.0	18
Washington	5.3	40
West Virginia	6.4	27
Wisconsin	6.1	31
Wyoming	9.7	1
50 States	n/a	
DC	9.9	
United States	6.6	

Rank in order by rate	
1	Wyoming
2	Louisiana
3	Mississippi
4	Arkansas
4	Tennessee
6	Indiana
7	Alabama
8	South Carolina
9	North Carolina
10	Maryland
11	Oklahoma
12	Georgia
13	Ohio
14	Michigan
14	South Dakota
16	Missouri
17	Illinois
18	Virginia
19	Delaware
19	Florida
19	Pennsylvania
22	Idaho
23	Kentucky
24	Arizona
24	Colorado
26	Kansas
27	West Virginia
28	Alaska
28	Nebraska
30	New Mexico
31	Maine
31	New York
31	Wisconsin
34	Nevada
35	Texas
36	Connecticut
36	Montana
36	Oregon
39	North Dakota
40	Washington
41	New Hampshire
41	Rhode Island
43	California
43	Iowa
43	Utah
46	New Jersey
47	Minnesota
48	Hawaii
48	Vermont
50	Massachusetts

Note: Ties in ranking reflect ties in actual values.

I-3 State Health Rankings, 2005

State	State health rankings	Rank
Alabama	-12.8	45
Alaska	-1.2	30
Arizona	-1.6	31
Arkansas	-16.1	47
California	6.0	22
Colorado	9.7	17
Connecticut	15.9	7
Delaware	-2.6	33
Florida	-8.6	40
Georgia	-10.2	43
Hawaii	17.0	5
Idaho	10.4	16
Illinois	0.9	28
Indiana	-2.1	32
Iowa	14.9	10
Kansas	5.8	23
Kentucky	-9.7	42
Louisiana	-18.4	49
Maine	15.5	8
Maryland	-3.6	34
Massachusetts	15.2	9
Michigan	0.3	29
Minnesota	22.1	1
Mississippi	-19.1	50
Missouri	-4.1	35
Montana	6.6	21
Nebraska	12.2	11
Nevada	-5.9	37
New Hampshire	18.1	3
New Jersey	10.6	15
New Mexico	-6.2	38
New York	1.2	26
North Carolina	-5.6	36
North Dakota	16.6	6
Ohio	1.1	27
Oklahoma	-11.4	44
Oregon	8.3	18
Pennsylvania	1.9	25
Rhode Island	11.5	12
South Carolina	-15.8	46
South Dakota	6.7	20
Tennessee	-17.1	48
Texas	-6.7	39
Utah	17.5	4
Vermont	21.3	2
Virginia	5.5	24
Washington	10.7	14
West Virginia	-9.3	41
Wisconsin	11.0	13
Wyoming	7.0	19
50 States	n/a	
DC	n/a	
United States	n/a	

Rank in order by ranking	
1	Minnesota
2	Vermont
3	New Hampshire
4	Utah
5	Hawaii
6	North Dakota
7	Connecticut
8	Maine
9	Massachusetts
10	Iowa
11	Nebraska
12	Rhode Island
13	Wisconsin
14	Washington
15	New Jersey
16	Idaho
17	Colorado
18	Oregon
19	Wyoming
20	South Dakota
21	Montana
22	California
23	Kansas
24	Virginia
25	Pennsylvania
26	New York
27	Ohio
28	Illinois
29	Michigan
30	Alaska
31	Arizona
32	Indiana
33	Delaware
34	Maryland
35	Missouri
36	North Carolina
37	Nevada
38	New Mexico
39	Texas
40	Florida
41	West Virginia
42	Kentucky
43	Georgia
44	Oklahoma
45	Alabama
46	South Carolina
47	Arkansas
48	Tennessee
49	Louisiana
50	Mississippi

Note: Ties in ranking reflect ties in actual values.

I-4 Percentage of Non-Elderly Population without Health Insurance, 2004

State	Percentage of non-elderly without health insurance	Rank
Alabama	15.2	30
Alaska	18.0	16
Arizona	19.7	8
Arkansas	19.1	12
California	20.8	6
Colorado	18.5	15
Connecticut	13.4	36
Delaware	16.5	21
Florida	23.6	3
Georgia	19.1	12
Hawaii	11.2	48
Idaho	16.8	20
Illinois	15.8	29
Indiana	15.9	27
Iowa	10.9	49
Kansas	12.5	45
Kentucky	16.3	23
Louisiana	19.6	9
Maine	11.7	47
Maryland	16.4	22
Massachusetts	13.2	37
Michigan	13.2	37
Minnesota	9.9	50
Mississippi	19.4	10
Missouri	14.4	33
Montana	22.3	5
Nebraska	13.0	40
Nevada	20.8	6
New Hampshire	13.2	37
New Jersey	17.1	18
New Mexico	23.8	2
New York	16.1	25
North Carolina	17.5	17
North Dakota	13.0	40
Ohio	13.0	40
Oklahoma	23.1	4
Oregon	18.9	14
Pennsylvania	14.0	34
Rhode Island	12.9	43
South Carolina	16.9	19
South Dakota	13.8	35
Tennessee	16.3	23
Texas	27.6	1
Utah	15.2	30
Vermont	12.9	43
Virginia	16.0	26
Washington	14.6	32
West Virginia	19.3	11
Wisconsin	11.9	46
Wyoming	15.9	27
50 States	n/a	
DC	14.9	
United States	17.8	

Rank in order by percentage	
1	Texas
2	New Mexico
3	Florida
4	Oklahoma
5	Montana
6	California
6	Nevada
8	Arizona
9	Louisiana
10	Mississippi
11	West Virginia
12	Arkansas
12	Georgia
14	Oregon
15	Colorado
16	Alaska
17	North Carolina
18	New Jersey
19	South Carolina
20	Idaho
21	Delaware
22	Maryland
23	Kentucky
23	Tennessee
25	New York
26	Virginia
27	Indiana
27	Wyoming
29	Illinois
30	Alabama
30	Utah
32	Washington
33	Missouri
34	Pennsylvania
35	South Dakota
36	Connecticut
37	Massachusetts
37	Michigan
37	New Hampshire
40	Nebraska
40	North Dakota
40	Ohio
43	Rhode Island
43	Vermont
45	Kansas
46	Wisconsin
47	Maine
48	Hawaii
49	Iowa
50	Minnesota

Note: Ties in ranking reflect ties in actual values.

I-5 Abortions, 2002

State	Abortions #	Per 1,000 births	Rank per 1,000 births
Alabama	12,249	208	24
Alaska	n/a	n/a	n/a
Arizona	10,677	122	37
Arkansas	5,316	142	34
California	n/a	n/a	n/a
Colorado	7,757	113	39
Connecticut	13,470	321	5
Delaware	4,493	405	4
Florida	87,964	428	3
Georgia	34,091	256	13
Hawaii	3,920	224	21
Idaho	829	40	46
Illinois	46,945	260	12
Indiana	10,937	129	35
Iowa	6,240	166	29
Kansas	11,765	299	9
Kentucky	3,502	65	45
Louisiana	10,451	161	30
Maine	2,315	171	28
Maryland	13,595	185	26
Massachusetts	25,249	313	7
Michigan	29,231	225	20
Minnesota	14,187	209	23
Mississippi	3,605	87	42
Missouri	8,201	109	40
Montana	2,248	203	25
Nebraska	3,775	149	33
Nevada	9,960	306	8
New Hampshire	n/a	n/a	n/a
New Jersey	32,854	286	11
New Mexico	5,069	183	27
New York	127,983	509	1
North Carolina	29,229	249	16
North Dakota	1,219	157	31
Ohio	35,830	241	18
Oklahoma	6,500	129	35
Oregon	13,172	291	10
Pennsylvania	35,167	246	17
Rhode Island	5,550	430	2
South Carolina	6,657	122	37
South Dakota	826	77	43
Tennessee	17,807	230	19
Texas	79,929	215	22
Utah	3,524	72	44
Vermont	1,635	256	13
Virginia	24,992	251	15
Washington	25,148	318	6
West Virginia	2,049	99	41
Wisconsin	10,489	153	32
Wyoming	10	n/a	n/a
50 States	848,611	n/a	
DC	5,511	735	
United States	854,122	246	

Rank in order per 1,000 births	
1	New York
2	Rhode Island
3	Florida
4	Delaware
5	Connecticut
6	Washington
7	Massachusetts
8	Nevada
9	Kansas
10	Oregon
11	New Jersey
12	Illinois
13	Georgia
13	Vermont
15	Virginia
16	North Carolina
17	Pennsylvania
18	Ohio
19	Tennessee
20	Michigan
21	Hawaii
22	Texas
23	Minnesota
24	Alabama
25	Montana
26	Maryland
27	New Mexico
28	Maine
29	Iowa
30	Louisiana
31	North Dakota
32	Wisconsin
33	Nebraska
34	Arkansas
35	Indiana
35	Oklahoma
37	Arizona
37	South Carolina
39	Colorado
40	Missouri
41	West Virginia
42	Mississippi
43	South Dakota
44	Utah
45	Kentucky
46	Idaho

Note: Ties in ranking reflect ties in actual values.

I-6 Alcohol Consumption Per Capita, 2003

State	Per capita consumption in gallons	Rank
Alabama	1.89	45
Alaska	2.43	13
Arizona	2.48	10
Arkansas	1.76	47
California	2.22	28
Colorado	2.60	7
Connecticut	2.22	28
Delaware	3.11	3
Florida	2.63	6
Georgia	2.11	35
Hawaii	2.39	18
Idaho	2.33	24
Illinois	2.34	23
Indiana	1.96	41
Iowa	2.05	37
Kansas	1.88	46
Kentucky	1.74	48
Louisiana	2.39	18
Maine	2.36	20
Maryland	2.11	35
Massachusetts	2.48	10
Michigan	2.13	34
Minnesota	2.41	15
Mississippi	2.14	33
Missouri	2.26	25
Montana	2.59	8
Nebraska	2.23	27
Nevada	3.63	2
New Hampshire	4.03	1
New Jersey	2.24	26
New Mexico	2.40	16
New York	1.93	43
North Carolina	2.00	40
North Dakota	2.56	9
Ohio	2.03	38
Oklahoma	1.93	43
Oregon	2.35	21
Pennsylvania	2.20	30
Rhode Island	2.42	14
South Carolina	2.35	21
South Dakota	2.40	16
Tennessee	1.96	41
Texas	2.19	31
Utah	1.31	50
Vermont	2.47	12
Virginia	2.03	38
Washington	2.19	31
West Virginia	1.71	49
Wisconsin	2.81	5
Wyoming	2.82	4
50 States	n/a	
DC	3.84	
United States	2.22	

Rank in order per capita

1	New Hampshire
2	Nevada
3	Delaware
4	Wyoming
5	Wisconsin
6	Florida
7	Colorado
8	Montana
9	North Dakota
10	Arizona
10	Massachusetts
12	Vermont
13	Alaska
14	Rhode Island
15	Minnesota
16	New Mexico
16	South Dakota
18	Hawaii
18	Louisiana
20	Maine
21	Oregon
21	South Carolina
23	Illinois
24	Idaho
25	Missouri
26	New Jersey
27	Nebraska
28	California
28	Connecticut
30	Pennsylvania
31	Texas
31	Washington
33	Mississippi
34	Michigan
35	Georgia
35	Maryland
37	Iowa
38	Ohio
38	Virginia
40	North Carolina
41	Indiana
41	Tennessee
43	New York
43	Oklahoma
45	Alabama
46	Kansas
47	Arkansas
48	Kentucky
49	West Virginia
50	Utah

Note: Ties in ranking reflect ties in actual values.

I-7 Percentage of Adult Smokers, 2004

State	Percentage of adult smokers	Rank
Alabama	24.8	7
Alaska	24.8	7
Arizona	18.5	44
Arkansas	25.5	6
California	14.7	48
Colorado	20.0	34
Connecticut	18.0	46
Delaware	24.3	11
Florida	20.2	32
Georgia	19.9	36
Hawaii	n/a	n/a
Idaho	17.4	47
Illinois	22.2	19
Indiana	24.8	7
Iowa	20.8	25
Kansas	19.8	39
Kentucky	27.5	1
Louisiana	23.5	14
Maine	20.9	24
Maryland	19.5	41
Massachusetts	18.4	45
Michigan	23.2	15
Minnesota	20.7	27
Mississippi	24.5	10
Missouri	24.0	13
Montana	20.4	28
Nebraska	20.2	32
Nevada	23.2	15
New Hampshire	21.6	22
New Jersey	18.8	43
New Mexico	20.3	30
New York	19.9	36
North Carolina	23.1	17
North Dakota	19.8	39
Ohio	25.8	5
Oklahoma	26.0	4
Oregon	20.0	34
Pennsylvania	22.7	18
Rhode Island	21.3	23
South Carolina	24.3	11
South Dakota	20.3	30
Tennessee	26.1	3
Texas	20.4	28
Utah	10.4	49
Vermont	19.9	36
Virginia	20.8	25
Washington	19.2	42
West Virginia	26.8	2
Wisconsin	21.9	20
Wyoming	21.7	21
50 States	n/a	
DC	20.8	
United States	20.8	

Rank in order by percentage	
1	Kentucky
2	West Virginia
3	Tennessee
4	Oklahoma
5	Ohio
6	Arkansas
7	Alabama
7	Alaska
7	Indiana
10	Mississippi
11	Delaware
11	South Carolina
13	Missouri
14	Louisiana
15	Michigan
15	Nevada
17	North Carolina
18	Pennsylvania
19	Illinois
20	Wisconsin
21	Wyoming
22	New Hampshire
23	Rhode Island
24	Maine
25	Iowa
25	Virginia
27	Minnesota
28	Montana
28	Texas
30	New Mexico
30	South Dakota
32	Florida
32	Nebraska
34	Colorado
34	Oregon
36	Georgia
36	New York
36	Vermont
39	Kansas
39	North Dakota
41	Maryland
42	Washington
43	New Jersey
44	Arizona
45	Massachusetts
46	Connecticut
47	Idaho
48	California
49	Utah

Note: Ties in ranking reflect ties in actual values.

I-8 Percentage of Population Obese, 2004

State	Percentage of population obese	Rank
Alabama	28.8	2
Alaska	23.6	21
Arizona	21.1	38
Arkansas	26.0	6
California	22.2	31
Colorado	16.7	50
Connecticut	19.6	46
Delaware	21.0	39
Florida	22.8	29
Georgia	24.7	15
Hawaii	20.9	41
Idaho	20.8	42
Illinois	22.9	28
Indiana	25.5	9
Iowa	23.5	22
Kansas	23.1	25
Kentucky	25.8	7
Louisiana	26.9	5
Maine	23.3	23
Maryland	23.9	19
Massachusetts	18.3	49
Michigan	25.4	10
Minnesota	22.6	30
Mississippi	29.4	1
Missouri	24.9	13
Montana	19.7	45
Nebraska	23.1	25
Nevada	21.0	39
New Hampshire	21.5	35
New Jersey	21.9	34
New Mexico	21.4	36
New York	22.0	33
North Carolina	24.2	17
North Dakota	24.5	16
Ohio	25.2	11
Oklahoma	24.8	14
Oregon	21.2	37
Pennsylvania	24.2	17
Rhode Island	18.9	47
South Carolina	25.0	12
South Dakota	23.8	20
Tennessee	27.1	4
Texas	25.7	8
Utah	20.3	44
Vermont	18.6	48
Virginia	23.0	27
Washington	22.1	32
West Virginia	27.6	3
Wisconsin	23.2	24
Wyoming	20.7	43
50 States	n/a	
DC	n/a	
United States	23.1	

Rank in order by percentage	
1	Mississippi
2	Alabama
3	West Virginia
4	Tennessee
5	Louisiana
6	Arkansas
7	Kentucky
8	Texas
9	Indiana
10	Michigan
11	Ohio
12	South Carolina
13	Missouri
14	Oklahoma
15	Georgia
16	North Dakota
17	North Carolina
17	Pennsylvania
19	Maryland
20	South Dakota
21	Alaska
22	Iowa
23	Maine
24	Wisconsin
25	Kansas
25	Nebraska
27	Virginia
28	Illinois
29	Florida
30	Minnesota
31	California
32	Washington
33	New York
34	New Jersey
35	New Hampshire
36	New Mexico
37	Oregon
38	Arizona
39	Delaware
39	Nevada
41	Hawaii
42	Idaho
43	Wyoming
44	Utah
45	Montana
46	Connecticut
47	Rhode Island
48	Vermont
49	Massachusetts
50	Colorado

Note: Ties in ranking reflect ties in actual values.

I-9 AIDS Cases, 2004

State	AIDS cases #	Rate per 100,000 residents	Rank by rate
Alabama	466	10.3	21
Alaska	55	8.4	25
Arizona	563	9.8	22
Arkansas	185	6.7	30
California	4,679	13.0	17
Colorado	338	7.3	27
Connecticut	643	18.4	8
Delaware	157	18.9	6
Florida	5,822	33.5	2
Georgia	1,640	18.6	7
Hawaii	136	10.8	19
Idaho	22	1.6	48
Illinois	1,679	13.2	13
Indiana	396	6.3	32
Iowa	64	2.2	47
Kansas	116	4.2	39
Kentucky	251	6.1	33
Louisiana	1,010	22.4	4
Maine	60	4.6	37
Maryland	1,451	26.1	3
Massachusetts	564	8.8	24
Michigan	655	6.5	31
Minnesota	218	4.3	38
Mississippi	479	16.5	10
Missouri	394	6.8	29
Montana	7	0.8	50
Nebraska	69	3.9	40
Nevada	305	13.1	14
New Hampshire	42	3.2	43
New Jersey	1,848	21.2	5
New Mexico	183	9.6	23
New York	7,641	39.7	1
North Carolina	1,137	13.3	12
North Dakota	17	2.7	45
Ohio	665	5.8	34
Oklahoma	195	5.5	35
Oregon	281	7.8	26
Pennsylvania	1,629	13.1	14
Rhode Island	132	12.2	18
South Carolina	759	18.1	9
South Dakota	12	1.6	48
Tennessee	774	13.1	14
Texas	3,298	14.7	11
Utah	79	3.3	42
Vermont	17	2.7	45
Virginia	796	10.7	20
Washington	444	7.2	28
West Virginia	93	5.1	36
Wisconsin	177	3.2	43
Wyoming	18	3.6	41
50 States	42,661	n/a	
DC	992	179.2	
United States	43,653	14.9	

Rank in order by rate	
1	New York
2	Florida
3	Maryland
4	Louisiana
5	New Jersey
6	Delaware
7	Georgia
8	Connecticut
9	South Carolina
10	Mississippi
11	Texas
12	North Carolina
13	Illinois
14	Nevada
14	Pennsylvania
14	Tennessee
17	California
18	Rhode Island
19	Hawaii
20	Virginia
21	Alabama
22	Arizona
23	New Mexico
24	Massachusetts
25	Alaska
26	Oregon
27	Colorado
28	Washington
29	Missouri
30	Arkansas
31	Michigan
32	Indiana
33	Kentucky
34	Ohio
35	Oklahoma
36	West Virginia
37	Maine
38	Minnesota
39	Kansas
40	Nebraska
41	Wyoming
42	Utah
43	New Hampshire
43	Wisconsin
45	North Dakota
45	Vermont
47	Iowa
48	Idaho
48	South Dakota
50	Montana

Note: Ties in ranking reflect ties in actual values.

I-10 Physicians Per 100,000 Population, 2005

State	Physicians per 100,000 population	Rank
Alabama	219	41
Alaska	232	35
Arizona	233	34
Arkansas	211	45
California	260	23
Colorado	270	17
Connecticut	359	5
Delaware	273	16
Florida	262	22
Georgia	227	36
Hawaii	306	9
Idaho	180	50
Illinois	283	13
Indiana	225	38
Iowa	215	43
Kansas	243	30
Kentucky	241	31
Louisiana	183	49
Maine	294	10
Maryland	405	2
Massachusetts	442	1
Michigan	291	11
Minnesota	280	14
Mississippi	191	48
Missouri	266	19
Montana	226	37
Nebraska	246	28
Nevada	204	46
New Hampshire	266	19
New Jersey	329	7
New Mexico	240	32
New York	376	3
North Carolina	256	27
North Dakota	244	29
Ohio	291	11
Oklahoma	212	44
Oregon	263	21
Pennsylvania	325	8
Rhode Island	366	4
South Carolina	239	33
South Dakota	225	38
Tennessee	268	18
Texas	222	40
Utah	218	42
Vermont	343	6
Virginia	274	15
Washington	259	26
West Virginia	260	23
Wisconsin	260	23
Wyoming	194	47
50 States	274	
DC	763	
United States	278	

Rank in order per 100,000 population	
1	Massachusetts
2	Maryland
3	New York
4	Rhode Island
5	Connecticut
6	Vermont
7	New Jersey
8	Pennsylvania
9	Hawaii
10	Maine
11	Ohio
11	Michigan
13	Illinois
14	Minnesota
15	Virginia
16	Delaware
17	Colorado
18	Tennessee
19	New Hampshire
19	Missouri
21	Oregon
22	Florida
23	California
23	Wisconsin
23	West Virginia
26	Washington
27	North Carolina
28	Nebraska
29	North Dakota
30	Kansas
31	Kentucky
32	New Mexico
33	South Carolina
34	Arizona
35	Alaska
36	Georgia
37	Montana
38	South Dakota
38	Indiana
40	Texas
41	Alabama
42	Utah
43	Iowa
44	Oklahoma
45	Arkansas
46	Nevada
47	Wyoming
48	Mississippi
49	Louisiana
50	Idaho

Note: Ties in ranking reflect ties in actual values.

I-11 Hospital Beds Per 1,000 Population, 2004

State	Hospital beds per 1,000 population	Rank
Alabama	3.4	14
Alaska	2.2	40
Arizona	1.9	46
Arkansas	3.5	12
California	2.0	45
Colorado	2.0	44
Connecticut	2.2	38
Delaware	2.4	36
Florida	2.9	22
Georgia	2.8	23
Hawaii	2.5	33
Idaho	2.5	34
Illinois	2.7	25
Indiana	3.0	20
Iowa	3.7	10
Kansas	3.8	9
Kentucky	3.7	11
Louisiana	3.8	8
Maine	2.7	26
Maryland	2.1	42
Massachusetts	2.5	31
Michigan	2.6	30
Minnesota	3.2	18
Mississippi	4.5	4
Missouri	3.3	16
Montana	4.7	3
Nebraska	4.2	5
Nevada	2.0	43
New Hampshire	2.2	41
New Jersey	2.5	32
New Mexico	1.9	47
New York	3.3	15
North Carolina	2.8	24
North Dakota	5.6	2
Ohio	2.9	21
Oklahoma	3.1	19
Oregon	1.8	49
Pennsylvania	3.2	17
Rhode Island	2.2	39
South Carolina	2.7	27
South Dakota	6.0	1
Tennessee	3.5	13
Texas	2.6	29
Utah	1.9	48
Vermont	2.4	35
Virginia	2.3	37
Washington	1.8	50
West Virginia	4.1	6
Wisconsin	2.6	28
Wyoming	4.0	7
50 States	2.7	
DC	6.2	
United States	2.8	

Rank in order per 1,000 population	
1	South Dakota
2	North Dakota
3	Montana
4	Mississippi
5	Nebraska
6	West Virginia
7	Wyoming
8	Louisiana
9	Kansas
10	Iowa
11	Kentucky
12	Arkansas
13	Tennessee
14	Alabama
15	New York
16	Missouri
17	Pennsylvania
18	Minnesota
19	Oklahoma
20	Indiana
21	Ohio
22	Florida
23	Georgia
24	North Carolina
25	Illinois
26	Maine
27	South Carolina
28	Wisconsin
29	Texas
30	Michigan
31	Massachusetts
32	New Jersey
33	Hawaii
34	Idaho
35	Vermont
36	Delaware
37	Virginia
38	Connecticut
39	Rhode Island
40	Alaska
41	New Hampshire
42	Maryland
43	Nevada
44	Colorado
45	California
46	Arizona
47	New Mexico
48	Utah
49	Oregon
50	Washington

Note: Numbers that appear to be identical are rounded and vary slightly in actual value. The rankings reflect the actual values before rounding. See the introduction for more details.

I-12 Medicaid Recipients, Mid-Year 2004

State	Medicaid recipients # (in thousands)	Percentage of population	Rank by percentage
Alabama	801	17.7	11
Alaska	97	14.7	22
Arizona	905	15.8	18
Arkansas	594	21.6	4
California	6,471	18.0	10
Colorado	378	8.2	46
Connecticut	402	11.5	39
Delaware	135	16.3	17
Florida	2,207	12.7	31
Georgia	1,323	15.0	20
Hawaii	190	15.1	19
Idaho	166	11.9	35
Illinois	1,740	13.7	27
Indiana	804	12.9	30
Iowa	285	9.6	42
Kansas	269	9.8	41
Kentucky	679	16.4	16
Louisiana	919	20.4	7
Maine	259	19.6	9
Maryland	696	12.5	33
Massachusetts	947	14.8	21
Michigan	1,410	13.9	26
Minnesota	569	11.2	40
Mississippi	638	22.0	3
Missouri	974	16.9	13
Montana	86	9.3	43
Nebraska	207	11.8	37
Nevada	169	7.3	50
New Hampshire	96	7.4	49
New Jersey	798	9.2	44
New Mexico	421	22.1	2
New York	4,023	20.9	6
North Carolina	1,112	13.0	28
North Dakota	52	8.3	45
Ohio	1,645	14.4	25
Oklahoma	519	14.7	23
Oregon	427	11.9	36
Pennsylvania	1,600	12.9	29
Rhode Island	181	16.7	14
South Carolina	846	20.1	8
South Dakota	98	12.7	32
Tennessee	1,345	22.8	1
Texas	2,692	12.0	34
Utah	189	7.9	48
Vermont	131	21.0	5
Virginia	607	8.1	47
Washington	1,081	17.4	12
West Virginia	298	16.4	15
Wisconsin	792	14.4	24
Wyoming	59	11.6	38
50 States	43,333	14.8	
DC	139	25.0	
United States*	44,356	15.1	

**Due to rounding or data sources, the 50-state total plus D.C. may not equal the U.S. total. Please see introduction.*

Rank in order by percentage	
1	Tennessee
2	New Mexico
3	Mississippi
4	Arkansas
5	Vermont
6	New York
7	Louisiana
8	South Carolina
9	Maine
10	California
11	Alabama
12	Washington
13	Missouri
14	Rhode Island
15	West Virginia
16	Kentucky
17	Delaware
18	Arizona
19	Hawaii
20	Georgia
21	Massachusetts
22	Alaska
23	Oklahoma
24	Wisconsin
25	Ohio
26	Michigan
27	Illinois
28	North Carolina
29	Pennsylvania
30	Indiana
31	Florida
32	South Dakota
33	Maryland
34	Texas
35	Idaho
36	Oregon
37	Nebraska
38	Wyoming
39	Connecticut
40	Minnesota
41	Kansas
42	Iowa
43	Montana
44	New Jersey
45	North Dakota
46	Colorado
47	Virginia
48	Utah
49	New Hampshire
50	Nevada

Note: Numbers that appear to be identical are rounded and vary slightly in actual value. The rankings reflect the actual values before rounding. See the introduction for more details.

I-13 Medicaid Recipients as a Percentage of Poverty Population, Mid-Year 2004

State	Recipients as a percentage of poverty population	Rank
Alabama	104.9	37
Alaska	163.8	5
Arizona	109.0	34
Arkansas	144.2	11
California	136.4	17
Colorado	84.1	46
Connecticut	115.6	30
Delaware	180.3	3
Florida	109.0	35
Georgia	116.2	29
Hawaii	181.3	2
Idaho	122.1	23
Illinois	113.5	32
Indiana	112.9	33
Iowa	90.7	41
Kansas	88.5	43
Kentucky	94.4	40
Louisiana	124.7	22
Maine	172.5	4
Maryland	127.7	19
Massachusetts	161.7	6
Michigan	106.8	36
Minnesota	158.9	7
Mississippi	119.9	25
Missouri	141.8	12
Montana	67.5	49
Nebraska	126.8	20
Nevada	65.4	50
New Hampshire	137.4	16
New Jersey	115.3	31
New Mexico	134.5	18
New York	141.4	13
North Carolina	90.7	42
North Dakota	86.0	45
Ohio	125.6	21
Oklahoma	139.5	14
Oregon	101.9	38
Pennsylvania	116.4	28
Rhode Island	149.2	9
South Carolina	137.8	15
South Dakota	96.8	39
Tennessee	144.8	10
Texas	73.3	48
Utah	80.0	47
Vermont	272.5	1
Virginia	88.2	44
Washington	154.2	8
West Virginia	117.4	27
Wisconsin	117.7	26
Wyoming	120.3	24
50 States	117.4	
DC	152.3	
United States	119.9	

Rank in order by percentage	
1	Vermont
2	Hawaii
3	Delaware
4	Maine
5	Alaska
6	Massachusetts
7	Minnesota
8	Washington
9	Rhode Island
10	Tennessee
11	Arkansas
12	Missouri
13	New York
14	Oklahoma
15	South Carolina
16	New Hampshire
17	California
18	New Mexico
19	Maryland
20	Nebraska
21	Ohio
22	Louisiana
23	Idaho
24	Wyoming
25	Mississippi
26	Wisconsin
27	West Virginia
28	Pennsylvania
29	Georgia
30	Connecticut
31	New Jersey
32	Illinois
33	Indiana
34	Arizona
35	Florida
36	Michigan
37	Alabama
38	Oregon
39	South Dakota
40	Kentucky
41	Iowa
42	North Carolina
43	Kansas
44	Virginia
45	North Dakota
46	Colorado
47	Utah
48	Texas
49	Montana
50	Nevada

Note: Numbers that appear to be identical are rounded and vary slightly in actual value. The rankings reflect the actual values before rounding. See the introduction for more details.

I-14 State and Local Spending for Health and Hospitals, FY 2002

State	Total spending $ (in millions)	Per capita $	Percentage of personal income	Rank per capita
Alabama	4,082	910	3.7	2
Alaska	263	408	1.3	32
Arizona	1,209	222	0.9	47
Arkansas	915	338	1.5	41
California	20,961	597	1.8	11
Colorado	2,040	453	1.4	22
Connecticut	1,903	550	1.3	14
Delaware	327	405	1.3	33
Florida	7,491	448	1.6	24
Georgia	4,832	564	2.0	13
Hawaii	652	524	1.9	16
Idaho	605	451	1.8	23
Illinois	5,199	413	1.3	31
Indiana	2,876	467	1.7	19
Iowa	1,886	642	2.4	9
Kansas	1,231	453	1.6	21
Kentucky	1,445	353	1.4	39
Louisiana	3,621	808	3.3	3
Maine	500	386	1.4	35
Maryland	1,490	273	0.8	45
Massachusetts	3,174	494	1.3	17
Michigan	5,347	532	1.8	15
Minnesota	1,965	391	1.2	34
Mississippi	2,140	745	3.4	5
Missouri	2,433	429	1.5	27
Montana	378	416	1.7	30
Nebraska	607	351	1.2	40
Nevada	923	425	1.5	28
New Hampshire	184	144	0.4	49
New Jersey	2,736	319	0.8	42
New Mexico	829	447	1.9	25
New York	13,008	679	1.9	7
North Carolina	6,087	732	2.7	6
North Dakota	104	164	0.6	48
Ohio	5,454	477	1.7	18
Oklahoma	1,305	374	1.5	37
Oregon	2,194	623	2.2	10
Pennsylvania	5,153	418	1.4	29
Rhode Island	299	279	0.9	44
South Carolina	3,143	765	3.1	4
South Dakota	171	224	0.8	46
Tennessee	3,300	569	2.1	12
Texas	10,104	464	1.6	20
Utah	858	371	1.5	38
Vermont	88	142	0.5	50
Virginia	3,184	437	1.4	26
Washington	4,013	661	2.1	8
West Virginia	516	287	1.2	43
Wisconsin	2,082	383	1.3	36
Wyoming	516	1,035	3.5	1
50 States	145,824	507	1.7	
DC	555	972	2.1	
United States	146,379	508	1.7	

Rank in order per capita	
1	Wyoming
2	Alabama
3	Louisiana
4	South Carolina
5	Mississippi
6	North Carolina
7	New York
8	Washington
9	Iowa
10	Oregon
11	California
12	Tennessee
13	Georgia
14	Connecticut
15	Michigan
16	Hawaii
17	Massachusetts
18	Ohio
19	Indiana
20	Texas
21	Kansas
22	Colorado
23	Idaho
24	Florida
25	New Mexico
26	Virginia
27	Missouri
28	Nevada
29	Pennsylvania
30	Montana
31	Illinois
32	Alaska
33	Delaware
34	Minnesota
35	Maine
36	Wisconsin
37	Oklahoma
38	Utah
39	Kentucky
40	Nebraska
41	Arkansas
42	New Jersey
43	West Virginia
44	Rhode Island
45	Maryland
46	South Dakota
47	Arizona
48	North Dakota
49	New Hampshire
50	Vermont

Note: Numbers that appear to be identical are rounded and vary slightly in actual value. The rankings reflect the actual values before rounding. See the introduction for more details.

I-15 State and Local Health and Hospital Spending as a Percentage of General Spending, FY 2002

State	Health and hospital spending as a percentage of general spending	Rank
Alabama	16.6	1
Alaska	3.1	47
Arizona	4.8	43
Arkansas	7.0	33
California	8.9	13
Colorado	7.5	26
Connecticut	7.9	23
Delaware	6.1	39
Florida	8.6	17
Georgia	10.7	9
Hawaii	7.9	24
Idaho	8.9	14
Illinois	7.0	31
Indiana	8.8	16
Iowa	11.0	8
Kansas	8.3	19
Kentucky	6.7	34
Louisiana	14.9	2
Maine	6.3	36
Maryland	4.7	44
Massachusetts	7.5	27
Michigan	8.8	15
Minnesota	5.6	40
Mississippi	13.9	3
Missouri	8.4	18
Montana	7.5	28
Nebraska	6.2	37
Nevada	7.8	25
New Hampshire	2.9	48
New Jersey	5.0	42
New Mexico	7.2	29
New York	8.1	22
North Carolina	13.7	4
North Dakota	2.7	49
Ohio	8.1	20
Oklahoma	7.2	30
Oregon	9.5	11
Pennsylvania	7.0	32
Rhode Island	4.4	45
South Carolina	13.2	6
South Dakota	4.4	46
Tennessee	11.4	7
Texas	9.1	12
Utah	6.7	35
Vermont	2.3	50
Virginia	8.1	21
Washington	10.4	10
West Virginia	5.2	41
Wisconsin	6.1	38
Wyoming	13.4	5
50 States	8.5	
DC	9.0	
United States	8.5	

Rank in order by percentage	
1	Alabama
2	Louisiana
3	Mississippi
4	North Carolina
5	Wyoming
6	South Carolina
7	Tennessee
8	Iowa
9	Georgia
10	Washington
11	Oregon
12	Texas
13	California
14	Idaho
15	Michigan
16	Indiana
17	Florida
18	Missouri
19	Kansas
20	Ohio
21	Virginia
22	New York
23	Connecticut
24	Hawaii
25	Nevada
26	Colorado
27	Massachusetts
28	Montana
29	New Mexico
30	Oklahoma
31	Illinois
32	Pennsylvania
33	Arkansas
34	Kentucky
35	Utah
36	Maine
37	Nebraska
38	Wisconsin
39	Delaware
40	Minnesota
41	West Virginia
42	New Jersey
43	Arizona
44	Maryland
45	Rhode Island
46	South Dakota
47	Alaska
48	New Hampshire
49	North Dakota
50	Vermont

Note: Numbers that appear to be identical are rounded and vary slightly in actual value. The rankings reflect the actual values before rounding. See the introduction for more details.

I-16 Per Capita Medicaid Spending, FY 2004

State	Per capita Medicaid spending $	Rank
Alabama	809	32
Alaska	1,358	5
Arizona	859	28
Arkansas	952	21
California	864	26
Colorado	579	47
Connecticut	1,140	11
Delaware	956	20
Florida	741	37
Georgia	1,045	16
Hawaii	725	43
Idaho	687	45
Illinois	798	33
Indiana	789	34
Iowa	771	36
Kansas	655	46
Kentucky	1,040	17
Louisiana	1,136	12
Maine	1,549	2
Maryland	850	29
Massachusetts	1,389	4
Michigan	889	25
Minnesota	1,105	13
Mississippi	1,180	8
Missouri	1,075	14
Montana	726	42
Nebraska	835	30
Nevada	445	50
New Hampshire	895	24
New Jersey	919	23
New Mexico	1,166	9
New York	2,165	1
North Carolina	979	19
North Dakota	773	35
Ohio	1,021	18
Oklahoma	736	39
Oregon	731	40
Pennsylvania	1,144	10
Rhode Island	1,538	3
South Carolina	948	22
South Dakota	738	38
Tennessee	1,197	7
Texas	725	44
Utah	524	49
Vermont	1,291	6
Virginia	528	48
Washington	860	27
West Virginia	1,075	15
Wisconsin	815	31
Wyoming	731	41
50 States	979	
DC	2,047	
United States	981	

Rank in order per capita	
1	New York
2	Maine
3	Rhode Island
4	Massachusetts
5	Alaska
6	Vermont
7	Tennessee
8	Mississippi
9	New Mexico
10	Pennsylvania
11	Connecticut
12	Louisiana
13	Minnesota
14	Missouri
15	West Virginia
16	Georgia
17	Kentucky
18	Ohio
19	North Carolina
20	Delaware
21	Arkansas
22	South Carolina
23	New Jersey
24	New Hampshire
25	Michigan
26	California
27	Washington
28	Arizona
29	Maryland
30	Nebraska
31	Wisconsin
32	Alabama
33	Illinois
34	Indiana
35	North Dakota
36	Iowa
37	Florida
38	South Dakota
39	Oklahoma
40	Oregon
41	Wyoming
42	Montana
43	Hawaii
44	Texas
45	Idaho
46	Kansas
47	Colorado
48	Virginia
49	Utah
50	Nevada

Note: Numbers that appear to be identical are rounded and vary slightly in actual value. The rankings reflect the actual values before rounding. See the introduction for more details.

I-17 Average Medicaid Spending Per Aged Recipient, FY 2001

State	Average spending per aged recipient $	Rank
Alabama	9,793	36
Alaska	14,807	17
Arizona	10,933	28
Arkansas	8,374	43
California	7,457	48
Colorado	12,768	23
Connecticut	24,127	1
Delaware	17,312	7
Florida	9,046	39
Georgia	8,249	45
Hawaii	8,518	42
Idaho	14,902	16
Illinois	13,233	22
Indiana	15,806	11
Iowa	13,864	20
Kansas	15,275	15
Kentucky	10,669	31
Louisiana	8,997	41
Maine	6,327	49
Maryland	15,508	13
Massachusetts	16,151	9
Michigan	11,584	26
Minnesota	19,500	5
Mississippi	8,060	46
Missouri	12,432	24
Montana	14,123	19
Nebraska	14,743	18
Nevada	9,026	40
New Hampshire	19,696	4
New Jersey	16,091	10
New Mexico	10,801	30
New York	21,804	2
North Carolina	10,646	32
North Dakota	16,366	8
Ohio	20,146	3
Oklahoma	10,474	33
Oregon	10,068	34
Pennsylvania	13,494	21
Rhode Island	18,049	6
South Carolina	8,315	44
South Dakota	11,417	27
Tennessee	5,179	50
Texas	9,462	38
Utah	10,812	29
Vermont	7,543	47
Virginia	9,933	35
Washington	9,716	37
West Virginia	12,348	25
Wisconsin	15,714	12
Wyoming	15,340	14
50 States	12,033	
DC	17,154	
United States	12,047	

Rank in order by $	
1	Connecticut
2	New York
3	Ohio
4	New Hampshire
5	Minnesota
6	Rhode Island
7	Delaware
8	North Dakota
9	Massachusetts
10	New Jersey
11	Indiana
12	Wisconsin
13	Maryland
14	Wyoming
15	Kansas
16	Idaho
17	Alaska
18	Nebraska
19	Montana
20	Iowa
21	Pennsylvania
22	Illinois
23	Colorado
24	Missouri
25	West Virginia
26	Michigan
27	South Dakota
28	Arizona
29	Utah
30	New Mexico
31	Kentucky
32	North Carolina
33	Oklahoma
34	Oregon
35	Virginia
36	Alabama
37	Washington
38	Texas
39	Florida
40	Nevada
41	Louisiana
42	Hawaii
43	Arkansas
44	South Carolina
45	Georgia
46	Mississippi
47	Vermont
48	California
49	Maine
50	Tennessee

I-18 Average Medicaid Spending Per Child, FY 2001

State	Average spending per child $	Rank
Alabama	929	50
Alaska	3,910	2
Arizona	1,949	22
Arkansas	1,973	20
California	1,482	41
Colorado	2,235	11
Connecticut	1,342	46
Delaware	2,723	6
Florida	1,656	38
Georgia	1,459	42
Hawaii	1,678	36
Idaho	1,859	24
Illinois	1,777	30
Indiana	1,595	40
Iowa	2,256	10
Kansas	1,752	32
Kentucky	2,146	15
Louisiana	1,445	44
Maine	4,404	1
Maryland	2,719	7
Massachusetts	2,156	13
Michigan	1,321	47
Minnesota	2,818	4
Mississippi	1,383	45
Missouri	1,650	39
Montana	2,488	8
Nebraska	1,859	25
Nevada	2,164	12
New Hampshire	2,809	5
New Jersey	1,996	19
New Mexico	2,033	18
New York	2,987	3
North Carolina	1,851	26
North Dakota	1,805	28
Ohio	1,804	29
Oklahoma	1,447	43
Oregon	1,728	34
Pennsylvania	2,038	17
Rhode Island	2,151	14
South Carolina	1,751	33
South Dakota	1,689	35
Tennessee	1,315	48
Texas	1,845	27
Utah	2,111	16
Vermont	2,485	9
Virginia	1,756	31
Washington	1,255	49
West Virginia	1,868	23
Wisconsin	1,674	37
Wyoming	1,954	21
50 States	1,814	
DC	2,712	
United States	1,817	

Rank in order by $	
1	Maine
2	Alaska
3	New York
4	Minnesota
5	New Hampshire
6	Delaware
7	Maryland
8	Montana
9	Vermont
10	Iowa
11	Colorado
12	Nevada
13	Massachusetts
14	Rhode Island
15	Kentucky
16	Utah
17	Pennsylvania
18	New Mexico
19	New Jersey
20	Arkansas
21	Wyoming
22	Arizona
23	West Virginia
24	Idaho
25	Nebraska
26	North Carolina
27	Texas
28	North Dakota
29	Ohio
30	Illinois
31	Virginia
32	Kansas
33	South Carolina
34	Oregon
35	South Dakota
36	Hawaii
37	Wisconsin
38	Florida
39	Missouri
40	Indiana
41	California
42	Georgia
43	Oklahoma
44	Louisiana
45	Mississippi
46	Connecticut
47	Michigan
48	Tennessee
49	Washington
50	Alabama

Note: Numbers that appear to be identical are rounded and vary slightly in actual value. The rankings reflect the actual values before rounding. See the introduction for more details.

I-19 Medicare Payment Per Hospital Day, FY 2003

State	Average payment per hospital day $	Rank
Alabama	3,999	12
Alaska	4,089	10
Arizona	5,057	4
Arkansas	3,067	37
California	7,100	2
Colorado	4,725	6
Connecticut	3,327	28
Delaware	2,537	48
Florida	4,903	5
Georgia	3,427	24
Hawaii	3,442	23
Idaho	3,199	34
Illinois	3,978	13
Indiana	2,980	41
Iowa	2,950	43
Kansas	3,661	16
Kentucky	3,028	38
Louisiana	3,599	20
Maine	2,960	42
Maryland	1,899	50
Massachusetts	3,010	40
Michigan	3,237	31
Minnesota	4,019	11
Mississippi	2,806	46
Missouri	3,657	17
Montana	3,023	39
Nebraska	4,344	9
Nevada	5,969	3
New Hampshire	3,250	30
New Jersey	7,256	1
New Mexico	3,507	21
New York	3,261	29
North Carolina	2,873	45
North Dakota	2,897	44
Ohio	3,349	27
Oklahoma	3,183	36
Oregon	3,601	19
Pennsylvania	4,693	7
Rhode Island	3,218	33
South Carolina	3,698	15
South Dakota	3,197	35
Tennessee	3,386	25
Texas	4,362	8
Utah	3,611	18
Vermont	2,548	47
Virginia	3,359	26
Washington	3,874	14
West Virginia	2,372	49
Wisconsin	3,443	22
Wyoming	3,228	32
50 States	4,037	
DC	4,311	
United States	3,999	

Rank in order by $	
1	New Jersey
2	California
3	Nevada
4	Arizona
5	Florida
6	Colorado
7	Pennsylvania
8	Texas
9	Nebraska
10	Alaska
11	Minnesota
12	Alabama
13	Illinois
14	Washington
15	South Carolina
16	Kansas
17	Missouri
18	Utah
19	Oregon
20	Louisiana
21	New Mexico
22	Wisconsin
23	Hawaii
24	Georgia
25	Tennessee
26	Virginia
27	Ohio
28	Connecticut
29	New York
30	New Hampshire
31	Michigan
32	Wyoming
33	Rhode Island
34	Idaho
35	South Dakota
36	Oklahoma
37	Arkansas
38	Kentucky
39	Montana
40	Massachusetts
41	Indiana
42	Maine
43	Iowa
44	North Dakota
45	North Carolina
46	Mississippi
47	Vermont
48	Delaware
49	West Virginia
50	Maryland

I-20 Hospital Expense Per Inpatient Day, 2004

State	Expense per inpatient day $	Rank
Alabama	1,945	49
Alaska	4,001	2
Arizona	2,487	34
Arkansas	2,102	46
California	2,924	21
Colorado	3,267	11
Connecticut	2,851	23
Delaware	2,689	29
Florida	2,336	43
Georgia	2,429	38
Hawaii	2,395	41
Idaho	3,211	12
Illinois	2,818	26
Indiana	2,851	22
Iowa	2,971	20
Kansas	2,525	33
Kentucky	2,281	45
Louisiana	1,978	48
Maine	3,398	8
Maryland	2,840	24
Massachusetts	3,570	6
Michigan	3,017	18
Minnesota	3,123	15
Mississippi	1,928	50
Missouri	2,829	25
Montana	3,026	17
Nebraska	2,752	28
Nevada	2,282	44
New Hampshire	3,705	5
New Jersey	2,422	39
New Mexico	2,979	19
New York	2,551	30
North Carolina	2,530	32
North Dakota	3,125	14
Ohio	3,088	16
Oklahoma	2,077	47
Oregon	3,716	4
Pennsylvania	2,475	37
Rhode Island	3,197	13
South Carolina	2,478	36
South Dakota	2,795	27
Tennessee	2,377	42
Texas	2,535	31
Utah	3,290	10
Vermont	4,288	1
Virginia	2,485	35
Washington	3,869	3
West Virginia	2,413	40
Wisconsin	3,501	7
Wyoming	3,385	9
50 States	2,684	
DC	3,024	
United States	2,685	

Rank in order by $	
1	Vermont
2	Alaska
3	Washington
4	Oregon
5	New Hampshire
6	Massachusetts
7	Wisconsin
8	Maine
9	Wyoming
10	Utah
11	Colorado
12	Idaho
13	Rhode Island
14	North Dakota
15	Minnesota
16	Ohio
17	Montana
18	Michigan
19	New Mexico
20	Iowa
21	California
22	Indiana
23	Connecticut
24	Maryland
25	Missouri
26	Illinois
27	South Dakota
28	Nebraska
29	Delaware
30	New York
31	Texas
32	North Carolina
33	Kansas
34	Arizona
35	Virginia
36	South Carolina
37	Pennsylvania
38	Georgia
39	New Jersey
40	West Virginia
41	Hawaii
42	Tennessee
43	Florida
44	Nevada
45	Kentucky
46	Arkansas
47	Oklahoma
48	Louisiana
49	Alabama
50	Mississippi

Note: Ties in ranking reflect ties in actual values.

I-21 Percentage of Population in Health Maintenance Organizations, 2005

State	Percentage of population in HMOs	Rank
Alabama	2.8	46
Alaska	0.0	50
Arizona	16.4	25
Arkansas	6.4	43
California	49.1	1
Colorado	25.6	12
Connecticut	36.1	4
Delaware	10.1	37
Florida	26.6	8
Georgia	16.4	25
Hawaii	37.4	2
Idaho	2.9	45
Illinois	15.7	30
Indiana	22.5	19
Iowa	10.9	33
Kansas	16.6	24
Kentucky	10.2	36
Louisiana	10.7	34
Maine	25.9	10
Maryland	28.0	6
Massachusetts	37.4	2
Michigan	26.3	9
Minnesota	25.4	13
Mississippi	0.1	49
Missouri	24.6	16
Montana	8.1	38
Nebraska	5.3	44
Nevada	25.2	14
New Hampshire	21.9	21
New Jersey	25.0	15
New Mexico	24.3	17
New York	24.0	18
North Carolina	10.5	35
North Dakota	0.4	48
Ohio	16.4	25
Oklahoma	7.1	41
Oregon	16.2	28
Pennsylvania	29.8	5
Rhode Island	25.9	10
South Carolina	7.1	41
South Dakota	7.9	40
Tennessee	14.4	31
Texas	11.8	32
Utah	21.3	22
Vermont	16.1	29
Virginia	22.2	20
Washington	18.1	23
West Virginia	8.1	38
Wisconsin	26.8	7
Wyoming	2.1	47
50 States	n/a	
DC	42.2	
United States	n/a	

Rank in order by percentage	
1	California
2	Hawaii
2	Massachusetts
4	Connecticut
5	Pennsylvania
6	Maryland
7	Wisconsin
8	Florida
9	Michigan
10	Maine
10	Rhode Island
12	Colorado
13	Minnesota
14	Nevada
15	New Jersey
16	Missouri
17	New Mexico
18	New York
19	Indiana
20	Virginia
21	New Hampshire
22	Utah
23	Washington
24	Kansas
25	Arizona
25	Georgia
25	Ohio
28	Oregon
29	Vermont
30	Illinois
31	Tennessee
32	Texas
33	Iowa
34	Louisiana
35	North Carolina
36	Kentucky
37	Delaware
38	Montana
38	West Virginia
40	South Dakota
41	Oklahoma
41	South Carolina
43	Arkansas
44	Nebraska
45	Idaho
46	Alabama
47	Wyoming
48	North Dakota
49	Mississippi
50	Alaska

Note: Ties in ranking reflect ties in actual values.

I-22 Prescription Drugs as a Percentage of State Medicaid Costs, FY 2002

State	Prescription drugs as a percentage of state Medicaid costs	Rank
Alabama	14.7	14
Alaska	12.3	25
Arizona	0.1	50
Arkansas	12.2	26
California	13.3	23
Colorado	8.2	46
Connecticut	10.4	39
Delaware	15.3	10
Florida	17.5	3
Georgia	14.0	20
Hawaii	11.9	29
Idaho	15.5	8
Illinois	14.6	15
Indiana	14.2	19
Iowa	11.0	34
Kansas	11.6	32
Kentucky	17.3	4
Louisiana	14.6	16
Maine	15.3	11
Maryland	8.2	45
Massachusetts	11.9	30
Michigan	8.9	44
Minnesota	7.0	47
Mississippi	19.7	1
Missouri	14.7	13
Montana	15.0	12
Nebraska	15.5	9
Nevada	10.8	36
New Hampshire	9.8	41
New Jersey	9.0	43
New Mexico	4.3	49
New York	10.1	40
North Carolina	16.5	6
North Dakota	11.5	33
Ohio	13.8	21
Oklahoma	12.7	24
Oregon	10.8	35
Pennsylvania	5.9	48
Rhode Island	9.2	42
South Carolina	13.7	22
South Dakota	12.0	28
Tennessee	15.7	7
Texas	11.8	31
Utah	14.3	17
Vermont	17.2	5
Virginia	12.1	27
Washington	10.5	38
West Virginia	17.5	2
Wisconsin	10.6	37
Wyoming	14.2	18
50 States	11.8	
DC	6.5	
United States	11.7	

Rank in order by percentage	
1	Mississippi
2	West Virginia
3	Florida
4	Kentucky
5	Vermont
6	North Carolina
7	Tennessee
8	Idaho
9	Nebraska
10	Delaware
11	Maine
12	Montana
13	Missouri
14	Alabama
15	Illinois
16	Louisiana
17	Utah
18	Wyoming
19	Indiana
20	Georgia
21	Ohio
22	South Carolina
23	California
24	Oklahoma
25	Alaska
26	Arkansas
27	Virginia
28	South Dakota
29	Hawaii
30	Massachusetts
31	Texas
32	Kansas
33	North Dakota
34	Iowa
35	Oregon
36	Nevada
37	Wisconsin
38	Washington
39	Connecticut
40	New York
41	New Hampshire
42	Rhode Island
43	New Jersey
44	Michigan
45	Maryland
46	Colorado
47	Minnesota
48	Pennsylvania
49	New Mexico
50	Arizona

Note: Numbers that appear to be identical are rounded and vary slightly in actual value. The rankings reflect the actual values before rounding. See the introduction for more details.

I-23 Percentage Change in Average Price and Sales of Retail Prescription Drugs, 2002–2003

State	Percentage change in price of prescription drugs %	Percentage change in sales of prescription drugs %	Rank by percentage change in price
Alabama	14.8	2.6	1
Alaska	8.7	9.9	6
Arizona	12.5	9.2	2
Arkansas	7.1	7.3	16
California	4.8	8.6	46
Colorado	5.9	3.5	25
Connecticut	6.3	6.1	21
Delaware	7.5	23.6	12
Florida	8.1	9.9	8
Georgia	7.5	8.0	12
Hawaii	9.9	21.9	4
Idaho	5.7	9.3	30
Illinois	6.3	-0.6	21
Indiana	6.8	5.0	20
Iowa	7.7	7.3	11
Kansas	5.7	-0.1	30
Kentucky	3.0	2.9	49
Louisiana	9.1	12.6	5
Maine	2.0	9.0	50
Maryland	8.3	10.5	7
Massachusetts	5.9	5.9	25
Michigan	5.6	7.8	33
Minnesota	6.1	10.5	23
Mississippi	5.2	3.7	39
Missouri	5.0	2.0	43
Montana	7.2	9.9	15
Nebraska	5.5	-2.1	35
Nevada	5.0	7.1	43
New Hampshire	5.9	11.9	25
New Jersey	7.8	21.5	9
New Mexico	3.6	5.5	48
New York	5.3	17.8	36
North Carolina	6.9	15.7	19
North Dakota	7.8	10.0	9
Ohio	5.1	6.2	41
Oklahoma	5.1	-4.4	41
Oregon	5.3	0.3	36
Pennsylvania	3.8	10.8	47
Rhode Island	7.3	4.9	14
South Carolina	5.7	14.7	30
South Dakota	5.2	8.9	39
Tennessee	11.9	-1.0	3
Texas	5.9	10.4	25
Utah	5.6	3.5	33
Vermont	7.1	10.4	16
Virginia	4.9	5.9	45
Washington	5.3	8.3	36
West Virginia	7.0	10.7	18
Wisconsin	5.8	5.6	29
Wyoming	6.1	7.9	23
50 States	n/a	n/a	
DC	14.5	17.4	
United States	6.7	8.3	

Rank in order by percentage	
1	Alabama
2	Arizona
3	Tennessee
4	Hawaii
5	Louisiana
6	Alaska
7	Maryland
8	Florida
9	New Jersey
9	North Dakota
11	Iowa
12	Delaware
12	Georgia
14	Rhode Island
15	Montana
16	Arkansas
16	Vermont
18	West Virginia
19	North Carolina
20	Indiana
21	Connecticut
21	Illinois
23	Minnesota
23	Wyoming
25	Colorado
25	Massachusetts
25	New Hampshire
25	Texas
29	Wisconsin
30	Idaho
30	Kansas
30	South Carolina
33	Michigan
33	Utah
35	Nebraska
36	New York
36	Oregon
36	Washington
39	Mississippi
39	South Dakota
41	Ohio
41	Oklahoma
43	Missouri
43	Nevada
45	Virginia
46	California
47	Pennsylvania
48	New Mexico
49	Kentucky
50	Maine

Note: Ties in ranking reflect ties in actual values.

Source Notes for Health (Section I)

I-1 Immunization Rates, 2004: Information on immunization is collected by the Centers for Disease Control and Prevention (CDC) as part of their National Immunization Survey and are available on the CDC Web site (www.cdc.gov).

I-2 Infant Mortality Rates, 2005: These data are collected by the Centers for Disease Control and Prevention and are available on the CDC Web site (www.cdc.gov). They cover deaths of all children under one year of age, expressed in relation to each one thousand live births. This statistic is considered one of the best indicators with which to compare health among states and local areas. Higher death rates are associated with poor health of the mother, absence of medical care during pregnancy, and lack of medical treatment for infants.

I-3 State Health Rankings, 2005: These scores and rankings are developed annually for the United Health Foundation. The results are published in *America's Health: State Health Rankings*. They reflect a composite of indicators, including unemployment, health practices (such as smoking), the availability of health services, and outcomes (such as death rates). Probably no two researchers would use identical lists to produce such rankings, but the state rankings would likely be similar. While decisions by states have some impact on health rankings, decisions on health practices by individual citizens have as much, or more, impact.

I-4 Percentage of Non-Elderly Population without Health Insurance, 2004: Most Americans get health insurance coverage through their employers. All Americans over age sixty-four are covered by Medicare. About 13 percent of the non-elderly, including all welfare recipients, get coverage paid for by state and federal governments through Medicaid. Non-elderly citizens who have no health insurance comprise 17.8 percent of the population. These data are part of a compilation titled "Table HI-6" from the Housing and Household Economic Statistics Division of the U.S. Census Bureau.

I-5 Abortions, 2002: This count comes from the Centers for Disease Control and Prevention (CDC) and available on its Web site (www.cdc.gov). The abortion rate compares the number of abortions with the number of live births.

I-6 Alcohol Consumption Per Capita, 2003: Some public health authorities consider high levels of alcoholic beverage consumption an indicator of poor health of a state's population. The data show the number of gallons of pure ethanol (typical liquor is about 43 percent ethanol or ethanol alcohol, wine 14 percent, and beer about 6 percent) consumed per resident age fourteen and over. The data are derived by dividing sales of alcoholic beverages by population. Those shown were developed by the Department of Health and Human Services (National Institute on Alcohol Abuse and Alcoholism) and are published on its Web site (www.niaaa.nih.gov). They are called "apparent" alcohol consumption because some alcoholic beverages are bought in one state for consumption by residents of another. This raises the apparent consumption of tourist-destination states, like Nevada, and states with low prices, like New Hampshire, which draw purchasers from other states.

I-7 Percentage of Adult Smokers, 2004: These estimates, results of sample surveys, are developed by the Behavioral Surveillance Branch of the Centers for Disease Control and Prevention (CDC) and are available on the CDC Web site (www.cdc.gov). They reflect the percentage of the population who have smoked 100 cigarettes in their lifetime and reported smoking every day or some days.

I-8 Percentage of Population Obese, 2004: These data are part of the Centers for Disease Control and Prevention's (CDC) behavioral risk factor surveillance system. The 2004 statistics are published in United Health Foundation's annual report *America's Health: State Health Rankings*. Different definitions of how high a person's body mass index (BMI) can be without being considered a health risk would produce different percentages for every state, but not appreciably affect the rankings. A person with a BMI of 30 or more is considered *obese*, while a BMI of 25 to 29.9 is considered *overweight*.

I-9 AIDS Cases, 2004: These data are developed by the Centers for Disease Control and Prevention (CDC) and reported in the *HIV/AIDS Surveillance Report* (vol. 16). They cover cases newly reported in calendar year 2004. The rate shown is cases per one hundred thousand residents. Because persons at most risk of contracting AIDS are predominantly found in larger metropolitan areas, states containing those areas typically show the highest rates.

I-10 Physicians Per 100,000 Population, 2005: This table shows the number of physicians in relation to population. Rural states will show below-average numbers in part because intensive medical care, such as that received from major hospitals, is often sought in nearby states with large metropolitan areas. The statistics are based on data from Medical Marketing Service, Inc. (www.mmslists.com).

I-11 Hospital Beds Per 1,000 Population, 2004: This table shows the number of community hospital beds in relation to population. The data come from *Hospital Statistics, 2006 Edition*, a publication of the American Hospital Association. As of 1998, the AHA state data no longer cover all hospitals. Thus, the data shown here reflect only community (non-federal, short-term, general and other special) hospitals.

I-12 Medicaid Recipients, Mid-Year 2004: Over forty-four million people receive health care through the Medicaid program each year. The federal government sets minimum standards for this program and pays about 60 percent of the costs nationwide through a formula that provides 50 percent of the costs in the most affluent states and up to 77 percent in the poorest states. Within federal guidelines, states set the rules for eligibility, the health services covered, and the amount of reimbursements to the providers of care.

The primary recipients are families that receive cash assistance from states through Temporary Assistance for Needy Families (TANF) or from the federal government through Supplemental Security Income (SSI). About 25 percent of Medicaid recipients are elderly or disabled. Also covered by Medicare, these so-called "dual-eligibles" receive supplemental coverage through the Medicaid program for specific services such as prescription drugs and long-term care. Though these populations make up only a quarter of Medicaid enrollment, they account for about 70 percent of Medicaid expenditures. In 2006, some prescription drug costs will shift to Medicare as the new Medicare prescription drug benefit goes into effect.

These data, reflecting a count as of June 30, 2004, come from tabulations of the Department of Health and Human Services Centers for Medicare and Medicaid Services (CMS) and are available on its Web site (www.cms.hhs.gov).

I-13 Medicaid Recipients as a Percentage of Poverty Population, Mid-Year 2004: These data, from the same source as Table I-12, relate the number of Medicaid recipients to the number of persons in households with income below federally defined poverty levels (see Table A-16). The differences among states are a good indication of how inclusive are the eligibility criteria set by the individual states.

I-14 State and Local Spending for Health and Hospitals, FY 2002: This table relates spending data to population and personal income in each state. The data come from the U.S. Census Bureau's electronic publication "State and Local Government Finance Estimates, by State," available on the bureau's Web site (www.census.gov). See notes to Table F-1 for more extensive information on the source of the data.

The spending includes public health activities plus the gross outlays of hospitals and nursing homes run by state and local governments, including costs defrayed by the charges hospitals make to patients and their health insurance providers. The largest outlays appear in states that rely heavily on government-owned hospitals.

I-15 State and Local Health and Hospital Spending as a Percentage of General Spending, FY 2002: This table shows the relative importance of health and hospital outlays in state and local budgets. It is derived by comparing this spending (see Table I-14) with total "general" spending. General spending includes essentially all other spending except municipal electric and other utilities and trust funds, such as those for workers' compensation.

I-16 Per Capita Medicaid Spending, FY 2004: These data, from the same source as the number of recipients in Table I-12, reflect the major impact that Medicaid costs are having on government budgets. The amounts shown reflect primarily federal grants spent by states, about 60 percent of the total with differences among the states, and state government matching funds. In a few states, particularly New York, some of the federally required state match is provided by local governments.

I-17 Average Medicaid Spending Per Aged Recipient, FY 2001: These data, from the same source as Table I-12, illustrate differences among the states in this component of Medicaid costs. They relate total spending on all Medicaid recipients age sixty-five and over to the number of recipients. Over half of the nursing home residents in the United States are having their bills paid by Medicaid. States differ in the extent and success of programs designed to encourage people to live at home and with relatives rather than enter nursing homes. Those programs typically provide visiting nurses and homemakers who assist frail elderly persons in their homes, thereby reducing the need for institutionalization.

I-18 Average Medicaid Spending Per Child, FY 2001: These data reflect the same concepts and come from the same source as those shown in Table I-17. Differences among states primarily reflect differences in how much doctors and other providers of health care are compensated for providing services.

I-19 Medicare Payment Per Hospital Day, FY 2003: These data are one way to measure health care cost differences among states. They reflect the cost of a day in short-stay hospitals as reimbursed by the federal Medicare program. The data come from the Centers for Medicare and Medicaid Services and are available on its Web site (www.cms.hhs.gov). These data include both the basic rate for staying in the hospital (see Table I-20) and charges for specific services.

I-20 Hospital Expense Per Inpatient Day, 2004: These data result from a comparison of inpatient days and hospital unit total expenses at community hospitals as reported by the American Hospital Association in the annual publication *Hospital Statistics*. See source for Table I-11.

I-21 Percentage of Population in Health Maintenance Organizations, 2005: Most Americans receive their health care by purchasing it from individual doctors, hospitals, pharmacies, and others. However, a percentage are served by health maintenance organizations that provide complete packages of care for one monthly fee. Many people believe that this approach to buying care will reduce health care costs because the service providers cannot increase their incomes by providing additional services. The statistics, reflecting enrollment in July 2005 as a percentage of population, come from HealthLeaders-InterStudy (Nashville, TN) and are published in *The Competitive Edge, January 2005.*

I-22 Prescription Drugs as a Percentage of State Medicaid Costs, FY 2002: In recent years there has been a significant jump in Medicaid spending. Rising health care costs, enrollment increases, and greater utilization help explain these increases. Prescription drug costs are also driving the growth in Medicaid spending. This table, from the same source as Table I-12, shows the percentage of state Medicaid spending that went towards prescription drugs in fiscal year 2002. In over three-quarters of the states, spending on prescription drugs was more than 10 percent of the total state cost for the program.

I-23 Percentage Change in Average Price and Sales of Retail Prescription Drugs, 2002–2003: This table shows year over year change in the average price of retail prescriptions filled, as well as year over year change in prescription drug sales. The data cover retail sales only, mail order prescriptions are not included. The statistics are produced by Verispan, L.L.C. for the Kaiser Family Foundation and are available on its Web site (statehealthfacts.org).

Crime and Law Enforcement

Overall, violent crime dropped by 0.5 percent in the first half of 2005, according to preliminary numbers from the Federal Bureau of Investigation. Violent crime, as a category, includes murder (up 2.1 percent), rape (down 4.7 percent), robbery (up 0.6 percent), and aggravated assault (down 0.7 percent).

Nationally, nonviolent crime also decreased compared to the previous year. There was considerable variation by region, however. Violent crime increased in the Midwest as did motor vehicle theft in the West.

2005 Crime Rates by Region

	Northeast	Midwest	South	West
Violent crime	-0.9	+3.5	-1.4	-1.9
Murder	+1.9	+4.9	+2.2	+0.2
Forcible rape	-5.7	-3.9	-5.8	-3.3
Robbery	+1.0	+3.0	+1.3	-1.9
Aggravated assault	-1.6	+4.8	-2.1	-1.8
Property crime	-4.2	-3.0	-3.3	-1.6
Burglary	-4.8	+0.8	-1.4	-0.5
Larceny-theft	-2.6	-3.6	-3.6	-3.6
Motor vehicle theft	-11.9	-5.2	-5.1	+4.5
Arson	-6.4	-7.4	-2.9	-7.0

Source: FBI Uniform Crime Reports

The nation's prison population rose by only 1.9 percent in 2004, much less than the 3.2 percent average annual increase since the end of 1995.

Female prisoners make up a small segment of inmate populations (7 percent in 2004), but one with a high growth rate. Since 1995, the number of male inmates has increased by 32 percent, while the number of female inmates has increased by 53 percent.

Change in Prisioners, by Gender

	Men	Women
Percent change 2003–2004	1.8	4.0
Average annual 1995–2004	3.1	4.8

Source: Bureau of Justice Statistics

J-1 Total Crime Rate, 2004

State	Crime rate (per 100,000 population)	Rank
Alabama	4,452	16
Alaska	4,017	22
Arizona	5,845	1
Arkansas	4,512	15
California	3,971	24
Colorado	4,293	21
Connecticut	2,914	39
Delaware	3,732	27
Florida	4,891	9
Georgia	4,721	13
Hawaii	5,047	5
Idaho	3,039	36
Illinois	3,729	28
Indiana	3,723	29
Iowa	3,176	34
Kansas	4,348	18
Kentucky	2,783	43
Louisiana	5,049	4
Maine	2,513	46
Maryland	4,341	19
Massachusetts	2,919	38
Michigan	3,548	31
Minnesota	3,309	32
Mississippi	3,774	26
Missouri	4,394	17
Montana	3,230	33
Nebraska	3,829	25
Nevada	4,823	11
New Hampshire	2,207	48
New Jersey	2,785	42
New Mexico	4,885	10
New York	2,640	45
North Carolina	4,608	14
North Dakota	1,996	50
Ohio	4,015	23
Oklahoma	4,743	12
Oregon	4,930	8
Pennsylvania	2,826	41
Rhode Island	3,132	35
South Carolina	5,289	2
South Dakota	2,105	49
Tennessee	5,002	7
Texas	5,035	6
Utah	4,322	20
Vermont	2,420	47
Virginia	2,952	37
Washington	5,193	3
West Virginia	2,777	44
Wisconsin	2,873	40
Wyoming	3,564	30
50 States	n/a	
DC	6,230	
United States	3,983	

Rank in order by rate	
1	Arizona
2	South Carolina
3	Washington
4	Louisiana
5	Hawaii
6	Texas
7	Tennessee
8	Oregon
9	Florida
10	New Mexico
11	Nevada
12	Oklahoma
13	Georgia
14	North Carolina
15	Arkansas
16	Alabama
17	Missouri
18	Kansas
19	Maryland
20	Utah
21	Colorado
22	Alaska
23	Ohio
24	California
25	Nebraska
26	Mississippi
27	Delaware
28	Illinois
29	Indiana
30	Wyoming
31	Michigan
32	Minnesota
33	Montana
34	Iowa
35	Rhode Island
36	Idaho
37	Virginia
38	Massachusetts
39	Connecticut
40	Wisconsin
41	Pennsylvania
42	New Jersey
43	Kentucky
44	West Virginia
45	New York
46	Maine
47	Vermont
48	New Hampshire
49	South Dakota
50	North Dakota

J-2 Violent Crime Rate, 2004

State	Violent crime rate (per 100,000 population)	Rank
Alabama	427	22
Alaska	635	7
Arizona	504	13
Arkansas	499	15
California	552	10
Colorado	374	25
Connecticut	286	34
Delaware	568	9
Florida	711	2
Georgia	456	19
Hawaii	254	39
Idaho	245	41
Illinois	543	11
Indiana	325	29
Iowa	271	37
Kansas	375	24
Kentucky	245	42
Louisiana	639	6
Maine	104	49
Maryland	701	3
Massachusetts	459	18
Michigan	490	17
Minnesota	270	38
Mississippi	295	32
Missouri	491	16
Montana	294	33
Nebraska	309	30
Nevada	616	8
New Hampshire	167	47
New Jersey	356	26
New Mexico	687	5
New York	442	21
North Carolina	448	20
North Dakota	79	50
Ohio	342	28
Oklahoma	501	14
Oregon	298	31
Pennsylvania	411	23
Rhode Island	247	40
South Carolina	784	1
South Dakota	172	46
Tennessee	695	4
Texas	541	12
Utah	236	43
Vermont	112	48
Virginia	276	35
Washington	344	27
West Virginia	271	36
Wisconsin	210	45
Wyoming	230	44
50 States	n/a	
DC	1,371	
United States	466	

Rank in order by rate	
1	South Carolina
2	Florida
3	Maryland
4	Tennessee
5	New Mexico
6	Louisiana
7	Alaska
8	Nevada
9	Delaware
10	California
11	Illinois
12	Texas
13	Arizona
14	Oklahoma
15	Arkansas
16	Missouri
17	Michigan
18	Massachusetts
19	Georgia
20	North Carolina
21	New York
22	Alabama
23	Pennsylvania
24	Kansas
25	Colorado
26	New Jersey
27	Washington
28	Ohio
29	Indiana
30	Nebraska
31	Oregon
32	Mississippi
33	Montana
34	Connecticut
35	Virginia
36	West Virginia
37	Iowa
38	Minnesota
39	Hawaii
40	Rhode Island
41	Idaho
42	Kentucky
43	Utah
44	Wyoming
45	Wisconsin
46	South Dakota
47	New Hampshire
48	Vermont
49	Maine
50	North Dakota

Note: Numbers that appear to be identical are rounded and vary slightly in actual value. The rankings reflect the actual values before rounding. See the introduction for more details.

J-3 Murder and Rape Rates, 2004

State	Murder rate (per 100,000 population)	Rape rate (per 100,000 population)	Rank by murder rate
Alabama	5.6	38.5	18
Alaska	5.6	85.1	18
Arizona	7.2	33.0	6
Arkansas	6.4	42.4	10
California	6.7	26.8	9
Colorado	4.4	42.5	29
Connecticut	2.6	20.7	34
Delaware	2.0	41.5	45
Florida	5.4	38.0	20
Georgia	6.9	27.0	7
Hawaii	2.6	26.4	34
Idaho	2.2	40.9	42
Illinois	6.1	33.2	14
Indiana	5.1	28.9	24
Iowa	1.6	26.7	47
Kansas	4.5	40.4	26
Kentucky	5.7	29.9	17
Louisiana	12.7	35.8	1
Maine	1.4	23.9	48
Maryland	9.4	23.7	2
Massachusetts	2.6	28.0	34
Michigan	6.4	54.2	10
Minnesota	2.2	41.6	42
Mississippi	7.8	40.0	4
Missouri	6.2	25.7	12
Montana	3.2	29.5	31
Nebraska	2.3	35.5	40
Nevada	7.4	40.9	5
New Hampshire	1.4	35.3	48
New Jersey	4.5	15.3	26
New Mexico	8.9	54.6	3
New York	4.6	18.8	25
North Carolina	6.2	27.4	12
North Dakota	1.4	25.1	48
Ohio	4.5	40.5	26
Oklahoma	5.3	44.2	21
Oregon	2.5	35.7	38
Pennsylvania	5.2	28.5	22
Rhode Island	2.4	29.6	39
South Carolina	6.9	40.9	7
South Dakota	2.3	43.8	40
Tennessee	5.9	37.6	16
Texas	6.1	37.3	14
Utah	1.9	39.1	46
Vermont	2.6	24.5	34
Virginia	5.2	23.7	22
Washington	3.1	46.1	32
West Virginia	3.7	17.6	30
Wisconsin	2.8	20.6	33
Wyoming	2.2	22.1	42
50 States	n/a	n/a	
DC	35.8	40.1	
United States	5.5	32.2	

Rank in order by murder rate	
1	Louisiana
2	Maryland
3	New Mexico
4	Mississippi
5	Nevada
6	Arizona
7	Georgia
7	South Carolina
9	California
10	Arkansas
10	Michigan
12	Missouri
12	North Carolina
14	Illinois
14	Texas
16	Tennessee
17	Kentucky
18	Alabama
18	Alaska
20	Florida
21	Oklahoma
22	Pennsylvania
22	Virginia
24	Indiana
25	New York
26	Kansas
26	New Jersey
26	Ohio
29	Colorado
30	West Virginia
31	Montana
32	Washington
33	Wisconsin
34	Connecticut
34	Hawaii
34	Massachusetts
34	Vermont
38	Oregon
39	Rhode Island
40	Nebraska
40	South Dakota
42	Idaho
42	Minnesota
42	Wyoming
45	Delaware
46	Utah
47	Iowa
48	Maine
48	New Hampshire
48	North Dakota

Note: Ties in ranking reflect ties in actual values.

J-4 Property Crime Rate, 2004

State	Property crime rate (per 100,000 population)	Rank
Alabama	4,025	16
Alaska	3,383	27
Arizona	5,341	1
Arkansas	4,013	17
California	3,419	25
Colorado	3,919	19
Connecticut	2,627	39
Delaware	3,164	30
Florida	4,180	13
Georgia	4,266	9
Hawaii	4,793	3
Idaho	2,794	36
Illinois	3,186	29
Indiana	3,398	26
Iowa	2,905	34
Kansas	3,974	18
Kentucky	2,538	40
Louisiana	4,410	7
Maine	2,410	45
Maryland	3,640	22
Massachusetts	2,460	42
Michigan	3,058	31
Minnesota	3,039	32
Mississippi	3,479	24
Missouri	3,904	20
Montana	2,936	33
Nebraska	3,521	23
Nevada	4,207	11
New Hampshire	2,040	48
New Jersey	2,429	43
New Mexico	4,198	12
New York	2,199	47
North Carolina	4,160	14
North Dakota	1,917	50
Ohio	3,673	21
Oklahoma	4,242	10
Oregon	4,631	4
Pennsylvania	2,415	44
Rhode Island	2,884	35
South Carolina	4,505	5
South Dakota	1,934	49
Tennessee	4,307	8
Texas	4,494	6
Utah	4,086	15
Vermont	2,308	46
Virginia	2,677	37
Washington	4,849	2
West Virginia	2,506	41
Wisconsin	2,663	38
Wyoming	3,334	28
50 States	n/a	
DC	4,859	
United States	3,517	

Rank in order by rate	
1	Arizona
2	Washington
3	Hawaii
4	Oregon
5	South Carolina
6	Texas
7	Louisiana
8	Tennessee
9	Georgia
10	Oklahoma
11	Nevada
12	New Mexico
13	Florida
14	North Carolina
15	Utah
16	Alabama
17	Arkansas
18	Kansas
19	Colorado
20	Missouri
21	Ohio
22	Maryland
23	Nebraska
24	Mississippi
25	California
26	Indiana
27	Alaska
28	Wyoming
29	Illinois
30	Delaware
31	Michigan
32	Minnesota
33	Montana
34	Iowa
35	Rhode Island
36	Idaho
37	Virginia
38	Wisconsin
39	Connecticut
40	Kentucky
41	West Virginia
42	Massachusetts
43	New Jersey
44	Pennsylvania
45	Maine
46	Vermont
47	New York
48	New Hampshire
49	South Dakota
50	North Dakota

J-5 Motor Vehicle Theft Rate, 2004

State	Motor vehicle theft rate (per 100,000 population)	Rank
Alabama	310	29
Alaska	342	23
Arizona	963	2
Arkansas	236	36
California	704	3
Colorado	523	7
Connecticut	315	28
Delaware	259	34
Florida	450	11
Georgia	501	9
Hawaii	683	5
Idaho	196	42
Illinois	317	26
Indiana	338	24
Iowa	183	43
Kansas	308	30
Kentucky	212	39
Louisiana	437	13
Maine	99	49
Maryland	645	6
Massachusetts	344	22
Michigan	500	10
Minnesota	265	33
Mississippi	271	32
Missouri	450	12
Montana	175	44
Nebraska	303	31
Nevada	970	1
New Hampshire	149	46
New Jersey	348	21
New Mexico	415	16
New York	213	38
North Carolina	316	27
North Dakota	143	47
Ohio	357	20
Oklahoma	368	19
Oregon	516	8
Pennsylvania	250	35
Rhode Island	377	17
South Carolina	373	18
South Dakota	110	48
Tennessee	419	14
Texas	418	15
Utah	320	25
Vermont	93	50
Virginia	233	37
Washington	697	4
West Virginia	206	41
Wisconsin	207	40
Wyoming	158	45
50 States	n/a	
DC	1,519	
United States	421	

Rank in order by rate	
1	Nevada
2	Arizona
3	California
4	Washington
5	Hawaii
6	Maryland
7	Colorado
8	Oregon
9	Georgia
10	Michigan
11	Florida
12	Missouri
13	Louisiana
14	Tennessee
15	Texas
16	New Mexico
17	Rhode Island
18	South Carolina
19	Oklahoma
20	Ohio
21	New Jersey
22	Massachusetts
23	Alaska
24	Indiana
25	Utah
26	Illinois
27	North Carolina
28	Connecticut
29	Alabama
30	Kansas
31	Nebraska
32	Mississippi
33	Minnesota
34	Delaware
35	Pennsylvania
36	Arkansas
37	Virginia
38	New York
39	Kentucky
40	Wisconsin
41	West Virginia
42	Idaho
43	Iowa
44	Montana
45	Wyoming
46	New Hampshire
47	North Dakota
48	South Dakota
49	Maine
50	Vermont

Note: Numbers that appear to be identical are rounded and vary slightly in actual value. The rankings reflect the actual values before rounding. See the introduction for more details.

J-6 Violent Crime Rate Change, 2000–2004

State	2000 violent crime rate (per 100,000 population)	Percentage increase in violent crime 2000–2004	Rank by percentage increase
Alabama	486	-12.3	38
Alaska	567	11.9	3
Arizona	532	-5.2	22
Arkansas	445	12.1	2
California	622	-11.2	34
Colorado	334	11.8	4
Connecticut	325	-11.8	37
Delaware	684	-16.9	45
Florida	812	-12.4	39
Georgia	505	-9.7	31
Hawaii	244	4.3	5
Idaho	253	-3.0	18
Illinois	657	-17.3	46
Indiana	349	-6.8	26
Iowa	266	1.7	8
Kansas	389	-3.8	20
Kentucky	295	-16.8	43
Louisiana	681	-6.2	25
Maine	110	-5.6	23
Maryland	787	-10.9	33
Massachusetts	476	-3.6	19
Michigan	555	-11.7	36
Minnesota	281	-4.0	21
Mississippi	361	-18.2	47
Missouri	490	0.1	10
Montana	241	n/a	n/a
Nebraska	328	-5.8	24
Nevada	524	17.5	1
New Hampshire	175	n/a	n/a
New Jersey	384	-7.3	28
New Mexico	758	-9.3	30
New York	554	-20.3	48
North Carolina	498	-10.0	32
North Dakota	81	-2.5	16
Ohio	334	2.3	7
Oklahoma	498	0.5	9
Oregon	351	-14.9	42
Pennsylvania	420	-2.1	14
Rhode Island	298	-16.9	44
South Carolina	805	-2.6	17
South Dakota	167	2.8	6
Tennessee	707	-1.7	13
Texas	545	-0.8	11
Utah	256	-7.7	29
Vermont	114	-1.3	12
Virginia	282	-2.2	15
Washington	370	-7.0	27
West Virginia	317	-14.3	41
Wisconsin	237	-11.5	35
Wyoming	267	-13.8	40
50 States	n/a	n/a	
DC	1,508	-9.1	
United States	506	-8.0	

Rank in order by percentage increase	
1	Nevada
2	Arkansas
3	Alaska
4	Colorado
5	Hawaii
6	South Dakota
7	Ohio
8	Iowa
9	Oklahoma
10	Missouri
11	Texas
12	Vermont
13	Tennessee
14	Pennsylvania
15	Virginia
16	North Dakota
17	South Carolina
18	Idaho
19	Massachusetts
20	Kansas
21	Minnesota
22	Arizona
23	Maine
24	Nebraska
25	Louisiana
26	Indiana
27	Washington
28	New Jersey
29	Utah
30	New Mexico
31	Georgia
32	North Carolina
33	Maryland
34	California
35	Wisconsin
36	Michigan
37	Connecticut
38	Alabama
39	Florida
40	Wyoming
41	West Virginia
42	Oregon
43	Kentucky
44	Rhode Island
45	Delaware
46	Illinois
47	Mississippi
48	New York

Note: Numbers that appear to be identical are rounded and vary slightly in actual value. The rankings reflect the actual values before rounding. See the introduction for more details.

J-7 Prisoners, 2004

State	Prisoners #	Rank
Alabama	25,887	16
Alaska	4,554	41
Arizona	32,515	13
Arkansas	13,807	28
California	166,556	2
Colorado	20,293	24
Connecticut	19,497	25
Delaware	6,927	35
Florida	85,533	3
Georgia	51,104	5
Hawaii	5,960	39
Idaho	6,375	37
Illinois	44,054	8
Indiana	24,008	18
Iowa	8,525	34
Kansas	8,966	32
Kentucky	17,814	26
Louisiana	36,939	10
Maine	2,024	47
Maryland	23,285	21
Massachusetts	10,144	31
Michigan	48,883	6
Minnesota	8,758	33
Mississippi	20,983	23
Missouri	31,081	14
Montana	3,877	43
Nebraska	4,130	42
Nevada	11,365	30
New Hampshire	2,448	46
New Jersey	26,757	15
New Mexico	6,379	36
New York	63,751	4
North Carolina	35,434	12
North Dakota	1,327	50
Ohio	44,806	7
Oklahoma	23,319	20
Oregon	13,183	29
Pennsylvania	40,963	9
Rhode Island	3,430	44
South Carolina	23,428	19
South Dakota	3,095	45
Tennessee	25,884	17
Texas	168,105	1
Utah	5,989	38
Vermont	1,968	49
Virginia	35,564	11
Washington	16,614	27
West Virginia	5,067	40
Wisconsin	22,966	22
Wyoming	1,980	48
50 States	1,316,301	
DC	n/a	
United States	1,316,301	

Rank in order by #	
1	Texas
2	California
3	Florida
4	New York
5	Georgia
6	Michigan
7	Ohio
8	Illinois
9	Pennsylvania
10	Louisiana
11	Virginia
12	North Carolina
13	Arizona
14	Missouri
15	New Jersey
16	Alabama
17	Tennessee
18	Indiana
19	South Carolina
20	Oklahoma
21	Maryland
22	Wisconsin
23	Mississippi
24	Colorado
25	Connecticut
26	Kentucky
27	Washington
28	Arkansas
29	Oregon
30	Nevada
31	Massachusetts
32	Kansas
33	Minnesota
34	Iowa
35	Delaware
36	New Mexico
37	Idaho
38	Utah
39	Hawaii
40	West Virginia
41	Alaska
42	Nebraska
43	Montana
44	Rhode Island
45	South Dakota
46	New Hampshire
47	Maine
48	Wyoming
49	Vermont
50	North Dakota

J-8 Change in Prisoners, 1995-2004

State	Percentage change in prisoners	Rank
Alabama	25.5	37
Alaska	28.9	32
Arizona	53.3	17
Arkansas	60.4	14
California	25.2	38
Colorado	83.4	7
Connecticut	27.1	34
Delaware	35.6	28
Florida	33.9	30
Georgia	49.5	18
Hawaii	61.2	13
Idaho	91.6	6
Illinois	17.0	43
Indiana	49.2	19
Iowa	44.3	23
Kansas	27.1	33
Kentucky	42.1	25
Louisiana	46.6	21
Maine	47.9	20
Maryland	11.0	44
Massachusetts	-16.7	50
Michigan	18.9	42
Minnesota	80.7	8
Mississippi	58.9	15
Missouri	62.3	12
Montana	93.9	5
Nebraska	34.3	29
Nevada	46.2	22
New Hampshire	21.5	40
New Jersey	-1.1	48
New Mexico	55.7	16
New York	-6.9	49
North Carolina	9.9	45
North Dakota	127.6	1
Ohio	0.3	47
Oklahoma	26.2	36
Oregon	102.1	4
Pennsylvania	26.3	35
Rhode Island	3.3	46
South Carolina	19.5	41
South Dakota	65.0	11
Tennessee	70.2	10
Texas	23.4	39
Utah	71.6	9
Vermont	38.5	27
Virginia	30.5	31
Washington	42.2	24
West Virginia	102.4	3
Wisconsin	108.4	2
Wyoming	41.9	26
50 States	28.5	
DC	n/a	
United States	27.3	

Rank in order by percentage	
1	North Dakota
2	Wisconsin
3	West Virginia
4	Oregon
5	Montana
6	Idaho
7	Colorado
8	Minnesota
9	Utah
10	Tennessee
11	South Dakota
12	Missouri
13	Hawaii
14	Arkansas
15	Mississippi
16	New Mexico
17	Arizona
18	Georgia
19	Indiana
20	Maine
21	Louisiana
22	Nevada
23	Iowa
24	Washington
25	Kentucky
26	Wyoming
27	Vermont
28	Delaware
29	Nebraska
30	Florida
31	Virginia
32	Alaska
33	Kansas
34	Connecticut
35	Pennsylvania
36	Oklahoma
37	Alabama
38	California
39	Texas
40	New Hampshire
41	South Carolina
42	Michigan
43	Illinois
44	Maryland
45	North Carolina
46	Rhode Island
47	Ohio
48	New Jersey
49	New York
50	Massachusetts

Note: Numbers that appear to be identical are rounded and vary slightly in actual value. The rankings reflect the actual values before rounding. See the introduction for more details.

J-9 Incarceration Rate, 2004

State	Incarceration rate (per 100,000 population)	Rank
Alabama	556	6
Alaska	398	24
Arizona	534	9
Arkansas	495	10
California	456	16
Colorado	438	18
Connecticut	377	29
Delaware	488	11
Florida	486	12
Georgia	574	5
Hawaii	329	34
Idaho	454	17
Illinois	346	32
Indiana	383	28
Iowa	288	39
Kansas	327	36
Kentucky	412	21
Louisiana	816	1
Maine	148	50
Maryland	406	22
Massachusetts	232	44
Michigan	483	13
Minnesota	171	49
Mississippi	669	3
Missouri	538	8
Montana	416	20
Nebraska	230	45
Nevada	474	14
New Hampshire	187	47
New Jersey	306	38
New Mexico	318	37
New York	331	33
North Carolina	357	31
North Dakota	195	46
Ohio	391	25
Oklahoma	649	4
Oregon	365	30
Pennsylvania	329	34
Rhode Island	175	48
South Carolina	539	7
South Dakota	399	23
Tennessee	437	19
Texas	694	2
Utah	246	42
Vermont	233	43
Virginia	473	15
Washington	264	41
West Virginia	277	40
Wisconsin	390	26
Wyoming	389	27
50 States	n/a	
DC	n/a	
United States	432	

Rank in order by rate	
1	Louisiana
2	Texas
3	Mississippi
4	Oklahoma
5	Georgia
6	Alabama
7	South Carolina
8	Missouri
9	Arizona
10	Arkansas
11	Delaware
12	Florida
13	Michigan
14	Nevada
15	Virginia
16	California
17	Idaho
18	Colorado
19	Tennessee
20	Montana
21	Kentucky
22	Maryland
23	South Dakota
24	Alaska
25	Ohio
26	Wisconsin
27	Wyoming
28	Indiana
29	Connecticut
30	Oregon
31	North Carolina
32	Illinois
33	New York
34	Hawaii
34	Pennsylvania
36	Kansas
37	New Mexico
38	New Jersey
39	Iowa
40	West Virginia
41	Washington
42	Utah
43	Vermont
44	Massachusetts
45	Nebraska
46	North Dakota
47	New Hampshire
48	Rhode Island
49	Minnesota
50	Maine

Note: Ties in ranking reflect ties in actual values.

J-10 Juvenile Violent Crime Index, 2003

State	Juvenile crime rate (per 100,000 youths)	Rank
Alabama	126	39
Alaska	243	19
Arizona	223	22
Arkansas	130	38
California	364	7
Colorado	231	20
Connecticut	290	12
Delaware	595	2
Florida	524	3
Georgia	266	15
Hawaii	197	28
Idaho	160	33
Illinois	944	1
Indiana	317	9
Iowa	251	17
Kansas	131	37
Kentucky	229	21
Louisiana	355	8
Maine	78	45
Maryland	505	4
Massachusetts	269	14
Michigan	166	32
Minnesota	176	31
Mississippi	136	36
Missouri	295	11
Montana	202	27
Nebraska	96	42
Nevada	n/a	n/a
New Hampshire	71	46
New Jersey	386	6
New Mexico	220	24
New York	264	16
North Carolina	310	10
North Dakota	45	48
Ohio	150	34
Oklahoma	217	25
Oregon	149	35
Pennsylvania	402	5
Rhode Island	288	13
South Carolina	47	47
South Dakota	108	40
Tennessee	223	22
Texas	185	29
Utah	216	26
Vermont	81	44
Virginia	106	41
Washington	246	18
West Virginia	40	49
Wisconsin	184	30
Wyoming	88	43
50 States	n/a	
DC	n/a	
United States	291	

Rank in order by rate	
n/a	Nevada
1	Illinois
2	Delaware
3	Florida
4	Maryland
5	Pennsylvania
6	New Jersey
7	California
8	Louisiana
9	Indiana
10	North Carolina
11	Missouri
12	Connecticut
13	Rhode Island
14	Massachusetts
15	Georgia
16	New York
17	Iowa
18	Washington
19	Alaska
20	Colorado
21	Kentucky
22	Arizona
22	Tennessee
24	New Mexico
25	Oklahoma
26	Utah
27	Montana
28	Hawaii
29	Texas
30	Wisconsin
31	Minnesota
32	Michigan
33	Idaho
34	Ohio
35	Oregon
36	Mississippi
37	Kansas
38	Arkansas
39	Alabama
40	South Dakota
41	Virginia
42	Nebraska
43	Wyoming
44	Vermont
45	Maine
46	New Hampshire
47	South Carolina
48	North Dakota
49	West Virginia

Note: Ties in ranking reflect ties in actual values.

J-11 State and Local Law Enforcement Employees, 2004

State	Law enforcement employees #	Per 10,000 population #	Rank per 10,000 population
Alabama	12,706	28.0	26
Alaska	1,660	25.3	38
Arizona	18,440	32.1	10
Arkansas	7,553	27.4	31
California	99,236	27.6	29
Colorado	13,372	29.1	21
Connecticut	10,911	31.1	13
Delaware	2,468	29.7	17
Florida	61,978	35.6	7
Georgia	25,505	28.9	23
Hawaii	3,661	29.0	22
Idaho	3,717	26.7	35
Illinois	46,093	36.3	4
Indiana	17,293	27.7	27
Iowa	7,637	25.8	37
Kansas	8,760	32.0	11
Kentucky	10,324	24.9	40
Louisiana	16,146	35.8	6
Maine	3,048	23.1	43
Maryland	16,612	29.9	16
Massachusetts	23,152	36.1	5
Michigan	24,514	24.2	41
Minnesota	10,443	20.5	48
Mississippi	8,628	29.7	18
Missouri	18,515	32.2	9
Montana	2,435	26.3	36
Nebraska	4,730	27.1	33
Nevada	6,860	29.4	19
New Hampshire	3,655	28.1	25
New Jersey	36,010	41.4	2
New Mexico	5,784	30.4	15
New York	85,813	44.6	1
North Carolina	23,307	27.3	32
North Dakota	1,437	22.7	47
Ohio	33,591	29.3	20
Oklahoma	11,252	31.9	12
Oregon	8,595	23.9	42
Pennsylvania	31,157	25.1	39
Rhode Island	2,988	27.7	28
South Carolina	13,683	32.6	8
South Dakota	1,780	23.1	45
Tennessee	18,182	30.8	14
Texas	62,056	27.6	30
Utah	5,520	23.1	44
Vermont	1,221	19.6	50
Virginia	20,130	27.0	34
Washington	14,216	22.9	46
West Virginia	3,629	20.0	49
Wisconsin	15,771	28.6	24
Wyoming	1,842	36.4	3
50 States	888,016	30.3	
DC	4,410	79.7	
United States	892,426	30.4	

Rank in order per 10,000 population	
1	New York
2	New Jersey
3	Wyoming
4	Illinois
5	Massachusetts
6	Louisiana
7	Florida
8	South Carolina
9	Missouri
10	Arizona
11	Kansas
12	Oklahoma
13	Connecticut
14	Tennessee
15	New Mexico
16	Maryland
17	Delaware
18	Mississippi
19	Nevada
20	Ohio
21	Colorado
22	Hawaii
23	Georgia
24	Wisconsin
25	New Hampshire
26	Alabama
27	Indiana
28	Rhode Island
29	California
30	Texas
31	Arkansas
32	North Carolina
33	Nebraska
34	Virginia
35	Idaho
36	Montana
37	Iowa
38	Alaska
39	Pennsylvania
40	Kentucky
41	Michigan
42	Oregon
43	Maine
44	Utah
45	South Dakota
46	Washington
47	North Dakota
48	Minnesota
49	West Virginia
50	Vermont

Note: Numbers that appear to be identical are rounded and vary slightly in actual value. The rankings reflect the actual values before rounding. See the introduction for more details.

J-12 State and Local Corrections Employees, 2004

State	Correction employees #	Per 10,000 population #	Rank per 10,000 population
Alabama	7,867	17.4	42
Alaska	1,840	28.1	9
Arizona	14,655	25.5	13
Arkansas	6,321	23.0	21
California	81,435	22.7	22
Colorado	9,923	21.6	27
Connecticut	7,473	21.3	30
Delaware	2,839	34.2	1
Florida	43,749	25.1	14
Georgia	27,504	31.2	3
Hawaii	2,376	18.8	36
Idaho	2,846	20.4	32
Illinois	24,415	19.2	35
Indiana	13,498	21.6	26
Iowa	4,473	15.1	47
Kansas	6,097	22.3	23
Kentucky	7,737	18.7	37
Louisiana	13,438	29.8	6
Maine	2,130	16.2	45
Maryland	15,150	27.3	11
Massachusetts	9,367	14.6	50
Michigan	23,248	23.0	20
Minnesota	8,662	17.0	43
Mississippi	5,924	20.4	33
Missouri	14,836	25.8	12
Montana	1,695	18.3	39
Nebraska	3,740	21.4	29
Nevada	5,670	24.3	16
New Hampshire	1,930	14.9	49
New Jersey	16,803	19.3	34
New Mexico	5,910	31.1	4
New York	58,286	30.3	5
North Carolina	23,606	27.6	10
North Dakota	944	14.9	48
Ohio	24,647	21.5	28
Oklahoma	6,531	18.5	38
Oregon	8,453	23.5	19
Pennsylvania	29,559	23.8	18
Rhode Island	1,716	15.9	46
South Carolina	10,239	24.4	15
South Dakota	1,292	16.8	44
Tennessee	12,956	22.0	24
Texas	70,241	31.2	2
Utah	4,981	20.8	31
Vermont	1,112	17.9	41
Virginia	21,007	28.2	8
Washington	13,604	21.9	25
West Virginia	3,270	18.0	40
Wisconsin	13,321	24.2	17
Wyoming	1,499	29.6	7
50 States	700,815	23.9	
DC	1,090	19.7	
United States	701,905	23.9	

Rank in order per 10,000 population	
1	Delaware
2	Texas
3	Georgia
4	New Mexico
5	New York
6	Louisiana
7	Wyoming
8	Virginia
9	Alaska
10	North Carolina
11	Maryland
12	Missouri
13	Arizona
14	Florida
15	South Carolina
16	Nevada
17	Wisconsin
18	Pennsylvania
19	Oregon
20	Michigan
21	Arkansas
22	California
23	Kansas
24	Tennessee
25	Washington
26	Indiana
27	Colorado
28	Ohio
29	Nebraska
30	Connecticut
31	Utah
32	Idaho
33	Mississippi
34	New Jersey
35	Illinois
36	Hawaii
37	Kentucky
38	Oklahoma
39	Montana
40	West Virginia
41	Vermont
42	Alabama
43	Minnesota
44	South Dakota
45	Maine
46	Rhode Island
47	Iowa
48	North Dakota
49	New Hampshire
50	Massachusetts

Note: Numbers that appear to be identical are rounded and vary slightly in actual value. The rankings reflect the actual values before rounding. See the introduction for more details.

J-13 State Corrections Spending, FY 2003

State	Corrections spending $ (in millions)	Corrections spending per prisoner $	Rank per prisoner
Alabama	309	10,563	49
Alaska	189	41,750	6
Arizona	638	20,468	38
Arkansas	179	13,681	48
California	5,344	32,489	20
Colorado	455	23,130	35
Connecticut	566	28,520	24
Delaware	186	27,377	27
Florida	1,614	20,278	39
Georgia	1,230	26,055	31
Hawaii	151	25,909	32
Idaho	135	22,932	36
Illinois	1,162	26,763	28
Indiana	639	27,700	26
Iowa	243	28,434	25
Kansas	263	28,800	23
Kentucky	371	22,320	37
Louisiana	589	16,340	44
Maine	114	56,632	2
Maryland	780	32,786	19
Massachusetts	821	80,238	1
Michigan	1,709	34,625	18
Minnesota	399	50,731	3
Mississippi	234	10,094	50
Missouri	481	15,873	46
Montana	96	26,519	29
Nebraska	140	34,653	17
Nevada	195	18,496	42
New Hampshire	74	30,403	22
New Jersey	1,172	43,015	4
New Mexico	222	35,674	14
New York	2,261	34,679	16
North Carolina	856	25,507	33
North Dakota	39	31,477	21
Ohio	1,601	35,754	13
Oklahoma	372	16,301	45
Oregon	461	36,256	12
Pennsylvania	1,453	35,534	15
Rhode Island	136	38,560	10
South Carolina	370	15,599	47
South Dakota	57	18,837	41
Tennessee	459	18,069	43
Texas	3,377	20,232	40
Utah	242	41,992	5
Vermont	79	40,638	8
Virginia	928	26,464	30
Washington	650	40,253	9
West Virginia	116	24,380	34
Wisconsin	853	37,720	11
Wyoming	77	41,132	7
50 States	35,087	27,053	
DC	n/a	n/a	
United States	35,087	27,053	

Rank in order per prisoner	
1	Massachusetts
2	Maine
3	Minnesota
4	New Jersey
5	Utah
6	Alaska
7	Wyoming
8	Vermont
9	Washington
10	Rhode Island
11	Wisconsin
12	Oregon
13	Ohio
14	New Mexico
15	Pennsylvania
16	New York
17	Nebraska
18	Michigan
19	Maryland
20	California
21	North Dakota
22	New Hampshire
23	Kansas
24	Connecticut
25	Iowa
26	Indiana
27	Delaware
28	Illinois
29	Montana
30	Virginia
31	Georgia
32	Hawaii
33	North Carolina
34	West Virginia
35	Colorado
36	Idaho
37	Kentucky
38	Arizona
39	Florida
40	Texas
41	South Dakota
42	Nevada
43	Tennessee
44	Louisiana
45	Oklahoma
46	Missouri
47	South Carolina
48	Arkansas
49	Alabama
50	Mississippi

J-14 Percentage Increase in State Corrections Spending, FY 2001-2003

State	Percentage increase in state corrections spending	Rank
Alabama	16.2	8
Alaska	n/a	n/a
Arizona	-1.1	36
Arkansas	8.5	17
California	-5.8	45
Colorado	3.4	26
Connecticut	8.0	18
Delaware	-1.6	39
Florida	3.2	27
Georgia	5.0	24
Hawaii	13.5	10
Idaho	8.0	19
Illinois	-1.4	37
Indiana	14.1	9
Iowa	-4.0	42
Kansas	-1.5	38
Kentucky	3.9	25
Louisiana	6.7	21
Maine	20.0	5
Maryland	5.5	23
Massachusetts	-10.9	48
Michigan	-2.8	41
Minnesota	2.3	28
Mississippi	1.3	32
Missouri	12.1	14
Montana	1.1	33
Nebraska	2.2	30
Nevada	21.9	4
New Hampshire	10.4	15
New Jersey	2.3	29
New Mexico	29.1	2
New York	-0.6	35
North Carolina	-4.9	44
North Dakota	18.2	7
Ohio	1.7	31
Oklahoma	0.5	34
Oregon	-8.7	46
Pennsylvania	7.3	20
Rhode Island	-8.7	47
South Carolina	-16.9	49
South Dakota	18.8	6
Tennessee	13.1	11
Texas	10.0	16
Utah	-2.0	40
Vermont	12.9	12
Virginia	-4.7	43
Washington	12.8	13
West Virginia	22.1	3
Wisconsin	6.1	22
Wyoming	32.8	1
50 States	2.1	
DC	n/a	
United States	2.1	

Rank in order by percentage	
1	Wyoming
2	New Mexico
3	West Virginia
4	Nevada
5	Maine
6	South Dakota
7	North Dakota
8	Alabama
9	Indiana
10	Hawaii
11	Tennessee
12	Vermont
13	Washington
14	Missouri
15	New Hampshire
16	Texas
17	Arkansas
18	Connecticut
19	Idaho
20	Pennsylvania
21	Louisiana
22	Wisconsin
23	Maryland
24	Georgia
25	Kentucky
26	Colorado
27	Florida
28	Minnesota
29	New Jersey
30	Nebraska
31	Ohio
32	Mississippi
33	Montana
34	Oklahoma
35	New York
36	Arizona
37	Illinois
38	Kansas
39	Delaware
40	Utah
41	Michigan
42	Iowa
43	Virginia
44	North Carolina
45	California
46	Oregon
47	Rhode Island
48	Massachusetts
49	South Carolina

Note: Numbers that appear to be identical are rounded and vary slightly in actual value. The rankings reflect the actual values before rounding. See the introduction for more details.

J-15 State and Local Spending for Law Enforcement, FY 2002

State	Law enforcement spending $ (in millions)	Law enforcement spending per capita $	Rank per capita
Alabama	1,171	261	46
Alaska	440	683	1
Arizona	2,381	436	12
Arkansas	773	285	39
California	19,159	546	3
Colorado	1,928	428	13
Connecticut	1,419	410	15
Delaware	436	540	4
Florida	7,758	464	8
Georgia	3,320	388	20
Hawaii	412	331	30
Idaho	470	350	28
Illinois	5,105	405	17
Indiana	1,736	282	40
Iowa	788	268	44
Kansas	839	309	36
Kentucky	1,142	279	41
Louisiana	1,659	370	24
Maine	326	252	48
Maryland	2,592	475	6
Massachusetts	2,566	399	18
Michigan	4,085	406	16
Minnesota	1,667	332	29
Mississippi	784	273	43
Missouri	1,834	323	32
Montana	292	321	34
Nebraska	525	304	37
Nevada	1,153	531	5
New Hampshire	327	256	47
New Jersey	4,026	469	7
New Mexico	781	421	14
New York	11,382	594	2
North Carolina	2,676	322	33
North Dakota	137	216	49
Ohio	4,228	370	23
Oklahoma	1,129	323	31
Oregon	1,600	454	10
Pennsylvania	4,899	397	19
Rhode Island	396	371	22
South Carolina	1,292	315	35
South Dakota	199	261	45
Tennessee	1,666	287	38
Texas	8,129	373	21
Utah	816	352	27
Vermont	172	278	42
Virginia	2,698	370	25
Washington	2,237	369	26
West Virginia	388	216	50
Wisconsin	2,448	450	11
Wyoming	231	464	9
50 States	118,615	412	
DC	559	978	
United States	119,174	413	

Rank in order per capita	
1	Alaska
2	New York
3	California
4	Delaware
5	Nevada
6	Maryland
7	New Jersey
8	Florida
9	Wyoming
10	Oregon
11	Wisconsin
12	Arizona
13	Colorado
14	New Mexico
15	Connecticut
16	Michigan
17	Illinois
18	Massachusetts
19	Pennsylvania
20	Georgia
21	Texas
22	Rhode Island
23	Ohio
24	Louisiana
25	Virginia
26	Washington
27	Utah
28	Idaho
29	Minnesota
30	Hawaii
31	Oklahoma
32	Missouri
33	North Carolina
34	Montana
35	South Carolina
36	Kansas
37	Nebraska
38	Tennessee
39	Arkansas
40	Indiana
41	Kentucky
42	Vermont
43	Mississippi
44	Iowa
45	South Dakota
46	Alabama
47	New Hampshire
48	Maine
49	North Dakota
50	West Virginia

Note: Numbers that appear to be identical are rounded and vary slightly in actual value. The rankings reflect the actual values before rounding. See the introduction for more details.

J-16 State and Local Law Enforcement Spending as a Percentage of General Spending, FY 2002

State	Law enforcement spending as a percentage of general spending	Rank
Alabama	4.76	45
Alaska	5.21	39
Arizona	9.43	2
Arkansas	5.91	28
California	8.14	6
Colorado	7.11	11
Connecticut	5.86	30
Delaware	8.14	5
Florida	8.91	3
Georgia	7.39	8
Hawaii	4.97	43
Idaho	6.91	15
Illinois	6.92	14
Indiana	5.29	37
Iowa	4.59	46
Kansas	5.64	34
Kentucky	5.29	38
Louisiana	6.82	18
Maine	4.11	48
Maryland	8.15	4
Massachusetts	6.06	25
Michigan	6.73	19
Minnesota	4.77	44
Mississippi	5.09	42
Missouri	6.31	22
Montana	5.78	32
Nebraska	5.39	36
Nevada	9.80	1
New Hampshire	5.15	40
New Jersey	7.40	7
New Mexico	6.83	17
New York	7.06	12
North Carolina	6.01	26
North Dakota	3.52	50
Ohio	6.31	23
Oklahoma	6.22	24
Oregon	6.96	13
Pennsylvania	6.68	20
Rhode Island	5.86	29
South Carolina	5.43	35
South Dakota	5.12	41
Tennessee	5.75	33
Texas	7.28	9
Utah	6.35	21
Vermont	4.51	47
Virginia	6.87	16
Washington	5.79	31
West Virginia	3.94	49
Wisconsin	7.20	10
Wyoming	6.00	27
50 States	6.88	
DC	9.04	
United States	6.89	

Rank in order by percentage	
1	Nevada
2	Arizona
3	Florida
4	Maryland
5	Delaware
6	California
7	New Jersey
8	Georgia
9	Texas
10	Wisconsin
11	Colorado
12	New York
13	Oregon
14	Illinois
15	Idaho
16	Virginia
17	New Mexico
18	Louisiana
19	Michigan
20	Pennsylvania
21	Utah
22	Missouri
23	Ohio
24	Oklahoma
25	Massachusetts
26	North Carolina
27	Wyoming
28	Arkansas
29	Rhode Island
30	Connecticut
31	Washington
32	Montana
33	Tennessee
34	Kansas
35	South Carolina
36	Nebraska
37	Indiana
38	Kentucky
39	Alaska
40	New Hampshire
41	South Dakota
42	Mississippi
43	Hawaii
44	Minnesota
45	Alabama
46	Iowa
47	Vermont
48	Maine
49	West Virginia
50	North Dakota

Note: Numbers that appear to be identical are rounded and vary slightly in actual value. The rankings reflect the actual values before rounding. See the introduction for more details.

Source Notes for Crime and Law Enforcement (Section J)

J-1 Total Crime Rate, 2004: This table reflects the total crime rate as derived from the uniform crime reporting system of the Federal Bureau of Investigation. The reports are compiled by individual law enforcement agencies throughout the nation and summarized in the FBI publication *Crime in the United States, 2004.* This report is available on the FBI Web site (www.fbi.gov).

Since 1960, the FBI has published a "Total Crime Index." The 2004 report (issued in November of 2005) does not contain this aggregate index but does contain the elements necessary to make the calculation. As explained in the summary in *Crime in the United States, 2003,* nearly 60 percent of crimes are classified as larceny-theft. Thus, "the Crime Index was driven upward by the offense with the highest number creating a bias against a jurisdiction with a high number of larceny-thefts, but a low number of other serious crimes such as murder and forcible rape." In light of this potential distortion, the bureau has suspended publication of the Crime Index. Until a more accurate Index is developed, *State Fact Finder* will continue to publish the calculated Crime Index, acknowledging the above caveat.

In addition, the crime rate statistics in Tables J-1 through J-6 inherently cover only crime known to law enforcement agencies, so they are often cited as "crime reported to the police." Certain crimes, such as murder and thefts for which victims seek insurance reimbursement, are almost always reported to police. Victims often fail to report other categories of crime, ranging from rape to thefts of small items. To capture information on crimes actually committed, the Department of Justice does a survey (known as the "victimization survey") of U.S. households. Because that survey is based on nationwide samples, data from it are not available on a state-by-state basis.

The FBI has worked for years to make the statistics reported from different states and cities more comparable. However, some significant differences remain. Some reflect differences among states in their criminal laws and crime reporting systems. Some reflect inherent differences among citizens in reporting crime that are in turn related to differences in perceptions of whether law enforcement authorities will be able to solve the crimes. Small thefts, for example, are often not reported in large cities but are commonly reported in some smaller communities.

J-2 Violent Crime Rate, 2004: Crimes fall into two major classes. Some, such as murder and assault, involve violence or the threat of violence. Others, such as auto theft and burglary, do not. This table, from the same source as Table J-1, shows the rates for all violent crimes combined.

J-3 Murder and Rape Rates, 2004: This table, from the same source as Table J-1, shows the rates for two specific crimes.

J-4 Property Crime Rate, 2004: This table, from the same source as Table J-1, shows the rates for crimes against property, such as burglary and auto theft.

J-5 Motor Vehicle Theft Rate, 2004: This table combines auto theft with theft of other vehicles, such as pickup trucks, using the same source as Table J-1.

J-6 Violent Crime Rate Change, 2000–2004: In the four-year period from 2000 to 2004 there was a nationwide decrease in the crime rate (crimes per one hundred thousand people) of 8.0 percent. The data come from the 2000 and 2004 editions of the Department of Justice's *Crime in the United States.* Because of changes in reporting procedures, 2000 rates in New Hampshire and Montana are not comparable to current rates.

J-7 Prisoners, 2004: This table shows the total number of prisoners held in state penal institutions at the end of 2004. These data are developed by the Department of Justice from statistical reports of state and federal corrections agencies. The data shown are available on the department's Web site (www.ojp.usdoj.gov). They reflect state prisoners only. Federal prisoners constitute about 12 percent of all prisoners. The count of total state prisoners covers only those sentenced for more than a year and thus excludes persons who are being held for short periods in local jails.

J-8 Change in Prisoners, 1995–2004: This table, from the same source as Table J-7, shows the percentage change in the number of prisoners, reflecting a net increase of 27.3 percent over this eight year period.

J-9 Incarceration Rate, 2004: This table measures the relationship between state prison populations (see Table J-7) and total population. While the national rate is equivalent to having 0.5 percent of the population in prison, the percentages are much higher for certain age and ethnic groups and for males.

J-10 Juvenile Violent Crime Index, 2003: This table is from the Web site of the Office of Juvenile Justice and Delinquency Prevention of the Department of Justice (www.ojjdp.ncjrs.org). It reflects the number of violent crime arrests during 2003 of youths between the ages of ten and seventeen per one hundred thousand youths in the population of each state.

J-11 State and Local Law Enforcement Employees, 2004: These statistics come from a U.S. Census Bureau survey of state and local government employment, *Public Employment in 2004.* The survey is available only on the bureau's Web site (www.census.gov).

J-12 State and Local Corrections Employees, 2004: This statistic comes from the same source as Table J-11.

J-13 State Corrections Spending, FY 2003: These data provide one way to look at the costs of maintaining prison systems in each state. The total spending shown is the general fund spending reported by state budget offices in the National Association of State Budget Officers' *2003 State Expenditure Report.* These general fund data showing about $35.1 billion for the fifty states exclude about $4.3 billion financed outside state general funds, primarily by bond funds used to finance prison construction. The per-inmate spending is the result of dividing the spending in fiscal year 2003 by the number of inmates in prison at the end of 2003.

The resulting calculation is somewhat arbitrary as it does not separately account for the supervision of inmates on parole, which is another major function of corrections agencies not associated directly with inmates in prison.

J-14 Percentage Increase in State Corrections Spending, FY 2001–2003: These data, from the same source as Table J-13, reflect the major impact that growing prison populations are having on state government budgets. Large deviations from one year to the next are often associated with large one-time expenditures for capital outlays in one of the years being compared. *State Fact Finder* has accounted for this by comparing spending over a two year interval.

J-15 State and Local Spending for Law Enforcement, FY 2002: This table relates spending on police and corrections to population in each state. The data come from the U.S. Census Bureau's electronic publication "State and Local Government Finance Estimates, by State," available on the bureau's Web site (www.census.gov). Population numbers, also from the U.S. Census Bureau, are as of July 1, 2002. See notes to Table F-1 for more extensive information on the source of the data.

J-16 State and Local Law Enforcement Spending as a Percentage of General Spending, FY 2002: This table shows the relative importance of law enforcement outlays in state and local budgets. It is derived by comparing this spending (see Table J-16) with total "general" spending. General spending includes essentially all other spending except municipal electric and other utilities and trust funds, such as those for workers' compensation.

Transportation

More of our time each year is devoted to commuting to work than to vacationing, according to Census Bureau survey data released in 2005. Each year Americans spend more than 100 hours commuting, which the bureau's report states "exceeds the two weeks of vacation time (80 hours) frequently taken by workers over the course of a year." Traffic congestion plays a role in commuting time, as does the distance between home and work. As expected, states with, or near, large metropolitan areas tend to have the longest commutes.

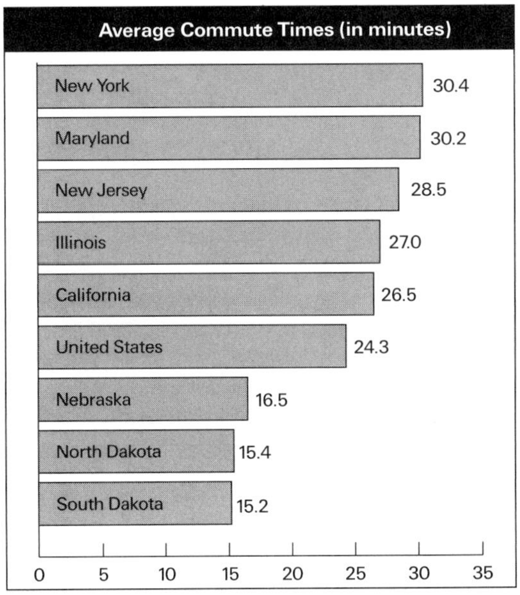

Source: U.S. Census Bureau

Having weathered the recent budget crisis, state governments are better positioned to take on issues such as traffic congestion. More funds for new road construction and upgrades are expected in 2006. Results in the November 2005 elections suggest that citizens are more willing to invest in transportation. Transportation measures passed in Maine, New Jersey, and New York, and in Washington voters refused to repeal a motor-fuel tax dedicated to transportation purposes. The story was different in Arkansas, where in a special late-year election, voters defeated a bond proposal for $575 million in interstate improvements. It should be noted that voter turnout was a mere 7 percent of registered voters.

K-1 Travel on Interstate Highways, 2004

State	Annual interstate vehicle-miles (in millions)	Percentage of travel on interstates	Rank by percentage
Alabama	12,939	21.9	38
Alaska	1,513	30.3	4
Arizona	13,111	22.9	33
Arkansas	8,021	25.3	22
California	89,829	27.3	17
Colorado	10,866	23.7	27
Connecticut	10,114	32.0	2
Delaware	1,410	15.2	50
Florida	33,409	17.0	49
Georgia	30,664	27.2	18
Hawaii	1,896	19.5	45
Idaho	3,357	22.8	34
Illinois	31,976	29.3	8
Indiana	16,125	22.2	35
Iowa	7,234	22.9	31
Kansas	6,931	23.8	26
Kentucky	12,708	26.9	19
Louisiana	12,475	28.0	14
Maine	3,123	20.9	40
Maryland	16,668	30.1	6
Massachusetts	16,567	30.2	5
Michigan	22,668	21.9	37
Minnesota	12,504	22.1	36
Mississippi	6,937	17.6	48
Missouri	18,185	26.4	21
Montana	2,837	25.3	23
Nebraska	3,968	20.7	42
Nevada	4,487	23.2	28
New Hampshire	3,050	23.1	29
New Jersey	14,279	19.6	43
New Mexico	6,955	29.0	10
New York	26,798	19.4	46
North Carolina	18,757	19.6	44
North Dakota	1,739	22.9	32
Ohio	32,665	29.3	9
Oklahoma	9,636	20.7	41
Oregon	8,751	24.6	24
Pennsylvania	25,709	23.8	25
Rhode Island	2,381	28.1	13
South Carolina	13,290	26.8	20
South Dakota	2,512	28.6	11
Tennessee	19,822	27.9	15
Texas	53,181	23.0	30
Utah	8,928	36.2	1
Vermont	1,683	21.4	39
Virginia	23,675	30.0	7
Washington	15,345	27.6	16
West Virginia	5,713	28.1	12
Wisconsin	10,670	17.7	47
Wyoming	2,878	31.1	3
50 States	720,939	24.4	
DC	442	11.8	
United States	721,381	24.4	

Rank in order by percentage	
1	Utah
2	Connecticut
3	Wyoming
4	Alaska
5	Massachusetts
6	Maryland
7	Virginia
8	Illinois
9	Ohio
10	New Mexico
11	South Dakota
12	West Virginia
13	Rhode Island
14	Louisiana
15	Tennessee
16	Washington
17	California
18	Georgia
19	Kentucky
20	South Carolina
21	Missouri
22	Arkansas
23	Montana
24	Oregon
25	Pennsylvania
26	Kansas
27	Colorado
28	Nevada
29	New Hampshire
30	Texas
31	Iowa
32	North Dakota
33	Arizona
34	Idaho
35	Indiana
36	Minnesota
37	Michigan
38	Alabama
39	Vermont
40	Maine
41	Oklahoma
42	Nebraska
43	New Jersey
44	North Carolina
45	Hawaii
46	New York
47	Wisconsin
48	Mississippi
49	Florida
50	Delaware

Note: Numbers that appear to be identical are rounded and vary slightly in actual value. The rankings reflect the actual values before rounding. See the introduction for more details.

K-2 Percentage of Interstate Mileage in "Unacceptable" Condition, 2004

State	Percentage of interstate mileage in "unacceptable" condition	Rank
Alabama	14.6	4
Alaska	2.0	23
Arizona	0.0	45
Arkansas	7.4	9
California	13.3	5
Colorado	3.1	18
Connecticut	4.6	14
Delaware	5.0	13
Florida	0.1	42
Georgia	0.0	45
Hawaii	20.4	1
Idaho	1.8	26
Illinois	2.0	23
Indiana	0.5	35
Iowa	4.4	15
Kansas	0.0	45
Kentucky	0.4	39
Louisiana	5.5	12
Maine	0.5	35
Maryland	7.6	8
Massachusetts	1.1	30
Michigan	10.4	6
Minnesota	1.3	29
Mississippi	1.9	25
Missouri	5.8	10
Montana	1.5	28
Nebraska	2.3	22
Nevada	0.5	35
New Hampshire	1.7	27
New Jersey	16.5	2
New Mexico	0.3	41
New York	14.7	3
North Carolina	5.7	11
North Dakota	0.0	45
Ohio	1.1	30
Oklahoma	4.3	16
Oregon	0.1	42
Pennsylvania	2.4	21
Rhode Island	0.0	45
South Carolina	0.1	42
South Dakota	0.7	33
Tennessee	0.4	39
Texas	0.7	33
Utah	2.9	19
Vermont	0.0	45
Virginia	1.1	30
Washington	8.5	7
West Virginia	0.5	35
Wisconsin	2.8	20
Wyoming	3.5	17
50 States	3.7	
DC	n/a	
United States	3.7	

Rank in order by percentage	
1	Hawaii
2	New Jersey
3	New York
4	Alabama
5	California
6	Michigan
7	Washington
8	Maryland
9	Arkansas
10	Missouri
11	North Carolina
12	Louisiana
13	Delaware
14	Connecticut
15	Iowa
16	Oklahoma
17	Wyoming
18	Colorado
19	Utah
20	Wisconsin
21	Pennsylvania
22	Nebraska
23	Alaska
23	Illinois
25	Mississippi
26	Idaho
27	New Hampshire
28	Montana
29	Minnesota
30	Ohio
30	Virginia
30	Massachusetts
33	Texas
33	South Dakota
35	Maine
35	West Virginia
35	Nevada
35	Indiana
39	Kentucky
39	Tennessee
41	New Mexico
42	Oregon
42	South Carolina
42	Florida
45	Arizona
45	Georgia
45	Kansas
45	North Dakota
45	Rhode Island
45	Vermont

Note: Ties in ranking reflect ties in actual values.

K-3 Deficient Bridges, 2004

State	Total deficient bridges #	Percentage of bridges deficient	Rank by percentage
Alabama	4,679	29.9	17
Alaska	353	29.7	18
Arizona	717	10.1	50
Arkansas	3,132	25.1	29
California	6,668	28.0	21
Colorado	1,387	17.0	45
Connecticut	1,363	32.7	13
Delaware	122	14.4	47
Florida	2,118	18.5	41
Georgia	2,948	20.4	39
Hawaii	513	46.7	3
Idaho	730	18.0	43
Illinois	4,361	17.0	46
Indiana	4,016	22.1	35
Iowa	6,958	27.9	22
Kansas	5,900	23.1	33
Kentucky	4,104	30.4	15
Louisiana	4,324	32.4	14
Maine	843	35.6	9
Maryland	1,479	29.2	19
Massachusetts	2,546	51.4	2
Michigan	3,121	28.9	20
Minnesota	1,633	12.5	48
Mississippi	4,697	27.9	23
Missouri	8,244	34.7	11
Montana	1,074	21.3	36
Nebraska	3,975	25.7	25
Nevada	198	12.3	49
New Hampshire	788	33.4	12
New Jersey	2,370	36.6	8
New Mexico	724	18.9	40
New York	6,552	37.9	5
North Carolina	5,196	30.0	16
North Dakota	1,062	23.6	31
Ohio	7,102	25.4	27
Oklahoma	8,757	37.6	6
Oregon	1,848	25.5	26
Pennsylvania	9,404	42.3	4
Rhode Island	405	54.1	1
South Carolina	2,130	23.1	32
South Dakota	1,490	25.0	30
Tennessee	4,499	22.9	34
Texas	10,195	20.8	37
Utah	506	18.0	42
Vermont	954	35.5	10
Virginia	3,348	25.4	28
Washington	2,056	27.3	24
West Virginia	2,555	37.1	7
Wisconsin	2,339	17.2	44
Wyoming	629	20.7	38
50 States	157,112	26.6	
DC	157	62.5	
United States*	158,318	26.7	

**Due to rounding or data sources, the 50-state total plus D.C. may not equal the U.S. total. Please see introduction.*

Rank in order by percentage	
1	Rhode Island
2	Massachusetts
3	Hawaii
4	Pennsylvania
5	New York
6	Oklahoma
7	West Virginia
8	New Jersey
9	Maine
10	Vermont
11	Missouri
12	New Hampshire
13	Connecticut
14	Louisiana
15	Kentucky
16	North Carolina
17	Alabama
18	Alaska
19	Maryland
20	Michigan
21	California
22	Iowa
23	Mississippi
24	Washington
25	Nebraska
26	Oregon
27	Ohio
28	Virginia
29	Arkansas
30	South Dakota
31	North Dakota
32	South Carolina
33	Kansas
34	Tennessee
35	Indiana
36	Montana
37	Texas
38	Wyoming
39	Georgia
40	New Mexico
41	Florida
42	Utah
43	Idaho
44	Wisconsin
45	Colorado
46	Illinois
47	Delaware
48	Minnesota
49	Nevada
50	Arizona

Note: Numbers that appear to be identical are rounded and vary slightly in actual value. The rankings reflect the actual values before rounding. See the introduction for more details.

K-4 Traffic Deaths Per 100 Million Vehicle-Miles, 2004

State	Traffic deaths per 100 million vehicle-miles	Rank
Alabama	1.95	13
Alaska	2.02	11
Arizona	2.01	12
Arkansas	2.22	3
California	1.25	35
Colorado	1.45	25
Connecticut	0.92	49
Delaware	1.44	26
Florida	1.65	18
Georgia	1.45	24
Hawaii	1.46	23
Idaho	1.77	16
Illinois	1.24	37
Indiana	1.30	31
Iowa	1.24	38
Kansas	1.58	21
Kentucky	2.04	8
Louisiana	2.03	9
Maine	1.30	32
Maryland	1.16	41
Massachusetts	0.87	50
Michigan	1.12	43
Minnesota	1.00	47
Mississippi	2.28	1
Missouri	1.64	19
Montana	2.04	6
Nebraska	1.32	28
Nevada	2.04	7
New Hampshire	1.29	33
New Jersey	1.00	46
New Mexico	2.18	4
New York	1.08	44
North Carolina	1.62	20
North Dakota	1.32	29
Ohio	1.15	42
Oklahoma	1.67	17
Oregon	1.28	34
Pennsylvania	1.38	27
Rhode Island	0.98	48
South Carolina	2.11	5
South Dakota	2.24	2
Tennessee	1.82	14
Texas	1.55	22
Utah	1.20	39
Vermont	1.25	36
Virginia	1.17	40
Washington	1.01	45
West Virginia	2.02	10
Wisconsin	1.31	30
Wyoming	1.77	15
50 States	1.44	
DC	1.15	
United States	1.44	

Rank in order by rate	
1	Mississippi
2	South Dakota
3	Arkansas
4	New Mexico
5	South Carolina
6	Montana
7	Nevada
8	Kentucky
9	Louisiana
10	West Virginia
11	Alaska
12	Arizona
13	Alabama
14	Tennessee
15	Wyoming
16	Idaho
17	Oklahoma
18	Florida
19	Missouri
20	North Carolina
21	Kansas
22	Texas
23	Hawaii
24	Georgia
25	Colorado
26	Delaware
27	Pennsylvania
28	Nebraska
29	North Dakota
30	Wisconsin
31	Indiana
32	Maine
33	New Hampshire
34	Oregon
35	California
36	Vermont
37	Illinois
38	Iowa
39	Utah
40	Virginia
41	Maryland
42	Ohio
43	Michigan
44	New York
45	Washington
46	New Jersey
47	Minnesota
48	Rhode Island
49	Connecticut
50	Massachusetts

Note: Numbers that appear to be identical are rounded and vary slightly in actual value. The rankings reflect the actual values before rounding. See the introduction for more details.

K-5 Percentage of Drivers Using Seat Belts, 2005

State	Percentage of drivers using seat belts	Rank
Alabama	82	23
Alaska	78	32
Arizona	94	4
Arkansas	68	45
California	93	5
Colorado	79	29
Connecticut	82	23
Delaware	84	19
Florida	74	39
Georgia	82	23
Hawaii	95	1
Idaho	76	35
Illinois	86	13
Indiana	81	26
Iowa	86	13
Kansas	69	43
Kentucky	67	46
Louisiana	78	32
Maine	76	35
Maryland	91	8
Massachusetts	65	47
Michigan	93	5
Minnesota	83	20
Mississippi	61	48
Missouri	77	34
Montana	80	27
Nebraska	79	29
Nevada	95	1
New Hampshire	n/a	n/a
New Jersey	86	13
New Mexico	90	9
New York	85	16
North Carolina	87	11
North Dakota	76	35
Ohio	79	29
Oklahoma	83	20
Oregon	93	5
Pennsylvania	83	20
Rhode Island	75	38
South Carolina	70	42
South Dakota	69	43
Tennessee	74	39
Texas	90	9
Utah	87	11
Vermont	85	16
Virginia	80	27
Washington	95	1
West Virginia	85	16
Wisconsin	73	41
Wyoming	n/a	n/a
50 States	n/a	
DC	89	
United States	82	

Rank in order by percentage	
1	Hawaii
1	Washington
1	Nevada
4	Arizona
5	Oregon
5	Michigan
5	California
8	Maryland
9	Texas
9	New Mexico
11	Utah
11	North Carolina
13	Illinois
13	New Jersey
13	Iowa
16	New York
16	West Virginia
16	Vermont
19	Delaware
20	Pennsylvania
20	Oklahoma
20	Minnesota
23	Alabama
23	Connecticut
23	Georgia
26	Indiana
27	Virginia
27	Montana
29	Colorado
29	Nebraska
29	Ohio
32	Alaska
32	Louisiana
34	Missouri
35	North Dakota
35	Idaho
35	Maine
38	Rhode Island
39	Tennessee
39	Florida
41	Wisconsin
42	South Carolina
43	Kansas
43	South Dakota
45	Arkansas
46	Kentucky
47	Massachusetts
48	Mississippi

Note: Ties in ranking reflect ties in actual values.

K-6 Vehicle-Miles Traveled Per Capita, 2004

State	Vehicle-miles traveled (in millions)	Vehicle-miles traveled per capita	Rank per capita
Alabama	59,035	13,031	4
Alaska	4,990	7,613	49
Arizona	57,336	9,982	33
Arkansas	31,648	11,497	14
California	328,917	9,164	39
Colorado	45,891	9,973	34
Connecticut	31,608	9,022	40
Delaware	9,301	11,201	20
Florida	196,444	11,292	18
Georgia	112,620	12,755	5
Hawaii	9,725	7,701	48
Idaho	14,729	10,572	28
Illinois	109,135	8,584	43
Indiana	72,713	11,657	13
Iowa	31,538	10,675	25
Kansas	29,172	10,664	26
Kentucky	47,322	11,414	15
Louisiana	44,607	9,878	37
Maine	14,948	11,348	17
Maryland	55,284	9,947	35
Massachusetts	54,771	8,536	44
Michigan	103,326	10,218	31
Minnesota	56,570	11,090	22
Mississippi	39,431	13,583	2
Missouri	68,994	11,989	10
Montana	11,207	12,091	8
Nebraska	19,171	10,972	23
Nevada	19,354	8,289	46
New Hampshire	13,216	10,170	32
New Jersey	72,844	8,374	45
New Mexico	23,942	12,579	7
New York	137,898	7,172	50
North Carolina	95,903	11,228	19
North Dakota	7,594	11,971	11
Ohio	111,654	9,744	38
Oklahoma	46,443	13,181	3
Oregon	35,598	9,903	36
Pennsylvania	108,070	8,711	42
Rhode Island	8,473	7,841	47
South Carolina	49,551	11,803	12
South Dakota	8,784	11,395	16
Tennessee	70,943	12,022	9
Texas	231,008	10,272	30
Utah	24,696	10,337	29
Vermont	7,855	12,641	6
Virginia	78,877	10,574	27
Washington	55,673	8,974	41
West Virginia	20,302	11,183	21
Wisconsin	60,399	10,964	24
Wyoming	9,261	18,283	1
50 States	2,958,771	10,095	
DC	3,742	6,760	
United States	2,962,513	10,088	

Rank in order per capita	
1	Wyoming
2	Mississippi
3	Oklahoma
4	Alabama
5	Georgia
6	Vermont
7	New Mexico
8	Montana
9	Tennessee
10	Missouri
11	North Dakota
12	South Carolina
13	Indiana
14	Arkansas
15	Kentucky
16	South Dakota
17	Maine
18	Florida
19	North Carolina
20	Delaware
21	West Virginia
22	Minnesota
23	Nebraska
24	Wisconsin
25	Iowa
26	Kansas
27	Virginia
28	Idaho
29	Utah
30	Texas
31	Michigan
32	New Hampshire
33	Arizona
34	Colorado
35	Maryland
36	Oregon
37	Louisiana
38	Ohio
39	California
40	Connecticut
41	Washington
42	Pennsylvania
43	Illinois
44	Massachusetts
45	New Jersey
46	Nevada
47	Rhode Island
48	Hawaii
49	Alaska
50	New York

K-7 Percentage of Workers Using Public Transportation, 2004

State	Percentage of workers using public transportation	Rank
Alabama	0.5	42
Alaska	1.0	32
Arizona	1.8	21
Arkansas	0.4	45
California	4.8	8
Colorado	2.5	16
Connecticut	3.9	10
Delaware	2.1	18
Florida	1.7	23
Georgia	2.1	18
Hawaii	5.5	6
Idaho	1.2	28
Illinois	8.0	5
Indiana	0.8	37
Iowa	1.0	32
Kansas	0.2	48
Kentucky	1.0	32
Louisiana	1.8	21
Maine	0.6	40
Maryland	8.3	3
Massachusetts	8.3	3
Michigan	0.9	35
Minnesota	2.9	14
Mississippi	0.2	48
Missouri	1.4	27
Montana	0.5	42
Nebraska	0.6	40
Nevada	3.8	11
New Hampshire	0.7	38
New Jersey	10.7	2
New Mexico	1.2	28
New York	25.1	1
North Carolina	0.9	35
North Dakota	0.4	45
Ohio	1.5	24
Oklahoma	0.4	45
Oregon	3.7	12
Pennsylvania	5.0	7
Rhode Island	2.2	17
South Carolina	0.5	42
South Dakota	0.2	48
Tennessee	0.7	38
Texas	1.5	24
Utah	2.6	15
Vermont	1.1	30
Virginia	3.5	13
Washington	4.3	9
West Virginia	1.1	30
Wisconsin	1.9	20
Wyoming	1.5	24
50 States	n/a	
DC	33.6	
United States	4.6	

Rank in order by percentage	
1	New York
2	New Jersey
3	Maryland
3	Massachusetts
5	Illinois
6	Hawaii
7	Pennsylvania
8	California
9	Washington
10	Connecticut
11	Nevada
12	Oregon
13	Virginia
14	Minnesota
15	Utah
16	Colorado
17	Rhode Island
18	Delaware
18	Georgia
20	Wisconsin
21	Arizona
21	Louisiana
23	Florida
24	Ohio
24	Texas
24	Wyoming
27	Missouri
28	Idaho
28	New Mexico
30	Vermont
30	West Virginia
32	Alaska
32	Iowa
32	Kentucky
35	Michigan
35	North Carolina
37	Indiana
38	New Hampshire
38	Tennessee
40	Maine
40	Nebraska
42	Alabama
42	Montana
42	South Carolina
45	Arkansas
45	North Dakota
45	Oklahoma
48	Kansas
48	Mississippi
48	South Dakota

Note: Ties in ranking reflect ties in actual values.

K-8 Road and Street Miles, 2004

State	Total road and street miles #	Total miles under state control #	Percentage under state control	Rank by percentage
Alabama	95,486	11,580	12.1	29
Alaska	14,108	5,636	39.9	6
Arizona	58,113	6,816	11.7	31
Arkansas	98,607	16,418	16.6	21
California	169,793	15,209	9.0	43
Colorado	87,094	9,113	10.5	38
Connecticut	21,144	3,718	17.6	18
Delaware	6,043	5,203	86.1	2
Florida	119,525	12,047	10.1	40
Georgia	116,915	17,943	15.3	25
Hawaii	4,318	940	21.8	15
Idaho	47,101	4,951	10.5	37
Illinois	138,626	16,123	11.6	32
Indiana	94,597	11,186	11.8	30
Iowa	113,836	8,881	7.8	48
Kansas	135,017	10,375	7.7	49
Kentucky	77,365	27,509	35.6	8
Louisiana	60,943	16,696	27.4	10
Maine	22,748	8,488	37.3	7
Maryland	30,810	5,136	16.7	20
Massachusetts	35,782	2,841	7.9	47
Michigan	122,381	9,720	7.9	46
Minnesota	131,937	11,833	9.0	42
Mississippi	74,127	10,887	14.7	26
Missouri	125,923	32,471	25.8	13
Montana	69,450	7,879	11.3	34
Nebraska	93,246	9,981	10.7	36
Nevada	33,976	5,449	16.0	22
New Hampshire	15,627	4,114	26.3	11
New Jersey	38,121	2,318	6.1	50
New Mexico	64,005	12,009	18.8	16
New York	113,343	15,033	13.3	28
North Carolina	102,666	78,871	76.8	4
North Dakota	86,781	7,382	8.5	45
Ohio	124,752	19,307	15.5	24
Oklahoma	112,713	12,280	10.9	35
Oregon	65,861	7,552	11.5	33
Pennsylvania	120,622	39,890	33.1	9
Rhode Island	6,419	1,103	17.2	19
South Carolina	66,249	41,532	62.7	5
South Dakota	83,548	7,851	9.4	41
Tennessee	88,989	13,809	15.5	23
Texas	303,176	79,624	26.3	12
Utah	42,712	5,858	13.7	27
Vermont	14,370	2,635	18.3	17
Virginia	71,534	57,515	80.4	3
Washington	81,218	7,046	8.7	44
West Virginia	37,012	33,971	91.8	1
Wisconsin	113,699	11,812	10.4	39
Wyoming	27,594	6,754	24.5	14
50 States	3,980,022	773,295	19.4	
DC	1,499	1,392	92.9	
United States	3,981,521	774,687	19.5	

Rank in order by percentage	
1	West Virginia
2	Delaware
3	Virginia
4	North Carolina
5	South Carolina
6	Alaska
7	Maine
8	Kentucky
9	Pennsylvania
10	Louisiana
11	New Hampshire
12	Texas
13	Missouri
14	Wyoming
15	Hawaii
16	New Mexico
17	Vermont
18	Connecticut
19	Rhode Island
20	Maryland
21	Arkansas
22	Nevada
23	Tennessee
24	Ohio
25	Georgia
26	Mississippi
27	Utah
28	New York
29	Alabama
30	Indiana
31	Arizona
32	Illinois
33	Oregon
34	Montana
35	Oklahoma
36	Nebraska
37	Idaho
38	Colorado
39	Wisconsin
40	Florida
41	South Dakota
42	Minnesota
43	California
44	Washington
45	North Dakota
46	Michigan
47	Massachusetts
48	Iowa
49	Kansas
50	New Jersey

Note: Numbers that appear to be identical are rounded and vary slightly in actual value. The rankings reflect the actual values before rounding. See the introduction for more details.

K-9 State and Local Highway Employees, 2004

State	Highway employees #	Per 10,000 population	Rank per 10,000 population
Alabama	11,544	25.5	16
Alaska	3,594	54.8	1
Arizona	8,159	14.2	45
Arkansas	7,362	26.7	14
California	42,640	11.9	50
Colorado	9,183	20.0	28
Connecticut	6,257	17.9	36
Delaware	2,164	26.1	15
Florida	23,075	13.3	46
Georgia	13,867	15.7	42
Hawaii	1,646	13.0	48
Idaho	3,368	24.2	18
Illinois	20,154	15.9	40
Indiana	10,586	17.0	37
Iowa	9,625	32.6	9
Kansas	9,327	34.1	7
Kentucky	8,285	20.0	27
Louisiana	10,504	23.3	21
Maine	4,145	31.5	11
Maryland	9,399	16.9	38
Massachusetts	10,341	16.1	39
Michigan	12,690	12.5	49
Minnesota	12,200	23.9	20
Mississippi	8,135	28.0	12
Missouri	13,765	23.9	19
Montana	3,503	37.8	3
Nebraska	5,642	32.3	10
Nevada	3,050	13.1	47
New Hampshire	3,583	27.6	13
New Jersey	18,421	21.2	24
New Mexico	4,056	21.3	23
New York	40,348	21.0	25
North Carolina	15,493	18.1	33
North Dakota	2,166	34.1	6
Ohio	21,767	19.0	32
Oklahoma	8,773	24.9	17
Oregon	7,152	19.9	29
Pennsylvania	24,181	19.5	30
Rhode Island	1,556	14.4	43
South Carolina	7,519	17.9	35
South Dakota	2,613	33.9	8
Tennessee	11,418	19.3	31
Texas	35,433	15.8	41
Utah	3,409	14.3	44
Vermont	2,128	34.2	5
Virginia	13,387	17.9	34
Washington	14,064	22.7	22
West Virginia	6,460	35.6	4
Wisconsin	11,481	20.8	26
Wyoming	2,584	51.0	2
50 States	542,202	18.5	
DC	440	7.9	
United States	542,642	18.5	

Rank in order per 10,000 population	
1	Alaska
2	Wyoming
3	Montana
4	West Virginia
5	Vermont
6	North Dakota
7	Kansas
8	South Dakota
9	Iowa
10	Nebraska
11	Maine
12	Mississippi
13	New Hampshire
14	Arkansas
15	Delaware
16	Alabama
17	Oklahoma
18	Idaho
19	Missouri
20	Minnesota
21	Louisiana
22	Washington
23	New Mexico
24	New Jersey
25	New York
26	Wisconsin
27	Kentucky
28	Colorado
29	Oregon
30	Pennsylvania
31	Tennessee
32	Ohio
33	North Carolina
34	Virginia
35	South Carolina
36	Connecticut
37	Indiana
38	Maryland
39	Massachusetts
40	Illinois
41	Texas
42	Georgia
43	Rhode Island
44	Utah
45	Arizona
46	Florida
47	Nevada
48	Hawaii
49	Michigan
50	California

Note: Numbers that appear to be identical are rounded and vary slightly in actual value. The rankings reflect the actual values before rounding. See the introduction for more details.

K-10 State and Local Public Transit Employees, 2004

State	Transit employees #	Per 10,000 population	Rank per 10,000 population
Alabama	281	0.6	43
Alaska	241	3.7	22
Arizona	287	0.5	46
Arkansas	231	0.8	40
California	33,582	9.4	6
Colorado	3,241	7.0	12
Connecticut	568	1.6	34
Delaware	640	7.7	10
Florida	7,628	4.4	19
Georgia	5,101	5.8	14
Hawaii	48	0.4	48
Idaho	35	0.3	50
Illinois	17,198	13.5	2
Indiana	1,649	2.6	25
Iowa	779	2.6	26
Kansas	318	1.2	36
Kentucky	1,045	2.5	29
Louisiana	1,435	3.2	24
Maine	102	0.8	42
Maryland	3,205	5.8	15
Massachusetts	5,843	9.1	7
Michigan	4,124	4.1	21
Minnesota	2,928	5.7	16
Mississippi	131	0.5	47
Missouri	3,335	5.8	13
Montana	170	1.8	32
Nebraska	452	2.6	28
Nevada	252	1.1	38
New Hampshire	107	0.8	41
New Jersey	11,188	12.9	3
New Mexico	646	3.4	23
New York	64,464	33.5	1
North Carolina	969	1.1	37
North Dakota	38	0.6	44
Ohio	6,523	5.7	17
Oklahoma	185	0.5	45
Oregon	3,211	8.9	8
Pennsylvania	13,312	10.7	5
Rhode Island	888	8.2	9
South Carolina	447	1.1	39
South Dakota	28	0.4	49
Tennessee	1,091	1.8	31
Texas	10,574	4.7	18
Utah	1,708	7.1	11
Vermont	151	2.4	30
Virginia	1,211	1.6	33
Washington	7,563	12.2	4
West Virginia	476	2.6	27
Wisconsin	2,363	4.3	20
Wyoming	69	1.4	35
50 States	222,061	7.6	
DC	9,836	177.7	
United States	231,897	7.9	

Rank in order per 10,000 population	
1	New York
2	Illinois
3	New Jersey
4	Washington
5	Pennsylvania
6	California
7	Massachusetts
8	Oregon
9	Rhode Island
10	Delaware
11	Utah
12	Colorado
13	Missouri
14	Georgia
15	Maryland
16	Minnesota
17	Ohio
18	Texas
19	Florida
20	Wisconsin
21	Michigan
22	Alaska
23	New Mexico
24	Louisiana
25	Indiana
26	Iowa
27	West Virginia
28	Nebraska
29	Kentucky
30	Vermont
31	Tennessee
32	Montana
33	Virginia
34	Connecticut
35	Wyoming
36	Kansas
37	North Carolina
38	Nevada
39	South Carolina
40	Arkansas
41	New Hampshire
42	Maine
43	Alabama
44	North Dakota
45	Oklahoma
46	Arizona
47	Mississippi
48	Hawaii
49	South Dakota
50	Idaho

Note: Numbers that appear to be identical are rounded and vary slightly in actual value. The rankings reflect the actual values before rounding. See the introduction for more details.

K-11 State and Local Spending for Highways, FY 2002

State	Highway spending $ (in millions)	Highway spending per capita $	Highway spending as a percentage of personal income	Rank per capita
Alabama	1,668	372	1.50	32
Alaska	916	1,422	4.55	1
Arizona	1,913	351	1.39	38
Arkansas	1,307	482	2.10	18
California	11,467	327	1.01	47
Colorado	2,836	629	1.88	5
Connecticut	1,224	354	0.84	37
Delaware	464	575	1.85	12
Florida	6,720	402	1.40	29
Georgia	2,939	343	1.23	41
Hawaii	419	336	1.19	45
Idaho	618	461	1.88	21
Illinois	5,676	450	1.38	22
Indiana	2,031	330	1.20	46
Iowa	1,762	600	2.20	7
Kansas	1,528	563	1.99	13
Kentucky	1,952	477	1.92	20
Louisiana	1,531	341	1.40	42
Maine	618	477	1.77	19
Maryland	1,855	340	0.97	43
Massachusetts	3,257	507	1.31	17
Michigan	3,219	320	1.09	48
Minnesota	2,681	534	1.64	16
Mississippi	1,236	430	1.97	26
Missouri	2,473	436	1.57	25
Montana	542	597	2.49	8
Nebraska	924	534	1.87	15
Nevada	1,271	585	2.00	10
New Hampshire	504	396	1.19	30
New Jersey	2,963	345	0.89	40
New Mexico	1,143	616	2.61	6
New York	7,078	369	1.04	33
North Carolina	3,017	363	1.34	35
North Dakota	461	726	2.80	4
Ohio	4,092	358	1.26	36
Oklahoma	1,544	442	1.75	23
Oregon	1,197	340	1.21	44
Pennsylvania	5,290	429	1.42	27
Rhode Island	331	310	1.04	49
South Carolina	1,491	363	1.46	34
South Dakota	580	762	2.85	3
Tennessee	1,773	306	1.15	50
Texas	7,527	346	1.22	39
Utah	1,017	439	1.83	24
Vermont	362	587	2.04	9
Virginia	3,102	425	1.33	28
Washington	2,376	392	1.23	31
West Virginia	1,041	577	2.50	11
Wisconsin	2,986	549	1.88	14
Wyoming	477	957	3.20	2
50 States	115,398	401	1.33	
DC	69	121	0.27	
United States	115,467	400	1.33	

Rank in order per capita	
1	Alaska
2	Wyoming
3	South Dakota
4	North Dakota
5	Colorado
6	New Mexico
7	Iowa
8	Montana
9	Vermont
10	Nevada
11	West Virginia
12	Delaware
13	Kansas
14	Wisconsin
15	Nebraska
16	Minnesota
17	Massachusetts
18	Arkansas
19	Maine
20	Kentucky
21	Idaho
22	Illinois
23	Oklahoma
24	Utah
25	Missouri
26	Mississippi
27	Pennsylvania
28	Virginia
29	Florida
30	New Hampshire
31	Washington
32	Alabama
33	New York
34	South Carolina
35	North Carolina
36	Ohio
37	Connecticut
38	Arizona
39	Texas
40	New Jersey
41	Georgia
42	Louisiana
43	Maryland
44	Oregon
45	Hawaii
46	Indiana
47	California
48	Michigan
49	Rhode Island
50	Tennessee

Note: Numbers that appear to be identical are rounded and vary slightly in actual value. The rankings reflect the actual values before rounding. See the introduction for more details.

K-12 State and Local Highway Spending as a Percentage of General Spending, FY 2002

State	Highway spending as a percentage of general spending	Rank
Alabama	6.78	32
Alaska	10.84	4
Arizona	7.58	30
Arkansas	10.00	11
California	4.87	49
Colorado	10.46	8
Connecticut	5.06	46
Delaware	8.67	18
Florida	7.72	26
Georgia	6.54	35
Hawaii	5.05	47
Idaho	9.09	15
Illinois	7.69	28
Indiana	6.19	38
Iowa	10.25	10
Kansas	10.27	9
Kentucky	9.04	16
Louisiana	6.29	36
Maine	7.77	25
Maryland	5.83	42
Massachusetts	7.69	27
Michigan	5.30	44
Minnesota	7.67	29
Mississippi	8.04	21
Missouri	8.51	19
Montana	10.74	6
Nebraska	9.48	14
Nevada	10.80	5
New Hampshire	7.95	22
New Jersey	5.45	43
New Mexico	10.00	12
New York	4.39	50
North Carolina	6.77	33
North Dakota	11.85	3
Ohio	6.10	41
Oklahoma	8.50	20
Oregon	5.21	45
Pennsylvania	7.22	31
Rhode Island	4.90	48
South Carolina	6.26	37
South Dakota	14.94	1
Tennessee	6.12	40
Texas	6.74	34
Utah	7.91	23
Vermont	9.52	13
Virginia	7.90	24
Washington	6.15	39
West Virginia	10.57	7
Wisconsin	8.78	17
Wyoming	12.38	2
50 States	6.69	
DC	1.12	
United States	6.67	

Rank in order by percentage	
1	South Dakota
2	Wyoming
3	North Dakota
4	Alaska
5	Nevada
6	Montana
7	West Virginia
8	Colorado
9	Kansas
10	Iowa
11	Arkansas
12	New Mexico
13	Vermont
14	Nebraska
15	Idaho
16	Kentucky
17	Wisconsin
18	Delaware
19	Missouri
20	Oklahoma
21	Mississippi
22	New Hampshire
23	Utah
24	Virginia
25	Maine
26	Florida
27	Massachusetts
28	Illinois
29	Minnesota
30	Arizona
31	Pennsylvania
32	Alabama
33	North Carolina
34	Texas
35	Georgia
36	Louisiana
37	South Carolina
38	Indiana
39	Washington
40	Tennessee
41	Ohio
42	Maryland
43	New Jersey
44	Michigan
45	Oregon
46	Connecticut
47	Hawaii
48	Rhode Island
49	California
50	New York

Note: Numbers that appear to be identical are rounded and vary slightly in actual value. The rankings reflect the actual values before rounding. See the introduction for more details.

Source Notes for Transportation (Section K)

K-1 Travel on Interstate Highways, 2004: Use of highways is measured by vehicle-miles (travel by one vehicle for one mile). By this measure, interstate highways account for nearly one-fourth of the nation's highway travel, according to calculations based on the Department of Transportation's *2004 Highway Statistics.* The federal government provides 90 percent of the money used to build interstates, but lower percentages for other highways. Having a large percentage of travel on interstates is good fiscal news as well as an indication of highway quality.

K-2 Percentage of Interstate Mileage in "Unacceptable" Condition, 2004: This table provides one measurement of pavement conditions. It is based on the International Roughness Index (IRI) which is an objective, equipment-based (as opposed to human observation) rating of the smoothness/bumpiness of interstate pavement. The IRI does not measure deterioration of other types. This table shows the percentage of interstate mileage given an IRI rating of 170 or above, the level identified as "unacceptable" in the Federal Highway Administration's *Conditions and Performance Report 1999.* The IRI data are from FHA's *2004 Highway Statistics.*

K-3 Deficient Bridges, 2004: This table shows the total number of deficient bridges on major highways in each state. Details appear in the complete inventory, *The Status of the Nation's Highway Bridges* to be published by the Department of Transportation (DOT) and updated biannually. The statistics are also posted on the DOT Web site (wwwcf.fhwa.dot.gov). Bridges can be classified as deficient as a result of deterioration, poor maintenance, or by original design (for example, too narrow for modern traffic).

K-4 Traffic Deaths Per 100 Million Vehicle-Miles, 2004: Relating deaths to total miles traveled is a common way of measuring the safety of highways. Many factors could affect the totals, including weather conditions, highway designs, congestion, and traffic law enforcement by the states. The figures come from the Department of Transportation (see notes to Table K-1).

K-5 Percentage of Drivers Using Seat Belts, 2005: These data come from periodic checks of safety belt usage, as reported by the Department of Transportation, National Highway Traffic Safety Administration in "Safety Belt Use in 2005" (www-nrd.nhtsa.dot.gov).

K-6 Vehicle-Miles Traveled Per Capita, 2004: Vehicle-miles of travel, as reported by the Department of Transportation in *2004 Highway Statistics,* show the intensity of use of state highway systems. Vehicle-miles per capita show that the average American travels 10,088 miles a year. Short distances between homes, stores, and offices plus mass transit make usage lowest in northern urban areas.

K-7 Percentage of Workers Using Public Transportation, 2004: This table shows the percentage of workers who used public transportation systems for their journeys to work in 2004. The estimates come from questions about transportation usage from the Census 2004 American Community Survey.

K-8 Road and Street Miles, 2004: These data, from the same source as Table K-1, reflect total road and street (as distinct from highway) miles. They show the percentage of these miles that are controlled and maintained by state governments. Some states, such as Delaware and Virginia, maintain many local service roads that are controlled and maintained by counties and municipalities in other states.

K-9 State and Local Highway Employees, 2004: This statistic comes from a U.S. Census Bureau survey of state and local government employment, *Public Employment in 2004.* It is available on the Internet at the bureau's Web site (www.census.gov). The data show the higher levels of employees, and thus costs, associated with maintaining highways in rural states.

K-10 State and Local Public Transit Employees, 2004: This statistic, from the same source as Table K-9, shows the higher levels of employees, and thus costs, associated with transit in urbanized states.

K-11 State and Local Spending for Highways, FY 2002: This table relates spending data to population and personal income in each state. The spending data, which cover local streets as well as state highways, come from the U.S. Census Bureau's electronic publication "State and Local Government Finance Estimates, by State," available on the bureau's Web site (www.census.gov). Population numbers, also from the census, are as of July 1, 2002, and personal income numbers are from the Department of Commerce. Based on census historical practices, *State Fact Finder* used calendar year 2001 numbers. See notes to Table F-1 for more extensive information on the source of the data.

K-12 State and Local Highway Spending as a Percentage of General Spending, FY 2002: This table shows the relative importance of highway outlays in state and local budgets. It is derived by comparing highway spending with total "general" spending (see notes to Table K-11). General spending includes essentially all other spending excepting municipal electric and other utilities and trust funds, such as those for workers' compensation.

Welfare

When the federal work-oriented welfare program, Temporary Assistance to Needy Families (TANF), was originally crafted in 1996, it was scheduled for reauthorization in 2002. That deadline passed without action and the program was given a short-term extension. It has been extended ten additional times; the latest extension occurred as Congress adjourned at the end of 2005. Controversies that have impeded reauthorization include disagreements over child care funding and how much recipients should be required to work. Also, there has been no compelling force, political or otherwise, to bring TANF reauthorization to the top of the docket. Yet, as part of the budget reconciliation bill, reauthorization is expected to go before Congress in early 2006.

TANF Spending in FY 2004

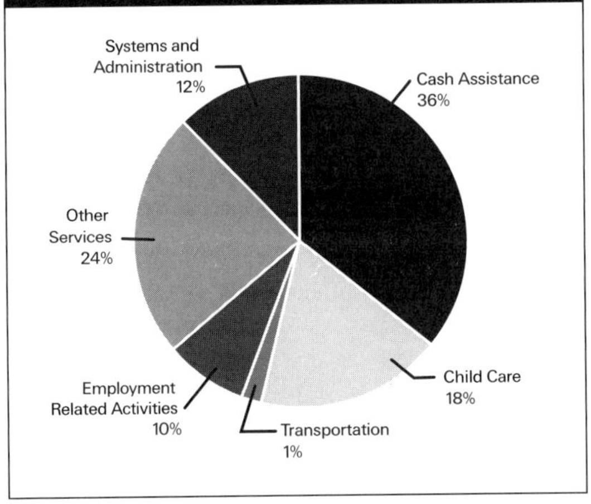

Source: U.S. Department of Health and Human Services, Administration for Children and Families

The share of persons eligible for income assistance who are actually receiving it has been on the decline. In the early 1990s approximately 80 percent of those eligible for cash assistance received it. In 2001, this figure was reduced to 48 percent. The share of the poverty population—not just those eligible for TANF—receiving cash assistance has also declined. In 1996, 33.3 percent of this group received assistance. By 2003, this percentage had fallen to 15.1 percent. Considering just child recipients, 57.8 percent of children in poverty were served by welfare in 1996. In 2003, this percentage was 31.1 percent.

L-1 Percentage of Births to Unwed Mothers, 2003

State	Percentage of births to unwed mothers	Rank
Alabama	35.0	20
Alaska	34.6	23
Arizona	41.5	5
Arkansas	38.0	10
California	33.5	29
Colorado	26.7	47
Connecticut	30.0	38
Delaware	41.9	4
Florida	39.9	7
Georgia	38.1	9
Hawaii	33.5	31
Idaho	22.3	49
Illinois	35.3	19
Indiana	37.1	12
Iowa	29.9	40
Kansas	31.6	35
Kentucky	33.8	28
Louisiana	47.5	2
Maine	33.5	30
Maryland	34.8	21
Massachusetts	27.8	45
Michigan	34.6	22
Minnesota	27.7	46
Mississippi	47.0	3
Missouri	35.6	17
Montana	32.2	33
Nebraska	29.7	41
Nevada	39.1	8
New Hampshire	24.8	48
New Jersey	29.3	42
New Mexico	48.4	1
New York	36.5	14
North Carolina	35.3	18
North Dakota	28.5	44
Ohio	36.2	15
Oklahoma	37.1	13
Oregon	31.7	34
Pennsylvania	33.9	27
Rhode Island	35.8	16
South Carolina	41.1	6
South Dakota	34.2	26
Tennessee	37.2	11
Texas	34.3	25
Utah	17.2	50
Vermont	30.0	39
Virginia	30.4	36
Washington	28.8	43
West Virginia	34.6	24
Wisconsin	30.4	37
Wyoming	32.6	32
50 States	34.6	
DC	53.6	
United States	34.6	

Rank in order by percentage	
1	New Mexico
2	Louisiana
3	Mississippi
4	Delaware
5	Arizona
6	South Carolina
7	Florida
8	Nevada
9	Georgia
10	Arkansas
11	Tennessee
12	Indiana
13	Oklahoma
14	New York
15	Ohio
16	Rhode Island
17	Missouri
18	North Carolina
19	Illinois
20	Alabama
21	Maryland
22	Michigan
23	Alaska
24	West Virginia
25	Texas
26	South Dakota
27	Pennsylvania
28	Kentucky
29	California
30	Maine
31	Hawaii
32	Wyoming
33	Montana
34	Oregon
35	Kansas
36	Virginia
37	Wisconsin
38	Connecticut
39	Vermont
40	Iowa
41	Nebraska
42	New Jersey
43	Washington
44	North Dakota
45	Massachusetts
46	Minnesota
47	Colorado
48	New Hampshire
49	Idaho
50	Utah

Note: Numbers that appear to be identical are rounded and vary slightly in actual value. The rankings reflect the actual values before rounding. See the introduction for more details.

L-2 Temporary Assistance for Needy Families (TANF) Recipients, 2005

State	Average monthly number of recipients	Average monthly number of families	Recipients as a percentage of population	Rank by percentage
Alabama	48,117	20,214	1.1	32
Alaska	13,342	4,814	2.0	8
Arizona	98,165	43,223	1.7	13
Arkansas	18,845	8,660	0.7	45
California	1,092,422	466,074	3.0	2
Colorado	38,060	15,903	0.8	39
Connecticut	39,812	19,608	1.1	30
Delaware	12,296	5,531	1.5	21
Florida	104,503	59,761	0.6	47
Georgia	87,979	41,155	1.0	33
Hawaii	20,713	8,169	1.6	17
Idaho	3,446	1,919	0.2	49
Illinois	97,736	38,887	0.8	42
Indiana	124,007	48,389	2.0	9
Iowa	42,942	17,738	1.5	22
Kansas	45,269	17,399	1.7	16
Kentucky	75,375	34,864	1.8	12
Louisiana	37,009	15,979	0.8	40
Maine	25,876	9,729	2.0	10
Maryland	54,658	23,091	1.0	34
Massachusetts	103,921	48,837	1.6	18
Michigan	216,726	81,329	2.1	6
Minnesota	73,880	29,301	1.4	23
Mississippi	33,795	15,763	1.2	28
Missouri	97,352	40,529	1.7	14
Montana	12,894	4,861	1.4	24
Nebraska	23,300	9,787	1.3	25
Nevada	15,531	6,794	0.7	46
New Hampshire	14,333	6,209	1.1	31
New Jersey	105,044	42,935	1.2	27
New Mexico	44,476	17,364	2.3	4
New York	322,681	141,446	1.7	15
North Carolina	65,919	33,201	0.8	41
North Dakota	7,242	2,832	1.1	29
Ohio	180,165	82,897	1.6	19
Oklahoma	26,448	11,630	0.8	44
Oregon	46,354	20,240	1.3	26
Pennsylvania	253,763	96,800	2.0	7
Rhode Island	27,157	10,763	2.5	3
South Carolina	34,955	15,506	0.8	38
South Dakota	5,871	2,744	0.8	43
Tennessee	185,246	70,379	3.1	1
Texas	195,944	85,092	0.9	36
Utah	23,016	9,164	1.0	35
Vermont	11,459	4,561	1.8	11
Virginia	28,126	9,869	0.4	48
Washington	140,461	58,311	2.3	5
West Virginia	27,219	11,963	1.5	20
Wisconsin	46,749	20,293	0.8	37
Wyoming	545	311	0.1	50
50 States	4,451,144	1,892,818	1.5	
DC	41,916	16,905	7.6	
United States*	4,547,143	1,928,544	1.5	

Due to rounding or data sources, the 50-state total plus D.C. may not equal the U.S. total. Please see introduction.

Rank in order by percentage	
1	Tennessee
2	California
3	Rhode Island
4	New Mexico
5	Washington
6	Michigan
7	Pennsylvania
8	Alaska
9	Indiana
10	Maine
11	Vermont
12	Kentucky
13	Arizona
14	Missouri
15	New York
16	Kansas
17	Hawaii
18	Massachusetts
19	Ohio
20	West Virginia
21	Delaware
22	Iowa
23	Minnesota
24	Montana
25	Nebraska
26	Oregon
27	New Jersey
28	Mississippi
29	North Dakota
30	Connecticut
31	New Hampshire
32	Alabama
33	Georgia
34	Maryland
35	Utah
36	Texas
37	Wisconsin
38	South Carolina
39	Colorado
40	Louisiana
41	North Carolina
42	Illinois
43	South Dakota
44	Oklahoma
45	Arkansas
46	Nevada
47	Florida
48	Virginia
49	Idaho
50	Wyoming

Note: Numbers that appear to be identical are rounded and vary slightly in actual value. The rankings reflect the actual values before rounding. See the introduction for more details.

L-3 Change in TANF/AFDC Recipients, FY 1996–2005

State	Average monthly AFDC recipients FY 1996	Percentage decrease FY 1996–2005	Rank by percentage decrease
Alabama	100,662	-52.2	36
Alaska	35,544	-62.5	22
Arizona	169,442	-42.1	43
Arkansas	56,343	-66.6	20
California	2,581,948	-57.7	25
Colorado	95,788	-60.3	24
Connecticut	159,246	-75.0	8
Delaware	23,654	-48.0	40
Florida	533,801	-80.4	6
Georgia	330,302	-73.4	9
Hawaii	66,482	-68.8	17
Idaho	21,780	-84.2	3
Illinois	642,644	-84.8	2
Indiana	142,604	-13.0	50
Iowa	86,146	-50.2	39
Kansas	63,783	-29.0	48
Kentucky	172,193	-56.2	29
Louisiana	228,115	-83.8	4
Maine	53,873	-52.0	38
Maryland	194,127	-71.8	12
Massachusetts	226,030	-54.0	33
Michigan	502,354	-56.9	26
Minnesota	169,744	-56.5	27
Mississippi	123,828	-72.7	10
Missouri	222,820	-56.3	28
Montana	29,130	-55.7	30
Nebraska	39,228	-40.6	46
Nevada	34,261	-54.7	32
New Hampshire	22,937	-37.5	47
New Jersey	275,637	-61.9	23
New Mexico	99,661	-55.4	31
New York	1,143,962	-71.8	13
North Carolina	267,326	-75.3	7
North Dakota	13,146	-44.9	42
Ohio	549,312	-67.2	19
Oklahoma	96,201	-72.5	11
Oregon	78,419	-40.9	45
Pennsylvania	531,059	-52.2	35
Rhode Island	56,560	-52.0	37
South Carolina	114,273	-69.4	16
South Dakota	15,896	-63.1	21
Tennessee	254,818	-27.3	49
Texas	649,018	-69.8	14
Utah	39,073	-41.1	44
Vermont	24,331	-52.9	34
Virginia	152,845	-81.6	5
Washington	268,927	-47.8	41
West Virginia	89,039	-69.4	15
Wisconsin	148,888	-68.6	18
Wyoming	11,398	-95.2	1
50 States	12,008,598	-62.9	
DC	69,292	-39.5	
United States*	12,242,125	-62.9	

**Due to rounding or data sources, the 50-state total plus D.C. may not equal the U.S. total. Please see introduction.*

Rank in order by percentage decrease	
1	Wyoming
2	Illinois
3	Idaho
4	Louisiana
5	Virginia
6	Florida
7	North Carolina
8	Connecticut
9	Georgia
10	Mississippi
11	Oklahoma
12	Maryland
13	New York
14	Texas
15	West Virginia
16	South Carolina
17	Hawaii
18	Wisconsin
19	Ohio
20	Arkansas
21	South Dakota
22	Alaska
23	New Jersey
24	Colorado
25	California
26	Michigan
27	Minnesota
28	Missouri
29	Kentucky
30	Montana
31	New Mexico
32	Nevada
33	Massachusetts
34	Vermont
35	Pennsylvania
36	Alabama
37	Rhode Island
38	Maine
39	Iowa
40	Delaware
41	Washington
42	North Dakota
43	Arizona
44	Utah
45	Oregon
46	Nebraska
47	New Hampshire
48	Kansas
49	Tennessee
50	Indiana

Note: Numbers that appear to be identical are rounded and vary slightly in actual value. The rankings reflect the actual values before rounding. See the introduction for more details.

L-4 Food Stamp Recipients, FY 2005

State	Food stamp recipients #	Recipients as a percentage of population	Rank by percentage
Alabama	539,892	11.9	12
Alaska	56,857	8.7	24
Arizona	556,592	9.7	17
Arkansas	376,308	13.7	6
California	1,991,121	5.5	43
Colorado	228,535	5.0	47
Connecticut	205,904	5.9	41
Delaware	62,334	7.5	27
Florida	1,268,620	7.3	30
Georgia	919,555	10.4	16
Hawaii	92,944	7.4	29
Idaho	92,936	6.7	35
Illinois	1,185,658	9.3	19
Indiana	554,776	8.9	21
Iowa	210,660	7.1	32
Kansas	179,643	6.6	38
Kentucky	573,731	13.8	5
Louisiana	743,772	16.5	1
Maine	157,266	11.9	11
Maryland	292,994	5.3	44
Massachusetts	392,052	6.1	40
Michigan	1,067,795	10.6	15
Minnesota	263,242	5.2	45
Mississippi	402,158	13.9	4
Missouri	772,398	13.4	7
Montana	81,942	8.8	23
Nebraska	117,435	6.7	34
Nevada	118,789	5.1	46
New Hampshire	52,791	4.1	50
New Jersey	399,383	4.6	49
New Mexico	240,204	12.6	8
New York	1,744,352	9.1	20
North Carolina	805,920	9.4	18
North Dakota	41,727	6.6	37
Ohio	1,014,775	8.9	22
Oklahoma	421,053	11.9	10
Oregon	428,213	11.9	13
Pennsylvania	1,056,104	8.5	25
Rhode Island	73,977	6.8	33
South Carolina	524,291	12.5	9
South Dakota	57,396	7.4	28
Tennessee	848,308	14.4	3
Texas	2,397,798	10.7	14
Utah	134,332	5.6	42
Vermont	45,295	7.3	31
Virginia	491,376	6.6	36
Washington	513,126	8.3	26
West Virginia	261,333	14.4	2
Wisconsin	349,467	6.3	39
Wyoming	24,636	4.9	48
50 States	25,431,766	8.7	
DC	90,988	16.4	
United States*	25,563,975	8.7	

Due to rounding or data sources, the 50-state total plus D.C. may not equal the U.S. total. Please see introduction.

Rank in order by percentage	
1	Louisiana
2	West Virginia
3	Tennessee
4	Mississippi
5	Kentucky
6	Arkansas
7	Missouri
8	New Mexico
9	South Carolina
10	Oklahoma
11	Maine
12	Alabama
13	Oregon
14	Texas
15	Michigan
16	Georgia
17	Arizona
18	North Carolina
19	Illinois
20	New York
21	Indiana
22	Ohio
23	Montana
24	Alaska
25	Pennsylvania
26	Washington
27	Delaware
28	South Dakota
29	Hawaii
30	Florida
31	Vermont
32	Iowa
33	Rhode Island
34	Nebraska
35	Idaho
36	Virginia
37	North Dakota
38	Kansas
39	Wisconsin
40	Massachusetts
41	Connecticut
42	Utah
43	California
44	Maryland
45	Minnesota
46	Nevada
47	Colorado
48	Wyoming
49	New Jersey
50	New Hampshire

Note: Numbers that appear to be identical are rounded and vary slightly in actual value. The rankings reflect the actual values before rounding. See the introduction for more details.

L-5 Supplemental Security Income (SSI) Recipients, 2004

State	SSI recipients #	Recipients as a percentage of population	Rank by percentage
Alabama	163,070	3.6	5
Alaska	10,773	1.6	32
Arizona	94,639	1.6	31
Arkansas	87,979	3.2	8
California	1,181,681	3.3	6
Colorado	54,223	1.2	47
Connecticut	51,538	1.5	40
Delaware	13,470	1.6	35
Florida	413,575	2.4	16
Georgia	200,169	2.3	18
Hawaii	22,256	1.8	28
Idaho	21,025	1.5	39
Illinois	255,462	2.0	25
Indiana	96,211	1.5	38
Iowa	42,656	1.4	41
Kansas	38,491	1.4	42
Kentucky	179,418	4.3	1
Louisiana	169,547	3.8	4
Maine	31,668	2.4	15
Maryland	92,817	1.7	30
Massachusetts	168,975	2.6	12
Michigan	219,194	2.2	20
Minnesota	70,788	1.4	43
Mississippi	125,241	4.3	2
Missouri	116,231	2.0	24
Montana	14,572	1.6	37
Nebraska	22,100	1.3	45
Nevada	32,281	1.4	44
New Hampshire	13,060	1.0	49
New Jersey	149,942	1.7	29
New Mexico	51,674	2.7	11
New York	625,841	3.3	7
North Carolina	195,819	2.3	17
North Dakota	7,943	1.3	46
Ohio	245,532	2.1	21
Oklahoma	77,172	2.2	19
Oregon	58,924	1.6	33
Pennsylvania	316,733	2.6	13
Rhode Island	29,645	2.7	9
South Carolina	105,323	2.5	14
South Dakota	12,494	1.6	36
Tennessee	160,554	2.7	10
Texas	472,563	2.1	22
Utah	21,686	0.9	50
Vermont	12,877	2.1	23
Virginia	134,634	1.8	27
Washington	112,008	1.8	26
West Virginia	76,017	4.2	3
Wisconsin	90,070	1.6	34
Wyoming	5,653	1.1	48
50 States	6,966,214	2.4	
DC	20,868	3.8	
United States*	6,987,845	2.4	

**Due to rounding or data sources, the 50-state total plus D.C. may not equal the U.S. total. Please see introduction.*

Rank in order by percentage	
1	Kentucky
2	Mississippi
3	West Virginia
4	Louisiana
5	Alabama
6	California
7	New York
8	Arkansas
9	Rhode Island
10	Tennessee
11	New Mexico
12	Massachusetts
13	Pennsylvania
14	South Carolina
15	Maine
16	Florida
17	North Carolina
18	Georgia
19	Oklahoma
20	Michigan
21	Ohio
22	Texas
23	Vermont
24	Missouri
25	Illinois
26	Washington
27	Virginia
28	Hawaii
29	New Jersey
30	Maryland
31	Arizona
32	Alaska
33	Oregon
34	Wisconsin
35	Delaware
36	South Dakota
37	Montana
38	Indiana
39	Idaho
40	Connecticut
41	Iowa
42	Kansas
43	Minnesota
44	Nevada
45	Nebraska
46	North Dakota
47	Colorado
48	Wyoming
49	New Hampshire
50	Utah

Note: Numbers that appear to be identical are rounded and vary slightly in actual value. The rankings reflect the actual values before rounding. See the introduction for more details.

L-6 Women, Infants, and Children (WIC) Recipients and Average Monthly Benefit, FY 2004

State	Average monthly WIC recipients #	Average monthly benefit $	Rank by benefit amount
Alabama	120,310	40.62	9
Alaska	26,616	44.13	3
Arizona	176,223	39.85	11
Arkansas	89,113	36.59	19
California	1,292,737	40.37	10
Colorado	83,409	35.91	24
Connecticut	52,130	41.07	6
Delaware	18,353	32.84	40
Florida	373,214	38.96	14
Georgia	259,992	35.34	26
Hawaii	33,221	51.83	1
Idaho	36,279	30.93	46
Illinois	275,833	40.97	7
Indiana	131,485	32.91	39
Iowa	66,188	32.74	41
Kansas	63,987	34.75	31
Kentucky	117,201	36.97	18
Louisiana	141,661	39.71	12
Maine	22,916	26.67	50
Maryland	107,542	33.04	38
Massachusetts	115,657	34.04	35
Michigan	222,077	32.52	43
Minnesota	116,677	34.29	34
Mississippi	102,738	36.45	21
Missouri	132,763	34.33	33
Montana	21,302	36.45	21
Nebraska	39,668	35.16	27
Nevada	46,355	33.46	37
New Hampshire	16,722	30.26	47
New Jersey	143,341	38.47	15
New Mexico	63,530	36.51	20
New York	473,058	44.30	2
North Carolina	218,930	37.16	16
North Dakota	14,117	40.84	8
Ohio	267,300	33.69	36
Oklahoma	116,145	32.30	44
Oregon	100,135	37.10	17
Pennsylvania	240,836	32.57	42
Rhode Island	22,780	35.08	28
South Carolina	106,784	35.76	25
South Dakota	21,608	34.99	29
Tennessee	155,394	39.62	13
Texas	867,586	31.49	45
Utah	66,848	29.07	49
Vermont	16,290	41.41	4
Virginia	131,832	34.55	32
Washington	159,233	41.23	5
West Virginia	50,436	36.22	23
Wisconsin	110,186	34.93	30
Wyoming	12,381	29.62	48
50 States	7,661,119	n/a	
DC	16,019	42.69	
United States*	7,904,435	37.54	

**Due to rounding or data sources, the 50-state total plus D.C. may not equal the U.S. total. Please see introduction.*

Rank in order by benefit amount	
1	Hawaii
2	New York
3	Alaska
4	Vermont
5	Washington
6	Connecticut
7	Illinois
8	North Dakota
9	Alabama
10	California
11	Arizona
12	Louisiana
13	Tennessee
14	Florida
15	New Jersey
16	North Carolina
17	Oregon
18	Kentucky
19	Arkansas
20	New Mexico
21	Mississippi
21	Montana
23	West Virginia
24	Colorado
25	South Carolina
26	Georgia
27	Nebraska
28	Rhode Island
29	South Dakota
30	Wisconsin
31	Kansas
32	Virginia
33	Missouri
34	Minnesota
35	Massachusetts
36	Ohio
37	Nevada
38	Maryland
39	Indiana
40	Delaware
41	Iowa
42	Pennsylvania
43	Michigan
44	Oklahoma
45	Texas
46	Idaho
47	New Hampshire
48	Wyoming
49	Utah
50	Maine

Note: Ties in ranking reflect ties in actual values.

L-7 National School Lunch Program (NSLP) Participants, FY 2005

State	NSLP participants #	Participation rate	Rank by rate
Alabama	565,605	76.1	4
Alaska	50,747	41.6	50
Arizona	578,297	60.2	30
Arkansas	339,390	70.8	12
California	2,851,442	45.8	47
Colorado	329,539	43.8	48
Connecticut	302,151	54.2	37
Delaware	81,025	67.9	14
Florida	1,518,103	58.1	32
Georgia	1,204,756	77.1	2
Hawaii	120,714	66.0	18
Idaho	155,786	66.4	17
Illinois	1,105,107	58.9	31
Indiana	690,546	71.1	11
Iowa	379,591	72.7	10
Kansas	325,538	66.0	19
Kentucky	534,580	75.5	6
Louisiana	612,519	79.2	1
Maine	107,627	54.0	38
Maryland	438,231	49.9	44
Massachusetts	548,777	55.6	34
Michigan	869,348	48.9	46
Minnesota	588,907	66.5	16
Mississippi	397,581	75.1	8
Missouri	624,178	64.8	22
Montana	78,394	53.8	39
Nebraska	228,945	75.5	5
Nevada	171,751	43.1	49
New Hampshire	113,080	50.2	43
New Jersey	629,681	49.1	45
New Mexico	210,634	62.3	26
New York	1,812,361	57.7	33
North Carolina	914,405	65.2	21
North Dakota	78,461	75.4	7
Ohio	1,059,886	55.2	36
Oklahoma	401,644	63.0	23
Oregon	289,229	53.5	41
Pennsylvania	1,118,435	60.7	29
Rhode Island	84,107	53.5	40
South Carolina	482,793	67.8	15
South Dakota	103,103	76.8	3
Tennessee	658,981	74.8	9
Texas	2,887,818	66.0	20
Utah	297,621	61.1	28
Vermont	55,208	55.4	35
Virginia	729,814	62.6	24
Washington	513,603	50.5	42
West Virginia	201,195	69.5	13
Wisconsin	582,100	62.4	25
Wyoming	51,210	61.2	27
50 States	29,074,546	n/a	
DC	46,964	63.1	
United States*	29,553,393	59.6	

**Due to rounding or data sources, the 50-state total plus D.C. may not equal the U.S. total. Please see introduction.*

Rank in order by rate	
1	Louisiana
2	Georgia
3	South Dakota
4	Alabama
5	Nebraska
6	Kentucky
7	North Dakota
8	Mississippi
9	Tennessee
10	Iowa
11	Indiana
12	Arkansas
13	West Virginia
14	Delaware
15	South Carolina
16	Minnesota
17	Idaho
18	Hawaii
19	Kansas
20	Texas
21	North Carolina
22	Missouri
23	Oklahoma
24	Virginia
25	Wisconsin
26	New Mexico
27	Wyoming
28	Utah
29	Pennsylvania
30	Arizona
31	Illinois
32	Florida
33	New York
34	Massachusetts
35	Vermont
36	Ohio
37	Connecticut
38	Maine
39	Montana
40	Rhode Island
41	Oregon
42	Washington
43	New Hampshire
44	Maryland
45	New Jersey
46	Michigan
47	California
48	Colorado
49	Nevada
50	Alaska

Note: Numbers that appear to be identical are rounded and vary slightly in actual value. The rankings reflect the actual values before rounding. See the introduction for more details.

L-8 Condition of Children Index, 2005

State	Condition of children index "child well-being" ranked from 1 (highest) to 50 (lowest)
Alabama	48
Alaska	36
Arizona	41
Arkansas	44
California	17
Colorado	26
Connecticut	11
Delaware	31
Florida	35
Georgia	39
Hawaii	24
Idaho	16
Illinois	28
Indiana	30
Iowa	8
Kansas	15
Kentucky	42
Louisiana	49
Maine	7
Maryland	19
Massachusetts	6
Michigan	25
Minnesota	3
Mississippi	50
Missouri	33
Montana	34
Nebraska	12
Nevada	32
New Hampshire	1
New Jersey	4
New Mexico	46
New York	20
North Carolina	40
North Dakota	5
Ohio	29
Oklahoma	38
Oregon	18
Pennsylvania	27
Rhode Island	22
South Carolina	45
South Dakota	21
Tennessee	43
Texas	37
Utah	9
Vermont	2
Virginia	13
Washington	14
West Virginia	47
Wisconsin	10
Wyoming	23
50 States	n/a
DC	n/a
United States	n/a

Rank in order by index ranked highest (1) to lowest (50)	
1	New Hampshire
2	Vermont
3	Minnesota
4	New Jersey
5	North Dakota
6	Massachusetts
7	Maine
8	Iowa
9	Utah
10	Wisconsin
11	Connecticut
12	Nebraska
13	Virginia
14	Washington
15	Kansas
16	Idaho
17	California
18	Oregon
19	Maryland
20	New York
21	South Dakota
22	Rhode Island
23	Wyoming
24	Hawaii
25	Michigan
26	Colorado
27	Pennsylvania
28	Illinois
29	Ohio
30	Indiana
31	Delaware
32	Nevada
33	Missouri
34	Montana
35	Florida
36	Alaska
37	Texas
38	Oklahoma
39	Georgia
40	North Carolina
41	Arizona
42	Kentucky
43	Tennessee
44	Arkansas
45	South Carolina
46	New Mexico
47	West Virginia
48	Alabama
49	Louisiana
50	Mississippi

L-9 Percentage of Families with Children Headed by a Single Parent, 2003

State	Percentage of families headed by single parent	Rank
Alabama	35	6
Alaska	31	17
Arizona	34	7
Arkansas	33	9
California	29	23
Colorado	26	39
Connecticut	28	28
Delaware	32	13
Florida	36	4
Georgia	33	9
Hawaii	30	19
Idaho	20	48
Illinois	29	23
Indiana	28	28
Iowa	23	44
Kansas	26	39
Kentucky	29	23
Louisiana	41	2
Maine	27	36
Maryland	32	13
Massachusetts	28	28
Michigan	30	19
Minnesota	23	44
Mississippi	42	1
Missouri	29	23
Montana	27	36
Nebraska	20	48
Nevada	30	19
New Hampshire	25	42
New Jersey	27	36
New Mexico	36	4
New York	34	7
North Carolina	33	9
North Dakota	23	44
Ohio	32	13
Oklahoma	29	23
Oregon	28	28
Pennsylvania	31	17
Rhode Island	32	13
South Carolina	37	3
South Dakota	22	47
Tennessee	33	9
Texas	28	28
Utah	17	50
Vermont	28	28
Virginia	28	28
Washington	28	28
West Virginia	30	19
Wisconsin	26	39
Wyoming	25	42
50 States	n/a	
DC	62	
United States	30	

Rank in order by percentage	
1	Mississippi
2	Louisiana
3	South Carolina
4	Florida
4	New Mexico
6	Alabama
7	Arizona
7	New York
9	Arkansas
9	Georgia
9	North Carolina
9	Tennessee
13	Delaware
13	Maryland
13	Ohio
13	Rhode Island
17	Alaska
17	Pennsylvania
19	Hawaii
19	Michigan
19	Nevada
19	West Virginia
23	California
23	Illinois
23	Kentucky
23	Missouri
23	Oklahoma
28	Connecticut
28	Indiana
28	Massachusetts
28	Oregon
28	Texas
28	Vermont
28	Virginia
28	Washington
36	Maine
36	Montana
36	New Jersey
39	Colorado
39	Kansas
39	Wisconsin
42	New Hampshire
42	Wyoming
44	Iowa
44	Minnesota
44	North Dakota
47	South Dakota
48	Idaho
48	Nebraska
50	Utah

Note: Ties in ranking reflect ties in actual values.

L-10 Average Monthly TANF Cash Assistance Per Family, FY 2004

State	Average monthly TANF payment $	Rank
Alabama	195	44
Alaska	733	4
Arizona	307	32
Arkansas	140	47
California	600	7
Colorado	373	21
Connecticut	508	10
Delaware	302	35
Florida	347	25
Georgia	254	40
Hawaii	820	3
Idaho	326	30
Illinois	258	39
Indiana	201	43
Iowa	364	23
Kansas	303	34
Kentucky	248	42
Louisiana	287	36
Maine	657	5
Maryland	360	24
Massachusetts	571	8
Michigan	420	16
Minnesota	406	18
Mississippi	142	46
Missouri	280	37
Montana	332	29
Nebraska	492	13
Nevada	305	33
New Hampshire	474	15
New Jersey	498	12
New Mexico	347	26
New York	899	2
North Carolina	264	38
North Dakota	339	28
Ohio	316	31
Oklahoma	250	41
Oregon	382	20
Pennsylvania	364	22
Rhode Island	533	9
South Carolina	89	49
South Dakota	342	27
Tennessee	138	48
Texas	169	45
Utah	419	17
Vermont	610	6
Virginia	988	1
Washington	480	14
West Virginia	388	19
Wisconsin	503	11
Wyoming	n/a	n/a
50 States	440	
DC	338	
United States	435	

Rank in order by $	
1	Virginia
2	New York
3	Hawaii
4	Alaska
5	Maine
6	Vermont
7	California
8	Massachusetts
9	Rhode Island
10	Connecticut
11	Wisconsin
12	New Jersey
13	Nebraska
14	Washington
15	New Hampshire
16	Michigan
17	Utah
18	Minnesota
19	West Virginia
20	Oregon
21	Colorado
22	Pennsylvania
23	Iowa
24	Maryland
25	Florida
26	New Mexico
27	South Dakota
28	North Dakota
29	Montana
30	Idaho
31	Ohio
32	Arizona
33	Nevada
34	Kansas
35	Delaware
36	Louisiana
37	Missouri
38	North Carolina
39	Illinois
40	Georgia
41	Oklahoma
42	Kentucky
43	Indiana
44	Alabama
45	Texas
46	Mississippi
47	Arkansas
48	Tennessee
49	South Carolina

Note: Numbers that appear to be identical are rounded and vary slightly in actual value. The rankings reflect the actual values before rounding. See the introduction for more details.

L-11 Assistance and Earnings of Three-Person TANF Family as a Percentage of Poverty-Level Income, 2003

State	Estimated assistance and earnings as a percentage of poverty-level income	Rank
Alabama	69.9	45
Alaska	103.2	3
Arizona	75.3	41
Arkansas	81.1	27
California	109.2	2
Colorado	79.4	36
Connecticut	117.8	1
Delaware	90.9	15
Florida	79.8	34
Georgia	73.6	44
Hawaii	102.1	5
Idaho	76.5	38
Illinois	83.5	21
Indiana	79.6	35
Iowa	83.5	21
Kansas	81.7	26
Kentucky	76.0	39
Louisiana	69.9	45
Maine	100.2	7
Maryland	81.1	27
Massachusetts	102.9	4
Michigan	84.3	20
Minnesota	95.2	10
Mississippi	69.9	45
Missouri	69.9	45
Montana	87.6	16
Nebraska	82.6	23
Nevada	69.9	45
New Hampshire	92.0	11
New Jersey	80.9	29
New Mexico	82.4	25
New York	91.9	12
North Carolina	76.0	39
North Dakota	85.2	18
Ohio	85.0	19
Oklahoma	77.0	37
Oregon	91.7	13
Pennsylvania	80.8	30
Rhode Island	97.7	8
South Carolina	74.9	43
South Dakota	80.8	30
Tennessee	80.1	32
Texas	69.9	45
Utah	86.4	17
Vermont	100.8	6
Virginia	91.3	14
Washington	96.9	9
West Virginia	80.1	32
Wisconsin	82.6	23
Wyoming	75.0	42
50 States	n/a	
DC	91.3	
United States	n/a	

Rank in order by percentage	
1	Connecticut
2	California
3	Alaska
4	Massachusetts
5	Hawaii
6	Vermont
7	Maine
8	Rhode Island
9	Washington
10	Minnesota
11	New Hampshire
12	New York
13	Oregon
14	Virginia
15	Delaware
16	Montana
17	Utah
18	North Dakota
19	Ohio
20	Michigan
21	Illinois
21	Iowa
23	Nebraska
23	Wisconsin
25	New Mexico
26	Kansas
27	Arkansas
27	Maryland
29	New Jersey
30	Pennsylvania
30	South Dakota
32	Tennessee
32	West Virginia
34	Florida
35	Indiana
36	Colorado
37	Oklahoma
38	Idaho
39	Kentucky
39	North Carolina
41	Arizona
42	Wyoming
43	South Carolina
44	Georgia
45	Alabama
45	Louisiana
45	Mississippi
45	Missouri
45	Nevada
45	Texas

Note: Ties in ranking reflect ties in actual values.

L-12 Supplemental Security Income (SSI) State Supplements, 2004

State	Average monthly SSI state supplements per recipient $	Rank
Alabama	56.31	29
Alaska	283.88	8
Arizona	50.00	35
Arkansas	23.29	43
California	220.09	13
Colorado	219.09	14
Connecticut	410.03	5
Delaware	124.80	17
Florida	69.22	27
Georgia	39.48	40
Hawaii	438.37	4
Idaho	55.34	30
Illinois	76.18	25
Indiana	260.53	10
Iowa	245.08	12
Kansas	18.25	47
Kentucky	313.16	7
Louisiana	18.71	46
Maine	18.89	45
Maryland	129.18	16
Massachusetts	81.24	22
Michigan	79.81	23
Minnesota	191.18	15
Mississippi	54.29	31
Missouri	250.09	11
Montana	78.65	24
Nebraska	93.16	21
Nevada	49.44	36
New Hampshire	51.99	33
New Jersey	44.67	37
New Mexico	100.00	19
New York	74.70	26
North Carolina	447.26	3
North Dakota	449.43	2
Ohio	50.50	34
Oklahoma	40.97	39
Oregon	99.03	20
Pennsylvania	38.14	41
Rhode Island	64.63	28
South Carolina	314.08	6
South Dakota	42.13	38
Tennessee	24.13	42
Texas	4.92	48
Utah	2.62	49
Vermont	54.07	32
Virginia	262.51	9
Washington	513.00	1
West Virginia	0.00	50
Wisconsin	100.70	18
Wyoming	20.00	44
50 States	n/a	
DC	188.20	
United States	131.34	

Rank in order by $	
1	Washington
2	North Dakota
3	North Carolina
4	Hawaii
5	Connecticut
6	South Carolina
7	Kentucky
8	Alaska
9	Virginia
10	Indiana
11	Missouri
12	Iowa
13	California
14	Colorado
15	Minnesota
16	Maryland
17	Delaware
18	Wisconsin
19	New Mexico
20	Oregon
21	Nebraska
22	Massachusetts
23	Michigan
24	Montana
25	Illinois
26	New York
27	Florida
28	Rhode Island
29	Alabama
30	Idaho
31	Mississippi
32	Vermont
33	New Hampshire
34	Ohio
35	Arizona
36	Nevada
37	New Jersey
38	South Dakota
39	Oklahoma
40	Georgia
41	Pennsylvania
42	Tennessee
43	Arkansas
44	Wyoming
45	Maine
46	Louisiana
47	Kansas
48	Texas
49	Utah
50	West Virginia

L-13 State Income Tax Liability of Typical Family in Poverty, 2004

State	Income tax liability $	Rank
Alabama	433	2
Alaska	n/a	n/a
Arizona	0	17
Arkansas	37	13
California	0	17
Colorado	0	17
Connecticut	0	17
Delaware	19	16
Florida	n/a	n/a
Georgia	67	11
Hawaii	346	3
Idaho	0	17
Illinois	68	10
Indiana	63	12
Iowa	0	17
Kansas	-557	35
Kentucky	455	1
Louisiana	135	7
Maine	0	17
Maryland	-637	37
Massachusetts	-612	36
Michigan	181	6
Minnesota	-1,076	39
Mississippi	20	15
Missouri	36	14
Montana	191	5
Nebraska	0	17
Nevada	n/a	n/a
New Hampshire	n/a	n/a
New Jersey	-816	38
New Mexico	-70	33
New York	-1,122	40
North Carolina	0	17
North Dakota	0	17
Ohio	86	9
Oklahoma	-34	31
Oregon	103	8
Pennsylvania	0	17
Rhode Island	-51	32
South Carolina	0	17
South Dakota	n/a	n/a
Tennessee	n/a	n/a
Texas	n/a	n/a
Utah	0	17
Vermont	-1,306	41
Virginia	0	17
Washington	n/a	n/a
West Virginia	272	4
Wisconsin	-408	34
Wyoming	n/a	n/a
50 States	n/a	
DC	-642	
United States	n/a	

Rank in order by $	
1	Kentucky
2	Alabama
3	Hawaii
4	West Virginia
5	Montana
6	Michigan
7	Louisiana
8	Oregon
9	Ohio
10	Illinois
11	Georgia
12	Indiana
13	Arkansas
14	Missouri
15	Mississippi
16	Delaware
17	Arizona
17	California
17	Colorado
17	Connecticut
17	Idaho
17	Iowa
17	Maine
17	Nebraska
17	North Carolina
17	North Dakota
17	Pennsylvania
17	South Carolina
17	Utah
17	Virginia
31	Oklahoma
32	Rhode Island
33	New Mexico
34	Wisconsin
35	Kansas
36	Massachusetts
37	Maryland
38	New Jersey
39	Minnesota
40	New York
41	Vermont

Note: Ties in ranking reflect ties in actual values.

L-14 Child Support Collections, FY 2004

State	Total collections $ (in thousands)	Per capita collections $	Rank per capita
Alabama	226,484	49.99	43
Alaska	82,113	125.28	3
Arizona	247,705	43.13	48
Arkansas	144,741	52.58	40
California	2,177,843	60.67	35
Colorado	217,201	47.20	45
Connecticut	226,643	64.69	29
Delaware	63,647	76.65	20
Florida	982,706	56.49	37
Georgia	465,377	52.71	39
Hawaii	80,829	64.01	30
Idaho	110,890	79.59	15
Illinois	511,215	40.21	49
Indiana	442,639	70.96	23
Iowa	280,399	94.91	10
Kansas	142,712	52.17	41
Kentucky	322,101	77.69	18
Louisiana	279,621	61.92	32
Maine	99,549	75.57	21
Maryland	427,575	76.93	19
Massachusetts	439,875	68.55	24
Michigan	1,414,388	139.86	2
Minnesota	567,377	111.23	4
Mississippi	182,009	62.70	31
Missouri	449,719	78.15	17
Montana	45,001	48.55	44
Nebraska	153,576	87.90	12
Nevada	107,715	46.13	46
New Hampshire	79,608	61.26	34
New Jersey	861,918	99.08	7
New Mexico	66,399	34.89	50
New York	1,312,113	68.24	25
North Carolina	527,373	61.74	33
North Dakota	57,670	90.91	11
Ohio	1,636,419	142.81	1
Oklahoma	154,023	43.71	47
Oregon	298,280	82.98	14
Pennsylvania	1,370,957	110.50	5
Rhode Island	54,655	50.58	42
South Carolina	235,648	56.13	38
South Dakota	55,767	72.34	22
Tennessee	382,290	64.78	28
Texas	1,502,576	66.81	26
Utah	140,597	58.85	36
Vermont	48,680	78.34	16
Virginia	495,051	66.36	27
Washington	591,199	95.30	9
West Virginia	158,469	87.29	13
Wisconsin	588,915	106.90	6
Wyoming	48,601	95.95	8
50 States	21,558,858	73.55	
DC	44,704	80.76	
United States*	21,861,259	74.45	

**Due to rounding or data sources, the 50-state total plus D.C. may not equal the U.S. total. Please see introduction.*

Rank in order per capita	
1	Ohio
2	Michigan
3	Alaska
4	Minnesota
5	Pennsylvania
6	Wisconsin
7	New Jersey
8	Wyoming
9	Washington
10	Iowa
11	North Dakota
12	Nebraska
13	West Virginia
14	Oregon
15	Idaho
16	Vermont
17	Missouri
18	Kentucky
19	Maryland
20	Delaware
21	Maine
22	South Dakota
23	Indiana
24	Massachusetts
25	New York
26	Texas
27	Virginia
28	Tennessee
29	Connecticut
30	Hawaii
31	Mississippi
32	Louisiana
33	North Carolina
34	New Hampshire
35	California
36	Utah
37	Florida
38	South Carolina
39	Georgia
40	Arkansas
41	Kansas
42	Rhode Island
43	Alabama
44	Montana
45	Colorado
46	Nevada
47	Oklahoma
48	Arizona
49	Illinois
50	New Mexico

L-15 Child Support Collections Per Dollar of Administrative Costs, FY 2004

State	Collections per dollar of costs $	Rank
Alabama	3.95	38
Alaska	4.50	29
Arizona	4.42	31
Arkansas	3.88	40
California	2.12	49
Colorado	3.55	43
Connecticut	3.20	46
Delaware	3.01	48
Florida	4.50	29
Georgia	4.67	26
Hawaii	8.70	1
Idaho	5.94	11
Illinois	3.22	45
Indiana	7.04	4
Iowa	5.59	13
Kansas	3.15	47
Kentucky	5.95	9
Louisiana	5.04	21
Maine	4.35	33
Maryland	4.57	27
Massachusetts	4.88	25
Michigan	5.42	15
Minnesota	4.10	36
Mississippi	7.96	2
Missouri	5.40	16
Montana	3.94	39
Nebraska	3.63	42
Nevada	3.31	44
New Hampshire	5.27	18
New Jersey	4.89	24
New Mexico	1.87	50
New York	4.31	34
North Carolina	5.01	22
North Dakota	5.37	17
Ohio	5.46	14
Oklahoma	3.64	41
Oregon	6.17	8
Pennsylvania	7.01	5
Rhode Island	5.01	22
South Carolina	7.00	6
South Dakota	7.49	3
Tennessee	5.16	19
Texas	5.95	9
Utah	4.08	37
Vermont	4.22	35
Virginia	6.33	7
Washington	4.52	28
West Virginia	4.42	31
Wisconsin	5.91	12
Wyoming	5.16	19
50 States	n/a	
DC	3.14	
United States	4.38	

Rank in order by $	
1	Hawaii
2	Mississippi
3	South Dakota
4	Indiana
5	Pennsylvania
6	South Carolina
7	Virginia
8	Oregon
9	Kentucky
9	Texas
11	Idaho
12	Wisconsin
13	Iowa
14	Ohio
15	Michigan
16	Missouri
17	North Dakota
18	New Hampshire
19	Tennessee
19	Wyoming
21	Louisiana
22	North Carolina
22	Rhode Island
24	New Jersey
25	Massachusetts
26	Georgia
27	Maryland
28	Washington
29	Alaska
29	Florida
31	Arizona
31	West Virginia
33	Maine
34	New York
35	Vermont
36	Minnesota
37	Utah
38	Alabama
39	Montana
40	Arkansas
41	Oklahoma
42	Nebraska
43	Colorado
44	Nevada
45	Illinois
46	Connecticut
47	Kansas
48	Delaware
49	California
50	New Mexico

Note: Ties in ranking reflect ties in actual values.

L-16 Children in Foster Care, FY 2003

State	Children in foster care #	Children in foster care per 10,000 children #	Rank per 10,000 children
Alabama	6,079	55	37
Alaska	2,040	108	3
Arizona	7,469	49	38
Arkansas	3,000	44	41
California	97,261	103	7
Colorado	8,754	76	24
Connecticut	6,742	81	21
Delaware	814	41	43
Florida	30,677	78	22
Georgia	13,578	59	33
Hawaii	2,967	100	9
Idaho	1,401	38	47
Illinois	21,608	67	29
Indiana	8,899	55	36
Iowa	5,011	72	25
Kansas	5,781	83	18
Kentucky	6,895	69	26
Louisiana	4,541	39	46
Maine	2,999	105	5
Maryland	11,521	84	17
Massachusetts	12,608	85	13
Michigan	21,376	84	16
Minnesota	7,330	59	34
Mississippi	2,812	37	48
Missouri	11,900	85	14
Montana	1,866	86	12
Nebraska	6,091	138	1
Nevada	3,599	62	30
New Hampshire	1,217	40	44
New Jersey	12,801	60	32
New Mexico	2,100	42	42
New York	37,067	82	19
North Carolina	9,534	46	40
North Dakota	1,238	84	15
Ohio	19,323	69	27
Oklahoma	9,194	105	4
Oregon	9,381	110	2
Pennsylvania	21,768	77	23
Rhode Island	2,334	96	10
South Carolina	4,894	48	39
South Dakota	1,580	81	20
Tennessee	9,487	68	28
Texas	22,191	36	49
Utah	2,033	27	50
Vermont	1,409	103	8
Virginia	7,046	39	45
Washington	9,213	62	31
West Virginia	4,069	104	6
Wisconsin	7,824	59	35
Wyoming	1,055	87	11
50 States	512,385	70	
DC	3,092	285	
United States*	523,085	72	

*Due to rounding or data sources, the 50-state total plus D.C. may not equal the U.S. total. Please see introduction.

Rank in order per 10,000 children	
1	Nebraska
2	Oregon
3	Alaska
4	Oklahoma
5	Maine
6	West Virginia
7	California
8	Vermont
9	Hawaii
10	Rhode Island
11	Wyoming
12	Montana
13	Massachusetts
14	Missouri
15	North Dakota
16	Michigan
17	Maryland
18	Kansas
19	New York
20	South Dakota
21	Connecticut
22	Florida
23	Pennsylvania
24	Colorado
25	Iowa
26	Kentucky
27	Ohio
28	Tennessee
29	Illinois
30	Nevada
31	Washington
32	New Jersey
33	Georgia
34	Minnesota
35	Wisconsin
36	Indiana
37	Alabama
38	Arizona
39	South Carolina
40	North Carolina
41	Arkansas
42	New Mexico
43	Delaware
44	New Hampshire
45	Virginia
46	Louisiana
47	Idaho
48	Mississippi
49	Texas
50	Utah

Note: Numbers that appear to be identical are rounded and vary slightly in actual value. The rankings reflect the actual values before rounding. See the introduction for more details.

L-17 State and Local Welfare Spending, FY 2002

State	Welfare spending $ (in millions)	Per capita $	Percentage of personal income	Rank per capita
Alabama	4,162	928	3.8	25
Alaska	1,035	1,608	5.1	2
Arizona	3,286	602	2.4	49
Arkansas	2,593	957	4.2	24
California	35,559	1,013	3.1	19
Colorado	2,823	626	1.9	48
Connecticut	3,472	1,003	2.4	20
Delaware	659	817	2.6	33
Florida	12,500	748	2.6	41
Georgia	6,159	720	2.6	44
Hawaii	1,141	917	3.2	27
Idaho	1,035	772	3.1	37
Illinois	9,861	783	2.4	36
Indiana	5,313	863	3.1	32
Iowa	2,682	913	3.3	29
Kansas	2,003	737	2.6	43
Kentucky	4,816	1,177	4.7	8
Louisiana	3,362	750	3.1	40
Maine	1,792	1,384	5.1	5
Maryland	4,737	868	2.5	31
Massachusetts	5,731	892	2.3	30
Michigan	9,837	979	3.3	22
Minnesota	7,473	1,489	4.6	4
Mississippi	3,236	1,127	5.2	11
Missouri	5,520	973	3.5	23
Montana	671	738	3.1	42
Nebraska	1,703	985	3.5	21
Nevada	1,120	515	1.8	50
New Hampshire	1,030	808	2.4	34
New Jersey	6,608	769	2.0	38
New Mexico	2,077	1,120	4.7	12
New York	32,503	1,697	4.8	1
North Carolina	7,657	920	3.4	26
North Dakota	664	1,047	4.0	16
Ohio	12,278	1,075	3.8	14
Oklahoma	3,192	914	3.6	28
Oregon	4,045	1,149	4.1	10
Pennsylvania	14,486	1,174	3.9	9
Rhode Island	1,667	1,558	5.2	3
South Carolina	4,374	1,065	4.3	15
South Dakota	605	795	3.0	35
Tennessee	6,458	1,114	4.2	13
Texas	14,903	684	2.4	46
Utah	1,595	689	2.9	45
Vermont	757	1,227	4.3	6
Virginia	4,674	641	2.0	47
Washington	6,198	1,021	3.2	18
West Virginia	2,139	1,187	5.1	7
Wisconsin	5,560	1,022	3.5	17
Wyoming	381	765	2.6	39
50 States	278,136	966	3.2	
DC	1,462	2,562	5.6	
United States	279,598	970	3.2	

Rank in order per capita	
1	New York
2	Alaska
3	Rhode Island
4	Minnesota
5	Maine
6	Vermont
7	West Virginia
8	Kentucky
9	Pennsylvania
10	Oregon
11	Mississippi
12	New Mexico
13	Tennessee
14	Ohio
15	South Carolina
16	North Dakota
17	Wisconsin
18	Washington
19	California
20	Connecticut
21	Nebraska
22	Michigan
23	Missouri
24	Arkansas
25	Alabama
26	North Carolina
27	Hawaii
28	Oklahoma
29	Iowa
30	Massachusetts
31	Maryland
32	Indiana
33	Delaware
34	New Hampshire
35	South Dakota
36	Illinois
37	Idaho
38	New Jersey
39	Wyoming
40	Louisiana
41	Florida
42	Montana
43	Kansas
44	Georgia
45	Utah
46	Texas
47	Virginia
48	Colorado
49	Arizona
50	Nevada

L-18 State and Local Welfare Spending as a Percentage of General Spending, FY 2002

State	Welfare spending as a percentage of general spending	Rank by percentage
Alabama	16.9	21
Alaska	12.3	45
Arizona	13.0	42
Arkansas	19.8	10
California	15.1	30
Colorado	10.4	48
Connecticut	14.3	33
Delaware	12.3	44
Florida	14.4	32
Georgia	13.7	36
Hawaii	13.8	35
Idaho	15.2	29
Illinois	13.4	39
Indiana	16.2	25
Iowa	15.6	27
Kansas	13.5	38
Kentucky	22.3	3
Louisiana	13.8	34
Maine	22.5	2
Maryland	14.9	31
Massachusetts	13.5	37
Michigan	16.2	24
Minnesota	21.4	6
Mississippi	21.0	7
Missouri	19.0	12
Montana	13.3	41
Nebraska	17.5	18
Nevada	9.5	50
New Hampshire	16.2	23
New Jersey	12.2	46
New Mexico	18.2	15
New York	20.2	8
North Carolina	17.2	19
North Dakota	17.1	20
Ohio	18.3	14
Oklahoma	17.6	17
Oregon	17.6	16
Pennsylvania	19.8	11
Rhode Island	24.7	1
South Carolina	18.4	13
South Dakota	15.6	28
Tennessee	22.3	4
Texas	13.4	40
Utah	12.4	43
Vermont	19.9	9
Virginia	11.9	47
Washington	16.0	26
West Virginia	21.7	5
Wisconsin	16.4	22
Wyoming	9.9	49
50 States	16.1	
DC	23.7	
United States	16.2	

Rank in order by percentage	
1	Rhode Island
2	Maine
3	Kentucky
4	Tennessee
5	West Virginia
6	Minnesota
7	Mississippi
8	New York
9	Vermont
10	Arkansas
11	Pennsylvania
12	Missouri
13	South Carolina
14	Ohio
15	New Mexico
16	Oregon
17	Oklahoma
18	Nebraska
19	North Carolina
20	North Dakota
21	Alabama
22	Wisconsin
23	New Hampshire
24	Michigan
25	Indiana
26	Washington
27	Iowa
28	South Dakota
29	Idaho
30	California
31	Maryland
32	Florida
33	Connecticut
34	Louisiana
35	Hawaii
36	Georgia
37	Massachusetts
38	Kansas
39	Illinois
40	Texas
41	Montana
42	Arizona
43	Utah
44	Delaware
45	Alaska
46	New Jersey
47	Virginia
48	Colorado
49	Wyoming
50	Nevada

Note: Numbers that appear to be identical are rounded and vary slightly in actual value. The rankings reflect the actual values before rounding. See the introduction for more details.

L-19 Average Monthly Administrative Costs Per TANF Case, FY 2004

State	Costs per case $	Rank
Alabama	51.77	37
Alaska	95.26	23
Arizona	53.70	35
Arkansas	49.92	40
California	102.80	19
Colorado	121.55	11
Connecticut	113.99	15
Delaware	56.07	33
Florida	98.86	21
Georgia	34.87	44
Hawaii	131.85	9
Idaho	121.09	12
Illinois	52.50	36
Indiana	55.61	34
Iowa	60.36	32
Kansas	50.48	39
Kentucky	35.01	43
Louisiana	136.07	8
Maine	14.11	48
Maryland	118.93	14
Massachusetts	51.50	38
Michigan	92.62	25
Minnesota	111.85	16
Mississippi	28.76	45
Missouri	40.02	41
Montana	106.69	17
Nebraska	6.96	49
Nevada	166.92	4
New Hampshire	120.94	13
New Jersey	105.31	18
New Mexico	28.19	46
New York	225.84	2
North Carolina	80.47	28
North Dakota	102.38	20
Ohio	79.68	29
Oklahoma	71.51	31
Oregon	143.28	6
Pennsylvania	98.05	22
Rhode Island	93.60	24
South Carolina	23.47	47
South Dakota	80.54	27
Tennessee	36.02	42
Texas	83.73	26
Utah	215.06	3
Vermont	131.63	10
Virginia	225.89	1
Washington	77.35	30
West Virginia	142.25	7
Wisconsin	165.68	5
Wyoming	n/a	n/a
50 States	95.70	
DC	84.10	
United States	94.21	

Rank in order by $	
1	Virginia
2	New York
3	Utah
4	Nevada
5	Wisconsin
6	Oregon
7	West Virginia
8	Louisiana
9	Hawaii
10	Vermont
11	Colorado
12	Idaho
13	New Hampshire
14	Maryland
15	Connecticut
16	Minnesota
17	Montana
18	New Jersey
19	California
20	North Dakota
21	Florida
22	Pennsylvania
23	Alaska
24	Rhode Island
25	Michigan
26	Texas
27	South Dakota
28	North Carolina
29	Ohio
30	Washington
31	Oklahoma
32	Iowa
33	Delaware
34	Indiana
35	Arizona
36	Illinois
37	Alabama
38	Massachusetts
39	Kansas
40	Arkansas
41	Missouri
42	Tennessee
43	Kentucky
44	Georgia
45	Mississippi
46	New Mexico
47	South Carolina
48	Maine
49	Nebraska

Source Notes for Welfare (Section L)

L-1 Percentage of Births to Unwed Mothers, 2003: These data come from state reports summarized by the National Center for Health Statistics in its *National Vital Statistics Report* (vol. 54, no. 2, September 8, 2005). The birth data, which come from hospitals, are highly reliable, but some states report the marital status of mothers somewhat differently.

L-2 TANF Recipients, Total and as a Percentage of Population, 2005: This table, from the Department of Health and Human Services Web site (www.acf.dhhs.gov), shows the total number of recipients and families receiving Temporary Assistance to Needy Families (TANF) as of March 2005. The table also expresses TANF recipients as a percentage of population. Because states set their own eligibility standards, states with high percentages of persons in poverty do not necessarily have a larger-than-average percentage.

L-3 Change in TANF/AFDC Recipients, FY 1996–2005: Under federal welfare reform legislation passed in 1996, states, during 1997 and 1998, made the transition from Aid to Families with Dependent Children (AFDC) to new programs. This table compares the 1996 average monthly number of recipients in each state with the 2005 average to show changes in welfare participation. The data come from the same source as Table L-2.

L-4 Food Stamp Recipients, Total and as a Percentage of Population, FY 2005: Unlike those for Temporary Assistance for Needy Families (TANF), food stamp standards of eligibility are uniform nationwide, so participation in this program tends to resemble closely the percentage of state population in poverty. The data are compiled by the U.S. Department of Agriculture, Food and Nutrition Service and are available on its Web site (www.fns.usda.gov).

L-5 SSI Recipients, Total and as a Percentage of Population, 2004: The Supplemental Security Income (SSI) program provides federal cash payments to persons eligible by reason of a combination of low-income and disability, blindness, or being over age sixty-four. The eligibility standards are uniform nationwide, as are the cash payments, except in about half the states that supplement the federal payments with state money (see Table L-12). The data, reflecting recipients at year-end 2003, were calculated from information posted on the Social Security Administration Web site (www.ssa.gov).

L-6 Women, Infants, and Children (WIC) Recipients and Average Monthly Benefit, FY 2004: WIC targets low-income, nutritionally at risk pregnant or breastfeeding women, infants, and children under age five. The program provides food aid, education, counseling, health screenings, and referrals to other social services. Participation and benefit data come from the same source as Table L-4.

L-7 National School Lunch Program (NSLP) Participants, FY 2005: Schools are required to offer free meals to children of households below 130 percent of the poverty level (reduced price meals are offered to those between 130 and 185 percent of the poverty level). These data, from the same source as Table L-4, show the number of children who participate, and express that number as a percentage of total enrollment in the schools and institutions that offer the program.

L-8 Condition of Children Index, 2005: This is a ranking of states (1 highest, 50 lowest) prepared by the Annie E. Casey Foundation based on ten indicators of health, income, education, and other factors. The details behind the rankings are found in *Kids Count Data Book* for 2005, the foundation's annual comprehensive publication.

L-9 Percentage of Families with Children Headed by a Single Parent, 2003: A large and growing number of American children do not live in households with two parents. These statistics (from *Kids Count*; see notes to Table L-8) include only children in households with a single parent present.

L-10 Average Monthly TANF Cash Assistance Per Family, FY 2004: These data show what a welfare family would receive to cover basic needs in a month. Assistance comes largely in the form of cash payments. Each state sets its own level of benefits. In addition to these cash payments, a typical welfare household might receive food stamps, assistance in paying heating and cooling bills, and free medical care under the Medicaid program. Some households would also receive additional cash as "emergency assistance" and reduced rents under various federal housing subsidy programs. For the source see Table L-2.

L-11 Assistance and Earnings of Three-Person TANF Family as a Percentage of Poverty-Level Income, 2003: These data are from a special compilation of the Congressional Research Service (CRS) and are included in the 2004 "Green Book" of the Ways and Means Committee of the U.S. House of Representatives (waysandmeans.house.gov). These data reflect assumed benefits and earnings for a single parent with two children working half-time at minimum wage in the thirteenth month of work. Assumed earnings from part-time minimum wage employment (approximately $5,000 annually in most states) and an assumed earned income credit are combined with TANF cash payments and food stamps. The total is compared with poverty level income, which, in 2003, was $15,260 for a family of three.

The TANF cash payments are set by the states (see notes to Table L-8). In the six states tied for the lowest rank TANF benefits are exhausted by the thirteenth month of work. Federally determined food stamp values differ from state to state, as greater amounts are provided in states with low cash welfare payments. The poverty level is uniform nationwide. CRS provides two numbers for the states of

California, Michigan, and New York. *State Fact Finder* included the data for Wayne County, Michigan, rather than Washtenaw County (86%), New York City rather than Suffolk County (98.9%), and those for Region 1 in California rather than Region 2 (109.2%).

L-12 SSI State Supplements, 2004: These data compare the extent to which states supplement benefits under the federal Supplemental Security Income (SSI) program. For a description of the program see the notes to Table L-5. The complex rules for determining who receives supplements and how large they are mean that the averages shown are not necessarily indicative of the average supplement received. Some states provide relatively large supplements to some beneficiaries and none to the rest. However, the extreme differences among states show marked differences in their willingness to add to federally funded benefits using their own funds. The data were calculated from information from the Social Security Administration provided to *State Fact Finder* in December, 2005.

L-13 State Income Tax Liability of Typical Family in Poverty, 2004: States have quite different approaches toward taxes on poor working families. The table illustrates these by showing how much state income tax a family of three making the 2004 poverty-level income ($15,071) would have to pay in tax on their 2004 income.

A few states, like the federal government, supplement the income of poverty-level families with a refundable credit indicated by the minus amounts shown in the table. Some states do not have income taxes (n/a on the table) or have a tax but do not make such families pay it (shown as zeros on the table). The others charge the taxes shown. The calculations were performed by the Center on Budget and Policy Priorities and are available on its Web site (www.cbpp.org).

L-14 Child Support Collections, FY 2004: Because large numbers of families on welfare consist of mothers and children who receive little or no child support from fathers, state and federal officials are intensifying efforts to ensure that fathers pay the support amounts they owe. The table provides an indication of the relative significance of the resulting child support payments in each state.

Collections are reported by the Department of Health and Human Services, Office of Child Support Enforcement (www.acf.dhhs.gov). The per capita amounts are those collections divided by each state's population on July 1, 2004. While most differences among states are real, some reflect the different degrees to which individual states enforce child support requirements through centralized systems.

L-15 Child Support Collections Per Dollar of Administrative Costs, FY 2004: Nationwide, it costs about 23 cents to collect every dollar of child support. These data, from the same source as Table L-14, indicate that the effectiveness of collections efforts varies considerably among the states.

L-16 Children in Foster Care, FY 2003: On the last day of fiscal year 2003, 523,062 children were in foster care. Most commonly, these are children who have been removed from their natural parent(s) because of suspected abuse or neglect. The count is from the Department of Health and Human Services, Administration for Children and Families (www.acf.hhs.gov). High rankings are not necessarily good or bad. Having large numbers of children in foster care for long periods is generally viewed as undesirable because the alternatives (adoption, return to natural parents) provide more stability for the child than do temporary homes with strangers. However, having small numbers may indicate that child welfare authorities are leaving abused and neglected children in homes where they should not be left.

L-17 State and Local Welfare Spending, FY 2002: This table relates spending data to population and personal income in each state. The data come from the U.S. Census Bureau's electronic publication "State and Local Government Finance Estimates, by State," available on the bureau's Web site (www.census.gov). Population numbers, also from the Census, are as of July 1, 2002, and personal income numbers are from the Department of Commerce. Based on census historical practices, *State Fact Finder* used calendar year 2001 numbers. See notes to Table F-1 for more extensive information on the source of the data. In addition to cash payments, the bureau's definition of welfare spending includes Medicaid and other payments to vendors, administrative costs, and welfare-related social services.

L-18 State and Local Welfare Spending as a Percentage of General Spending, FY 2002: These data (see notes to Table L-17) show the importance of welfare spending relative to total spending of state and local governments for "general" activities, a category that excludes spending for certain trust funds such as unemployment compensation and municipal utilities.

L-19 Average Monthly Administrative Costs Per TANF Case, FY 2004: In fiscal year 2004 the average monthly costs of administering welfare run about $94 per case, with substantial variation among the states. The information comes from unpublished tabulations by the Department of Health and Human Services, Administration for Children and Families (see notes to Table L-2).

Technology

The high-tech industry continues to experience job losses, but those numbers are getting smaller and smaller. In 2002, the sector lost 612,000 jobs; in 2004, this figure was estimated to be 25,300.

U.S. High-Tech Unemployment Rates

	2003	2004
Electrical Engineers	6.8	2.2
Math & Computer Occupations (General)	5.9	4.4
Computer Programmers	6.7	5.9

Source: American Electronics Association

Each year Darrell M. West of the Taubman Center for Public Policy at Brown University analyses state government Web sites and issues a ranking report with his findings. In 2005, after examining an average of thirty-one Web sites for each state, West found Utah to be the state with the best e-government performance. Maine, New Jersey, North Carolina, and Michigan filled the rest of the top five spots. (Wyoming was ranked as the state with the worst e-government performance.) West explains some of the features that led to Utah's top rating:

> The Utah site was our most highly rated in 2005. The site is very easy to navigate with the state's most popular online services front and center on the home page. A toolbar is located at the top of each page and links every department back to the home page. . . . Other features on the state home page include an option to chat live with online support, take a user survey, and look at current news publications, along with weather and traffic updates. At the bottom of the page, the site also offers a Utah Alerts option that gives citizens the option of receiving timely alerts through email or mobile phones about homeland security, AMBER alerts, statewide weather-related emergencies, and more. The home page also has clear links to executive, judicial, and legislative pages as well as a link to a clear privacy policy at the bottom of the page.

M-1 Percentage of Households with Computers, 2003

State	Percentage with computers	Rank
Alabama	53.9	47
Alaska	73.4	2
Arizona	64.5	19
Arkansas	49.8	49
California	66.3	13
Colorado	70.3	5
Connecticut	69.2	6
Delaware	64.4	20
Florida	61.1	29
Georgia	60.7	30
Hawaii	63.3	24
Idaho	69.1	7
Illinois	60.1	33
Indiana	59.7	37
Iowa	64.6	18
Kansas	63.6	23
Kentucky	58.4	40
Louisiana	52.5	48
Maine	67.9	9
Maryland	66.2	14
Massachusetts	64.2	21
Michigan	59.9	34
Minnesota	68.0	8
Mississippi	48.8	50
Missouri	60.6	31
Montana	59.8	36
Nebraska	66.4	12
Nevada	61.3	28
New Hampshire	71.7	3
New Jersey	65.2	17
New Mexico	54.1	46
New York	59.9	34
North Carolina	57.9	41
North Dakota	61.5	27
Ohio	58.8	39
Oklahoma	55.3	43
Oregon	67.1	10
Pennsylvania	60.2	32
Rhode Island	62.3	25
South Carolina	55.2	44
South Dakota	62.2	26
Tennessee	56.8	42
Texas	59.1	38
Utah	74.1	1
Vermont	65.6	15
Virginia	67.0	11
Washington	71.4	4
West Virginia	54.7	45
Wisconsin	63.8	22
Wyoming	65.5	16
50 States	n/a	
DC	59.5	
United States	61.8	

Rank in order by percentage	
1	Utah
2	Alaska
3	New Hampshire
4	Washington
5	Colorado
6	Connecticut
7	Idaho
8	Minnesota
9	Maine
10	Oregon
11	Virginia
12	Nebraska
13	California
14	Maryland
15	Vermont
16	Wyoming
17	New Jersey
18	Iowa
19	Arizona
20	Delaware
21	Massachusetts
22	Wisconsin
23	Kansas
24	Hawaii
25	Rhode Island
26	South Dakota
27	North Dakota
28	Nevada
29	Florida
30	Georgia
31	Missouri
32	Pennsylvania
33	Illinois
34	Michigan
34	New York
36	Montana
37	Indiana
38	Texas
39	Ohio
40	Kentucky
41	North Carolina
42	Tennessee
43	Oklahoma
44	South Carolina
45	West Virginia
46	New Mexico
47	Alabama
48	Louisiana
49	Arkansas
50	Mississippi

Note: Ties in ranking reflect ties in actual values.

M-2 Percentage of Households with Internet Access, 2003

State	Percentage using Internet	Rank
Alabama	45.8	46
Alaska	68.5	1
Arizona	55.3	24
Arkansas	42.3	49
California	59.6	11
Colorado	63.4	3
Connecticut	62.9	4
Delaware	56.9	19
Florida	55.7	22
Georgia	53.7	29
Hawaii	54.9	26
Idaho	56.4	20
Illinois	51.2	38
Indiana	51.2	38
Iowa	57.0	18
Kansas	54.3	28
Kentucky	49.9	41
Louisiana	44.1	48
Maine	58.1	13
Maryland	59.4	12
Massachusetts	58.1	13
Michigan	52.0	35
Minnesota	61.7	7
Mississippi	39.5	50
Missouri	53.0	33
Montana	50.8	40
Nebraska	55.8	21
Nevada	55.3	24
New Hampshire	65.5	2
New Jersey	60.2	10
New Mexico	44.8	47
New York	53.3	32
North Carolina	51.3	37
North Dakota	53.6	31
Ohio	52.4	34
Oklahoma	48.3	43
Oregon	61.1	8
Pennsylvania	54.7	27
Rhode Island	55.7	22
South Carolina	45.9	45
South Dakota	53.7	29
Tennessee	49.0	42
Texas	51.8	36
Utah	62.6	5
Vermont	58.0	15
Virginia	60.4	9
Washington	62.3	6
West Virginia	47.4	44
Wisconsin	57.5	17
Wyoming	57.9	16
50 States	n/a	
DC	53.2	
United States	54.7	

Rank in order by percentage	
1	Alaska
2	New Hampshire
3	Colorado
4	Connecticut
5	Utah
6	Washington
7	Minnesota
8	Oregon
9	Virginia
10	New Jersey
11	California
12	Maryland
13	Maine
13	Massachusetts
15	Vermont
16	Wyoming
17	Wisconsin
18	Iowa
19	Delaware
20	Idaho
21	Nebraska
22	Florida
22	Rhode Island
24	Arizona
24	Nevada
26	Hawaii
27	Pennsylvania
28	Kansas
29	Georgia
29	South Dakota
31	North Dakota
32	New York
33	Missouri
34	Ohio
35	Michigan
36	Texas
37	North Carolina
38	Illinois
38	Indiana
40	Montana
41	Kentucky
42	Tennessee
43	Oklahoma
44	West Virginia
45	South Carolina
46	Alabama
47	New Mexico
48	Louisiana
49	Arkansas
50	Mississippi

Note: Ties in ranking reflect ties in actual values.

M-3 Percentage of Zip Codes with Broadband Telecommunications Service, 2004

State	Percentage of zip codes with at least one subscriber	Number of broadband providers	Rank by percentage
Alabama	93	27	35
Alaska	96	8	30
Arizona	99	26	6
Arkansas	90	17	38
California	99	46	6
Colorado	97	22	23
Connecticut	100	18	1
Delaware	98	7	16
Florida	99	39	6
Georgia	99	53	6
Hawaii	90	n/a	38
Idaho	93	17	35
Illinois	97	46	23
Indiana	98	35	16
Iowa	86	61	48
Kansas	90	41	38
Kentucky	90	30	38
Louisiana	98	22	16
Maine	94	15	33
Maryland	99	21	6
Massachusetts	100	21	1
Michigan	99	32	6
Minnesota	90	51	38
Mississippi	97	20	23
Missouri	90	37	38
Montana	87	20	47
Nebraska	90	29	38
Nevada	98	18	16
New Hampshire	100	17	1
New Jersey	100	18	1
New Mexico	90	16	38
New York	100	39	1
North Carolina	99	33	6
North Dakota	85	22	49
Ohio	99	38	6
Oklahoma	94	26	33
Oregon	96	29	30
Pennsylvania	97	41	23
Rhode Island	99	8	6
South Carolina	97	26	23
South Dakota	78	23	50
Tennessee	97	36	23
Texas	98	54	16
Utah	93	20	35
Vermont	99	11	6
Virginia	97	25	23
Washington	98	31	16
West Virginia	88	14	46
Wisconsin	98	40	16
Wyoming	96	8	30
50 States	n/a	n/a	
DC	100	10	
United States	95	552	

Rank in order by percentage	
1	Connecticut
1	Massachusetts
1	New Hampshire
1	New Jersey
1	New York
6	Arizona
6	California
6	Florida
6	Georgia
6	Maryland
6	Michigan
6	North Carolina
6	Ohio
6	Rhode Island
6	Vermont
16	Delaware
16	Indiana
16	Louisiana
16	Nevada
16	Texas
16	Washington
16	Wisconsin
23	Colorado
23	Illinois
23	Mississippi
23	Pennsylvania
23	South Carolina
23	Tennessee
23	Virginia
30	Alaska
30	Oregon
30	Wyoming
33	Maine
33	Oklahoma
35	Alabama
35	Idaho
35	Utah
38	Arkansas
38	Hawaii
38	Kansas
38	Kentucky
38	Minnesota
38	Missouri
38	Nebraska
38	New Mexico
46	West Virginia
47	Montana
48	Iowa
49	North Dakota
50	South Dakota

Note: Ties in ranking reflect ties in actual values.

M-4 High-Tech Jobs, 2003

State	Employment in the high-tech industry	High-tech employment per 1,000 private sector workers	Rank per 1,000 workers
Alabama	69,589	47	22
Alaska	8,818	41	30
Arizona	109,448	58	14
Arkansas	27,098	29	44
California	915,516	74	6
Colorado	162,217	91	1
Connecticut	69,231	50	20
Delaware	18,736	54	17
Florida	258,801	42	28
Georgia	167,565	53	19
Hawaii	13,249	29	42
Idaho	34,052	73	7
Illinois	210,635	43	26
Indiana	67,692	28	46
Iowa	39,002	33	36
Kansas	55,770	53	18
Kentucky	43,220	30	40
Louisiana	37,281	25	48
Maine	15,580	32	38
Maryland	154,945	78	4
Massachusetts	235,584	86	3
Michigan	183,218	50	21
Minnesota	124,866	57	16
Mississippi	18,955	22	50
Missouri	87,113	40	31
Montana	10,006	32	37
Nebraska	30,174	42	29
Nevada	28,066	30	41
New Hampshire	35,081	67	9
New Jersey	202,587	62	11
New Mexico	43,821	77	5
New York	305,338	45	24
North Carolina	136,015	44	25
North Dakota	9,525	38	32
Ohio	158,770	35	34
Oklahoma	40,278	36	33
Oregon	81,436	62	12
Pennsylvania	203,756	43	27
Rhode Island	18,468	45	23
South Carolina	42,470	29	43
South Dakota	9,344	32	39
Tennessee	63,089	29	45
Texas	445,973	59	13
Utah	48,525	57	15
Vermont	15,488	63	10
Virginia	244,213	88	2
Washington	150,801	70	8
West Virginia	14,241	26	47
Wisconsin	77,228	33	35
Wyoming	4,365	24	49
50 States	5,547,239	n/a	
DC	33,286	79	
United States*	5,584,713	52	

**Due to rounding or data sources, the 50-state total plus D.C. may not equal the U.S. total. Please see introduction.*

Rank in order per 1,000 workers	
1	Colorado
2	Virginia
3	Massachusetts
4	Maryland
5	New Mexico
6	California
7	Idaho
8	Washington
9	New Hampshire
10	Vermont
11	New Jersey
12	Oregon
13	Texas
14	Arizona
15	Utah
16	Minnesota
17	Delaware
18	Kansas
19	Georgia
20	Connecticut
21	Michigan
22	Alabama
23	Rhode Island
24	New York
25	North Carolina
26	Illinois
27	Pennsylvania
28	Florida
29	Nebraska
30	Alaska
31	Missouri
32	North Dakota
33	Oklahoma
34	Ohio
35	Wisconsin
36	Iowa
37	Montana
38	Maine
39	South Dakota
40	Kentucky
41	Nevada
42	Hawaii
43	South Carolina
44	Arkansas
45	Tennessee
46	Indiana
47	West Virginia
48	Louisiana
49	Wyoming
50	Mississippi

Note: Numbers that appear to be identical are rounded and vary slightly in actual value. The rankings reflect the actual values before rounding. See the introduction for more details.

M-5 Percentage Change in High-Tech Employment, 2002–2003

State	Percentage change in high-tech employment	Rank
Alabama	-0.1	5
Alaska	1.3	1
Arizona	-5.7	32
Arkansas	-0.5	6
California	-6.9	38
Colorado	-8.3	48
Connecticut	-7.5	46
Delaware	-5.3	29
Florida	-3.4	20
Georgia	-5.9	34
Hawaii	-1.9	11
Idaho	-3.3	19
Illinois	-7.5	45
Indiana	-4.5	26
Iowa	-3.8	25
Kansas	-5.6	31
Kentucky	-3.8	24
Louisiana	-3.2	18
Maine	-7.9	47
Maryland	-2.3	13
Massachusetts	-7.3	44
Michigan	-3.5	22
Minnesota	-6.9	39
Mississippi	-5.2	28
Missouri	-1.2	8
Montana	-2.7	14
Nebraska	-12.2	50
Nevada	-0.0	4
New Hampshire	-7.2	42
New Jersey	-6.7	35
New Mexico	-2.8	15
New York	-7.2	43
North Carolina	-7.1	41
North Dakota	0.2	2
Ohio	-5.8	33
Oklahoma	-5.4	30
Oregon	-7.1	40
Pennsylvania	-6.8	36
Rhode Island	-0.6	7
South Carolina	-2.1	12
South Dakota	-3.0	17
Tennessee	-3.5	21
Texas	-6.9	37
Utah	-1.6	9
Vermont	-9.5	49
Virginia	-1.7	10
Washington	-3.7	23
West Virginia	-4.8	27
Wisconsin	-2.9	16
Wyoming	0.0	3
50 States	-5.6	
DC	-0.4	
United States	-5.6	

Rank in order by percentage	
1	Alaska
2	North Dakota
3	Wyoming
4	Nevada
5	Alabama
6	Arkansas
7	Rhode Island
8	Missouri
9	Utah
10	Virginia
11	Hawaii
12	South Carolina
13	Maryland
14	Montana
15	New Mexico
16	Wisconsin
17	South Dakota
18	Louisiana
19	Idaho
20	Florida
21	Tennessee
22	Michigan
23	Washington
24	Kentucky
25	Iowa
26	Indiana
27	West Virginia
28	Mississippi
29	Delaware
30	Oklahoma
31	Kansas
32	Arizona
33	Ohio
34	Georgia
35	New Jersey
36	Pennsylvania
37	Texas
38	California
39	Minnesota
40	Oregon
41	North Carolina
42	New Hampshire
43	New York
44	Massachusetts
45	Illinois
46	Connecticut
47	Maine
48	Colorado
49	Vermont
50	Nebraska

Note: Numbers that appear to be identical are rounded and vary slightly in actual value. The rankings reflect the actual values before rounding. See the introduction for more details.

M-6 State Government Web Site Ratings, 2005

State	Web site rating	Rank
Alabama	31.9	48
Alaska	29.2	49
Arizona	40.9	28
Arkansas	50.4	11
California	33.8	46
Colorado	49.1	13
Connecticut	44.1	19
Delaware	51.9	7
Florida	39.7	31
Georgia	38.2	33
Hawaii	37.2	37
Idaho	47.8	15
Illinois	36.9	38
Indiana	44.0	20
Iowa	39.5	32
Kansas	41.1	27
Kentucky	38.1	34
Louisiana	33.8	46
Maine	61.3	2
Maryland	39.9	30
Massachusetts	51.4	8
Michigan	53.0	5
Minnesota	35.5	42
Mississippi	50.7	9
Missouri	36.5	39
Montana	41.5	26
Nebraska	43.2	23
Nevada	50.5	10
New Hampshire	46.8	17
New Jersey	59.5	3
New Mexico	34.4	45
New York	49.0	14
North Carolina	59.0	4
North Dakota	47.7	16
Ohio	43.6	21
Oklahoma	34.8	44
Oregon	49.2	12
Pennsylvania	43.3	22
Rhode Island	36.5	39
South Carolina	34.9	43
South Dakota	43.0	24
Tennessee	52.2	6
Texas	45.8	18
Utah	62.1	1
Vermont	36.0	41
Virginia	37.6	35
Washington	41.9	25
West Virginia	37.4	36
Wisconsin	40.1	29
Wyoming	28.4	50
50 States	n/a	
DC	n/a	
United States	n/a	

Rank in order by rating	
1	Utah
2	Maine
3	New Jersey
4	North Carolina
5	Michigan
6	Tennessee
7	Delaware
8	Massachusetts
9	Mississippi
10	Nevada
11	Arkansas
12	Oregon
13	Colorado
14	New York
15	Idaho
16	North Dakota
17	New Hampshire
18	Texas
19	Connecticut
20	Indiana
21	Ohio
22	Pennsylvania
23	Nebraska
24	South Dakota
25	Washington
26	Montana
27	Kansas
28	Arizona
29	Wisconsin
30	Maryland
31	Florida
32	Iowa
33	Georgia
34	Kentucky
35	Virginia
36	West Virginia
37	Hawaii
38	Illinois
39	Missouri
39	Rhode Island
41	Vermont
42	Minnesota
43	South Carolina
44	Oklahoma
45	New Mexico
46	California
46	Louisiana
48	Alabama
49	Alaska
50	Wyoming

Note: Ties in ranking reflect ties in actual values.

M-7 Average Number of Online Services Available on State Government Web Sites, 2005

State	Average number of online services	Rank
Alabama	1.6	47
Alaska	1.8	46
Arizona	5.1	27
Arkansas	28.4	4
California	1.1	49
Colorado	14.7	11
Connecticut	6.9	22
Delaware	12.8	13
Florida	6.3	23
Georgia	4.9	30
Hawaii	4.5	31
Idaho	25.3	5
Illinois	1.4	48
Indiana	5.8	26
Iowa	7.5	20
Kansas	7.3	21
Kentucky	5.0	29
Louisiana	2.1	45
Maine	30.9	2
Maryland	8.8	18
Massachusetts	17.7	8
Michigan	15.4	10
Minnesota	2.3	43
Mississippi	22.1	7
Missouri	2.8	40
Montana	5.9	25
Nebraska	29.2	3
Nevada	13.6	12
New Hampshire	11.0	16
New Jersey	17.4	9
New Mexico	3.6	34
New York	11.2	14
North Carolina	24.7	6
North Dakota	11.2	15
Ohio	4.4	32
Oklahoma	5.1	28
Oregon	10.1	17
Pennsylvania	2.8	41
Rhode Island	3.5	35
South Carolina	2.4	42
South Dakota	3.3	36
Tennessee	6.2	24
Texas	3.1	37
Utah	42.9	1
Vermont	4.0	33
Virginia	2.2	44
Washington	2.9	39
West Virginia	8.0	19
Wisconsin	2.9	38
Wyoming	0.1	50
50 States	n/a	
DC	n/a	
United States	22.1	

Rank in order by number	
1	Utah
2	Maine
3	Nebraska
4	Arkansas
5	Idaho
6	North Carolina
7	Mississippi
8	Massachusetts
9	New Jersey
10	Michigan
11	Colorado
12	Nevada
13	Delaware
14	New York
15	North Dakota
16	New Hampshire
17	Oregon
18	Maryland
19	West Virginia
20	Iowa
21	Kansas
22	Connecticut
23	Florida
24	Tennessee
25	Montana
26	Indiana
27	Arizona
28	Oklahoma
29	Kentucky
30	Georgia
31	Hawaii
32	Ohio
33	Vermont
34	New Mexico
35	Rhode Island
36	South Dakota
37	Texas
38	Wisconsin
39	Washington
40	Missouri
41	Pennsylvania
42	South Carolina
43	Minnesota
44	Virginia
45	Louisiana
46	Alaska
47	Alabama
48	Illinois
49	California
50	Wyoming

Note: Numbers that appear to be identical are rounded and vary slightly in actual value. The rankings reflect the actual values before rounding. See the introduction for more details.

M-8 Students Per Computer, 2004

State	Students per instructional computer	Rank
Alabama	4.8	6
Alaska	3.3	31
Arizona	3.9	16
Arkansas	3.4	29
California	5.1	2
Colorado	4.2	11
Connecticut	3.7	22
Delaware	n/a	n/a
Florida	3.5	27
Georgia	3.8	21
Hawaii	3.9	16
Idaho	3.3	31
Illinois	3.9	16
Indiana	3.2	36
Iowa	3.1	40
Kansas	2.7	43
Kentucky	3.7	22
Louisiana	4.9	5
Maine	2.2	47
Maryland	4.7	7
Massachusetts	3.9	16
Michigan	3.9	16
Minnesota	3.3	31
Mississippi	5.1	2
Missouri	3.3	31
Montana	2.7	43
Nebraska	2.7	43
Nevada	5.7	1
New Hampshire	4.5	9
New Jersey	3.7	22
New Mexico	3.2	36
New York	4.2	11
North Carolina	4.1	13
North Dakota	2.7	43
Ohio	3.2	36
Oklahoma	3.0	41
Oregon	4.5	9
Pennsylvania	3.6	25
Rhode Island	4.6	8
South Carolina	4.0	15
South Dakota	1.7	49
Tennessee	4.1	13
Texas	3.3	31
Utah	5.1	2
Vermont	3.5	27
Virginia	3.2	36
Washington	3.6	25
West Virginia	3.4	29
Wisconsin	2.8	42
Wyoming	2.1	48
50 States	n/a	
DC	3.3	
United States	3.8	

Rank in order by number	
1	Nevada
2	California
2	Mississippi
2	Utah
5	Louisiana
6	Alabama
7	Maryland
8	Rhode Island
9	New Hampshire
9	Oregon
11	Colorado
11	New York
13	North Carolina
13	Tennessee
15	South Carolina
16	Arizona
16	Hawaii
16	Illinois
16	Massachusetts
16	Michigan
21	Georgia
22	Connecticut
22	Kentucky
22	New Jersey
25	Pennsylvania
25	Washington
27	Florida
27	Vermont
29	Arkansas
29	West Virginia
31	Alaska
31	Idaho
31	Minnesota
31	Missouri
31	Texas
36	Indiana
36	New Mexico
36	Ohio
36	Virginia
40	Iowa
41	Oklahoma
42	Wisconsin
43	Kansas
43	Montana
43	Nebraska
43	North Dakota
47	Maine
48	Wyoming
49	South Dakota

Note: Ties in ranking reflect ties in actual values.

M-9 Students Per Internet-Connected Computer, 2004

State	Students per Internet-connected instructional computer	Rank
Alabama	4.9	8
Alaska	3.5	34
Arizona	4.3	18
Arkansas	3.5	34
California	5.8	2
Colorado	4.8	10
Connecticut	4.4	15
Delaware	n/a	n/a
Florida	4.0	24
Georgia	4.1	21
Hawaii	4.4	15
Idaho	3.6	31
Illinois	4.3	18
Indiana	3.5	34
Iowa	3.3	41
Kansas	2.9	44
Kentucky	4.0	24
Louisiana	5.1	5
Maine	2.5	47
Maryland	5.1	5
Massachusetts	4.8	10
Michigan	4.1	21
Minnesota	3.8	29
Mississippi	4.6	13
Missouri	3.3	41
Montana	3.1	43
Nebraska	2.9	44
Nevada	6.1	1
New Hampshire	5.2	3
New Jersey	4.1	21
New Mexico	3.6	31
New York	4.9	8
North Carolina	4.4	15
North Dakota	2.8	46
Ohio	3.6	31
Oklahoma	3.5	34
Oregon	5.0	7
Pennsylvania	4.0	24
Rhode Island	4.8	10
South Carolina	4.0	24
South Dakota	1.9	49
Tennessee	4.6	13
Texas	3.7	30
Utah	5.2	3
Vermont	4.3	18
Virginia	3.5	34
Washington	4.0	24
West Virginia	3.4	40
Wisconsin	3.5	34
Wyoming	2.5	47
50 States	n/a	
DC	4.2	
United States	4.1	

Rank in order by number	
1	Nevada
2	California
3	Utah
3	New Hampshire
5	Louisiana
5	Maryland
7	Oregon
8	Alabama
8	New York
10	Rhode Island
10	Massachusetts
10	Colorado
13	Mississippi
13	Tennessee
15	Hawaii
15	Connecticut
15	North Carolina
18	Arizona
18	Vermont
18	Illinois
21	Michigan
21	Georgia
21	New Jersey
24	Florida
24	Washington
24	Kentucky
24	Pennsylvania
24	South Carolina
29	Minnesota
30	Texas
31	Idaho
31	Ohio
31	New Mexico
34	Alaska
34	Oklahoma
34	Indiana
34	Virginia
34	Arkansas
34	Wisconsin
40	West Virginia
41	Iowa
41	Missouri
43	Montana
44	Nebraska
44	Kansas
46	North Dakota
47	Wyoming
47	Maine
49	South Dakota

Note: Ties in ranking reflect ties in actual values.

M-10 Percentage of Public Libraries with Internet Access, FY 2002

State	Percentage of libraries with Internet access	Rank
Alabama	99.5	22
Alaska	88.2	46
Arizona	100.0	1
Arkansas	100.0	1
California	99.4	24
Colorado	98.3	36
Connecticut	95.9	40
Delaware	100.0	1
Florida	100.0	1
Georgia	100.0	1
Hawaii	100.0	1
Idaho	98.1	37
Illinois	99.4	24
Indiana	98.7	32
Iowa	97.2	39
Kansas	95.0	42
Kentucky	100.0	1
Louisiana	100.0	1
Maine	91.6	44
Maryland	100.0	1
Massachusetts	99.2	28
Michigan	99.5	22
Minnesota	99.3	27
Mississippi	100.0	1
Missouri	95.3	41
Montana	98.7	32
Nebraska	85.1	48
Nevada	100.0	1
New Hampshire	90.4	45
New Jersey	99.4	24
New Mexico	93.3	43
New York	99.9	20
North Carolina	100.0	1
North Dakota	84.1	49
Ohio	100.0	1
Oklahoma	99.1	31
Oregon	99.2	28
Pennsylvania	99.8	21
Rhode Island	100.0	1
South Carolina	100.0	1
South Dakota	85.6	47
Tennessee	98.4	34
Texas	97.8	38
Utah	100.0	1
Vermont	80.4	50
Virginia	100.0	1
Washington	98.4	34
West Virginia	100.0	1
Wisconsin	99.2	28
Wyoming	100.0	1
50 States	n/a	
DC	100.0	
United States	97.1	

Rank in order by percentage	
1	Arizona
1	Arkansas
1	Delaware
1	Florida
1	Georgia
1	Hawaii
1	Kentucky
1	Louisiana
1	Maryland
1	Mississippi
1	Nevada
1	North Carolina
1	Ohio
1	Rhode Island
1	South Carolina
1	Utah
1	Virginia
1	West Virginia
1	Wyoming
20	New York
21	Pennsylvania
22	Alabama
22	Michigan
24	California
24	Illinois
24	New Jersey
27	Minnesota
28	Massachusetts
28	Oregon
28	Wisconsin
31	Oklahoma
32	Indiana
32	Montana
34	Tennessee
34	Washington
36	Colorado
37	Idaho
38	Texas
39	Iowa
40	Connecticut
41	Missouri
42	Kansas
43	New Mexico
44	Maine
45	New Hampshire
46	Alaska
47	South Dakota
48	Nebraska
49	North Dakota
50	Vermont

Note: Ties in ranking reflect ties in actual values.

Source Notes for Technology (Section M)

M-1 Percentage of Households with Computers, 2003: In 1995, the National Telecommunication and Information Administration (NTIA), an agency of the Department of Commerce, began publishing a series of reports on access to technology in the United States based on data from the U.S. Census Bureau's Current Population Survey. The statistics on computer ownership come from the U.S. Census Bureau interviews with approximately 57,000 sample households. They are available on the bureau's Web site (www.census.gov).

M-2 Percentage of Households with Internet Access, 2003: This table is from the same source as cited in the notes to Table M-1.

M-3 Percentage of Zip Codes with Broadband Telecommunications Service, 2004: High-speed, high-capacity, "always on" broadband telecommunications services allow large amounts of information to be transmitted quickly, providing at least the promise of increased productivity. The majority of these services are supplied by cable lines and digital subscriber lines (DSL), a small percentage come from satellite, wireless, and other technologies. As many who live in rural areas know, broadband service is not yet universally available.

The Federal Communications Commission (FCC) began tracking access to broadband services in 1998. While it does not count individual subscribers, the FCC does keep statistics on the number of broadband providers in each zip code. This information for 2004 is provided in the table. The first column shows the percentage of zip codes in each state that have one or more subscribers to one or more broadband services. According to the FCC report from which the data is culled ("High-Speed Services for Internet Access: Status as of December 31, 2004"), 99 percent of the U.S. population resides in those zip codes. Because access can vary greatly within a zip code—cable lines tend to be laid in residential rather than business and industrial areas, and one neighbor can be offered DSL while another is not—presumptions about access should be made with caution. The second column of the table shows the number of companies that supply broadband service within each state, providing some indication of competition in the broadband market.

M-4 High-Tech Jobs, 2003: The recognized authority on employment statistics—the Bureau of Labor Statistics (BLS)—does not currently release "high-tech" industry data for states, but the bureau does assign every category of job an employment code (North American Industrial Classification System, or NAICS code). In order to create this table, the American Electronics Association (AeA) sifted through these NAICS codes to create its own definition of the high-tech industry. In *Cyberstates 2005,* the source of the data in this table, AeA calls their definition "a solid, yet conservative, representation of the core components of today's high-tech industry." It includes high-tech manufacturing, communications services, and software and computer-related services. It does not include the biotechnology industry (due to the difficulty of separating "tech" from "bio" activities), temporary employees, consultants, or freelance workers. High-technology is not an easy industry to isolate. Other groups are bound to develop differing definitions.

Cyberstates 2005 also includes detailed state-level information on high-tech wages, establishments,and payroll, as well as information on trade, venture capital investments, and research and development expenditures.

M-5 Percentage Change in High-Tech Employment, 2002–2003: Overall high-tech employment dropped by 5.6 percent between 2002 and 2003, reflecting a loss of 333,033 jobs. The total U.S. private sector saw employment drop by 0.46 percent over the same period. For source, see notes to Table M-4.

M-6 State Government Web Site Ratings, 2005: Citing the Internet as an important means for governments to deliver information and services to citizens, Daniel M. West, Director of the Taubman Center for Public Policy at Brown University, has taken on the task of rating "e-government." West's report, "State and Federal E-Government in the United States, 2005," published on www.InsidePolitics.org, analyzes 1,620 government Web sites from a "citizen's perspective." A variety of measures were used to evaluate web sites. These include the presence of online services, publications and databases, security and privacy measures, handicap accessibility, readability, and other services such as foreign language translation, digital signatures, credit card payments, and comment forms. Each state was given a score out of a possible 100. Utah topped the scale with a score of 62.1.

M-7: Average Number of Online Services Available on State Government Web Sites, 2005: State and federal governments are offering more services online. Some examples of available online services are vehicle registration, driver's license renewal, registering to vote, ordering birth or death certificates, filing consumer complaints, and filing business and payroll taxes. These data, from the same source as Table M-6, show the average number of online services offered on state government Web sites.

M-8: Students Per Computer, 2004: This table is one measure of student access to technology in public schools. The data are from *Education Week's* "Technology Counts 2005" (www.edweek.org), which includes additional information on how computers and the Internet are used in the classroom. For more information on the capacity to use technology see also, the National Center for Education Statistics' report,

"Teachers' Tools for the 21st Century: A Report on Teachers' Use of Technology."

M-9: Students Per Internet-Connected Computer, 2004: See notes to Table M-4.

M-10: Percentage of Public Libraries with Internet Access, FY 2002: From the U.S. Department of Education's *Public Libraries Survey, Fiscal Year 2002,* these data show that most of the public libraries in the country have access to the Internet (97.1%).

State Rankings

Alabama

Population - Section A

Population 2005	23
Population 2004	23
Population Change 2003–2004	34
Population Change 1994–2004	36
Population 2015	43
Population 2025	24
Percentage 65 and Over	17
Percentage 17 and Under	28
Median Age	22
Percentage African American	6
Percentage American Indian	28
Percentage Asian American	44
Percentage Hispanic	42
Percentage White (Non-Hispanic)	32
Percentage Mixed-Race	46
Percentage in Poverty	3
Child Poverty Rate	2
Percentage Female	6
Birth Rates	32
Death Rates	3
Population Density	26
Legal Immigrants FY 2004	40
Unauthorized Immigrants	31

Economies - Section B

Personal Income, 2004	24
Gross State Product	45
Per Capita Personal Income	41
Personal Income from Wages and Salaries	35
Average Annual Pay	31
Average Hourly Earnings	36
Value Added in Manufacturing	24
Cost of Living	40
Average Annual Pay in Manufacturing	39
Average Annual Pay in Retailing	35
Labor Force	47
Unemployment Rate	40
Employment Rate	11
Government Employment	13
Manufacturing Employment	7
Fortune 500 Companies	35
Forbes 500 Companies	19
Tourism Spending Per Capita	44
Exports Per Capita	29
Housing Permits	27
Percentage Change in Home Prices	39
Net Farm Income	13
Financial Institution Assets	8
Bankruptcy Filings	2
Patents Issued	43
WC Disability Payment	28
Average Weekly UC Benefit	50
Economic Momentum	24
One-year Employment Change	34
Manufacturing Employment Change	7
Home Ownership	2
Annual Electricity Use Per Residential Customer	3
Cost Per Kwh	8
New Companies	45

Geography - Section C

Total Land Area	28
Federally Owned Land	38
State Park Acreage	42
State Park Visitors	46
Population Not Active	5
Hunters with Firearms	21
Registered Boats	17
State Spending for the Arts	29
Energy Consumption Per Capita	9
Toxic Chemical Release Per Capita	12
Hazardous Waste Sites	28
Drinking Water Quality	49
Expired Water Pollution Permits	32
Air Pollution Emissions	15

Government - Section D

Members of United States House	22
State Legislators	27
Legislators Per Million Population	29
Units of Government	31
Legislators Compensation	48
Female Legislators	49
Turnover in Legislatures	n/a
Term Limits	n/a
Legislative Session Length	13
Democrats in State Legislatures	9
Governors' Power Rating	46
Number of Statewide Elected Officials	9
State and Local Government Employees	12
State and Local Average Salaries	37
Local Employment	32
Local Spending Accountability	26
Registered Voters	29
Percentage of Population Voting	39
Statewide Initiatives	n/a
Campaign Costs Per Vote	8

Federal Impacts - Section E

Per Capita Federal Spending	9
Increase in Federal Spending	15
Per Capita Federal Grant Spending	22
Per Capita Federal Spending on Procurement	7
Per Capita Federal Spending on Payments to Individuals	6
Per Capita Federal Spending on Social Security and Medicare	4
Social Security Benefits	43
Federal Spending on Employee Wages and Salaries	18
Per Capita Federal Defense Spending	7
Per Capita Homeland Security Grants	28
Federal Grant Spending Per Dollar of State Tax Revenue	9
General Revenue from Federal Government	13
Federal Tax Burden Per Capita	43
Federal Spending Per Dollar of Taxes Paid	6
Highway Charges Returned to States	21
Terms of Trade	16
Federal Personal Income Taxes	39
Federal Share of Medicaid	9

Taxes - Section F

Tax Revenue	48
Per Capita Tax Revenue	50
Tax Effort	45
Tax Capacity	46
Percentage Change in Taxes	24
Property Taxes as a Percentage of Income	50
Property Taxes Per Capita	50
Property Tax Revenue as a Percentage of 3-tax Revenue	48
Sales Taxes as a Percentage of Income	16
Sales Taxes Per Capita	26
Sales Tax Revenue as a Percentage of 3-tax Revenue	8
Sales Tax Rate	38
Income Taxes as a Percentage of Income	36
Income Taxes Per Capita	37
Income Tax Revenue as a Percentage of 3-tax Revenue	28
Highest Personal Income Rate	40
Corporate Income Taxes	21
Motor Fuel Taxes	36
Motor Vehicle Fees	35
Tobacco Taxes	38
Taxes on High-Income Families	38
Taxes in the Largest City in Each State	29
Progressivity of Taxes	41
Per Capita Estate Tax Revenue	39

Revenues and Finances - Section G

Per Capita Total Revenue	39
Per Capita General Revenue	35

"Own-Source" General Revenue	40
Per Capita Non-Tax Revenue	7
Per Capita Total Spending	31
General Spending as a Percentage of Income	15
Per Capita General Spending	30
Change in General Expenditures	8
State Government General Revenue	33
State Government General Spending	32
State Government General Fund Spending	24
State and Local Debt	41
Debt as a Percentage of Revenue	30
Per Capita Full Faith and Credit Debt	30
Bond Ratings	3
State Solvency Index	27
Pension Plan Assets	37
State Reserves	9
Capital Outlays and Interest	34
State Budget Process Quality	40
Relative State Spending "Needs"	40
Structural Deficits	37

Education - Section H

Math Proficiency, Eighth Grade	49
Reading Proficiency, Eighth Grade	46
AFQT Ranks	46
SAT Scores	n/a
ACT Scores	21
Population over 25 with a High School Diploma	42
Students in Private Schools	24
High School Dropout Rates	42
Pupil-Teacher Ratio	19
Public School Enrollment	25
Library Holdings Per Capita	40
Children with Disabilities	39
Education Spending Per Capita	38
Education Spending as a Percentage of General Spending	29
Spending Per Pupil	42
Average Teacher Salary	46
Sources of School Funds	36
State Aid Per Pupil	28
Per Capita Higher Education Spending	21
Higher Education Spending as a Percentage of General Spending	16
Public Higher Education Enrollment	29
Per Pupil Support of Higher Education	11
In-State Tuition and Fees	29
Out-of-State Tuition and Fees	34
Change in Tuition and Fees	13
Affordability Index	45
Average Professor Salary	36
Education Employees	33
R and D Spending	5
Library Operating Spending	46
Head Start Spending	44

Health - Section I

Immunization Rates	26
Infant Mortality Rates	7
State Health Rankings	45
Population without Health Insurance	30
Abortions	24
Alcohol Consumption	45
Percentage of Adult Smokers	7
Percentage Obese	2
AIDS Cases	21
Physicians Per 100,000 Population	41
Hospital Beds Per 1,000 Population	14
Medicaid Recipients	11
Medicaid Recipients as a Percentage of Poverty Population	37
Health and Hospital Spending	2
Health and Hospital Spending as a Percentage of General Spending	1
Per Capita Medicaid Spending	32
Medicaid Spending Per Aged	36
Medicaid Spending Per Child	50
Medicare Payment Per Hospital Day	12
Hospital Expense Per Inpatient Day	49
Population in HMOs	46
Prescription Drugs as a Percentage of Medicaid Costs	14
Percentage Change in Average Price of Prescription Drugs	1

Crime - Section J

Crime Rate	16
Violent Crime Rate	22
Murder Rate	18
Property Crime Rate	16
Motor Vehicle Theft Rate	29
Violent Crime Rate Change	38
Prisoners	16
Change in Prisoners	37
Incarceration Rate	6
Juvenile Violent Crime Rate	39
Law Enforcement Employees	26
Corrections Employees	42
State Corrections Spending	49
Increase in State Corrections Spending	8
Law Enforcement Spending	46
Law Enforcement Spending as a Percentage of General Spending	45

Transportation - Section K

Travel on Interstates	38
Interstate Mileage in "Unacceptable" Condition	4
Deficient Bridges	17
Traffic Deaths	13
Seat Belt Use	23
Vehicle-Miles Traveled Per Capita	4
Use of Public Transportation	42
Road and Street Miles	29
Highway Employees	16
Public Transit Employees	43
Highway Spending Per Capita	32
Highway Spending as a Percentage of General Spending	32

Welfare - Section L

Births to Unwed Mothers	20
TANF Recipients	32
Change in TANF/AFDC Recipients	36
Food Stamp Recipients	12
SSI Recipients	5
WIC Average Monthly Benefit	9
NSLP Recipients	4
Condition of Children Index	48
Families with Single Parent	6
Average Monthly TANF Payments	44
Welfare as a Percentage of Poverty-Level Income	45
State Supplements of SSI	29
State Income Tax Liability of Typical Family in Poverty	2
Child Support Collections	43
Child Support Collections Per Dollar of Administrative Costs	38
Children in Foster Care	37
Welfare Spending Per Capita	25
Welfare Spending as a Percentage of General Spending	21
Administrative Costs Per TANF Case	37

Technology - Section M

Households with Computers	47
Percentage Using Internet	46
Zip Codes with Broadband Service	35
High-Tech Jobs	22
Change in High-Tech Jobs	5
State Government Web Site Ratings	48
Number of Online Government Services	47
Students Per Computer	6
Students Per Internet-Connected Computer	8
Libraries with Internet Access	22

Alaska

Population - Section A

Population 2005	47
Population 2004	47
Population Change 2003–2004	17
Population Change 1994–2004	22
Population 2015	13
Population 2025	46
Percentage 65 and Over	50
Percentage 17 and Under	2
Median Age	48
Percentage African American	34
Percentage American Indian	1
Percentage Asian American	9
Percentage Hispanic	28
Percentage White (Non-Hispanic)	35
Percentage Mixed-Race	2
Percentage in Poverty	43
Child Poverty Rate	40
Percentage Female	50
Birth Rates	6
Death Rates	23
Population Density	50
Legal Immigrants FY 2004	44
Unauthorized Immigrants	40

Economies - Section B

Personal Income, 2004	47
Gross State Product	3
Per Capita Personal Income	16
Personal Income from Wages and Salaries	6
Average Annual Pay	15
Average Hourly Earnings	29
Value Added in Manufacturing	48
Cost of Living	6
Average Annual Pay in Manufacturing	46
Average Annual Pay in Retailing	10
Labor Force	22
Unemployment Rate	3
Employment Rate	48
Government Employment	1
Manufacturing Employment	45
Fortune 500 Companies	n/a
Forbes 500 Companies	n/a
Tourism Spending Per Capita	8
Exports Per Capita	2
Housing Permits	41
Percentage Change in Home Prices	23
Net Farm Income	50
Financial Institution Assets	49
Bankruptcy Filings	50
Patents Issued	46
WC Disability Payment	10
Average Weekly UC Benefit	47
Economic Momentum	20
One-year Employment Change	23
Manufacturing Employment Change	3
Home Ownership	42
Annual Electricity Use Per Residential Customer	40
Cost Per Kwh	38
New Companies	26

Geography - Section C

Total Land Area	1
Federally Owned Land	1
State Park Acreage	1
State Park Visitors	5
Population Not Active	35
Hunters with Firearms	n/a
Registered Boats	45
State Spending for the Arts	28
Energy Consumption Per Capita	1
Toxic Chemical Release Per Capita	1
Hazardous Waste Sites	43
Drinking Water Quality	3
Expired Water Pollution Permits	8
Air Pollution Emissions	47

Government - Section D

Members of United States House	44
State Legislators	49
Legislators Per Million Population	9
Units of Government	30
Legislators Compensation	20
Female Legislators	32
Turnover in Legislatures	22
Term Limits	n/a
Legislative Session Length	8
Democrats in State Legislatures	41
Governors' Power Rating	1
Number of Statewide Elected Officials	45
State and Local Government Employees	2
State and Local Average Salaries	6
Local Employment	48
Local Spending Accountability	40
Registered Voters	1
Percentage of Population Voting	6
Statewide Initiatives	n/a
Campaign Costs Per Vote	6

Federal Impacts - Section E

Per Capita Federal Spending	1
Increase in Federal Spending	1
Per Capita Federal Grant Spending	1
Per Capita Federal Spending on Procurement	5
Per Capita Federal Spending on Payments to Individuals	49
Per Capita Federal Spending on Social Security and Medicare	50
Social Security Benefits	42
Federal Spending on Employee Wages and Salaries	1
Per Capita Federal Defense Spending	2
Per Capita Homeland Security Grants	4
Federal Grant Spending Per Dollar of State Tax Revenue	1
General Revenue from Federal Government	18
Federal Tax Burden Per Capita	20
Federal Spending Per Dollar of Taxes Paid	2
Highway Charges Returned to States	1
Terms of Trade	1
Federal Personal Income Taxes	13
Federal Share of Medicaid	37

Taxes - Section F

Tax Revenue	28
Per Capita Tax Revenue	16
Tax Effort	40
Tax Capacity	11
Percentage Change in Taxes	50
Property Taxes as a Percentage of Income	7
Property Taxes Per Capita	10
Property Tax Revenue as a Percentage of 3-tax Revenue	2
Sales Taxes as a Percentage of Income	47
Sales Taxes Per Capita	46
Sales Tax Revenue as a Percentage of 3-tax Revenue	45
Sales Tax Rate	n/a
Income Taxes as a Percentage of Income	n/a
Income Taxes Per Capita	n/a
Income Tax Revenue as a Percentage of 3-tax Revenue	n/a
Highest Personal Income Rate	n/a
Corporate Income Taxes	1
Motor Fuel Taxes	49
Motor Vehicle Fees	19
Tobacco Taxes	5
Taxes on High-Income Families	49
Taxes in the Largest City in Each State	48
Progressivity of Taxes	46
Per Capita Estate Tax Revenue	47

Revenues and Finances - Section G

Per Capita Total Revenue	1
Per Capita General Revenue	1

"Own-Source" General Revenue	1
Per Capita Non-Tax Revenue	1
Per Capita Total Spending	1
General Spending as a Percentage of Income	1
Per Capita General Spending	1
Change in General Expenditures	48
State Government General Revenue	1
State Government General Spending	1
State Government General Fund Spending	2
State and Local Debt	1
Debt as a Percentage of Revenue	3
Per Capita Full Faith and Credit Debt	5
Bond Ratings	3
State Solvency Index	1
Pension Plan Assets	7
State Reserves	1
Capital Outlays and Interest	1
State Budget Process Quality	45
Relative State Spending "Needs"	49
Structural Deficits	42

Education - Section H

Math Proficiency, Eighth Grade	29
Reading Proficiency, Eighth Grade	34
AFQT Ranks	4
SAT Scores	6
ACT Scores	n/a
Population over 25 with a High School Diploma	8
Students in Private Schools	44
High School Dropout Rates	38
Pupil-Teacher Ratio	11
Public School Enrollment	2
Library Holdings Per Capita	19
Children with Disabilities	35
Education Spending Per Capita	1
Education Spending as a Percentage of General Spending	50
Spending Per Pupil	10
Average Teacher Salary	10
Sources of School Funds	46
State Aid Per Pupil	7
Per Capita Higher Education Spending	6
Higher Education Spending as a Percentage of General Spending	49
Public Higher Education Enrollment	47
Per Pupil Support of Higher Education	1
In-State Tuition and Fees	45
Out-of-State Tuition and Fees	45
Change in Tuition and Fees	50
Affordability Index	19
Average Professor Salary	44
Education Employees	3
R and D Spending	10
Library Operating Spending	10
Head Start Spending	11

Health - Section I

Immunization Rates	50
Infant Mortality Rates	28
State Health Rankings	30
Population without Health Insurance	16
Abortions	n/a
Alcohol Consumption	13
Percentage of Adult Smokers	7
Percentage Obese	21
AIDS Cases	25
Physicians Per 100,000 Population	35
Hospital Beds Per 1,000 Population	40
Medicaid Recipients	22
Medicaid Recipients as a Percentage of Poverty Population	5
Health and Hospital Spending	32
Health and Hospital Spending as a Percentage of General Spending	47
Per Capita Medicaid Spending	5
Medicaid Spending Per Aged	17
Medicaid Spending Per Child	2
Medicare Payment Per Hospital Day	10
Hospital Expense Per Inpatient Day	2
Population in HMOs	50
Prescription Drugs as a Percentage of Medicaid Costs	25
Percentage Change in Average Price of Prescription Drugs	6

Crime - Section J

Crime Rate	22
Violent Crime Rate	7
Murder Rate	18
Property Crime Rate	27
Motor Vehicle Theft Rate	23
Violent Crime Rate Change	3
Prisoners	41
Change in Prisoners	32
Incarceration Rate	24
Juvenile Violent Crime Rate	19
Law Enforcement Employees	38
Corrections Employees	9
State Corrections Spending	6
Increase in State Corrections Spending	n/a
Law Enforcement Spending	1
Law Enforcement Spending as a Percentage of General Spending	39

Transportation - Section K

Travel on Interstates	4
Interstate Mileage in "Unacceptable" Condition	23
Deficient Bridges	18
Traffic Deaths	11
Seat Belt Use	32
Vehicle-Miles Traveled Per Capita	49
Use of Public Transportation	32
Road and Street Miles	6
Highway Employees	1
Public Transit Employees	22
Highway Spending Per Capita	1
Highway Spending as a Percentage of General Spending	4

Welfare - Section L

Births to Unwed Mothers	23
TANF Recipients	8
Change in TANF/AFDC Recipients	22
Food Stamp Recipients	24
SSI Recipients	32
WIC Average Monthly Benefit	3
NSLP Recipients	50
Condition of Children Index	36
Families with Single Parent	17
Average Monthly TANF Payments	4
Welfare as a Percentage of Poverty-Level Income	3
State Supplements of SSI	8
State Income Tax Liability of Typical Family in Poverty	n/a
Child Support Collections	3
Child Support Collections Per Dollar of Administrative Costs	29
Children in Foster Care	3
Welfare Spending Per Capita	2
Welfare Spending as a Percentage of General Spending	45
Administrative Costs Per TANF Case	23

Technology - Section M

Households with Computers	2
Percentage Using Internet	1
Zip Codes with Broadband Service	30
High-Tech Jobs	30
Change in High-Tech Jobs	1
State Government Web Site Ratings	49
Number of Online Government Services	46
Students Per Computer	31
Students Per Internet-Connected Computer	34
Libraries with Internet Access	46

Arizona

Population - Section A

Population 2005	17
Population 2004	18
Population Change 2003–2004	2
Population Change 1994–2004	2
Population 2015	2
Population 2025	12
Percentage 65 and Over	26
Percentage 17 and Under	4
Median Age	46
Percentage African American	35
Percentage American Indian	7
Percentage Asian American	22
Percentage Hispanic	4
Percentage White (Non-Hispanic)	42
Percentage Mixed-Race	12
Percentage in Poverty	12
Child Poverty Rate	8
Percentage Female	44
Birth Rates	3
Death Rates	33
Population Density	36
Legal Immigrants FY 2004	11
Unauthorized Immigrants	6

Economies - Section B

Personal Income, 2004	22
Gross State Product	36
Per Capita Personal Income	38
Personal Income from Wages and Salaries	22
Average Annual Pay	21
Average Hourly Earnings	37
Value Added in Manufacturing	36
Cost of Living	19
Average Annual Pay in Manufacturing	7
Average Annual Pay in Retailing	8
Labor Force	40
Unemployment Rate	26
Employment Rate	25
Government Employment	32
Manufacturing Employment	40
Fortune 500 Companies	34
Forbes 500 Companies	38
Tourism Spending Per Capita	23
Exports Per Capita	22
Housing Permits	2
Percentage Change in Home Prices	12
Net Farm Income	22
Financial Institution Assets	42
Bankruptcy Filings	22
Patents Issued	20
WC Disability Payment	49
Average Weekly UC Benefit	48
Economic Momentum	2
One-year Employment Change	2
Manufacturing Employment Change	29
Home Ownership	40
Annual Electricity Use Per Residential Customer	14
Cost Per Kwh	35
New Companies	43

Geography - Section C

Total Land Area	6
Federally Owned Land	4
State Park Acreage	38
State Park Visitors	50
Population Not Active	18
Hunters with Firearms	34
Registered Boats	30
State Spending for the Arts	33
Energy Consumption Per Capita	43
Toxic Chemical Release Per Capita	34
Hazardous Waste Sites	41
Drinking Water Quality	8
Expired Water Pollution Permits	11
Air Pollution Emissions	31

Government - Section D

Members of United States House	18
State Legislators	43
Legislators Per Million Population	42
Units of Government	42
Legislators Compensation	21
Female Legislators	3
Turnover in Legislatures	8
Term Limits	4
Legislative Session Length	14
Democrats in State Legislatures	39
Governors' Power Rating	29
Number of Statewide Elected Officials	34
State and Local Government Employees	47
State and Local Average Salaries	21
Local Employment	10
Local Spending Accountability	37
Registered Voters	40
Percentage of Population Voting	44
Statewide Initiatives	n/a
Campaign Costs Per Vote	35

Federal Impacts - Section E

Per Capita Federal Spending	24
Increase in Federal Spending	4
Per Capita Federal Grant Spending	30
Per Capita Federal Spending on Procurement	6
Per Capita Federal Spending on Payments to Individuals	40
Per Capita Federal Spending on Social Security and Medicare	36
Social Security Benefits	16
Federal Spending on Employee Wages and Salaries	29
Per Capita Federal Defense Spending	6
Per Capita Homeland Security Grants	35
Federal Grant Spending Per Dollar of State Tax Revenue	34
General Revenue from Federal Government	23
Federal Tax Burden Per Capita	37
Federal Spending Per Dollar of Taxes Paid	21
Highway Charges Returned to States	43
Terms of Trade	22
Federal Personal Income Taxes	31
Federal Share of Medicaid	13

Taxes - Section F

Tax Revenue	19
Per Capita Tax Revenue	36
Tax Effort	41
Tax Capacity	23
Percentage Change in Taxes	3
Property Taxes as a Percentage of Income	26
Property Taxes Per Capita	33
Property Tax Revenue as a Percentage of 3-tax Revenue	31
Sales Taxes as a Percentage of Income	8
Sales Taxes Per Capita	9
Sales Tax Revenue as a Percentage of 3-tax Revenue	13
Sales Tax Rate	22
Income Taxes as a Percentage of Income	40
Income Taxes Per Capita	39
Income Tax Revenue as a Percentage of 3-tax Revenue	40
Highest Personal Income Rate	30
Corporate Income Taxes	28
Motor Fuel Taxes	36
Motor Vehicle Fees	49
Tobacco Taxes	14
Taxes on High-Income Families	39
Taxes in the Largest City in Each State	42
Progressivity of Taxes	19
Per Capita Estate Tax Revenue	29

Revenues and Finances - Section G

Per Capita Total Revenue	40
Per Capita General Revenue	50

"Own-Source" General Revenue	47
Per Capita Non-Tax Revenue	50
Per Capita Total Spending	46
General Spending as a Percentage of Income	40
Per Capita General Spending	50
Change in General Expenditures	10
State Government General Revenue	47
State Government General Spending	47
State Government General Fund Spending	27
State and Local Debt	27
Debt as a Percentage of Revenue	23
Per Capita Full Faith and Credit Debt	26
Bond Ratings	n/a
State Solvency Index	14
Pension Plan Assets	42
State Reserves	15
Capital Outlays and Interest	16
State Budget Process Quality	46
Relative State Spending "Needs"	41
Structural Deficits	49

Education - Section H

Math Proficiency, Eighth Grade	35
Reading Proficiency, Eighth Grade	42
AFQT Ranks	23
SAT Scores	2
ACT Scores	n/a
Population over 25 with a High School Diploma	37
Students in Private Schools	46
High School Dropout Rates	33
Pupil-Teacher Ratio	2
Public School Enrollment	8
Library Holdings Per Capita	50
Children with Disabilities	43
Education Spending Per Capita	49
Education Spending as a Percentage of General Spending	27
Spending Per Pupil	49
Average Teacher Salary	27
Sources of School Funds	27
State Aid Per Pupil	39
Per Capita Higher Education Spending	36
Higher Education Spending as a Percentage of General Spending	21
Public Higher Education Enrollment	2
Per Pupil Support of Higher Education	46
In-State Tuition and Fees	35
Out-of-State Tuition and Fees	31
Change in Tuition and Fees	8
Affordability Index	35
Average Professor Salary	24
Education Employees	45
R and D Spending	13
Library Operating Spending	34
Head Start Spending	9

Health - Section I

Immunization Rates	38
Infant Mortality Rates	24
State Health Rankings	31
Population without Health Insurance	8
Abortions	37
Alcohol Consumption	10
Percentage of Adult Smokers	44
Percentage Obese	38
AIDS Cases	22
Physicians Per 100,000 Population	34
Hospital Beds Per 1,000 Population	46
Medicaid Recipients	18
Medicaid Recipients as a Percentage of Poverty Population	34
Health and Hospital Spending	47
Health and Hospital Spending as a Percentage of General Spending	43
Per Capita Medicaid Spending	28
Medicaid Spending Per Aged	28
Medicaid Spending Per Child	22
Medicare Payment Per Hospital Day	4
Hospital Expense Per Inpatient Day	34
Population in HMOs	25
Prescription Drugs as a Percentage of Medicaid Costs	50
Percentage Change in Average Price of Prescription Drugs	2

Crime - Section J

Crime Rate	1
Violent Crime Rate	13
Murder Rate	6
Property Crime Rate	1
Motor Vehicle Theft Rate	2
Violent Crime Rate Change	22
Prisoners	13
Change in Prisoners	17
Incarceration Rate	9
Juvenile Violent Crime Rate	22
Law Enforcement Employees	10
Corrections Employees	13
State Corrections Spending	38
Increase in State Corrections Spending	36
Law Enforcement Spending	12
Law Enforcement Spending as a Percentage of General Spending	2

Transportation - Section K

Travel on Interstates	33
Interstate Mileage in "Unacceptable" Condition	45
Deficient Bridges	50
Traffic Deaths	12
Seat Belt Use	4
Vehicle-Miles Traveled Per Capita	33
Use of Public Transportation	21
Road and Street Miles	31
Highway Employees	45
Public Transit Employees	46
Highway Spending Per Capita	38
Highway Spending as a Percentage of General Spending	30

Welfare - Section L

Births to Unwed Mothers	5
TANF Recipients	13
Change in TANF/AFDC Recipients	43
Food Stamp Recipients	17
SSI Recipients	31
WIC Average Monthly Benefit	11
NSLP Recipients	30
Condition of Children Index	41
Families with Single Parent	7
Average Monthly TANF Payments	32
Welfare as a Percentage of Poverty-Level Income	41
State Supplements of SSI	35
State Income Tax Liability of Typical Family in Poverty	17
Child Support Collections	48
Child Support Collections Per Dollar of Administrative Costs	31
Children in Foster Care	38
Welfare Spending Per Capita	49
Welfare Spending as a Percentage of General Spending	42
Administrative Costs Per TANF Case	35

Technology - Section M

Households with Computers	19
Percentage Using Internet	24
Zip Codes with Broadband Service	6
High-Tech Jobs	14
Change in High-Tech Jobs	32
State Government Web Site Ratings	28
Number of Online Government Services	27
Students Per Computer	16
Students Per Internet-Connected Computer	18
Libraries with Internet Access	1

Arkansas

Population - Section A

Population 2005	32
Population 2004	32
Population Change 2003–2004	20
Population Change 1994–2004	21
Population 2015	23
Population 2025	32
Percentage 65 and Over	9
Percentage 17 and Under	22
Median Age	29
Percentage African American	12
Percentage American Indian	21
Percentage Asian American	41
Percentage Hispanic	29
Percentage White (Non-Hispanic)	27
Percentage Mixed-Race	30
Percentage in Poverty	8
Child Poverty Rate	6
Percentage Female	18
Birth Rates	21
Death Rates	9
Population Density	34
Legal Immigrants FY 2004	37
Unauthorized Immigrants	30

Economies - Section B

Personal Income, 2004	33
Gross State Product	48
Per Capita Personal Income	48
Personal Income from Wages and Salaries	39
Average Annual Pay	45
Average Hourly Earnings	44
Value Added in Manufacturing	10
Cost of Living	48
Average Annual Pay in Manufacturing	48
Average Annual Pay in Retailing	49
Labor Force	43
Unemployment Rate	11
Employment Rate	40
Government Employment	20
Manufacturing Employment	3
Fortune 500 Companies	17
Forbes 500 Companies	29
Tourism Spending Per Capita	35
Exports Per Capita	43
Housing Permits	30
Percentage Change in Home Prices	35
Net Farm Income	6
Financial Institution Assets	32
Bankruptcy Filings	3
Patents Issued	49
WC Disability Payment	44
Average Weekly UC Benefit	36
Economic Momentum	27
One-year Employment Change	35
Manufacturing Employment Change	34
Home Ownership	37
Annual Electricity Use Per Residential Customer	15
Cost Per Kwh	14
New Companies	22

Geography - Section C

Total Land Area	27
Federally Owned Land	20
State Park Acreage	41
State Park Visitors	14
Population Not Active	7
Hunters with Firearms	4
Registered Boats	26
State Spending for the Arts	39
Energy Consumption Per Capita	11
Toxic Chemical Release Per Capita	21
Hazardous Waste Sites	38
Drinking Water Quality	9
Expired Water Pollution Permits	45
Air Pollution Emissions	33

Government - Section D

Members of United States House	31
State Legislators	30
Legislators Per Million Population	19
Units of Government	13
Legislators Compensation	31
Female Legislators	38
Turnover in Legislatures	7
Term Limits	13
Legislative Session Length	n/a
Democrats in State Legislatures	4
Governors' Power Rating	39
Number of Statewide Elected Officials	22
State and Local Government Employees	25
State and Local Average Salaries	48
Local Employment	41
Local Spending Accountability	47
Registered Voters	33
Percentage of Population Voting	49
Statewide Initiatives	n/a
Campaign Costs Per Vote	36

Federal Impacts - Section E

Per Capita Federal Spending	28
Increase in Federal Spending	19
Per Capita Federal Grant Spending	16
Per Capita Federal Spending on Procurement	50
Per Capita Federal Spending on Payments to Individuals	7
Per Capita Federal Spending on Social Security and Medicare	10
Social Security Benefits	48
Federal Spending on Employee Wages and Salaries	38
Per Capita Federal Defense Spending	41
Per Capita Homeland Security Grants	19
Federal Grant Spending Per Dollar of State Tax Revenue	22
General Revenue from Federal Government	11
Federal Tax Burden Per Capita	47
Federal Spending Per Dollar of Taxes Paid	13
Highway Charges Returned to States	18
Terms of Trade	10
Federal Personal Income Taxes	48
Federal Share of Medicaid	2

Taxes - Section F

Tax Revenue	22
Per Capita Tax Revenue	45
Tax Effort	36
Tax Capacity	47
Percentage Change in Taxes	16
Property Taxes as a Percentage of Income	48
Property Taxes Per Capita	49
Property Tax Revenue as a Percentage of 3-tax Revenue	49
Sales Taxes as a Percentage of Income	5
Sales Taxes Per Capita	12
Sales Tax Revenue as a Percentage of 3-tax Revenue	9
Sales Tax Rate	10
Income Taxes as a Percentage of Income	22
Income Taxes Per Capita	32
Income Tax Revenue as a Percentage of 3-tax Revenue	22
Highest Personal Income Rate	13
Corporate Income Taxes	27
Motor Fuel Taxes	22
Motor Vehicle Fees	30
Tobacco Taxes	29
Taxes on High-Income Families	23
Taxes in the Largest City in Each State	27
Progressivity of Taxes	15
Per Capita Estate Tax Revenue	41

Revenues and Finances - Section G

Per Capita Total Revenue	50
Per Capita General Revenue	48

"Own-Source" General Revenue	49
Per Capita Non-Tax Revenue	48
Per Capita Total Spending	50
General Spending as a Percentage of Income	23
Per Capita General Spending	49
Change in General Expenditures	20
State Government General Revenue	24
State Government General Spending	23
State Government General Fund Spending	7
State and Local Debt	49
Debt as a Percentage of Revenue	45
Per Capita Full Faith and Credit Debt	41
Bond Ratings	3
State Solvency Index	22
Pension Plan Assets	32
State Reserves	48
Capital Outlays and Interest	50
State Budget Process Quality	42
Relative State Spending "Needs"	34
Structural Deficits	32

Education - Section H

Math Proficiency, Eighth Grade	38
Reading Proficiency, Eighth Grade	36
AFQT Ranks	45
SAT Scores	n/a
ACT Scores	19
Population over 25 with a High School Diploma	48
Students in Private Schools	39
High School Dropout Rates	26
Pupil-Teacher Ratio	36
Public School Enrollment	20
Library Holdings Per Capita	37
Children with Disabilities	21
Education Spending Per Capita	45
Education Spending as a Percentage of General Spending	16
Spending Per Pupil	48
Average Teacher Salary	34
Sources of School Funds	33
State Aid Per Pupil	25
Per Capita Higher Education Spending	30
Higher Education Spending as a Percentage of General Spending	19
Public Higher Education Enrollment	43
Per Pupil Support of Higher Education	9
In-State Tuition and Fees	27
Out-of-State Tuition and Fees	36
Change in Tuition and Fees	18
Affordability Index	25
Average Professor Salary	37
Education Employees	23
R and D Spending	50
Library Operating Spending	49
Head Start Spending	49

Health - Section I

Immunization Rates	20
Infant Mortality Rates	4
State Health Rankings	47
Population without Health Insurance	12
Abortions	34
Alcohol Consumption	47
Percentage of Adult Smokers	6
Percentage Obese	6
AIDS Cases	30
Physicians Per 100,000 Population	45
Hospital Beds Per 1,000 Population	12
Medicaid Recipients	4
Medicaid Recipients as a Percentage of Poverty Population	11
Health and Hospital Spending	41
Health and Hospital Spending as a Percentage of General Spending	33
Per Capita Medicaid Spending	21
Medicaid Spending Per Aged	43
Medicaid Spending Per Child	20
Medicare Payment Per Hospital Day	37
Hospital Expense Per Inpatient Day	46
Population in HMOs	43
Prescription Drugs as a Percentage of Medicaid Costs	26
Percentage Change in Average Price of Prescription Drugs	16

Crime - Section J

Crime Rate	15
Violent Crime Rate	15
Murder Rate	10
Property Crime Rate	17
Motor Vehicle Theft Rate	36
Violent Crime Rate Change	2
Prisoners	28
Change in Prisoners	14
Incarceration Rate	10
Juvenile Violent Crime Rate	38
Law Enforcement Employees	31
Corrections Employees	21
State Corrections Spending	48
Increase in State Corrections Spending	17
Law Enforcement Spending	39
Law Enforcement Spending as a Percentage of General Spending	28

Transportation - Section K

Travel on Interstates	22
Interstate Mileage in "Unacceptable" Condition	9
Deficient Bridges	29
Traffic Deaths	3
Seat Belt Use	45
Vehicle-Miles Traveled Per Capita	14
Use of Public Transportation	45
Road and Street Miles	21
Highway Employees	14
Public Transit Employees	40
Highway Spending Per Capita	18
Highway Spending as a Percentage of General Spending	11

Welfare - Section L

Births to Unwed Mothers	10
TANF Recipients	45
Change in TANF/AFDC Recipients	20
Food Stamp Recipients	6
SSI Recipients	8
WIC Average Monthly Benefit	19
NSLP Recipients	12
Condition of Children Index	44
Families with Single Parent	9
Average Monthly TANF Payments	47
Welfare as a Percentage of Poverty-Level Income	27
State Supplements of SSI	43
State Income Tax Liability of Typical Family in Poverty	13
Child Support Collections	40
Child Support Collections Per Dollar of Administrative Costs	40
Children in Foster Care	41
Welfare Spending Per Capita	24
Welfare Spending as a Percentage of General Spending	10
Administrative Costs Per TANF Case	40

Technology - Section M

Households with Computers	49
Percentage Using Internet	49
Zip Codes with Broadband Service	38
High-Tech Jobs	44
Change in High-Tech Jobs	6
State Government Web Site Ratings	11
Number of Online Government Services	4
Students Per Computer	29
Students Per Internet-Connected Computer	34
Libraries with Internet Access	1

California

Population - Section A

Population 2005	1
Population 2004	1
Population Change 2003–2004	12
Population Change 1994–2004	13
Population 2015	12
Population 2025	1
Percentage 65 and Over	45
Percentage 17 and Under	5
Median Age	45
Percentage African American	26
Percentage American Indian	16
Percentage Asian American	2
Percentage Hispanic	2
Percentage White (Non-Hispanic)	48
Percentage Mixed-Race	6
Percentage in Poverty	16
Child Poverty Rate	15
Percentage Female	42
Birth Rates	7
Death Rates	n/a
Population Density	11
Legal Immigrants FY 2004	1
Unauthorized Immigrants	1

Economies - Section B

Personal Income, 2004	1
Gross State Product	11
Per Capita Personal Income	11
Personal Income from Wages and Salaries	18
Average Annual Pay	5
Average Hourly Earnings	25
Value Added in Manufacturing	34
Cost of Living	2
Average Annual Pay in Manufacturing	4
Average Annual Pay in Retailing	1
Labor Force	38
Unemployment Rate	24
Employment Rate	27
Government Employment	33
Manufacturing Employment	25
Fortune 500 Companies	22
Forbes 500 Companies	14
Tourism Spending Per Capita	19
Exports Per Capita	13
Housing Permits	28
Percentage Change in Home Prices	1
Net Farm Income	1
Financial Institution Assets	20
Bankruptcy Filings	45
Patents Issued	4
WC Disability Payment	9
Average Weekly UC Benefit	11
Economic Momentum	19
One-year Employment Change	19
Manufacturing Employment Change	27
Home Ownership	49
Annual Electricity Use Per Residential Customer	49
Cost Per Kwh	50
New Companies	15

Geography - Section C

Total Land Area	3
Federally Owned Land	3
State Park Acreage	3
State Park Visitors	25
Population Not Active	25
Hunters with Firearms	45
Registered Boats	3
State Spending for the Arts	50
Energy Consumption Per Capita	48
Toxic Chemical Release Per Capita	46
Hazardous Waste Sites	3
Drinking Water Quality	37
Expired Water Pollution Permits	20
Air Pollution Emissions	2

Government - Section D

Members of United States House	1
State Legislators	35
Legislators Per Million Population	50
Units of Government	41
Legislators Compensation	1
Female Legislators	10
Turnover in Legislatures	9
Term Limits	13
Legislative Session Length	1
Democrats in State Legislatures	11
Governors' Power Rating	35
Number of Statewide Elected Officials	6
State and Local Government Employees	45
State and Local Average Salaries	1
Local Employment	5
Local Spending Accountability	43
Registered Voters	38
Percentage of Population Voting	30
Statewide Initiatives	1
Campaign Costs Per Vote	17

Federal Impacts - Section E

Per Capita Federal Spending	34
Increase in Federal Spending	30
Per Capita Federal Grant Spending	23
Per Capita Federal Spending on Procurement	15
Per Capita Federal Spending on Payments to Individuals	45
Per Capita Federal Spending on Social Security and Medicare	41
Social Security Benefits	26
Federal Spending on Employee Wages and Salaries	31
Per Capita Federal Defense Spending	20
Per Capita Homeland Security Grants	50
Federal Grant Spending Per Dollar of State Tax Revenue	36
General Revenue from Federal Government	28
Federal Tax Burden Per Capita	7
Federal Spending Per Dollar of Taxes Paid	43
Highway Charges Returned to States	24
Terms of Trade	40
Federal Personal Income Taxes	11
Federal Share of Medicaid	39

Taxes - Section F

Tax Revenue	17
Per Capita Tax Revenue	9
Tax Effort	23
Tax Capacity	8
Percentage Change in Taxes	7
Property Taxes as a Percentage of Income	36
Property Taxes Per Capita	30
Property Tax Revenue as a Percentage of 3-tax Revenue	37
Sales Taxes as a Percentage of Income	24
Sales Taxes Per Capita	14
Sales Tax Revenue as a Percentage of 3-tax Revenue	24
Sales Tax Rate	7
Income Taxes as a Percentage of Income	13
Income Taxes Per Capita	9
Income Tax Revenue as a Percentage of 3-tax Revenue	12
Highest Personal Income Rate	3
Corporate Income Taxes	6
Motor Fuel Taxes	36
Motor Vehicle Fees	24
Tobacco Taxes	21
Taxes on High-Income Families	4
Taxes in the Largest City in Each State	15
Progressivity of Taxes	27
Per Capita Estate Tax Revenue	8

Revenues and Finances - Section G

Per Capita Total Revenue	6
Per Capita General Revenue	7

"Own-Source" General Revenue	9
Per Capita Non-Tax Revenue	11
Per Capita Total Spending	4
General Spending as a Percentage of Income	24
Per Capita General Spending	6
Change in General Expenditures	5
State Government General Revenue	19
State Government General Spending	10
State Government General Fund Spending	22
State and Local Debt	15
Debt as a Percentage of Revenue	26
Per Capita Full Faith and Credit Debt	27
Bond Ratings	6
State Solvency Index	25
Pension Plan Assets	2
State Reserves	19
Capital Outlays and Interest	24
State Budget Process Quality	35
Relative State Spending "Needs"	48
Structural Deficits	14

Education - Section H

Math Proficiency, Eighth Grade	44
Reading Proficiency, Eighth Grade	49
AFQT Ranks	40
SAT Scores	10
ACT Scores	n/a
Population over 25 with a High School Diploma	44
Students in Private Schools	23
High School Dropout Rates	31
Pupil-Teacher Ratio	3
Public School Enrollment	6
Library Holdings Per Capita	40
Children with Disabilities	50
Education Spending Per Capita	16
Education Spending as a Percentage of General Spending	39
Spending Per Pupil	31
Average Teacher Salary	2
Sources of School Funds	44
State Aid Per Pupil	9
Per Capita Higher Education Spending	25
Higher Education Spending as a Percentage of General Spending	38
Public Higher Education Enrollment	10
Per Pupil Support of Higher Education	23
In-State Tuition and Fees	33
Out-of-State Tuition and Fees	3
Change in Tuition and Fees	6
Affordability Index	1
Average Professor Salary	4
Education Employees	46
R and D Spending	7
Library Operating Spending	26
Head Start Spending	6

Health - Section I

Immunization Rates	26
Infant Mortality Rates	43
State Health Rankings	22
Population without Health Insurance	6
Abortions	n/a
Alcohol Consumption	28
Percentage of Adult Smokers	48
Percentage Obese	31
AIDS Cases	17
Physicians Per 100,000 Population	23
Hospital Beds Per 1,000 Population	45
Medicaid Recipients	10
Medicaid Recipients as a Percentage of Poverty Population	17
Health and Hospital Spending	11
Health and Hospital Spending as a Percentage of General Spending	13
Per Capita Medicaid Spending	26
Medicaid Spending Per Aged	48
Medicaid Spending Per Child	41
Medicare Payment Per Hospital Day	2
Hospital Expense Per Inpatient Day	21
Population in HMOs	1
Prescription Drugs as a Percentage of Medicaid Costs	23
Percentage Change in Average Price of Prescription Drugs	46

Crime - Section J

Crime Rate	24
Violent Crime Rate	10
Murder Rate	9
Property Crime Rate	25
Motor Vehicle Theft Rate	3
Violent Crime Rate Change	34
Prisoners	2
Change in Prisoners	38
Incarceration Rate	16
Juvenile Violent Crime Rate	7
Law Enforcement Employees	29
Corrections Employees	22
State Corrections Spending	20
Increase in State Corrections Spending	45
Law Enforcement Spending	3
Law Enforcement Spending as a Percentage of General Spending	6

Transportation - Section K

Travel on Interstates	17
Interstate Mileage in "Unacceptable" Condition	5
Deficient Bridges	21
Traffic Deaths	35
Seat Belt Use	5
Vehicle-Miles Traveled Per Capita	39
Use of Public Transportation	8
Road and Street Miles	43
Highway Employees	50
Public Transit Employees	6
Highway Spending Per Capita	47
Highway Spending as a Percentage of General Spending	49

Welfare - Section L

Births to Unwed Mothers	29
TANF Recipients	2
Change in TANF/AFDC Recipients	25
Food Stamp Recipients	43
SSI Recipients	6
WIC Average Monthly Benefit	10
NSLP Recipients	47
Condition of Children Index	17
Families with Single Parent	23
Average Monthly TANF Payments	7
Welfare as a Percentage of Poverty-Level Income	2
State Supplements of SSI	13
State Income Tax Liability of Typical Family in Poverty	17
Child Support Collections	35
Child Support Collections Per Dollar of Administrative Costs	49
Children in Foster Care	7
Welfare Spending Per Capita	19
Welfare Spending as a Percentage of General Spending	30
Administrative Costs Per TANF Case	19

Technology - Section M

Households with Computers	13
Percentage Using Internet	11
Zip Codes with Broadband Service	6
High-Tech Jobs	6
Change in High-Tech Jobs	38
State Government Web Site Ratings	46
Number of Online Government Services	49
Students Per Computer	2
Students Per Internet-Connected Computer	2
Libraries with Internet Access	24

Colorado

Population - Section A

Population 2005	22
Population 2004	22
Population Change 2003–2004	14
Population Change 1994–2004	3
Population 2015	21
Population 2025	22
Percentage 65 and Over	47
Percentage 17 and Under	13
Median Age	43
Percentage African American	33
Percentage American Indian	17
Percentage Asian American	19
Percentage Hispanic	6
Percentage White (Non-Hispanic)	30
Percentage Mixed-Race	8
Percentage in Poverty	34
Child Poverty Rate	41
Percentage Female	48
Birth Rates	7
Death Rates	35
Population Density	37
Legal Immigrants FY 2004	18
Unauthorized Immigrants	10

Economies - Section B

Personal Income, 2004	21
Gross State Product	10
Per Capita Personal Income	9
Personal Income from Wages and Salaries	19
Average Annual Pay	12
Average Hourly Earnings	22
Value Added in Manufacturing	42
Cost of Living	24
Average Annual Pay in Manufacturing	8
Average Annual Pay in Retailing	12
Labor Force	10
Unemployment Rate	22
Employment Rate	29
Government Employment	30
Manufacturing Employment	41
Fortune 500 Companies	12
Forbes 500 Companies	18
Tourism Spending Per Capita	10
Exports Per Capita	40
Housing Permits	9
Percentage Change in Home Prices	32
Net Farm Income	23
Financial Institution Assets	44
Bankruptcy Filings	18
Patents Issued	8
WC Disability Payment	21
Average Weekly UC Benefit	7
Economic Momentum	14
One-year Employment Change	11
Manufacturing Employment Change	43
Home Ownership	30
Annual Electricity Use Per Residential Customer	39
Cost Per Kwh	30
New Companies	4

Geography - Section C

Total Land Area	8
Federally Owned Land	11
State Park Acreage	8
State Park Visitors	23
Population Not Active	42
Hunters with Firearms	36
Registered Boats	34
State Spending for the Arts	48
Energy Consumption Per Capita	39
Toxic Chemical Release Per Capita	40
Hazardous Waste Sites	20
Drinking Water Quality	30
Expired Water Pollution Permits	26
Air Pollution Emissions	27

Government - Section D

Members of United States House	22
State Legislators	42
Legislators Per Million Population	38
Units of Government	20
Legislators Compensation	17
Female Legislators	7
Turnover in Legislatures	15
Term Limits	4
Legislative Session Length	9
Democrats in State Legislatures	20
Governors' Power Rating	17
Number of Statewide Elected Officials	34
State and Local Government Employees	30
State and Local Average Salaries	15
Local Employment	14
Local Spending Accountability	3
Registered Voters	10
Percentage of Population Voting	14
Statewide Initiatives	n/a
Campaign Costs Per Vote	44

Federal Impacts - Section E

Per Capita Federal Spending	33
Increase in Federal Spending	33
Per Capita Federal Grant Spending	46
Per Capita Federal Spending on Procurement	13
Per Capita Federal Spending on Payments to Individuals	48
Per Capita Federal Spending on Social Security and Medicare	48
Social Security Benefits	28
Federal Spending on Employee Wages and Salaries	11
Per Capita Federal Defense Spending	12
Per Capita Homeland Security Grants	29
Federal Grant Spending Per Dollar of State Tax Revenue	35
General Revenue from Federal Government	46
Federal Tax Burden Per Capita	9
Federal Spending Per Dollar of Taxes Paid	41
Highway Charges Returned to States	27
Terms of Trade	46
Federal Personal Income Taxes	12
Federal Share of Medicaid	39

Taxes - Section F

Tax Revenue	45
Per Capita Tax Revenue	19
Tax Effort	26
Tax Capacity	15
Percentage Change in Taxes	4
Property Taxes as a Percentage of Income	34
Property Taxes Per Capita	25
Property Tax Revenue as a Percentage of 3-tax Revenue	29
Sales Taxes as a Percentage of Income	30
Sales Taxes Per Capita	16
Sales Tax Revenue as a Percentage of 3-tax Revenue	23
Sales Tax Rate	45
Income Taxes as a Percentage of Income	30
Income Taxes Per Capita	17
Income Tax Revenue as a Percentage of 3-tax Revenue	21
Highest Personal Income Rate	34
Corporate Income Taxes	39
Motor Fuel Taxes	20
Motor Vehicle Fees	28
Tobacco Taxes	22
Taxes on High-Income Families	41
Taxes in the Largest City in Each State	40
Progressivity of Taxes	17
Per Capita Estate Tax Revenue	17

Revenues and Finances - Section G

Per Capita Total Revenue	35
Per Capita General Revenue	22

"Own-Source" General Revenue	11
Per Capita Non-Tax Revenue	6
Per Capita Total Spending	16
General Spending as a Percentage of Income	43
Per Capita General Spending	20
Change in General Expenditures	1
State Government General Revenue	45
State Government General Spending	46
State Government General Fund Spending	49
State and Local Debt	16
Debt as a Percentage of Revenue	15
Per Capita Full Faith and Credit Debt	22
Bond Ratings	n/a
State Solvency Index	33
Pension Plan Assets	27
State Reserves	46
Capital Outlays and Interest	7
State Budget Process Quality	14
Relative State Spending "Needs"	20
Structural Deficits	35

Education · Section H

Math Proficiency, Eighth Grade	20
Reading Proficiency, Eighth Grade	19
AFQT Ranks	10
SAT Scores	n/a
ACT Scores	21
Population over 25 with a High School Diploma	16
Students in Private Schools	38
High School Dropout Rates	31
Pupil-Teacher Ratio	9
Public School Enrollment	14
Library Holdings Per Capita	29
Children with Disabilities	49
Education Spending Per Capita	29
Education Spending as a Percentage of General Spending	32
Spending Per Pupil	24
Average Teacher Salary	23
Sources of School Funds	14
State Aid Per Pupil	37
Per Capita Higher Education Spending	19
Higher Education Spending as a Percentage of General Spending	23
Public Higher Education Enrollment	11
Per Pupil Support of Higher Education	49
In-State Tuition and Fees	42
Out-of-State Tuition and Fees	5
Change in Tuition and Fees	48
Affordability Index	11
Average Professor Salary	14
Education Employees	39
R and D Spending	12
Library Operating Spending	9
Head Start Spending	27

Health · Section I

Immunization Rates	44
Infant Mortality Rates	24
State Health Rankings	17
Population without Health Insurance	15
Abortions	39
Alcohol Consumption	7
Percentage of Adult Smokers	34
Percentage Obese	50
AIDS Cases	27
Physicians Per 100,000 Population	17
Hospital Beds Per 1,000 Population	44
Medicaid Recipients	46
Medicaid Recipients as a Percentage of Poverty Population	46
Health and Hospital Spending	22
Health and Hospital Spending as a Percentage of General Spending	26
Per Capita Medicaid Spending	47
Medicaid Spending Per Aged	23
Medicaid Spending Per Child	11
Medicare Payment Per Hospital Day	6
Hospital Expense Per Inpatient Day	11
Population in HMOs	12
Prescription Drugs as a Percentage of Medicaid Costs	46
Percentage Change in Average Price of Prescription Drugs	25

Crime · Section J

Crime Rate	21
Violent Crime Rate	25
Murder Rate	29
Property Crime Rate	19
Motor Vehicle Theft Rate	7
Violent Crime Rate Change	4
Prisoners	24
Change in Prisoners	7
Incarceration Rate	18
Juvenile Violent Crime Rate	20
Law Enforcement Employees	21
Corrections Employees	27
State Corrections Spending	35
Increase in State Corrections Spending	26
Law Enforcement Spending	13
Law Enforcement Spending as a Percentage of General Spending	11

Transportation · Section K

Travel on Interstates	27
Interstate Mileage in "Unacceptable" Condition	18
Deficient Bridges	45
Traffic Deaths	25
Seat Belt Use	29
Vehicle-Miles Traveled Per Capita	34
Use of Public Transportation	16
Road and Street Miles	38
Highway Employees	28
Public Transit Employees	12
Highway Spending Per Capita	5
Highway Spending as a Percentage of General Spending	8

Welfare · Section L

Births to Unwed Mothers	47
TANF Recipients	39
Change in TANF/AFDC Recipients	24
Food Stamp Recipients	47
SSI Recipients	47
WIC Average Monthly Benefit	24
NSLP Recipients	48
Condition of Children Index	26
Families with Single Parent	39
Average Monthly TANF Payments	21
Welfare as a Percentage of Poverty-Level Income	36
State Supplements of SSI	14
State Income Tax Liability of Typical Family in Poverty	17
Child Support Collections	45
Child Support Collections Per Dollar of Administrative Costs	43
Children in Foster Care	24
Welfare Spending Per Capita	48
Welfare Spending as a Percentage of General Spending	48
Administrative Costs Per TANF Case	11

Technology · Section M

Households with Computers	5
Percentage Using Internet	3
Zip Codes with Broadband Service	23
High-Tech Jobs	1
Change in High-Tech Jobs	48
State Government Web Site Ratings	13
Number of Online Government Services	11
Students Per Computer	11
Students Per Internet-Connected Computer	10
Libraries with Internet Access	36

Connecticut

Population - Section A

Population 2005	29
Population 2004	29
Population Change 2003–2004	39
Population Change 1994–2004	39
Population 2015	39
Population 2025	30
Percentage 65 and Over	12
Percentage 17 and Under	31
Median Age	8
Percentage African American	21
Percentage American Indian	37
Percentage Asian American	15
Percentage Hispanic	11
Percentage White (Non-Hispanic)	28
Percentage Mixed-Race	20
Percentage in Poverty	34
Child Poverty Rate	38
Percentage Female	7
Birth Rates	44
Death Rates	46
Population Density	4
Legal Immigrants FY 2004	15
Unauthorized Immigrants	27

Economies - Section B

Personal Income, 2004	23
Gross State Product	2
Per Capita Personal Income	1
Personal Income from Wages and Salaries	26
Average Annual Pay	1
Average Hourly Earnings	3
Value Added in Manufacturing	17
Cost of Living	7
Average Annual Pay in Manufacturing	1
Average Annual Pay in Retailing	2
Labor Force	25
Unemployment Rate	20
Employment Rate	31
Government Employment	41
Manufacturing Employment	19
Fortune 500 Companies	1
Forbes 500 Companies	1
Tourism Spending Per Capita	14
Exports Per Capita	18
Housing Permits	47
Percentage Change in Home Prices	15
Net Farm Income	45
Financial Institution Assets	26
Bankruptcy Filings	46
Patents Issued	9
WC Disability Payment	4
Average Weekly UC Benefit	8
Economic Momentum	29
One-year Employment Change	26
Manufacturing Employment Change	26
Home Ownership	26
Annual Electricity Use Per Residential Customer	34
Cost Per Kwh	42
New Companies	33

Geography - Section C

Total Land Area	48
Federally Owned Land	49
State Park Acreage	16
State Park Visitors	31
Population Not Active	40
Hunters with Firearms	48
Registered Boats	31
State Spending for the Arts	5
Energy Consumption Per Capita	45
Toxic Chemical Release Per Capita	47
Hazardous Waste Sites	23
Drinking Water Quality	16
Expired Water Pollution Permits	10
Air Pollution Emissions	41

Government - Section D

Members of United States House	27
State Legislators	9
Legislators Per Million Population	17
Units of Government	37
Legislators Compensation	19
Female Legislators	14
Turnover in Legislatures	34
Term Limits	n/a
Legislative Session Length	23
Democrats in State Legislatures	7
Governors' Power Rating	17
Number of Statewide Elected Officials	22
State and Local Government Employees	39
State and Local Average Salaries	4
Local Employment	37
Local Spending Accountability	7
Registered Voters	22
Percentage of Population Voting	12
Statewide Initiatives	n/a
Campaign Costs Per Vote	32

Federal Impacts - Section E

Per Capita Federal Spending	8
Increase in Federal Spending	5
Per Capita Federal Grant Spending	21
Per Capita Federal Spending on Procurement	4
Per Capita Federal Spending on Payments to Individuals	27
Per Capita Federal Spending on Social Security and Medicare	6
Social Security Benefits	2
Federal Spending on Employee Wages and Salaries	45
Per Capita Federal Defense Spending	4
Per Capita Homeland Security Grants	22
Federal Grant Spending Per Dollar of State Tax Revenue	46
General Revenue from Federal Government	43
Federal Tax Burden Per Capita	1
Federal Spending Per Dollar of Taxes Paid	48
Highway Charges Returned to States	12
Terms of Trade	49
Federal Personal Income Taxes	1
Federal Share of Medicaid	39

Taxes - Section F

Tax Revenue	27
Per Capita Tax Revenue	2
Tax Effort	2
Tax Capacity	2
Percentage Change in Taxes	48
Property Taxes as a Percentage of Income	8
Property Taxes Per Capita	2
Property Tax Revenue as a Percentage of 3-tax Revenue	11
Sales Taxes as a Percentage of Income	40
Sales Taxes Per Capita	8
Sales Tax Revenue as a Percentage of 3-tax Revenue	39
Sales Tax Rate	10
Income Taxes as a Percentage of Income	21
Income Taxes Per Capita	5
Income Tax Revenue as a Percentage of 3-tax Revenue	26
Highest Personal Income Rate	31
Corporate Income Taxes	41
Motor Fuel Taxes	11
Motor Vehicle Fees	18
Tobacco Taxes	6
Taxes on High-Income Families	2
Taxes in the Largest City in Each State	4
Progressivity of Taxes	33
Per Capita Estate Tax Revenue	14

Revenues and Finances - Section G

Per Capita Total Revenue	5
Per Capita General Revenue	6

"Own-Source" General Revenue	5
Per Capita Non-Tax Revenue	49
Per Capita Total Spending	7
General Spending as a Percentage of Income	48
Per Capita General Spending	4
Change in General Expenditures	32
State Government General Revenue	11
State Government General Spending	8
State Government General Fund Spending	23
State and Local Debt	4
Debt as a Percentage of Revenue	8
Per Capita Full Faith and Credit Debt	1
Bond Ratings	4
State Solvency Index	50
Pension Plan Assets	11
State Reserves	35
Capital Outlays and Interest	14
State Budget Process Quality	15
Relative State Spending "Needs"	26
Structural Deficits	5

Education - Section H

Math Proficiency, Eighth Grade	20
Reading Proficiency, Eighth Grade	23
AFQT Ranks	29
SAT Scores	8
ACT Scores	n/a
Population over 25 with a High School Diploma	13
Students in Private Schools	16
High School Dropout Rates	10
Pupil-Teacher Ratio	41
Public School Enrollment	18
Library Holdings Per Capita	9
Children with Disabilities	40
Education Spending Per Capita	9
Education Spending as a Percentage of General Spending	40
Spending Per Pupil	3
Average Teacher Salary	1
Sources of School Funds	9
State Aid Per Pupil	18
Per Capita Higher Education Spending	43
Higher Education Spending as a Percentage of General Spending	47
Public Higher Education Enrollment	42
Per Pupil Support of Higher Education	14
In-State Tuition and Fees	12
Out-of-State Tuition and Fees	11
Change in Tuition and Fees	33
Affordability Index	27
Average Professor Salary	3
Education Employees	15
R and D Spending	6
Library Operating Spending	5
Head Start Spending	19

Health - Section I

Immunization Rates	7
Infant Mortality Rates	36
State Health Rankings	7
Population without Health Insurance	36
Abortions	5
Alcohol Consumption	28
Percentage of Adult Smokers	46
Percentage Obese	46
AIDS Cases	8
Physicians Per 100,000 Population	5
Hospital Beds Per 1,000 Population	38
Medicaid Recipients	39
Medicaid Recipients as a Percentage of Poverty Population	30
Health and Hospital Spending	14
Health and Hospital Spending as a Percentage of General Spending	23
Per Capita Medicaid Spending	11
Medicaid Spending Per Aged	1
Medicaid Spending Per Child	46
Medicare Payment Per Hospital Day	28
Hospital Expense Per Inpatient Day	23
Population in HMOs	4
Prescription Drugs as a Percentage of Medicaid Costs	39
Percentage Change in Average Price of Prescription Drugs	21

Crime - Section J

Crime Rate	39
Violent Crime Rate	34
Murder Rate	34
Property Crime Rate	39
Motor Vehicle Theft Rate	28
Violent Crime Rate Change	37
Prisoners	25
Change in Prisoners	34
Incarceration Rate	29
Juvenile Violent Crime Rate	12
Law Enforcement Employees	13
Corrections Employees	30
State Corrections Spending	24
Increase in State Corrections Spending	18
Law Enforcement Spending	15
Law Enforcement Spending as a Percentage of General Spending	30

Transportation - Section K

Travel on Interstates	2
Interstate Mileage in "Unacceptable" Condition	14
Deficient Bridges	13
Traffic Deaths	49
Seat Belt Use	23
Vehicle-Miles Traveled Per Capita	40
Use of Public Transportation	10
Road and Street Miles	18
Highway Employees	36
Public Transit Employees	34
Highway Spending Per Capita	37
Highway Spending as a Percentage of General Spending	46

Welfare - Section L

Births to Unwed Mothers	38
TANF Recipients	30
Change in TANF/AFDC Recipients	8
Food Stamp Recipients	41
SSI Recipients	40
WIC Average Monthly Benefit	6
NSLP Recipients	37
Condition of Children Index	11
Families with Single Parent	28
Average Monthly TANF Payments	10
Welfare as a Percentage of Poverty-Level Income	1
State Supplements of SSI	5
State Income Tax Liability of Typical Family in Poverty	17
Child Support Collections	29
Child Support Collections Per Dollar of Administrative Costs	46
Children in Foster Care	21
Welfare Spending Per Capita	20
Welfare Spending as a Percentage of General Spending	33
Administrative Costs Per TANF Case	15

Technology - Section M

Households with Computers	6
Percentage Using Internet	4
Zip Codes with Broadband Service	1
High-Tech Jobs	20
Change in High-Tech Jobs	46
State Government Web Site Ratings	19
Number of Online Government Services	22
Students Per Computer	22
Students Per Internet-Connected Computer	15
Libraries with Internet Access	40

Delaware

Population - Section A

Population 2005	45
Population 2004	45
Population Change 2003–2004	8
Population Change 1994–2004	10
Population 2015	15
Population 2025	45
Percentage 65 and Over	19
Percentage 17 and Under	39
Median Age	16
Percentage African American	8
Percentage American Indian	32
Percentage Asian American	18
Percentage Hispanic	25
Percentage White (Non-Hispanic)	31
Percentage Mixed-Race	22
Percentage in Poverty	45
Child Poverty Rate	33
Percentage Female	13
Birth Rates	21
Death Rates	22
Population Density	6
Legal Immigrants FY 2004	41
Unauthorized Immigrants	38

Economies - Section B

Personal Income, 2004	44
Gross State Product	1
Per Capita Personal Income	10
Personal Income from Wages and Salaries	1
Average Annual Pay	7
Average Hourly Earnings	7
Value Added in Manufacturing	31
Cost of Living	18
Average Annual Pay in Manufacturing	12
Average Annual Pay in Retailing	20
Labor Force	18
Unemployment Rate	38
Employment Rate	13
Government Employment	46
Manufacturing Employment	38
Fortune 500 Companies	8
Forbes 500 Companies	7
Tourism Spending Per Capita	39
Exports Per Capita	15
Housing Permits	10
Percentage Change in Home Prices	14
Net Farm Income	38
Financial Institution Assets	2
Bankruptcy Filings	36
Patents Issued	10
WC Disability Payment	39
Average Weekly UC Benefit	30
Economic Momentum	16
One-year Employment Change	14
Manufacturing Employment Change	49
Home Ownership	3
Annual Electricity Use Per Residential Customer	22
Cost Per Kwh	23
New Companies	10

Geography - Section C

Total Land Area	49
Federally Owned Land	48
State Park Acreage	47
State Park Visitors	9
Population Not Active	28
Hunters with Firearms	18
Registered Boats	43
State Spending for the Arts	6
Energy Consumption Per Capita	21
Toxic Chemical Release Per Capita	19
Hazardous Waste Sites	23
Drinking Water Quality	21
Expired Water Pollution Permits	4
Air Pollution Emissions	48

Government - Section D

Members of United States House	44
State Legislators	48
Legislators Per Million Population	11
Units of Government	21
Legislators Compensation	11
Female Legislators	2
Turnover in Legislatures	42
Term Limits	n/a
Legislative Session Length	3
Democrats in State Legislatures	30
Governors' Power Rating	26
Number of Statewide Elected Officials	22
State and Local Government Employees	16
State and Local Average Salaries	18
Local Employment	49
Local Spending Accountability	46
Registered Voters	13
Percentage of Population Voting	24
Statewide Initiatives	n/a
Campaign Costs Per Vote	33

Federal Impacts - Section E

Per Capita Federal Spending	39
Increase in Federal Spending	31
Per Capita Federal Grant Spending	26
Per Capita Federal Spending on Procurement	49
Per Capita Federal Spending on Payments to Individuals	25
Per Capita Federal Spending on Social Security and Medicare	21
Social Security Benefits	5
Federal Spending on Employee Wages and Salaries	33
Per Capita Federal Defense Spending	32
Per Capita Homeland Security Grants	6
Federal Grant Spending Per Dollar of State Tax Revenue	45
General Revenue from Federal Government	45
Federal Tax Burden Per Capita	13
Federal Spending Per Dollar of Taxes Paid	40
Highway Charges Returned to States	9
Terms of Trade	35
Federal Personal Income Taxes	15
Federal Share of Medicaid	38

Taxes - Section F

Tax Revenue	15
Per Capita Tax Revenue	13
Tax Effort	39
Tax Capacity	3
Percentage Change in Taxes	20
Property Taxes as a Percentage of Income	49
Property Taxes Per Capita	43
Property Tax Revenue as a Percentage of 3-tax Revenue	40
Sales Taxes as a Percentage of Income	49
Sales Taxes Per Capita	49
Sales Tax Revenue as a Percentage of 3-tax Revenue	47
Sales Tax Rate	n/a
Income Taxes as a Percentage of Income	12
Income Taxes Per Capita	8
Income Tax Revenue as a Percentage of 3-tax Revenue	1
Highest Personal Income Rate	24
Corporate Income Taxes	2
Motor Fuel Taxes	18
Motor Vehicle Fees	38
Tobacco Taxes	32
Taxes on High-Income Families	37
Taxes in the Largest City in Each State	39
Progressivity of Taxes	18
Per Capita Estate Tax Revenue	1

Revenues and Finances - Section G

Per Capita Total Revenue	4
Per Capita General Revenue	4

"Own-Source" General Revenue	4
Per Capita Non-Tax Revenue	3
Per Capita Total Spending	13
General Spending as a Percentage of Income	20
Per Capita General Spending	8
Change in General Expenditures	33
State Government General Revenue	3
State Government General Spending	5
State Government General Fund Spending	5
State and Local Debt	8
Debt as a Percentage of Revenue	19
Per Capita Full Faith and Credit Debt	18
Bond Ratings	1
State Solvency Index	8
Pension Plan Assets	15
State Reserves	2
Capital Outlays and Interest	11
State Budget Process Quality	21
Relative State Spending "Needs"	13
Structural Deficits	6

Education · Section H

Math Proficiency, Eighth Grade	20
Reading Proficiency, Eighth Grade	17
AFQT Ranks	36
SAT Scores	20
ACT Scores	n/a
Population over 25 with a High School Diploma	30
Students in Private Schools	1
High School Dropout Rates	38
Pupil-Teacher Ratio	25
Public School Enrollment	50
Library Holdings Per Capita	44
Children with Disabilities	14
Education Spending Per Capita	4
Education Spending as a Percentage of General Spending	19
Spending Per Pupil	6
Average Teacher Salary	12
Sources of School Funds	43
State Aid Per Pupil	4
Per Capita Higher Education Spending	5
Higher Education Spending as a Percentage of General Spending	10
Public Higher Education Enrollment	19
Per Pupil Support of Higher Education	18
In-State Tuition and Fees	8
Out-of-State Tuition and Fees	21
Change in Tuition and Fees	30
Affordability Index	35
Average Professor Salary	9
Education Employees	38
R and D Spending	39
Library Operating Spending	37
Head Start Spending	50

Health · Section I

Immunization Rates	13
Infant Mortality Rates	19
State Health Rankings	33
Population without Health Insurance	21
Abortions	4
Alcohol Consumption	3
Percentage of Adult Smokers	11
Percentage Obese	39
AIDS Cases	6
Physicians Per 100,000 Population	16
Hospital Beds Per 1,000 Population	36
Medicaid Recipients	17
Medicaid Recipients as a Percentage of Poverty Population	3
Health and Hospital Spending	33
Health and Hospital Spending as a Percentage of General Spending	39
Per Capita Medicaid Spending	20
Medicaid Spending Per Aged	7
Medicaid Spending Per Child	6
Medicare Payment Per Hospital Day	48
Hospital Expense Per Inpatient Day	29
Population in HMOs	37
Prescription Drugs as a Percentage of Medicaid Costs	10
Percentage Change in Average Price of Prescription Drugs	12

Crime · Section J

Crime Rate	27
Violent Crime Rate	9
Murder Rate	45
Property Crime Rate	30
Motor Vehicle Theft Rate	34
Violent Crime Rate Change	45
Prisoners	35
Change in Prisoners	28
Incarceration Rate	11
Juvenile Violent Crime Rate	2
Law Enforcement Employees	17
Corrections Employees	1
State Corrections Spending	27
Increase in State Corrections Spending	39
Law Enforcement Spending	4
Law Enforcement Spending as a Percentage of General Spending	5

Transportation · Section K

Travel on Interstates	50
Interstate Mileage in "Unacceptable" Condition	13
Deficient Bridges	47
Traffic Deaths	26
Seat Belt Use	19
Vehicle-Miles Traveled Per Capita	20
Use of Public Transportation	18
Road and Street Miles	2
Highway Employees	15
Public Transit Employees	10
Highway Spending Per Capita	12
Highway Spending as a Percentage of General Spending	18

Welfare · Section L

Births to Unwed Mothers	4
TANF Recipients	21
Change in TANF/AFDC Recipients	40
Food Stamp Recipients	27
SSI Recipients	35
WIC Average Monthly Benefit	40
NSLP Recipients	14
Condition of Children Index	31
Families with Single Parent	13
Average Monthly TANF Payments	35
Welfare as a Percentage of Poverty-Level Income	15
State Supplements of SSI	17
State Income Tax Liability of Typical Family in Poverty	16
Child Support Collections	20
Child Support Collections Per Dollar of Administrative Costs	48
Children in Foster Care	43
Welfare Spending Per Capita	33
Welfare Spending as a Percentage of General Spending	44
Administrative Costs Per TANF Case	33

Technology · Section M

Households with Computers	20
Percentage Using Internet	19
Zip Codes with Broadband Service	16
High-Tech Jobs	17
Change in High-Tech Jobs	29
State Government Web Site Ratings	7
Number of Online Government Services	13
Students Per Computer	n/a
Students Per Internet-Connected Computer	n/a
Libraries with Internet Access	1

Florida

Population - Section A

Population 2005	4
Population 2004	4
Population Change 2003–2004	3
Population Change 1994–2004	5
Population 2015	3
Population 2025	3
Percentage 65 and Over	1
Percentage 17 and Under	42
Median Age	5
Percentage African American	13
Percentage American Indian	31
Percentage Asian American	24
Percentage Hispanic	7
Percentage White (Non-Hispanic)	39
Percentage Mixed-Race	28
Percentage in Poverty	23
Child Poverty Rate	25
Percentage Female	19
Birth Rates	41
Death Rates	39
Population Density	8
Legal Immigrants FY 2004	4
Unauthorized Immigrants	5

Economies - Section B

Personal Income, 2004	4
Gross State Product	38
Per Capita Personal Income	24
Personal Income from Wages and Salaries	43
Average Annual Pay	25
Average Hourly Earnings	43
Value Added in Manufacturing	46
Cost of Living	20
Average Annual Pay in Manufacturing	27
Average Annual Pay in Retailing	14
Labor Force	36
Unemployment Rate	49
Employment Rate	2
Government Employment	45
Manufacturing Employment	44
Fortune 500 Companies	30
Forbes 500 Companies	39
Tourism Spending Per Capita	4
Exports Per Capita	30
Housing Permits	3
Percentage Change in Home Prices	5
Net Farm Income	11
Financial Institution Assets	47
Bankruptcy Filings	30
Patents Issued	30
WC Disability Payment	25
Average Weekly UC Benefit	38
Economic Momentum	3
One-year Employment Change	5
Manufacturing Employment Change	17
Home Ownership	23
Annual Electricity Use Per Residential Customer	4
Cost Per Kwh	32
New Companies	6

Geography - Section C

Total Land Area	26
Federally Owned Land	18
State Park Acreage	4
State Park Visitors	43
Population Not Active	22
Hunters with Firearms	38
Registered Boats	1
State Spending for the Arts	20
Energy Consumption Per Capita	44
Toxic Chemical Release Per Capita	37
Hazardous Waste Sites	6
Drinking Water Quality	33
Expired Water Pollution Permits	19
Air Pollution Emissions	3

Government - Section D

Members of United States House	4
State Legislators	18
Legislators Per Million Population	48
Units of Government	48
Legislators Compensation	18
Female Legislators	22
Turnover in Legislatures	32
Term Limits	4
Legislative Session Length	30
Democrats in State Legislatures	44
Governors' Power Rating	17
Number of Statewide Elected Officials	15
State and Local Government Employees	46
State and Local Average Salaries	22
Local Employment	6
Local Spending Accountability	4
Registered Voters	25
Percentage of Population Voting	19
Statewide Initiatives	n/a
Campaign Costs Per Vote	47

Federal Impacts - Section E

Per Capita Federal Spending	29
Increase in Federal Spending	26
Per Capita Federal Grant Spending	48
Per Capita Federal Spending on Procurement	33
Per Capita Federal Spending on Payments to Individuals	5
Per Capita Federal Spending on Social Security and Medicare	3
Social Security Benefits	22
Federal Spending on Employee Wages and Salaries	32
Per Capita Federal Defense Spending	26
Per Capita Homeland Security Grants	47
Federal Grant Spending Per Dollar of State Tax Revenue	38
General Revenue from Federal Government	44
Federal Tax Burden Per Capita	18
Federal Spending Per Dollar of Taxes Paid	32
Highway Charges Returned to States	34
Terms of Trade	43
Federal Personal Income Taxes	18
Federal Share of Medicaid	28

Taxes - Section F

Tax Revenue	44
Per Capita Tax Revenue	34
Tax Effort	42
Tax Capacity	18
Percentage Change in Taxes	17
Property Taxes as a Percentage of Income	19
Property Taxes Per Capita	21
Property Tax Revenue as a Percentage of 3-tax Revenue	14
Sales Taxes as a Percentage of Income	10
Sales Taxes Per Capita	6
Sales Tax Revenue as a Percentage of 3-tax Revenue	5
Sales Tax Rate	10
Income Taxes as a Percentage of Income	n/a
Income Taxes Per Capita	n/a
Income Tax Revenue as a Percentage of 3-tax Revenue	n/a
Highest Personal Income Rate	n/a
Corporate Income Taxes	20
Motor Fuel Taxes	46
Motor Vehicle Fees	22
Tobacco Taxes	43
Taxes on High-Income Families	48
Taxes in the Largest City in Each State	49
Progressivity of Taxes	6
Per Capita Estate Tax Revenue	2

Revenues and Finances - Section G

Per Capita Total Revenue	37
Per Capita General Revenue	39

"Own-Source" General Revenue	29
Per Capita Non-Tax Revenue	14
Per Capita Total Spending	43
General Spending as a Percentage of Income	41
Per Capita General Spending	41
Change in General Expenditures	29
State Government General Revenue	50
State Government General Spending	50
State Government General Fund Spending	45
State and Local Debt	22
Debt as a Percentage of Revenue	16
Per Capita Full Faith and Credit Debt	40
Bond Ratings	2
State Solvency Index	12
Pension Plan Assets	10
State Reserves	6
Capital Outlays and Interest	15
State Budget Process Quality	13
Relative State Spending "Needs"	5
Structural Deficits	45

Education - Section H

Math Proficiency, Eighth Grade	35
Reading Proficiency, Eighth Grade	41
AFQT Ranks	37
SAT Scores	22
ACT Scores	n/a
Population over 25 with a High School Diploma	33
Students in Private Schools	17
High School Dropout Rates	49
Pupil-Teacher Ratio	12
Public School Enrollment	45
Library Holdings Per Capita	48
Children with Disabilities	19
Education Spending Per Capita	50
Education Spending as a Percentage of General Spending	47
Spending Per Pupil	40
Average Teacher Salary	31
Sources of School Funds	19
State Aid Per Pupil	41
Per Capita Higher Education Spending	50
Higher Education Spending as a Percentage of General Spending	46
Public Higher Education Enrollment	39
Per Pupil Support of Higher Education	30
In-State Tuition and Fees	49
Out-of-State Tuition and Fees	25
Change in Tuition and Fees	43
Affordability Index	33
Average Professor Salary	22
Education Employees	47
R and D Spending	35
Library Operating Spending	32
Head Start Spending	15

Health - Section I

Immunization Rates	3
Infant Mortality Rates	19
State Health Rankings	40
Population without Health Insurance	3
Abortions	3
Alcohol Consumption	6
Percentage of Adult Smokers	32
Percentage Obese	29
AIDS Cases	2
Physicians Per 100,000 Population	22
Hospital Beds Per 1,000 Population	22
Medicaid Recipients	31
Medicaid Recipients as a Percentage of Poverty Population	35
Health and Hospital Spending	24
Health and Hospital Spending as a Percentage of General Spending	17
Per Capita Medicaid Spending	37
Medicaid Spending Per Aged	39
Medicaid Spending Per Child	38
Medicare Payment Per Hospital Day	5
Hospital Expense Per Inpatient Day	43
Population in HMOs	8
Prescription Drugs as a Percentage of Medicaid Costs	3
Percentage Change in Average Price of Prescription Drugs	8

Crime - Section J

Crime Rate	9
Violent Crime Rate	2
Murder Rate	20
Property Crime Rate	13
Motor Vehicle Theft Rate	11
Violent Crime Rate Change	39
Prisoners	3
Change in Prisoners	30
Incarceration Rate	12
Juvenile Violent Crime Rate	3
Law Enforcement Employees	7
Corrections Employees	14
State Corrections Spending	39
Increase in State Corrections Spending	27
Law Enforcement Spending	8
Law Enforcement Spending as a Percentage of General Spending	3

Transportation - Section K

Travel on Interstates	49
Interstate Mileage in "Unacceptable" Condition	42
Deficient Bridges	41
Traffic Deaths	18
Seat Belt Use	39
Vehicle-Miles Traveled Per Capita	18
Use of Public Transportation	23
Road and Street Miles	40
Highway Employees	46
Public Transit Employees	19
Highway Spending Per Capita	29
Highway Spending as a Percentage of General Spending	26

Welfare - Section L

Births to Unwed Mothers	7
TANF Recipients	47
Change in TANF/AFDC Recipients	6
Food Stamp Recipients	30
SSI Recipients	16
WIC Average Monthly Benefit	14
NSLP Recipients	32
Condition of Children Index	35
Families with Single Parent	4
Average Monthly TANF Payments	25
Welfare as a Percentage of Poverty-Level Income	34
State Supplements of SSI	27
State Income Tax Liability of Typical Family in Poverty	n/a
Child Support Collections	37
Child Support Collections Per Dollar of Administrative Costs	29
Children in Foster Care	22
Welfare Spending Per Capita	41
Welfare Spending as a Percentage of General Spending	32
Administrative Costs Per TANF Case	21

Technology - Section M

Households with Computers	29
Percentage Using Internet	22
Zip Codes with Broadband Service	6
High-Tech Jobs	28
Change in High-Tech Jobs	20
State Government Web Site Ratings	31
Number of Online Government Services	23
Students Per Computer	27
Students Per Internet-Connected Computer	24
Libraries with Internet Access	1

Georgia

Population - Section A

Population 2005	9
Population 2004	9
Population Change 2003–2004	5
Population Change 1994–2004	4
Population 2015	8
Population 2025	9
Percentage 65 and Over	48
Percentage 17 and Under	7
Median Age	47
Percentage African American	3
Percentage American Indian	40
Percentage Asian American	17
Percentage Hispanic	21
Percentage White (Non-Hispanic)	44
Percentage Mixed-Race	36
Percentage in Poverty	18
Child Poverty Rate	12
Percentage Female	32
Birth Rates	5
Death Rates	8
Population Density	18
Legal Immigrants FY 2004	14
Unauthorized Immigrants	7

Economies - Section B

Personal Income, 2004	12
Gross State Product	21
Per Capita Personal Income	32
Personal Income from Wages and Salaries	5
Average Annual Pay	18
Average Hourly Earnings	39
Value Added in Manufacturing	23
Cost of Living	42
Average Annual Pay in Manufacturing	34
Average Annual Pay in Retailing	18
Labor Force	30
Unemployment Rate	18
Employment Rate	33
Government Employment	29
Manufacturing Employment	22
Fortune 500 Companies	14
Forbes 500 Companies	25
Tourism Spending Per Capita	22
Exports Per Capita	26
Housing Permits	5
Percentage Change in Home Prices	34
Net Farm Income	8
Financial Institution Assets	16
Bankruptcy Filings	5
Patents Issued	31
WC Disability Payment	47
Average Weekly UC Benefit	29
Economic Momentum	21
One-year Employment Change	45
Manufacturing Employment Change	39
Home Ownership	32
Annual Electricity Use Per Residential Customer	10
Cost Per Kwh	6
New Companies	16

Geography - Section C

Total Land Area	21
Federally Owned Land	26
State Park Acreage	32
State Park Visitors	41
Population Not Active	10
Hunters with Firearms	16
Registered Boats	14
State Spending for the Arts	41
Energy Consumption Per Capita	26
Toxic Chemical Release Per Capita	22
Hazardous Waste Sites	22
Drinking Water Quality	45
Expired Water Pollution Permits	22
Air Pollution Emissions	8

Government - Section D

Members of United States House	9
State Legislators	3
Legislators Per Million Population	32
Units of Government	36
Legislators Compensation	25
Female Legislators	33
Turnover in Legislatures	12
Term Limits	n/a
Legislative Session Length	27
Democrats in State Legislatures	32
Governors' Power Rating	35
Number of Statewide Elected Officials	2
State and Local Government Employees	20
State and Local Average Salaries	33
Local Employment	7
Local Spending Accountability	10
Registered Voters	44
Percentage of Population Voting	43
Statewide Initiatives	n/a
Campaign Costs Per Vote	24

Federal Impacts - Section E

Per Capita Federal Spending	41
Increase in Federal Spending	23
Per Capita Federal Grant Spending	39
Per Capita Federal Spending on Procurement	32
Per Capita Federal Spending on Payments to Individuals	44
Per Capita Federal Spending on Social Security and Medicare	45
Social Security Benefits	36
Federal Spending on Employee Wages and Salaries	13
Per Capita Federal Defense Spending	22
Per Capita Homeland Security Grants	42
Federal Grant Spending Per Dollar of State Tax Revenue	25
General Revenue from Federal Government	31
Federal Tax Burden Per Capita	24
Federal Spending Per Dollar of Taxes Paid	36
Highway Charges Returned to States	31
Terms of Trade	31
Federal Personal Income Taxes	24
Federal Share of Medicaid	24

Taxes - Section F

Tax Revenue	34
Per Capita Tax Revenue	28
Tax Effort	29
Tax Capacity	23
Percentage Change in Taxes	8
Property Taxes as a Percentage of Income	33
Property Taxes Per Capita	34
Property Tax Revenue as a Percentage of 3-tax Revenue	36
Sales Taxes as a Percentage of Income	19
Sales Taxes Per Capita	23
Sales Tax Revenue as a Percentage of 3-tax Revenue	21
Sales Tax Rate	38
Income Taxes as a Percentage of Income	16
Income Taxes Per Capita	20
Income Tax Revenue as a Percentage of 3-tax Revenue	16
Highest Personal Income Rate	22
Corporate Income Taxes	25
Motor Fuel Taxes	50
Motor Vehicle Fees	38
Tobacco Taxes	40
Taxes on High-Income Families	10
Taxes in the Largest City in Each State	12
Progressivity of Taxes	15
Per Capita Estate Tax Revenue	24

Revenues and Finances - Section G

Per Capita Total Revenue	44
Per Capita General Revenue	40

"Own-Source" General Revenue	34
Per Capita Non-Tax Revenue	37
Per Capita Total Spending	37
General Spending as a Percentage of Income	36
Per Capita General Spending	40
Change in General Expenditures	27
State Government General Revenue	46
State Government General Spending	43
State Government General Fund Spending	39
State and Local Debt	43
Debt as a Percentage of Revenue	36
Per Capita Full Faith and Credit Debt	20
Bond Ratings	1
State Solvency Index	11
Pension Plan Assets	26
State Reserves	24
Capital Outlays and Interest	17
State Budget Process Quality	1
Relative State Spending "Needs"	45
Structural Deficits	39

Education - Section H

Math Proficiency, Eighth Grade	38
Reading Proficiency, Eighth Grade	39
AFQT Ranks	44
SAT Scores	24
ACT Scores	n/a
Population over 25 with a High School Diploma	35
Students in Private Schools	35
High School Dropout Rates	47
Pupil-Teacher Ratio	27
Public School Enrollment	7
Library Holdings Per Capita	44
Children with Disabilities	41
Education Spending Per Capita	27
Education Spending as a Percentage of General Spending	5
Spending Per Pupil	23
Average Teacher Salary	17
Sources of School Funds	21
State Aid Per Pupil	27
Per Capita Higher Education Spending	42
Higher Education Spending as a Percentage of General Spending	37
Public Higher Education Enrollment	46
Per Pupil Support of Higher Education	13
In-State Tuition and Fees	46
Out-of-State Tuition and Fees	27
Change in Tuition and Fees	47
Affordability Index	27
Average Professor Salary	34
Education Employees	7
R and D Spending	28
Library Operating Spending	39
Head Start Spending	21

Health - Section I

Immunization Rates	11
Infant Mortality Rates	12
State Health Rankings	43
Population without Health Insurance	12
Abortions	13
Alcohol Consumption	35
Percentage of Adult Smokers	36
Percentage Obese	15
AIDS Cases	7
Physicians Per 100,000 Population	36
Hospital Beds Per 1,000 Population	23
Medicaid Recipients	20
Medicaid Recipients as a Percentage of Poverty Population	29
Health and Hospital Spending	13
Health and Hospital Spending as a Percentage of General Spending	9
Per Capita Medicaid Spending	16
Medicaid Spending Per Aged	45
Medicaid Spending Per Child	42
Medicare Payment Per Hospital Day	24
Hospital Expense Per Inpatient Day	38
Population in HMOs	25
Prescription Drugs as a Percentage of Medicaid Costs	20
Percentage Change in Average Price of Prescription Drugs	12

Crime - Section J

Crime Rate	13
Violent Crime Rate	19
Murder Rate	7
Property Crime Rate	9
Motor Vehicle Theft Rate	9
Violent Crime Rate Change	31
Prisoners	5
Change in Prisoners	18
Incarceration Rate	5
Juvenile Violent Crime Rate	15
Law Enforcement Employees	23
Corrections Employees	3
State Corrections Spending	31
Increase in State Corrections Spending	24
Law Enforcement Spending	20
Law Enforcement Spending as a Percentage of General Spending	8

Transportation - Section K

Travel on Interstates	18
Interstate Mileage in "Unacceptable" Condition	45
Deficient Bridges	39
Traffic Deaths	24
Seat Belt Use	23
Vehicle-Miles Traveled Per Capita	5
Use of Public Transportation	18
Road and Street Miles	25
Highway Employees	42
Public Transit Employees	14
Highway Spending Per Capita	41
Highway Spending as a Percentage of General Spending	35

Welfare - Section L

Births to Unwed Mothers	9
TANF Recipients	33
Change in TANF/AFDC Recipients	9
Food Stamp Recipients	16
SSI Recipients	18
WIC Average Monthly Benefit	26
NSLP Recipients	2
Condition of Children Index	39
Families with Single Parent	9
Average Monthly TANF Payments	40
Welfare as a Percentage of Poverty-Level Income	44
State Supplements of SSI	40
State Income Tax Liability of Typical Family in Poverty	11
Child Support Collections	39
Child Support Collections Per Dollar of Administrative Costs	26
Children in Foster Care	33
Welfare Spending Per Capita	44
Welfare Spending as a Percentage of General Spending	36
Administrative Costs Per TANF Case	44

Technology - Section M

Households with Computers	30
Percentage Using Internet	29
Zip Codes with Broadband Service	6
High-Tech Jobs	19
Change in High-Tech Jobs	34
State Government Web Site Ratings	33
Number of Online Government Services	30
Students Per Computer	21
Students Per Internet-Connected Computer	21
Libraries with Internet Access	1

Hawaii

Population - Section A

Population 2005	42
Population 2004	42
Population Change 2003–2004	16
Population Change 1994–2004	35
Population 2015	20
Population 2025	41
Percentage 65 and Over	11
Percentage 17 and Under	35
Median Age	13
Percentage African American	40
Percentage American Indian	36
Percentage Asian American	1
Percentage Hispanic	18
Percentage White (Non-Hispanic)	50
Percentage Mixed-Race	1
Percentage in Poverty	46
Child Poverty Rate	47
Percentage Female	41
Birth Rates	16
Death Rates	48
Population Density	13
Legal Immigrants FY 2004	23
Unauthorized Immigrants	42

Economies - Section B

Personal Income, 2004	40
Gross State Product	17
Per Capita Personal Income	19
Personal Income from Wages and Salaries	9
Average Annual Pay	24
Average Hourly Earnings	47
Value Added in Manufacturing	50
Cost of Living	1
Average Annual Pay in Manufacturing	50
Average Annual Pay in Retailing	15
Labor Force	33
Unemployment Rate	50
Employment Rate	1
Government Employment	9
Manufacturing Employment	50
Fortune 500 Companies	n/a
Forbes 500 Companies	34
Tourism Spending Per Capita	2
Exports Per Capita	50
Housing Permits	19
Percentage Change in Home Prices	4
Net Farm Income	42
Financial Institution Assets	12
Bankruptcy Filings	49
Patents Issued	47
WC Disability Payment	26
Average Weekly UC Benefit	2
Economic Momentum	6
One-year Employment Change	7
Manufacturing Employment Change	40
Home Ownership	48
Annual Electricity Use Per Residential Customer	42
Cost Per Kwh	44
New Companies	24

Geography - Section C

Total Land Area	47
Federally Owned Land	31
State Park Acreage	46
State Park Visitors	3
Population Not Active	n/a
Hunters with Firearms	n/a
Registered Boats	50
State Spending for the Arts	1
Energy Consumption Per Capita	47
Toxic Chemical Release Per Capita	44
Hazardous Waste Sites	45
Drinking Water Quality	47
Expired Water Pollution Permits	17
Air Pollution Emissions	49

Government - Section D

Members of United States House	39
State Legislators	46
Legislators Per Million Population	14
Units of Government	50
Legislators Compensation	14
Female Legislators	12
Turnover in Legislatures	29
Term Limits	n/a
Legislative Session Length	10
Democrats in State Legislatures	3
Governors' Power Rating	29
Number of Statewide Elected Officials	45
State and Local Government Employees	24
State and Local Average Salaries	19
Local Employment	50
Local Spending Accountability	5
Registered Voters	41
Percentage of Population Voting	50
Statewide Initiatives	n/a
Campaign Costs Per Vote	5

Federal Impacts - Section E

Per Capita Federal Spending	5
Increase in Federal Spending	21
Per Capita Federal Grant Spending	15
Per Capita Federal Spending on Procurement	8
Per Capita Federal Spending on Payments to Individuals	31
Per Capita Federal Spending on Social Security and Medicare	38
Social Security Benefits	23
Federal Spending on Employee Wages and Salaries	2
Per Capita Federal Defense Spending	3
Per Capita Homeland Security Grants	9
Federal Grant Spending Per Dollar of State Tax Revenue	48
General Revenue from Federal Government	34
Federal Tax Burden Per Capita	31
Federal Spending Per Dollar of Taxes Paid	9
Highway Charges Returned to States	7
Terms of Trade	18
Federal Personal Income Taxes	23
Federal Share of Medicaid	29

Taxes - Section F

Tax Revenue	4
Per Capita Tax Revenue	11
Tax Effort	27
Tax Capacity	4
Percentage Change in Taxes	47
Property Taxes as a Percentage of Income	45
Property Taxes Per Capita	44
Property Tax Revenue as a Percentage of 3-tax Revenue	50
Sales Taxes as a Percentage of Income	1
Sales Taxes Per Capita	2
Sales Tax Revenue as a Percentage of 3-tax Revenue	10
Sales Tax Rate	38
Income Taxes as a Percentage of Income	9
Income Taxes Per Capita	12
Income Tax Revenue as a Percentage of 3-tax Revenue	20
Highest Personal Income Rate	7
Corporate Income Taxes	43
Motor Fuel Taxes	44
Motor Vehicle Fees	11
Tobacco Taxes	10
Taxes on High-Income Families	31
Taxes in the Largest City in Each State	28
Progressivity of Taxes	25
Per Capita Estate Tax Revenue	27

Revenues and Finances - Section G

Per Capita Total Revenue	26
Per Capita General Revenue	17

"Own-Source" General Revenue	15
Per Capita Non-Tax Revenue	34
Per Capita Total Spending	10
General Spending as a Percentage of Income	8
Per Capita General Spending	7
Change in General Expenditures	50
State Government General Revenue	6
State Government General Spending	4
State Government General Fund Spending	6
State and Local Debt	11
Debt as a Percentage of Revenue	7
Per Capita Full Faith and Credit Debt	3
Bond Ratings	3
State Solvency Index	48
Pension Plan Assets	18
State Reserves	11
Capital Outlays and Interest	10
State Budget Process Quality	12
Relative State Spending "Needs"	1
Structural Deficits	47

Education - Section H

Math Proficiency, Eighth Grade	47
Reading Proficiency, Eighth Grade	50
AFQT Ranks	48
SAT Scores	19
ACT Scores	n/a
Population over 25 with a High School Diploma	18
Students in Private Schools	2
High School Dropout Rates	34
Pupil-Teacher Ratio	14
Public School Enrollment	49
Library Holdings Per Capita	32
Children with Disabilities	42
Education Spending Per Capita	40
Education Spending as a Percentage of General Spending	49
Spending Per Pupil	21
Average Teacher Salary	18
Sources of School Funds	50
State Aid Per Pupil	2
Per Capita Higher Education Spending	18
Higher Education Spending as a Percentage of General Spending	29
Public Higher Education Enrollment	37
Per Pupil Support of Higher Education	3
In-State Tuition and Fees	43
Out-of-State Tuition and Fees	47
Change in Tuition and Fees	46
Affordability Index	7
Average Professor Salary	27
Education Employees	37
R and D Spending	17
Library Operating Spending	36
Head Start Spending	13

Health - Section I

Immunization Rates	29
Infant Mortality Rates	48
State Health Rankings	5
Population without Health Insurance	48
Abortions	21
Alcohol Consumption	18
Percentage of Adult Smokers	n/a
Percentage Obese	41
AIDS Cases	19
Physicians Per 100,000 Population	9
Hospital Beds Per 1,000 Population	33
Medicaid Recipients	19
Medicaid Recipients as a Percentage of Poverty Population	2
Health and Hospital Spending	16
Health and Hospital Spending as a Percentage of General Spending	24
Per Capita Medicaid Spending	43
Medicaid Spending Per Aged	42
Medicaid Spending Per Child	36
Medicare Payment Per Hospital Day	23
Hospital Expense Per Inpatient Day	41
Population in HMOs	2
Prescription Drugs as a Percentage of Medicaid Costs	29
Percentage Change in Average Price of Prescription Drugs	4

Crime - Section J

Crime Rate	5
Violent Crime Rate	39
Murder Rate	34
Property Crime Rate	3
Motor Vehicle Theft Rate	5
Violent Crime Rate Change	5
Prisoners	39
Change in Prisoners	13
Incarceration Rate	34
Juvenile Violent Crime Rate	28
Law Enforcement Employees	22
Corrections Employees	36
State Corrections Spending	32
Increase in State Corrections Spending	10
Law Enforcement Spending	30
Law Enforcement Spending as a Percentage of General Spending	43

Transportation - Section K

Travel on Interstates	45
Interstate Mileage in "Unacceptable" Condition	1
Deficient Bridges	3
Traffic Deaths	23
Seat Belt Use	1
Vehicle-Miles Traveled Per Capita	48
Use of Public Transportation	6
Road and Street Miles	15
Highway Employees	48
Public Transit Employees	48
Highway Spending Per Capita	45
Highway Spending as a Percentage of General Spending	47

Welfare - Section L

Births to Unwed Mothers	31
TANF Recipients	17
Change in TANF/AFDC Recipients	17
Food Stamp Recipients	29
SSI Recipients	28
WIC Average Monthly Benefit	1
NSLP Recipients	18
Condition of Children Index	24
Families with Single Parent	19
Average Monthly TANF Payments	3
Welfare as a Percentage of Poverty-Level Income	5
State Supplements of SSI	4
State Income Tax Liability of Typical Family in Poverty	3
Child Support Collections	30
Child Support Collections Per Dollar of Administrative Costs	1
Children in Foster Care	9
Welfare Spending Per Capita	27
Welfare Spending as a Percentage of General Spending	35
Administrative Costs Per TANF Case	9

Technology - Section M

Households with Computers	24
Percentage Using Internet	26
Zip Codes with Broadband Service	38
High-Tech Jobs	42
Change in High-Tech Jobs	11
State Government Web Site Ratings	37
Number of Online Government Services	31
Students Per Computer	16
Students Per Internet-Connected Computer	15
Libraries with Internet Access	1

Idaho

Population - Section A

Population 2005	39
Population 2004	39
Population Change 2003–2004	4
Population Change 1994–2004	7
Population 2015	6
Population 2025	37
Percentage 65 and Over	41
Percentage 17 and Under	6
Median Age	44
Percentage African American	49
Percentage American Indian	10
Percentage Asian American	39
Percentage Hispanic	15
Percentage White (Non-Hispanic)	10
Percentage Mixed-Race	19
Percentage in Poverty	36
Child Poverty Rate	37
Percentage Female	45
Birth Rates	4
Death Rates	29
Population Density	44
Legal Immigrants FY 2004	38
Unauthorized Immigrants	35

Economies - Section B

Personal Income, 2004	42
Gross State Product	44
Per Capita Personal Income	46
Personal Income from Wages and Salaries	44
Average Annual Pay	46
Average Hourly Earnings	35
Value Added in Manufacturing	30
Cost of Living	35
Average Annual Pay in Manufacturing	33
Average Annual Pay in Retailing	32
Labor Force	19
Unemployment Rate	48
Employment Rate	3
Government Employment	14
Manufacturing Employment	28
Fortune 500 Companies	24
Forbes 500 Companies	16
Tourism Spending Per Capita	25
Exports Per Capita	27
Housing Permits	4
Percentage Change in Home Prices	25
Net Farm Income	18
Financial Institution Assets	50
Bankruptcy Filings	13
Patents Issued	1
WC Disability Payment	43
Average Weekly UC Benefit	35
Economic Momentum	4
One-year Employment Change	3
Manufacturing Employment Change	6
Home Ownership	12
Annual Electricity Use Per Residential Customer	20
Cost Per Kwh	40
New Companies	1

Geography - Section C

Total Land Area	11
Federally Owned Land	9
State Park Acreage	43
State Park Visitors	29
Population Not Active	38
Hunters with Firearms	3
Registered Boats	36
State Spending for the Arts	34
Energy Consumption Per Capita	19
Toxic Chemical Release Per Capita	6
Hazardous Waste Sites	43
Drinking Water Quality	14
Expired Water Pollution Permits	2
Air Pollution Emissions	34

Government - Section D

Members of United States House	39
State Legislators	39
Legislators Per Million Population	10
Units of Government	8
Legislators Compensation	28
Female Legislators	17
Turnover in Legislatures	19
Term Limits	n/a
Legislative Session Length	26
Democrats in State Legislatures	49
Governors' Power Rating	26
Number of Statewide Elected Officials	6
State and Local Government Employees	23
State and Local Average Salaries	41
Local Employment	27
Local Spending Accountability	30
Registered Voters	43
Percentage of Population Voting	28
Statewide Initiatives	n/a
Campaign Costs Per Vote	37

Federal Impacts - Section E

Per Capita Federal Spending	36
Increase in Federal Spending	16
Per Capita Federal Grant Spending	35
Per Capita Federal Spending on Procurement	19
Per Capita Federal Spending on Payments to Individuals	42
Per Capita Federal Spending on Social Security and Medicare	44
Social Security Benefits	32
Federal Spending on Employee Wages and Salaries	28
Per Capita Federal Defense Spending	42
Per Capita Homeland Security Grants	12
Federal Grant Spending Per Dollar of State Tax Revenue	31
General Revenue from Federal Government	27
Federal Tax Burden Per Capita	39
Federal Spending Per Dollar of Taxes Paid	18
Highway Charges Returned to States	11
Terms of Trade	21
Federal Personal Income Taxes	47
Federal Share of Medicaid	7

Taxes - Section F

Tax Revenue	36
Per Capita Tax Revenue	43
Tax Effort	22
Tax Capacity	44
Percentage Change in Taxes	30
Property Taxes as a Percentage of Income	30
Property Taxes Per Capita	36
Property Tax Revenue as a Percentage of 3-tax Revenue	27
Sales Taxes as a Percentage of Income	33
Sales Taxes Per Capita	43
Sales Tax Revenue as a Percentage of 3-tax Revenue	25
Sales Tax Rate	10
Income Taxes as a Percentage of Income	19
Income Taxes Per Capita	29
Income Tax Revenue as a Percentage of 3-tax Revenue	17
Highest Personal Income Rate	10
Corporate Income Taxes	33
Motor Fuel Taxes	11
Motor Vehicle Fees	10
Tobacco Taxes	30
Taxes on High-Income Families	18
Taxes in the Largest City in Each State	33
Progressivity of Taxes	4
Per Capita Estate Tax Revenue	5

Revenues and Finances - Section G

Per Capita Total Revenue	49
Per Capita General Revenue	47

"Own-Source" General Revenue	42
Per Capita Non-Tax Revenue	26
Per Capita Total Spending	47
General Spending as a Percentage of Income	25
Per Capita General Spending	46
Change in General Expenditures	13
State Government General Revenue	41
State Government General Spending	39
State Government General Fund Spending	33
State and Local Debt	50
Debt as a Percentage of Revenue	48
Per Capita Full Faith and Credit Debt	45
Bond Ratings	n/a
State Solvency Index	9
Pension Plan Assets	33
State Reserves	14
Capital Outlays and Interest	46
State Budget Process Quality	47
Relative State Spending "Needs"	37
Structural Deficits	46

Education - Section H

Math Proficiency, Eighth Grade	20
Reading Proficiency, Eighth Grade	23
AFQT Ranks	7
SAT Scores	n/a
ACT Scores	13
Population over 25 with a High School Diploma	19
Students in Private Schools	48
High School Dropout Rates	2
Pupil-Teacher Ratio	8
Public School Enrollment	4
Library Holdings Per Capita	23
Children with Disabilities	48
Education Spending Per Capita	41
Education Spending as a Percentage of General Spending	21
Spending Per Pupil	44
Average Teacher Salary	29
Sources of School Funds	38
State Aid Per Pupil	34
Per Capita Higher Education Spending	33
Higher Education Spending as a Percentage of General Spending	26
Public Higher Education Enrollment	32
Per Pupil Support of Higher Education	15
In-State Tuition and Fees	41
Out-of-State Tuition and Fees	42
Change in Tuition and Fees	28
Affordability Index	10
Average Professor Salary	48
Education Employees	28
R and D Spending	33
Library Operating Spending	33
Head Start Spending	10

Health - Section I

Immunization Rates	33
Infant Mortality Rates	22
State Health Rankings	16
Population without Health Insurance	20
Abortions	46
Alcohol Consumption	24
Percentage of Adult Smokers	47
Percentage Obese	42
AIDS Cases	48
Physicians Per 100,000 Population	50
Hospital Beds Per 1,000 Population	34
Medicaid Recipients	35
Medicaid Recipients as a Percentage of Poverty Population	23
Health and Hospital Spending	23
Health and Hospital Spending as a Percentage of General Spending	14
Per Capita Medicaid Spending	45
Medicaid Spending Per Aged	16
Medicaid Spending Per Child	24
Medicare Payment Per Hospital Day	34
Hospital Expense Per Inpatient Day	12
Population in HMOs	45
Prescription Drugs as a Percentage of Medicaid Costs	8
Percentage Change in Average Price of Prescription Drugs	30

Crime - Section J

Crime Rate	36
Violent Crime Rate	41
Murder Rate	42
Property Crime Rate	36
Motor Vehicle Theft Rate	42
Violent Crime Rate Change	18
Prisoners	37
Change in Prisoners	6
Incarceration Rate	17
Juvenile Violent Crime Rate	33
Law Enforcement Employees	35
Corrections Employees	32
State Corrections Spending	36
Increase in State Corrections Spending	19
Law Enforcement Spending	28
Law Enforcement Spending as a Percentage of General Spending	15

Transportation - Section K

Travel on Interstates	34
Interstate Mileage in "Unacceptable" Condition	26
Deficient Bridges	43
Traffic Deaths	16
Seat Belt Use	35
Vehicle-Miles Traveled Per Capita	28
Use of Public Transportation	28
Road and Street Miles	37
Highway Employees	18
Public Transit Employees	50
Highway Spending Per Capita	21
Highway Spending as a Percentage of General Spending	15

Welfare - Section L

Births to Unwed Mothers	49
TANF Recipients	49
Change in TANF/AFDC Recipients	3
Food Stamp Recipients	35
SSI Recipients	39
WIC Average Monthly Benefit	46
NSLP Recipients	17
Condition of Children Index	16
Families with Single Parent	48
Average Monthly TANF Payments	30
Welfare as a Percentage of Poverty-Level Income	38
State Supplements of SSI	30
State Income Tax Liability of Typical Family in Poverty	17
Child Support Collections	15
Child Support Collections Per Dollar of Administrative Costs	11
Children in Foster Care	47
Welfare Spending Per Capita	37
Welfare Spending as a Percentage of General Spending	29
Administrative Costs Per TANF Case	12

Technology - Section M

Households with Computers	7
Percentage Using Internet	20
Zip Codes with Broadband Service	35
High-Tech Jobs	7
Change in High-Tech Jobs	19
State Government Web Site Ratings	15
Number of Online Government Services	5
Students Per Computer	31
Students Per Internet-Connected Computer	31
Libraries with Internet Access	37

Illinois

Population - Section A

Population 2005	5
Population 2004	5
Population Change 2003–2004	36
Population Change 1994–2004	31
Population 2015	42
Population 2025	5
Percentage 65 and Over	38
Percentage 17 and Under	14
Median Age	39
Percentage African American	14
Percentage American Indian	41
Percentage Asian American	11
Percentage Hispanic	10
Percentage White (Non-Hispanic)	36
Percentage Mixed-Race	33
Percentage in Poverty	20
Child Poverty Rate	19
Percentage Female	21
Birth Rates	16
Death Rates	n/a
Population Density	12
Legal Immigrants FY 2004	6
Unauthorized Immigrants	4

Economies - Section B

Personal Income, 2004	5
Gross State Product	14
Per Capita Personal Income	13
Personal Income from Wages and Salaries	10
Average Annual Pay	8
Average Hourly Earnings	23
Value Added in Manufacturing	16
Cost of Living	30
Average Annual Pay in Manufacturing	15
Average Annual Pay in Retailing	17
Labor Force	31
Unemployment Rate	8
Employment Rate	43
Government Employment	43
Manufacturing Employment	20
Fortune 500 Companies	6
Forbes 500 Companies	4
Tourism Spending Per Capita	20
Exports Per Capita	17
Housing Permits	42
Percentage Change in Home Prices	24
Net Farm Income	4
Financial Institution Assets	13
Bankruptcy Filings	19
Patents Issued	19
WC Disability Payment	3
Average Weekly UC Benefit	13
Economic Momentum	49
One-year Employment Change	43
Manufacturing Employment Change	36
Home Ownership	20
Annual Electricity Use Per Residential Customer	36
Cost Per Kwh	20
New Companies	42

Geography - Section C

Total Land Area	24
Federally Owned Land	35
State Park Acreage	6
State Park Visitors	15
Population Not Active	13
Hunters with Firearms	39
Registered Boats	10
State Spending for the Arts	9
Energy Consumption Per Capita	35
Toxic Chemical Release Per Capita	29
Hazardous Waste Sites	9
Drinking Water Quality	19
Expired Water Pollution Permits	30
Air Pollution Emissions	7

Government - Section D

Members of United States House	5
State Legislators	13
Legislators Per Million Population	44
Units of Government	15
Legislators Compensation	5
Female Legislators	16
Turnover in Legislatures	44
Term Limits	n/a
Legislative Session Length	n/a
Democrats in State Legislatures	18
Governors' Power Rating	8
Number of Statewide Elected Officials	22
State and Local Government Employees	43
State and Local Average Salaries	14
Local Employment	2
Local Spending Accountability	24
Registered Voters	21
Percentage of Population Voting	26
Statewide Initiatives	n/a
Campaign Costs Per Vote	20

Federal Impacts - Section E

Per Capita Federal Spending	45
Increase in Federal Spending	38
Per Capita Federal Grant Spending	42
Per Capita Federal Spending on Procurement	40
Per Capita Federal Spending on Payments to Individuals	35
Per Capita Federal Spending on Social Security and Medicare	24
Social Security Benefits	8
Federal Spending on Employee Wages and Salaries	37
Per Capita Federal Defense Spending	43
Per Capita Homeland Security Grants	46
Federal Grant Spending Per Dollar of State Tax Revenue	42
General Revenue from Federal Government	40
Federal Tax Burden Per Capita	10
Federal Spending Per Dollar of Taxes Paid	45
Highway Charges Returned to States	48
Terms of Trade	45
Federal Personal Income Taxes	9
Federal Share of Medicaid	39

Taxes - Section F

Tax Revenue	29
Per Capita Tax Revenue	14
Tax Effort	15
Tax Capacity	16
Percentage Change in Taxes	28
Property Taxes as a Percentage of Income	13
Property Taxes Per Capita	11
Property Tax Revenue as a Percentage of 3-tax Revenue	9
Sales Taxes as a Percentage of Income	34
Sales Taxes Per Capita	21
Sales Tax Revenue as a Percentage of 3-tax Revenue	31
Sales Tax Rate	7
Income Taxes as a Percentage of Income	37
Income Taxes Per Capita	31
Income Tax Revenue as a Percentage of 3-tax Revenue	37
Highest Personal Income Rate	41
Corporate Income Taxes	11
Motor Fuel Taxes	27
Motor Vehicle Fees	6
Tobacco Taxes	19
Taxes on High-Income Families	24
Taxes in the Largest City in Each State	13
Progressivity of Taxes	40
Per Capita Estate Tax Revenue	6

Revenues and Finances - Section G

Per Capita Total Revenue	32
Per Capita General Revenue	29

"Own-Source" General Revenue	26
Per Capita Non-Tax Revenue	45
Per Capita Total Spending	19
General Spending as a Percentage of Income	44
Per Capita General Spending	23
Change in General Expenditures	19
State Government General Revenue	44
State Government General Spending	41
State Government General Fund Spending	48
State and Local Debt	13
Debt as a Percentage of Revenue	9
Per Capita Full Faith and Credit Debt	8
Bond Ratings	4
State Solvency Index	46
Pension Plan Assets	21
State Reserves	40
Capital Outlays and Interest	12
State Budget Process Quality	3
Relative State Spending "Needs"	27
Structural Deficits	17

Education - Section H

Math Proficiency, Eighth Grade	31
Reading Proficiency, Eighth Grade	23
AFQT Ranks	28
SAT Scores	n/a
ACT Scores	19
Population over 25 with a High School Diploma	29
Students in Private Schools	13
High School Dropout Rates	14
Pupil-Teacher Ratio	16
Public School Enrollment	17
Library Holdings Per Capita	16
Children with Disabilities	16
Education Spending Per Capita	24
Education Spending as a Percentage of General Spending	25
Spending Per Pupil	15
Average Teacher Salary	6
Sources of School Funds	1
State Aid Per Pupil	48
Per Capita Higher Education Spending	32
Higher Education Spending as a Percentage of General Spending	35
Public Higher Education Enrollment	15
Per Pupil Support of Higher Education	37
In-State Tuition and Fees	10
Out-of-State Tuition and Fees	6
Change in Tuition and Fees	9
Affordability Index	4
Average Professor Salary	12
Education Employees	36
R and D Spending	34
Library Operating Spending	4
Head Start Spending	34

Health - Section I

Immunization Rates	13
Infant Mortality Rates	17
State Health Rankings	28
Population without Health Insurance	29
Abortions	12
Alcohol Consumption	23
Percentage of Adult Smokers	19
Percentage Obese	28
AIDS Cases	13
Physicians Per 100,000 Population	13
Hospital Beds Per 1,000 Population	25
Medicaid Recipients	27
Medicaid Recipients as a Percentage of Poverty Population	32
Health and Hospital Spending	31
Health and Hospital Spending as a Percentage of General Spending	31
Per Capita Medicaid Spending	33
Medicaid Spending Per Aged	22
Medicaid Spending Per Child	30
Medicare Payment Per Hospital Day	13
Hospital Expense Per Inpatient Day	26
Population in HMOs	30
Prescription Drugs as a Percentage of Medicaid Costs	15
Percentage Change in Average Price of Prescription Drugs	21

Crime - Section J

Crime Rate	28
Violent Crime Rate	11
Murder Rate	14
Property Crime Rate	29
Motor Vehicle Theft Rate	26
Violent Crime Rate Change	46
Prisoners	8
Change in Prisoners	43
Incarceration Rate	32
Juvenile Violent Crime Rate	1
Law Enforcement Employees	4
Corrections Employees	35
State Corrections Spending	28
Increase in State Corrections Spending	37
Law Enforcement Spending	17
Law Enforcement Spending as a Percentage of General Spending	14

Transportation - Section K

Travel on Interstates	8
Interstate Mileage in "Unacceptable" Condition	23
Deficient Bridges	46
Traffic Deaths	37
Seat Belt Use	13
Vehicle-Miles Traveled Per Capita	43
Use of Public Transportation	5
Road and Street Miles	32
Highway Employees	40
Public Transit Employees	2
Highway Spending Per Capita	22
Highway Spending as a Percentage of General Spending	28

Welfare - Section L

Births to Unwed Mothers	19
TANF Recipients	42
Change in TANF/AFDC Recipients	2
Food Stamp Recipients	19
SSI Recipients	25
WIC Average Monthly Benefit	7
NSLP Recipients	31
Condition of Children Index	28
Families with Single Parent	23
Average Monthly TANF Payments	39
Welfare as a Percentage of Poverty-Level Income	21
State Supplements of SSI	25
State Income Tax Liability of Typical Family in Poverty	10
Child Support Collections	49
Child Support Collections Per Dollar of Administrative Costs	45
Children in Foster Care	29
Welfare Spending Per Capita	36
Welfare Spending as a Percentage of General Spending	39
Administrative Costs Per TANF Case	36

Technology - Section M

Households with Computers	33
Percentage Using Internet	38
Zip Codes with Broadband Service	23
High-Tech Jobs	26
Change in High-Tech Jobs	45
State Government Web Site Ratings	38
Number of Online Government Services	48
Students Per Computer	16
Students Per Internet-Connected Computer	18
Libraries with Internet Access	24

Indiana

Population - Section A

Population 2005	15
Population 2004	14
Population Change 2003–2004	33
Population Change 1994–2004	27
Population 2015	34
Population 2025	18
Percentage 65 and Over	30
Percentage 17 and Under	12
Median Age	38
Percentage African American	22
Percentage American Indian	45
Percentage Asian American	37
Percentage Hispanic	30
Percentage White (Non-Hispanic)	15
Percentage Mixed-Race	32
Percentage in Poverty	23
Child Poverty Rate	17
Percentage Female	25
Birth Rates	20
Death Rates	14
Population Density	17
Legal Immigrants FY 2004	24
Unauthorized Immigrants	24

Economies - Section B

Personal Income, 2004	16
Gross State Product	30
Per Capita Personal Income	33
Personal Income from Wages and Salaries	21
Average Annual Pay	30
Average Hourly Earnings	5
Value Added in Manufacturing	1
Cost of Living	32
Average Annual Pay in Manufacturing	17
Average Annual Pay in Retailing	36
Labor Force	28
Unemployment Rate	19
Employment Rate	32
Government Employment	42
Manufacturing Employment	1
Fortune 500 Companies	29
Forbes 500 Companies	26
Tourism Spending Per Capita	49
Exports Per Capita	8
Housing Permits	25
Percentage Change in Home Prices	50
Net Farm Income	12
Financial Institution Assets	28
Bankruptcy Filings	4
Patents Issued	25
WC Disability Payment	31
Average Weekly UC Benefit	16
Economic Momentum	48
One-year Employment Change	40
Manufacturing Employment Change	21
Home Ownership	7
Annual Electricity Use Per Residential Customer	24
Cost Per Kwh	13
New Companies	46

Geography - Section C

Total Land Area	38
Federally Owned Land	39
State Park Acreage	18
State Park Visitors	17
Population Not Active	12
Hunters with Firearms	33
Registered Boats	21
State Spending for the Arts	35
Energy Consumption Per Capita	7
Toxic Chemical Release Per Capita	8
Hazardous Waste Sites	14
Drinking Water Quality	18
Expired Water Pollution Permits	9
Air Pollution Emissions	11

Government - Section D

Members of United States House	14
State Legislators	19
Legislators Per Million Population	34
Units of Government	17
Legislators Compensation	36
Female Legislators	36
Turnover in Legislatures	38
Term Limits	n/a
Legislative Session Length	28
Democrats in State Legislatures	33
Governors' Power Rating	39
Number of Statewide Elected Officials	9
State and Local Government Employees	35
State and Local Average Salaries	28
Local Employment	17
Local Spending Accountability	16
Registered Voters	9
Percentage of Population Voting	42
Statewide Initiatives	n/a
Campaign Costs Per Vote	22

Federal Impacts - Section E

Per Capita Federal Spending	44
Increase in Federal Spending	22
Per Capita Federal Grant Spending	47
Per Capita Federal Spending on Procurement	34
Per Capita Federal Spending on Payments to Individuals	29
Per Capita Federal Spending on Social Security and Medicare	22
Social Security Benefits	7
Federal Spending on Employee Wages and Salaries	48
Per Capita Federal Defense Spending	35
Per Capita Homeland Security Grants	36
Federal Grant Spending Per Dollar of State Tax Revenue	33
General Revenue from Federal Government	38
Federal Tax Burden Per Capita	30
Federal Spending Per Dollar of Taxes Paid	35
Highway Charges Returned to States	48
Terms of Trade	36
Federal Personal Income Taxes	29
Federal Share of Medicaid	19

Taxes - Section F

Tax Revenue	33
Per Capita Tax Revenue	29
Tax Effort	31
Tax Capacity	30
Percentage Change in Taxes	42
Property Taxes as a Percentage of Income	16
Property Taxes Per Capita	19
Property Tax Revenue as a Percentage of 3-tax Revenue	16
Sales Taxes as a Percentage of Income	38
Sales Taxes Per Capita	42
Sales Tax Revenue as a Percentage of 3-tax Revenue	34
Sales Tax Rate	10
Income Taxes as a Percentage of Income	25
Income Taxes Per Capita	24
Income Tax Revenue as a Percentage of 3-tax Revenue	25
Highest Personal Income Rate	38
Corporate Income Taxes	10
Motor Fuel Taxes	36
Motor Vehicle Fees	46
Tobacco Taxes	31
Taxes on High-Income Families	16
Taxes in the Largest City in Each State	9
Progressivity of Taxes	39
Per Capita Estate Tax Revenue	45

Revenues and Finances - Section G

Per Capita Total Revenue	36
Per Capita General Revenue	36

"Own-Source" General Revenue	32
Per Capita Non-Tax Revenue	21
Per Capita Total Spending	44
General Spending as a Percentage of Income	33
Per Capita General Spending	38
Change in General Expenditures	12
State Government General Revenue	39
State Government General Spending	42
State Government General Fund Spending	41
State and Local Debt	44
Debt as a Percentage of Revenue	40
Per Capita Full Faith and Credit Debt	48
Bond Ratings	n/a
State Solvency Index	20
Pension Plan Assets	45
State Reserves	37
Capital Outlays and Interest	43
State Budget Process Quality	49
Relative State Spending "Needs"	14
Structural Deficits	28

Education - Section H

Math Proficiency, Eighth Grade	16
Reading Proficiency, Eighth Grade	29
AFQT Ranks	13
SAT Scores	15
ACT Scores	n/a
Population over 25 with a High School Diploma	26
Students in Private Schools	21
High School Dropout Rates	23
Pupil-Teacher Ratio	10
Public School Enrollment	21
Library Holdings Per Capita	9
Children with Disabilities	5
Education Spending Per Capita	30
Education Spending as a Percentage of General Spending	13
Spending Per Pupil	20
Average Teacher Salary	16
Sources of School Funds	23
State Aid Per Pupil	20
Per Capita Higher Education Spending	24
Higher Education Spending as a Percentage of General Spending	18
Public Higher Education Enrollment	27
Per Pupil Support of Higher Education	20
In-State Tuition and Fees	16
Out-of-State Tuition and Fees	14
Change in Tuition and Fees	43
Affordability Index	7
Average Professor Salary	18
Education Employees	34
R and D Spending	43
Library Operating Spending	3
Head Start Spending	35

Health - Section I

Immunization Rates	40
Infant Mortality Rates	6
State Health Rankings	32
Population without Health Insurance	27
Abortions	35
Alcohol Consumption	41
Percentage of Adult Smokers	7
Percentage Obese	9
AIDS Cases	32
Physicians Per 100,000 Population	38
Hospital Beds Per 1,000 Population	20
Medicaid Recipients	30
Medicaid Recipients as a Percentage of Poverty Population	33
Health and Hospital Spending	19
Health and Hospital Spending as a Percentage of General Spending	16
Per Capita Medicaid Spending	34
Medicaid Spending Per Aged	11
Medicaid Spending Per Child	40
Medicare Payment Per Hospital Day	41
Hospital Expense Per Inpatient Day	22
Population in HMOs	19
Prescription Drugs as a Percentage of Medicaid Costs	19
Percentage Change in Average Price of Prescription Drugs	20

Crime - Section J

Crime Rate	29
Violent Crime Rate	29
Murder Rate	24
Property Crime Rate	26
Motor Vehicle Theft Rate	24
Violent Crime Rate Change	26
Prisoners	18
Change in Prisoners	19
Incarceration Rate	28
Juvenile Violent Crime Rate	9
Law Enforcement Employees	27
Corrections Employees	26
State Corrections Spending	26
Increase in State Corrections Spending	9
Law Enforcement Spending	40
Law Enforcement Spending as a Percentage of General Spending	37

Transportation - Section K

Travel on Interstates	35
Interstate Mileage in "Unacceptable" Condition	35
Deficient Bridges	35
Traffic Deaths	31
Seat Belt Use	26
Vehicle-Miles Traveled Per Capita	13
Use of Public Transportation	37
Road and Street Miles	30
Highway Employees	37
Public Transit Employees	25
Highway Spending Per Capita	46
Highway Spending as a Percentage of General Spending	38

Welfare - Section L

Births to Unwed Mothers	12
TANF Recipients	9
Change in TANF/AFDC Recipients	50
Food Stamp Recipients	21
SSI Recipients	38
WIC Average Monthly Benefit	39
NSLP Recipients	11
Condition of Children Index	30
Families with Single Parent	28
Average Monthly TANF Payments	43
Welfare as a Percentage of Poverty-Level Income	35
State Supplements of SSI	10
State Income Tax Liability of Typical Family in Poverty	12
Child Support Collections	23
Child Support Collections Per Dollar of Administrative Costs	4
Children in Foster Care	36
Welfare Spending Per Capita	32
Welfare Spending as a Percentage of General Spending	25
Administrative Costs Per TANF Case	34

Technology - Section M

Households with Computers	37
Percentage Using Internet	38
Zip Codes with Broadband Service	16
High-Tech Jobs	46
Change in High-Tech Jobs	26
State Government Web Site Ratings	20
Number of Online Government Services	26
Students Per Computer	36
Students Per Internet-Connected Computer	34
Libraries with Internet Access	32

Iowa

Population - Section A

Population 2005	30
Population 2004	30
Population Change 2003–2004	40
Population Change 1994–2004	46
Population 2015	45
Population 2025	34
Percentage 65 and Over	5
Percentage 17 and Under	41
Median Age	13
Percentage African American	39
Percentage American Indian	35
Percentage Asian American	31
Percentage Hispanic	34
Percentage White (Non-Hispanic)	5
Percentage Mixed-Race	45
Percentage in Poverty	32
Child Poverty Rate	36
Percentage Female	28
Birth Rates	36
Death Rates	41
Population Density	33
Legal Immigrants FY 2004	29
Unauthorized Immigrants	31

Economies - Section B

Personal Income, 2004	30
Gross State Product	26
Per Capita Personal Income	27
Personal Income from Wages and Salaries	36
Average Annual Pay	36
Average Hourly Earnings	19
Value Added in Manufacturing	3
Cost of Living	29
Average Annual Pay in Manufacturing	29
Average Annual Pay in Retailing	44
Labor Force	7
Unemployment Rate	33
Employment Rate	18
Government Employment	28
Manufacturing Employment	6
Fortune 500 Companies	33
Forbes 500 Companies	32
Tourism Spending Per Capita	29
Exports Per Capita	23
Housing Permits	32
Percentage Change in Home Prices	41
Net Farm Income	3
Financial Institution Assets	27
Bankruptcy Filings	31
Patents Issued	24
WC Disability Payment	1
Average Weekly UC Benefit	17
Economic Momentum	44
One-year Employment Change	30
Manufacturing Employment Change	13
Home Ownership	17
Annual Electricity Use Per Residential Customer	30
Cost Per Kwh	1
New Companies	50

Geography - Section C

Total Land Area	23
Federally Owned Land	42
State Park Acreage	37
State Park Visitors	7
Population Not Active	32
Hunters with Firearms	26
Registered Boats	20
State Spending for the Arts	40
Energy Consumption Per Capita	14
Toxic Chemical Release Per Capita	25
Hazardous Waste Sites	34
Drinking Water Quality	39
Expired Water Pollution Permits	14
Air Pollution Emissions	26

Government - Section D

Members of United States House	27
State Legislators	19
Legislators Per Million Population	18
Units of Government	10
Legislators Compensation	22
Female Legislators	29
Turnover in Legislatures	31
Term Limits	n/a
Legislative Session Length	14
Democrats in State Legislatures	27
Governors' Power Rating	14
Number of Statewide Elected Officials	9
State and Local Government Employees	9
State and Local Average Salaries	25
Local Employment	21
Local Spending Accountability	21
Registered Voters	5
Percentage of Population Voting	7
Statewide Initiatives	n/a
Campaign Costs Per Vote	21

Federal Impacts - Section E

Per Capita Federal Spending	32
Increase in Federal Spending	49
Per Capita Federal Grant Spending	37
Per Capita Federal Spending on Procurement	39
Per Capita Federal Spending on Payments to Individuals	13
Per Capita Federal Spending on Social Security and Medicare	19
Social Security Benefits	24
Federal Spending on Employee Wages and Salaries	47
Per Capita Federal Defense Spending	45
Per Capita Homeland Security Grants	21
Federal Grant Spending Per Dollar of State Tax Revenue	21
General Revenue from Federal Government	26
Federal Tax Burden Per Capita	35
Federal Spending Per Dollar of Taxes Paid	29
Highway Charges Returned to States	29
Terms of Trade	26
Federal Personal Income Taxes	37
Federal Share of Medicaid	17

Taxes - Section F

Tax Revenue	24
Per Capita Tax Revenue	26
Tax Effort	32
Tax Capacity	28
Percentage Change in Taxes	41
Property Taxes as a Percentage of Income	14
Property Taxes Per Capita	17
Property Tax Revenue as a Percentage of 3-tax Revenue	17
Sales Taxes as a Percentage of Income	27
Sales Taxes Per Capita	33
Sales Tax Revenue as a Percentage of 3-tax Revenue	30
Sales Tax Rate	25
Income Taxes as a Percentage of Income	32
Income Taxes Per Capita	30
Income Tax Revenue as a Percentage of 3-tax Revenue	33
Highest Personal Income Rate	28
Corporate Income Taxes	45
Motor Fuel Taxes	26
Motor Vehicle Fees	2
Tobacco Taxes	41
Taxes on High-Income Families	25
Taxes in the Largest City in Each State	19
Progressivity of Taxes	27
Per Capita Estate Tax Revenue	32

Revenues and Finances - Section G

Per Capita Total Revenue	25
Per Capita General Revenue	24

"Own-Source" General Revenue 21
Per Capita Non-Tax Revenue 9
Per Capita Total Spending 28
General Spending as a Percentage of Income 17
Per Capita General Spending 24
Change in General Expenditures 36
State Government General Revenue 27
State Government General Spending 25
State Government General Fund Spending 11
State and Local Debt 48
Debt as a Percentage of Revenue 50
Per Capita Full Faith and Credit Debt 38
Bond Ratings n/a
State Solvency Index 19
Pension Plan Assets 46
State Reserves 29
Capital Outlays and Interest 27
State Budget Process Quality 16
Relative State Spending "Needs" 2
Structural Deficits 26

Education - Section H

Math Proficiency, Eighth Grade 10
Reading Proficiency, Eighth Grade 12
AFQT Ranks 16
SAT Scores n/a
ACT Scores 3
Population over 25 with a High School Diploma 9
Students in Private Schools 27
High School Dropout Rates 6
Pupil-Teacher Ratio 36
Public School Enrollment 23
Library Holdings Per Capita 14
Children with Disabilities 17
Education Spending Per Capita 14
Education Spending as a Percentage of General Spending 12
Spending Per Pupil 36
Average Teacher Salary 40
Sources of School Funds 20
State Aid Per Pupil 30
Per Capita Higher Education Spending 3
Higher Education Spending as a Percentage of General Spending 2
Public Higher Education Enrollment 5
Per Pupil Support of Higher Education 31
In-State Tuition and Fees 19
Out-of-State Tuition and Fees 23
Change in Tuition and Fees 24
Affordability Index 25
Average Professor Salary 22
Education Employees 13
R and D Spending 32
Library Operating Spending 25
Head Start Spending 42

Health - Section I

Immunization Rates 8
Infant Mortality Rates 43
State Health Rankings 10
Population without Health Insurance 49
Abortions 29
Alcohol Consumption 37
Percentage of Adult Smokers 25
Percentage Obese 22
AIDS Cases 47
Physicians Per 100,000 Population 43
Hospital Beds Per 1,000 Population 10
Medicaid Recipients 42
Medicaid Recipients as a Percentage of Poverty Population 41
Health and Hospital Spending 9
Health and Hospital Spending as a Percentage of General Spending 8
Per Capita Medicaid Spending 36
Medicaid Spending Per Aged 20
Medicaid Spending Per Child 10
Medicare Payment Per Hospital Day 43
Hospital Expense Per Inpatient Day 20
Population in HMOs 33
Prescription Drugs as a Percentage of Medicaid Costs 34
Percentage Change in Average Price of Prescription Drugs 11

Crime - Section J

Crime Rate 34
Violent Crime Rate 37
Murder Rate 47
Property Crime Rate 34
Motor Vehicle Theft Rate 43
Violent Crime Rate Change 8
Prisoners 34
Change in Prisoners 23
Incarceration Rate 39
Juvenile Violent Crime Rate 17
Law Enforcement Employees 37
Corrections Employees 47
State Corrections Spending 25
Increase in State Corrections Spending 42
Law Enforcement Spending 44
Law Enforcement Spending as a Percentage of General Spending 46

Transportation - Section K

Travel on Interstates 31
Interstate Mileage in "Unacceptable" Condition 15
Deficient Bridges 22
Traffic Deaths 38
Seat Belt Use 13
Vehicle-Miles Traveled Per Capita 25
Use of Public Transportation 32
Road and Street Miles 48
Highway Employees 9
Public Transit Employees 26
Highway Spending Per Capita 7
Highway Spending as a Percentage of General Spending 10

Welfare - Section L

Births to Unwed Mothers 40
TANF Recipients 22
Change in TANF/AFDC Recipients 39
Food Stamp Recipients 32
SSI Recipients 41
WIC Average Monthly Benefit 41
NSLP Recipients 10
Condition of Children Index 8
Families with Single Parent 44
Average Monthly TANF Payments 23
Welfare as a Percentage of Poverty-Level Income 21
State Supplements of SSI 12
State Income Tax Liability of Typical Family in Poverty 17
Child Support Collections 10
Child Support Collections Per Dollar of Administrative Costs 13
Children in Foster Care 25
Welfare Spending Per Capita 29
Welfare Spending as a Percentage of General Spending 27
Administrative Costs Per TANF Case 32

Technology - Section M

Households with Computers 18
Percentage Using Internet 18
Zip Codes with Broadband Service 48
High-Tech Jobs 36
Change in High-Tech Jobs 25
State Government Web Site Ratings 32
Number of Online Government Services 20
Students Per Computer 40
Students Per Internet-Connected Computer 41
Libraries with Internet Access 39

Kansas

Population - Section A

Population 2005	33
Population 2004	33
Population Change 2003–2004	42
Population Change 1994–2004	37
Population 2015	35
Population 2025	35
Percentage 65 and Over	23
Percentage 17 and Under	17
Median Age	34
Percentage African American	30
Percentage American Indian	18
Percentage Asian American	23
Percentage Hispanic	17
Percentage White (Non-Hispanic)	21
Percentage Mixed-Race	9
Percentage in Poverty	29
Child Poverty Rate	28
Percentage Female	35
Birth Rates	13
Death Rates	26
Population Density	40
Legal Immigrants FY 2004	28
Unauthorized Immigrants	21

Economies - Section B

Personal Income, 2004	31
Gross State Product	31
Per Capita Personal Income	26
Personal Income from Wages and Salaries	27
Average Annual Pay	34
Average Hourly Earnings	14
Value Added in Manufacturing	15
Cost of Living	37
Average Annual Pay in Manufacturing	24
Average Annual Pay in Retailing	38
Labor Force	13
Unemployment Rate	25
Employment Rate	26
Government Employment	17
Manufacturing Employment	13
Fortune 500 Companies	32
Forbes 500 Companies	28
Tourism Spending Per Capita	38
Exports Per Capita	24
Housing Permits	39
Percentage Change in Home Prices	37
Net Farm Income	19
Financial Institution Assets	23
Bankruptcy Filings	20
Patents Issued	29
WC Disability Payment	45
Average Weekly UC Benefit	12
Economic Momentum	35
One-year Employment Change	38
Manufacturing Employment Change	20
Home Ownership	35
Annual Electricity Use Per Residential Customer	27
Cost Per Kwh	24
New Companies	41

Geography - Section C

Total Land Area	13
Federally Owned Land	36
State Park Acreage	45
State Park Visitors	22
Population Not Active	23
Hunters with Firearms	27
Registered Boats	33
State Spending for the Arts	37
Energy Consumption Per Capita	15
Toxic Chemical Release Per Capita	28
Hazardous Waste Sites	38
Drinking Water Quality	20
Expired Water Pollution Permits	43
Air Pollution Emissions	25

Government - Section D

Members of United States House	31
State Legislators	17
Legislators Per Million Population	13
Units of Government	5
Legislators Compensation	41
Female Legislators	8
Turnover in Legislatures	14
Term Limits	n/a
Legislative Session Length	14
Democrats in State Legislatures	43
Governors' Power Rating	32
Number of Statewide Elected Officials	22
State and Local Government Employees	4
State and Local Average Salaries	35
Local Employment	9
Local Spending Accountability	14
Registered Voters	26
Percentage of Population Voting	27
Statewide Initiatives	n/a
Campaign Costs Per Vote	12

Federal Impacts - Section E

Per Capita Federal Spending	30
Increase in Federal Spending	47
Per Capita Federal Grant Spending	43
Per Capita Federal Spending on Procurement	22
Per Capita Federal Spending on Payments to Individuals	21
Per Capita Federal Spending on Social Security and Medicare	23
Social Security Benefits	13
Federal Spending on Employee Wages and Salaries	16
Per Capita Federal Defense Spending	23
Per Capita Homeland Security Grants	18
Federal Grant Spending Per Dollar of State Tax Revenue	27
General Revenue from Federal Government	29
Federal Tax Burden Per Capita	27
Federal Spending Per Dollar of Taxes Paid	25
Highway Charges Returned to States	17
Terms of Trade	34
Federal Personal Income Taxes	27
Federal Share of Medicaid	25

Taxes - Section F

Tax Revenue	26
Per Capita Tax Revenue	25
Tax Effort	16
Tax Capacity	34
Percentage Change in Taxes	38
Property Taxes as a Percentage of Income	20
Property Taxes Per Capita	24
Property Tax Revenue as a Percentage of 3-tax Revenue	24
Sales Taxes as a Percentage of Income	18
Sales Taxes Per Capita	20
Sales Tax Revenue as a Percentage of 3-tax Revenue	22
Sales Tax Rate	24
Income Taxes as a Percentage of Income	26
Income Taxes Per Capita	23
Income Tax Revenue as a Percentage of 3-tax Revenue	29
Highest Personal Income Rate	21
Corporate Income Taxes	40
Motor Fuel Taxes	14
Motor Vehicle Fees	30
Tobacco Taxes	24
Taxes on High-Income Families	35
Taxes in the Largest City in Each State	41
Progressivity of Taxes	5
Per Capita Estate Tax Revenue	23

Revenues and Finances - Section G

Per Capita Total Revenue	30
Per Capita General Revenue	31

"Own-Source" General Revenue	31
Per Capita Non-Tax Revenue	35
Per Capita Total Spending	36
General Spending as a Percentage of Income	34
Per Capita General Spending	31
Change in General Expenditures	35
State Government General Revenue	36
State Government General Spending	36
State Government General Fund Spending	32
State and Local Debt	36
Debt as a Percentage of Revenue	31
Per Capita Full Faith and Credit Debt	21
Bond Ratings	n/a
State Solvency Index	32
Pension Plan Assets	50
State Reserves	17
Capital Outlays and Interest	37
State Budget Process Quality	39
Relative State Spending "Needs"	25
Structural Deficits	24

Education - Section H

Math Proficiency, Eighth Grade	10
Reading Proficiency, Eighth Grade	12
AFQT Ranks	18
SAT Scores	n/a
ACT Scores	6
Population over 25 with a High School Diploma	11
Students in Private Schools	31
High School Dropout Rates	16
Pupil-Teacher Ratio	33
Public School Enrollment	10
Library Holdings Per Capita	4
Children with Disabilities	33
Education Spending Per Capita	28
Education Spending as a Percentage of General Spending	14
Spending Per Pupil	35
Average Teacher Salary	41
Sources of School Funds	30
State Aid Per Pupil	17
Per Capita Higher Education Spending	14
Higher Education Spending as a Percentage of General Spending	9
Public Higher Education Enrollment	6
Per Pupil Support of Higher Education	25
In-State Tuition and Fees	34
Out-of-State Tuition and Fees	33
Change in Tuition and Fees	11
Affordability Index	18
Average Professor Salary	32
Education Employees	5
R and D Spending	48
Library Operating Spending	11
Head Start Spending	46

Health - Section I

Immunization Rates	42
Infant Mortality Rates	26
State Health Rankings	23
Population without Health Insurance	45
Abortions	9
Alcohol Consumption	46
Percentage of Adult Smokers	39
Percentage Obese	25
AIDS Cases	39
Physicians Per 100,000 Population	30
Hospital Beds Per 1,000 Population	9
Medicaid Recipients	41
Medicaid Recipients as a Percentage of Poverty Population	43
Health and Hospital Spending	21
Health and Hospital Spending as a Percentage of General Spending	19
Per Capita Medicaid Spending	46
Medicaid Spending Per Aged	15
Medicaid Spending Per Child	32
Medicare Payment Per Hospital Day	16
Hospital Expense Per Inpatient Day	33
Population in HMOs	24
Prescription Drugs as a Percentage of Medicaid Costs	32
Percentage Change in Average Price of Prescription Drugs	30

Crime - Section J

Crime Rate	18
Violent Crime Rate	24
Murder Rate	26
Property Crime Rate	18
Motor Vehicle Theft Rate	30
Violent Crime Rate Change	20
Prisoners	32
Change in Prisoners	33
Incarceration Rate	36
Juvenile Violent Crime Rate	37
Law Enforcement Employees	11
Corrections Employees	23
State Corrections Spending	23
Increase in State Corrections Spending	38
Law Enforcement Spending	36
Law Enforcement Spending as a Percentage of General Spending	34

Transportation - Section K

Travel on Interstates	26
Interstate Mileage in "Unacceptable" Condition	45
Deficient Bridges	33
Traffic Deaths	21
Seat Belt Use	43
Vehicle-Miles Traveled Per Capita	26
Use of Public Transportation	48
Road and Street Miles	49
Highway Employees	7
Public Transit Employees	36
Highway Spending Per Capita	13
Highway Spending as a Percentage of General Spending	9

Welfare - Section L

Births to Unwed Mothers	35
TANF Recipients	16
Change in TANF/AFDC Recipients	48
Food Stamp Recipients	38
SSI Recipients	42
WIC Average Monthly Benefit	31
NSLP Recipients	19
Condition of Children Index	15
Families with Single Parent	39
Average Monthly TANF Payments	34
Welfare as a Percentage of Poverty-Level Income	26
State Supplements of SSI	47
State Income Tax Liability of Typical Family in Poverty	35
Child Support Collections	41
Child Support Collections Per Dollar of Administrative Costs	47
Children in Foster Care	18
Welfare Spending Per Capita	43
Welfare Spending as a Percentage of General Spending	38
Administrative Costs Per TANF Case	39

Technology - Section M

Households with Computers	23
Percentage Using Internet	28
Zip Codes with Broadband Service	38
High-Tech Jobs	18
Change in High-Tech Jobs	31
State Government Web Site Ratings	27
Number of Online Government Services	21
Students Per Computer	43
Students Per Internet-Connected Computer	44
Libraries with Internet Access	42

Kentucky

Population - Section A

Population 2005	26
Population 2004	26
Population Change 2003–2004	28
Population Change 1994–2004	26
Population 2015	32
Population 2025	27
Percentage 65 and Over	27
Percentage 17 and Under	36
Median Age	19
Percentage African American	25
Percentage American Indian	48
Percentage Asian American	42
Percentage Hispanic	45
Percentage White (Non-Hispanic)	8
Percentage Mixed-Race	39
Percentage in Poverty	2
Child Poverty Rate	3
Percentage Female	20
Birth Rates	29
Death Rates	6
Population Density	22
Legal Immigrants FY 2004	31
Unauthorized Immigrants	37

Economies - Section B

Personal Income, 2004	27
Gross State Product	40
Per Capita Personal Income	44
Personal Income from Wages and Salaries	25
Average Annual Pay	33
Average Hourly Earnings	16
Value Added in Manufacturing	9
Cost of Living	36
Average Annual Pay in Manufacturing	23
Average Annual Pay in Retailing	37
Labor Force	46
Unemployment Rate	9
Employment Rate	42
Government Employment	25
Manufacturing Employment	11
Fortune 500 Companies	23
Forbes 500 Companies	37
Tourism Spending Per Capita	41
Exports Per Capita	7
Housing Permits	33
Percentage Change in Home Prices	42
Net Farm Income	26
Financial Institution Assets	38
Bankruptcy Filings	10
Patents Issued	41
WC Disability Payment	27
Average Weekly UC Benefit	26
Economic Momentum	41
One-year Employment Change	28
Manufacturing Employment Change	19
Home Ownership	14
Annual Electricity Use Per Residential Customer	9
Cost Per Kwh	12
New Companies	44

Geography - Section C

Total Land Area	36
Federally Owned Land	27
State Park Acreage	40
State Park Visitors	32
Population Not Active	2
Hunters with Firearms	9
Registered Boats	28
State Spending for the Arts	17
Energy Consumption Per Capita	6
Toxic Chemical Release Per Capita	15
Hazardous Waste Sites	23
Drinking Water Quality	23
Expired Water Pollution Permits	7
Air Pollution Emissions	19

Government - Section D

Members of United States House	25
State Legislators	29
Legislators Per Million Population	26
Units of Government	25
Legislators Compensation	30
Female Legislators	48
Turnover in Legislatures	33
Term Limits	n/a
Legislative Session Length	14
Democrats in State Legislatures	22
Governors' Power Rating	26
Number of Statewide Elected Officials	9
State and Local Government Employees	17
State and Local Average Salaries	38
Local Employment	38
Local Spending Accountability	33
Registered Voters	19
Percentage of Population Voting	35
Statewide Initiatives	n/a
Campaign Costs Per Vote	27

Federal Impacts - Section E

Per Capita Federal Spending	18
Increase in Federal Spending	20
Per Capita Federal Grant Spending	18
Per Capita Federal Spending on Procurement	17
Per Capita Federal Spending on Payments to Individuals	20
Per Capita Federal Spending on Social Security and Medicare	14
Social Security Benefits	45
Federal Spending on Employee Wages and Salaries	17
Per Capita Federal Defense Spending	18
Per Capita Homeland Security Grants	25
Federal Grant Spending Per Dollar of State Tax Revenue	23
General Revenue from Federal Government	14
Federal Tax Burden Per Capita	41
Federal Spending Per Dollar of Taxes Paid	10
Highway Charges Returned to States	34
Terms of Trade	13
Federal Personal Income Taxes	40
Federal Share of Medicaid	11

Taxes - Section F

Tax Revenue	16
Per Capita Tax Revenue	37
Tax Effort	21
Tax Capacity	43
Percentage Change in Taxes	29
Property Taxes as a Percentage of Income	43
Property Taxes Per Capita	45
Property Tax Revenue as a Percentage of 3-tax Revenue	44
Sales Taxes as a Percentage of Income	21
Sales Taxes Per Capita	34
Sales Tax Revenue as a Percentage of 3-tax Revenue	20
Sales Tax Rate	10
Income Taxes as a Percentage of Income	5
Income Taxes Per Capita	14
Income Tax Revenue as a Percentage of 3-tax Revenue	5
Highest Personal Income Rate	22
Corporate Income Taxes	19
Motor Fuel Taxes	41
Motor Vehicle Fees	46
Tobacco Taxes	44
Taxes on High-Income Families	15
Taxes in the Largest City in Each State	14
Progressivity of Taxes	34
Per Capita Estate Tax Revenue	37

Revenues and Finances - Section G

Per Capita Total Revenue	41
Per Capita General Revenue	38

"Own-Source" General Revenue	44
Per Capita Non-Tax Revenue	40
Per Capita Total Spending	38
General Spending as a Percentage of Income	21
Per Capita General Spending	39
Change in General Expenditures	21
State Government General Revenue	22
State Government General Spending	22
State Government General Fund Spending	10
State and Local Debt	7
Debt as a Percentage of Revenue	2
Per Capita Full Faith and Credit Debt	44
Bond Ratings	n/a
State Solvency Index	30
Pension Plan Assets	39
State Reserves	37
Capital Outlays and Interest	25
State Budget Process Quality	26
Relative State Spending "Needs"	28
Structural Deficits	30

Education - Section H

Math Proficiency, Eighth Grade	35
Reading Proficiency, Eighth Grade	23
AFQT Ranks	42
SAT Scores	n/a
ACT Scores	16
Population over 25 with a High School Diploma	43
Students in Private Schools	20
High School Dropout Rates	35
Pupil-Teacher Ratio	16
Public School Enrollment	41
Library Holdings Per Capita	40
Children with Disabilities	6
Education Spending Per Capita	47
Education Spending as a Percentage of General Spending	43
Spending Per Pupil	28
Average Teacher Salary	33
Sources of School Funds	39
State Aid Per Pupil	15
Per Capita Higher Education Spending	23
Higher Education Spending as a Percentage of General Spending	14
Public Higher Education Enrollment	23
Per Pupil Support of Higher Education	12
In-State Tuition and Fees	30
Out-of-State Tuition and Fees	40
Change in Tuition and Fees	4
Affordability Index	14
Average Professor Salary	35
Education Employees	9
R and D Spending	49
Library Operating Spending	40
Head Start Spending	37

Health - Section I

Immunization Rates	43
Infant Mortality Rates	23
State Health Rankings	42
Population without Health Insurance	23
Abortions	45
Alcohol Consumption	48
Percentage of Adult Smokers	1
Percentage Obese	7
AIDS Cases	33
Physicians Per 100,000 Population	31
Hospital Beds Per 1,000 Population	11
Medicaid Recipients	16
Medicaid Recipients as a Percentage of Poverty Population	40
Health and Hospital Spending	39
Health and Hospital Spending as a Percentage of General Spending	34
Per Capita Medicaid Spending	17
Medicaid Spending Per Aged	31
Medicaid Spending Per Child	15
Medicare Payment Per Hospital Day	38
Hospital Expense Per Inpatient Day	45
Population in HMOs	36
Prescription Drugs as a Percentage of Medicaid Costs	4
Percentage Change in Average Price of Prescription Drugs	49

Crime - Section J

Crime Rate	43
Violent Crime Rate	42
Murder Rate	17
Property Crime Rate	40
Motor Vehicle Theft Rate	39
Violent Crime Rate Change	43
Prisoners	26
Change in Prisoners	25
Incarceration Rate	21
Juvenile Violent Crime Rate	21
Law Enforcement Employees	40
Corrections Employees	37
State Corrections Spending	37
Increase in State Corrections Spending	25
Law Enforcement Spending	41
Law Enforcement Spending as a Percentage of General Spending	38

Transportation - Section K

Travel on Interstates	19
Interstate Mileage in "Unacceptable" Condition	39
Deficient Bridges	15
Traffic Deaths	8
Seat Belt Use	46
Vehicle-Miles Traveled Per Capita	15
Use of Public Transportation	32
Road and Street Miles	8
Highway Employees	27
Public Transit Employees	29
Highway Spending Per Capita	20
Highway Spending as a Percentage of General Spending	16

Welfare - Section L

Births to Unwed Mothers	28
TANF Recipients	12
Change in TANF/AFDC Recipients	29
Food Stamp Recipients	5
SSI Recipients	1
WIC Average Monthly Benefit	18
NSLP Recipients	6
Condition of Children Index	42
Families with Single Parent	23
Average Monthly TANF Payments	42
Welfare as a Percentage of Poverty-Level Income	39
State Supplements of SSI	7
State Income Tax Liability of Typical Family in Poverty	1
Child Support Collections	18
Child Support Collections Per Dollar of Administrative Costs	9
Children in Foster Care	26
Welfare Spending Per Capita	8
Welfare Spending as a Percentage of General Spending	3
Administrative Costs Per TANF Case	43

Technology - Section M

Households with Computers	40
Percentage Using Internet	41
Zip Codes with Broadband Service	38
High-Tech Jobs	40
Change in High-Tech Jobs	24
State Government Web Site Ratings	34
Number of Online Government Services	29
Students Per Computer	22
Students Per Internet-Connected Computer	24
Libraries with Internet Access	1

Louisiana

Population - Section A

Population 2005	24
Population 2004	24
Population Change 2003–2004	37
Population Change 1994–2004	45
Population 2015	40
Population 2025	25
Percentage 65 and Over	39
Percentage 17 and Under	11
Median Age	40
Percentage African American	2
Percentage American Indian	23
Percentage Asian American	33
Percentage Hispanic	38
Percentage White (Non-Hispanic)	40
Percentage Mixed-Race	49
Percentage in Poverty	4
Child Poverty Rate	10
Percentage Female	9
Birth Rates	13
Death Rates	2
Population Density	23
Legal Immigrants FY 2004	34
Unauthorized Immigrants	40

Economies - Section B

Personal Income, 2004	25
Gross State Product	39
Per Capita Personal Income	42
Personal Income from Wages and Salaries	38
Average Annual Pay	38
Average Hourly Earnings	12
Value Added in Manufacturing	22
Cost of Living	26
Average Annual Pay in Manufacturing	16
Average Annual Pay in Retailing	43
Labor Force	50
Unemployment Rate	1
Employment Rate	50
Government Employment	4
Manufacturing Employment	35
Fortune 500 Companies	39
Forbes 500 Companies	35
Tourism Spending Per Capita	11
Exports Per Capita	5
Housing Permits	36
Percentage Change in Home Prices	33
Net Farm Income	30
Financial Institution Assets	34
Bankruptcy Filings	15
Patents Issued	45
WC Disability Payment	46
Average Weekly UC Benefit	46
Economic Momentum	42
One-year Employment Change	47
Manufacturing Employment Change	38
Home Ownership	33
Annual Electricity Use Per Residential Customer	1
Cost Per Kwh	43
New Companies	39

Geography - Section C

Total Land Area	33
Federally Owned Land	25
State Park Acreage	44
State Park Visitors	48
Population Not Active	2
Hunters with Firearms	11
Registered Boats	15
State Spending for the Arts	15
Energy Consumption Per Capita	3
Toxic Chemical Release Per Capita	11
Hazardous Waste Sites	34
Drinking Water Quality	26
Expired Water Pollution Permits	25
Air Pollution Emissions	18

Government - Section D

Members of United States House	22
State Legislators	25
Legislators Per Million Population	27
Units of Government	45
Legislators Compensation	24
Female Legislators	34
Turnover in Legislatures	n/a
Term Limits	1
Legislative Session Length	23
Democrats in State Legislatures	8
Governors' Power Rating	29
Number of Statewide Elected Officials	9
State and Local Government Employees	8
State and Local Average Salaries	47
Local Employment	35
Local Spending Accountability	15
Registered Voters	24
Percentage of Population Voting	32
Statewide Initiatives	n/a
Campaign Costs Per Vote	3

Federal Impacts - Section E

Per Capita Federal Spending	25
Increase in Federal Spending	41
Per Capita Federal Grant Spending	14
Per Capita Federal Spending on Procurement	28
Per Capita Federal Spending on Payments to Individuals	14
Per Capita Federal Spending on Social Security and Medicare	11
Social Security Benefits	49
Federal Spending on Employee Wages and Salaries	30
Per Capita Federal Defense Spending	27
Per Capita Homeland Security Grants	27
Federal Grant Spending Per Dollar of State Tax Revenue	11
General Revenue from Federal Government	17
Federal Tax Burden Per Capita	46
Federal Spending Per Dollar of Taxes Paid	14
Highway Charges Returned to States	38
Terms of Trade	12
Federal Personal Income Taxes	42
Federal Share of Medicaid	8

Taxes - Section F

Tax Revenue	10
Per Capita Tax Revenue	31
Tax Effort	20
Tax Capacity	45
Percentage Change in Taxes	14
Property Taxes as a Percentage of Income	44
Property Taxes Per Capita	46
Property Tax Revenue as a Percentage of 3-tax Revenue	47
Sales Taxes as a Percentage of Income	2
Sales Taxes Per Capita	4
Sales Tax Revenue as a Percentage of 3-tax Revenue	4
Sales Tax Rate	38
Income Taxes as a Percentage of Income	38
Income Taxes Per Capita	38
Income Tax Revenue as a Percentage of 3-tax Revenue	38
Highest Personal Income Rate	36
Corporate Income Taxes	32
Motor Fuel Taxes	28
Motor Vehicle Fees	29
Tobacco Taxes	41
Taxes on High-Income Families	21
Taxes in the Largest City in Each State	35
Progressivity of Taxes	2
Per Capita Estate Tax Revenue	46

Revenues and Finances - Section G

Per Capita Total Revenue	22
Per Capita General Revenue	21

Louisiana

"Own-Source" General Revenue	27
Per Capita Non-Tax Revenue	12
Per Capita Total Spending	35
General Spending as a Percentage of Income	14
Per Capita General Spending	33
Change in General Expenditures	44
State Government General Revenue	21
State Government General Spending	34
State Government General Fund Spending	17
State and Local Debt	31
Debt as a Percentage of Revenue	32
Per Capita Full Faith and Credit Debt	33
Bond Ratings	6
State Solvency Index	35
Pension Plan Assets	25
State Reserves	30
Capital Outlays and Interest	39
State Budget Process Quality	6
Relative State Spending "Needs"	47
Structural Deficits	19

Education - Section H

Math Proficiency, Eighth Grade	46
Reading Proficiency, Eighth Grade	44
AFQT Ranks	49
SAT Scores	n/a
ACT Scores	24
Population over 25 with a High School Diploma	49
Students in Private Schools	3
High School Dropout Rates	35
Pupil-Teacher Ratio	27
Public School Enrollment	27
Library Holdings Per Capita	32
Children with Disabilities	29
Education Spending Per Capita	43
Education Spending as a Percentage of General Spending	36
Spending Per Pupil	34
Average Teacher Salary	43
Sources of School Funds	32
State Aid Per Pupil	31
Per Capita Higher Education Spending	40
Higher Education Spending as a Percentage of General Spending	39
Public Higher Education Enrollment	31
Per Pupil Support of Higher Education	7
In-State Tuition and Fees	40
Out-of-State Tuition and Fees	46
Change in Tuition and Fees	35
Affordability Index	27
Average Professor Salary	42
Education Employees	17
R and D Spending	42
Library Operating Spending	31
Head Start Spending	41

Health - Section I

Immunization Rates	45
Infant Mortality Rates	2
State Health Rankings	49
Population without Health Insurance	9
Abortions	30
Alcohol Consumption	18
Percentage of Adult Smokers	14
Percentage Obese	5
AIDS Cases	4
Physicians Per 100,000 Population	49
Hospital Beds Per 1,000 Population	8
Medicaid Recipients	7
Medicaid Recipients as a Percentage of Poverty Population	22
Health and Hospital Spending	3
Health and Hospital Spending as a Percentage of General Spending	2
Per Capita Medicaid Spending	12
Medicaid Spending Per Aged	41
Medicaid Spending Per Child	44
Medicare Payment Per Hospital Day	20
Hospital Expense Per Inpatient Day	48
Population in HMOs	34
Prescription Drugs as a Percentage of Medicaid Costs	16
Percentage Change in Average Price of Prescription Drugs	5

Crime - Section J

Crime Rate	4
Violent Crime Rate	6
Murder Rate	1
Property Crime Rate	7
Motor Vehicle Theft Rate	13
Violent Crime Rate Change	25
Prisoners	10
Change in Prisoners	21
Incarceration Rate	1
Juvenile Violent Crime Rate	8
Law Enforcement Employees	6
Corrections Employees	6
State Corrections Spending	44
Increase in State Corrections Spending	21
Law Enforcement Spending	24
Law Enforcement Spending as a Percentage of General Spending	18

Transportation - Section K

Travel on Interstates	14
Interstate Mileage in "Unacceptable" Condition	12
Deficient Bridges	14
Traffic Deaths	9
Seat Belt Use	32
Vehicle-Miles Traveled Per Capita	37
Use of Public Transportation	21
Road and Street Miles	10
Highway Employees	21
Public Transit Employees	24
Highway Spending Per Capita	42
Highway Spending as a Percentage of General Spending	36

Welfare - Section L

Births to Unwed Mothers	2
TANF Recipients	40
Change in TANF/AFDC Recipients	4
Food Stamp Recipients	1
SSI Recipients	4
WIC Average Monthly Benefit	12
NSLP Recipients	1
Condition of Children Index	49
Families with Single Parent	2
Average Monthly TANF Payments	36
Welfare as a Percentage of Poverty-Level Income	45
State Supplements of SSI	46
State Income Tax Liability of Typical Family in Poverty	7
Child Support Collections	32
Child Support Collections Per Dollar of Administrative Costs	21
Children in Foster Care	46
Welfare Spending Per Capita	40
Welfare Spending as a Percentage of General Spending	34
Administrative Costs Per TANF Case	8

Technology - Section M

Households with Computers	48
Percentage Using Internet	48
Zip Codes with Broadband Service	16
High-Tech Jobs	48
Change in High-Tech Jobs	18
State Government Web Site Ratings	46
Number of Online Government Services	45
Students Per Computer	5
Students Per Internet-Connected Computer	5
Libraries with Internet Access	1

Maine

Population - Section A

Population 2005	40
Population 2004	40
Population Change 2003–2004	32
Population Change 1994–2004	38
Population 2015	30
Population 2025	42
Percentage 65 and Over	6
Percentage 17 and Under	49
Median Age	1
Percentage African American	46
Percentage American Indian	26
Percentage Asian American	43
Percentage Hispanic	49
Percentage White (Non-Hispanic)	1
Percentage Mixed-Race	44
Percentage in Poverty	23
Child Poverty Rate	31
Percentage Female	14
Birth Rates	49
Death Rates	27
Population Density	38
Legal Immigrants FY 2004	42
Unauthorized Immigrants	43

Economies - Section B

Personal Income, 2004	41
Gross State Product	41
Per Capita Personal Income	34
Personal Income from Wages and Salaries	41
Average Annual Pay	37
Average Hourly Earnings	10
Value Added in Manufacturing	29
Cost of Living	n/a
Average Annual Pay in Manufacturing	35
Average Annual Pay in Retailing	33
Labor Force	11
Unemployment Rate	17
Employment Rate	34
Government Employment	26
Manufacturing Employment	29
Fortune 500 Companies	n/a
Forbes 500 Companies	36
Tourism Spending Per Capita	33
Exports Per Capita	37
Housing Permits	21
Percentage Change in Home Prices	13
Net Farm Income	44
Financial Institution Assets	10
Bankruptcy Filings	44
Patents Issued	39
WC Disability Payment	40
Average Weekly UC Benefit	32
Economic Momentum	43
One-year Employment Change	44
Manufacturing Employment Change	46
Home Ownership	10
Annual Electricity Use Per Residential Customer	50
Cost Per Kwh	4
New Companies	21

Geography - Section C

Total Land Area	39
Federally Owned Land	44
State Park Acreage	30
State Park Visitors	35
Population Not Active	31
Hunters with Firearms	14
Registered Boats	35
State Spending for the Arts	31
Energy Consumption Per Capita	16
Toxic Chemical Release Per Capita	38
Hazardous Waste Sites	30
Drinking Water Quality	2
Expired Water Pollution Permits	34
Air Pollution Emissions	44

Government - Section D

Members of United States House	39
State Legislators	10
Legislators Per Million Population	6
Units of Government	11
Legislators Compensation	39
Female Legislators	23
Turnover in Legislatures	1
Term Limits	4
Legislative Session Length	12
Democrats in State Legislatures	24
Governors' Power Rating	17
Number of Statewide Elected Officials	48
State and Local Government Employees	14
State and Local Average Salaries	36
Local Employment	19
Local Spending Accountability	1
Registered Voters	n/a
Percentage of Population Voting	2
Statewide Initiatives	4
Campaign Costs Per Vote	29

Federal Impacts - Section E

Per Capita Federal Spending	13
Increase in Federal Spending	14
Per Capita Federal Grant Spending	11
Per Capita Federal Spending on Procurement	12
Per Capita Federal Spending on Payments to Individuals	19
Per Capita Federal Spending on Social Security and Medicare	18
Social Security Benefits	46
Federal Spending on Employee Wages and Salaries	23
Per Capita Federal Defense Spending	8
Per Capita Homeland Security Grants	11
Federal Grant Spending Per Dollar of State Tax Revenue	18
General Revenue from Federal Government	20
Federal Tax Burden Per Capita	33
Federal Spending Per Dollar of Taxes Paid	16
Highway Charges Returned to States	43
Terms of Trade	9
Federal Personal Income Taxes	35
Federal Share of Medicaid	20

Taxes - Section F

Tax Revenue	2
Per Capita Tax Revenue	8
Tax Effort	4
Tax Capacity	35
Percentage Change in Taxes	12
Property Taxes as a Percentage of Income	1
Property Taxes Per Capita	4
Property Tax Revenue as a Percentage of 3-tax Revenue	8
Sales Taxes as a Percentage of Income	29
Sales Taxes Per Capita	35
Sales Tax Revenue as a Percentage of 3-tax Revenue	41
Sales Tax Rate	25
Income Taxes as a Percentage of Income	11
Income Taxes Per Capita	15
Income Tax Revenue as a Percentage of 3-tax Revenue	27
Highest Personal Income Rate	6
Corporate Income Taxes	31
Motor Fuel Taxes	10
Motor Vehicle Fees	30
Tobacco Taxes	17
Taxes on High-Income Families	7
Taxes in the Largest City in Each State	11
Progressivity of Taxes	10
Per Capita Estate Tax Revenue	10

Revenues and Finances - Section G

Per Capita Total Revenue	20
Per Capita General Revenue	11

"Own-Source" General Revenue	14
Per Capita Non-Tax Revenue	38
Per Capita Total Spending	24
General Spending as a Percentage of Income	13
Per Capita General Spending	17
Change in General Expenditures	26
State Government General Revenue	10
State Government General Spending	12
State Government General Fund Spending	12
State and Local Debt	26
Debt as a Percentage of Revenue	29
Per Capita Full Faith and Credit Debt	36
Bond Ratings	4
State Solvency Index	38
Pension Plan Assets	9
State Reserves	42
Capital Outlays and Interest	48
State Budget Process Quality	31
Relative State Spending "Needs"	4
Structural Deficits	10

Education - Section H

Math Proficiency, Eighth Grade	20
Reading Proficiency, Eighth Grade	2
AFQT Ranks	12
SAT Scores	14
ACT Scores	n/a
Population over 25 with a High School Diploma	27
Students in Private Schools	29
High School Dropout Rates	23
Pupil-Teacher Ratio	47
Public School Enrollment	44
Library Holdings Per Capita	1
Children with Disabilities	2
Education Spending Per Capita	35
Education Spending as a Percentage of General Spending	45
Spending Per Pupil	7
Average Teacher Salary	37
Sources of School Funds	15
State Aid Per Pupil	23
Per Capita Higher Education Spending	46
Higher Education Spending as a Percentage of General Spending	44
Public Higher Education Enrollment	45
Per Pupil Support of Higher Education	26
In-State Tuition and Fees	17
Out-of-State Tuition and Fees	24
Change in Tuition and Fees	32
Affordability Index	46
Average Professor Salary	37
Education Employees	4
R and D Spending	40
Library Operating Spending	29
Head Start Spending	29

Health - Section I

Immunization Rates	17
Infant Mortality Rates	31
State Health Rankings	8
Population without Health Insurance	47
Abortions	28
Alcohol Consumption	20
Percentage of Adult Smokers	24
Percentage Obese	23
AIDS Cases	37
Physicians Per 100,000 Population	10
Hospital Beds Per 1,000 Population	26
Medicaid Recipients	9
Medicaid Recipients as a Percentage of Poverty Population	4
Health and Hospital Spending	35
Health and Hospital Spending as a Percentage of General Spending	36
Per Capita Medicaid Spending	2
Medicaid Spending Per Aged	49
Medicaid Spending Per Child	1
Medicare Payment Per Hospital Day	42
Hospital Expense Per Inpatient Day	8
Population in HMOs	10
Prescription Drugs as a Percentage of Medicaid Costs	11
Percentage Change in Average Price of Prescription Drugs	50

Crime - Section J

Crime Rate	46
Violent Crime Rate	49
Murder Rate	48
Property Crime Rate	45
Motor Vehicle Theft Rate	49
Violent Crime Rate Change	23
Prisoners	47
Change in Prisoners	20
Incarceration Rate	50
Juvenile Violent Crime Rate	45
Law Enforcement Employees	43
Corrections Employees	45
State Corrections Spending	2
Increase in State Corrections Spending	5
Law Enforcement Spending	48
Law Enforcement Spending as a Percentage of General Spending	48

Transportation - Section K

Travel on Interstates	40
Interstate Mileage in "Unacceptable" Condition	35
Deficient Bridges	9
Traffic Deaths	32
Seat Belt Use	35
Vehicle-Miles Traveled Per Capita	17
Use of Public Transportation	40
Road and Street Miles	7
Highway Employees	11
Public Transit Employees	42
Highway Spending Per Capita	19
Highway Spending as a Percentage of General Spending	25

Welfare - Section L

Births to Unwed Mothers	30
TANF Recipients	10
Change in TANF/AFDC Recipients	38
Food Stamp Recipients	11
SSI Recipients	15
WIC Average Monthly Benefit	50
NSLP Recipients	38
Condition of Children Index	7
Families with Single Parent	36
Average Monthly TANF Payments	5
Welfare as a Percentage of Poverty-Level Income	7
State Supplements of SSI	45
State Income Tax Liability of Typical Family in Poverty	17
Child Support Collections	21
Child Support Collections Per Dollar of Administrative Costs	33
Children in Foster Care	5
Welfare Spending Per Capita	5
Welfare Spending as a Percentage of General Spending	2
Administrative Costs Per TANF Case	48

Technology - Section M

Households with Computers	9
Percentage Using Internet	13
Zip Codes with Broadband Service	33
High-Tech Jobs	38
Change in High-Tech Jobs	47
State Government Web Site Ratings	2
Number of Online Government Services	2
Students Per Computer	47
Students Per Internet-Connected Computer	47
Libraries with Internet Access	44

Maryland

Population - Section A

Population 2005	19
Population 2004	19
Population Change 2003–2004	24
Population Change 1994–2004	19
Population 2015	14
Population 2025	17
Percentage 65 and Over	40
Percentage 17 and Under	15
Median Age	28
Percentage African American	5
Percentage American Indian	39
Percentage Asian American	7
Percentage Hispanic	27
Percentage White (Non-Hispanic)	46
Percentage Mixed-Race	14
Percentage in Poverty	39
Child Poverty Rate	43
Percentage Female	4
Birth Rates	25
Death Rates	17
Population Density	5
Legal Immigrants FY 2004	9
Unauthorized Immigrants	19

Economies - Section B

Personal Income, 2004	14
Gross State Product	15
Per Capita Personal Income	4
Personal Income from Wages and Salaries	42
Average Annual Pay	6
Average Hourly Earnings	11
Value Added in Manufacturing	44
Cost of Living	8
Average Annual Pay in Manufacturing	6
Average Annual Pay in Retailing	9
Labor Force	16
Unemployment Rate	37
Employment Rate	14
Government Employment	15
Manufacturing Employment	43
Fortune 500 Companies	28
Forbes 500 Companies	22
Tourism Spending Per Capita	24
Exports Per Capita	44
Housing Permits	38
Percentage Change in Home Prices	6
Net Farm Income	35
Financial Institution Assets	45
Bankruptcy Filings	27
Patents Issued	23
WC Disability Payment	11
Average Weekly UC Benefit	24
Economic Momentum	17
One-year Employment Change	10
Manufacturing Employment Change	48
Home Ownership	24
Annual Electricity Use Per Residential Customer	13
Cost Per Kwh	33
New Companies	11

Geography - Section C

Total Land Area	42
Federally Owned Land	45
State Park Acreage	12
State Park Visitors	30
Population Not Active	28
Hunters with Firearms	37
Registered Boats	24
State Spending for the Arts	7
Energy Consumption Per Capita	41
Toxic Chemical Release Per Capita	36
Hazardous Waste Sites	20
Drinking Water Quality	40
Expired Water Pollution Permits	33
Air Pollution Emissions	28

Government - Section D

Members of United States House	18
State Legislators	8
Legislators Per Million Population	25
Units of Government	49
Legislators Compensation	10
Female Legislators	1
Turnover in Legislatures	n/a
Term Limits	n/a
Legislative Session Length	21
Democrats in State Legislatures	5
Governors' Power Rating	8
Number of Statewide Elected Officials	41
State and Local Government Employees	40
State and Local Average Salaries	9
Local Employment	36
Local Spending Accountability	2
Registered Voters	34
Percentage of Population Voting	22
Statewide Initiatives	n/a
Campaign Costs Per Vote	49

Federal Impacts - Section E

Per Capita Federal Spending	3
Increase in Federal Spending	6
Per Capita Federal Grant Spending	20
Per Capita Federal Spending on Procurement	2
Per Capita Federal Spending on Payments to Individuals	8
Per Capita Federal Spending on Social Security and Medicare	35
Social Security Benefits	15
Federal Spending on Employee Wages and Salaries	4
Per Capita Federal Defense Spending	5
Per Capita Homeland Security Grants	32
Federal Grant Spending Per Dollar of State Tax Revenue	41
General Revenue from Federal Government	42
Federal Tax Burden Per Capita	8
Federal Spending Per Dollar of Taxes Paid	17
Highway Charges Returned to States	27
Terms of Trade	37
Federal Personal Income Taxes	5
Federal Share of Medicaid	39

Taxes - Section F

Tax Revenue	20
Per Capita Tax Revenue	7
Tax Effort	11
Tax Capacity	17
Percentage Change in Taxes	6
Property Taxes as a Percentage of Income	32
Property Taxes Per Capita	16
Property Tax Revenue as a Percentage of 3-tax Revenue	35
Sales Taxes as a Percentage of Income	44
Sales Taxes Per Capita	40
Sales Tax Revenue as a Percentage of 3-tax Revenue	44
Sales Tax Rate	25
Income Taxes as a Percentage of Income	2
Income Taxes Per Capita	2
Income Tax Revenue as a Percentage of 3-tax Revenue	3
Highest Personal Income Rate	33
Corporate Income Taxes	26
Motor Fuel Taxes	16
Motor Vehicle Fees	7
Tobacco Taxes	17
Taxes on High-Income Families	8
Taxes in the Largest City in Each State	5
Progressivity of Taxes	9
Per Capita Estate Tax Revenue	15

Revenues and Finances - Section G

Per Capita Total Revenue	21
Per Capita General Revenue	18

Maryland

"Own-Source" General Revenue	10
Per Capita Non-Tax Revenue	42
Per Capita Total Spending	29
General Spending as a Percentage of Income	47
Per Capita General Spending	25
Change in General Expenditures	15
State Government General Revenue	29
State Government General Spending	27
State Government General Fund Spending	38
State and Local Debt	30
Debt as a Percentage of Revenue	33
Per Capita Full Faith and Credit Debt	16
Bond Ratings	1
State Solvency Index	31
Pension Plan Assets	13
State Reserves	7
Capital Outlays and Interest	30
State Budget Process Quality	11
Relative State Spending "Needs"	17
Structural Deficits	11

Education - Section H

Math Proficiency, Eighth Grade	31
Reading Proficiency, Eighth Grade	29
AFQT Ranks	35
SAT Scores	10
ACT Scores	n/a
Population over 25 with a High School Diploma	24
Students in Private Schools	5
High School Dropout Rates	14
Pupil-Teacher Ratio	22
Public School Enrollment	37
Library Holdings Per Capita	24
Children with Disabilities	38
Education Spending Per Capita	13
Education Spending as a Percentage of General Spending	9
Spending Per Pupil	11
Average Teacher Salary	11
Sources of School Funds	7
State Aid Per Pupil	32
Per Capita Higher Education Spending	15
Higher Education Spending as a Percentage of General Spending	15
Public Higher Education Enrollment	26
Per Pupil Support of Higher Education	27
In-State Tuition and Fees	11
Out-of-State Tuition and Fees	12
Change in Tuition and Fees	21
Affordability Index	27
Average Professor Salary	8
Education Employees	41
R and D Spending	2
Library Operating Spending	14
Head Start Spending	12

Health - Section I

Immunization Rates	40
Infant Mortality Rates	10
State Health Rankings	34
Population without Health Insurance	22
Abortions	26
Alcohol Consumption	35
Percentage of Adult Smokers	41
Percentage Obese	19
AIDS Cases	3
Physicians Per 100,000 Population	2
Hospital Beds Per 1,000 Population	42
Medicaid Recipients	33
Medicaid Recipients as a Percentage of Poverty Population	19
Health and Hospital Spending	45
Health and Hospital Spending as a Percentage of General Spending	44
Per Capita Medicaid Spending	29
Medicaid Spending Per Aged	13
Medicaid Spending Per Child	7
Medicare Payment Per Hospital Day	50
Hospital Expense Per Inpatient Day	24
Population in HMOs	6
Prescription Drugs as a Percentage of Medicaid Costs	45
Percentage Change in Average Price of Prescription Drugs	7

Crime - Section J

Crime Rate	19
Violent Crime Rate	3
Murder Rate	2
Property Crime Rate	22
Motor Vehicle Theft Rate	6
Violent Crime Rate Change	33
Prisoners	21
Change in Prisoners	44
Incarceration Rate	22
Juvenile Violent Crime Rate	4
Law Enforcement Employees	16
Corrections Employees	11
State Corrections Spending	19
Increase in State Corrections Spending	23
Law Enforcement Spending	6
Law Enforcement Spending as a Percentage of General Spending	4

Transportation - Section K

Travel on Interstates	6
Interstate Mileage in "Unacceptable" Condition	8
Deficient Bridges	19
Traffic Deaths	41
Seat Belt Use	8
Vehicle-Miles Traveled Per Capita	35
Use of Public Transportation	3
Road and Street Miles	20
Highway Employees	38
Public Transit Employees	15
Highway Spending Per Capita	43
Highway Spending as a Percentage of General Spending	42

Welfare - Section L

Births to Unwed Mothers	21
TANF Recipients	34
Change in TANF/AFDC Recipients	12
Food Stamp Recipients	44
SSI Recipients	30
WIC Average Monthly Benefit	38
NSLP Recipients	44
Condition of Children Index	19
Families with Single Parent	13
Average Monthly TANF Payments	24
Welfare as a Percentage of Poverty-Level Income	27
State Supplements of SSI	16
State Income Tax Liability of Typical Family in Poverty	37
Child Support Collections	19
Child Support Collections Per Dollar of Administrative Costs	27
Children in Foster Care	17
Welfare Spending Per Capita	31
Welfare Spending as a Percentage of General Spending	31
Administrative Costs Per TANF Case	14

Technology - Section M

Households with Computers	14
Percentage Using Internet	12
Zip Codes with Broadband Service	6
High-Tech Jobs	4
Change in High-Tech Jobs	13
State Government Web Site Ratings	30
Number of Online Government Services	18
Students Per Computer	7
Students Per Internet-Connected Computer	5
Libraries with Internet Access	1

Massachusetts

Population - Section A

Population 2005	13
Population 2004	13
Population Change 2003–2004	50
Population Change 1994–2004	43
Population 2015	31
Population 2025	16
Percentage 65 and Over	13
Percentage 17 and Under	44
Median Age	11
Percentage African American	27
Percentage American Indian	44
Percentage Asian American	8
Percentage Hispanic	19
Percentage White (Non-Hispanic)	22
Percentage Mixed-Race	23
Percentage in Poverty	43
Child Poverty Rate	46
Percentage Female	3
Birth Rates	41
Death Rates	37
Population Density	3
Legal Immigrants FY 2004	7
Unauthorized Immigrants	15

Economies - Section B

Personal Income, 2004	10
Gross State Product	4
Per Capita Personal Income	2
Personal Income from Wages and Salaries	3
Average Annual Pay	3
Average Hourly Earnings	8
Value Added in Manufacturing	18
Cost of Living	4
Average Annual Pay in Manufacturing	2
Average Annual Pay in Retailing	5
Labor Force	20
Unemployment Rate	30
Employment Rate	21
Government Employment	49
Manufacturing Employment	30
Fortune 500 Companies	19
Forbes 500 Companies	9
Tourism Spending Per Capita	32
Exports Per Capita	10
Housing Permits	46
Percentage Change in Home Prices	11
Net Farm Income	46
Financial Institution Assets	9
Bankruptcy Filings	47
Patents Issued	3
WC Disability Payment	5
Average Weekly UC Benefit	1
Economic Momentum	46
One-year Employment Change	46
Manufacturing Employment Change	31
Home Ownership	46
Annual Electricity Use Per Residential Customer	43
Cost Per Kwh	47
New Companies	27

Geography - Section C

Total Land Area	45
Federally Owned Land	47
State Park Acreage	9
State Park Visitors	39
Population Not Active	37
Hunters with Firearms	46
Registered Boats	29
State Spending for the Arts	11
Energy Consumption Per Capita	46
Toxic Chemical Release Per Capita	48
Hazardous Waste Sites	11
Drinking Water Quality	28
Expired Water Pollution Permits	13
Air Pollution Emissions	29

Government - Section D

Members of United States House	13
State Legislators	6
Legislators Per Million Population	28
Units of Government	40
Legislators Compensation	7
Female Legislators	19
Turnover in Legislatures	41
Term Limits	n/a
Legislative Session Length	n/a
Democrats in State Legislatures	1
Governors' Power Rating	17
Number of Statewide Elected Officials	22
State and Local Government Employees	41
State and Local Average Salaries	8
Local Employment	16
Local Spending Accountability	34
Registered Voters	15
Percentage of Population Voting	16
Statewide Initiatives	n/a
Campaign Costs Per Vote	19

Federal Impacts - Section E

Per Capita Federal Spending	12
Increase in Federal Spending	34
Per Capita Federal Grant Spending	7
Per Capita Federal Spending on Procurement	9
Per Capita Federal Spending on Payments to Individuals	18
Per Capita Federal Spending on Social Security and Medicare	5
Social Security Benefits	17
Federal Spending on Employee Wages and Salaries	36
Per Capita Federal Defense Spending	16
Per Capita Homeland Security Grants	38
Federal Grant Spending Per Dollar of State Tax Revenue	49
General Revenue from Federal Government	49
Federal Tax Burden Per Capita	2
Federal Spending Per Dollar of Taxes Paid	44
Highway Charges Returned to States	19
Terms of Trade	33
Federal Personal Income Taxes	3
Federal Share of Medicaid	39

Taxes - Section F

Tax Revenue	40
Per Capita Tax Revenue	4
Tax Effort	10
Tax Capacity	7
Percentage Change in Taxes	35
Property Taxes as a Percentage of Income	17
Property Taxes Per Capita	8
Property Tax Revenue as a Percentage of 3-tax Revenue	15
Sales Taxes as a Percentage of Income	45
Sales Taxes Per Capita	44
Sales Tax Revenue as a Percentage of 3-tax Revenue	46
Sales Tax Rate	25
Income Taxes as a Percentage of Income	8
Income Taxes Per Capita	3
Income Tax Revenue as a Percentage of 3-tax Revenue	6
Highest Personal Income Rate	29
Corporate Income Taxes	8
Motor Fuel Taxes	24
Motor Vehicle Fees	30
Tobacco Taxes	6
Taxes on High-Income Families	20
Taxes in the Largest City in Each State	17
Progressivity of Taxes	23
Per Capita Estate Tax Revenue	4

Revenues and Finances - Section G

Per Capita Total Revenue	13
Per Capita General Revenue	14

"Own-Source" General Revenue	8
Per Capita Non-Tax Revenue	28
Per Capita Total Spending	8
General Spending as a Percentage of Income	45
Per Capita General Spending	9
Change in General Expenditures	37
State Government General Revenue	18
State Government General Spending	17
State Government General Fund Spending	44
State and Local Debt	3
Debt as a Percentage of Revenue	1
Per Capita Full Faith and Credit Debt	4
Bond Ratings	3
State Solvency Index	49
Pension Plan Assets	19
State Reserves	15
Capital Outlays and Interest	4
State Budget Process Quality	7
Relative State Spending "Needs"	11
Structural Deficits	2

Education - Section H

Math Proficiency, Eighth Grade	1
Reading Proficiency, Eighth Grade	1
AFQT Ranks	21
SAT Scores	5
ACT Scores	n/a
Population over 25 with a High School Diploma	28
Students in Private Schools	11
High School Dropout Rates	26
Pupil-Teacher Ratio	31
Public School Enrollment	43
Library Holdings Per Capita	2
Children with Disabilities	8
Education Spending Per Capita	20
Education Spending as a Percentage of General Spending	44
Spending Per Pupil	4
Average Teacher Salary	7
Sources of School Funds	11
State Aid Per Pupil	16
Per Capita Higher Education Spending	48
Higher Education Spending as a Percentage of General Spending	48
Public Higher Education Enrollment	7
Per Pupil Support of Higher Education	48
In-State Tuition and Fees	6
Out-of-State Tuition and Fees	16
Change in Tuition and Fees	29
Affordability Index	35
Average Professor Salary	1
Education Employees	25
R and D Spending	4
Library Operating Spending	12
Head Start Spending	7

Health - Section I

Immunization Rates	1
Infant Mortality Rates	50
State Health Rankings	9
Population without Health Insurance	37
Abortions	7
Alcohol Consumption	10
Percentage of Adult Smokers	45
Percentage Obese	49
AIDS Cases	24
Physicians Per 100,000 Population	1
Hospital Beds Per 1,000 Population	31
Medicaid Recipients	21
Medicaid Recipients as a Percentage of Poverty Population	6
Health and Hospital Spending	17
Health and Hospital Spending as a Percentage of General Spending	27
Per Capita Medicaid Spending	4
Medicaid Spending Per Aged	9
Medicaid Spending Per Child	13
Medicare Payment Per Hospital Day	40
Hospital Expense Per Inpatient Day	6
Population in HMOs	2
Prescription Drugs as a Percentage of Medicaid Costs	30
Percentage Change in Average Price of Prescription Drugs	25

Crime - Section J

Crime Rate	38
Violent Crime Rate	18
Murder Rate	34
Property Crime Rate	42
Motor Vehicle Theft Rate	22
Violent Crime Rate Change	19
Prisoners	31
Change in Prisoners	50
Incarceration Rate	44
Juvenile Violent Crime Rate	14
Law Enforcement Employees	5
Corrections Employees	50
State Corrections Spending	1
Increase in State Corrections Spending	48
Law Enforcement Spending	18
Law Enforcement Spending as a Percentage of General Spending	25

Transportation - Section K

Travel on Interstates	5
Interstate Mileage in "Unacceptable" Condition	30
Deficient Bridges	2
Traffic Deaths	50
Seat Belt Use	47
Vehicle-Miles Traveled Per Capita	44
Use of Public Transportation	3
Road and Street Miles	47
Highway Employees	39
Public Transit Employees	7
Highway Spending Per Capita	17
Highway Spending as a Percentage of General Spending	27

Welfare - Section L

Births to Unwed Mothers	45
TANF Recipients	18
Change in TANF/AFDC Recipients	33
Food Stamp Recipients	40
SSI Recipients	12
WIC Average Monthly Benefit	35
NSLP Recipients	34
Condition of Children Index	6
Families with Single Parent	28
Average Monthly TANF Payments	8
Welfare as a Percentage of Poverty-Level Income	4
State Supplements of SSI	22
State Income Tax Liability of Typical Family in Poverty	36
Child Support Collections	24
Child Support Collections Per Dollar of Administrative Costs	25
Children in Foster Care	13
Welfare Spending Per Capita	30
Welfare Spending as a Percentage of General Spending	37
Administrative Costs Per TANF Case	38

Technology - Section M

Households with Computers	21
Percentage Using Internet	13
Zip Codes with Broadband Service	1
High-Tech Jobs	3
Change in High-Tech Jobs	44
State Government Web Site Ratings	8
Number of Online Government Services	8
Students Per Computer	16
Students Per Internet-Connected Computer	10
Libraries with Internet Access	28

Michigan

Population - Section A

Population 2005	8
Population 2004	8
Population Change 2003–2004	44
Population Change 1994–2004	42
Population 2015	33
Population 2025	10
Percentage 65 and Over	31
Percentage 17 and Under	16
Median Age	29
Percentage African American	16
Percentage American Indian	24
Percentage Asian American	20
Percentage Hispanic	33
Percentage White (Non-Hispanic)	25
Percentage Mixed-Race	17
Percentage in Poverty	16
Child Poverty Rate	13
Percentage Female	22
Birth Rates	36
Death Rates	20
Population Density	15
Legal Immigrants FY 2004	12
Unauthorized Immigrants	16

Economies - Section B

Personal Income, 2004	9
Gross State Product	28
Per Capita Personal Income	22
Personal Income from Wages and Salaries	15
Average Annual Pay	11
Average Hourly Earnings	1
Value Added in Manufacturing	5
Cost of Living	22
Average Annual Pay in Manufacturing	5
Average Annual Pay in Retailing	22
Labor Force	35
Unemployment Rate	5
Employment Rate	46
Government Employment	36
Manufacturing Employment	5
Fortune 500 Companies	11
Forbes 500 Companies	20
Tourism Spending Per Capita	47
Exports Per Capita	6
Housing Permits	34
Percentage Change in Home Prices	40
Net Farm Income	27
Financial Institution Assets	25
Bankruptcy Filings	17
Patents Issued	11
WC Disability Payment	18
Average Weekly UC Benefit	10
Economic Momentum	50
One-year Employment Change	50
Manufacturing Employment Change	45
Home Ownership	4
Annual Electricity Use Per Residential Customer	41
Cost Per Kwh	22
New Companies	36

Geography - Section C

Total Land Area	22
Federally Owned Land	14
State Park Acreage	11
State Park Visitors	27
Population Not Active	26
Hunters with Firearms	15
Registered Boats	2
State Spending for the Arts	13
Energy Consumption Per Capita	34
Toxic Chemical Release Per Capita	31
Hazardous Waste Sites	5
Drinking Water Quality	42
Expired Water Pollution Permits	31
Air Pollution Emissions	9

Government - Section D

Members of United States House	8
State Legislators	23
Legislators Per Million Population	43
Units of Government	29
Legislators Compensation	2
Female Legislators	27
Turnover in Legislatures	3
Term Limits	13
Legislative Session Length	n/a
Democrats in State Legislatures	29
Governors' Power Rating	17
Number of Statewide Elected Officials	41
State and Local Government Employees	44
State and Local Average Salaries	12
Local Employment	13
Local Spending Accountability	48
Registered Voters	3
Percentage of Population Voting	10
Statewide Initiatives	n/a
Campaign Costs Per Vote	42

Federal Impacts - Section E

Per Capita Federal Spending	46
Increase in Federal Spending	32
Per Capita Federal Grant Spending	40
Per Capita Federal Spending on Procurement	46
Per Capita Federal Spending on Payments to Individuals	26
Per Capita Federal Spending on Social Security and Medicare	9
Social Security Benefits	3
Federal Spending on Employee Wages and Salaries	49
Per Capita Federal Defense Spending	49
Per Capita Homeland Security Grants	43
Federal Grant Spending Per Dollar of State Tax Revenue	37
General Revenue from Federal Government	25
Federal Tax Burden Per Capita	19
Federal Spending Per Dollar of Taxes Paid	38
Highway Charges Returned to States	38
Terms of Trade	39
Federal Personal Income Taxes	20
Federal Share of Medicaid	32

Taxes - Section F

Tax Revenue	25
Per Capita Tax Revenue	22
Tax Effort	12
Tax Capacity	20
Percentage Change in Taxes	43
Property Taxes as a Percentage of Income	18
Property Taxes Per Capita	18
Property Tax Revenue as a Percentage of 3-tax Revenue	21
Sales Taxes as a Percentage of Income	32
Sales Taxes Per Capita	31
Sales Tax Revenue as a Percentage of 3-tax Revenue	28
Sales Tax Rate	10
Income Taxes as a Percentage of Income	34
Income Taxes Per Capita	27
Income Tax Revenue as a Percentage of 3-tax Revenue	30
Highest Personal Income Rate	35
Corporate Income Taxes	5
Motor Fuel Taxes	33
Motor Vehicle Fees	n/a
Tobacco Taxes	3
Taxes on High-Income Families	13
Taxes in the Largest City in Each State	8
Progressivity of Taxes	35
Per Capita Estate Tax Revenue	22

Revenues and Finances - Section G

Per Capita Total Revenue	18
Per Capita General Revenue	23

"Own-Source" General Revenue	20
Per Capita Non-Tax Revenue	22
Per Capita Total Spending	20
General Spending as a Percentage of Income	27
Per Capita General Spending	19
Change in General Expenditures	41
State Government General Revenue	17
State Government General Spending	14
State Government General Fund Spending	31
State and Local Debt	23
Debt as a Percentage of Revenue	25
Per Capita Full Faith and Credit Debt	17
Bond Ratings	3
State Solvency Index	28
Pension Plan Assets	16
State Reserves	48
Capital Outlays and Interest	31
State Budget Process Quality	2
Relative State Spending "Needs"	42
Structural Deficits	15

Education - Section H

Math Proficiency, Eighth Grade	33
Reading Proficiency, Eighth Grade	29
AFQT Ranks	25
SAT Scores	n/a
ACT Scores	10
Population over 25 with a High School Diploma	19
Students in Private Schools	25
High School Dropout Rates	16
Pupil-Teacher Ratio	7
Public School Enrollment	12
Library Holdings Per Capita	21
Children with Disabilities	31
Education Spending Per Capita	7
Education Spending as a Percentage of General Spending	3
Spending Per Pupil	19
Average Teacher Salary	3
Sources of School Funds	41
State Aid Per Pupil	3
Per Capita Higher Education Spending	7
Higher Education Spending as a Percentage of General Spending	7
Public Higher Education Enrollment	18
Per Pupil Support of Higher Education	41
In-State Tuition and Fees	13
Out-of-State Tuition and Fees	1
Change in Tuition and Fees	12
Affordability Index	19
Average Professor Salary	2
Education Employees	30
R and D Spending	30
Library Operating Spending	18
Head Start Spending	39

Health - Section I

Immunization Rates	30
Infant Mortality Rates	14
State Health Rankings	29
Population without Health Insurance	37
Abortions	20
Alcohol Consumption	34
Percentage of Adult Smokers	15
Percentage Obese	10
AIDS Cases	31
Physicians Per 100,000 Population	11
Hospital Beds Per 1,000 Population	30
Medicaid Recipients	26
Medicaid Recipients as a Percentage of Poverty Population	36
Health and Hospital Spending	15
Health and Hospital Spending as a Percentage of General Spending	15
Per Capita Medicaid Spending	25
Medicaid Spending Per Aged	26
Medicaid Spending Per Child	47
Medicare Payment Per Hospital Day	31
Hospital Expense Per Inpatient Day	18
Population in HMOs	9
Prescription Drugs as a Percentage of Medicaid Costs	44
Percentage Change in Average Price of Prescription Drugs	33

Crime - Section J

Crime Rate	31
Violent Crime Rate	17
Murder Rate	10
Property Crime Rate	31
Motor Vehicle Theft Rate	10
Violent Crime Rate Change	36
Prisoners	6
Change in Prisoners	42
Incarceration Rate	13
Juvenile Violent Crime Rate	32
Law Enforcement Employees	41
Corrections Employees	20
State Corrections Spending	18
Increase in State Corrections Spending	41
Law Enforcement Spending	16
Law Enforcement Spending as a Percentage of General Spending	19

Transportation - Section K

Travel on Interstates	37
Interstate Mileage in "Unacceptable" Condition	6
Deficient Bridges	20
Traffic Deaths	43
Seat Belt Use	5
Vehicle-Miles Traveled Per Capita	31
Use of Public Transportation	35
Road and Street Miles	46
Highway Employees	49
Public Transit Employees	21
Highway Spending Per Capita	48
Highway Spending as a Percentage of General Spending	44

Welfare - Section L

Births to Unwed Mothers	22
TANF Recipients	6
Change in TANF/AFDC Recipients	26
Food Stamp Recipients	15
SSI Recipients	20
WIC Average Monthly Benefit	43
NSLP Recipients	46
Condition of Children Index	25
Families with Single Parent	19
Average Monthly TANF Payments	16
Welfare as a Percentage of Poverty-Level Income	20
State Supplements of SSI	23
State Income Tax Liability of Typical Family in Poverty	6
Child Support Collections	2
Child Support Collections Per Dollar of Administrative Costs	15
Children in Foster Care	16
Welfare Spending Per Capita	22
Welfare Spending as a Percentage of General Spending	24
Administrative Costs Per TANF Case	25

Technology - Section M

Households with Computers	34
Percentage Using Internet	35
Zip Codes with Broadband Service	6
High-Tech Jobs	21
Change in High-Tech Jobs	22
State Government Web Site Ratings	5
Number of Online Government Services	10
Students Per Computer	16
Students Per Internet-Connected Computer	21
Libraries with Internet Access	22

Minnesota

Population · Section A

Population 2005	21
Population 2004	21
Population Change 2003–2004	26
Population Change 1994–2004	20
Population 2015	17
Population 2025	20
Percentage 65 and Over	35
Percentage 17 and Under	25
Median Age	29
Percentage African American	32
Percentage American Indian	15
Percentage Asian American	13
Percentage Hispanic	35
Percentage White (Non-Hispanic)	12
Percentage Mixed-Race	18
Percentage in Poverty	49
Child Poverty Rate	48
Percentage Female	34
Birth Rates	23
Death Rates	47
Population Density	31
Legal Immigrants FY 2004	16
Unauthorized Immigrants	18

Economies · Section B

Personal Income, 2004	17
Gross State Product	9
Per Capita Personal Income	8
Personal Income from Wages and Salaries	2
Average Annual Pay	10
Average Hourly Earnings	18
Value Added in Manufacturing	11
Cost of Living	23
Average Annual Pay in Manufacturing	14
Average Annual Pay in Retailing	25
Labor Force	1
Unemployment Rate	44
Employment Rate	7
Government Employment	37
Manufacturing Employment	14
Fortune 500 Companies	2
Forbes 500 Companies	2
Tourism Spending Per Capita	30
Exports Per Capita	16
Housing Permits	13
Percentage Change in Home Prices	17
Net Farm Income	9
Financial Institution Assets	37
Bankruptcy Filings	40
Patents Issued	5
WC Disability Payment	13
Average Weekly UC Benefit	6
Economic Momentum	31
One-year Employment Change	20
Manufacturing Employment Change	14
Home Ownership	5
Annual Electricity Use Per Residential Customer	33
Cost Per Kwh	15
New Companies	32

Geography · Section C

Total Land Area	14
Federally Owned Land	17
State Park Acreage	15
State Park Visitors	40
Population Not Active	49
Hunters with Firearms	20
Registered Boats	4
State Spending for the Arts	8
Energy Consumption Per Capita	23
Toxic Chemical Release Per Capita	39
Hazardous Waste Sites	18
Drinking Water Quality	48
Expired Water Pollution Permits	38
Air Pollution Emissions	13

Government · Section D

Members of United States House	18
State Legislators	5
Legislators Per Million Population	23
Units of Government	9
Legislators Compensation	16
Female Legislators	13
Turnover in Legislatures	18
Term Limits	n/a
Legislative Session Length	25
Democrats in State Legislatures	25
Governors' Power Rating	8
Number of Statewide Elected Officials	34
State and Local Government Employees	31
State and Local Average Salaries	11
Local Employment	15
Local Spending Accountability	41
Registered Voters	35
Percentage of Population Voting	1
Statewide Initiatives	n/a
Campaign Costs Per Vote	50

Federal Impacts · Section E

Per Capita Federal Spending	49
Increase in Federal Spending	48
Per Capita Federal Grant Spending	36
Per Capita Federal Spending on Procurement	45
Per Capita Federal Spending on Payments to Individuals	43
Per Capita Federal Spending on Social Security and Medicare	39
Social Security Benefits	19
Federal Spending on Employee Wages and Salaries	46
Per Capita Federal Defense Spending	46
Per Capita Homeland Security Grants	30
Federal Grant Spending Per Dollar of State Tax Revenue	47
General Revenue from Federal Government	41
Federal Tax Burden Per Capita	12
Federal Spending Per Dollar of Taxes Paid	47
Highway Charges Returned to States	50
Terms of Trade	41
Federal Personal Income Taxes	14
Federal Share of Medicaid	39

Taxes · Section F

Tax Revenue	7
Per Capita Tax Revenue	5
Tax Effort	7
Tax Capacity	13
Percentage Change in Taxes	40
Property Taxes as a Percentage of Income	24
Property Taxes Per Capita	14
Property Tax Revenue as a Percentage of 3-tax Revenue	32
Sales Taxes as a Percentage of Income	26
Sales Taxes Per Capita	15
Sales Tax Revenue as a Percentage of 3-tax Revenue	32
Sales Tax Rate	4
Income Taxes as a Percentage of Income	6
Income Taxes Per Capita	4
Income Tax Revenue as a Percentage of 3-tax Revenue	10
Highest Personal Income Rate	9
Corporate Income Taxes	12
Motor Fuel Taxes	28
Motor Vehicle Fees	1
Tobacco Taxes	36
Taxes on High-Income Families	22
Taxes in the Largest City in Each State	23
Progressivity of Taxes	6
Per Capita Estate Tax Revenue	38

Revenues and Finances · Section G

Per Capita Total Revenue	7
Per Capita General Revenue	5

"Own-Source" General Revenue	6
Per Capita Non-Tax Revenue	8
Per Capita Total Spending	6
General Spending as a Percentage of Income	19
Per Capita General Spending	5
Change in General Expenditures	16
State Government General Revenue	13
State Government General Spending	9
State Government General Fund Spending	25
State and Local Debt	14
Debt as a Percentage of Revenue	22
Per Capita Full Faith and Credit Debt	9
Bond Ratings	2
State Solvency Index	24
Pension Plan Assets	38
State Reserves	28
Capital Outlays and Interest	8
State Budget Process Quality	5
Relative State Spending "Needs"	24
Structural Deficits	21

Education · Section H

Math Proficiency, Eighth Grade	2
Reading Proficiency, Eighth Grade	9
AFQT Ranks	8
SAT Scores	n/a
ACT Scores	1
Population over 25 with a High School Diploma	1
Students in Private Schools	18
High School Dropout Rates	4
Pupil-Teacher Ratio	15
Public School Enrollment	19
Library Holdings Per Capita	21
Children with Disabilities	34
Education Spending Per Capita	11
Education Spending as a Percentage of General Spending	41
Spending Per Pupil	18
Average Teacher Salary	15
Sources of School Funds	47
State Aid Per Pupil	5
Per Capita Higher Education Spending	22
Higher Education Spending as a Percentage of General Spending	40
Public Higher Education Enrollment	13
Per Pupil Support of Higher Education	24
In-State Tuition and Fees	9
Out-of-State Tuition and Fees	10
Change in Tuition and Fees	45
Affordability Index	3
Average Professor Salary	18
Education Employees	22
R and D Spending	29
Library Operating Spending	16
Head Start Spending	28

Health · Section I

Immunization Rates	12
Infant Mortality Rates	47
State Health Rankings	1
Population without Health Insurance	50
Abortions	23
Alcohol Consumption	15
Percentage of Adult Smokers	27
Percentage Obese	30
AIDS Cases	38
Physicians Per 100,000 Population	14
Hospital Beds Per 1,000 Population	18
Medicaid Recipients	40
Medicaid Recipients as a Percentage of Poverty Population	7
Health and Hospital Spending	34
Health and Hospital Spending as a Percentage of General Spending	40
Per Capita Medicaid Spending	13
Medicaid Spending Per Aged	5
Medicaid Spending Per Child	4
Medicare Payment Per Hospital Day	11
Hospital Expense Per Inpatient Day	15
Population in HMOs	13
Prescription Drugs as a Percentage of Medicaid Costs	47
Percentage Change in Average Price of Prescription Drugs	23

Crime · Section J

Crime Rate	32
Violent Crime Rate	38
Murder Rate	42
Property Crime Rate	32
Motor Vehicle Theft Rate	33
Violent Crime Rate Change	21
Prisoners	33
Change in Prisoners	8
Incarceration Rate	49
Juvenile Violent Crime Rate	31
Law Enforcement Employees	48
Corrections Employees	43
State Corrections Spending	3
Increase in State Corrections Spending	28
Law Enforcement Spending	29
Law Enforcement Spending as a Percentage of General Spending	44

Transportation · Section K

Travel on Interstates	36
Interstate Mileage in "Unacceptable" Condition	29
Deficient Bridges	48
Traffic Deaths	47
Seat Belt Use	20
Vehicle-Miles Traveled Per Capita	22
Use of Public Transportation	14
Road and Street Miles	42
Highway Employees	20
Public Transit Employees	16
Highway Spending Per Capita	16
Highway Spending as a Percentage of General Spending	29

Welfare · Section L

Births to Unwed Mothers	46
TANF Recipients	23
Change in TANF/AFDC Recipients	27
Food Stamp Recipients	45
SSI Recipients	43
WIC Average Monthly Benefit	34
NSLP Recipients	16
Condition of Children Index	3
Families with Single Parent	44
Average Monthly TANF Payments	18
Welfare as a Percentage of Poverty-Level Income	10
State Supplements of SSI	15
State Income Tax Liability of Typical Family in Poverty	39
Child Support Collections	4
Child Support Collections Per Dollar of Administrative Costs	36
Children in Foster Care	34
Welfare Spending Per Capita	4
Welfare Spending as a Percentage of General Spending	6
Administrative Costs Per TANF Case	16

Technology · Section M

Households with Computers	8
Percentage Using Internet	7
Zip Codes with Broadband Service	38
High-Tech Jobs	16
Change in High-Tech Jobs	39
State Government Web Site Ratings	42
Number of Online Government Services	43
Students Per Computer	31
Students Per Internet-Connected Computer	29
Libraries with Internet Access	27

Mississippi

Population - Section A

Population 2005	31
Population 2004	31
Population Change 2003–2004	27
Population Change 1994–2004	25
Population 2015	38
Population 2025	33
Percentage 65 and Over	32
Percentage 17 and Under	10
Median Age	42
Percentage African American	1
Percentage American Indian	29
Percentage Asian American	45
Percentage Hispanic	46
Percentage White (Non-Hispanic)	45
Percentage Mixed-Race	50
Percentage in Poverty	1
Child Poverty Rate	1
Percentage Female	8
Birth Rates	12
Death Rates	1
Population Density	32
Legal Immigrants FY 2004	43
Unauthorized Immigrants	39

Economies - Section B

Personal Income, 2004	34
Gross State Product	50
Per Capita Personal Income	50
Personal Income from Wages and Salaries	46
Average Annual Pay	48
Average Hourly Earnings	48
Value Added in Manufacturing	28
Cost of Living	41
Average Annual Pay in Manufacturing	49
Average Annual Pay in Retailing	48
Labor Force	48
Unemployment Rate	2
Employment Rate	49
Government Employment	5
Manufacturing Employment	4
Fortune 500 Companies	n/a
Forbes 500 Companies	44
Tourism Spending Per Capita	16
Exports Per Capita	41
Housing Permits	37
Percentage Change in Home Prices	47
Net Farm Income	17
Financial Institution Assets	33
Bankruptcy Filings	9
Patents Issued	50
WC Disability Payment	50
Average Weekly UC Benefit	49
Economic Momentum	25
One-year Employment Change	21
Manufacturing Employment Change	18
Home Ownership	11
Annual Electricity Use Per Residential Customer	5
Cost Per Kwh	21
New Companies	40

Geography - Section C

Total Land Area	31
Federally Owned Land	22
State Park Acreage	48
State Park Visitors	45
Population Not Active	1
Hunters with Firearms	25
Registered Boats	23
State Spending for the Arts	36
Energy Consumption Per Capita	12
Toxic Chemical Release Per Capita	16
Hazardous Waste Sites	45
Drinking Water Quality	50
Expired Water Pollution Permits	46
Air Pollution Emissions	30

Government - Section D

Members of United States House	31
State Legislators	14
Legislators Per Million Population	15
Units of Government	26
Legislators Compensation	40
Female Legislators	47
Turnover in Legislatures	n/a
Term Limits	n/a
Legislative Session Length	21
Democrats in State Legislatures	12
Governors' Power Rating	44
Number of Statewide Elected Officials	6
State and Local Government Employees	6
State and Local Average Salaries	50
Local Employment	29
Local Spending Accountability	39
Registered Voters	n/a
Percentage of Population Voting	46
Statewide Initiatives	n/a
Campaign Costs Per Vote	9

Federal Impacts - Section E

Per Capita Federal Spending	17
Increase in Federal Spending	40
Per Capita Federal Grant Spending	13
Per Capita Federal Spending on Procurement	23
Per Capita Federal Spending on Payments to Individuals	11
Per Capita Federal Spending on Social Security and Medicare	15
Social Security Benefits	50
Federal Spending on Employee Wages and Salaries	24
Per Capita Federal Defense Spending	17
Per Capita Homeland Security Grants	20
Federal Grant Spending Per Dollar of State Tax Revenue	6
General Revenue from Federal Government	2
Federal Tax Burden Per Capita	50
Federal Spending Per Dollar of Taxes Paid	3
Highway Charges Returned to States	43
Terms of Trade	5
Federal Personal Income Taxes	50
Federal Share of Medicaid	1

Taxes - Section F

Tax Revenue	23
Per Capita Tax Revenue	48
Tax Effort	17
Tax Capacity	49
Percentage Change in Taxes	26
Property Taxes as a Percentage of Income	37
Property Taxes Per Capita	41
Property Tax Revenue as a Percentage of 3-tax Revenue	39
Sales Taxes as a Percentage of Income	7
Sales Taxes Per Capita	18
Sales Tax Revenue as a Percentage of 3-tax Revenue	11
Sales Tax Rate	1
Income Taxes as a Percentage of Income	39
Income Taxes Per Capita	40
Income Tax Revenue as a Percentage of 3-tax Revenue	39
Highest Personal Income Rate	31
Corporate Income Taxes	22
Motor Fuel Taxes	35
Motor Vehicle Fees	42
Tobacco Taxes	48
Taxes on High-Income Families	33
Taxes in the Largest City in Each State	32
Progressivity of Taxes	14
Per Capita Estate Tax Revenue	42

Revenues and Finances - Section G

Per Capita Total Revenue	38
Per Capita General Revenue	33

"Own-Source" General Revenue	46
Per Capita Non-Tax Revenue	25
Per Capita Total Spending	39
General Spending as a Percentage of Income	4
Per Capita General Spending	36
Change in General Expenditures	22
State Government General Revenue	20
State Government General Spending	21
State Government General Fund Spending	9
State and Local Debt	47
Debt as a Percentage of Revenue	47
Per Capita Full Faith and Credit Debt	19
Bond Ratings	4
State Solvency Index	42
Pension Plan Assets	48
State Reserves	43
Capital Outlays and Interest	49
State Budget Process Quality	37
Relative State Spending "Needs"	44
Structural Deficits	36

Education - Section H

Math Proficiency, Eighth Grade	49
Reading Proficiency, Eighth Grade	47
AFQT Ranks	50
SAT Scores	n/a
ACT Scores	25
Population over 25 with a High School Diploma	39
Students in Private Schools	22
High School Dropout Rates	45
Pupil-Teacher Ratio	18
Public School Enrollment	13
Library Holdings Per Capita	37
Children with Disabilities	28
Education Spending Per Capita	44
Education Spending as a Percentage of General Spending	33
Spending Per Pupil	46
Average Teacher Salary	48
Sources of School Funds	37
State Aid Per Pupil	33
Per Capita Higher Education Spending	16
Higher Education Spending as a Percentage of General Spending	8
Public Higher Education Enrollment	40
Per Pupil Support of Higher Education	6
In-State Tuition and Fees	36
Out-of-State Tuition and Fees	50
Change in Tuition and Fees	40
Affordability Index	35
Average Professor Salary	33
Education Employees	10
R and D Spending	9
Library Operating Spending	50
Head Start Spending	47

Health - Section I

Immunization Rates	13
Infant Mortality Rates	3
State Health Rankings	50
Population without Health Insurance	10
Abortions	42
Alcohol Consumption	33
Percentage of Adult Smokers	10
Percentage Obese	1
AIDS Cases	10
Physicians Per 100,000 Population	48
Hospital Beds Per 1,000 Population	4
Medicaid Recipients	3
Medicaid Recipients as a Percentage of Poverty Population	25
Health and Hospital Spending	5
Health and Hospital Spending as a Percentage of General Spending	3
Per Capita Medicaid Spending	8
Medicaid Spending Per Aged	46
Medicaid Spending Per Child	45
Medicare Payment Per Hospital Day	46
Hospital Expense Per Inpatient Day	50
Population in HMOs	49
Prescription Drugs as a Percentage of Medicaid Costs	1
Percentage Change in Average Price of Prescription Drugs	39

Crime - Section J

Crime Rate	26
Violent Crime Rate	32
Murder Rate	4
Property Crime Rate	24
Motor Vehicle Theft Rate	32
Violent Crime Rate Change	47
Prisoners	23
Change in Prisoners	15
Incarceration Rate	3
Juvenile Violent Crime Rate	36
Law Enforcement Employees	18
Corrections Employees	33
State Corrections Spending	50
Increase in State Corrections Spending	32
Law Enforcement Spending	43
Law Enforcement Spending as a Percentage of General Spending	42

Transportation - Section K

Travel on Interstates	48
Interstate Mileage in "Unacceptable" Condition	25
Deficient Bridges	23
Traffic Deaths	1
Seat Belt Use	48
Vehicle-Miles Traveled Per Capita	2
Use of Public Transportation	48
Road and Street Miles	26
Highway Employees	12
Public Transit Employees	47
Highway Spending Per Capita	26
Highway Spending as a Percentage of General Spending	21

Welfare - Section L

Births to Unwed Mothers	3
TANF Recipients	28
Change in TANF/AFDC Recipients	10
Food Stamp Recipients	4
SSI Recipients	2
WIC Average Monthly Benefit	21
NSLP Recipients	8
Condition of Children Index	50
Families with Single Parent	1
Average Monthly TANF Payments	46
Welfare as a Percentage of Poverty-Level Income	45
State Supplements of SSI	31
State Income Tax Liability of Typical Family in Poverty	15
Child Support Collections	31
Child Support Collections Per Dollar of Administrative Costs	2
Children in Foster Care	48
Welfare Spending Per Capita	11
Welfare Spending as a Percentage of General Spending	7
Administrative Costs Per TANF Case	45

Technology - Section M

Households with Computers	50
Percentage Using Internet	50
Zip Codes with Broadband Service	23
High-Tech Jobs	50
Change in High-Tech Jobs	28
State Government Web Site Ratings	9
Number of Online Government Services	7
Students Per Computer	2
Students Per Internet-Connected Computer	13
Libraries with Internet Access	1

Missouri

Population - Section A

Population 2005	18
Population 2004	17
Population Change 2003–2004	31
Population Change 1994–2004	24
Population 2015	28
Population 2025	19
Percentage 65 and Over	15
Percentage 17 and Under	29
Median Age	19
Percentage African American	19
Percentage American Indian	30
Percentage Asian American	34
Percentage Hispanic	39
Percentage White (Non-Hispanic)	18
Percentage Mixed-Race	24
Percentage in Poverty	20
Child Poverty Rate	22
Percentage Female	15
Birth Rates	26
Death Rates	13
Population Density	28
Legal Immigrants FY 2004	22
Unauthorized Immigrants	34

Economies - Section B

Personal Income, 2004	20
Gross State Product	34
Per Capita Personal Income	31
Personal Income from Wages and Salaries	17
Average Annual Pay	27
Average Hourly Earnings	15
Value Added in Manufacturing	14
Cost of Living	38
Average Annual Pay in Manufacturing	26
Average Annual Pay in Retailing	34
Labor Force	23
Unemployment Rate	29
Employment Rate	22
Government Employment	35
Manufacturing Employment	21
Fortune 500 Companies	15
Forbes 500 Companies	12
Tourism Spending Per Capita	26
Exports Per Capita	35
Housing Permits	31
Percentage Change in Home Prices	29
Net Farm Income	10
Financial Institution Assets	30
Bankruptcy Filings	16
Patents Issued	33
WC Disability Payment	20
Average Weekly UC Benefit	45
Economic Momentum	40
One-year Employment Change	33
Manufacturing Employment Change	16
Home Ownership	21
Annual Electricity Use Per Residential Customer	19
Cost Per Kwh	36
New Companies	30

Geography - Section C

Total Land Area	18
Federally Owned Land	21
State Park Acreage	22
State Park Visitors	16
Population Not Active	14
Hunters with Firearms	19
Registered Boats	13
State Spending for the Arts	49
Energy Consumption Per Capita	29
Toxic Chemical Release Per Capita	18
Hazardous Waste Sites	16
Drinking Water Quality	11
Expired Water Pollution Permits	12
Air Pollution Emissions	12

Government - Section D

Members of United States House	14
State Legislators	7
Legislators Per Million Population	24
Units of Government	12
Legislators Compensation	15
Female Legislators	26
Turnover in Legislatures	13
Term Limits	4
Legislative Session Length	5
Democrats in State Legislatures	38
Governors' Power Rating	17
Number of Statewide Elected Officials	22
State and Local Government Employees	29
State and Local Average Salaries	42
Local Employment	25
Local Spending Accountability	17
Registered Voters	2
Percentage of Population Voting	17
Statewide Initiatives	n/a
Campaign Costs Per Vote	37

Federal Impacts - Section E

Per Capita Federal Spending	15
Increase in Federal Spending	35
Per Capita Federal Grant Spending	24
Per Capita Federal Spending on Procurement	10
Per Capita Federal Spending on Payments to Individuals	10
Per Capita Federal Spending on Social Security and Medicare	13
Social Security Benefits	30
Federal Spending on Employee Wages and Salaries	25
Per Capita Federal Defense Spending	9
Per Capita Homeland Security Grants	33
Federal Grant Spending Per Dollar of State Tax Revenue	14
General Revenue from Federal Government	15
Federal Tax Burden Per Capita	28
Federal Spending Per Dollar of Taxes Paid	19
Highway Charges Returned to States	34
Terms of Trade	24
Federal Personal Income Taxes	30
Federal Share of Medicaid	21

Taxes - Section F

Tax Revenue	39
Per Capita Tax Revenue	35
Tax Effort	33
Tax Capacity	33
Percentage Change in Taxes	32
Property Taxes as a Percentage of Income	39
Property Taxes Per Capita	37
Property Tax Revenue as a Percentage of 3-tax Revenue	38
Sales Taxes as a Percentage of Income	22
Sales Taxes Per Capita	27
Sales Tax Revenue as a Percentage of 3-tax Revenue	19
Sales Tax Rate	37
Income Taxes as a Percentage of Income	23
Income Taxes Per Capita	22
Income Tax Revenue as a Percentage of 3-tax Revenue	19
Highest Personal Income Rate	36
Corporate Income Taxes	36
Motor Fuel Taxes	42
Motor Vehicle Fees	16
Tobacco Taxes	49
Taxes on High-Income Families	27
Taxes in the Largest City in Each State	20
Progressivity of Taxes	26
Per Capita Estate Tax Revenue	7

Revenues and Finances - Section G

Per Capita Total Revenue	43
Per Capita General Revenue	44

"Own-Source" General Revenue	45
Per Capita Non-Tax Revenue	47
Per Capita Total Spending	45
General Spending as a Percentage of Income	39
Per Capita General Spending	44
Change in General Expenditures	11
State Government General Revenue	42
State Government General Spending	44
State Government General Fund Spending	42
State and Local Debt	40
Debt as a Percentage of Revenue	28
Per Capita Full Faith and Credit Debt	39
Bond Ratings	1
State Solvency Index	26
Pension Plan Assets	14
State Reserves	24
Capital Outlays and Interest	35
State Budget Process Quality	18
Relative State Spending "Needs"	15
Structural Deficits	27

Education - Section H

Math Proficiency, Eighth Grade	34
Reading Proficiency, Eighth Grade	19
AFQT Ranks	30
SAT Scores	n/a
ACT Scores	7
Population over 25 with a High School Diploma	21
Students in Private Schools	14
High School Dropout Rates	22
Pupil-Teacher Ratio	41
Public School Enrollment	38
Library Holdings Per Capita	18
Children with Disabilities	12
Education Spending Per Capita	37
Education Spending as a Percentage of General Spending	18
Spending Per Pupil	37
Average Teacher Salary	42
Sources of School Funds	5
State Aid Per Pupil	45
Per Capita Higher Education Spending	41
Higher Education Spending as a Percentage of General Spending	32
Public Higher Education Enrollment	16
Per Pupil Support of Higher Education	44
In-State Tuition and Fees	14
Out-of-State Tuition and Fees	22
Change in Tuition and Fees	15
Affordability Index	27
Average Professor Salary	29
Education Employees	31
R and D Spending	19
Library Operating Spending	22
Head Start Spending	33

Health - Section I

Immunization Rates	18
Infant Mortality Rates	16
State Health Rankings	35
Population without Health Insurance	33
Abortions	40
Alcohol Consumption	25
Percentage of Adult Smokers	13
Percentage Obese	13
AIDS Cases	29
Physicians Per 100,000 Population	19
Hospital Beds Per 1,000 Population	16
Medicaid Recipients	13
Medicaid Recipients as a Percentage of Poverty Population	12
Health and Hospital Spending	27
Health and Hospital Spending as a Percentage of General Spending	18
Per Capita Medicaid Spending	14
Medicaid Spending Per Aged	24
Medicaid Spending Per Child	39
Medicare Payment Per Hospital Day	17
Hospital Expense Per Inpatient Day	25
Population in HMOs	16
Prescription Drugs as a Percentage of Medicaid Costs	13
Percentage Change in Average Price of Prescription Drugs	43

Crime - Section J

Crime Rate	17
Violent Crime Rate	16
Murder Rate	12
Property Crime Rate	20
Motor Vehicle Theft Rate	12
Violent Crime Rate Change	10
Prisoners	14
Change in Prisoners	12
Incarceration Rate	8
Juvenile Violent Crime Rate	11
Law Enforcement Employees	9
Corrections Employees	12
State Corrections Spending	46
Increase in State Corrections Spending	14
Law Enforcement Spending	32
Law Enforcement Spending as a Percentage of General Spending	22

Transportation - Section K

Travel on Interstates	21
Interstate Mileage in "Unacceptable" Condition	10
Deficient Bridges	11
Traffic Deaths	19
Seat Belt Use	34
Vehicle-Miles Traveled Per Capita	10
Use of Public Transportation	27
Road and Street Miles	13
Highway Employees	19
Public Transit Employees	13
Highway Spending Per Capita	25
Highway Spending as a Percentage of General Spending	19

Welfare - Section L

Births to Unwed Mothers	17
TANF Recipients	14
Change in TANF/AFDC Recipients	28
Food Stamp Recipients	7
SSI Recipients	24
WIC Average Monthly Benefit	33
NSLP Recipients	22
Condition of Children Index	33
Families with Single Parent	23
Average Monthly TANF Payments	37
Welfare as a Percentage of Poverty-Level Income	45
State Supplements of SSI	11
State Income Tax Liability of Typical Family in Poverty	14
Child Support Collections	17
Child Support Collections Per Dollar of Administrative Costs	16
Children in Foster Care	14
Welfare Spending Per Capita	23
Welfare Spending as a Percentage of General Spending	12
Administrative Costs Per TANF Case	41

Technology - Section M

Households with Computers	31
Percentage Using Internet	33
Zip Codes with Broadband Service	38
High-Tech Jobs	31
Change in High-Tech Jobs	8
State Government Web Site Ratings	39
Number of Online Government Services	40
Students Per Computer	31
Students Per Internet-Connected Computer	41
Libraries with Internet Access	41

Montana

Population - Section A

Population 2005	44
Population 2004	44
Population Change 2003–2004	19
Population Change 1994–2004	28
Population 2015	24
Population 2025	44
Percentage 65 and Over	10
Percentage 17 and Under	46
Median Age	4
Percentage African American	50
Percentage American Indian	5
Percentage Asian American	50
Percentage Hispanic	40
Percentage White (Non-Hispanic)	7
Percentage Mixed-Race	11
Percentage in Poverty	14
Child Poverty Rate	26
Percentage Female	39
Birth Rates	43
Death Rates	24
Population Density	48
Legal Immigrants FY 2004	49
Unauthorized Immigrants	43

Economies - Section B

Personal Income, 2004	45
Gross State Product	47
Per Capita Personal Income	40
Personal Income from Wages and Salaries	49
Average Annual Pay	50
Average Hourly Earnings	26
Value Added in Manufacturing	49
Cost of Living	21
Average Annual Pay in Manufacturing	45
Average Annual Pay in Retailing	42
Labor Force	15
Unemployment Rate	34
Employment Rate	17
Government Employment	8
Manufacturing Employment	47
Fortune 500 Companies	n/a
Forbes 500 Companies	n/a
Tourism Spending Per Capita	5
Exports Per Capita	49
Housing Permits	35
Percentage Change in Home Prices	19
Net Farm Income	32
Financial Institution Assets	31
Bankruptcy Filings	32
Patents Issued	35
WC Disability Payment	42
Average Weekly UC Benefit	44
Economic Momentum	15
One-year Employment Change	17
Manufacturing Employment Change	10
Home Ownership	21
Annual Electricity Use Per Residential Customer	32
Cost Per Kwh	7
New Companies	5

Geography - Section C

Total Land Area	4
Federally Owned Land	8
State Park Acreage	39
State Park Visitors	38
Population Not Active	40
Hunters with Firearms	2
Registered Boats	40
State Spending for the Arts	45
Energy Consumption Per Capita	13
Toxic Chemical Release Per Capita	5
Hazardous Waste Sites	23
Drinking Water Quality	17
Expired Water Pollution Permits	1
Air Pollution Emissions	38

Government - Section D

Members of United States House	44
State Legislators	19
Legislators Per Million Population	5
Units of Government	6
Legislators Compensation	42
Female Legislators	20
Turnover in Legislatures	5
Term Limits	4
Legislative Session Length	n/a
Democrats in State Legislatures	23
Governors' Power Rating	17
Number of Statewide Elected Officials	15
State and Local Government Employees	13
State and Local Average Salaries	45
Local Employment	39
Local Spending Accountability	38
Registered Voters	18
Percentage of Population Voting	20
Statewide Initiatives	n/a
Campaign Costs Per Vote	31

Federal Impacts - Section E

Per Capita Federal Spending	14
Increase in Federal Spending	50
Per Capita Federal Grant Spending	9
Per Capita Federal Spending on Procurement	35
Per Capita Federal Spending on Payments to Individuals	9
Per Capita Federal Spending on Social Security and Medicare	29
Social Security Benefits	37
Federal Spending on Employee Wages and Salaries	12
Per Capita Federal Defense Spending	36
Per Capita Homeland Security Grants	7
Federal Grant Spending Per Dollar of State Tax Revenue	5
General Revenue from Federal Government	1
Federal Tax Burden Per Capita	42
Federal Spending Per Dollar of Taxes Paid	7
Highway Charges Returned to States	3
Terms of Trade	6
Federal Personal Income Taxes	45
Federal Share of Medicaid	6

Taxes - Section F

Tax Revenue	38
Per Capita Tax Revenue	47
Tax Effort	44
Tax Capacity	31
Percentage Change in Taxes	46
Property Taxes as a Percentage of Income	12
Property Taxes Per Capita	22
Property Tax Revenue as a Percentage of 3-tax Revenue	5
Sales Taxes as a Percentage of Income	46
Sales Taxes Per Capita	48
Sales Tax Revenue as a Percentage of 3-tax Revenue	48
Sales Tax Rate	n/a
Income Taxes as a Percentage of Income	27
Income Taxes Per Capita	35
Income Tax Revenue as a Percentage of 3-tax Revenue	14
Highest Personal Income Rate	19
Corporate Income Taxes	18
Motor Fuel Taxes	5
Motor Vehicle Fees	41
Tobacco Taxes	4
Taxes on High-Income Families	36
Taxes in the Largest City in Each State	46
Progressivity of Taxes	8
Per Capita Estate Tax Revenue	36

Revenues and Finances - Section G

Per Capita Total Revenue	24
Per Capita General Revenue	27

"Own-Source" General Revenue	41
Per Capita Non-Tax Revenue	18
Per Capita Total Spending	34
General Spending as a Percentage of Income	11
Per Capita General Spending	28
Change in General Expenditures	45
State Government General Revenue	15
State Government General Spending	18
State Government General Fund Spending	14
State and Local Debt	39
Debt as a Percentage of Revenue	37
Per Capita Full Faith and Credit Debt	46
Bond Ratings	4
State Solvency Index	16
Pension Plan Assets	40
State Reserves	3
Capital Outlays and Interest	38
State Budget Process Quality	24
Relative State Spending "Needs"	35
Structural Deficits	17

Education - Section H

Math Proficiency, Eighth Grade	6
Reading Proficiency, Eighth Grade	5
AFQT Ranks	19
SAT Scores	n/a
ACT Scores	4
Population over 25 with a High School Diploma	2
Students in Private Schools	40
High School Dropout Rates	10
Pupil-Teacher Ratio	33
Public School Enrollment	32
Library Holdings Per Capita	25
Children with Disabilities	36
Education Spending Per Capita	32
Education Spending as a Percentage of General Spending	22
Spending Per Pupil	27
Average Teacher Salary	44
Sources of School Funds	29
State Aid Per Pupil	26
Per Capita Higher Education Spending	28
Higher Education Spending as a Percentage of General Spending	28
Public Higher Education Enrollment	41
Per Pupil Support of Higher Education	39
In-State Tuition and Fees	31
Out-of-State Tuition and Fees	32
Change in Tuition and Fees	23
Affordability Index	48
Average Professor Salary	50
Education Employees	16
R and D Spending	36
Library Operating Spending	44
Head Start Spending	22

Health - Section I

Immunization Rates	35
Infant Mortality Rates	36
State Health Rankings	21
Population without Health Insurance	5
Abortions	25
Alcohol Consumption	8
Percentage of Adult Smokers	28
Percentage Obese	45
AIDS Cases	50
Physicians Per 100,000 Population	37
Hospital Beds Per 1,000 Population	3
Medicaid Recipients	43
Medicaid Recipients as a Percentage of Poverty Population	49
Health and Hospital Spending	30
Health and Hospital Spending as a Percentage of General Spending	28
Per Capita Medicaid Spending	42
Medicaid Spending Per Aged	19
Medicaid Spending Per Child	8
Medicare Payment Per Hospital Day	39
Hospital Expense Per Inpatient Day	17
Population in HMOs	38
Prescription Drugs as a Percentage of Medicaid Costs	12
Percentage Change in Average Price of Prescription Drugs	15

Crime - Section J

Crime Rate	33
Violent Crime Rate	33
Murder Rate	31
Property Crime Rate	33
Motor Vehicle Theft Rate	44
Violent Crime Rate Change	n/a
Prisoners	43
Change in Prisoners	5
Incarceration Rate	20
Juvenile Violent Crime Rate	27
Law Enforcement Employees	36
Corrections Employees	39
State Corrections Spending	29
Increase in State Corrections Spending	33
Law Enforcement Spending	34
Law Enforcement Spending as a Percentage of General Spending	32

Transportation - Section K

Travel on Interstates	23
Interstate Mileage in "Unacceptable" Condition	28
Deficient Bridges	36
Traffic Deaths	6
Seat Belt Use	27
Vehicle-Miles Traveled Per Capita	8
Use of Public Transportation	42
Road and Street Miles	34
Highway Employees	3
Public Transit Employees	32
Highway Spending Per Capita	8
Highway Spending as a Percentage of General Spending	6

Welfare - Section L

Births to Unwed Mothers	33
TANF Recipients	24
Change in TANF/AFDC Recipients	30
Food Stamp Recipients	23
SSI Recipients	37
WIC Average Monthly Benefit	21
NSLP Recipients	39
Condition of Children Index	34
Families with Single Parent	36
Average Monthly TANF Payments	29
Welfare as a Percentage of Poverty-Level Income	16
State Supplements of SSI	24
State Income Tax Liability of Typical Family in Poverty	5
Child Support Collections	44
Child Support Collections Per Dollar of Administrative Costs	39
Children in Foster Care	12
Welfare Spending Per Capita	42
Welfare Spending as a Percentage of General Spending	41
Administrative Costs Per TANF Case	17

Technology - Section M

Households with Computers	36
Percentage Using Internet	40
Zip Codes with Broadband Service	47
High-Tech Jobs	37
Change in High-Tech Jobs	14
State Government Web Site Ratings	26
Number of Online Government Services	25
Students Per Computer	43
Students Per Internet-Connected Computer	43
Libraries with Internet Access	32

Nebraska

Population - Section A

Population 2005	38
Population 2004	38
Population Change 2003–2004	35
Population Change 1994–2004	32
Population 2015	46
Population 2025	38
Percentage 65 and Over	16
Percentage 17 and Under	18
Median Age	35
Percentage African American	31
Percentage American Indian	19
Percentage Asian American	29
Percentage Hispanic	20
Percentage White (Non-Hispanic)	14
Percentage Mixed-Race	31
Percentage in Poverty	41
Child Poverty Rate	45
Percentage Female	31
Birth Rates	10
Death Rates	31
Population Density	42
Legal Immigrants FY 2004	35
Unauthorized Immigrants	31

Economies - Section B

Personal Income, 2004	36
Gross State Product	20
Per Capita Personal Income	20
Personal Income from Wages and Salaries	29
Average Annual Pay	40
Average Hourly Earnings	28
Value Added in Manufacturing	21
Cost of Living	43
Average Annual Pay in Manufacturing	44
Average Annual Pay in Retailing	45
Labor Force	5
Unemployment Rate	42
Employment Rate	9
Government Employment	23
Manufacturing Employment	24
Fortune 500 Companies	9
Forbes 500 Companies	17
Tourism Spending Per Capita	27
Exports Per Capita	36
Housing Permits	26
Percentage Change in Home Prices	48
Net Farm Income	5
Financial Institution Assets	15
Bankruptcy Filings	23
Patents Issued	37
WC Disability Payment	33
Average Weekly UC Benefit	40
Economic Momentum	45
One-year Employment Change	39
Manufacturing Employment Change	30
Home Ownership	29
Annual Electricity Use Per Residential Customer	23
Cost Per Kwh	26
New Companies	37

Geography - Section C

Total Land Area	15
Federally Owned Land	34
State Park Acreage	24
State Park Visitors	6
Population Not Active	30
Hunters with Firearms	13
Registered Boats	37
State Spending for the Arts	32
Energy Consumption Per Capita	22
Toxic Chemical Release Per Capita	10
Hazardous Waste Sites	30
Drinking Water Quality	1
Expired Water Pollution Permits	44
Air Pollution Emissions	37

Government - Section D

Members of United States House	34
State Legislators	50
Legislators Per Million Population	30
Units of Government	3
Legislators Compensation	35
Female Legislators	21
Turnover in Legislatures	25
Term Limits	4
Legislative Session Length	18
Democrats in State Legislatures	n/a
Governors' Power Rating	8
Number of Statewide Elected Officials	22
State and Local Government Employees	3
State and Local Average Salaries	29
Local Employment	26
Local Spending Accountability	6
Registered Voters	11
Percentage of Population Voting	25
Statewide Initiatives	n/a
Campaign Costs Per Vote	48

Federal Impacts - Section E

Per Capita Federal Spending	31
Increase in Federal Spending	44
Per Capita Federal Grant Spending	31
Per Capita Federal Spending on Procurement	47
Per Capita Federal Spending on Payments to Individuals	16
Per Capita Federal Spending on Social Security and Medicare	34
Social Security Benefits	27
Federal Spending on Employee Wages and Salaries	22
Per Capita Federal Defense Spending	33
Per Capita Homeland Security Grants	13
Federal Grant Spending Per Dollar of State Tax Revenue	30
General Revenue from Federal Government	36
Federal Tax Burden Per Capita	26
Federal Spending Per Dollar of Taxes Paid	30
Highway Charges Returned to States	22
Terms of Trade	28
Federal Personal Income Taxes	32
Federal Share of Medicaid	27

Taxes - Section F

Tax Revenue	14
Per Capita Tax Revenue	20
Tax Effort	28
Tax Capacity	22
Percentage Change in Taxes	36
Property Taxes as a Percentage of Income	15
Property Taxes Per Capita	15
Property Tax Revenue as a Percentage of 3-tax Revenue	20
Sales Taxes as a Percentage of Income	23
Sales Taxes Per Capita	28
Sales Tax Revenue as a Percentage of 3-tax Revenue	27
Sales Tax Rate	23
Income Taxes as a Percentage of Income	28
Income Taxes Per Capita	25
Income Tax Revenue as a Percentage of 3-tax Revenue	31
Highest Personal Income Rate	15
Corporate Income Taxes	29
Motor Fuel Taxes	8
Motor Vehicle Fees	42
Tobacco Taxes	27
Taxes on High-Income Families	14
Taxes in the Largest City in Each State	21
Progressivity of Taxes	20
Per Capita Estate Tax Revenue	20

Revenues and Finances - Section G

Per Capita Total Revenue	8
Per Capita General Revenue	26

"Own-Source" General Revenue	17
Per Capita Non-Tax Revenue	23
Per Capita Total Spending	14
General Spending as a Percentage of Income	31
Per Capita General Spending	27
Change in General Expenditures	42
State Government General Revenue	25
State Government General Spending	33
State Government General Fund Spending	28
State and Local Debt	34
Debt as a Percentage of Revenue	43
Per Capita Full Faith and Credit Debt	37
Bond Ratings	n/a
State Solvency Index	10
Pension Plan Assets	30
State Reserves	4
Capital Outlays and Interest	9
State Budget Process Quality	28
Relative State Spending "Needs"	12
Structural Deficits	31

Education - Section H

Math Proficiency, Eighth Grade	10
Reading Proficiency, Eighth Grade	12
AFQT Ranks	15
SAT Scores	n/a
ACT Scores	4
Population over 25 with a High School Diploma	4
Students in Private Schools	10
High School Dropout Rates	10
Pupil-Teacher Ratio	36
Public School Enrollment	22
Library Holdings Per Capita	8
Children with Disabilities	10
Education Spending Per Capita	15
Education Spending as a Percentage of General Spending	4
Spending Per Pupil	33
Average Teacher Salary	38
Sources of School Funds	8
State Aid Per Pupil	44
Per Capita Higher Education Spending	11
Higher Education Spending as a Percentage of General Spending	6
Public Higher Education Enrollment	8
Per Pupil Support of Higher Education	16
In-State Tuition and Fees	25
Out-of-State Tuition and Fees	30
Change in Tuition and Fees	17
Affordability Index	15
Average Professor Salary	26
Education Employees	14
R and D Spending	44
Library Operating Spending	24
Head Start Spending	23

Health - Section I

Immunization Rates	32
Infant Mortality Rates	28
State Health Rankings	11
Population without Health Insurance	40
Abortions	33
Alcohol Consumption	27
Percentage of Adult Smokers	32
Percentage Obese	25
AIDS Cases	40
Physicians Per 100,000 Population	28
Hospital Beds Per 1,000 Population	5
Medicaid Recipients	37
Medicaid Recipients as a Percentage of Poverty Population	20
Health and Hospital Spending	40
Health and Hospital Spending as a Percentage of General Spending	37
Per Capita Medicaid Spending	30
Medicaid Spending Per Aged	18
Medicaid Spending Per Child	25
Medicare Payment Per Hospital Day	9
Hospital Expense Per Inpatient Day	28
Population in HMOs	44
Prescription Drugs as a Percentage of Medicaid Costs	9
Percentage Change in Average Price of Prescription Drugs	35

Crime - Section J

Crime Rate	25
Violent Crime Rate	30
Murder Rate	40
Property Crime Rate	23
Motor Vehicle Theft Rate	31
Violent Crime Rate Change	24
Prisoners	42
Change in Prisoners	29
Incarceration Rate	45
Juvenile Violent Crime Rate	42
Law Enforcement Employees	33
Corrections Employees	29
State Corrections Spending	17
Increase in State Corrections Spending	30
Law Enforcement Spending	37
Law Enforcement Spending as a Percentage of General Spending	36

Transportation - Section K

Travel on Interstates	42
Interstate Mileage in "Unacceptable" Condition	22
Deficient Bridges	25
Traffic Deaths	28
Seat Belt Use	29
Vehicle-Miles Traveled Per Capita	23
Use of Public Transportation	40
Road and Street Miles	36
Highway Employees	10
Public Transit Employees	28
Highway Spending Per Capita	15
Highway Spending as a Percentage of General Spending	14

Welfare - Section L

Births to Unwed Mothers	41
TANF Recipients	25
Change in TANF/AFDC Recipients	46
Food Stamp Recipients	34
SSI Recipients	45
WIC Average Monthly Benefit	27
NSLP Recipients	5
Condition of Children Index	12
Families with Single Parent	48
Average Monthly TANF Payments	13
Welfare as a Percentage of Poverty-Level Income	23
State Supplements of SSI	21
State Income Tax Liability of Typical Family in Poverty	17
Child Support Collections	12
Child Support Collections Per Dollar of Administrative Costs	42
Children in Foster Care	1
Welfare Spending Per Capita	21
Welfare Spending as a Percentage of General Spending	18
Administrative Costs Per TANF Case	49

Technology - Section M

Households with Computers	12
Percentage Using Internet	21
Zip Codes with Broadband Service	38
High-Tech Jobs	29
Change in High-Tech Jobs	50
State Government Web Site Ratings	23
Number of Online Government Services	3
Students Per Computer	43
Students Per Internet-Connected Computer	44
Libraries with Internet Access	48

Nevada

Population - Section A

Population 2005	35
Population 2004	35
Population Change 2003–2004	1
Population Change 1994–2004	1
Population 2015	1
Population 2025	28
Percentage 65 and Over	44
Percentage 17 and Under	9
Median Age	41
Percentage African American	24
Percentage American Indian	11
Percentage Asian American	6
Percentage Hispanic	5
Percentage White (Non-Hispanic)	41
Percentage Mixed-Race	5
Percentage in Poverty	31
Child Poverty Rate	32
Percentage Female	49
Birth Rates	9
Death Rates	11
Population Density	43
Legal Immigrants FY 2004	20
Unauthorized Immigrants	13

Economies - Section B

Personal Income, 2004	32
Gross State Product	12
Per Capita Personal Income	17
Personal Income from Wages and Salaries	11
Average Annual Pay	20
Average Hourly Earnings	34
Value Added in Manufacturing	47
Cost of Living	11
Average Annual Pay in Manufacturing	28
Average Annual Pay in Retailing	4
Labor Force	21
Unemployment Rate	36
Employment Rate	15
Government Employment	50
Manufacturing Employment	48
Fortune 500 Companies	26
Forbes 500 Companies	23
Tourism Spending Per Capita	1
Exports Per Capita	39
Housing Permits	1
Percentage Change in Home Prices	3
Net Farm Income	41
Financial Institution Assets	19
Bankruptcy Filings	12
Patents Issued	28
WC Disability Payment	24
Average Weekly UC Benefit	20
Economic Momentum	1
One-year Employment Change	1
Manufacturing Employment Change	2
Home Ownership	44
Annual Electricity Use Per Residential Customer	25
Cost Per Kwh	49
New Companies	7

Geography - Section C

Total Land Area	7
Federally Owned Land	2
State Park Acreage	26
State Park Visitors	33
Population Not Active	18
Hunters with Firearms	44
Registered Boats	41
State Spending for the Arts	27
Energy Consumption Per Capita	37
Toxic Chemical Release Per Capita	2
Hazardous Waste Sites	49
Drinking Water Quality	25
Expired Water Pollution Permits	46
Air Pollution Emissions	42

Government - Section D

Members of United States House	34
State Legislators	47
Legislators Per Million Population	31
Units of Government	46
Legislators Compensation	44
Female Legislators	3
Turnover in Legislatures	10
Term Limits	1
Legislative Session Length	n/a
Democrats in State Legislatures	16
Governors' Power Rating	42
Number of Statewide Elected Officials	22
State and Local Government Employees	50
State and Local Average Salaries	10
Local Employment	12
Local Spending Accountability	23
Registered Voters	45
Percentage of Population Voting	41
Statewide Initiatives	n/a
Campaign Costs Per Vote	39

Federal Impacts - Section E

Per Capita Federal Spending	50
Increase in Federal Spending	2
Per Capita Federal Grant Spending	50
Per Capita Federal Spending on Procurement	31
Per Capita Federal Spending on Payments to Individuals	47
Per Capita Federal Spending on Social Security and Medicare	46
Social Security Benefits	11
Federal Spending on Employee Wages and Salaries	35
Per Capita Federal Defense Spending	37
Per Capita Homeland Security Grants	16
Federal Grant Spending Per Dollar of State Tax Revenue	50
General Revenue from Federal Government	50
Federal Tax Burden Per Capita	15
Federal Spending Per Dollar of Taxes Paid	46
Highway Charges Returned to States	46
Terms of Trade	47
Federal Personal Income Taxes	8
Federal Share of Medicaid	34

Taxes - Section F

Tax Revenue	30
Per Capita Tax Revenue	24
Tax Effort	50
Tax Capacity	1
Percentage Change in Taxes	2
Property Taxes as a Percentage of Income	35
Property Taxes Per Capita	32
Property Tax Revenue as a Percentage of 3-tax Revenue	34
Sales Taxes as a Percentage of Income	4
Sales Taxes Per Capita	3
Sales Tax Revenue as a Percentage of 3-tax Revenue	1
Sales Tax Rate	4
Income Taxes as a Percentage of Income	n/a
Income Taxes Per Capita	n/a
Income Tax Revenue as a Percentage of 3-tax Revenue	n/a
Highest Personal Income Rate	n/a
Corporate Income Taxes	n/a
Motor Fuel Taxes	18
Motor Vehicle Fees	21
Tobacco Taxes	23
Taxes on High-Income Families	47
Taxes in the Largest City in Each State	47
Progressivity of Taxes	50
Per Capita Estate Tax Revenue	13

Revenues and Finances - Section G

Per Capita Total Revenue	29
Per Capita General Revenue	37

"Own-Source" General Revenue	22
Per Capita Non-Tax Revenue	17
Per Capita Total Spending	30
General Spending as a Percentage of Income	38
Per Capita General Spending	34
Change in General Expenditures	4
State Government General Revenue	49
State Government General Spending	49
State Government General Fund Spending	50
State and Local Debt	6
Debt as a Percentage of Revenue	4
Per Capita Full Faith and Credit Debt	2
Bond Ratings	2
State Solvency Index	39
Pension Plan Assets	4
State Reserves	21
Capital Outlays and Interest	6
State Budget Process Quality	17
Relative State Spending "Needs"	32
Structural Deficits	50

Education - Section H

Math Proficiency, Eighth Grade	43
Reading Proficiency, Eighth Grade	44
AFQT Ranks	22
SAT Scores	12
ACT Scores	n/a
Population over 25 with a High School Diploma	32
Students in Private Schools	47
High School Dropout Rates	48
Pupil-Teacher Ratio	5
Public School Enrollment	9
Library Holdings Per Capita	44
Children with Disabilities	46
Education Spending Per Capita	46
Education Spending as a Percentage of General Spending	46
Spending Per Pupil	45
Average Teacher Salary	25
Sources of School Funds	2
State Aid Per Pupil	50
Per Capita Higher Education Spending	49
Higher Education Spending as a Percentage of General Spending	45
Public Higher Education Enrollment	49
Per Pupil Support of Higher Education	8
In-State Tuition and Fees	50
Out-of-State Tuition and Fees	43
Change in Tuition and Fees	40
Affordability Index	33
Average Professor Salary	10
Education Employees	50
R and D Spending	26
Library Operating Spending	23
Head Start Spending	3

Health - Section I

Immunization Rates	49
Infant Mortality Rates	34
State Health Rankings	37
Population without Health Insurance	6
Abortions	8
Alcohol Consumption	2
Percentage of Adult Smokers	15
Percentage Obese	39
AIDS Cases	14
Physicians Per 100,000 Population	46
Hospital Beds Per 1,000 Population	43
Medicaid Recipients	50
Medicaid Recipients as a Percentage of Poverty Population	50
Health and Hospital Spending	28
Health and Hospital Spending as a Percentage of General Spending	25
Per Capita Medicaid Spending	50
Medicaid Spending Per Aged	40
Medicaid Spending Per Child	12
Medicare Payment Per Hospital Day	3
Hospital Expense Per Inpatient Day	44
Population in HMOs	14
Prescription Drugs as a Percentage of Medicaid Costs	36
Percentage Change in Average Price of Prescription Drugs	43

Crime - Section J

Crime Rate	11
Violent Crime Rate	8
Murder Rate	5
Property Crime Rate	11
Motor Vehicle Theft Rate	1
Violent Crime Rate Change	1
Prisoners	30
Change in Prisoners	22
Incarceration Rate	14
Juvenile Violent Crime Rate	n/a
Law Enforcement Employees	19
Corrections Employees	16
State Corrections Spending	42
Increase in State Corrections Spending	4
Law Enforcement Spending	5
Law Enforcement Spending as a Percentage of General Spending	1

Transportation - Section K

Travel on Interstates	28
Interstate Mileage in "Unacceptable" Condition	35
Deficient Bridges	49
Traffic Deaths	7
Seat Belt Use	1
Vehicle-Miles Traveled Per Capita	46
Use of Public Transportation	11
Road and Street Miles	22
Highway Employees	47
Public Transit Employees	38
Highway Spending Per Capita	10
Highway Spending as a Percentage of General Spending	5

Welfare - Section L

Births to Unwed Mothers	8
TANF Recipients	46
Change in TANF/AFDC Recipients	32
Food Stamp Recipients	46
SSI Recipients	44
WIC Average Monthly Benefit	37
NSLP Recipients	49
Condition of Children Index	32
Families with Single Parent	19
Average Monthly TANF Payments	33
Welfare as a Percentage of Poverty-Level Income	45
State Supplements of SSI	36
State Income Tax Liability of Typical Family in Poverty	n/a
Child Support Collections	46
Child Support Collections Per Dollar of Administrative Costs	44
Children in Foster Care	30
Welfare Spending Per Capita	50
Welfare Spending as a Percentage of General Spending	50
Administrative Costs Per TANF Case	4

Technology - Section M

Households with Computers	28
Percentage Using Internet	24
Zip Codes with Broadband Service	16
High-Tech Jobs	41
Change in High-Tech Jobs	4
State Government Web Site Ratings	10
Number of Online Government Services	12
Students Per Computer	1
Students Per Internet-Connected Computer	1
Libraries with Internet Access	1

New Hampshire

Population - Section A

Population 2005	41
Population 2004	41
Population Change 2003–2004	23
Population Change 1994–2004	14
Population 2015	10
Population 2025	40
Percentage 65 and Over	37
Percentage 17 and Under	38
Median Age	7
Percentage African American	42
Percentage American Indian	46
Percentage Asian American	28
Percentage Hispanic	43
Percentage White (Non-Hispanic)	4
Percentage Mixed-Race	42
Percentage in Poverty	50
Child Poverty Rate	50
Percentage Female	29
Birth Rates	48
Death Rates	45
Population Density	19
Legal Immigrants FY 2004	39
Unauthorized Immigrants	43

Economies - Section B

Personal Income, 2004	38
Gross State Product	16
Per Capita Personal Income	6
Personal Income from Wages and Salaries	37
Average Annual Pay	14
Average Hourly Earnings	21
Value Added in Manufacturing	20
Cost of Living	n/a
Average Annual Pay in Manufacturing	11
Average Annual Pay in Retailing	11
Labor Force	3
Unemployment Rate	43
Employment Rate	8
Government Employment	44
Manufacturing Employment	16
Fortune 500 Companies	31
Forbes 500 Companies	43
Tourism Spending Per Capita	9
Exports Per Capita	31
Housing Permits	20
Percentage Change in Home Prices	9
Net Farm Income	48
Financial Institution Assets	18
Bankruptcy Filings	42
Patents Issued	7
WC Disability Payment	2
Average Weekly UC Benefit	23
Economic Momentum	18
One-year Employment Change	13
Manufacturing Employment Change	12
Home Ownership	14
Annual Electricity Use Per Residential Customer	44
Cost Per Kwh	48
New Companies	17

Geography - Section C

Total Land Area	44
Federally Owned Land	32
State Park Acreage	14
State Park Visitors	26
Population Not Active	43
Hunters with Firearms	22
Registered Boats	32
State Spending for the Arts	38
Energy Consumption Per Capita	42
Toxic Chemical Release Per Capita	41
Hazardous Waste Sites	19
Drinking Water Quality	6
Expired Water Pollution Permits	6
Air Pollution Emissions	45

Government - Section D

Members of United States House	39
State Legislators	1
Legislators Per Million Population	1
Units of Government	19
Legislators Compensation	49
Female Legislators	11
Turnover in Legislatures	6
Term Limits	n/a
Legislative Session Length	2
Democrats in State Legislatures	42
Governors' Power Rating	46
Number of Statewide Elected Officials	48
State and Local Government Employees	36
State and Local Average Salaries	26
Local Employment	24
Local Spending Accountability	20
Registered Voters	16
Percentage of Population Voting	4
Statewide Initiatives	n/a
Campaign Costs Per Vote	30

Federal Impacts - Section E

Per Capita Federal Spending	42
Increase in Federal Spending	8
Per Capita Federal Grant Spending	32
Per Capita Federal Spending on Procurement	27
Per Capita Federal Spending on Payments to Individuals	41
Per Capita Federal Spending on Social Security and Medicare	33
Social Security Benefits	12
Federal Spending on Employee Wages and Salaries	41
Per Capita Federal Defense Spending	29
Per Capita Homeland Security Grants	10
Federal Grant Spending Per Dollar of State Tax Revenue	24
General Revenue from Federal Government	35
Federal Tax Burden Per Capita	4
Federal Spending Per Dollar of Taxes Paid	49
Highway Charges Returned to States	15
Terms of Trade	44
Federal Personal Income Taxes	6
Federal Share of Medicaid	39

Taxes - Section F

Tax Revenue	49
Per Capita Tax Revenue	27
Tax Effort	49
Tax Capacity	6
Percentage Change in Taxes	10
Property Taxes as a Percentage of Income	2
Property Taxes Per Capita	3
Property Tax Revenue as a Percentage of 3-tax Revenue	1
Sales Taxes as a Percentage of Income	48
Sales Taxes Per Capita	47
Sales Tax Revenue as a Percentage of 3-tax Revenue	49
Sales Tax Rate	n/a
Income Taxes as a Percentage of Income	42
Income Taxes Per Capita	42
Income Tax Revenue as a Percentage of 3-tax Revenue	42
Highest Personal Income Rate	n/a
Corporate Income Taxes	3
Motor Fuel Taxes	32
Motor Vehicle Fees	23
Tobacco Taxes	35
Taxes on High-Income Families	43
Taxes in the Largest City in Each State	38
Progressivity of Taxes	44
Per Capita Estate Tax Revenue	16

Revenues and Finances - Section G

Per Capita Total Revenue	46
Per Capita General Revenue	45

"Own-Source" General Revenue	36
Per Capita Non-Tax Revenue	44
Per Capita Total Spending	49
General Spending as a Percentage of Income	50
Per Capita General Spending	48
Change in General Expenditures	46
State Government General Revenue	37
State Government General Spending	38
State Government General Fund Spending	47
State and Local Debt	18
Debt as a Percentage of Revenue	12
Per Capita Full Faith and Credit Debt	23
Bond Ratings	3
State Solvency Index	34
Pension Plan Assets	44
State Reserves	24
Capital Outlays and Interest	44
State Budget Process Quality	50
Relative State Spending "Needs"	6
Structural Deficits	3

Education - Section H

Math Proficiency, Eighth Grade	7
Reading Proficiency, Eighth Grade	2
AFQT Ranks	1
SAT Scores	4
ACT Scores	n/a
Population over 25 with a High School Diploma	6
Students in Private Schools	19
High School Dropout Rates	16
Pupil-Teacher Ratio	40
Public School Enrollment	31
Library Holdings Per Capita	7
Children with Disabilities	18
Education Spending Per Capita	36
Education Spending as a Percentage of General Spending	7
Spending Per Pupil	12
Average Teacher Salary	24
Sources of School Funds	25
State Aid Per Pupil	14
Per Capita Higher Education Spending	45
Higher Education Spending as a Percentage of General Spending	34
Public Higher Education Enrollment	36
Per Pupil Support of Higher Education	50
In-State Tuition and Fees	4
Out-of-State Tuition and Fees	8
Change in Tuition and Fees	38
Affordability Index	50
Average Professor Salary	16
Education Employees	11
R and D Spending	16
Library Operating Spending	19
Head Start Spending	8

Health - Section I

Immunization Rates	5
Infant Mortality Rates	41
State Health Rankings	3
Population without Health Insurance	37
Abortions	n/a
Alcohol Consumption	1
Percentage of Adult Smokers	22
Percentage Obese	35
AIDS Cases	43
Physicians Per 100,000 Population	19
Hospital Beds Per 1,000 Population	41
Medicaid Recipients	49
Medicaid Recipients as a Percentage of Poverty Population	16
Health and Hospital Spending	49
Health and Hospital Spending as a Percentage of General Spending	48
Per Capita Medicaid Spending	24
Medicaid Spending Per Aged	4
Medicaid Spending Per Child	5
Medicare Payment Per Hospital Day	30
Hospital Expense Per Inpatient Day	5
Population in HMOs	21
Prescription Drugs as a Percentage of Medicaid Costs	41
Percentage Change in Average Price of Prescription Drugs	25

Crime - Section J

Crime Rate	48
Violent Crime Rate	47
Murder Rate	48
Property Crime Rate	48
Motor Vehicle Theft Rate	46
Violent Crime Rate Change	n/a
Prisoners	46
Change in Prisoners	40
Incarceration Rate	47
Juvenile Violent Crime Rate	46
Law Enforcement Employees	25
Corrections Employees	49
State Corrections Spending	22
Increase in State Corrections Spending	15
Law Enforcement Spending	47
Law Enforcement Spending as a Percentage of General Spending	40

Transportation - Section K

Travel on Interstates	29
Interstate Mileage in "Unacceptable" Condition	27
Deficient Bridges	12
Traffic Deaths	33
Seat Belt Use	n/a
Vehicle-Miles Traveled Per Capita	32
Use of Public Transportation	38
Road and Street Miles	11
Highway Employees	13
Public Transit Employees	41
Highway Spending Per Capita	30
Highway Spending as a Percentage of General Spending	22

Welfare - Section L

Births to Unwed Mothers	48
TANF Recipients	31
Change in TANF/AFDC Recipients	47
Food Stamp Recipients	50
SSI Recipients	49
WIC Average Monthly Benefit	47
NSLP Recipients	43
Condition of Children Index	1
Families with Single Parent	42
Average Monthly TANF Payments	15
Welfare as a Percentage of Poverty-Level Income	11
State Supplements of SSI	33
State Income Tax Liability of Typical Family in Poverty	n/a
Child Support Collections	34
Child Support Collections Per Dollar of Administrative Costs	18
Children in Foster Care	44
Welfare Spending Per Capita	34
Welfare Spending as a Percentage of General Spending	23
Administrative Costs Per TANF Case	13

Technology - Section M

Households with Computers	3
Percentage Using Internet	2
Zip Codes with Broadband Service	1
High-Tech Jobs	9
Change in High-Tech Jobs	42
State Government Web Site Ratings	17
Number of Online Government Services	16
Students Per Computer	9
Students Per Internet-Connected Computer	3
Libraries with Internet Access	45

New Jersey

Population - Section A

Population 2005	10
Population 2004	10
Population Change 2003–2004	29
Population Change 1994–2004	23
Population 2015	27
Population 2025	11
Percentage 65 and Over	24
Percentage 17 and Under	20
Median Age	15
Percentage African American	15
Percentage American Indian	42
Percentage Asian American	3
Percentage Hispanic	9
Percentage White (Non-Hispanic)	38
Percentage Mixed-Race	25
Percentage in Poverty	47
Child Poverty Rate	49
Percentage Female	10
Birth Rates	26
Death Rates	30
Population Density	1
Legal Immigrants FY 2004	5
Unauthorized Immigrants	8

Economies - Section B

Personal Income, 2004	7
Gross State Product	5
Per Capita Personal Income	3
Personal Income from Wages and Salaries	32
Average Annual Pay	4
Average Hourly Earnings	24
Value Added in Manufacturing	27
Cost of Living	3
Average Annual Pay in Manufacturing	3
Average Annual Pay in Retailing	3
Labor Force	29
Unemployment Rate	35
Employment Rate	16
Government Employment	34
Manufacturing Employment	37
Fortune 500 Companies	4
Forbes 500 Companies	6
Tourism Spending Per Capita	21
Exports Per Capita	25
Housing Permits	44
Percentage Change in Home Prices	7
Net Farm Income	40
Financial Institution Assets	24
Bankruptcy Filings	33
Patents Issued	13
WC Disability Payment	22
Average Weekly UC Benefit	4
Economic Momentum	30
One-year Employment Change	25
Manufacturing Employment Change	47
Home Ownership	39
Annual Electricity Use Per Residential Customer	38
Cost Per Kwh	41
New Companies	9

Geography - Section C

Total Land Area	46
Federally Owned Land	46
State Park Acreage	7
State Park Visitors	37
Population Not Active	11
Hunters with Firearms	43
Registered Boats	22
State Spending for the Arts	2
Energy Consumption Per Capita	38
Toxic Chemical Release Per Capita	43
Hazardous Waste Sites	1
Drinking Water Quality	46
Expired Water Pollution Permits	20
Air Pollution Emissions	21

Government - Section D

Members of United States House	9
State Legislators	35
Legislators Per Million Population	45
Units of Government	38
Legislators Compensation	8
Female Legislators	41
Turnover in Legislatures	n/a
Term Limits	n/a
Legislative Session Length	n/a
Democrats in State Legislatures	13
Governors' Power Rating	1
Number of Statewide Elected Officials	48
State and Local Government Employees	19
State and Local Average Salaries	2
Local Employment	28
Local Spending Accountability	8
Registered Voters	23
Percentage of Population Voting	21
Statewide Initiatives	n/a
Campaign Costs Per Vote	15

Federal Impacts - Section E

Per Capita Federal Spending	38
Increase in Federal Spending	42
Per Capita Federal Grant Spending	41
Per Capita Federal Spending on Procurement	30
Per Capita Federal Spending on Payments to Individuals	30
Per Capita Federal Spending on Social Security and Medicare	12
Social Security Benefits	1
Federal Spending on Employee Wages and Salaries	42
Per Capita Federal Defense Spending	38
Per Capita Homeland Security Grants	40
Federal Grant Spending Per Dollar of State Tax Revenue	43
General Revenue from Federal Government	47
Federal Tax Burden Per Capita	3
Federal Spending Per Dollar of Taxes Paid	50
Highway Charges Returned to States	31
Terms of Trade	50
Federal Personal Income Taxes	2
Federal Share of Medicaid	39

Taxes - Section F

Tax Revenue	21
Per Capita Tax Revenue	3
Tax Effort	6
Tax Capacity	5
Percentage Change in Taxes	15
Property Taxes as a Percentage of Income	3
Property Taxes Per Capita	1
Property Tax Revenue as a Percentage of 3-tax Revenue	3
Sales Taxes as a Percentage of Income	43
Sales Taxes Per Capita	30
Sales Tax Revenue as a Percentage of 3-tax Revenue	43
Sales Tax Rate	10
Income Taxes as a Percentage of Income	35
Income Taxes Per Capita	16
Income Tax Revenue as a Percentage of 3-tax Revenue	36
Highest Personal Income Rate	5
Corporate Income Taxes	7
Motor Fuel Taxes	46
Motor Vehicle Fees	4
Tobacco Taxes	2
Taxes on High-Income Families	5
Taxes in the Largest City in Each State	3
Progressivity of Taxes	42
Per Capita Estate Tax Revenue	9

Revenues and Finances - Section G

Per Capita Total Revenue	15
Per Capita General Revenue	8

"Own-Source" General Revenue	7
Per Capita Non-Tax Revenue	33
Per Capita Total Spending	11
General Spending as a Percentage of Income	49
Per Capita General Spending	12
Change in General Expenditures	40
State Government General Revenue	14
State Government General Spending	24
State Government General Fund Spending	43
State and Local Debt	12
Debt as a Percentage of Revenue	14
Per Capita Full Faith and Credit Debt	14
Bond Ratings	4
State Solvency Index	23
Pension Plan Assets	34
State Reserves	47
Capital Outlays and Interest	26
State Budget Process Quality	9
Relative State Spending "Needs"	18
Structural Deficits	3

Education - Section H

Math Proficiency, Eighth Grade	10
Reading Proficiency, Eighth Grade	5
AFQT Ranks	41
SAT Scores	13
ACT Scores	n/a
Population over 25 with a High School Diploma	22
Students in Private Schools	8
High School Dropout Rates	1
Pupil-Teacher Ratio	44
Public School Enrollment	28
Library Holdings Per Capita	16
Children with Disabilities	4
Education Spending Per Capita	5
Education Spending as a Percentage of General Spending	11
Spending Per Pupil	1
Average Teacher Salary	4
Sources of School Funds	4
State Aid Per Pupil	21
Per Capita Higher Education Spending	38
Higher Education Spending as a Percentage of General Spending	42
Public Higher Education Enrollment	50
Per Pupil Support of Higher Education	10
In-State Tuition and Fees	5
Out-of-State Tuition and Fees	26
Change in Tuition and Fees	31
Affordability Index	6
Average Professor Salary	6
Education Employees	12
R and D Spending	23
Library Operating Spending	7
Head Start Spending	5

Health - Section I

Immunization Rates	26
Infant Mortality Rates	46
State Health Rankings	15
Population without Health Insurance	18
Abortions	11
Alcohol Consumption	26
Percentage of Adult Smokers	43
Percentage Obese	34
AIDS Cases	5
Physicians Per 100,000 Population	7
Hospital Beds Per 1,000 Population	32
Medicaid Recipients	44
Medicaid Recipients as a Percentage of Poverty Population	31
Health and Hospital Spending	42
Health and Hospital Spending as a Percentage of General Spending	42
Per Capita Medicaid Spending	23
Medicaid Spending Per Aged	10
Medicaid Spending Per Child	19
Medicare Payment Per Hospital Day	1
Hospital Expense Per Inpatient Day	39
Population in HMOs	15
Prescription Drugs as a Percentage of Medicaid Costs	43
Percentage Change in Average Price of Prescription Drugs	9

Crime - Section J

Crime Rate	42
Violent Crime Rate	26
Murder Rate	26
Property Crime Rate	43
Motor Vehicle Theft Rate	21
Violent Crime Rate Change	28
Prisoners	15
Change in Prisoners	48
Incarceration Rate	38
Juvenile Violent Crime Rate	6
Law Enforcement Employees	2
Corrections Employees	34
State Corrections Spending	4
Increase in State Corrections Spending	29
Law Enforcement Spending	7
Law Enforcement Spending as a Percentage of General Spending	7

Transportation - Section K

Travel on Interstates	43
Interstate Mileage in "Unacceptable" Condition	2
Deficient Bridges	8
Traffic Deaths	46
Seat Belt Use	13
Vehicle-Miles Traveled Per Capita	45
Use of Public Transportation	2
Road and Street Miles	50
Highway Employees	24
Public Transit Employees	3
Highway Spending Per Capita	40
Highway Spending as a Percentage of General Spending	43

Welfare - Section L

Births to Unwed Mothers	42
TANF Recipients	27
Change in TANF/AFDC Recipients	23
Food Stamp Recipients	49
SSI Recipients	29
WIC Average Monthly Benefit	15
NSLP Recipients	45
Condition of Children Index	4
Families with Single Parent	36
Average Monthly TANF Payments	12
Welfare as a Percentage of Poverty-Level Income	29
State Supplements of SSI	37
State Income Tax Liability of Typical Family in Poverty	38
Child Support Collections	7
Child Support Collections Per Dollar of Administrative Costs	24
Children in Foster Care	32
Welfare Spending Per Capita	38
Welfare Spending as a Percentage of General Spending	46
Administrative Costs Per TANF Case	18

Technology - Section M

Households with Computers	17
Percentage Using Internet	10
Zip Codes with Broadband Service	1
High-Tech Jobs	11
Change in High-Tech Jobs	35
State Government Web Site Ratings	3
Number of Online Government Services	9
Students Per Computer	22
Students Per Internet-Connected Computer	21
Libraries with Internet Access	24

New Mexico

Population - Section A

Population 2005	36
Population 2004	36
Population Change 2003–2004	10
Population Change 1994–2004	17
Population 2015	25
Population 2025	36
Percentage 65 and Over	36
Percentage 17 and Under	8
Median Age	37
Percentage African American	38
Percentage American Indian	2
Percentage Asian American	35
Percentage Hispanic	1
Percentage White (Non-Hispanic)	49
Percentage Mixed-Race	16
Percentage in Poverty	5
Child Poverty Rate	4
Percentage Female	24
Birth Rates	11
Death Rates	25
Population Density	45
Legal Immigrants FY 2004	33
Unauthorized Immigrants	27

Economies - Section B

Personal Income, 2004	37
Gross State Product	43
Per Capita Personal Income	47
Personal Income from Wages and Salaries	33
Average Annual Pay	41
Average Hourly Earnings	46
Value Added in Manufacturing	45
Cost of Living	13
Average Annual Pay in Manufacturing	38
Average Annual Pay in Retailing	28
Labor Force	41
Unemployment Rate	15
Employment Rate	36
Government Employment	2
Manufacturing Employment	46
Fortune 500 Companies	n/a
Forbes 500 Companies	46
Tourism Spending Per Capita	7
Exports Per Capita	45
Housing Permits	22
Percentage Change in Home Prices	27
Net Farm Income	29
Financial Institution Assets	46
Bankruptcy Filings	24
Patents Issued	27
WC Disability Payment	35
Average Weekly UC Benefit	37
Economic Momentum	8
One-year Employment Change	12
Manufacturing Employment Change	22
Home Ownership	28
Annual Electricity Use Per Residential Customer	47
Cost Per Kwh	16
New Companies	19

Geography - Section C

Total Land Area	5
Federally Owned Land	6
State Park Acreage	31
State Park Visitors	28
Population Not Active	34
Hunters with Firearms	12
Registered Boats	47
State Spending for the Arts	25
Energy Consumption Per Capita	20
Toxic Chemical Release Per Capita	32
Hazardous Waste Sites	30
Drinking Water Quality	12
Expired Water Pollution Permits	16
Air Pollution Emissions	32

Government - Section D

Members of United States House	34
State Legislators	38
Legislators Per Million Population	16
Units of Government	18
Legislators Compensation	50
Female Legislators	9
Turnover in Legislatures	28
Term Limits	n/a
Legislative Session Length	35
Democrats in State Legislatures	14
Governors' Power Rating	14
Number of Statewide Elected Officials	15
State and Local Government Employees	5
State and Local Average Salaries	44
Local Employment	45
Local Spending Accountability	50
Registered Voters	39
Percentage of Population Voting	36
Statewide Initiatives	n/a
Campaign Costs Per Vote	11

Federal Impacts - Section E

Per Capita Federal Spending	4
Increase in Federal Spending	13
Per Capita Federal Grant Spending	4
Per Capita Federal Spending on Procurement	3
Per Capita Federal Spending on Payments to Individuals	32
Per Capita Federal Spending on Social Security and Medicare	43
Social Security Benefits	47
Federal Spending on Employee Wages and Salaries	6
Per Capita Federal Defense Spending	15
Per Capita Homeland Security Grants	15
Federal Grant Spending Per Dollar of State Tax Revenue	15
General Revenue from Federal Government	7
Federal Tax Burden Per Capita	49
Federal Spending Per Dollar of Taxes Paid	1
Highway Charges Returned to States	16
Terms of Trade	2
Federal Personal Income Taxes	46
Federal Share of Medicaid	4

Taxes - Section F

Tax Revenue	9
Per Capita Tax Revenue	38
Tax Effort	18
Tax Capacity	41
Percentage Change in Taxes	44
Property Taxes as a Percentage of Income	46
Property Taxes Per Capita	48
Property Tax Revenue as a Percentage of 3-tax Revenue	46
Sales Taxes as a Percentage of Income	6
Sales Taxes Per Capita	11
Sales Tax Revenue as a Percentage of 3-tax Revenue	7
Sales Tax Rate	25
Income Taxes as a Percentage of Income	33
Income Taxes Per Capita	36
Income Tax Revenue as a Percentage of 3-tax Revenue	32
Highest Personal Income Rate	16
Corporate Income Taxes	23
Motor Fuel Taxes	34
Motor Vehicle Fees	13
Tobacco Taxes	20
Taxes on High-Income Families	30
Taxes in the Largest City in Each State	31
Progressivity of Taxes	12
Per Capita Estate Tax Revenue	30

Revenues and Finances - Section G

Per Capita Total Revenue	19
Per Capita General Revenue	19

New Mexico

"Own-Source" General Revenue	33
Per Capita Non-Tax Revenue	16
Per Capita Total Spending	23
General Spending as a Percentage of Income	2
Per Capita General Spending	16
Change in General Expenditures	30
State Government General Revenue	8
State Government General Spending	7
State Government General Fund Spending	4
State and Local Debt	32
Debt as a Percentage of Revenue	35
Per Capita Full Faith and Credit Debt	34
Bond Ratings	2
State Solvency Index	3
Pension Plan Assets	28
State Reserves	8
Capital Outlays and Interest	33
State Budget Process Quality	8
Relative State Spending "Needs"	50
Structural Deficits	40

Education - Section H

Math Proficiency, Eighth Grade	48
Reading Proficiency, Eighth Grade	47
AFQT Ranks	43
SAT Scores	n/a
ACT Scores	23
Population over 25 with a High School Diploma	40
Students in Private Schools	37
High School Dropout Rates	42
Pupil-Teacher Ratio	23
Public School Enrollment	11
Library Holdings Per Capita	32
Children with Disabilities	13
Education Spending Per Capita	10
Education Spending as a Percentage of General Spending	17
Spending Per Pupil	25
Average Teacher Salary	39
Sources of School Funds	48
State Aid Per Pupil	6
Per Capita Higher Education Spending	4
Higher Education Spending as a Percentage of General Spending	4
Public Higher Education Enrollment	9
Per Pupil Support of Higher Education	5
In-State Tuition and Fees	44
Out-of-State Tuition and Fees	35
Change in Tuition and Fees	33
Affordability Index	15
Average Professor Salary	45
Education Employees	19
R and D Spending	1
Library Operating Spending	41
Head Start Spending	25

Health - Section I

Immunization Rates	22
Infant Mortality Rates	30
State Health Rankings	38
Population without Health Insurance	2
Abortions	27
Alcohol Consumption	16
Percentage of Adult Smokers	30
Percentage Obese	36
AIDS Cases	23
Physicians Per 100,000 Population	32
Hospital Beds Per 1,000 Population	47
Medicaid Recipients	2
Medicaid Recipients as a Percentage of Poverty Population	18
Health and Hospital Spending	25
Health and Hospital Spending as a Percentage of General Spending	29
Per Capita Medicaid Spending	9
Medicaid Spending Per Aged	30
Medicaid Spending Per Child	18
Medicare Payment Per Hospital Day	21
Hospital Expense Per Inpatient Day	19
Population in HMOs	17
Prescription Drugs as a Percentage of Medicaid Costs	49
Percentage Change in Average Price of Prescription Drugs	48

Crime - Section J

Crime Rate	10
Violent Crime Rate	5
Murder Rate	3
Property Crime Rate	12
Motor Vehicle Theft Rate	16
Violent Crime Rate Change	30
Prisoners	36
Change in Prisoners	16
Incarceration Rate	37
Juvenile Violent Crime Rate	24
Law Enforcement Employees	15
Corrections Employees	4
State Corrections Spending	14
Increase in State Corrections Spending	2
Law Enforcement Spending	14
Law Enforcement Spending as a Percentage of General Spending	17

Transportation - Section K

Travel on Interstates	10
Interstate Mileage in "Unacceptable" Condition	41
Deficient Bridges	40
Traffic Deaths	4
Seat Belt Use	9
Vehicle-Miles Traveled Per Capita	7
Use of Public Transportation	28
Road and Street Miles	16
Highway Employees	23
Public Transit Employees	23
Highway Spending Per Capita	6
Highway Spending as a Percentage of General Spending	12

Welfare - Section L

Births to Unwed Mothers	1
TANF Recipients	4
Change in TANF/AFDC Recipients	31
Food Stamp Recipients	8
SSI Recipients	11
WIC Average Monthly Benefit	20
NSLP Recipients	26
Condition of Children Index	46
Families with Single Parent	4
Average Monthly TANF Payments	26
Welfare as a Percentage of Poverty-Level Income	25
State Supplements of SSI	19
State Income Tax Liability of Typical Family in Poverty	33
Child Support Collections	50
Child Support Collections Per Dollar of Administrative Costs	50
Children in Foster Care	42
Welfare Spending Per Capita	12
Welfare Spending as a Percentage of General Spending	15
Administrative Costs Per TANF Case	46

Technology - Section M

Households with Computers	46
Percentage Using Internet	47
Zip Codes with Broadband Service	38
High-Tech Jobs	5
Change in High-Tech Jobs	15
State Government Web Site Ratings	45
Number of Online Government Services	34
Students Per Computer	36
Students Per Internet-Connected Computer	31
Libraries with Internet Access	43

New York

Population - Section A

Population 2005	3
Population 2004	3
Population Change 2003–2004	49
Population Change 1994–2004	44
Population 2015	47
Population 2025	4
Percentage 65 and Over	22
Percentage 17 and Under	32
Median Age	19
Percentage African American	10
Percentage American Indian	27
Percentage Asian American	4
Percentage Hispanic	8
Percentage White (Non-Hispanic)	43
Percentage Mixed-Race	15
Percentage in Poverty	9
Child Poverty Rate	7
Percentage Female	2
Birth Rates	32
Death Rates	44
Population Density	7
Legal Immigrants FY 2004	2
Unauthorized Immigrants	3

Economies - Section B

Personal Income, 2004	2
Gross State Product	7
Per Capita Personal Income	5
Personal Income from Wages and Salaries	4
Average Annual Pay	2
Average Hourly Earnings	6
Value Added in Manufacturing	40
Cost of Living	5
Average Annual Pay in Manufacturing	13
Average Annual Pay in Retailing	7
Labor Force	42
Unemployment Rate	21
Employment Rate	30
Government Employment	21
Manufacturing Employment	42
Fortune 500 Companies	3
Forbes 500 Companies	3
Tourism Spending Per Capita	36
Exports Per Capita	20
Housing Permits	49
Percentage Change in Home Prices	10
Net Farm Income	33
Financial Institution Assets	7
Bankruptcy Filings	37
Patents Issued	15
WC Disability Payment	48
Average Weekly UC Benefit	14
Economic Momentum	39
One-year Employment Change	36
Manufacturing Employment Change	44
Home Ownership	50
Annual Electricity Use Per Residential Customer	48
Cost Per Kwh	2
New Companies	14

Geography - Section C

Total Land Area	30
Federally Owned Land	43
State Park Acreage	2
State Park Visitors	20
Population Not Active	7
Hunters with Firearms	30
Registered Boats	7
State Spending for the Arts	4
Energy Consumption Per Capita	49
Toxic Chemical Release Per Capita	45
Hazardous Waste Sites	4
Drinking Water Quality	43
Expired Water Pollution Permits	39
Air Pollution Emissions	5

Government - Section D

Members of United States House	3
State Legislators	4
Legislators Per Million Population	47
Units of Government	34
Legislators Compensation	3
Female Legislators	25
Turnover in Legislatures	39
Term Limits	n/a
Legislative Session Length	n/a
Democrats in State Legislatures	10
Governors' Power Rating	1
Number of Statewide Elected Officials	41
State and Local Government Employees	10
State and Local Average Salaries	3
Local Employment	1
Local Spending Accountability	25
Registered Voters	6
Percentage of Population Voting	31
Statewide Initiatives	n/a
Campaign Costs Per Vote	1

Federal Impacts - Section E

Per Capita Federal Spending	22
Increase in Federal Spending	25
Per Capita Federal Grant Spending	3
Per Capita Federal Spending on Procurement	43
Per Capita Federal Spending on Payments to Individuals	23
Per Capita Federal Spending on Social Security and Medicare	8
Social Security Benefits	4
Federal Spending on Employee Wages and Salaries	44
Per Capita Federal Defense Spending	48
Per Capita Homeland Security Grants	48
Federal Grant Spending Per Dollar of State Tax Revenue	16
General Revenue from Federal Government	21
Federal Tax Burden Per Capita	5
Federal Spending Per Dollar of Taxes Paid	42
Highway Charges Returned to States	13
Terms of Trade	14
Federal Personal Income Taxes	4
Federal Share of Medicaid	39

Taxes - Section F

Tax Revenue	1
Per Capita Tax Revenue	1
Tax Effort	1
Tax Capacity	14
Percentage Change in Taxes	39
Property Taxes as a Percentage of Income	11
Property Taxes Per Capita	5
Property Tax Revenue as a Percentage of 3-tax Revenue	25
Sales Taxes as a Percentage of Income	36
Sales Taxes Per Capita	17
Sales Tax Revenue as a Percentage of 3-tax Revenue	42
Sales Tax Rate	36
Income Taxes as a Percentage of Income	1
Income Taxes Per Capita	1
Income Tax Revenue as a Percentage of 3-tax Revenue	4
Highest Personal Income Rate	11
Corporate Income Taxes	4
Motor Fuel Taxes	17
Motor Vehicle Fees	36
Tobacco Taxes	8
Taxes on High-Income Families	1
Taxes in the Largest City in Each State	2
Progressivity of Taxes	3
Per Capita Estate Tax Revenue	3

Revenues and Finances - Section G

Per Capita Total Revenue	2
Per Capita General Revenue	3

"Own-Source" General Revenue	2
Per Capita Non-Tax Revenue	15
Per Capita Total Spending	2
General Spending as a Percentage of Income	5
Per Capita General Spending	2
Change in General Expenditures	47
State Government General Revenue	5
State Government General Spending	6
State Government General Fund Spending	29
State and Local Debt	2
Debt as a Percentage of Revenue	5
Per Capita Full Faith and Credit Debt	6
Bond Ratings	5
State Solvency Index	45
Pension Plan Assets	1
State Reserves	45
Capital Outlays and Interest	2
State Budget Process Quality	20
Relative State Spending "Needs"	36
Structural Deficits	11

Education - Section H

Math Proficiency, Eighth Grade	28
Reading Proficiency, Eighth Grade	19
AFQT Ranks	34
SAT Scores	17
ACT Scores	n/a
Population over 25 with a High School Diploma	34
Students in Private Schools	6
High School Dropout Rates	42
Pupil-Teacher Ratio	44
Public School Enrollment	47
Library Holdings Per Capita	9
Children with Disabilities	11
Education Spending Per Capita	3
Education Spending as a Percentage of General Spending	48
Spending Per Pupil	2
Average Teacher Salary	5
Sources of School Funds	17
State Aid Per Pupil	11
Per Capita Higher Education Spending	47
Higher Education Spending as a Percentage of General Spending	50
Public Higher Education Enrollment	22
Per Pupil Support of Higher Education	29
In-State Tuition and Fees	23
Out-of-State Tuition and Fees	38
Change in Tuition and Fees	49
Affordability Index	21
Average Professor Salary	17
Education Employees	20
R and D Spending	22
Library Operating Spending	2
Head Start Spending	2

Health - Section I

Immunization Rates	24
Infant Mortality Rates	31
State Health Rankings	26
Population without Health Insurance	25
Abortions	1
Alcohol Consumption	43
Percentage of Adult Smokers	36
Percentage Obese	33
AIDS Cases	1
Physicians Per 100,000 Population	3
Hospital Beds Per 1,000 Population	15
Medicaid Recipients	6
Medicaid Recipients as a Percentage of Poverty Population	13
Health and Hospital Spending	7
Health and Hospital Spending as a Percentage of General Spending	22
Per Capita Medicaid Spending	1
Medicaid Spending Per Aged	2
Medicaid Spending Per Child	3
Medicare Payment Per Hospital Day	29
Hospital Expense Per Inpatient Day	30
Population in HMOs	18
Prescription Drugs as a Percentage of Medicaid Costs	40
Percentage Change in Average Price of Prescription Drugs	36

Crime - Section J

Crime Rate	45
Violent Crime Rate	21
Murder Rate	25
Property Crime Rate	47
Motor Vehicle Theft Rate	38
Violent Crime Rate Change	48
Prisoners	4
Change in Prisoners	49
Incarceration Rate	33
Juvenile Violent Crime Rate	16
Law Enforcement Employees	1
Corrections Employees	5
State Corrections Spending	16
Increase in State Corrections Spending	35
Law Enforcement Spending	2
Law Enforcement Spending as a Percentage of General Spending	12

Transportation - Section K

Travel on Interstates	46
Interstate Mileage in "Unacceptable" Condition	3
Deficient Bridges	5
Traffic Deaths	44
Seat Belt Use	16
Vehicle-Miles Traveled Per Capita	50
Use of Public Transportation	1
Road and Street Miles	28
Highway Employees	25
Public Transit Employees	1
Highway Spending Per Capita	33
Highway Spending as a Percentage of General Spending	50

Welfare - Section L

Births to Unwed Mothers	14
TANF Recipients	15
Change in TANF/AFDC Recipients	13
Food Stamp Recipients	20
SSI Recipients	7
WIC Average Monthly Benefit	2
NSLP Recipients	33
Condition of Children Index	20
Families with Single Parent	7
Average Monthly TANF Payments	2
Welfare as a Percentage of Poverty-Level Income	12
State Supplements of SSI	26
State Income Tax Liability of Typical Family in Poverty	40
Child Support Collections	25
Child Support Collections Per Dollar of Administrative Costs	34
Children in Foster Care	19
Welfare Spending Per Capita	1
Welfare Spending as a Percentage of General Spending	8
Administrative Costs Per TANF Case	2

Technology - Section M

Households with Computers	34
Percentage Using Internet	32
Zip Codes with Broadband Service	1
High-Tech Jobs	24
Change in High-Tech Jobs	43
State Government Web Site Ratings	14
Number of Online Government Services	14
Students Per Computer	11
Students Per Internet-Connected Computer	8
Libraries with Internet Access	20

North Carolina

Population - Section A

Population 2005	11
Population 2004	11
Population Change 2003–2004	9
Population Change 1994–2004	9
Population 2015	5
Population 2025	8
Percentage 65 and Over	33
Percentage 17 and Under	19
Median Age	35
Percentage African American	7
Percentage American Indian	14
Percentage Asian American	27
Percentage Hispanic	24
Percentage White (Non-Hispanic)	34
Percentage Mixed-Race	38
Percentage in Poverty	11
Child Poverty Rate	14
Percentage Female	23
Birth Rates	19
Death Rates	12
Population Density	16
Legal Immigrants FY 2004	19
Unauthorized Immigrants	9

Economies - Section B

Personal Income, 2004	13
Gross State Product	18
Per Capita Personal Income	36
Personal Income from Wages and Salaries	12
Average Annual Pay	28
Average Hourly Earnings	41
Value Added in Manufacturing	4
Cost of Living	27
Average Annual Pay in Manufacturing	32
Average Annual Pay in Retailing	29
Labor Force	34
Unemployment Rate	16
Employment Rate	35
Government Employment	27
Manufacturing Employment	10
Fortune 500 Companies	20
Forbes 500 Companies	27
Tourism Spending Per Capita	34
Exports Per Capita	28
Housing Permits	6
Percentage Change in Home Prices	44
Net Farm Income	7
Financial Institution Assets	4
Bankruptcy Filings	34
Patents Issued	26
WC Disability Payment	17
Average Weekly UC Benefit	22
Economic Momentum	12
One-year Employment Change	22
Manufacturing Employment Change	37
Home Ownership	36
Annual Electricity Use Per Residential Customer	11
Cost Per Kwh	18
New Companies	28

Geography - Section C

Total Land Area	29
Federally Owned Land	13
State Park Acreage	19
State Park Visitors	42
Population Not Active	15
Hunters with Firearms	24
Registered Boats	11
State Spending for the Arts	30
Energy Consumption Per Capita	33
Toxic Chemical Release Per Capita	20
Hazardous Waste Sites	11
Drinking Water Quality	13
Expired Water Pollution Permits	28
Air Pollution Emissions	10

Government - Section D

Members of United States House	9
State Legislators	15
Legislators Per Million Population	40
Units of Government	43
Legislators Compensation	32
Female Legislators	24
Turnover in Legislatures	20
Term Limits	n/a
Legislative Session Length	20
Democrats in State Legislatures	19
Governors' Power Rating	44
Number of Statewide Elected Officials	3
State and Local Government Employees	34
State and Local Average Salaries	27
Local Employment	23
Local Spending Accountability	36
Registered Voters	20
Percentage of Population Voting	38
Statewide Initiatives	n/a
Campaign Costs Per Vote	40

Federal Impacts - Section E

Per Capita Federal Spending	35
Increase in Federal Spending	9
Per Capita Federal Grant Spending	27
Per Capita Federal Spending on Procurement	44
Per Capita Federal Spending on Payments to Individuals	34
Per Capita Federal Spending on Social Security and Medicare	32
Social Security Benefits	33
Federal Spending on Employee Wages and Salaries	15
Per Capita Federal Defense Spending	24
Per Capita Homeland Security Grants	41
Federal Grant Spending Per Dollar of State Tax Revenue	29
General Revenue from Federal Government	22
Federal Tax Burden Per Capita	32
Federal Spending Per Dollar of Taxes Paid	26
Highway Charges Returned to States	41
Terms of Trade	23
Federal Personal Income Taxes	34
Federal Share of Medicaid	18

Taxes - Section F

Tax Revenue	35
Per Capita Tax Revenue	32
Tax Effort	35
Tax Capacity	25
Percentage Change in Taxes	13
Property Taxes as a Percentage of Income	40
Property Taxes Per Capita	38
Property Tax Revenue as a Percentage of 3-tax Revenue	41
Sales Taxes as a Percentage of Income	31
Sales Taxes Per Capita	36
Sales Tax Revenue as a Percentage of 3-tax Revenue	29
Sales Tax Rate	34
Income Taxes as a Percentage of Income	7
Income Taxes Per Capita	13
Income Tax Revenue as a Percentage of 3-tax Revenue	8
Highest Personal Income Rate	7
Corporate Income Taxes	16
Motor Fuel Taxes	7
Motor Vehicle Fees	38
Tobacco Taxes	44
Taxes on High-Income Families	19
Taxes in the Largest City in Each State	22
Progressivity of Taxes	11
Per Capita Estate Tax Revenue	26

Revenues and Finances - Section G

Per Capita Total Revenue	31
Per Capita General Revenue	34

"Own-Source" General Revenue	35
Per Capita Non-Tax Revenue	31
Per Capita Total Spending	33
General Spending as a Percentage of Income	30
Per Capita General Spending	37
Change in General Expenditures	9
State Government General Revenue	35
State Government General Spending	35
State Government General Fund Spending	36
State and Local Debt	42
Debt as a Percentage of Revenue	41
Per Capita Full Faith and Credit Debt	35
Bond Ratings	2
State Solvency Index	5
Pension Plan Assets	29
State Reserves	33
Capital Outlays and Interest	36
State Budget Process Quality	41
Relative State Spending "Needs"	33
Structural Deficits	34

Education - Section H

Math Proficiency, Eighth Grade	16
Reading Proficiency, Eighth Grade	36
AFQT Ranks	38
SAT Scores	16
ACT Scores	n/a
Population over 25 with a High School Diploma	46
Students in Private Schools	36
High School Dropout Rates	38
Pupil-Teacher Ratio	27
Public School Enrollment	34
Library Holdings Per Capita	40
Children with Disabilities	27
Education Spending Per Capita	39
Education Spending as a Percentage of General Spending	28
Spending Per Pupil	38
Average Teacher Salary	26
Sources of School Funds	45
State Aid Per Pupil	24
Per Capita Higher Education Spending	20
Higher Education Spending as a Percentage of General Spending	11
Public Higher Education Enrollment	33
Per Pupil Support of Higher Education	4
In-State Tuition and Fees	39
Out-of-State Tuition and Fees	19
Change in Tuition and Fees	10
Affordability Index	11
Average Professor Salary	7
Education Employees	44
R and D Spending	25
Library Operating Spending	42
Head Start Spending	16

Health - Section I

Immunization Rates	36
Infant Mortality Rates	9
State Health Rankings	36
Population without Health Insurance	17
Abortions	16
Alcohol Consumption	40
Percentage of Adult Smokers	17
Percentage Obese	17
AIDS Cases	12
Physicians Per 100,000 Population	27
Hospital Beds Per 1,000 Population	24
Medicaid Recipients	28
Medicaid Recipients as a Percentage of Poverty Population	42
Health and Hospital Spending	6
Health and Hospital Spending as a Percentage of General Spending	4
Per Capita Medicaid Spending	19
Medicaid Spending Per Aged	32
Medicaid Spending Per Child	26
Medicare Payment Per Hospital Day	45
Hospital Expense Per Inpatient Day	32
Population in HMOs	35
Prescription Drugs as a Percentage of Medicaid Costs	6
Percentage Change in Average Price of Prescription Drugs	19

Crime - Section J

Crime Rate	14
Violent Crime Rate	20
Murder Rate	12
Property Crime Rate	14
Motor Vehicle Theft Rate	27
Violent Crime Rate Change	32
Prisoners	12
Change in Prisoners	45
Incarceration Rate	31
Juvenile Violent Crime Rate	10
Law Enforcement Employees	32
Corrections Employees	10
State Corrections Spending	33
Increase in State Corrections Spending	44
Law Enforcement Spending	33
Law Enforcement Spending as a Percentage of General Spending	26

Transportation - Section K

Travel on Interstates	44
Interstate Mileage in "Unacceptable" Condition	11
Deficient Bridges	16
Traffic Deaths	20
Seat Belt Use	11
Vehicle-Miles Traveled Per Capita	19
Use of Public Transportation	35
Road and Street Miles	4
Highway Employees	33
Public Transit Employees	37
Highway Spending Per Capita	35
Highway Spending as a Percentage of General Spending	33

Welfare - Section L

Births to Unwed Mothers	18
TANF Recipients	41
Change in TANF/AFDC Recipients	7
Food Stamp Recipients	18
SSI Recipients	17
WIC Average Monthly Benefit	16
NSLP Recipients	21
Condition of Children Index	40
Families with Single Parent	9
Average Monthly TANF Payments	38
Welfare as a Percentage of Poverty-Level Income	39
State Supplements of SSI	3
State Income Tax Liability of Typical Family in Poverty	17
Child Support Collections	33
Child Support Collections Per Dollar of Administrative Costs	22
Children in Foster Care	40
Welfare Spending Per Capita	26
Welfare Spending as a Percentage of General Spending	19
Administrative Costs Per TANF Case	28

Technology - Section M

Households with Computers	41
Percentage Using Internet	37
Zip Codes with Broadband Service	6
High-Tech Jobs	25
Change in High-Tech Jobs	41
State Government Web Site Ratings	4
Number of Online Government Services	6
Students Per Computer	13
Students Per Internet-Connected Computer	15
Libraries with Internet Access	1

North Dakota

Population - Section A

Population 2005	48
Population 2004	48
Population Change 2003–2004	48
Population Change 1994–2004	50
Population 2015	50
Population 2025	49
Percentage 65 and Over	4
Percentage 17 and Under	47
Median Age	9
Percentage African American	47
Percentage American Indian	6
Percentage Asian American	47
Percentage Hispanic	47
Percentage White (Non-Hispanic)	6
Percentage Mixed-Race	40
Percentage in Poverty	40
Child Poverty Rate	39
Percentage Female	43
Birth Rates	40
Death Rates	42
Population Density	47
Legal Immigrants FY 2004	48
Unauthorized Immigrants	43

Economies - Section B

Personal Income, 2004	49
Gross State Product	32
Per Capita Personal Income	37
Personal Income from Wages and Salaries	16
Average Annual Pay	47
Average Hourly Earnings	32
Value Added in Manufacturing	41
Cost of Living	39
Average Annual Pay in Manufacturing	43
Average Annual Pay in Retailing	47
Labor Force	6
Unemployment Rate	46
Employment Rate	5
Government Employment	6
Manufacturing Employment	39
Fortune 500 Companies	n/a
Forbes 500 Companies	13
Tourism Spending Per Capita	13
Exports Per Capita	32
Housing Permits	24
Percentage Change in Home Prices	28
Net Farm Income	28
Financial Institution Assets	17
Bankruptcy Filings	39
Patents Issued	44
WC Disability Payment	34
Average Weekly UC Benefit	33
Economic Momentum	26
One-year Employment Change	32
Manufacturing Employment Change	9
Home Ownership	34
Annual Electricity Use Per Residential Customer	18
Cost Per Kwh	27
New Companies	38

Geography - Section C

Total Land Area	17
Federally Owned Land	28
State Park Acreage	49
State Park Visitors	36
Population Not Active	32
Hunters with Firearms	1
Registered Boats	42
State Spending for the Arts	23
Energy Consumption Per Capita	4
Toxic Chemical Release Per Capita	9
Hazardous Waste Sites	50
Drinking Water Quality	29
Expired Water Pollution Permits	46
Air Pollution Emissions	39

Government - Section D

Members of United States House	44
State Legislators	26
Legislators Per Million Population	3
Units of Government	1
Legislators Compensation	33
Female Legislators	38
Turnover in Legislatures	40
Term Limits	n/a
Legislative Session Length	n/a
Democrats in State Legislatures	45
Governors' Power Rating	6
Number of Statewide Elected Officials	1
State and Local Government Employees	7
State and Local Average Salaries	32
Local Employment	47
Local Spending Accountability	27
Registered Voters	n/a
Percentage of Population Voting	15
Statewide Initiatives	n/a
Campaign Costs Per Vote	44

Federal Impacts - Section E

Per Capita Federal Spending	6
Increase in Federal Spending	46
Per Capita Federal Grant Spending	5
Per Capita Federal Spending on Procurement	26
Per Capita Federal Spending on Payments to Individuals	1
Per Capita Federal Spending on Social Security and Medicare	25
Social Security Benefits	41
Federal Spending on Employee Wages and Salaries	5
Per Capita Federal Defense Spending	14
Per Capita Homeland Security Grants	3
Federal Grant Spending Per Dollar of State Tax Revenue	7
General Revenue from Federal Government	6
Federal Tax Burden Per Capita	38
Federal Spending Per Dollar of Taxes Paid	5
Highway Charges Returned to States	5
Terms of Trade	4
Federal Personal Income Taxes	38
Federal Share of Medicaid	14

Taxes - Section F

Tax Revenue	18
Per Capita Tax Revenue	30
Tax Effort	34
Tax Capacity	27
Percentage Change in Taxes	49
Property Taxes as a Percentage of Income	23
Property Taxes Per Capita	31
Property Tax Revenue as a Percentage of 3-tax Revenue	19
Sales Taxes as a Percentage of Income	17
Sales Taxes Per Capita	25
Sales Tax Revenue as a Percentage of 3-tax Revenue	16
Sales Tax Rate	25
Income Taxes as a Percentage of Income	41
Income Taxes Per Capita	41
Income Tax Revenue as a Percentage of 3-tax Revenue	41
Highest Personal Income Rate	27
Corporate Income Taxes	17
Motor Fuel Taxes	24
Motor Vehicle Fees	5
Tobacco Taxes	37
Taxes on High-Income Families	40
Taxes in the Largest City in Each State	36
Progressivity of Taxes	38
Per Capita Estate Tax Revenue	43

Revenues and Finances - Section G

Per Capita Total Revenue	10
Per Capita General Revenue	9

"Own-Source" General Revenue	25
Per Capita Non-Tax Revenue	5
Per Capita Total Spending	27
General Spending as a Percentage of Income	7
Per Capita General Spending	18
Change in General Expenditures	43
State Government General Revenue	9
State Government General Spending	13
State Government General Fund Spending	19
State and Local Debt	33
Debt as a Percentage of Revenue	42
Per Capita Full Faith and Credit Debt	43
Bond Ratings	n/a
State Solvency Index	4
Pension Plan Assets	41
State Reserves	5
Capital Outlays and Interest	20
State Budget Process Quality	36
Relative State Spending "Needs"	38
Structural Deficits	13

Education - Section H

Math Proficiency, Eighth Grade	3
Reading Proficiency, Eighth Grade	2
AFQT Ranks	6
SAT Scores	n/a
ACT Scores	13
Population over 25 with a High School Diploma	12
Students in Private Schools	41
High School Dropout Rates	2
Pupil-Teacher Ratio	43
Public School Enrollment	36
Library Holdings Per Capita	13
Children with Disabilities	22
Education Spending Per Capita	23
Education Spending as a Percentage of General Spending	30
Spending Per Pupil	41
Average Teacher Salary	49
Sources of School Funds	13
State Aid Per Pupil	47
Per Capita Higher Education Spending	2
Higher Education Spending as a Percentage of General Spending	3
Public Higher Education Enrollment	3
Per Pupil Support of Higher Education	17
In-State Tuition and Fees	26
Out-of-State Tuition and Fees	44
Change in Tuition and Fees	3
Affordability Index	35
Average Professor Salary	43
Education Employees	26
R and D Spending	31
Library Operating Spending	45
Head Start Spending	17

Health - Section I

Immunization Rates	23
Infant Mortality Rates	39
State Health Rankings	6
Population without Health Insurance	40
Abortions	31
Alcohol Consumption	9
Percentage of Adult Smokers	39
Percentage Obese	16
AIDS Cases	45
Physicians Per 100,000 Population	29
Hospital Beds Per 1,000 Population	2
Medicaid Recipients	45
Medicaid Recipients as a Percentage of Poverty Population	45
Health and Hospital Spending	48
Health and Hospital Spending as a Percentage of General Spending	49
Per Capita Medicaid Spending	35
Medicaid Spending Per Aged	8
Medicaid Spending Per Child	28
Medicare Payment Per Hospital Day	44
Hospital Expense Per Inpatient Day	14
Population in HMOs	48
Prescription Drugs as a Percentage of Medicaid Costs	33
Percentage Change in Average Price of Prescription Drugs	9

Crime - Section J

Crime Rate	50
Violent Crime Rate	50
Murder Rate	48
Property Crime Rate	50
Motor Vehicle Theft Rate	47
Violent Crime Rate Change	16
Prisoners	50
Change in Prisoners	1
Incarceration Rate	46
Juvenile Violent Crime Rate	48
Law Enforcement Employees	47
Corrections Employees	48
State Corrections Spending	21
Increase in State Corrections Spending	7
Law Enforcement Spending	49
Law Enforcement Spending as a Percentage of General Spending	50

Transportation - Section K

Travel on Interstates	32
Interstate Mileage in "Unacceptable" Condition	45
Deficient Bridges	31
Traffic Deaths	29
Seat Belt Use	35
Vehicle-Miles Traveled Per Capita	11
Use of Public Transportation	45
Road and Street Miles	45
Highway Employees	6
Public Transit Employees	44
Highway Spending Per Capita	4
Highway Spending as a Percentage of General Spending	3

Welfare - Section L

Births to Unwed Mothers	44
TANF Recipients	29
Change in TANF/AFDC Recipients	42
Food Stamp Recipients	37
SSI Recipients	46
WIC Average Monthly Benefit	8
NSLP Recipients	7
Condition of Children Index	5
Families with Single Parent	44
Average Monthly TANF Payments	28
Welfare as a Percentage of Poverty-Level Income	18
State Supplements of SSI	2
State Income Tax Liability of Typical Family in Poverty	17
Child Support Collections	11
Child Support Collections Per Dollar of Administrative Costs	17
Children in Foster Care	15
Welfare Spending Per Capita	16
Welfare Spending as a Percentage of General Spending	20
Administrative Costs Per TANF Case	20

Technology - Section M

Households with Computers	27
Percentage Using Internet	31
Zip Codes with Broadband Service	49
High-Tech Jobs	32
Change in High-Tech Jobs	2
State Government Web Site Ratings	16
Number of Online Government Services	15
Students Per Computer	43
Students Per Internet-Connected Computer	46
Libraries with Internet Access	49

Ohio

Population - Section A

Population 2005	7
Population 2004	7
Population Change 2003–2004	47
Population Change 1994–2004	47
Population 2015	48
Population 2025	7
Percentage 65 and Over	14
Percentage 17 and Under	26
Median Age	16
Percentage African American	17
Percentage American Indian	47
Percentage Asian American	32
Percentage Hispanic	41
Percentage White (Non-Hispanic)	17
Percentage Mixed-Race	27
Percentage in Poverty	23
Child Poverty Rate	24
Percentage Female	11
Birth Rates	34
Death Rates	15
Population Density	9
Legal Immigrants FY 2004	17
Unauthorized Immigrants	26

Economies - Section B

Personal Income, 2004	8
Gross State Product	29
Per Capita Personal Income	25
Personal Income from Wages and Salaries	13
Average Annual Pay	22
Average Hourly Earnings	2
Value Added in Manufacturing	6
Cost of Living	25
Average Annual Pay in Manufacturing	18
Average Annual Pay in Retailing	27
Labor Force	27
Unemployment Rate	7
Employment Rate	44
Government Employment	39
Manufacturing Employment	8
Fortune 500 Companies	5
Forbes 500 Companies	8
Tourism Spending Per Capita	48
Exports Per Capita	14
Housing Permits	43
Percentage Change in Home Prices	46
Net Farm Income	21
Financial Institution Assets	5
Bankruptcy Filings	7
Patents Issued	17
WC Disability Payment	19
Average Weekly UC Benefit	25
Economic Momentum	47
One-year Employment Change	48
Manufacturing Employment Change	25
Home Ownership	18
Annual Electricity Use Per Residential Customer	28
Cost Per Kwh	19
New Companies	48

Geography - Section C

Total Land Area	35
Federally Owned Land	40
State Park Acreage	20
State Park Visitors	10
Population Not Active	24
Hunters with Firearms	41
Registered Boats	8
State Spending for the Arts	19
Energy Consumption Per Capita	24
Toxic Chemical Release Per Capita	14
Hazardous Waste Sites	13
Drinking Water Quality	35
Expired Water Pollution Permits	24
Air Pollution Emissions	4

Government - Section D

Members of United States House	7
State Legislators	32
Legislators Per Million Population	46
Units of Government	27
Legislators Compensation	6
Female Legislators	30
Turnover in Legislatures	26
Term Limits	4
Legislative Session Length	n/a
Democrats in State Legislatures	40
Governors' Power Rating	6
Number of Statewide Elected Officials	15
State and Local Government Employees	27
State and Local Average Salaries	20
Local Employment	4
Local Spending Accountability	29
Registered Voters	8
Percentage of Population Voting	11
Statewide Initiatives	3
Campaign Costs Per Vote	43

Federal Impacts - Section E

Per Capita Federal Spending	37
Increase in Federal Spending	37
Per Capita Federal Grant Spending	34
Per Capita Federal Spending on Procurement	36
Per Capita Federal Spending on Payments to Individuals	28
Per Capita Federal Spending on Social Security and Medicare	16
Social Security Benefits	21
Federal Spending on Employee Wages and Salaries	43
Per Capita Federal Defense Spending	39
Per Capita Homeland Security Grants	44
Federal Grant Spending Per Dollar of State Tax Revenue	28
General Revenue from Federal Government	30
Federal Tax Burden Per Capita	29
Federal Spending Per Dollar of Taxes Paid	31
Highway Charges Returned to States	47
Terms of Trade	27
Federal Personal Income Taxes	26
Federal Share of Medicaid	26

Taxes - Section F

Tax Revenue	11
Per Capita Tax Revenue	18
Tax Effort	13
Tax Capacity	32
Percentage Change in Taxes	21
Property Taxes as a Percentage of Income	22
Property Taxes Per Capita	23
Property Tax Revenue as a Percentage of 3-tax Revenue	30
Sales Taxes as a Percentage of Income	37
Sales Taxes Per Capita	37
Sales Tax Revenue as a Percentage of 3-tax Revenue	38
Sales Tax Rate	10
Income Taxes as a Percentage of Income	4
Income Taxes Per Capita	7
Income Tax Revenue as a Percentage of 3-tax Revenue	7
Highest Personal Income Rate	12
Corporate Income Taxes	24
Motor Fuel Taxes	9
Motor Vehicle Fees	15
Tobacco Taxes	12
Taxes on High-Income Families	12
Taxes in the Largest City in Each State	16
Progressivity of Taxes	31
Per Capita Estate Tax Revenue	48

Revenues and Finances - Section G

Per Capita Total Revenue	16
Per Capita General Revenue	25

"Own-Source" General Revenue	19
Per Capita Non-Tax Revenue	32
Per Capita Total Spending	17
General Spending as a Percentage of Income	28
Per Capita General Spending	22
Change in General Expenditures	14
State Government General Revenue	32
State Government General Spending	29
State Government General Fund Spending	21
State and Local Debt	37
Debt as a Percentage of Revenue	39
Per Capita Full Faith and Credit Debt	28
Bond Ratings	2
State Solvency Index	43
Pension Plan Assets	31
State Reserves	43
Capital Outlays and Interest	29
State Budget Process Quality	34
Relative State Spending "Needs"	21
Structural Deficits	25

Education - Section H

Math Proficiency, Eighth Grade	15
Reading Proficiency, Eighth Grade	12
AFQT Ranks	20
SAT Scores	n/a
ACT Scores	10
Population over 25 with a High School Diploma	17
Students in Private Schools	12
High School Dropout Rates	26
Pupil-Teacher Ratio	13
Public School Enrollment	26
Library Holdings Per Capita	9
Children with Disabilities	30
Education Spending Per Capita	22
Education Spending as a Percentage of General Spending	23
Spending Per Pupil	16
Average Teacher Salary	13
Sources of School Funds	18
State Aid Per Pupil	19
Per Capita Higher Education Spending	34
Higher Education Spending as a Percentage of General Spending	36
Public Higher Education Enrollment	38
Per Pupil Support of Higher Education	33
In-State Tuition and Fees	3
Out-of-State Tuition and Fees	15
Change in Tuition and Fees	2
Affordability Index	43
Average Professor Salary	15
Education Employees	29
R and D Spending	21
Library Operating Spending	1
Head Start Spending	45

Health - Section I

Immunization Rates	30
Infant Mortality Rates	13
State Health Rankings	27
Population without Health Insurance	40
Abortions	18
Alcohol Consumption	38
Percentage of Adult Smokers	5
Percentage Obese	11
AIDS Cases	34
Physicians Per 100,000 Population	11
Hospital Beds Per 1,000 Population	21
Medicaid Recipients	25
Medicaid Recipients as a Percentage of Poverty Population	21
Health and Hospital Spending	18
Health and Hospital Spending as a Percentage of General Spending	20
Per Capita Medicaid Spending	18
Medicaid Spending Per Aged	3
Medicaid Spending Per Child	29
Medicare Payment Per Hospital Day	27
Hospital Expense Per Inpatient Day	16
Population in HMOs	25
Prescription Drugs as a Percentage of Medicaid Costs	21
Percentage Change in Average Price of Prescription Drugs	41

Crime - Section J

Crime Rate	23
Violent Crime Rate	28
Murder Rate	26
Property Crime Rate	21
Motor Vehicle Theft Rate	20
Violent Crime Rate Change	7
Prisoners	7
Change in Prisoners	47
Incarceration Rate	25
Juvenile Violent Crime Rate	34
Law Enforcement Employees	20
Corrections Employees	28
State Corrections Spending	13
Increase in State Corrections Spending	31
Law Enforcement Spending	23
Law Enforcement Spending as a Percentage of General Spending	23

Transportation - Section K

Travel on Interstates	9
Interstate Mileage in "Unacceptable" Condition	30
Deficient Bridges	27
Traffic Deaths	42
Seat Belt Use	29
Vehicle-Miles Traveled Per Capita	38
Use of Public Transportation	24
Road and Street Miles	24
Highway Employees	32
Public Transit Employees	17
Highway Spending Per Capita	36
Highway Spending as a Percentage of General Spending	41

Welfare - Section L

Births to Unwed Mothers	15
TANF Recipients	19
Change in TANF/AFDC Recipients	19
Food Stamp Recipients	22
SSI Recipients	21
WIC Average Monthly Benefit	36
NSLP Recipients	36
Condition of Children Index	29
Families with Single Parent	13
Average Monthly TANF Payments	31
Welfare as a Percentage of Poverty-Level Income	19
State Supplements of SSI	34
State Income Tax Liability of Typical Family in Poverty	9
Child Support Collections	1
Child Support Collections Per Dollar of Administrative Costs	14
Children in Foster Care	27
Welfare Spending Per Capita	14
Welfare Spending as a Percentage of General Spending	14
Administrative Costs Per TANF Case	29

Technology - Section M

Households with Computers	39
Percentage Using Internet	34
Zip Codes with Broadband Service	6
High-Tech Jobs	34
Change in High-Tech Jobs	33
State Government Web Site Ratings	21
Number of Online Government Services	32
Students Per Computer	36
Students Per Internet-Connected Computer	31
Libraries with Internet Access	1

Oklahoma

Population · Section A

Population 2005	28
Population 2004	28
Population Change 2003–2004	38
Population Change 1994–2004	29
Population 2015	37
Population 2025	29
Percentage 65 and Over	18
Percentage 17 and Under	24
Median Age	32
Percentage African American	23
Percentage American Indian	4
Percentage Asian American	30
Percentage Hispanic	23
Percentage White (Non-Hispanic)	29
Percentage Mixed-Race	3
Percentage in Poverty	32
Child Poverty Rate	30
Percentage Female	30
Birth Rates	13
Death Rates	7
Population Density	35
Legal Immigrants FY 2004	32
Unauthorized Immigrants	22

Economies · Section B

Personal Income, 2004	29
Gross State Product	46
Per Capita Personal Income	39
Personal Income from Wages and Salaries	47
Average Annual Pay	43
Average Hourly Earnings	38
Value Added in Manufacturing	37
Cost of Living	47
Average Annual Pay in Manufacturing	42
Average Annual Pay in Retailing	41
Labor Force	44
Unemployment Rate	27
Employment Rate	24
Government Employment	7
Manufacturing Employment	31
Fortune 500 Companies	25
Forbes 500 Companies	31
Tourism Spending Per Capita	46
Exports Per Capita	47
Housing Permits	40
Percentage Change in Home Prices	38
Net Farm Income	20
Financial Institution Assets	29
Bankruptcy Filings	8
Patents Issued	36
WC Disability Payment	38
Average Weekly UC Benefit	39
Economic Momentum	22
One-year Employment Change	15
Manufacturing Employment Change	35
Home Ownership	30
Annual Electricity Use Per Residential Customer	12
Cost Per Kwh	29
New Companies	29

Geography · Section C

Total Land Area	19
Federally Owned Land	24
State Park Acreage	34
State Park Visitors	13
Population Not Active	6
Hunters with Firearms	17
Registered Boats	25
State Spending for the Arts	14
Energy Consumption Per Capita	8
Toxic Chemical Release Per Capita	35
Hazardous Waste Sites	38
Drinking Water Quality	7
Expired Water Pollution Permits	35
Air Pollution Emissions	22

Government · Section D

Members of United States House	27
State Legislators	22
Legislators Per Million Population	21
Units of Government	16
Legislators Compensation	12
Female Legislators	44
Turnover in Legislatures	2
Term Limits	1
Legislative Session Length	10
Democrats in State Legislatures	28
Governors' Power Rating	46
Number of Statewide Elected Officials	9
State and Local Government Employees	18
State and Local Average Salaries	49
Local Employment	33
Local Spending Accountability	35
Registered Voters	30
Percentage of Population Voting	37
Statewide Initiatives	4
Campaign Costs Per Vote	25

Federal Impacts · Section E

Per Capita Federal Spending	21
Increase in Federal Spending	29
Per Capita Federal Grant Spending	25
Per Capita Federal Spending on Procurement	24
Per Capita Federal Spending on Payments to Individuals	12
Per Capita Federal Spending on Social Security and Medicare	20
Social Security Benefits	39
Federal Spending on Employee Wages and Salaries	9
Per Capita Federal Defense Spending	19
Per Capita Homeland Security Grants	23
Federal Grant Spending Per Dollar of State Tax Revenue	20
General Revenue from Federal Government	19
Federal Tax Burden Per Capita	45
Federal Spending Per Dollar of Taxes Paid	12
Highway Charges Returned to States	31
Terms of Trade	17
Federal Personal Income Taxes	43
Federal Share of Medicaid	12

Taxes · Section F

Tax Revenue	37
Per Capita Tax Revenue	42
Tax Effort	19
Tax Capacity	48
Percentage Change in Taxes	23
Property Taxes as a Percentage of Income	47
Property Taxes Per Capita	47
Property Tax Revenue as a Percentage of 3-tax Revenue	45
Sales Taxes as a Percentage of Income	20
Sales Taxes Per Capita	32
Sales Tax Revenue as a Percentage of 3-tax Revenue	17
Sales Tax Rate	35
Income Taxes as a Percentage of Income	17
Income Taxes Per Capita	28
Income Tax Revenue as a Percentage of 3-tax Revenue	11
Highest Personal Income Rate	18
Corporate Income Taxes	37
Motor Fuel Taxes	43
Motor Vehicle Fees	2
Tobacco Taxes	16
Taxes on High-Income Families	32
Taxes in the Largest City in Each State	24
Progressivity of Taxes	32
Per Capita Estate Tax Revenue	50

Revenues and Finances · Section G

Per Capita Total Revenue	42
Per Capita General Revenue	42

"Own-Source" General Revenue	39
Per Capita Non-Tax Revenue	27
Per Capita Total Spending	42
General Spending as a Percentage of Income	26
Per Capita General Spending	42
Change in General Expenditures	3
State Government General Revenue	34
State Government General Spending	31
State Government General Fund Spending	20
State and Local Debt	46
Debt as a Percentage of Revenue	44
Per Capita Full Faith and Credit Debt	47
Bond Ratings	4
State Solvency Index	41
Pension Plan Assets	24
State Reserves	18
Capital Outlays and Interest	40
State Budget Process Quality	19
Relative State Spending "Needs"	30
Structural Deficits	8

Education - Section H

Math Proficiency, Eighth Grade	41
Reading Proficiency, Eighth Grade	33
AFQT Ranks	30
SAT Scores	n/a
ACT Scores	16
Population over 25 with a High School Diploma	35
Students in Private Schools	45
High School Dropout Rates	30
Pupil-Teacher Ratio	20
Public School Enrollment	5
Library Holdings Per Capita	36
Children with Disabilities	20
Education Spending Per Capita	31
Education Spending as a Percentage of General Spending	10
Spending Per Pupil	47
Average Teacher Salary	47
Sources of School Funds	34
State Aid Per Pupil	38
Per Capita Higher Education Spending	17
Higher Education Spending as a Percentage of General Spending	5
Public Higher Education Enrollment	17
Per Pupil Support of Higher Education	32
In-State Tuition and Fees	37
Out-of-State Tuition and Fees	41
Change in Tuition and Fees	20
Affordability Index	21
Average Professor Salary	41
Education Employees	21
R and D Spending	46
Library Operating Spending	35
Head Start Spending	48

Health - Section I

Immunization Rates	48
Infant Mortality Rates	11
State Health Rankings	44
Population without Health Insurance	4
Abortions	35
Alcohol Consumption	43
Percentage of Adult Smokers	4
Percentage Obese	14
AIDS Cases	35
Physicians Per 100,000 Population	44
Hospital Beds Per 1,000 Population	19
Medicaid Recipients	23
Medicaid Recipients as a Percentage of Poverty Population	14
Health and Hospital Spending	37
Health and Hospital Spending as a Percentage of General Spending	30
Per Capita Medicaid Spending	39
Medicaid Spending Per Aged	33
Medicaid Spending Per Child	43
Medicare Payment Per Hospital Day	36
Hospital Expense Per Inpatient Day	47
Population in HMOs	41
Prescription Drugs as a Percentage of Medicaid Costs	24
Percentage Change in Average Price of Prescription Drugs	41

Crime - Section J

Crime Rate	12
Violent Crime Rate	14
Murder Rate	21
Property Crime Rate	10
Motor Vehicle Theft Rate	19
Violent Crime Rate Change	9
Prisoners	20
Change in Prisoners	36
Incarceration Rate	4
Juvenile Violent Crime Rate	25
Law Enforcement Employees	12
Corrections Employees	38
State Corrections Spending	45
Increase in State Corrections Spending	34
Law Enforcement Spending	31
Law Enforcement Spending as a Percentage of General Spending	24

Transportation - Section K

Travel on Interstates	41
Interstate Mileage in "Unacceptable" Condition	16
Deficient Bridges	6
Traffic Deaths	17
Seat Belt Use	20
Vehicle-Miles Traveled Per Capita	3
Use of Public Transportation	45
Road and Street Miles	35
Highway Employees	17
Public Transit Employees	45
Highway Spending Per Capita	23
Highway Spending as a Percentage of General Spending	20

Welfare - Section L

Births to Unwed Mothers	13
TANF Recipients	44
Change in TANF/AFDC Recipients	11
Food Stamp Recipients	10
SSI Recipients	19
WIC Average Monthly Benefit	44
NSLP Recipients	23
Condition of Children Index	38
Families with Single Parent	23
Average Monthly TANF Payments	41
Welfare as a Percentage of Poverty-Level Income	37
State Supplements of SSI	39
State Income Tax Liability of Typical Family in Poverty	31
Child Support Collections	47
Child Support Collections Per Dollar of Administrative Costs	41
Children in Foster Care	4
Welfare Spending Per Capita	28
Welfare Spending as a Percentage of General Spending	17
Administrative Costs Per TANF Case	31

Technology - Section M

Households with Computers	43
Percentage Using Internet	43
Zip Codes with Broadband Service	33
High-Tech Jobs	33
Change in High-Tech Jobs	30
State Government Web Site Ratings	44
Number of Online Government Services	28
Students Per Computer	41
Students Per Internet-Connected Computer	34
Libraries with Internet Access	31

Oregon

Population - Section A

Population 2005	27
Population 2004	27
Population Change 2003–2004	22
Population Change 1994–2004	12
Population 2015	16
Population 2025	26
Percentage 65 and Over	25
Percentage 17 and Under	34
Median Age	22
Percentage African American	41
Percentage American Indian	12
Percentage Asian American	12
Percentage Hispanic	14
Percentage White (Non-Hispanic)	20
Percentage Mixed-Race	7
Percentage in Poverty	22
Child Poverty Rate	28
Percentage Female	36
Birth Rates	38
Death Rates	28
Population Density	39
Legal Immigrants FY 2004	21
Unauthorized Immigrants	14

Economies - Section B

Personal Income, 2004	28
Gross State Product	33
Per Capita Personal Income	30
Personal Income from Wages and Salaries	28
Average Annual Pay	23
Average Hourly Earnings	27
Value Added in Manufacturing	19
Cost of Living	14
Average Annual Pay in Manufacturing	19
Average Annual Pay in Retailing	19
Labor Force	26
Unemployment Rate	6
Employment Rate	45
Government Employment	31
Manufacturing Employment	15
Fortune 500 Companies	37
Forbes 500 Companies	40
Tourism Spending Per Capita	31
Exports Per Capita	11
Housing Permits	15
Percentage Change in Home Prices	21
Net Farm Income	24
Financial Institution Assets	48
Bankruptcy Filings	11
Patents Issued	6
WC Disability Payment	6
Average Weekly UC Benefit	18
Economic Momentum	13
One-year Employment Change	6
Manufacturing Employment Change	1
Home Ownership	38
Annual Electricity Use Per Residential Customer	21
Cost Per Kwh	39
New Companies	12

Geography - Section C

Total Land Area	10
Federally Owned Land	5
State Park Acreage	29
State Park Visitors	1
Population Not Active	47
Hunters with Firearms	31
Registered Boats	27
State Spending for the Arts	47
Energy Consumption Per Capita	36
Toxic Chemical Release Per Capita	27
Hazardous Waste Sites	34
Drinking Water Quality	4
Expired Water Pollution Permits	3
Air Pollution Emissions	20

Government - Section D

Members of United States House	27
State Legislators	43
Legislators Per Million Population	33
Units of Government	22
Legislators Compensation	27
Female Legislators	15
Turnover in Legislatures	11
Term Limits	n/a
Legislative Session Length	n/a
Democrats in State Legislatures	26
Governors' Power Rating	32
Number of Statewide Elected Officials	22
State and Local Government Employees	42
State and Local Average Salaries	17
Local Employment	34
Local Spending Accountability	42
Registered Voters	31
Percentage of Population Voting	5
Statewide Initiatives	n/a
Campaign Costs Per Vote	23

Federal Impacts - Section E

Per Capita Federal Spending	43
Increase in Federal Spending	27
Per Capita Federal Grant Spending	33
Per Capita Federal Spending on Procurement	48
Per Capita Federal Spending on Payments to Individuals	33
Per Capita Federal Spending on Social Security and Medicare	31
Social Security Benefits	14
Federal Spending on Employee Wages and Salaries	40
Per Capita Federal Defense Spending	50
Per Capita Homeland Security Grants	24
Federal Grant Spending Per Dollar of State Tax Revenue	2
General Revenue from Federal Government	3
Federal Tax Burden Per Capita	25
Federal Spending Per Dollar of Taxes Paid	33
Highway Charges Returned to States	23
Terms of Trade	30
Federal Personal Income Taxes	33
Federal Share of Medicaid	22

Taxes - Section F

Tax Revenue	46
Per Capita Tax Revenue	41
Tax Effort	46
Tax Capacity	12
Percentage Change in Taxes	45
Property Taxes as a Percentage of Income	25
Property Taxes Per Capita	27
Property Tax Revenue as a Percentage of 3-tax Revenue	13
Sales Taxes as a Percentage of Income	50
Sales Taxes Per Capita	50
Sales Tax Revenue as a Percentage of 3-tax Revenue	50
Sales Tax Rate	n/a
Income Taxes as a Percentage of Income	3
Income Taxes Per Capita	6
Income Tax Revenue as a Percentage of 3-tax Revenue	2
Highest Personal Income Rate	4
Corporate Income Taxes	34
Motor Fuel Taxes	14
Motor Vehicle Fees	42
Tobacco Taxes	14
Taxes on High-Income Families	9
Taxes in the Largest City in Each State	7
Progressivity of Taxes	29
Per Capita Estate Tax Revenue	33

Revenues and Finances - Section G

Per Capita Total Revenue	11
Per Capita General Revenue	13

"Own-Source" General Revenue	28
Per Capita Non-Tax Revenue	4
Per Capita Total Spending	9
General Spending as a Percentage of Income	10
Per Capita General Spending	10
Change in General Expenditures	18
State Government General Revenue	28
State Government General Spending	26
State Government General Fund Spending	16
State and Local Debt	24
Debt as a Percentage of Revenue	27
Per Capita Full Faith and Credit Debt	12
Bond Ratings	4
State Solvency Index	15
Pension Plan Assets	3
State Reserves	32
Capital Outlays and Interest	28
State Budget Process Quality	22
Relative State Spending "Needs"	31
Structural Deficits	43

Education - Section H

Math Proficiency, Eighth Grade	16
Reading Proficiency, Eighth Grade	27
AFQT Ranks	3
SAT Scores	3
ACT Scores	n/a
Population over 25 with a High School Diploma	24
Students in Private Schools	33
High School Dropout Rates	16
Pupil-Teacher Ratio	4
Public School Enrollment	40
Library Holdings Per Capita	27
Children with Disabilities	32
Education Spending Per Capita	17
Education Spending as a Percentage of General Spending	37
Spending Per Pupil	30
Average Teacher Salary	14
Sources of School Funds	28
State Aid Per Pupil	22
Per Capita Higher Education Spending	9
Higher Education Spending as a Percentage of General Spending	17
Public Higher Education Enrollment	28
Per Pupil Support of Higher Education	42
In-State Tuition and Fees	20
Out-of-State Tuition and Fees	18
Change in Tuition and Fees	14
Affordability Index	46
Average Professor Salary	47
Education Employees	48
R and D Spending	37
Library Operating Spending	8
Head Start Spending	32

Health - Section I

Immunization Rates	38
Infant Mortality Rates	36
State Health Rankings	18
Population without Health Insurance	14
Abortions	10
Alcohol Consumption	21
Percentage of Adult Smokers	34
Percentage Obese	37
AIDS Cases	26
Physicians Per 100,000 Population	21
Hospital Beds Per 1,000 Population	49
Medicaid Recipients	36
Medicaid Recipients as a Percentage of Poverty Population	38
Health and Hospital Spending	10
Health and Hospital Spending as a Percentage of General Spending	11
Per Capita Medicaid Spending	40
Medicaid Spending Per Aged	34
Medicaid Spending Per Child	34
Medicare Payment Per Hospital Day	19
Hospital Expense Per Inpatient Day	4
Population in HMOs	28
Prescription Drugs as a Percentage of Medicaid Costs	35
Percentage Change in Average Price of Prescription Drugs	36

Crime - Section J

Crime Rate	8
Violent Crime Rate	31
Murder Rate	38
Property Crime Rate	4
Motor Vehicle Theft Rate	8
Violent Crime Rate Change	42
Prisoners	29
Change in Prisoners	4
Incarceration Rate	30
Juvenile Violent Crime Rate	35
Law Enforcement Employees	42
Corrections Employees	19
State Corrections Spending	12
Increase in State Corrections Spending	46
Law Enforcement Spending	10
Law Enforcement Spending as a Percentage of General Spending	13

Transportation - Section K

Travel on Interstates	24
Interstate Mileage in "Unacceptable" Condition	42
Deficient Bridges	26
Traffic Deaths	34
Seat Belt Use	5
Vehicle-Miles Traveled Per Capita	36
Use of Public Transportation	12
Road and Street Miles	33
Highway Employees	29
Public Transit Employees	8
Highway Spending Per Capita	44
Highway Spending as a Percentage of General Spending	45

Welfare - Section L

Births to Unwed Mothers	34
TANF Recipients	26
Change in TANF/AFDC Recipients	45
Food Stamp Recipients	13
SSI Recipients	33
WIC Average Monthly Benefit	17
NSLP Recipients	41
Condition of Children Index	18
Families with Single Parent	28
Average Monthly TANF Payments	20
Welfare as a Percentage of Poverty-Level Income	13
State Supplements of SSI	20
State Income Tax Liability of Typical Family in Poverty	8
Child Support Collections	14
Child Support Collections Per Dollar of Administrative Costs	8
Children in Foster Care	2
Welfare Spending Per Capita	10
Welfare Spending as a Percentage of General Spending	16
Administrative Costs Per TANF Case	6

Technology - Section M

Households with Computers	10
Percentage Using Internet	8
Zip Codes with Broadband Service	30
High-Tech Jobs	12
Change in High-Tech Jobs	40
State Government Web Site Ratings	12
Number of Online Government Services	17
Students Per Computer	9
Students Per Internet-Connected Computer	7
Libraries with Internet Access	28

Pennsylvania

Population - Section A

Population 2005	6
Population 2004	6
Population Change 2003–2004	45
Population Change 1994–2004	48
Population 2015	44
Population 2025	6
Percentage 65 and Over	3
Percentage 17 and Under	43
Median Age	5
Percentage African American	20
Percentage American Indian	50
Percentage Asian American	21
Percentage Hispanic	32
Percentage White (Non-Hispanic)	19
Percentage Mixed-Race	43
Percentage in Poverty	30
Child Poverty Rate	23
Percentage Female	5
Birth Rates	46
Death Rates	21
Population Density	10
Legal Immigrants FY 2004	13
Unauthorized Immigrants	20

Economies - Section B

Personal Income, 2004	6
Gross State Product	25
Per Capita Personal Income	18
Personal Income from Wages and Salaries	30
Average Annual Pay	16
Average Hourly Earnings	31
Value Added in Manufacturing	13
Cost of Living	15
Average Annual Pay in Manufacturing	20
Average Annual Pay in Retailing	26
Labor Force	32
Unemployment Rate	28
Employment Rate	23
Government Employment	48
Manufacturing Employment	18
Fortune 500 Companies	10
Forbes 500 Companies	10
Tourism Spending Per Capita	45
Exports Per Capita	33
Housing Permits	45
Percentage Change in Home Prices	18
Net Farm Income	25
Financial Institution Assets	14
Bankruptcy Filings	29
Patents Issued	22
WC Disability Payment	14
Average Weekly UC Benefit	9
Economic Momentum	34
One-year Employment Change	31
Manufacturing Employment Change	41
Home Ownership	8
Annual Electricity Use Per Residential Customer	29
Cost Per Kwh	34
New Companies	31

Geography - Section C

Total Land Area	32
Federally Owned Land	33
State Park Acreage	10
State Park Visitors	19
Population Not Active	17
Hunters with Firearms	10
Registered Boats	12
State Spending for the Arts	12
Energy Consumption Per Capita	31
Toxic Chemical Release Per Capita	23
Hazardous Waste Sites	2
Drinking Water Quality	36
Expired Water Pollution Permits	36
Air Pollution Emissions	6

Government - Section D

Members of United States House	5
State Legislators	2
Legislators Per Million Population	39
Units of Government	23
Legislators Compensation	4
Female Legislators	46
Turnover in Legislatures	43
Term Limits	n/a
Legislative Session Length	n/a
Democrats in State Legislatures	31
Governors' Power Rating	14
Number of Statewide Elected Officials	34
State and Local Government Employees	49
State and Local Average Salaries	13
Local Employment	20
Local Spending Accountability	32
Registered Voters	17
Percentage of Population Voting	23
Statewide Initiatives	n/a
Campaign Costs Per Vote	14

Federal Impacts - Section E

Per Capita Federal Spending	19
Increase in Federal Spending	39
Per Capita Federal Grant Spending	19
Per Capita Federal Spending on Procurement	29
Per Capita Federal Spending on Payments to Individuals	4
Per Capita Federal Spending on Social Security and Medicare	2
Social Security Benefits	10
Federal Spending on Employee Wages and Salaries	39
Per Capita Federal Defense Spending	34
Per Capita Homeland Security Grants	45
Federal Grant Spending Per Dollar of State Tax Revenue	26
General Revenue from Federal Government	24
Federal Tax Burden Per Capita	17
Federal Spending Per Dollar of Taxes Paid	27
Highway Charges Returned to States	13
Terms of Trade	29
Federal Personal Income Taxes	19
Federal Share of Medicaid	33

Taxes - Section F

Tax Revenue	31
Per Capita Tax Revenue	21
Tax Effort	9
Tax Capacity	37
Percentage Change in Taxes	37
Property Taxes as a Percentage of Income	29
Property Taxes Per Capita	28
Property Tax Revenue as a Percentage of 3-tax Revenue	23
Sales Taxes as a Percentage of Income	41
Sales Taxes Per Capita	39
Sales Tax Revenue as a Percentage of 3-tax Revenue	33
Sales Tax Rate	10
Income Taxes as a Percentage of Income	20
Income Taxes Per Capita	18
Income Tax Revenue as a Percentage of 3-tax Revenue	13
Highest Personal Income Rate	39
Corporate Income Taxes	13
Motor Fuel Taxes	2
Motor Vehicle Fees	17
Tobacco Taxes	11
Taxes on High-Income Families	3
Taxes in the Largest City in Each State	1
Progressivity of Taxes	37
Per Capita Estate Tax Revenue	44

Revenues and Finances - Section G

Per Capita Total Revenue	27
Per Capita General Revenue	20

"Own-Source" General Revenue	18
Per Capita Non-Tax Revenue	20
Per Capita Total Spending	18
General Spending as a Percentage of Income	32
Per Capita General Spending	21
Change in General Expenditures	23
State Government General Revenue	26
State Government General Spending	30
State Government General Fund Spending	37
State and Local Debt	10
Debt as a Percentage of Revenue	6
Per Capita Full Faith and Credit Debt	11
Bond Ratings	3
State Solvency Index	21
Pension Plan Assets	12
State Reserves	41
Capital Outlays and Interest	22
State Budget Process Quality	25
Relative State Spending "Needs"	7
Structural Deficits	15

Education - Section H

Math Proficiency, Eighth Grade	20
Reading Proficiency, Eighth Grade	12
AFQT Ranks	23
SAT Scores	21
ACT Scores	n/a
Population over 25 with a High School Diploma	30
Students in Private Schools	4
High School Dropout Rates	13
Pupil-Teacher Ratio	23
Public School Enrollment	48
Library Holdings Per Capita	35
Children with Disabilities	15
Education Spending Per Capita	33
Education Spending as a Percentage of General Spending	35
Spending Per Pupil	13
Average Teacher Salary	9
Sources of School Funds	6
State Aid Per Pupil	35
Per Capita Higher Education Spending	39
Higher Education Spending as a Percentage of General Spending	41
Public Higher Education Enrollment	30
Per Pupil Support of Higher Education	43
In-State Tuition and Fees	2
Out-of-State Tuition and Fees	7
Change in Tuition and Fees	24
Affordability Index	15
Average Professor Salary	11
Education Employees	43
R and D Spending	14
Library Operating Spending	30
Head Start Spending	14

Health - Section I

Immunization Rates	10
Infant Mortality Rates	19
State Health Rankings	25
Population without Health Insurance	34
Abortions	17
Alcohol Consumption	30
Percentage of Adult Smokers	18
Percentage Obese	17
AIDS Cases	14
Physicians Per 100,000 Population	8
Hospital Beds Per 1,000 Population	17
Medicaid Recipients	29
Medicaid Recipients as a Percentage of Poverty Population	28
Health and Hospital Spending	29
Health and Hospital Spending as a Percentage of General Spending	32
Per Capita Medicaid Spending	10
Medicaid Spending Per Aged	21
Medicaid Spending Per Child	17
Medicare Payment Per Hospital Day	7
Hospital Expense Per Inpatient Day	37
Population in HMOs	5
Prescription Drugs as a Percentage of Medicaid Costs	48
Percentage Change in Average Price of Prescription Drugs	47

Crime - Section J

Crime Rate	41
Violent Crime Rate	23
Murder Rate	22
Property Crime Rate	44
Motor Vehicle Theft Rate	35
Violent Crime Rate Change	14
Prisoners	9
Change in Prisoners	35
Incarceration Rate	34
Juvenile Violent Crime Rate	5
Law Enforcement Employees	39
Corrections Employees	18
State Corrections Spending	15
Increase in State Corrections Spending	20
Law Enforcement Spending	19
Law Enforcement Spending as a Percentage of General Spending	20

Transportation - Section K

Travel on Interstates	25
Interstate Mileage in "Unacceptable" Condition	21
Deficient Bridges	4
Traffic Deaths	27
Seat Belt Use	20
Vehicle-Miles Traveled Per Capita	42
Use of Public Transportation	7
Road and Street Miles	9
Highway Employees	30
Public Transit Employees	5
Highway Spending Per Capita	27
Highway Spending as a Percentage of General Spending	31

Welfare - Section L

Births to Unwed Mothers	27
TANF Recipients	7
Change in TANF/AFDC Recipients	35
Food Stamp Recipients	25
SSI Recipients	13
WIC Average Monthly Benefit	42
NSLP Recipients	29
Condition of Children Index	27
Families with Single Parent	17
Average Monthly TANF Payments	22
Welfare as a Percentage of Poverty-Level Income	30
State Supplements of SSI	41
State Income Tax Liability of Typical Family in Poverty	17
Child Support Collections	5
Child Support Collections Per Dollar of Administrative Costs	5
Children in Foster Care	23
Welfare Spending Per Capita	9
Welfare Spending as a Percentage of General Spending	11
Administrative Costs Per TANF Case	22

Technology - Section M

Households with Computers	32
Percentage Using Internet	27
Zip Codes with Broadband Service	23
High-Tech Jobs	27
Change in High-Tech Jobs	36
State Government Web Site Ratings	22
Number of Online Government Services	41
Students Per Computer	25
Students Per Internet-Connected Computer	24
Libraries with Internet Access	21

Rhode Island

Population - Section A

Population 2005	43
Population 2004	43
Population Change 2003–2004	41
Population Change 1994–2004	34
Population 2015	29
Population 2025	43
Percentage 65 and Over	8
Percentage 17 and Under	45
Median Age	11
Percentage African American	28
Percentage American Indian	25
Percentage Asian American	16
Percentage Hispanic	13
Percentage White (Non-Hispanic)	23
Percentage Mixed-Race	13
Percentage in Poverty	27
Child Poverty Rate	18
Percentage Female	1
Birth Rates	44
Death Rates	34
Population Density	2
Legal Immigrants FY 2004	30
Unauthorized Immigrants	36

Economies - Section B

Personal Income, 2004	43
Gross State Product	22
Per Capita Personal Income	15
Personal Income from Wages and Salaries	40
Average Annual Pay	19
Average Hourly Earnings	50
Value Added in Manufacturing	32
Cost of Living	9
Average Annual Pay in Manufacturing	36
Average Annual Pay in Retailing	16
Labor Force	12
Unemployment Rate	12
Employment Rate	39
Government Employment	47
Manufacturing Employment	23
Fortune 500 Companies	16
Forbes 500 Companies	5
Tourism Spending Per Capita	40
Exports Per Capita	48
Housing Permits	50
Percentage Change in Home Prices	2
Net Farm Income	49
Financial Institution Assets	3
Bankruptcy Filings	38
Patents Issued	16
WC Disability Payment	12
Average Weekly UC Benefit	3
Economic Momentum	36
One-year Employment Change	29
Manufacturing Employment Change	50
Home Ownership	47
Annual Electricity Use Per Residential Customer	46
Cost Per Kwh	46
New Companies	13

Geography - Section C

Total Land Area	50
Federally Owned Land	50
State Park Acreage	50
State Park Visitors	18
Population Not Active	18
Hunters with Firearms	47
Registered Boats	46
State Spending for the Arts	3
Energy Consumption Per Capita	50
Toxic Chemical Release Per Capita	49
Hazardous Waste Sites	30
Drinking Water Quality	34
Expired Water Pollution Permits	15
Air Pollution Emissions	50

Government - Section D

Members of United States House	39
State Legislators	37
Legislators Per Million Population	8
Units of Government	44
Legislators Compensation	34
Female Legislators	37
Turnover in Legislatures	30
Term Limits	n/a
Legislative Session Length	4
Democrats in State Legislatures	2
Governors' Power Rating	49
Number of Statewide Elected Officials	34
State and Local Government Employees	48
State and Local Average Salaries	5
Local Employment	46
Local Spending Accountability	12
Registered Voters	14
Percentage of Population Voting	34
Statewide Initiatives	n/a
Campaign Costs Per Vote	10

Federal Impacts - Section E

Per Capita Federal Spending	20
Increase in Federal Spending	45
Per Capita Federal Grant Spending	8
Per Capita Federal Spending on Procurement	41
Per Capita Federal Spending on Payments to Individuals	15
Per Capita Federal Spending on Social Security and Medicare	7
Social Security Benefits	18
Federal Spending on Employee Wages and Salaries	19
Per Capita Federal Defense Spending	28
Per Capita Homeland Security Grants	8
Federal Grant Spending Per Dollar of State Tax Revenue	13
General Revenue from Federal Government	12
Federal Tax Burden Per Capita	16
Federal Spending Per Dollar of Taxes Paid	28
Highway Charges Returned to States	2
Terms of Trade	15
Federal Personal Income Taxes	17
Federal Share of Medicaid	35

Taxes - Section F

Tax Revenue	6
Per Capita Tax Revenue	12
Tax Effort	3
Tax Capacity	38
Percentage Change in Taxes	22
Property Taxes as a Percentage of Income	6
Property Taxes Per Capita	7
Property Tax Revenue as a Percentage of 3-tax Revenue	10
Sales Taxes as a Percentage of Income	25
Sales Taxes Per Capita	24
Sales Tax Revenue as a Percentage of 3-tax Revenue	35
Sales Tax Rate	1
Income Taxes as a Percentage of Income	18
Income Taxes Per Capita	19
Income Tax Revenue as a Percentage of 3-tax Revenue	34
Highest Personal Income Rate	1
Corporate Income Taxes	46
Motor Fuel Taxes	1
Motor Vehicle Fees	24
Tobacco Taxes	1
Taxes on High-Income Families	6
Taxes in the Largest City in Each State	6
Progressivity of Taxes	23
Per Capita Estate Tax Revenue	11

Revenues and Finances - Section G

Per Capita Total Revenue	14
Per Capita General Revenue	12

"Own-Source" General Revenue	16
Per Capita Non-Tax Revenue	46
Per Capita Total Spending	12
General Spending as a Percentage of Income	22
Per Capita General Spending	13
Change in General Expenditures	17
State Government General Revenue	7
State Government General Spending	11
State Government General Fund Spending	13
State and Local Debt	9
Debt as a Percentage of Revenue	13
Per Capita Full Faith and Credit Debt	24
Bond Ratings	4
State Solvency Index	47
Pension Plan Assets	8
State Reserves	34
Capital Outlays and Interest	47
State Budget Process Quality	10
Relative State Spending "Needs"	8
Structural Deficits	20

Education - Section H

Math Proficiency, Eighth Grade	38
Reading Proficiency, Eighth Grade	29
AFQT Ranks	25
SAT Scores	17
ACT Scores	n/a
Population over 25 with a High School Diploma	45
Students in Private Schools	7
High School Dropout Rates	16
Pupil-Teacher Ratio	49
Public School Enrollment	46
Library Holdings Per Capita	14
Children with Disabilities	1
Education Spending Per Capita	26
Education Spending as a Percentage of General Spending	42
Spending Per Pupil	8
Average Teacher Salary	8
Sources of School Funds	3
State Aid Per Pupil	42
Per Capita Higher Education Spending	44
Higher Education Spending as a Percentage of General Spending	43
Public Higher Education Enrollment	4
Per Pupil Support of Higher Education	45
In-State Tuition and Fees	15
Out-of-State Tuition and Fees	13
Change in Tuition and Fees	22
Affordability Index	48
Average Professor Salary	40
Education Employees	42
R and D Spending	8
Library Operating Spending	13
Head Start Spending	26

Health - Section I

Immunization Rates	2
Infant Mortality Rates	41
State Health Rankings	12
Population without Health Insurance	43
Abortions	2
Alcohol Consumption	14
Percentage of Adult Smokers	23
Percentage Obese	47
AIDS Cases	18
Physicians Per 100,000 Population	4
Hospital Beds Per 1,000 Population	39
Medicaid Recipients	14
Medicaid Recipients as a Percentage of Poverty Population	9
Health and Hospital Spending	44
Health and Hospital Spending as a Percentage of General Spending	45
Per Capita Medicaid Spending	3
Medicaid Spending Per Aged	6
Medicaid Spending Per Child	14
Medicare Payment Per Hospital Day	33
Hospital Expense Per Inpatient Day	13
Population in HMOs	10
Prescription Drugs as a Percentage of Medicaid Costs	42
Percentage Change in Average Price of Prescription Drugs	14

Crime - Section J

Crime Rate	35
Violent Crime Rate	40
Murder Rate	39
Property Crime Rate	35
Motor Vehicle Theft Rate	17
Violent Crime Rate Change	44
Prisoners	44
Change in Prisoners	46
Incarceration Rate	48
Juvenile Violent Crime Rate	13
Law Enforcement Employees	28
Corrections Employees	46
State Corrections Spending	10
Increase in State Corrections Spending	47
Law Enforcement Spending	22
Law Enforcement Spending as a Percentage of General Spending	29

Transportation - Section K

Travel on Interstates	13
Interstate Mileage in "Unacceptable" Condition	45
Deficient Bridges	1
Traffic Deaths	48
Seat Belt Use	38
Vehicle-Miles Traveled Per Capita	47
Use of Public Transportation	17
Road and Street Miles	19
Highway Employees	43
Public Transit Employees	9
Highway Spending Per Capita	49
Highway Spending as a Percentage of General Spending	48

Welfare - Section L

Births to Unwed Mothers	16
TANF Recipients	3
Change in TANF/AFDC Recipients	37
Food Stamp Recipients	33
SSI Recipients	9
WIC Average Monthly Benefit	28
NSLP Recipients	40
Condition of Children Index	22
Families with Single Parent	13
Average Monthly TANF Payments	9
Welfare as a Percentage of Poverty-Level Income	8
State Supplements of SSI	28
State Income Tax Liability of Typical Family in Poverty	32
Child Support Collections	42
Child Support Collections Per Dollar of Administrative Costs	22
Children in Foster Care	10
Welfare Spending Per Capita	3
Welfare Spending as a Percentage of General Spending	1
Administrative Costs Per TANF Case	24

Technology - Section M

Households with Computers	25
Percentage Using Internet	22
Zip Codes with Broadband Service	6
High-Tech Jobs	23
Change in High-Tech Jobs	7
State Government Web Site Ratings	39
Number of Online Government Services	35
Students Per Computer	8
Students Per Internet-Connected Computer	10
Libraries with Internet Access	1

South Carolina

Population - Section A

Population 2005	25
Population 2004	25
Population Change 2003–2004	13
Population Change 1994–2004	15
Population 2015	18
Population 2025	23
Percentage 65 and Over	29
Percentage 17 and Under	23
Median Age	26
Percentage African American	4
Percentage American Indian	34
Percentage Asian American	38
Percentage Hispanic	36
Percentage White (Non-Hispanic)	37
Percentage Mixed-Race	47
Percentage in Poverty	10
Child Poverty Rate	9
Percentage Female	12
Birth Rates	29
Death Rates	10
Population Density	21
Legal Immigrants FY 2004	36
Unauthorized Immigrants	29

Economies - Section B

Personal Income, 2004	26
Gross State Product	42
Per Capita Personal Income	43
Personal Income from Wages and Salaries	31
Average Annual Pay	39
Average Hourly Earnings	30
Value Added in Manufacturing	7
Cost of Living	31
Average Annual Pay in Manufacturing	37
Average Annual Pay in Retailing	31
Labor Force	39
Unemployment Rate	4
Employment Rate	47
Government Employment	16
Manufacturing Employment	12
Fortune 500 Companies	38
Forbes 500 Companies	41
Tourism Spending Per Capita	18
Exports Per Capita	9
Housing Permits	7
Percentage Change in Home Prices	36
Net Farm Income	31
Financial Institution Assets	41
Bankruptcy Filings	43
Patents Issued	38
WC Disability Payment	29
Average Weekly UC Benefit	41
Economic Momentum	33
One-year Employment Change	49
Manufacturing Employment Change	42
Home Ownership	6
Annual Electricity Use Per Residential Customer	7
Cost Per Kwh	3
New Companies	25

Geography - Section C

Total Land Area	40
Federally Owned Land	37
State Park Acreage	33
State Park Visitors	34
Population Not Active	21
Hunters with Firearms	32
Registered Boats	9
State Spending for the Arts	24
Energy Consumption Per Capita	18
Toxic Chemical Release Per Capita	17
Hazardous Waste Sites	16
Drinking Water Quality	22
Expired Water Pollution Permits	42
Air Pollution Emissions	24

Government - Section D

Members of United States House	25
State Legislators	15
Legislators Per Million Population	22
Units of Government	35
Legislators Compensation	38
Female Legislators	50
Turnover in Legislatures	36
Term Limits	n/a
Legislative Session Length	6
Democrats in State Legislatures	35
Governors' Power Rating	42
Number of Statewide Elected Officials	3
State and Local Government Employees	15
State and Local Average Salaries	40
Local Employment	31
Local Spending Accountability	22
Registered Voters	42
Percentage of Population Voting	48
Statewide Initiatives	n/a
Campaign Costs Per Vote	4

Federal Impacts - Section E

Per Capita Federal Spending	27
Increase in Federal Spending	18
Per Capita Federal Grant Spending	29
Per Capita Federal Spending on Procurement	18
Per Capita Federal Spending on Payments to Individuals	24
Per Capita Federal Spending on Social Security and Medicare	27
Social Security Benefits	34
Federal Spending on Employee Wages and Salaries	20
Per Capita Federal Defense Spending	21
Per Capita Homeland Security Grants	26
Federal Grant Spending Per Dollar of State Tax Revenue	10
General Revenue from Federal Government	16
Federal Tax Burden Per Capita	40
Federal Spending Per Dollar of Taxes Paid	15
Highway Charges Returned to States	29
Terms of Trade	20
Federal Personal Income Taxes	41
Federal Share of Medicaid	10

Taxes - Section F

Tax Revenue	41
Per Capita Tax Revenue	46
Tax Effort	38
Tax Capacity	42
Percentage Change in Taxes	19
Property Taxes as a Percentage of Income	27
Property Taxes Per Capita	35
Property Tax Revenue as a Percentage of 3-tax Revenue	22
Sales Taxes as a Percentage of Income	35
Sales Taxes Per Capita	45
Sales Tax Revenue as a Percentage of 3-tax Revenue	26
Sales Tax Rate	25
Income Taxes as a Percentage of Income	29
Income Taxes Per Capita	34
Income Tax Revenue as a Percentage of 3-tax Revenue	23
Highest Personal Income Rate	13
Corporate Income Taxes	44
Motor Fuel Taxes	44
Motor Vehicle Fees	46
Tobacco Taxes	50
Taxes on High-Income Families	17
Taxes in the Largest City in Each State	34
Progressivity of Taxes	1
Per Capita Estate Tax Revenue	34

Revenues and Finances - Section G

Per Capita Total Revenue	23
Per Capita General Revenue	41

"Own-Source" General Revenue	43
Per Capita Non-Tax Revenue	19
Per Capita Total Spending	21
General Spending as a Percentage of Income	9
Per Capita General Spending	26
Change in General Expenditures	2
State Government General Revenue	31
State Government General Spending	19
State Government General Fund Spending	15
State and Local Debt	21
Debt as a Percentage of Revenue	20
Per Capita Full Faith and Credit Debt	15
Bond Ratings	1
State Solvency Index	40
Pension Plan Assets	49
State Reserves	19
Capital Outlays and Interest	18
State Budget Process Quality	29
Relative State Spending "Needs"	23
Structural Deficits	38

Education - Section H

Math Proficiency, Eighth Grade	20
Reading Proficiency, Eighth Grade	39
AFQT Ranks	47
SAT Scores	24
ACT Scores	n/a
Population over 25 with a High School Diploma	38
Students in Private Schools	30
High School Dropout Rates	50
Pupil-Teacher Ratio	31
Public School Enrollment	30
Library Holdings Per Capita	37
Children with Disabilities	7
Education Spending Per Capita	25
Education Spending as a Percentage of General Spending	24
Spending Per Pupil	26
Average Teacher Salary	28
Sources of School Funds	22
State Aid Per Pupil	29
Per Capita Higher Education Spending	31
Higher Education Spending as a Percentage of General Spending	33
Public Higher Education Enrollment	44
Per Pupil Support of Higher Education	40
In-State Tuition and Fees	7
Out-of-State Tuition and Fees	20
Change in Tuition and Fees	5
Affordability Index	43
Average Professor Salary	30
Education Employees	24
R and D Spending	41
Library Operating Spending	38
Head Start Spending	36

Health - Section I

Immunization Rates	33
Infant Mortality Rates	8
State Health Rankings	46
Population without Health Insurance	19
Abortions	37
Alcohol Consumption	21
Percentage of Adult Smokers	11
Percentage Obese	12
AIDS Cases	9
Physicians Per 100,000 Population	33
Hospital Beds Per 1,000 Population	27
Medicaid Recipients	8
Medicaid Recipients as a Percentage of Poverty Population	15
Health and Hospital Spending	4
Health and Hospital Spending as a Percentage of General Spending	6
Per Capita Medicaid Spending	22
Medicaid Spending Per Aged	44
Medicaid Spending Per Child	33
Medicare Payment Per Hospital Day	15
Hospital Expense Per Inpatient Day	36
Population in HMOs	41
Prescription Drugs as a Percentage of Medicaid Costs	22
Percentage Change in Average Price of Prescription Drugs	30

Crime - Section J

Crime Rate	2
Violent Crime Rate	1
Murder Rate	7
Property Crime Rate	5
Motor Vehicle Theft Rate	18
Violent Crime Rate Change	17
Prisoners	19
Change in Prisoners	41
Incarceration Rate	7
Juvenile Violent Crime Rate	47
Law Enforcement Employees	8
Corrections Employees	15
State Corrections Spending	47
Increase in State Corrections Spending	49
Law Enforcement Spending	35
Law Enforcement Spending as a Percentage of General Spending	35

Transportation - Section K

Travel on Interstates	20
Interstate Mileage in "Unacceptable" Condition	42
Deficient Bridges	32
Traffic Deaths	5
Seat Belt Use	42
Vehicle-Miles Traveled Per Capita	12
Use of Public Transportation	42
Road and Street Miles	5
Highway Employees	35
Public Transit Employees	39
Highway Spending Per Capita	34
Highway Spending as a Percentage of General Spending	37

Welfare - Section L

Births to Unwed Mothers	6
TANF Recipients	38
Change in TANF/AFDC Recipients	16
Food Stamp Recipients	9
SSI Recipients	14
WIC Average Monthly Benefit	25
NSLP Recipients	15
Condition of Children Index	45
Families with Single Parent	3
Average Monthly TANF Payments	49
Welfare as a Percentage of Poverty-Level Income	43
State Supplements of SSI	6
State Income Tax Liability of Typical Family in Poverty	17
Child Support Collections	38
Child Support Collections Per Dollar of Administrative Costs	6
Children in Foster Care	39
Welfare Spending Per Capita	15
Welfare Spending as a Percentage of General Spending	13
Administrative Costs Per TANF Case	47

Technology - Section M

Households with Computers	44
Percentage Using Internet	45
Zip Codes with Broadband Service	23
High-Tech Jobs	43
Change in High-Tech Jobs	12
State Government Web Site Ratings	43
Number of Online Government Services	42
Students Per Computer	15
Students Per Internet-Connected Computer	24
Libraries with Internet Access	1

South Dakota

Population - Section A

Population 2005	46
Population 2004	46
Population Change 2003–2004	25
Population Change 1994–2004	40
Population 2015	41
Population 2025	47
Percentage 65 and Over	7
Percentage 17 and Under	21
Median Age	22
Percentage African American	45
Percentage American Indian	3
Percentage Asian American	46
Percentage Hispanic	44
Percentage White (Non-Hispanic)	11
Percentage Mixed-Race	29
Percentage in Poverty	15
Child Poverty Rate	16
Percentage Female	37
Birth Rates	16
Death Rates	32
Population Density	46
Legal Immigrants FY 2004	46
Unauthorized Immigrants	43

Economies - Section B

Personal Income, 2004	46
Gross State Product	24
Per Capita Personal Income	29
Personal Income from Wages and Salaries	48
Average Annual Pay	49
Average Hourly Earnings	49
Value Added in Manufacturing	38
Cost of Living	33
Average Annual Pay in Manufacturing	47
Average Annual Pay in Retailing	46
Labor Force	8
Unemployment Rate	41
Employment Rate	10
Government Employment	11
Manufacturing Employment	27
Fortune 500 Companies	n/a
Forbes 500 Companies	n/a
Tourism Spending Per Capita	12
Exports Per Capita	46
Housing Permits	17
Percentage Change in Home Prices	31
Net Farm Income	14
Financial Institution Assets	1
Bankruptcy Filings	41
Patents Issued	42
WC Disability Payment	41
Average Weekly UC Benefit	43
Economic Momentum	37
One-year Employment Change	16
Manufacturing Employment Change	5
Home Ownership	41
Annual Electricity Use Per Residential Customer	26
Cost Per Kwh	25
New Companies	49

Geography - Section C

Total Land Area	16
Federally Owned Land	16
State Park Acreage	28
State Park Visitors	2
Population Not Active	39
Hunters with Firearms	5
Registered Boats	44
State Spending for the Arts	26
Energy Consumption Per Capita	28
Toxic Chemical Release Per Capita	24
Hazardous Waste Sites	47
Drinking Water Quality	24
Expired Water Pollution Permits	18
Air Pollution Emissions	43

Government - Section D

Members of United States House	44
State Legislators	39
Legislators Per Million Population	7
Units of Government	2
Legislators Compensation	46
Female Legislators	40
Turnover in Legislatures	4
Term Limits	4
Legislative Session Length	28
Democrats in State Legislatures	46
Governors' Power Rating	8
Number of Statewide Elected Officials	15
State and Local Government Employees	22
State and Local Average Salaries	46
Local Employment	30
Local Spending Accountability	11
Registered Voters	4
Percentage of Population Voting	8
Statewide Initiatives	n/a
Campaign Costs Per Vote	2

Federal Impacts - Section E

Per Capita Federal Spending	10
Increase in Federal Spending	43
Per Capita Federal Grant Spending	10
Per Capita Federal Spending on Procurement	38
Per Capita Federal Spending on Payments to Individuals	3
Per Capita Federal Spending on Social Security and Medicare	30
Social Security Benefits	44
Federal Spending on Employee Wages and Salaries	8
Per Capita Federal Defense Spending	30
Per Capita Homeland Security Grants	5
Federal Grant Spending Per Dollar of State Tax Revenue	3
General Revenue from Federal Government	5
Federal Tax Burden Per Capita	36
Federal Spending Per Dollar of Taxes Paid	11
Highway Charges Returned to States	6
Terms of Trade	8
Federal Personal Income Taxes	36
Federal Share of Medicaid	15

Taxes - Section F

Tax Revenue	47
Per Capita Tax Revenue	44
Tax Effort	47
Tax Capacity	29
Percentage Change in Taxes	18
Property Taxes as a Percentage of Income	21
Property Taxes Per Capita	29
Property Tax Revenue as a Percentage of 3-tax Revenue	12
Sales Taxes as a Percentage of Income	15
Sales Taxes Per Capita	13
Sales Tax Revenue as a Percentage of 3-tax Revenue	6
Sales Tax Rate	38
Income Taxes as a Percentage of Income	n/a
Income Taxes Per Capita	n/a
Income Tax Revenue as a Percentage of 3-tax Revenue	n/a
Highest Personal Income Rate	n/a
Corporate Income Taxes	35
Motor Fuel Taxes	20
Motor Vehicle Fees	13
Tobacco Taxes	34
Taxes on High-Income Families	46
Taxes in the Largest City in Each State	45
Progressivity of Taxes	49
Per Capita Estate Tax Revenue	35

Revenues and Finances - Section G

Per Capita Total Revenue	48
Per Capita General Revenue	43

"Own-Source" General Revenue	48
Per Capita Non-Tax Revenue	41
Per Capita Total Spending	48
General Spending as a Percentage of Income	35
Per Capita General Spending	45
Change in General Expenditures	39
State Government General Revenue	38
State Government General Spending	40
State Government General Fund Spending	26
State and Local Debt	35
Debt as a Percentage of Revenue	24
Per Capita Full Faith and Credit Debt	42
Bond Ratings	n/a
State Solvency Index	7
Pension Plan Assets	22
State Reserves	10
Capital Outlays and Interest	23
State Budget Process Quality	23
Relative State Spending "Needs"	10
Structural Deficits	29

Education - Section H

Math Proficiency, Eighth Grade	3
Reading Proficiency, Eighth Grade	5
AFQT Ranks	17
SAT Scores	n/a
ACT Scores	8
Population over 25 with a High School Diploma	23
Students in Private Schools	32
High School Dropout Rates	4
Pupil-Teacher Ratio	39
Public School Enrollment	33
Library Holdings Per Capita	5
Children with Disabilities	23
Education Spending Per Capita	42
Education Spending as a Percentage of General Spending	26
Spending Per Pupil	32
Average Teacher Salary	50
Sources of School Funds	16
State Aid Per Pupil	49
Per Capita Higher Education Spending	37
Higher Education Spending as a Percentage of General Spending	31
Public Higher Education Enrollment	14
Per Pupil Support of Higher Education	36
In-State Tuition and Fees	28
Out-of-State Tuition and Fees	48
Change in Tuition and Fees	39
Affordability Index	40
Average Professor Salary	49
Education Employees	8
R and D Spending	47
Library Operating Spending	27
Head Start Spending	40

Health - Section I

Immunization Rates	6
Infant Mortality Rates	14
State Health Rankings	20
Population without Health Insurance	35
Abortions	43
Alcohol Consumption	16
Percentage of Adult Smokers	30
Percentage Obese	20
AIDS Cases	48
Physicians Per 100,000 Population	38
Hospital Beds Per 1,000 Population	1
Medicaid Recipients	32
Medicaid Recipients as a Percentage of Poverty Population	39
Health and Hospital Spending	46
Health and Hospital Spending as a Percentage of General Spending	46
Per Capita Medicaid Spending	38
Medicaid Spending Per Aged	27
Medicaid Spending Per Child	35
Medicare Payment Per Hospital Day	35
Hospital Expense Per Inpatient Day	27
Population in HMOs	40
Prescription Drugs as a Percentage of Medicaid Costs	28
Percentage Change in Average Price of Prescription Drugs	39

Crime - Section J

Crime Rate	49
Violent Crime Rate	46
Murder Rate	40
Property Crime Rate	49
Motor Vehicle Theft Rate	48
Violent Crime Rate Change	6
Prisoners	45
Change in Prisoners	11
Incarceration Rate	23
Juvenile Violent Crime Rate	40
Law Enforcement Employees	45
Corrections Employees	44
State Corrections Spending	41
Increase in State Corrections Spending	6
Law Enforcement Spending	45
Law Enforcement Spending as a Percentage of General Spending	41

Transportation - Section K

Travel on Interstates	11
Interstate Mileage in "Unacceptable" Condition	33
Deficient Bridges	30
Traffic Deaths	2
Seat Belt Use	43
Vehicle-Miles Traveled Per Capita	16
Use of Public Transportation	48
Road and Street Miles	41
Highway Employees	8
Public Transit Employees	49
Highway Spending Per Capita	3
Highway Spending as a Percentage of General Spending	1

Welfare - Section L

Births to Unwed Mothers	26
TANF Recipients	43
Change in TANF/AFDC Recipients	21
Food Stamp Recipients	28
SSI Recipients	36
WIC Average Monthly Benefit	29
NSLP Recipients	3
Condition of Children Index	21
Families with Single Parent	47
Average Monthly TANF Payments	27
Welfare as a Percentage of Poverty-Level Income	30
State Supplements of SSI	38
State Income Tax Liability of Typical Family in Poverty	n/a
Child Support Collections	22
Child Support Collections Per Dollar of Administrative Costs	3
Children in Foster Care	20
Welfare Spending Per Capita	35
Welfare Spending as a Percentage of General Spending	28
Administrative Costs Per TANF Case	27

Technology - Section M

Households with Computers	26
Percentage Using Internet	29
Zip Codes with Broadband Service	50
High-Tech Jobs	39
Change in High-Tech Jobs	17
State Government Web Site Ratings	24
Number of Online Government Services	36
Students Per Computer	49
Students Per Internet-Connected Computer	49
Libraries with Internet Access	47

Tennessee

Population - Section A

Population 2005	16
Population 2004	16
Population Change 2003–2004	18
Population Change 1994–2004	18
Population 2015	19
Population 2025	15
Percentage 65 and Over	28
Percentage 17 and Under	37
Median Age	22
Percentage African American	11
Percentage American Indian	43
Percentage Asian American	36
Percentage Hispanic	37
Percentage White (Non-Hispanic)	24
Percentage Mixed-Race	41
Percentage in Poverty	7
Child Poverty Rate	11
Percentage Female	17
Birth Rates	26
Death Rates	5
Population Density	20
Legal Immigrants FY 2004	25
Unauthorized Immigrants	22

Economies - Section B

Personal Income, 2004	19
Gross State Product	27
Per Capita Personal Income	35
Personal Income from Wages and Salaries	20
Average Annual Pay	26
Average Hourly Earnings	45
Value Added in Manufacturing	8
Cost of Living	46
Average Annual Pay in Manufacturing	30
Average Annual Pay in Retailing	21
Labor Force	45
Unemployment Rate	23
Employment Rate	28
Government Employment	38
Manufacturing Employment	9
Fortune 500 Companies	27
Forbes 500 Companies	30
Tourism Spending Per Capita	17
Exports Per Capita	12
Housing Permits	16
Percentage Change in Home Prices	43
Net Farm Income	36
Financial Institution Assets	21
Bankruptcy Filings	1
Patents Issued	34
WC Disability Payment	23
Average Weekly UC Benefit	42
Economic Momentum	28
One-year Employment Change	41
Manufacturing Employment Change	28
Home Ownership	27
Annual Electricity Use Per Residential Customer	2
Cost Per Kwh	37
New Companies	23

Geography - Section C

Total Land Area	34
Federally Owned Land	30
State Park Acreage	23
State Park Visitors	8
Population Not Active	4
Hunters with Firearms	29
Registered Boats	18
State Spending for the Arts	18
Energy Consumption Per Capita	17
Toxic Chemical Release Per Capita	13
Hazardous Waste Sites	28
Drinking Water Quality	44
Expired Water Pollution Permits	23
Air Pollution Emissions	14

Government - Section D

Members of United States House	14
State Legislators	32
Legislators Per Million Population	37
Units of Government	39
Legislators Compensation	26
Female Legislators	34
Turnover in Legislatures	35
Term Limits	n/a
Legislative Session Length	18
Democrats in State Legislatures	21
Governors' Power Rating	8
Number of Statewide Elected Officials	45
State and Local Government Employees	32
State and Local Average Salaries	39
Local Employment	11
Local Spending Accountability	18
Registered Voters	28
Percentage of Population Voting	40
Statewide Initiatives	n/a
Campaign Costs Per Vote	26

Federal Impacts - Section E

Per Capita Federal Spending	16
Increase in Federal Spending	11
Per Capita Federal Grant Spending	17
Per Capita Federal Spending on Procurement	11
Per Capita Federal Spending on Payments to Individuals	22
Per Capita Federal Spending on Social Security and Medicare	17
Social Security Benefits	40
Federal Spending on Employee Wages and Salaries	34
Per Capita Federal Defense Spending	40
Per Capita Homeland Security Grants	34
Federal Grant Spending Per Dollar of State Tax Revenue	8
General Revenue from Federal Government	10
Federal Tax Burden Per Capita	34
Federal Spending Per Dollar of Taxes Paid	20
Highway Charges Returned to States	41
Terms of Trade	19
Federal Personal Income Taxes	28
Federal Share of Medicaid	16

Taxes - Section F

Tax Revenue	50
Per Capita Tax Revenue	49
Tax Effort	48
Tax Capacity	36
Percentage Change in Taxes	25
Property Taxes as a Percentage of Income	41
Property Taxes Per Capita	40
Property Tax Revenue as a Percentage of 3-tax Revenue	33
Sales Taxes as a Percentage of Income	9
Sales Taxes Per Capita	10
Sales Tax Revenue as a Percentage of 3-tax Revenue	2
Sales Tax Rate	1
Income Taxes as a Percentage of Income	43
Income Taxes Per Capita	43
Income Tax Revenue as a Percentage of 3-tax Revenue	43
Highest Personal Income Rate	n/a
Corporate Income Taxes	14
Motor Fuel Taxes	23
Motor Vehicle Fees	37
Tobacco Taxes	47
Taxes on High-Income Families	45
Taxes in the Largest City in Each State	44
Progressivity of Taxes	48
Per Capita Estate Tax Revenue	49

Revenues and Finances - Section G

Per Capita Total Revenue	33
Per Capita General Revenue	49

"Own-Source" General Revenue	50
Per Capita Non-Tax Revenue	43
Per Capita Total Spending	32
General Spending as a Percentage of Income	37
Per Capita General Spending	47
Change in General Expenditures	31
State Government General Revenue	43
State Government General Spending	45
State Government General Fund Spending	35
State and Local Debt	45
Debt as a Percentage of Revenue	46
Per Capita Full Faith and Credit Debt	25
Bond Ratings	3
State Solvency Index	13
Pension Plan Assets	17
State Reserves	23
Capital Outlays and Interest	45
State Budget Process Quality	32
Relative State Spending "Needs"	22
Structural Deficits	44

Education - Section H

Math Proficiency, Eighth Grade	41
Reading Proficiency, Eighth Grade	34
AFQT Ranks	32
SAT Scores	n/a
ACT Scores	15
Population over 25 with a High School Diploma	40
Students in Private Schools	26
High School Dropout Rates	45
Pupil-Teacher Ratio	20
Public School Enrollment	35
Library Holdings Per Capita	48
Children with Disabilities	37
Education Spending Per Capita	48
Education Spending as a Percentage of General Spending	38
Spending Per Pupil	43
Average Teacher Salary	30
Sources of School Funds	24
State Aid Per Pupil	43
Per Capita Higher Education Spending	35
Higher Education Spending as a Percentage of General Spending	25
Public Higher Education Enrollment	48
Per Pupil Support of Higher Education	22
In-State Tuition and Fees	32
Out-of-State Tuition and Fees	28
Change in Tuition and Fees	35
Affordability Index	42
Average Professor Salary	24
Education Employees	35
R and D Spending	27
Library Operating Spending	47
Head Start Spending	18

Health - Section I

Immunization Rates	25
Infant Mortality Rates	4
State Health Rankings	48
Population without Health Insurance	23
Abortions	19
Alcohol Consumption	41
Percentage of Adult Smokers	3
Percentage Obese	4
AIDS Cases	14
Physicians Per 100,000 Population	18
Hospital Beds Per 1,000 Population	13
Medicaid Recipients	1
Medicaid Recipients as a Percentage of Poverty Population	10
Health and Hospital Spending	12
Health and Hospital Spending as a Percentage of General Spending	7
Per Capita Medicaid Spending	7
Medicaid Spending Per Aged	50
Medicaid Spending Per Child	48
Medicare Payment Per Hospital Day	25
Hospital Expense Per Inpatient Day	42
Population in HMOs	31
Prescription Drugs as a Percentage of Medicaid Costs	7
Percentage Change in Average Price of Prescription Drugs	3

Crime - Section J

Crime Rate	7
Violent Crime Rate	4
Murder Rate	16
Property Crime Rate	8
Motor Vehicle Theft Rate	14
Violent Crime Rate Change	13
Prisoners	17
Change in Prisoners	10
Incarceration Rate	19
Juvenile Violent Crime Rate	22
Law Enforcement Employees	14
Corrections Employees	24
State Corrections Spending	43
Increase in State Corrections Spending	11
Law Enforcement Spending	38
Law Enforcement Spending as a Percentage of General Spending	33

Transportation - Section K

Travel on Interstates	15
Interstate Mileage in "Unacceptable" Condition	39
Deficient Bridges	34
Traffic Deaths	14
Seat Belt Use	39
Vehicle-Miles Traveled Per Capita	9
Use of Public Transportation	38
Road and Street Miles	23
Highway Employees	31
Public Transit Employees	31
Highway Spending Per Capita	50
Highway Spending as a Percentage of General Spending	40

Welfare - Section L

Births to Unwed Mothers	11
TANF Recipients	1
Change in TANF/AFDC Recipients	49
Food Stamp Recipients	3
SSI Recipients	10
WIC Average Monthly Benefit	13
NSLP Recipients	9
Condition of Children Index	43
Families with Single Parent	9
Average Monthly TANF Payments	48
Welfare as a Percentage of Poverty-Level Income	32
State Supplements of SSI	42
State Income Tax Liability of Typical Family in Poverty	n/a
Child Support Collections	28
Child Support Collections Per Dollar of Administrative Costs	19
Children in Foster Care	28
Welfare Spending Per Capita	13
Welfare Spending as a Percentage of General Spending	4
Administrative Costs Per TANF Case	42

Technology - Section M

Households with Computers	42
Percentage Using Internet	42
Zip Codes with Broadband Service	23
High-Tech Jobs	45
Change in High-Tech Jobs	21
State Government Web Site Ratings	6
Number of Online Government Services	24
Students Per Computer	13
Students Per Internet-Connected Computer	13
Libraries with Internet Access	34

Texas

Population - Section A

Population 2005	2
Population 2004	2
Population Change 2003–2004	6
Population Change 1994–2004	8
Population 2015	4
Population 2025	2
Percentage 65 and Over	46
Percentage 17 and Under	3
Median Age	49
Percentage African American	18
Percentage American Indian	22
Percentage Asian American	14
Percentage Hispanic	3
Percentage White (Non-Hispanic)	47
Percentage Mixed-Race	35
Percentage in Poverty	5
Child Poverty Rate	5
Percentage Female	38
Birth Rates	2
Death Rates	16
Population Density	27
Legal Immigrants FY 2004	3
Unauthorized Immigrants	2

Economies - Section B

Personal Income, 2004	3
Gross State Product	19
Per Capita Personal Income	28
Personal Income from Wages and Salaries	23
Average Annual Pay	17
Average Hourly Earnings	42
Value Added in Manufacturing	33
Cost of Living	45
Average Annual Pay in Manufacturing	10
Average Annual Pay in Retailing	13
Labor Force	37
Unemployment Rate	10
Employment Rate	41
Government Employment	22
Manufacturing Employment	32
Fortune 500 Companies	13
Forbes 500 Companies	15
Tourism Spending Per Capita	37
Exports Per Capita	4
Housing Permits	12
Percentage Change in Home Prices	45
Net Farm Income	2
Financial Institution Assets	43
Bankruptcy Filings	35
Patents Issued	21
WC Disability Payment	37
Average Weekly UC Benefit	21
Economic Momentum	10
One-year Employment Change	27
Manufacturing Employment Change	24
Home Ownership	45
Annual Electricity Use Per Residential Customer	6
Cost Per Kwh	17
New Companies	35

Geography - Section C

Total Land Area	2
Federally Owned Land	15
State Park Acreage	5
State Park Visitors	49
Population Not Active	9
Hunters with Firearms	28
Registered Boats	5
State Spending for the Arts	46
Energy Consumption Per Capita	5
Toxic Chemical Release Per Capita	26
Hazardous Waste Sites	8
Drinking Water Quality	32
Expired Water Pollution Permits	28
Air Pollution Emissions	1

Government - Section D

Members of United States House	2
State Legislators	11
Legislators Per Million Population	49
Units of Government	33
Legislators Compensation	45
Female Legislators	31
Turnover in Legislatures	37
Term Limits	n/a
Legislative Session Length	n/a
Democrats in State Legislatures	34
Governors' Power Rating	35
Number of Statewide Elected Officials	34
State and Local Government Employees	21
State and Local Average Salaries	31
Local Employment	3
Local Spending Accountability	9
Registered Voters	12
Percentage of Population Voting	47
Statewide Initiatives	n/a
Campaign Costs Per Vote	7

Federal Impacts - Section E

Per Capita Federal Spending	40
Increase in Federal Spending	17
Per Capita Federal Grant Spending	44
Per Capita Federal Spending on Procurement	14
Per Capita Federal Spending on Payments to Individuals	46
Per Capita Federal Spending on Social Security and Medicare	47
Social Security Benefits	38
Federal Spending on Employee Wages and Salaries	26
Per Capita Federal Defense Spending	10
Per Capita Homeland Security Grants	49
Federal Grant Spending Per Dollar of State Tax Revenue	17
General Revenue from Federal Government	32
Federal Tax Burden Per Capita	22
Federal Spending Per Dollar of Taxes Paid	34
Highway Charges Returned to States	34
Terms of Trade	38
Federal Personal Income Taxes	21
Federal Share of Medicaid	23

Taxes - Section F

Tax Revenue	42
Per Capita Tax Revenue	33
Tax Effort	37
Tax Capacity	39
Percentage Change in Taxes	5
Property Taxes as a Percentage of Income	10
Property Taxes Per Capita	13
Property Tax Revenue as a Percentage of 3-tax Revenue	6
Sales Taxes as a Percentage of Income	14
Sales Taxes Per Capita	7
Sales Tax Revenue as a Percentage of 3-tax Revenue	12
Sales Tax Rate	7
Income Taxes as a Percentage of Income	n/a
Income Taxes Per Capita	n/a
Income Tax Revenue as a Percentage of 3-tax Revenue	n/a
Highest Personal Income Rate	n/a
Corporate Income Taxes	n/a
Motor Fuel Taxes	28
Motor Vehicle Fees	8
Tobacco Taxes	39
Taxes on High-Income Families	44
Taxes in the Largest City in Each State	43
Progressivity of Taxes	43
Per Capita Estate Tax Revenue	25

Revenues and Finances - Section G

Per Capita Total Revenue	47
Per Capita General Revenue	46

"Own-Source" General Revenue	37
Per Capita Non-Tax Revenue	39
Per Capita Total Spending	41
General Spending as a Percentage of Income	42
Per Capita General Spending	43
Change in General Expenditures	6
State Government General Revenue	48
State Government General Spending	48
State Government General Fund Spending	46
State and Local Debt	19
Debt as a Percentage of Revenue	11
Per Capita Full Faith and Credit Debt	13
Bond Ratings	2
State Solvency Index	6
Pension Plan Assets	36
State Reserves	13
Capital Outlays and Interest	19
State Budget Process Quality	29
Relative State Spending "Needs"	46
Structural Deficits	32

Education - Section H

Math Proficiency, Eighth Grade	20
Reading Proficiency, Eighth Grade	36
AFQT Ranks	33
SAT Scores	23
ACT Scores	n/a
Population over 25 with a High School Diploma	50
Students in Private Schools	42
High School Dropout Rates	35
Pupil-Teacher Ratio	25
Public School Enrollment	3
Library Holdings Per Capita	44
Children with Disabilities	47
Education Spending Per Capita	19
Education Spending as a Percentage of General Spending	1
Spending Per Pupil	39
Average Teacher Salary	32
Sources of School Funds	12
State Aid Per Pupil	46
Per Capita Higher Education Spending	26
Higher Education Spending as a Percentage of General Spending	13
Public Higher Education Enrollment	34
Per Pupil Support of Higher Education	21
In-State Tuition and Fees	21
Out-of-State Tuition and Fees	29
Change in Tuition and Fees	1
Affordability Index	7
Average Professor Salary	20
Education Employees	6
R and D Spending	20
Library Operating Spending	43
Head Start Spending	24

Health - Section I

Immunization Rates	46
Infant Mortality Rates	35
State Health Rankings	39
Population without Health Insurance	1
Abortions	22
Alcohol Consumption	31
Percentage of Adult Smokers	28
Percentage Obese	8
AIDS Cases	11
Physicians Per 100,000 Population	40
Hospital Beds Per 1,000 Population	29
Medicaid Recipients	34
Medicaid Recipients as a Percentage of Poverty Population	48
Health and Hospital Spending	20
Health and Hospital Spending as a Percentage of General Spending	12
Per Capita Medicaid Spending	44
Medicaid Spending Per Aged	38
Medicaid Spending Per Child	27
Medicare Payment Per Hospital Day	8
Hospital Expense Per Inpatient Day	31
Population in HMOs	32
Prescription Drugs as a Percentage of Medicaid Costs	31
Percentage Change in Average Price of Prescription Drugs	25

Crime - Section J

Crime Rate	6
Violent Crime Rate	12
Murder Rate	14
Property Crime Rate	6
Motor Vehicle Theft Rate	15
Violent Crime Rate Change	11
Prisoners	1
Change in Prisoners	39
Incarceration Rate	2
Juvenile Violent Crime Rate	29
Law Enforcement Employees	30
Corrections Employees	2
State Corrections Spending	40
Increase in State Corrections Spending	16
Law Enforcement Spending	21
Law Enforcement Spending as a Percentage of General Spending	9

Transportation - Section K

Travel on Interstates	30
Interstate Mileage in "Unacceptable" Condition	33
Deficient Bridges	37
Traffic Deaths	22
Seat Belt Use	9
Vehicle-Miles Traveled Per Capita	30
Use of Public Transportation	24
Road and Street Miles	12
Highway Employees	41
Public Transit Employees	18
Highway Spending Per Capita	39
Highway Spending as a Percentage of General Spending	34

Welfare - Section L

Births to Unwed Mothers	25
TANF Recipients	36
Change in TANF/AFDC Recipients	14
Food Stamp Recipients	14
SSI Recipients	22
WIC Average Monthly Benefit	45
NSLP Recipients	20
Condition of Children Index	37
Families with Single Parent	28
Average Monthly TANF Payments	45
Welfare as a Percentage of Poverty-Level Income	45
State Supplements of SSI	48
State Income Tax Liability of Typical Family in Poverty	n/a
Child Support Collections	26
Child Support Collections Per Dollar of Administrative Costs	9
Children in Foster Care	49
Welfare Spending Per Capita	46
Welfare Spending as a Percentage of General Spending	40
Administrative Costs Per TANF Case	26

Technology - Section M

Households with Computers	38
Percentage Using Internet	36
Zip Codes with Broadband Service	16
High-Tech Jobs	13
Change in High-Tech Jobs	37
State Government Web Site Ratings	18
Number of Online Government Services	37
Students Per Computer	31
Students Per Internet-Connected Computer	30
Libraries with Internet Access	38

Utah

Population - Section A

Population 2005	34
Population 2004	34
Population Change 2003–2004	7
Population Change 1994–2004	6
Population 2015	7
Population 2025	31
Percentage 65 and Over	49
Percentage 17 and Under	1
Median Age	50
Percentage African American	43
Percentage American Indian	13
Percentage Asian American	26
Percentage Hispanic	12
Percentage White (Non-Hispanic)	16
Percentage Mixed-Race	21
Percentage in Poverty	36
Child Poverty Rate	35
Percentage Female	46
Birth Rates	1
Death Rates	36
Population Density	41
Legal Immigrants FY 2004	27
Unauthorized Immigrants	17

Economies - Section B

Personal Income, 2004	35
Gross State Product	37
Per Capita Personal Income	45
Personal Income from Wages and Salaries	7
Average Annual Pay	35
Average Hourly Earnings	40
Value Added in Manufacturing	35
Cost of Living	34
Average Annual Pay in Manufacturing	41
Average Annual Pay in Retailing	30
Labor Force	24
Unemployment Rate	31
Employment Rate	20
Government Employment	19
Manufacturing Employment	26
Fortune 500 Companies	36
Forbes 500 Companies	42
Tourism Spending Per Capita	28
Exports Per Capita	21
Housing Permits	8
Percentage Change in Home Prices	49
Net Farm Income	37
Financial Institution Assets	6
Bankruptcy Filings	6
Patents Issued	18
WC Disability Payment	30
Average Weekly UC Benefit	19
Economic Momentum	5
One-year Employment Change	4
Manufacturing Employment Change	8
Home Ownership	8
Annual Electricity Use Per Residential Customer	35
Cost Per Kwh	11
New Companies	3

Geography - Section C

Total Land Area	12
Federally Owned Land	7
State Park Acreage	21
State Park Visitors	24
Population Not Active	48
Hunters with Firearms	42
Registered Boats	38
State Spending for the Arts	16
Energy Consumption Per Capita	32
Toxic Chemical Release Per Capita	3
Hazardous Waste Sites	23
Drinking Water Quality	27
Expired Water Pollution Permits	46
Air Pollution Emissions	36

Government - Section D

Members of United States House	34
State Legislators	41
Legislators Per Million Population	20
Units of Government	32
Legislators Compensation	47
Female Legislators	28
Turnover in Legislatures	23
Term Limits	n/a
Legislative Session Length	34
Democrats in State Legislatures	47
Governors' Power Rating	5
Number of Statewide Elected Officials	34
State and Local Government Employees	33
State and Local Average Salaries	30
Local Employment	44
Local Spending Accountability	31
Registered Voters	36
Percentage of Population Voting	33
Statewide Initiatives	n/a
Campaign Costs Per Vote	34

Federal Impacts - Section E

Per Capita Federal Spending	47
Increase in Federal Spending	10
Per Capita Federal Grant Spending	45
Per Capita Federal Spending on Procurement	20
Per Capita Federal Spending on Payments to Individuals	50
Per Capita Federal Spending on Social Security and Medicare	49
Social Security Benefits	25
Federal Spending on Employee Wages and Salaries	14
Per Capita Federal Defense Spending	11
Per Capita Homeland Security Grants	17
Federal Grant Spending Per Dollar of State Tax Revenue	32
General Revenue from Federal Government	33
Federal Tax Burden Per Capita	44
Federal Spending Per Dollar of Taxes Paid	22
Highway Charges Returned to States	24
Terms of Trade	25
Federal Personal Income Taxes	44
Federal Share of Medicaid	5

Taxes - Section F

Tax Revenue	13
Per Capita Tax Revenue	39
Tax Effort	25
Tax Capacity	40
Percentage Change in Taxes	11
Property Taxes as a Percentage of Income	38
Property Taxes Per Capita	39
Property Tax Revenue as a Percentage of 3-tax Revenue	42
Sales Taxes as a Percentage of Income	12
Sales Taxes Per Capita	19
Sales Tax Revenue as a Percentage of 3-tax Revenue	18
Sales Tax Rate	33
Income Taxes as a Percentage of Income	14
Income Taxes Per Capita	21
Income Tax Revenue as a Percentage of 3-tax Revenue	18
Highest Personal Income Rate	26
Corporate Income Taxes	38
Motor Fuel Taxes	13
Motor Vehicle Fees	34
Tobacco Taxes	26
Taxes on High-Income Families	26
Taxes in the Largest City in Each State	18
Progressivity of Taxes	22
Per Capita Estate Tax Revenue	31

Revenues and Finances - Section G

Per Capita Total Revenue	28
Per Capita General Revenue	30

"Own-Source" General Revenue	30
Per Capita Non-Tax Revenue	10
Per Capita Total Spending	25
General Spending as a Percentage of Income	12
Per Capita General Spending	29
Change in General Expenditures	7
State Government General Revenue	30
State Government General Spending	28
State Government General Fund Spending	30
State and Local Debt	17
Debt as a Percentage of Revenue	18
Per Capita Full Faith and Credit Debt	32
Bond Ratings	1
State Solvency Index	29
Pension Plan Assets	20
State Reserves	37
Capital Outlays and Interest	13
State Budget Process Quality	3
Relative State Spending "Needs"	43
Structural Deficits	41

Education - Section H

Math Proficiency, Eighth Grade	29
Reading Proficiency, Eighth Grade	28
AFQT Ranks	11
SAT Scores	n/a
ACT Scores	8
Population over 25 with a High School Diploma	5
Students in Private Schools	49
High School Dropout Rates	6
Pupil-Teacher Ratio	1
Public School Enrollment	1
Library Holdings Per Capita	29
Children with Disabilities	44
Education Spending Per Capita	12
Education Spending as a Percentage of General Spending	2
Spending Per Pupil	50
Average Teacher Salary	36
Sources of School Funds	35
State Aid Per Pupil	36
Per Capita Higher Education Spending	1
Higher Education Spending as a Percentage of General Spending	1
Public Higher Education Enrollment	1
Per Pupil Support of Higher Education	38
In-State Tuition and Fees	47
Out-of-State Tuition and Fees	37
Change in Tuition and Fees	24
Affordability Index	2
Average Professor Salary	28
Education Employees	40
R and D Spending	18
Library Operating Spending	21
Head Start Spending	31

Health - Section I

Immunization Rates	46
Infant Mortality Rates	43
State Health Rankings	4
Population without Health Insurance	30
Abortions	44
Alcohol Consumption	50
Percentage of Adult Smokers	49
Percentage Obese	44
AIDS Cases	42
Physicians Per 100,000 Population	42
Hospital Beds Per 1,000 Population	48
Medicaid Recipients	48
Medicaid Recipients as a Percentage of Poverty Population	47
Health and Hospital Spending	38
Health and Hospital Spending as a Percentage of General Spending	35
Per Capita Medicaid Spending	49
Medicaid Spending Per Aged	29
Medicaid Spending Per Child	16
Medicare Payment Per Hospital Day	18
Hospital Expense Per Inpatient Day	10
Population in HMOs	22
Prescription Drugs as a Percentage of Medicaid Costs	17
Percentage Change in Average Price of Prescription Drugs	33

Crime - Section J

Crime Rate	20
Violent Crime Rate	43
Murder Rate	46
Property Crime Rate	15
Motor Vehicle Theft Rate	25
Violent Crime Rate Change	29
Prisoners	38
Change in Prisoners	9
Incarceration Rate	42
Juvenile Violent Crime Rate	26
Law Enforcement Employees	44
Corrections Employees	31
State Corrections Spending	5
Increase in State Corrections Spending	40
Law Enforcement Spending	27
Law Enforcement Spending as a Percentage of General Spending	21

Transportation - Section K

Travel on Interstates	1
Interstate Mileage in "Unacceptable" Condition	19
Deficient Bridges	42
Traffic Deaths	39
Seat Belt Use	11
Vehicle-Miles Traveled Per Capita	29
Use of Public Transportation	15
Road and Street Miles	27
Highway Employees	44
Public Transit Employees	11
Highway Spending Per Capita	24
Highway Spending as a Percentage of General Spending	23

Welfare - Section L

Births to Unwed Mothers	50
TANF Recipients	35
Change in TANF/AFDC Recipients	44
Food Stamp Recipients	42
SSI Recipients	50
WIC Average Monthly Benefit	49
NSLP Recipients	28
Condition of Children Index	9
Families with Single Parent	50
Average Monthly TANF Payments	17
Welfare as a Percentage of Poverty-Level Income	17
State Supplements of SSI	49
State Income Tax Liability of Typical Family in Poverty	17
Child Support Collections	36
Child Support Collections Per Dollar of Administrative Costs	37
Children in Foster Care	50
Welfare Spending Per Capita	45
Welfare Spending as a Percentage of General Spending	43
Administrative Costs Per TANF Case	3

Technology - Section M

Households with Computers	1
Percentage Using Internet	5
Zip Codes with Broadband Service	35
High-Tech Jobs	15
Change in High-Tech Jobs	9
State Government Web Site Ratings	1
Number of Online Government Services	1
Students Per Computer	2
Students Per Internet-Connected Computer	3
Libraries with Internet Access	1

Vermont

Population - Section A

Population 2005	49
Population 2004	49
Population Change 2003–2004	43
Population Change 1994–2004	33
Population 2015	22
Population 2025	48
Percentage 65 and Over	20
Percentage 17 and Under	48
Median Age	2
Percentage African American	48
Percentage American Indian	33
Percentage Asian American	40
Percentage Hispanic	48
Percentage White (Non-Hispanic)	2
Percentage Mixed-Race	34
Percentage in Poverty	48
Child Poverty Rate	44
Percentage Female	26
Birth Rates	49
Death Rates	43
Population Density	30
Legal Immigrants FY 2004	45
Unauthorized Immigrants	43

Economies - Section B

Personal Income, 2004	48
Gross State Product	35
Per Capita Personal Income	23
Personal Income from Wages and Salaries	34
Average Annual Pay	32
Average Hourly Earnings	33
Value Added in Manufacturing	12
Cost of Living	10
Average Annual Pay in Manufacturing	21
Average Annual Pay in Retailing	23
Labor Force	2
Unemployment Rate	45
Employment Rate	6
Government Employment	24
Manufacturing Employment	17
Fortune 500 Companies	n/a
Forbes 500 Companies	33
Tourism Spending Per Capita	6
Exports Per Capita	1
Housing Permits	29
Percentage Change in Home Prices	16
Net Farm Income	43
Financial Institution Assets	35
Bankruptcy Filings	48
Patents Issued	2
WC Disability Payment	7
Average Weekly UC Benefit	15
Economic Momentum	23
One-year Employment Change	18
Manufacturing Employment Change	15
Home Ownership	25
Annual Electricity Use Per Residential Customer	45
Cost Per Kwh	31
New Companies	18

Geography - Section C

Total Land Area	43
Federally Owned Land	41
State Park Acreage	35
State Park Visitors	44
Population Not Active	45
Hunters with Firearms	23
Registered Boats	48
State Spending for the Arts	22
Energy Consumption Per Capita	40
Toxic Chemical Release Per Capita	50
Hazardous Waste Sites	34
Drinking Water Quality	5
Expired Water Pollution Permits	37
Air Pollution Emissions	46

Government - Section D

Members of United States House	44
State Legislators	12
Legislators Per Million Population	2
Units of Government	7
Legislators Compensation	37
Female Legislators	3
Turnover in Legislatures	17
Term Limits	n/a
Legislative Session Length	7
Democrats in State Legislatures	15
Governors' Power Rating	50
Number of Statewide Elected Officials	15
State and Local Government Employees	11
State and Local Average Salaries	24
Local Employment	42
Local Spending Accountability	49
Registered Voters	7
Percentage of Population Voting	9
Statewide Initiatives	n/a
Campaign Costs Per Vote	46

Federal Impacts - Section E

Per Capita Federal Spending	23
Increase in Federal Spending	12
Per Capita Federal Grant Spending	6
Per Capita Federal Spending on Procurement	21
Per Capita Federal Spending on Payments to Individuals	37
Per Capita Federal Spending on Social Security and Medicare	28
Social Security Benefits	31
Federal Spending on Employee Wages and Salaries	27
Per Capita Federal Defense Spending	25
Per Capita Homeland Security Grants	2
Federal Grant Spending Per Dollar of State Tax Revenue	19
General Revenue from Federal Government	8
Federal Tax Burden Per Capita	23
Federal Spending Per Dollar of Taxes Paid	23
Highway Charges Returned to States	4
Terms of Trade	11
Federal Personal Income Taxes	25
Federal Share of Medicaid	30

Taxes - Section F

Tax Revenue	12
Per Capita Tax Revenue	17
Tax Effort	14
Tax Capacity	21
Percentage Change in Taxes	27
Property Taxes as a Percentage of Income	5
Property Taxes Per Capita	9
Property Tax Revenue as a Percentage of 3-tax Revenue	7
Sales Taxes as a Percentage of Income	39
Sales Taxes Per Capita	38
Sales Tax Revenue as a Percentage of 3-tax Revenue	40
Sales Tax Rate	10
Income Taxes as a Percentage of Income	31
Income Taxes Per Capita	26
Income Tax Revenue as a Percentage of 3-tax Revenue	35
Highest Personal Income Rate	2
Corporate Income Taxes	30
Motor Fuel Taxes	28
Motor Vehicle Fees	12
Tobacco Taxes	13
Taxes on High-Income Families	28
Taxes in the Largest City in Each State	25
Progressivity of Taxes	21
Per Capita Estate Tax Revenue	12

Revenues and Finances - Section G

Per Capita Total Revenue	12
Per Capita General Revenue	10

"Own-Source" General Revenue	24
Per Capita Non-Tax Revenue	36
Per Capita Total Spending	22
General Spending as a Percentage of Income	18
Per Capita General Spending	15
Change in General Expenditures	28
State Government General Revenue	4
State Government General Spending	2
State Government General Fund Spending	18
State and Local Debt	25
Debt as a Percentage of Revenue	34
Per Capita Full Faith and Credit Debt	29
Bond Ratings	2
State Solvency Index	17
Pension Plan Assets	43
State Reserves	35
Capital Outlays and Interest	41
State Budget Process Quality	48
Relative State Spending "Needs"	3
Structural Deficits	9

Education · Section H

Math Proficiency, Eighth Grade	3
Reading Proficiency, Eighth Grade	5
AFQT Ranks	2
SAT Scores	7
ACT Scores	n/a
Population over 25 with a High School Diploma	6
Students in Private Schools	15
High School Dropout Rates	6
Pupil-Teacher Ratio	50
Public School Enrollment	42
Library Holdings Per Capita	5
Children with Disabilities	25
Education Spending Per Capita	6
Education Spending as a Percentage of General Spending	8
Spending Per Pupil	5
Average Teacher Salary	21
Sources of School Funds	49
State Aid Per Pupil	1
Per Capita Higher Education Spending	10
Higher Education Spending as a Percentage of General Spending	12
Public Higher Education Enrollment	20
Per Pupil Support of Higher Education	47
In-State Tuition and Fees	1
Out-of-State Tuition and Fees	2
Change in Tuition and Fees	37
Affordability Index	27
Average Professor Salary	31
Education Employees	2
R and D Spending	15
Library Operating Spending	28
Head Start Spending	4

Health · Section I

Immunization Rates	4
Infant Mortality Rates	48
State Health Rankings	2
Population without Health Insurance	43
Abortions	13
Alcohol Consumption	12
Percentage of Adult Smokers	36
Percentage Obese	48
AIDS Cases	45
Physicians Per 100,000 Population	6
Hospital Beds Per 1,000 Population	35
Medicaid Recipients	5
Medicaid Recipients as a Percentage of Poverty Population	1
Health and Hospital Spending	50
Health and Hospital Spending as a Percentage of General Spending	50
Per Capita Medicaid Spending	6
Medicaid Spending Per Aged	47
Medicaid Spending Per Child	9
Medicare Payment Per Hospital Day	47
Hospital Expense Per Inpatient Day	1
Population in HMOs	29
Prescription Drugs as a Percentage of Medicaid Costs	5
Percentage Change in Average Price of Prescription Drugs	16

Crime · Section J

Crime Rate	47
Violent Crime Rate	48
Murder Rate	34
Property Crime Rate	46
Motor Vehicle Theft Rate	50
Violent Crime Rate Change	12
Prisoners	49
Change in Prisoners	27
Incarceration Rate	43
Juvenile Violent Crime Rate	44
Law Enforcement Employees	50
Corrections Employees	41
State Corrections Spending	8
Increase in State Corrections Spending	12
Law Enforcement Spending	42
Law Enforcement Spending as a Percentage of General Spending	47

Transportation · Section K

Travel on Interstates	39
Interstate Mileage in "Unacceptable" Condition	45
Deficient Bridges	10
Traffic Deaths	36
Seat Belt Use	16
Vehicle-Miles Traveled Per Capita	6
Use of Public Transportation	30
Road and Street Miles	17
Highway Employees	5
Public Transit Employees	30
Highway Spending Per Capita	9
Highway Spending as a Percentage of General Spending	13

Welfare · Section L

Births to Unwed Mothers	39
TANF Recipients	11
Change in TANF/AFDC Recipients	34
Food Stamp Recipients	31
SSI Recipients	23
WIC Average Monthly Benefit	4
NSLP Recipients	35
Condition of Children Index	2
Families with Single Parent	28
Average Monthly TANF Payments	6
Welfare as a Percentage of Poverty-Level Income	6
State Supplements of SSI	32
State Income Tax Liability of Typical Family in Poverty	41
Child Support Collections	16
Child Support Collections Per Dollar of Administrative Costs	35
Children in Foster Care	8
Welfare Spending Per Capita	6
Welfare Spending as a Percentage of General Spending	9
Administrative Costs Per TANF Case	10

Technology · Section M

Households with Computers	15
Percentage Using Internet	15
Zip Codes with Broadband Service	6
High-Tech Jobs	10
Change in High-Tech Jobs	49
State Government Web Site Ratings	41
Number of Online Government Services	33
Students Per Computer	27
Students Per Internet-Connected Computer	18
Libraries with Internet Access	50

Virginia

Population - Section A

Population 2005	12
Population 2004	12
Population Change 2003–2004	11
Population Change 1994–2004	16
Population 2015	9
Population 2025	13
Percentage 65 and Over	42
Percentage 17 and Under	27
Median Age	26
Percentage African American	9
Percentage American Indian	38
Percentage Asian American	10
Percentage Hispanic	26
Percentage White (Non-Hispanic)	33
Percentage Mixed-Race	10
Percentage in Poverty	42
Child Poverty Rate	41
Percentage Female	27
Birth Rates	24
Death Rates	18
Population Density	14
Legal Immigrants FY 2004	8
Unauthorized Immigrants	12

Economies - Section B

Personal Income, 2004	11
Gross State Product	8
Per Capita Personal Income	7
Personal Income from Wages and Salaries	8
Average Annual Pay	9
Average Hourly Earnings	17
Value Added in Manufacturing	25
Cost of Living	16
Average Annual Pay in Manufacturing	31
Average Annual Pay in Retailing	24
Labor Force	17
Unemployment Rate	47
Employment Rate	4
Government Employment	18
Manufacturing Employment	36
Fortune 500 Companies	7
Forbes 500 Companies	11
Tourism Spending Per Capita	15
Exports Per Capita	38
Housing Permits	11
Percentage Change in Home Prices	8
Net Farm Income	34
Financial Institution Assets	11
Bankruptcy Filings	26
Patents Issued	32
WC Disability Payment	16
Average Weekly UC Benefit	27
Economic Momentum	9
One-year Employment Change	24
Manufacturing Employment Change	33
Home Ownership	13
Annual Electricity Use Per Residential Customer	8
Cost Per Kwh	10
New Companies	20

Geography - Section C

Total Land Area	37
Federally Owned Land	19
State Park Acreage	36
State Park Visitors	47
Population Not Active	27
Hunters with Firearms	40
Registered Boats	19
State Spending for the Arts	42
Energy Consumption Per Capita	30
Toxic Chemical Release Per Capita	30
Hazardous Waste Sites	14
Drinking Water Quality	10
Expired Water Pollution Permits	27
Air Pollution Emissions	16

Government - Section D

Members of United States House	12
State Legislators	27
Legislators Per Million Population	41
Units of Government	47
Legislators Compensation	23
Female Legislators	43
Turnover in Legislatures	n/a
Term Limits	n/a
Legislative Session Length	30
Democrats in State Legislatures	37
Governors' Power Rating	35
Number of Statewide Elected Officials	44
State and Local Government Employees	26
State and Local Average Salaries	23
Local Employment	22
Local Spending Accountability	28
Registered Voters	27
Percentage of Population Voting	29
Statewide Initiatives	n/a
Campaign Costs Per Vote	13

Federal Impacts - Section E

Per Capita Federal Spending	2
Increase in Federal Spending	3
Per Capita Federal Grant Spending	49
Per Capita Federal Spending on Procurement	1
Per Capita Federal Spending on Payments to Individuals	17
Per Capita Federal Spending on Social Security and Medicare	42
Social Security Benefits	29
Federal Spending on Employee Wages and Salaries	3
Per Capita Federal Defense Spending	1
Per Capita Homeland Security Grants	39
Federal Grant Spending Per Dollar of State Tax Revenue	44
General Revenue from Federal Government	48
Federal Tax Burden Per Capita	14
Federal Spending Per Dollar of Taxes Paid	8
Highway Charges Returned to States	38
Terms of Trade	48
Federal Personal Income Taxes	7
Federal Share of Medicaid	39

Taxes - Section F

Tax Revenue	43
Per Capita Tax Revenue	23
Tax Effort	30
Tax Capacity	19
Percentage Change in Taxes	9
Property Taxes as a Percentage of Income	31
Property Taxes Per Capita	26
Property Tax Revenue as a Percentage of 3-tax Revenue	26
Sales Taxes as a Percentage of Income	42
Sales Taxes Per Capita	41
Sales Tax Revenue as a Percentage of 3-tax Revenue	37
Sales Tax Rate	38
Income Taxes as a Percentage of Income	15
Income Taxes Per Capita	10
Income Tax Revenue as a Percentage of 3-tax Revenue	9
Highest Personal Income Rate	25
Corporate Income Taxes	42
Motor Fuel Taxes	40
Motor Vehicle Fees	27
Tobacco Taxes	44
Taxes on High-Income Families	34
Taxes in the Largest City in Each State	26
Progressivity of Taxes	35
Per Capita Estate Tax Revenue	19

Revenues and Finances - Section G

Per Capita Total Revenue	45
Per Capita General Revenue	32

"Own-Source" General Revenue	23
Per Capita Non-Tax Revenue	24
Per Capita Total Spending	40
General Spending as a Percentage of Income	46
Per Capita General Spending	35
Change in General Expenditures	25
State Government General Revenue	40
State Government General Spending	37
State Government General Fund Spending	40
State and Local Debt	28
Debt as a Percentage of Revenue	21
Per Capita Full Faith and Credit Debt	31
Bond Ratings	1
State Solvency Index	18
Pension Plan Assets	35
State Reserves	24
Capital Outlays and Interest	32
State Budget Process Quality	42
Relative State Spending "Needs"	16
Structural Deficits	23

Education - Section H

Math Proficiency, Eighth Grade	10
Reading Proficiency, Eighth Grade	9
AFQT Ranks	27
SAT Scores	9
ACT Scores	n/a
Population over 25 with a High School Diploma	15
Students in Private Schools	28
High School Dropout Rates	16
Pupil-Teacher Ratio	48
Public School Enrollment	24
Library Holdings Per Capita	29
Children with Disabilities	26
Education Spending Per Capita	21
Education Spending as a Percentage of General Spending	6
Spending Per Pupil	22
Average Teacher Salary	20
Sources of School Funds	10
State Aid Per Pupil	40
Per Capita Higher Education Spending	27
Higher Education Spending as a Percentage of General Spending	22
Public Higher Education Enrollment	24
Per Pupil Support of Higher Education	28
In-State Tuition and Fees	18
Out-of-State Tuition and Fees	4
Change in Tuition and Fees	19
Affordability Index	11
Average Professor Salary	4
Education Employees	18
R and D Spending	3
Library Operating Spending	20
Head Start Spending	20

Health - Section I

Immunization Rates	19
Infant Mortality Rates	18
State Health Rankings	24
Population without Health Insurance	26
Abortions	15
Alcohol Consumption	38
Percentage of Adult Smokers	25
Percentage Obese	27
AIDS Cases	20
Physicians Per 100,000 Population	15
Hospital Beds Per 1,000 Population	37
Medicaid Recipients	47
Medicaid Recipients as a Percentage of Poverty Population	44
Health and Hospital Spending	26
Health and Hospital Spending as a Percentage of General Spending	21
Per Capita Medicaid Spending	48
Medicaid Spending Per Aged	35
Medicaid Spending Per Child	31
Medicare Payment Per Hospital Day	26
Hospital Expense Per Inpatient Day	35
Population in HMOs	20
Prescription Drugs as a Percentage of Medicaid Costs	27
Percentage Change in Average Price of Prescription Drugs	45

Crime - Section J

Crime Rate	37
Violent Crime Rate	35
Murder Rate	22
Property Crime Rate	37
Motor Vehicle Theft Rate	37
Violent Crime Rate Change	15
Prisoners	11
Change in Prisoners	31
Incarceration Rate	15
Juvenile Violent Crime Rate	41
Law Enforcement Employees	34
Corrections Employees	8
State Corrections Spending	30
Increase in State Corrections Spending	43
Law Enforcement Spending	25
Law Enforcement Spending as a Percentage of General Spending	16

Transportation - Section K

Travel on Interstates	7
Interstate Mileage in "Unacceptable" Condition	30
Deficient Bridges	28
Traffic Deaths	40
Seat Belt Use	27
Vehicle-Miles Traveled Per Capita	27
Use of Public Transportation	13
Road and Street Miles	3
Highway Employees	34
Public Transit Employees	33
Highway Spending Per Capita	28
Highway Spending as a Percentage of General Spending	24

Welfare - Section L

Births to Unwed Mothers	36
TANF Recipients	48
Change in TANF/AFDC Recipients	5
Food Stamp Recipients	36
SSI Recipients	27
WIC Average Monthly Benefit	32
NSLP Recipients	24
Condition of Children Index	13
Families with Single Parent	28
Average Monthly TANF Payments	1
Welfare as a Percentage of Poverty-Level Income	14
State Supplements of SSI	9
State Income Tax Liability of Typical Family in Poverty	17
Child Support Collections	27
Child Support Collections Per Dollar of Administrative Costs	7
Children in Foster Care	45
Welfare Spending Per Capita	47
Welfare Spending as a Percentage of General Spending	47
Administrative Costs Per TANF Case	1

Technology - Section M

Households with Computers	11
Percentage Using Internet	9
Zip Codes with Broadband Service	23
High-Tech Jobs	2
Change in High-Tech Jobs	10
State Government Web Site Ratings	35
Number of Online Government Services	44
Students Per Computer	36
Students Per Internet-Connected Computer	34
Libraries with Internet Access	1

Washington

Population - Section A

Population 2005	14
Population 2004	15
Population Change 2003–2004	15
Population Change 1994–2004	11
Population 2015	11
Population 2025	14
Percentage 65 and Over	43
Percentage 17 and Under	30
Median Age	33
Percentage African American	36
Percentage American Indian	9
Percentage Asian American	5
Percentage Hispanic	16
Percentage White (Non-Hispanic)	26
Percentage Mixed-Race	4
Percentage in Poverty	27
Child Poverty Rate	27
Percentage Female	40
Birth Rates	34
Death Rates	38
Population Density	25
Legal Immigrants FY 2004	10
Unauthorized Immigrants	11

Economies - Section B

Personal Income, 2004	15
Gross State Product	13
Per Capita Personal Income	12
Personal Income from Wages and Salaries	24
Average Annual Pay	13
Average Hourly Earnings	4
Value Added in Manufacturing	26
Cost of Living	12
Average Annual Pay in Manufacturing	9
Average Annual Pay in Retailing	6
Labor Force	14
Unemployment Rate	14
Employment Rate	37
Government Employment	12
Manufacturing Employment	33
Fortune 500 Companies	21
Forbes 500 Companies	21
Tourism Spending Per Capita	42
Exports Per Capita	3
Housing Permits	14
Percentage Change in Home Prices	20
Net Farm Income	15
Financial Institution Assets	36
Bankruptcy Filings	21
Patents Issued	12
WC Disability Payment	8
Average Weekly UC Benefit	5
Economic Momentum	11
One-year Employment Change	9
Manufacturing Employment Change	11
Home Ownership	43
Annual Electricity Use Per Residential Customer	17
Cost Per Kwh	45
New Companies	2

Geography - Section C

Total Land Area	20
Federally Owned Land	12
State Park Acreage	13
State Park Visitors	4
Population Not Active	46
Hunters with Firearms	35
Registered Boats	16
State Spending for the Arts	44
Energy Consumption Per Capita	27
Toxic Chemical Release Per Capita	42
Hazardous Waste Sites	7
Drinking Water Quality	15
Expired Water Pollution Permits	5
Air Pollution Emissions	23

Government - Section D

Members of United States House	14
State Legislators	24
Legislators Per Million Population	36
Units of Government	28
Legislators Compensation	13
Female Legislators	3
Turnover in Legislatures	21
Term Limits	n/a
Legislative Session Length	30
Democrats in State Legislatures	17
Governors' Power Rating	17
Number of Statewide Elected Officials	3
State and Local Government Employees	38
State and Local Average Salaries	7
Local Employment	40
Local Spending Accountability	19
Registered Voters	37
Percentage of Population Voting	13
Statewide Initiatives	2
Campaign Costs Per Vote	41

Federal Impacts - Section E

Per Capita Federal Spending	26
Increase in Federal Spending	24
Per Capita Federal Grant Spending	28
Per Capita Federal Spending on Procurement	16
Per Capita Federal Spending on Payments to Individuals	36
Per Capita Federal Spending on Social Security and Medicare	40
Social Security Benefits	6
Federal Spending on Employee Wages and Salaries	10
Per Capita Federal Defense Spending	13
Per Capita Homeland Security Grants	37
Federal Grant Spending Per Dollar of State Tax Revenue	40
General Revenue from Federal Government	39
Federal Tax Burden Per Capita	6
Federal Spending Per Dollar of Taxes Paid	37
Highway Charges Returned to States	24
Terms of Trade	42
Federal Personal Income Taxes	10
Federal Share of Medicaid	39

Taxes - Section F

Tax Revenue	32
Per Capita Tax Revenue	15
Tax Effort	24
Tax Capacity	10
Percentage Change in Taxes	33
Property Taxes as a Percentage of Income	28
Property Taxes Per Capita	20
Property Tax Revenue as a Percentage of 3-tax Revenue	28
Sales Taxes as a Percentage of Income	3
Sales Taxes Per Capita	1
Sales Tax Revenue as a Percentage of 3-tax Revenue	3
Sales Tax Rate	4
Income Taxes as a Percentage of Income	n/a
Income Taxes Per Capita	n/a
Income Tax Revenue as a Percentage of 3-tax Revenue	n/a
Highest Personal Income Rate	n/a
Corporate Income Taxes	n/a
Motor Fuel Taxes	4
Motor Vehicle Fees	20
Tobacco Taxes	9
Taxes on High-Income Families	42
Taxes in the Largest City in Each State	37
Progressivity of Taxes	47
Per Capita Estate Tax Revenue	18

Revenues and Finances - Section G

Per Capita Total Revenue	9
Per Capita General Revenue	15

"Own-Source" General Revenue	12
Per Capita Non-Tax Revenue	13
Per Capita Total Spending	5
General Spending as a Percentage of Income	29
Per Capita General Spending	11
Change in General Expenditures	38
State Government General Revenue	23
State Government General Spending	20
State Government General Fund Spending	34
State and Local Debt	5
Debt as a Percentage of Revenue	10
Per Capita Full Faith and Credit Debt	7
Bond Ratings	2
State Solvency Index	37
Pension Plan Assets	5
State Reserves	22
Capital Outlays and Interest	5
State Budget Process Quality	33
Relative State Spending "Needs"	19
Structural Deficits	48

Education - Section H

Math Proficiency, Eighth Grade	7
Reading Proficiency, Eighth Grade	19
AFQT Ranks	5
SAT Scores	1
ACT Scores	n/a
Population over 25 with a High School Diploma	10
Students in Private Schools	34
High School Dropout Rates	41
Pupil-Teacher Ratio	6
Public School Enrollment	15
Library Holdings Per Capita	25
Children with Disabilities	45
Education Spending Per Capita	18
Education Spending as a Percentage of General Spending	31
Spending Per Pupil	29
Average Teacher Salary	19
Sources of School Funds	42
State Aid Per Pupil	13
Per Capita Higher Education Spending	13
Higher Education Spending as a Percentage of General Spending	24
Public Higher Education Enrollment	25
Per Pupil Support of Higher Education	19
In-State Tuition and Fees	24
Out-of-State Tuition and Fees	17
Change in Tuition and Fees	27
Affordability Index	21
Average Professor Salary	21
Education Employees	49
R and D Spending	11
Library Operating Spending	6
Head Start Spending	1

Health - Section I

Immunization Rates	37
Infant Mortality Rates	40
State Health Rankings	14
Population without Health Insurance	32
Abortions	6
Alcohol Consumption	31
Percentage of Adult Smokers	42
Percentage Obese	32
AIDS Cases	28
Physicians Per 100,000 Population	26
Hospital Beds Per 1,000 Population	50
Medicaid Recipients	12
Medicaid Recipients as a Percentage of Poverty Population	8
Health and Hospital Spending	8
Health and Hospital Spending as a Percentage of General Spending	10
Per Capita Medicaid Spending	27
Medicaid Spending Per Aged	37
Medicaid Spending Per Child	49
Medicare Payment Per Hospital Day	14
Hospital Expense Per Inpatient Day	3
Population in HMOs	23
Prescription Drugs as a Percentage of Medicaid Costs	38
Percentage Change in Average Price of Prescription Drugs	36

Crime - Section J

Crime Rate	3
Violent Crime Rate	27
Murder Rate	32
Property Crime Rate	2
Motor Vehicle Theft Rate	4
Violent Crime Rate Change	27
Prisoners	27
Change in Prisoners	24
Incarceration Rate	41
Juvenile Violent Crime Rate	18
Law Enforcement Employees	46
Corrections Employees	25
State Corrections Spending	9
Increase in State Corrections Spending	13
Law Enforcement Spending	26
Law Enforcement Spending as a Percentage of General Spending	31

Transportation - Section K

Travel on Interstates	16
Interstate Mileage in "Unacceptable" Condition	7
Deficient Bridges	24
Traffic Deaths	45
Seat Belt Use	1
Vehicle-Miles Traveled Per Capita	41
Use of Public Transportation	9
Road and Street Miles	44
Highway Employees	22
Public Transit Employees	4
Highway Spending Per Capita	31
Highway Spending as a Percentage of General Spending	39

Welfare - Section L

Births to Unwed Mothers	43
TANF Recipients	5
Change in TANF/AFDC Recipients	41
Food Stamp Recipients	26
SSI Recipients	26
WIC Average Monthly Benefit	5
NSLP Recipients	42
Condition of Children Index	14
Families with Single Parent	28
Average Monthly TANF Payments	14
Welfare as a Percentage of Poverty-Level Income	9
State Supplements of SSI	1
State Income Tax Liability of Typical Family in Poverty	n/a
Child Support Collections	9
Child Support Collections Per Dollar of Administrative Costs	28
Children in Foster Care	31
Welfare Spending Per Capita	18
Welfare Spending as a Percentage of General Spending	26
Administrative Costs Per TANF Case	30

Technology - Section M

Households with Computers	4
Percentage Using Internet	6
Zip Codes with Broadband Service	16
High-Tech Jobs	8
Change in High-Tech Jobs	23
State Government Web Site Ratings	25
Number of Online Government Services	39
Students Per Computer	25
Students Per Internet-Connected Computer	24
Libraries with Internet Access	34

West Virginia

Population - Section A

Population 2005	37
Population 2004	37
Population Change 2003–2004	46
Population Change 1994–2004	49
Population 2015	49
Population 2025	39
Percentage 65 and Over	2
Percentage 17 and Under	50
Median Age	3
Percentage African American	37
Percentage American Indian	49
Percentage Asian American	49
Percentage Hispanic	50
Percentage White (Non-Hispanic)	3
Percentage Mixed-Race	48
Percentage in Poverty	13
Child Poverty Rate	19
Percentage Female	16
Birth Rates	47
Death Rates	4
Population Density	29
Legal Immigrants FY 2004	47
Unauthorized Immigrants	43

Economies - Section B

Personal Income, 2004	39
Gross State Product	49
Per Capita Personal Income	49
Personal Income from Wages and Salaries	50
Average Annual Pay	44
Average Hourly Earnings	13
Value Added in Manufacturing	39
Cost of Living	44
Average Annual Pay in Manufacturing	25
Average Annual Pay in Retailing	50
Labor Force	49
Unemployment Rate	13
Employment Rate	38
Government Employment	10
Manufacturing Employment	34
Fortune 500 Companies	n/a
Forbes 500 Companies	45
Tourism Spending Per Capita	50
Exports Per Capita	34
Housing Permits	48
Percentage Change in Home Prices	30
Net Farm Income	47
Financial Institution Assets	40
Bankruptcy Filings	14
Patents Issued	48
WC Disability Payment	36
Average Weekly UC Benefit	34
Economic Momentum	32
One-year Employment Change	37
Manufacturing Employment Change	32
Home Ownership	1
Annual Electricity Use Per Residential Customer	16
Cost Per Kwh	28
New Companies	34

Geography - Section C

Total Land Area	41
Federally Owned Land	29
State Park Acreage	17
State Park Visitors	12
Population Not Active	16
Hunters with Firearms	7
Registered Boats	39
State Spending for the Arts	10
Energy Consumption Per Capita	10
Toxic Chemical Release Per Capita	4
Hazardous Waste Sites	41
Drinking Water Quality	31
Expired Water Pollution Permits	41
Air Pollution Emissions	35

Government - Section D

Members of United States House	34
State Legislators	31
Legislators Per Million Population	12
Units of Government	24
Legislators Compensation	29
Female Legislators	42
Turnover in Legislatures	27
Term Limits	n/a
Legislative Session Length	30
Democrats in State Legislatures	6
Governors' Power Rating	1
Number of Statewide Elected Officials	22
State and Local Government Employees	28
State and Local Average Salaries	43
Local Employment	43
Local Spending Accountability	44
Registered Voters	32
Percentage of Population Voting	45
Statewide Initiatives	n/a
Campaign Costs Per Vote	16

Federal Impacts - Section E

Per Capita Federal Spending	11
Increase in Federal Spending	36
Per Capita Federal Grant Spending	12
Per Capita Federal Spending on Procurement	37
Per Capita Federal Spending on Payments to Individuals	2
Per Capita Federal Spending on Social Security and Medicare	1
Social Security Benefits	35
Federal Spending on Employee Wages and Salaries	21
Per Capita Federal Defense Spending	47
Per Capita Homeland Security Grants	14
Federal Grant Spending Per Dollar of State Tax Revenue	12
General Revenue from Federal Government	4
Federal Tax Burden Per Capita	48
Federal Spending Per Dollar of Taxes Paid	4
Highway Charges Returned to States	8
Terms of Trade	3
Federal Personal Income Taxes	49
Federal Share of Medicaid	3

Taxes - Section F

Tax Revenue	8
Per Capita Tax Revenue	40
Tax Effort	8
Tax Capacity	50
Percentage Change in Taxes	31
Property Taxes as a Percentage of Income	42
Property Taxes Per Capita	42
Property Tax Revenue as a Percentage of 3-tax Revenue	43
Sales Taxes as a Percentage of Income	11
Sales Taxes Per Capita	22
Sales Tax Revenue as a Percentage of 3-tax Revenue	14
Sales Tax Rate	10
Income Taxes as a Percentage of Income	24
Income Taxes Per Capita	33
Income Tax Revenue as a Percentage of 3-tax Revenue	24
Highest Personal Income Rate	20
Corporate Income Taxes	9
Motor Fuel Taxes	5
Motor Vehicle Fees	24
Tobacco Taxes	32
Taxes on High-Income Families	29
Taxes in the Largest City in Each State	30
Progressivity of Taxes	30
Per Capita Estate Tax Revenue	40

Revenues and Finances - Section G

Per Capita Total Revenue	17
Per Capita General Revenue	28

"Own-Source" General Revenue	38
Per Capita Non-Tax Revenue	30
Per Capita Total Spending	26
General Spending as a Percentage of Income	6
Per Capita General Spending	32
Change in General Expenditures	49
State Government General Revenue	12
State Government General Spending	15
State Government General Fund Spending	1
State and Local Debt	38
Debt as a Percentage of Revenue	38
Per Capita Full Faith and Credit Debt	49
Bond Ratings	4
State Solvency Index	44
Pension Plan Assets	47
State Reserves	11
Capital Outlays and Interest	42
State Budget Process Quality	38
Relative State Spending "Needs"	29
Structural Deficits	6

Education - Section H

Math Proficiency, Eighth Grade	44
Reading Proficiency, Eighth Grade	42
AFQT Ranks	39
SAT Scores	n/a
ACT Scores	16
Population over 25 with a High School Diploma	46
Students in Private Schools	43
High School Dropout Rates	26
Pupil-Teacher Ratio	35
Public School Enrollment	39
Library Holdings Per Capita	27
Children with Disabilities	3
Education Spending Per Capita	34
Education Spending as a Percentage of General Spending	20
Spending Per Pupil	17
Average Teacher Salary	45
Sources of School Funds	40
State Aid Per Pupil	10
Per Capita Higher Education Spending	29
Higher Education Spending as a Percentage of General Spending	27
Public Higher Education Enrollment	35
Per Pupil Support of Higher Education	34
In-State Tuition and Fees	38
Out-of-State Tuition and Fees	39
Change in Tuition and Fees	15
Affordability Index	40
Average Professor Salary	45
Education Employees	27
R and D Spending	24
Library Operating Spending	48
Head Start Spending	43

Health - Section I

Immunization Rates	9
Infant Mortality Rates	27
State Health Rankings	41
Population without Health Insurance	11
Abortions	41
Alcohol Consumption	49
Percentage of Adult Smokers	2
Percentage Obese	3
AIDS Cases	36
Physicians Per 100,000 Population	23
Hospital Beds Per 1,000 Population	6
Medicaid Recipients	15
Medicaid Recipients as a Percentage of Poverty Population	27
Health and Hospital Spending	43
Health and Hospital Spending as a Percentage of General Spending	41
Per Capita Medicaid Spending	15
Medicaid Spending Per Aged	25
Medicaid Spending Per Child	23
Medicare Payment Per Hospital Day	49
Hospital Expense Per Inpatient Day	40
Population in HMOs	38
Prescription Drugs as a Percentage of Medicaid Costs	2
Percentage Change in Average Price of Prescription Drugs	18

Crime - Section J

Crime Rate	44
Violent Crime Rate	36
Murder Rate	30
Property Crime Rate	41
Motor Vehicle Theft Rate	41
Violent Crime Rate Change	41
Prisoners	40
Change in Prisoners	3
Incarceration Rate	40
Juvenile Violent Crime Rate	49
Law Enforcement Employees	49
Corrections Employees	40
State Corrections Spending	34
Increase in State Corrections Spending	3
Law Enforcement Spending	50
Law Enforcement Spending as a Percentage of General Spending	49

Transportation - Section K

Travel on Interstates	12
Interstate Mileage in "Unacceptable" Condition	35
Deficient Bridges	7
Traffic Deaths	10
Seat Belt Use	16
Vehicle-Miles Traveled Per Capita	21
Use of Public Transportation	30
Road and Street Miles	1
Highway Employees	4
Public Transit Employees	27
Highway Spending Per Capita	11
Highway Spending as a Percentage of General Spending	7

Welfare - Section L

Births to Unwed Mothers	24
TANF Recipients	20
Change in TANF/AFDC Recipients	15
Food Stamp Recipients	2
SSI Recipients	3
WIC Average Monthly Benefit	23
NSLP Recipients	13
Condition of Children Index	47
Families with Single Parent	19
Average Monthly TANF Payments	19
Welfare as a Percentage of Poverty-Level Income	32
State Supplements of SSI	50
State Income Tax Liability of Typical Family in Poverty	4
Child Support Collections	13
Child Support Collections Per Dollar of Administrative Costs	31
Children in Foster Care	6
Welfare Spending Per Capita	7
Welfare Spending as a Percentage of General Spending	5
Administrative Costs Per TANF Case	7

Technology - Section M

Households with Computers	45
Percentage Using Internet	44
Zip Codes with Broadband Service	46
High-Tech Jobs	47
Change in High-Tech Jobs	27
State Government Web Site Ratings	36
Number of Online Government Services	19
Students Per Computer	29
Students Per Internet-Connected Computer	40
Libraries with Internet Access	1

Wisconsin

Population - Section A

Population 2005	20
Population 2004	20
Population Change 2003–2004	30
Population Change 1994–2004	30
Population 2015	26
Population 2025	21
Percentage 65 and Over	21
Percentage 17 and Under	33
Median Age	16
Percentage African American	29
Percentage American Indian	20
Percentage Asian American	25
Percentage Hispanic	31
Percentage White (Non-Hispanic)	13
Percentage Mixed-Race	37
Percentage in Poverty	19
Child Poverty Rate	19
Percentage Female	33
Birth Rates	39
Death Rates	40
Population Density	24
Legal Immigrants FY 2004	26
Unauthorized Immigrants	25

Economies - Section B

Personal Income, 2004	18
Gross State Product	23
Per Capita Personal Income	21
Personal Income from Wages and Salaries	14
Average Annual Pay	29
Average Hourly Earnings	20
Value Added in Manufacturing	2
Cost of Living	28
Average Annual Pay in Manufacturing	22
Average Annual Pay in Retailing	39
Labor Force	9
Unemployment Rate	32
Employment Rate	19
Government Employment	40
Manufacturing Employment	2
Fortune 500 Companies	18
Forbes 500 Companies	24
Tourism Spending Per Capita	43
Exports Per Capita	19
Housing Permits	18
Percentage Change in Home Prices	26
Net Farm Income	16
Financial Institution Assets	22
Bankruptcy Filings	25
Patents Issued	14
WC Disability Payment	15
Average Weekly UC Benefit	28
Economic Momentum	38
One-year Employment Change	42
Manufacturing Employment Change	23
Home Ownership	14
Annual Electricity Use Per Residential Customer	37
Cost Per Kwh	9
New Companies	47

Geography - Section C

Total Land Area	25
Federally Owned Land	23
State Park Acreage	25
State Park Visitors	21
Population Not Active	43
Hunters with Firearms	8
Registered Boats	6
State Spending for the Arts	43
Energy Consumption Per Capita	25
Toxic Chemical Release Per Capita	33
Hazardous Waste Sites	10
Drinking Water Quality	41
Expired Water Pollution Permits	40
Air Pollution Emissions	17

Government - Section D

Members of United States House	18
State Legislators	32
Legislators Per Million Population	35
Units of Government	14
Legislators Compensation	9
Female Legislators	18
Turnover in Legislatures	24
Term Limits	n/a
Legislative Session Length	n/a
Democrats in State Legislatures	36
Governors' Power Rating	32
Number of Statewide Elected Officials	15
State and Local Government Employees	37
State and Local Average Salaries	16
Local Employment	8
Local Spending Accountability	45
Registered Voters	n/a
Percentage of Population Voting	3
Statewide Initiatives	n/a
Campaign Costs Per Vote	28

Federal Impacts - Section E

Per Capita Federal Spending	48
Increase in Federal Spending	28
Per Capita Federal Grant Spending	38
Per Capita Federal Spending on Procurement	42
Per Capita Federal Spending on Payments to Individuals	39
Per Capita Federal Spending on Social Security and Medicare	26
Social Security Benefits	9
Federal Spending on Employee Wages and Salaries	50
Per Capita Federal Defense Spending	44
Per Capita Homeland Security Grants	31
Federal Grant Spending Per Dollar of State Tax Revenue	39
General Revenue from Federal Government	37
Federal Tax Burden Per Capita	21
Federal Spending Per Dollar of Taxes Paid	39
Highway Charges Returned to States	19
Terms of Trade	32
Federal Personal Income Taxes	22
Federal Share of Medicaid	31

Taxes - Section F

Tax Revenue	5
Per Capita Tax Revenue	10
Tax Effort	5
Tax Capacity	26
Percentage Change in Taxes	34
Property Taxes as a Percentage of Income	9
Property Taxes Per Capita	12
Property Tax Revenue as a Percentage of 3-tax Revenue	18
Sales Taxes as a Percentage of Income	28
Sales Taxes Per Capita	29
Sales Tax Revenue as a Percentage of 3-tax Revenue	36
Sales Tax Rate	25
Income Taxes as a Percentage of Income	10
Income Taxes Per Capita	11
Income Tax Revenue as a Percentage of 3-tax Revenue	15
Highest Personal Income Rate	17
Corporate Income Taxes	15
Motor Fuel Taxes	3
Motor Vehicle Fees	9
Tobacco Taxes	25
Taxes on High-Income Families	11
Taxes in the Largest City in Each State	10
Progressivity of Taxes	13
Per Capita Estate Tax Revenue	28

Revenues and Finances - Section G

Per Capita Total Revenue	34
Per Capita General Revenue	16

"Own-Source" General Revenue	13
Per Capita Non-Tax Revenue	29
Per Capita Total Spending	15
General Spending as a Percentage of Income	16
Per Capita General Spending	14
Change in General Expenditures	34
State Government General Revenue	16
State Government General Spending	16
State Government General Fund Spending	8
State and Local Debt	20
Debt as a Percentage of Revenue	17
Per Capita Full Faith and Credit Debt	10
Bond Ratings	4
State Solvency Index	36
Pension Plan Assets	6
State Reserves	48
Capital Outlays and Interest	21
State Budget Process Quality	44
Relative State Spending "Needs"	9
Structural Deficits	22

Education - Section H

Math Proficiency, Eighth Grade	7
Reading Proficiency, Eighth Grade	17
AFQT Ranks	13
SAT Scores	n/a
ACT Scores	2
Population over 25 with a High School Diploma	13
Students in Private Schools	9
High School Dropout Rates	6
Pupil-Teacher Ratio	30
Public School Enrollment	29
Library Holdings Per Capita	19
Children with Disabilities	24
Education Spending Per Capita	8
Education Spending as a Percentage of General Spending	15
Spending Per Pupil	14
Average Teacher Salary	22
Sources of School Funds	26
State Aid Per Pupil	12
Per Capita Higher Education Spending	12
Higher Education Spending as a Percentage of General Spending	20
Public Higher Education Enrollment	21
Per Pupil Support of Higher Education	35
In-State Tuition and Fees	22
Out-of-State Tuition and Fees	9
Change in Tuition and Fees	7
Affordability Index	5
Average Professor Salary	13
Education Employees	32
R and D Spending	38
Library Operating Spending	17
Head Start Spending	38

Health - Section I

Immunization Rates	16
Infant Mortality Rates	31
State Health Rankings	13
Population without Health Insurance	46
Abortions	32
Alcohol Consumption	5
Percentage of Adult Smokers	20
Percentage Obese	24
AIDS Cases	43
Physicians Per 100,000 Population	23
Hospital Beds Per 1,000 Population	28
Medicaid Recipients	24
Medicaid Recipients as a Percentage of Poverty Population	26
Health and Hospital Spending	36
Health and Hospital Spending as a Percentage of General Spending	38
Per Capita Medicaid Spending	31
Medicaid Spending Per Aged	12
Medicaid Spending Per Child	37
Medicare Payment Per Hospital Day	22
Hospital Expense Per Inpatient Day	7
Population in HMOs	7
Prescription Drugs as a Percentage of Medicaid Costs	37
Percentage Change in Average Price of Prescription Drugs	29

Crime - Section J

Crime Rate	40
Violent Crime Rate	45
Murder Rate	33
Property Crime Rate	38
Motor Vehicle Theft Rate	40
Violent Crime Rate Change	35
Prisoners	22
Change in Prisoners	2
Incarceration Rate	26
Juvenile Violent Crime Rate	30
Law Enforcement Employees	24
Corrections Employees	17
State Corrections Spending	11
Increase in State Corrections Spending	22
Law Enforcement Spending	11
Law Enforcement Spending as a Percentage of General Spending	10

Transportation - Section K

Travel on Interstates	47
Interstate Mileage in "Unacceptable" Condition	20
Deficient Bridges	44
Traffic Deaths	30
Seat Belt Use	41
Vehicle-Miles Traveled Per Capita	24
Use of Public Transportation	20
Road and Street Miles	39
Highway Employees	26
Public Transit Employees	20
Highway Spending Per Capita	14
Highway Spending as a Percentage of General Spending	17

Welfare - Section L

Births to Unwed Mothers	37
TANF Recipients	37
Change in TANF/AFDC Recipients	18
Food Stamp Recipients	39
SSI Recipients	34
WIC Average Monthly Benefit	30
NSLP Recipients	25
Condition of Children Index	10
Families with Single Parent	39
Average Monthly TANF Payments	11
Welfare as a Percentage of Poverty-Level Income	23
State Supplements of SSI	18
State Income Tax Liability of Typical Family in Poverty	34
Child Support Collections	6
Child Support Collections Per Dollar of Administrative Costs	12
Children in Foster Care	35
Welfare Spending Per Capita	17
Welfare Spending as a Percentage of General Spending	22
Administrative Costs Per TANF Case	5

Technology - Section M

Households with Computers	22
Percentage Using Internet	17
Zip Codes with Broadband Service	16
High-Tech Jobs	35
Change in High-Tech Jobs	16
State Government Web Site Ratings	29
Number of Online Government Services	38
Students Per Computer	42
Students Per Internet-Connected Computer	34
Libraries with Internet Access	28

Wyoming

Population - Section A

Population 2005	50
Population 2004	50
Population Change 2003–2004	21
Population Change 1994–2004	41
Population 2015	36
Population 2025	50
Percentage 65 and Over	34
Percentage 17 and Under	40
Median Age	10
Percentage African American	44
Percentage American Indian	8
Percentage Asian American	48
Percentage Hispanic	22
Percentage White (Non-Hispanic)	9
Percentage Mixed-Race	26
Percentage in Poverty	36
Child Poverty Rate	33
Percentage Female	47
Birth Rates	29
Death Rates	19
Population Density	49
Legal Immigrants FY 2004	50
Unauthorized Immigrants	43

Economies - Section B

Personal Income, 2004	50
Gross State Product	6
Per Capita Personal Income	14
Personal Income from Wages and Salaries	45
Average Annual Pay	42
Average Hourly Earnings	9
Value Added in Manufacturing	43
Cost of Living	17
Average Annual Pay in Manufacturing	40
Average Annual Pay in Retailing	40
Labor Force	4
Unemployment Rate	39
Employment Rate	12
Government Employment	3
Manufacturing Employment	49
Fortune 500 Companies	n/a
Forbes 500 Companies	n/a
Tourism Spending Per Capita	3
Exports Per Capita	42
Housing Permits	23
Percentage Change in Home Prices	22
Net Farm Income	39
Financial Institution Assets	39
Bankruptcy Filings	28
Patents Issued	40
WC Disability Payment	32
Average Weekly UC Benefit	31
Economic Momentum	7
One-year Employment Change	8
Manufacturing Employment Change	4
Home Ownership	19
Annual Electricity Use Per Residential Customer	31
Cost Per Kwh	5
New Companies	8

Geography - Section C

Total Land Area	9
Federally Owned Land	10
State Park Acreage	27
State Park Visitors	11
Population Not Active	36
Hunters with Firearms	6
Registered Boats	49
State Spending for the Arts	21
Energy Consumption Per Capita	2
Toxic Chemical Release Per Capita	7
Hazardous Waste Sites	47
Drinking Water Quality	38
Expired Water Pollution Permits	46
Air Pollution Emissions	40

Government - Section D

Members of United States House	44
State Legislators	43
Legislators Per Million Population	4
Units of Government	4
Legislators Compensation	43
Female Legislators	45
Turnover in Legislatures	16
Term Limits	n/a
Legislative Session Length	36
Democrats in State Legislatures	48
Governors' Power Rating	39
Number of Statewide Elected Officials	22
State and Local Government Employees	1
State and Local Average Salaries	34
Local Employment	18
Local Spending Accountability	13
Registered Voters	46
Percentage of Population Voting	18
Statewide Initiatives	n/a
Campaign Costs Per Vote	18

Federal Impacts - Section E

Per Capita Federal Spending	7
Increase in Federal Spending	7
Per Capita Federal Grant Spending	2
Per Capita Federal Spending on Procurement	25
Per Capita Federal Spending on Payments to Individuals	38
Per Capita Federal Spending on Social Security and Medicare	37
Social Security Benefits	20
Federal Spending on Employee Wages and Salaries	7
Per Capita Federal Defense Spending	31
Per Capita Homeland Security Grants	1
Federal Grant Spending Per Dollar of State Tax Revenue	4
General Revenue from Federal Government	9
Federal Tax Burden Per Capita	11
Federal Spending Per Dollar of Taxes Paid	24
Highway Charges Returned to States	10
Terms of Trade	7
Federal Personal Income Taxes	16
Federal Share of Medicaid	36

Taxes - Section F

Tax Revenue	3
Per Capita Tax Revenue	6
Tax Effort	43
Tax Capacity	9
Percentage Change in Taxes	1
Property Taxes as a Percentage of Income	4
Property Taxes Per Capita	6
Property Tax Revenue as a Percentage of 3-tax Revenue	4
Sales Taxes as a Percentage of Income	13
Sales Taxes Per Capita	5
Sales Tax Revenue as a Percentage of 3-tax Revenue	15
Sales Tax Rate	38
Income Taxes as a Percentage of Income	n/a
Income Taxes Per Capita	n/a
Income Tax Revenue as a Percentage of 3-tax Revenue	n/a
Highest Personal Income Rate	n/a
Corporate Income Taxes	n/a
Motor Fuel Taxes	48
Motor Vehicle Fees	42
Tobacco Taxes	28
Taxes on High-Income Families	50
Taxes in the Largest City in Each State	50
Progressivity of Taxes	44
Per Capita Estate Tax Revenue	21

Revenues and Finances - Section G

Per Capita Total Revenue	3
Per Capita General Revenue	2

"Own-Source" General Revenue	3
Per Capita Non-Tax Revenue	2
Per Capita Total Spending	3
General Spending as a Percentage of Income	3
Per Capita General Spending	3
Change in General Expenditures	24
State Government General Revenue	2
State Government General Spending	3
State Government General Fund Spending	3
State and Local Debt	29
Debt as a Percentage of Revenue	49
Per Capita Full Faith and Credit Debt	50
Bond Ratings	n/a
State Solvency Index	2
Pension Plan Assets	23
State Reserves	31
Capital Outlays and Interest	3
State Budget Process Quality	27
Relative State Spending "Needs"	39
Structural Deficits	1

Education - Section H

Math Proficiency, Eighth Grade	16
Reading Proficiency, Eighth Grade	9
AFQT Ranks	9
SAT Scores	n/a
ACT Scores	10
Population over 25 with a High School Diploma	2
Students in Private Schools	50
High School Dropout Rates	23
Pupil-Teacher Ratio	46
Public School Enrollment	16
Library Holdings Per Capita	2
Children with Disabilities	9
Education Spending Per Capita	2
Education Spending as a Percentage of General Spending	34
Spending Per Pupil	9
Average Teacher Salary	35
Sources of School Funds	31
State Aid Per Pupil	8
Per Capita Higher Education Spending	8
Higher Education Spending as a Percentage of General Spending	30
Public Higher Education Enrollment	12
Per Pupil Support of Higher Education	2
In-State Tuition and Fees	48
Out-of-State Tuition and Fees	49
Change in Tuition and Fees	42
Affordability Index	21
Average Professor Salary	39
Education Employees	1
R and D Spending	45
Library Operating Spending	15
Head Start Spending	30

Health - Section I

Immunization Rates	20
Infant Mortality Rates	1
State Health Rankings	19
Population without Health Insurance	27
Abortions	n/a
Alcohol Consumption	4
Percentage of Adult Smokers	21
Percentage Obese	43
AIDS Cases	41
Physicians Per 100,000 Population	47
Hospital Beds Per 1,000 Population	7
Medicaid Recipients	38
Medicaid Recipients as a Percentage of Poverty Population	24
Health and Hospital Spending	1
Health and Hospital Spending as a Percentage of General Spending	5
Per Capita Medicaid Spending	41
Medicaid Spending Per Aged	14
Medicaid Spending Per Child	21
Medicare Payment Per Hospital Day	32
Hospital Expense Per Inpatient Day	9
Population in HMOs	47
Prescription Drugs as a Percentage of Medicaid Costs	18
Percentage Change in Average Price of Prescription Drugs	23

Crime - Section J

Crime Rate	30
Violent Crime Rate	44
Murder Rate	42
Property Crime Rate	28
Motor Vehicle Theft Rate	45
Violent Crime Rate Change	40
Prisoners	48
Change in Prisoners	26
Incarceration Rate	27
Juvenile Violent Crime Rate	43
Law Enforcement Employees	3
Corrections Employees	7
State Corrections Spending	7
Increase in State Corrections Spending	1
Law Enforcement Spending	9
Law Enforcement Spending as a Percentage of General Spending	27

Transportation - Section K

Travel on Interstates	3
Interstate Mileage in "Unacceptable" Condition	17
Deficient Bridges	38
Traffic Deaths	15
Seat Belt Use	n/a
Vehicle-Miles Traveled Per Capita	1
Use of Public Transportation	24
Road and Street Miles	14
Highway Employees	2
Public Transit Employees	35
Highway Spending Per Capita	2
Highway Spending as a Percentage of General Spending	2

Welfare - Section L

Births to Unwed Mothers	32
TANF Recipients	50
Change in TANF/AFDC Recipients	1
Food Stamp Recipients	48
SSI Recipients	48
WIC Average Monthly Benefit	48
NSLP Recipients	27
Condition of Children Index	23
Families with Single Parent	42
Average Monthly TANF Payments	n/a
Welfare as a Percentage of Poverty-Level Income	42
State Supplements of SSI	44
State Income Tax Liability of Typical Family in Poverty	n/a
Child Support Collections	8
Child Support Collections Per Dollar of Administrative Costs	19
Children in Foster Care	11
Welfare Spending Per Capita	39
Welfare Spending as a Percentage of General Spending	49
Administrative Costs Per TANF Case	n/a

Technology - Section M

Households with Computers	16
Percentage Using Internet	16
Zip Codes with Broadband Service	30
High-Tech Jobs	49
Change in High-Tech Jobs	3
State Government Web Site Ratings	50
Number of Online Government Services	50
Students Per Computer	48
Students Per Internet-Connected Computer	47
Libraries with Internet Access	1

Index